THE

CHEROKEE LAND LOTTERY,

CONTAINING

95 - 1141

A NUMERICAL LIST OF THE NAMES OF THE FORTUNATE
DRAWERS IN SAID LOTTERY,

WITH

AN ENGRAVED MAP OF EACH DISTRICT.

BY JAMES F. SMITH,

OF MILLEDGEVILLE, GEO.

NEW-YORK:

PRINTED BY HARPER & BROTHERS,

NO. 82 CLIFF-STREET.

1838.

New Material Copyrighted
October, 1968
The Rev. Silas Emmett Lucas, Jr.

Reprinted 1991

SOUTHERN HISTORICAL PRESS, INC.
c/o The Rev. Silas Emmett Lucas, Jr.
275 West Broad Street
Greenville, South Carolina 29601

ISBN 0-89308- 033-0

PUBLISHER'S PREFACE to the 1991 REPRINT

Due to rising printing costs on books of over 300 pages we have reformatted the arrangement of the contents of this edition so as to decrease the total nmber of pages but to not omit any of the material appearing in the 1832 edition. We have therefore taken the sixty individual maps showing each District and Section covered in this Land Lottery and put them in a map section following the listing of fortunate drawers of land and immediately before the full name index. These sixty maps were originally scattered throughout the book in the midst of the text pertaining to their said Districts and Sections. This original format added sixty blank, unnumbered pages to the map section which increased the page count of the book significantly.

CONTENTS OF THE MAP SECTION

23.	23rd District, 2nd Section	— Cass & Cherokee Counties
24.	24th District, 2nd Section	— Murray & Gilmer Counties
25.	25th District, 2nd Section	— Murray & Gilmer Counties
26.	26th District, 2nd Section	— Murray & Gilmer Counties
27.	27th District, 2nd Section	— Murray & Gilmer Counties
28.	5th District, 3rd Section	— Cass County
29.	6th District, 3rd Section	— Cass County
30.	7th District, 3rd Section	— Murray County
31.	8th District, 3rd Section	— Murray County
32.	9th District, 3rd Section	— Murray County
33.	10th District, 3rd Section	— Murray County
34.	11th District, 3rd Section	— Murray County
35.	12th District, 3rd Section	— Murray County
36.	13th District, 3rd Section	— Murray County
37.	14th District, 3rd Section	— Murray County
38.	15th District, 3rd Section	— Cass County
39.	16th District, 3rd Section	— Cass County
40.	22nd District, 3rd Section	— Floyd County
41.	23rd District, 3rd Section	— Floyd County
42.	24th District, 3rd Section	— Floyd County
43.	25th District, 3rd Section	— Walker County
44.	26th District, 3rd Section	— Walker County
45.	27th District, 3rd Section	— Walker County
46.	28th District, 3rd Section	— Walker County
47.	4th District, 4th Section	— Floyd County
48.	5th District, 4th Section	— Floyd County
49.	6th District, 4th Section	— Walker County
50.	7th District, 4th Section	— Walker County
51.	8th District, 4th Section	— Walker County
52.	9th District, 4th Section	— Walker County
53.	10th District, 4th Section	— Walker County
54.	11th District, 4th Section	— Walker County
55.	12th District, 4th Section	— Walker County
56.	13th District, 4th Section	— Walker County
57.	14th District, 4th Section	— Floyd County
58.	15th District, 4th Section	— Floyd County
59.	18th District, 4th Section	— Walker County
60.	19th District, 4th Section	— Walker County

PREFACE

THE undersigned offers to the public in the following pages a work which, he trusts, will not only be acceptable, but highly valuable to many of his fellow-citizens.

The numerous and constant inquiries at the printing establishments and public offices for something of a similar character, induced him, some months since, to engage in its compilation, and, after much labour, he now presents it to the judgment of an enlightened community, confident that its merits will be justly appreciated.

It contains the names and residence of all the fortunate drawers in the *Land Lottery* of the Cherokee country, arranged by districts in numerical order, and a map of each district, all carefully copied from the originals in the Executive Department and the office of the Surveyor General, designating also the lots which have been granted.

He has given the quality of the lots in some instances, but not generally, deeming it altogether unimportant, from the well known inaccuracy of the surveyors in classing their value, and from the additional fact that very few individuals engage in contracts for real estate until they are enabled by personal observation to place a proper estimate upon the premises.

By reference to the numerical list, the drawer's name and residence can be readily ascertained, while the maps will give a pretty correct idea of the watercourses and local situation of any particular lot, as well as whether it has been granted or not.

To those who drew land in this lottery—who are desirous of obtaining settlements in that section of the state—and more particularly to those who are extensively engaged in the purchase and sale of lots, this work is particularly recommended.

The materials for publication having been prepared principally by himself, and the printing having been executed under his personal superintendence, he feels assured that its accuracy may be relied on.

In conclusion, he deems it due to his subscribers and the public to offer an explanation for the delay in bringing out the work, which has been occasioned by circumstances beyond his control; to wit, the fulfilment of other imperious obligations, which engrossed a longer portion of his time than he could reasonably have anticipated; for which, he entertains no doubt, due allowance will be made.

JAMES F. SMITH.

Milledgeville, Geo., April 19, 1838.

FOREWORD

The last, or 1832 Land Lottery of Georgia, made available for distribution and settlement that part of the Cherokee Indian Nation which was in Georgia. This was a large area generally north of the Chattahoochee River in the north west and north central parts of the state. There were two distinct areas involved in this Lottery. One part was the area referred to as the gold lots, lying along the south boundary of the subject area, and the other part was referred to as the land lots. This book deals only with the land lots as shown on the map following the Foreword.

Georgia's western and northern boundary had been established in 1802 by the cession of her western territory, from the Chattahoochee River to the Mississippi, to the United States. Although this cession had provided for the peaceful removal of all Indians within these boundaries, in 1828, the Cherokee still remained. Despite the fact the Cherokee were a peaceful and agricultural people, in that year Georgia extended her jurisdiction over them and named the area Cherokee County. Shortly thereafter, the General Assembly, by the Acts of December 21, 1830 and December 24, 1831, authorized the land to be surveyed and distributed by Lottery to citizens of Georgia. In 1832 the surveyors laid off the area in four sections, the sections into land districts about nine miles square, and the land districts into land lots of 40 and 160 acres respectively.

While the surveying was being carried out, those persons who had lived in Georgia three years immediately prior to the Acts of the General Assembly, registered to draw in the Lottery in their counties of residence. Their names, together with the numbers of the lots and districts, were sent to Milledgeville, then the capital of the state, and on specified days tickets from two wheels or drums were drawn simultaneously, one from the wheel holding the name tickets and one from the drum holding the land lot tickets. In this way, a person knew which lot he had drawn and if he subsequently paid to the state a grant fee of $18.00, a grant was issued to the lot he had drawn. This grant from the State of Georgia was his title to the lot and from that time he could do whatever he wished with his property, although the state did not require that he live on it or cultivate it.

Revolutionary War veterans were given extra draws and were indicated by the letters "R.S." written after their names. Many other classifications are indicated by initials, such as widows, insane, orphans, idiots, illegitimates, etc. Ordinary married men with their families, or bachelors, etc, are not designated by any initial. All citizens participating in this and other Lotteries had to take only an ORAL oath when they registered to draw. Consequently, there are no written records as to what they may have said about themselves and their families.

Immediately after the Lottery of 1832 was held, the whole area of Cherokee County was divided into ten counties, i.e., Cass (which was renamed Bartow in 1861), Cherokee, Cobb, Floyd, Forsyth, Gilmer, Lumpkin, Murray, Paulding and Union, all of which were created in 1832. However, the original survey and grant records in the Surveyor General Department of the Office of the Secretary of State, always use the name of the original county—Cherokee.

The 1832 Land Lottery opened up the last area within the present boundaries of Georgia, which heretofore had not been available to the white settlers and was participated in by more persons than any other Lottery.

In spite of the distributing of the lands in the area, it was not fully settled at first. It was not until a Treaty with the United States and the Cherokee Nation on December 29, 1835 held at New Echota in Georgia, that the Cherokee finally agreed to leave their lands and move west beyond the Mississippi River. Soon after Georgians came in in large numbers and not an Indian was left within her boundaries.

TENNESSEE   NORTH CAROLINA

4th. Section | 3rd. Section | 2nd. Section | 1st. Section

| 19 | 10 | 9 | 28 | 11 | 10 | 27 | 9 | 8 | 8 | 9 | 17 | 18 |

| 18 | 11 | 8 | 27 | 12 | 9 | 26 | 10 | 7 | 7 | 10 | 16 | 19 |

MURRAY COUNTY

UNION COUNTY

GILMER COUNTY

| 12 | 7 | 26 | 13 | 8 | 25 | 11 | 6 | 6 | 11 |

| 13 | 6 | 25 | 14 | 7 | 24 | 12 | 5 | 5 | 12 | 15 |

LUMPKIN COUNTY

| 14 | 5 | 24 | 15 | 6 | 23 | 13 | 4 | 4 | 13 |

CHEROKEE COUNTY

FLOYD COUNTY

| 15 | 4 | 23 | 16 | 5 | 22 | 14 | 3 | 3 | 14 |

CASS COUNTY

FORSYTH COUNTY

| 16 | 3 | 22 | 17 | 4 | 21 | 15 | 2 | 2 |

| 17 | 2 | 21 | 18 | 3 | 20 | 16 | 1 | 1 |

PAULDING COUNTY   COBB COUNTY

| 1 | 20 | 19 | 2 | 19 | 17 |

| 1 | 18 |

ALABAMA

THE LAND AREA OF THE CHEROKEE LOTTERY

The numbered squares showing dots are the gold districts and the
numbered squares without the dots are the land districts. This book
shows only those who drew lots in the land districts. The ten counties
shown are those created in 1832 immediately after the Land Lottery.
The broken lines show the boundaries of the ten counties.

©

EXPLANATION OF ABBREVIATIONS.

sol., soldier.
s. i. w., soldier of Indian war.
s. l. w., soldier of late war.
r. s., revolutionary soldier.
sol. 1784–97, soldier between the years 1784 and 1797.
s. s., soldier by substitute.
m. s., militia soldier.
wid'r., widower.
w., widow.
w. r. s., widow of revolutionary soldier.
w. s. i. w., widow of soldier of Indian war.
w. s. l. w., widow of soldier of late war.
w. of sol., widow of soldier.
d. sol. l. w., daughter of soldier of late war.
h. d. l. w., husband died last war.
f. d. l. w., father died last war.
or., orphan.
ors., orphans.
mi., minor.
lun., lunatic.
id., idiot.
h. a., husband absent.
f. a., father absent.
h. of f., head of family.
d. and d., deaf and dumb.
(fr.), fractional lots.
Cher., Cherokee.
b. m., by mother.
f. in p., father in penitentiary.
c. r., cross roads.

Note—All names marked * were granted previous to the first day of January, 1838.

CHEROKEE LAND LOTTERY.

SIXTH DISTRICT, FIRST SECTION, CHEROKEE.

1 Arthur Turner, Summerlin's, Bulloch.*
2 Miles Shepherd, Hitchcock's, Muscogee.
3 Absalom Ogletree, Ball's, Monroe.
4 Aaron Palmer, Chastain's, Habersham.
5 Thomas Duren, sol., Newman's, Thomas.*
6 William A. Stewart, 559th, Walton.
7 George W. Bowen, Wolfskin's, Oglethorpe.
8 Edmund Bradley, Curry's, Merriwether.
9 David Martin, Martin's, Hall.
10 William C. Paramore, 271st, M'Intosh.*
11 Mary Mays, w. of sol., M'Dowell's, Lincoln.
12 George Barlow, Swinney's, Laurens.
13 Charles L. Dupree, 277th, Morgan.*
14 Hannah Reid, w., Herndon's, Hall.
15 William M. Halsey, Morton's, De Kalb.
16 Absalom R. Allen, Reid's, Gwinnett.
17 Robert W. M'Keen, 398th, Richmond.
18 Ebenezer C. Hatcher, 318th, Baldwin.*
19 Jesse Duncan, M'Linn's, Butts.
20 Jonathan M'Kay, Smith's, Henry.
21 John K. Miller, 49th, Emanuel.
22 Alexander Johnson, Morrison's, Montgomery.
23 Walter Dubois, Valleau's, Chatham.
24 Murdock Chisholm, Ellsworth's, Bibb.
25 John Anthony, Compton's, Fayette.
26 George Fausett, sol., M'Culler's, Newton.
27 James Blair, r. s., Whitehead's, Habersham.
28 James Bell's ors., 122d, Richmond.
29 John J. Jones, Allen's, Bibb.
30 Ray Whitfield, Brown's, Habersham.
31 David Pruett, Reid's, Gwinnett.
32 Daniel Freyermath, Sanderlin's, Chatham.
33 Jacob Canyers, Dupree's, Washington.*
34 Thomas Ogletree, Griffin's, Fayette.*
35 Sarah Ann Turner, w., Duke's, Carroll.
36 John C. Rogers, Candler's, Bibb.
37 William Durham, 138th, Greene.
38 Joseph Riley's ors., Martin's, Stewart.

2

39 Joseph Holden, Brock's, Habersham.*
40 Ezekiel E. Park, 320th, Baldwin.*
41 James Bell's ors., 122d, Richmond.
42 Jemimah Monk, or., Folsom's, Lowndes.*
43 Thomas Echols's ors., 168th, Wilkes.*
44 John Tomberlin, sol., Smith's, Wilkinson.
45 Jane Willis, w., Willis's, Franklin.
46 John Houze, Belcher's, Jasper.
47 Benjamin Lane, Davis's, Clarke.
48 Thomas Gardner, Ellsworth's, Bibb.
49 David M. Smith, Crawford's, Franklin.
50 Harrison Walker, Evans's, Fayette.*
51 Elijah V. Echols, Higginbotham's, Rabun.
52 John Jolly, Holley's, Franklin.
53 Robert Barks, Barks's, Stewart.
54 Lovick Merritt, or., 364th, Jasper.
55 Frederic Mathews, M'Gehee's, Troup.*
56 Elizabeth Hillyer, h. a., Talley's, Troup.
57 Delana Hawkins, or., Smith's, Houston.
58 Elizabeth Gray, w., Head's, Butts.
59 Presley Jones, Hampton's, Newton.
60 John Wallace, Herndon's, Hall.
61 John C. Wynn, sol., Groover's, Thomas.
62 Robert Orr, Roberts's, Hall.
63 John Turner, r. s., 374th, Putnam.
64 Robert Ellitt, s. l. w., Moore's, Randolph.
65 Christopher Stanton, Price's, Hall.
66 Robert J. Patterson, 71st, Burke.*
67 Nathaniel Dent's ors., Taylor's, Putnam.
68 Charles F. Patillo, Smith's, Houston.
69 Joshua Spence, Jones's, Thomas.
70 William H. Wiley, Alberson's, Walton.
71 Samuel H. Beman, 138th, Greene.
72 Henry J. Valleau, sol., Cleland's, Chatham.
73 Mariah Chambless, w., Davis's, Jones.
74 James B. Head, Loveless's, Gwinnett.
75 Josiah F. Thomas, sol., Sanderlin's, Chatham.
76 Jethro Oshields, Lay's, Jackson.*
77 Sampson Massey's ors., Williams's, Washington.
78 Simon Carrell, Neal's, Campbell.
79 James Hays, 589th, Upson.*
80 Paul M. Otwell, Allison's, Pike.*
81 Mary Flakes, w., Pace's, Putnam.
82 James M'Mellon, Hart's, Jones.
83 R. J., I. F., and Wm. J. Kelly, 559th, Walton.
84 Seaborn Camp, Allen's, Henry.
85 John White, Espy's, Clarke.

86 William P. Wilson, Slater's, Bulloch.
87 Ebenezer B. Vernon, 561st, Upson.
88 Stephen Felker, 419th, Walton.
89 Noe Mathews, sol., Hitchcock's, Muscogee.
90 Murdock M'Leod, sol., Ellis's, Pulaski.*
91 Elizabeth Neyle, or., 3d, Chatham.
92 Eleanor Blalock, w. r. s., 588th, Upson.
93 William Moss's ors., Wood's, Jefferson.
94 Silas Tanner, M'Linn's, Butts.
95 Jesse Ammoy, Copeland's, Houston.
96 Amanda G. Noalas, or., 9th, Effingham.
97 Isaac Cain, Johnson's, De Kalb.
98 Alexander Houghton, s. l. w., Head's, Butts.
99 Martin Lowe, Arrington's, Merriwether.*
100 Jesse Hunter, 36th, Scriven.
101 Riley Sizemore, 119th, Richmond.*
102 Stephen Satterwhite, sol., Sims's, Troup.*
103 Isaac Johnson, Pearce's, Houston.*
104 William Baber, M'Gill's, Lincoln.
105 William Youngblood, 374th, Putnam.
106 George Vinson, s. l. w., Everett's, Washington.
107 George Murray, 123d, Richmond.
108 Salze Gordon, w., Gunn's, Jones.
109 Hardy Hays, Trout's, Hall.
110 James H. Smith, Loveless's, Gwinnett.
111 James R. Lockett, 603d, Taliaferro.
112 Benjamin Philips's ors., Wynn's, Gwinnett.
113 Robert Richardson, 160th, Greene.
114 Wiley Bishop, Sen., Daniel's, Hall.
115 Elisha King, sol., 105th, Baldwin.
116 Benjamin King, May's, Monroe.
117 William Harige, Smith's, Henry.*
118 Jacob Homker, Hobkerk's, Camden.*
119 James F. Linder, 6th, Chatham.*
120 James Smithart, Taylor's, Houston.
121 John T. Barnes, or., Groce's, Bibb.
122 Isaac Bolton's or., 166th, Wilkes.
123 John Steele, 406th, Gwinnett.
124 Jacob Beardin, sol., Whelchel's, Hall.*
125 James Wilkes, Watson's, Marion.
126 James M. Killgore, 250th, Walton.
127 Jas. Key Kendall, r. s., Stephens's, Habersham.*
128 Martin L. Ruff, Dearing's, Henry.
129 Levi Loveless, Loveless's, Gwinnett.
130 Wiatt Parham, Madden's, Pike.*
131 Robt. and Jincey Adcock, f. a., Maguire's, Morgan.
132 John S. Harry, Allen's, Henry.

133 Robert M. Fields, Brown's, Habersham.
134 Jacob Paul, Bryan's, Monroe.
135 Jeremiah Hendrix, Sewell's, Franklin.
136 Samuel Worthy, Rhodes's, De Kalb.
137 James S. Thomas, or., 114th, Hancock.
138 Richard Hooper, Jr., Chandler's, Franklin.
139 David M. Crockett, Cleggs's, Walton.
140 Solomon Arnstorff, sol., 9th, Effingham.*
141 Catharine Langley,w. s. i. w., Hyrnes's, Chatham.
142 Hubbard Carnes, Jr., Keener's, Rabun.
143 Moses Caps, Lawrence's, Pike.
144 Chinchell Gibson, May's, Monroe.*
145 Jesse Keaton, Robison's, Washington.*
146 Solomon Scott, Levritt's, Lincoln.
147 John M. Dunn, Perry's, Habersham.
148 David Robertson, Salem, Baldwin.
149 William Murphy, Mizell's, Talbot.
150 John Robinson, sol., Walker's, Harris.*
151 David Pruitt, Reid's, Gwinnett.
152 Thomas Squires, 1st, Chatham.*
153 John L. Nickolson, Talley's, Troup.
154 William T. Ansley, 146th, Greene.
155 James W. Harkness, Berry's, Butts.
156 William Matthews, r. s., Riden's, Jackson.
157 Wright Williams, Mangum's, Franklin.
158 William M'Collum, Jones's, Habersham.
159 Berry A. Ruark, Wood's, Morgan.
160 Thomas M. Wilson's ors., Riden's, Jackson.
161 James Norton, Chambers's, Gwinnett.
162 William Conner, sol., Southwell's, Tatnall.
163 William Lansford, Compton's, Fayette.
164 Jesse Russell's ors., Burk's, Stewart.
165 James Wofford, 2d 'section, Cherokee.
166 Reuben Vining, Vining's, Putnam.*
167 Doct. John Carter, 120th, Richmond.
168 Gasham Stewart's ors., Park's, Walton.
169 Isaac Evans, Covington's, Pike.*
170 James W. Shankle, M'Ginnis's, Jackson.
171 James M. Anderson, Walden's, Pulaski.
172 Richard Y. Loffton, Camp's, Baker.*
173 Thomas D. Carr's ors./ Few's, Muscogee.
174 Elisha Hubboard, sol., Wood's, Morgan.
175 Silas M. Johnson, sol., Hampton's, Newton.
176 Louisa Long, w., Candler's, Bibb.
177 David Furlow, sol., 143d, Greene.
178 Stephen Godwin, 720th, Decatur.*
179 William Lord, M'Ginnis's, Jackson.
180 Richard Gregory, r. s., Hargrove's, Oglethorpe.

181 James R. Bailey, Seal's, Elbert.
182 Edmund Glawns's ors., Collier's, Monroe.
183 Alexander Stewart, House's, Henry.
184 Burton Hepburn, 320th, Baldwin.
185 Isaac Bentley, s. l. w., Hatson's, Newton.
186 John Spence, Arrington's, Merriwether.
187 Daniel Fowler, Woodruff's, Campbell.
188 Samuel Wright, Bivins's, Jones.
189 Jesse Holt, Wellingham's, Harris.*
190 John Hass, 320th, Baldwin.
191 John Stephens, 117th, Hancock.
192 Henry Byrd, s. l. w., 600th, Richmond.
193 James L. Burney, 295th, Jasper.*
194 Uriah Laney, Martin's, Newton.
195 Anson Reynolds, Hendon's, Carroll.
196 Allen Andrews, Smith's, Franklin.
197 John Collatt's ors., Allen's, Henry.
198 John Frinks, Bailey's, Camden.
199 Allen G. Holley, Chandler's, Franklin.
200 Samuel Horton, Hughes's, Habersham.*
201 Edward Horn's ors., 277th, Morgan.
202 Stephen Boutwell, Camp's, Baker.*
203 Robert Hemphill's ors., Hammond's, Franklin.
204 John C. Perkins, Crawford's, Morgan.
205 Samuel Warden, r. s., Morgan's, Madison.*
206 Bradley Kinbrough, m. s., 160th, Greene.
207 Thomas Grubbs, Allen's, Bibb.
208 Joshua Daughtry, 574th, Early.
209 Watson Patman's ors., Hines's, Coweta.*
210 Wilson F. Blackstock, Heard's, De Kalb.
211 David Walker's ors., 175th, Wilkes.
212 John Clark, sol., Collier's, Monroe.
213 David Adams, Derrick's, Henry.
214 Johnston Wiley, Willis's, Franklin.
215 John Hollis, Maguire's, Morgan.
216 Frances Barrett, or., 122d, Richmond.
217 John E. Loyd, Sen., s. l. w., Coxe's, Talbot.
218 John Purcell, Sen., sol., Field's, Habersham.
219 Eli Huggins, Moseley's, Coweta.
220 Mary Ann Rhodes, w., 574th, Early.
221 Patrick G. Dickey, Peterson's, Burke.
222 William Roberson, Morrison's, Appling.
223 Benajah Hardy, Williams's, Jasper.
224 Rice B. Greene, Jr., 406th, Gwinnett.
225 Daniel M'Farland's ors., 561st, Upson.
226 Thomas Sparks, sol., Phillips's, Jasper.
227 Middleton Sharbutt, Sen., Taylor's, Putnam.
228 Nancy Wynne, w., Bushe's, Pulaski.

229 Jeremiah Davis, Peavy's, Bulloch.*
230 Benjamin Crisler, Seal's, Elbert.
231 Caleb Downey, Barker's, Gwinnett.
232 James Hudgins, Dyer's, Habersham.
233 Mary M. Clements, w., Coxe's, Morgan.
234 Burton Kent, Madden's, Pike.
235 Henry F. David, David's, Franklin.*
236 William Burden, Bostick's, Twiggs.
237 John Gilbert, Seas's, Madison.*
238 Samuel Willson, r. s., 34th, Scriven.
239 James Boatright, Moseley's, Coweta.
240 Mary Oglesby, w., 11th, Effingham.
241 William C. Hurpes's ors., Bishop's, Henry.
242 Sampson G. Williams, M'Craney's, Lowndes.
243 George Wortham, Buck-branch, Clarke.
244 Owen H. Fort, Whitfield's, Washington.*
245 William C. Davis, Prophett's, Newton.
246 Claborn Sandridge, r. s., Seal's, Elbert.
247 John J. Hudson, Gunn's, Jefferson.
248 Moses Weaver, 510th, Early.
249 James D. Gray, Jack's, Clarke.
250 James Watwood, Mobley's, De Kalb.
251 Jethro Oshields, Lay's, Jackson.*
252 Benjamin D. Mays, M'Millon's, Lincoln.*
253 Joseph Nicolan, 27th, Glynn.
254 Remsom Harwell, Clark's, Morgan.
255 George Taylor, Jr., Jones's, Habersham.
256 Tabitha Ann Guiton, or., Barwick's, Washington.
257 William Miher's ors., Lightfoot's, Washington.
258 David Brownin, Groover's, Thomas.*
259 Martin W. Berry, M. Brown's, Habersham.
260 Jacob Oxford, Hughes's, Habersham.
261 Simpson M'Clendon, 364th, Jasper.
262 William S. Faller, Huchinson's, Columbia.
263 Lucy Windham, w. r. s., Downs's, Warren.
264 George A. F. Allen, Roberson's, Putnam.
265 Mary Rutherford, w. r. s., Barker's, Gwinnett.
266 William Straham, Hand's, Applin.
267 William Sinquefield, Hannah's, Jefferson.
268 Edmund Collins, Ross's, Monroe.*
269 John Keenum, Herndon's, Hall.
270 Cassander Chambers, w., Daniels's, Hall.
271 Isabella Estes, w. r. s., M'Clendon's, Putnam.
272 Curtis King, sol., of Greene, 141st, Taliaferro.
273 Robert Pope, Wolfskin's, Oglethorpe.*
274 P. W. Hubbard, of Cherokee, Latimer's, De Kalb.
275 John R. M'Lewreath, Williams's, Decatur.
276 Hiram Ansley, Gunn's, Jones.

277 James F. Turner, sol., M'Korkle's, Jasper.
278 Moses Sadler, Killen's, Decatur.
279 Sally Knoulman, w., Bragaw's, Oglethorpe.
280 Norman M. Crow, Barker's, Gwinnett.
281 Thomas Greer's ors., 466th, Monroe.
282 John B. Tuggle, 294th, Jasper.
283 Delila Fletcher, w., Hill's, Stewart.*
284 Elisha B. Prichard, Butt's, Monroe.
285 Starling Cook, Williams's, Washington.
286 Richard Winters's ors., 245th, Jackson.
287 Lawrence Joyner, Will's, Twiggs.*
288 Moses Daniel, Mitchell's, Pulaski.
289 Moses Beard, r. s., Athens, Clarke.
290 Richard Simmons, r. s., 404th, Gwinnett.
291 Margaret S. Holland, w., Robinson's, Putnam.
292 James Walling, Hamilton's, Hall.
293 John C. Smith, Allen's, Monroe.
294 Thomas Hampton, sol., Harralson's, Troup.*
295 Isaac Coalson, Hatton's, Baker.
296 Adam Bird, Allen's, Monroe.
297 Thomas W. Rice, sol., Houston's, Chatham.*
298 James B. Holt, 374th, Putnam.
299 Joseph Randolph, Atkinson's, Coweta.*
300 Albin Ryland, Downs's, Warren.*
301 Sophia Young, Walker's, Columbia.
302 James M. Rowzee, Taylor's, Elbert.
303 Elijah Eckles, sol., 166th, Wilkes.
304 Stephen Clayton, Sen., r. s., Burgess's, Carroll.
305 John Mills, Park's, Walton.
306 Robert Sharly, Deane's, Clarke.
307 John D. Warner's ors., Carswell's, Jefferson.
308 Warren Coiles, or., Hardman's, Oglethorpe.
309 John M'Donald, Simmons's, Crawford.
310 Archibald Buye, 35th, Scriven.*
311 Allen W. Prior, Wilson's, Pike.*
312 John M. Mullins, Price's, Hall.*
313 William Jones, Wood's, Morgan.
314 Nancy Ivy, w., Folsom's, Lowndes.
315 Georgia Mulvy, w., 22d, M'Intosh.
316 Couthvy Campbell, or., 27th, Glynn.*
317 James Livermon, sol., Sealey's, Talbot.*
318 Mary Martindale, w., Huey's, Harris.
319 Thomas Jones, Griffin's, Fayette.
320 Seaborn J. Vann, Bushe's, Burke.*
321 Henry W. Beauford, Willson's, Jasper.
322 John Hembey, Phillips's, Talbot.
323 Jacob Freeman, Chastain's, Habersham.
324 John Williamson, Camp's, Baker.

1 Sarah Moore, w., Parham's, Warren.
2 William T. Nelums, Clark's, Elbert.*
3 John G. Town's or., Wilson's, Pike.*
4 David Dickson, Hampton's, Newton.
5 James Cook's ors., Curry's, Wilkinson.
6 Arthur G. Holmes, Dean's, Clarke.
7 William Carter, widower, 7th, Chatham.*
8 Robert Shearman, Jr., Freeman's, Jasper.
9 William Wallace's ors., Hearn's, Butts.
10 Henry Hodges, 687th, Lee.*
11 David Smith, Talley's, Troup.
12 Archibald Martin, Martin's, Jones.*
13 Thomas Williams, Coffee's, Rabun.
14 Overton Arnold, 419th, Walton.
15 Hardy Mattox, sol., Coxe's, Morgan.
16 Benjamin F. Kenrick, 600th, Richmond.
17 George Dodds, 404th, Gwinnett.
18 Henry Blanchett, Williams's, Decatur.*
19 Thomas A. Banks, sol., Clark's, Elbert.*
20 William Strawder, 601st, Taliaferro.
21 John Dormany, Bryan's, Pulaski.
22 John Clay, Haygood's, Washington.*
23 John Denton, Valleau's, Chatham.
24 John Russell, Arrington's, Merriwether.
25 Stephen Daniel, Martin's, Newton.
26 Hugh L. Irwin, Barron's, Houston.*
27 William Harmon, Hall's, Butts.
28 Sarah Harvey, w. r. s., 470th, Upson.
29 John M. Chalmers, 2d section, Cherokee.
30 Hardy Levritt, sol., Levritt's, Lincoln.*
31 Thomas Smith's ors., Phillips's, Talbot.
32 John T. Freeman, 37th, Scriven.
33 Stephen K. Crambey, Martin's, Pike.
34 Peter Strozer, 166th, Wilkes.*
35 James Brooks, Baugh's, Jackson.
36 Elhanan Wells, Price's, Hall.
37 Isom Batton, Folsom's, Lowndes.
38 John Clary's ors., Cleland's, Chatham.
39 William A. Slaton, or., Lester's, Monroe.
40 Jacob Evans, Bryant's, Burke.
41 Archibald Clement's ors., Prescott's, Twiggs.

42 William B. Glenn, Robinson's, Washington.
43 John W. Lewis, 574th, Early.
44 •John Sharpe, sol., Hill's, Baldwin.*
45 Alice Deadwyler, w., Wilhite's, Elbert.
46 William Beasley, sen., Holton's, Emanuel.
47 Jesse Acock, Lockhart's, Bulloch.
48 John Blount's ors., Ross's, Monroe.
49 Jeremiah Salmons, Kelley's, Elbert.
50 Frances Holcombe, w. r. s., 1st, Chatham.
51 Thomas Hampton, Hampton's, Newton.
52 Sampson Stallings, Walkerk's, Harris.
53 Peny Pruitt, w., Martin's, Newton.*
54 Dennis Duncan, Baugh's, Jackson.
55 Asa Weems, Hammond's, Franklin.
56 Elizabeth Hathorn, w., Rook's, Putnam.
57 Boley Embrey, M'Ginnis's, Jackson.
58 Samuel Wallace's ors., Chambers's, Gwinnett.
59 Catharine C. Ernst, w., 9th, Effingham.
60 Alfred C. Boon, Atkison's, Coweta.*
61 Mary Thomas, f. a., Ware's, Coweta.
62 James B. Wooten, Moseley's, Coweta.*
63 William Hinton, Newsom's, Warren.
64 William Cole, 55th, Emanuel.*
65 Miller Grieve, 320th, Baldwin.
66 Eli R. Callaway's ors., Bragaw's, Oglethorpe.
67 Willis Bobo, Stowers's, Elbert.
68 Gabriel Parker's ors., Sam Streetman's, Twiggs.
69 Samuel Chancey, s. l. w., Morgan's, Appling.
70 Elijah Boyed, 72d, Burke.
71 James S. Daniel, sol., 104th, Hancock.
72 Charles M'Common, Hood's, Henry.
73 Richard B. Rucker, Durham's, Talbot.
74 William Driskill, Dawson's, Jasper.
75 Moses Park, Walker's, Harris.
76 Cornelius Bradley, Jr., Curry's, Wilkinson.
77 Joseph W. Hopkins, Newsom's, Warren.
78 Benj. Bagley, mi., f. a., Sinquefield's, Washington.
79 Young Davis, 24th, M'Intosh.
80 Samuel Barrett, Moseley's, Coweta.
81 Roberson H. Turner, Kelly's, Jasper.
82 John Daniel's ors., 104th, Hancock.
83 John T. Ezzard, Hamilton's, Gwinnett.
84 S. D. Jenkins, s. l. w., Williams's, Washington.
85 Oliver Taylor, Maguire's, Gwinnett.
86 Mary Wheeler, w. r. s., White's, Franklin.
87 James Wilson, 2d section, Cherokee. *
88 Jacob Cleonkloy, Lamberth's, Fayette.

89 Josiah Hardy, M'Linn's, Butts.
90 Thomas Hick's ors., 588th, Upson.
91 Jacob B. Heldebrand, Foote's, De Kalb.
92 Duncan Locklear, Gittens's, Fayette.*
93 Archibald Moon, Riden's, Jackson.*
94 Henry Johnson's ors., Davis's, Jones.
95 Nancy Parker, w., Cook's, Telfair.
96 Burrell Murphy, Simmons's, Crawford.
97 Edward W. Pew, Roberts's, Hall.
98 Richard Smith's ors., Lester's, Monroe.
99 Samuel Dingler, or., Night's, Morgan.
100 James Rosseau's ors., 320th, Baldwin.
101 Nancy Duke, w., Night's, Morgan.
102 James Ford, Hatton's, Baker.
103 Benjamin Yarbrough's ors., Smith's, Wilkinson.*
104 Ferdinand Duke, Brackett's, Newton.
105 Robert Pate's ors., Carswell's, Jefferson.
106 Polly Cash, w., Johnson's, De Kalb.
107 Miranda Fort, Edwards's, Talbot.*
108 John Henricks, 27th, M'Intosh.*
109 Lawrence Kirk, Bustin's, Pike.*
110 John Franklin, Crawford's, Morgan.
111 Theophilus J. Hill, 419th, Walton.
112 Sampson Gibson, s. l. w., M'Clain's, Newton
113 Gustavus A. Parker, 120th, Richmond.*
114 John J. Kemp, Bivins's, Jones.
115 Milton A. Browder, Whipple's, Wilkinson.*
116 Seaton Winn, Graves's, Lincoln.
117 William Hodges, Sims's, Troup.*
118 David Howell, Martin's, Pike.
119 Valentine Etherington, Marshall's, Crawford.
120 William W. Perry, M'Ginnis's, Jackson.
121 Susannah Marshall, w., Tankersley's, Columbia.
122 Rowland Parham's ors., Ross's, Monroe.
123 Frances Barron, w. r. s., 589th, Upson.
124 William Stoker, Neal's, Campbell.
125 Martha Murphy, w. r. s., 177th, Wilkes.
126 Allen Finley, Tuggle's, Merriwether.
127 Abel Roberts, M'Millon's, Lincoln.
128 Sarah Smith, w., Howard's, Oglethorpe.
129 Alexander Lemon, Peurifoy's, Henry.
130 James Henson, Foote's, De Kalb.
131 Benjamin F. Porter, 4th section, Cherokee.
132 James Sanders, Whisenhunt's, Carroll.
133 John Patterson, Jr., Stewart's, Troup.
134 Willis W. M. Dowdy, Guice's, Oglethorpe.*
135 George White, Valleau's, Chatham.*

136 Miles Smith, s. l. w., Ware's, Coweta.
137 Isaac Waldrop, Compton's, Fayette.
138 William Holton, Barron's, Houston.*
139 Jonathan Pinian's ors., Blackstock's, Hall.
140 James Farmer's ors., 69th, Burke.
141 Washington Huff's or., 165th, Wilkes.
142 Alexander Hogan, Whisenhunt's, Carroll.
143 Joshua B. Harper, Hutson's, Newton.*
144 Eldridge B. Thomas, 559th, Walton.
145 William Meador, Lay's, De Kalb.
146 Joseph Grimsley, sol., 510th, Early.
147 William B. Parham, Harris's, Crawford.
148 Thomas B. Duncan, Liddell's, Jackson.
149 Elsey Rowell, w., 398th, Richmond.
150 Edward Bryan, Rainey's, Twiggs.*
151 William Conine, Evans's, Fayette.
152 John C. Durr, Wood's, Jefferson.
153 Daniel Horton, Everitt's, Washington.
154 William Yates, Griffin's, De Kalb.
155 William Williamson, s. l. w., Hobbs's, Laurens.*
156 John Willis's ors., Canning's, Elbert.
157 Thomas Landreth, s. l. w., Gorley's, Putnam.
158 William Liddell, Wynn's, Gwinnett.
159 Winney Huff, w. s. i. w., Green's, Oglethorpe.
160 John M. Ellington, Collier's, Monroe.
161 Morgan Gardner, 49th, Emanuel.*
162 Archibald G. Janes, 606th, Taliaferro.*
163 Parrey Hicks, Hood's, Henry.*
164 Barrington King, sol., 271st, M'Intosh.
165 Thomas Hall's ors., Hall's, Oglethorpe.
166 John Forshe, Everett's, Washington.
167 Richard H. Cocroft, 138th, Greene.
168 Solomon Harrell, s.l. w., Williams's, Washington.*
169 Thomas W. Bachelor, Miller's, Jackson.
170 Richard L. Powell, Dyer's, Habersham.
171 James K. Byers, Stephens's, Habersham.
172 Jeremiah Newman, Derrick's, Henry.
173 William Rieves, Dobbs's, Hall.
174 Benjamin Taylor, 293d, Jasper.*
175 Riley Durden, 320th, Baldwin.
176 William Cone, Everitt's, Washington.
177 Benjamin E. Mobley, Griffin's, Burke.
178 Elbert Herren's three orphans, Mobley's, De Kalb.
179 Wyett R. Singleton, Smith's, Henry.
180 James Russell, Jr., Peurifoy's, Henry.
181 James Rylee, Sen., r. s., Blackstock's, Hall.
182 Ann Elizabeth Rolls, w., 2d, Chatham.*

183 Daniel Clark, Walker's, Houston.*
184 Charles Howard, 537th, Upson.
185 Nancy Harper, h. a., Camp's, Warren.
186 Zachariah K. Wilson, Miller's, Jackson.
187 John A. Wynn, Wheeler's, Pulaski.
188 Solomon Cook, Lightfoot's, Washington.*
189 Hinchey Lary, Norris's, Monroe.
190 Benjamin Maddox's ors., 603d, Taliaferro.
191 Luke Johnston, Collins's, Henry.*
192 John Deavours, Seay's, Hall.
193 Abraham Mills, or., 516th, Dooly.*
194 Archibald Hill, Mitchell's, Marion.
195 Thomas W. Bellah, Waltzes's, Morgan.
196 John Westbrook, r. s., Mangum's, Franklin.
197 David S. Watts, 601st, Taliaferro.
198 John York's ors., Phillips's, Talbot.
199 Mary Jones, w., Jack's, Clarke.
200 Asa Thompson, 271st, M'Intosh.*
201 Paul Hagler, Woodruff's, Campbell.
202 Charles Crawford, Leveritt's, Lincoln.
203 Peterson Hubbard, Thompson's, Henry.
204 John Coleman, Roberts's, Hall.
205 Thomas P. Dailey, Chisholm's, Morgan.
206 Jane C. Watts, w., 693d, Heard.
207 John Hitchcock, sol., Smith's, Campbell.*
208 Hilliard J. Thompson, Talley's, Troup.*
209 William C. Wortham, Payne's, Merriwether.*
210 Alexander Craig, Hood's, Henry.
211 Thomas Cavenaugh, 2d, Chatham.*
212 John J. Barnes, Phillips's, Talbot.
213 Allen Wheeler, Waller's, Putnam.
214 James M'Mullen, Mimm's, Fayette.
215 Elisha Barber, Duke's, Carroll.*
216 Alexander Brown, Thomas's, Clarke.
217 Vincent F. Freeman, Young's, Jefferson.*
218 Francis Foster, m. s., 160th, Greene.
219 James Davis, Sen., s. l. w., Nichols's, Fayette.
220 Absala Ellis, w., Wright's, Tatnall.*
221 Cyrus Dobbs, Clinton's, Campbell.
222 Peter Tatum, sol., 574th, Early.*
223 James R. Hines, 362d, Jasper.
224 Joseph B. Battle, 111th, Hancock.
225 Mary Crawley, w., Smith's, Henry.*
226 Silas Phillips, 574th, Early.
227 Andrew Orr, Nesbit's, Newton.
228 William Robertson, Mizell's, Talbot.
229 John Caps, Atkinson's, Coweta.

230 Jesse C. Bouchelle, Athens, Clarke.*
231 Rebecca Allison, w., Moseley's, Wilkes.
232 Henry Smith, Bustin's, Pike.
233 Gilbert Faulkner, Talley's, Troup.
234 Eldridge Harris Cox, or., 510th, Early.
235 William C. White, Morton's, De Kalb.
236 Riley Griffin, Payne's, Merriwether.
237 Daniel Wooten, Blackstock's, Hall.
238 Jacob White, s. l. w., Mobley's, De Kalb.*
239 James Scott, r. s., Baker's, Liberty.
240 Jane Hatcher, w., Whipple's, Wilkinson.
241 Littleberry Broach's ors., Colley's, Madison.
242 Amos Huguly, 175th, Wilkes.
243 Fashaw Long, Smith's, Liberty.*
244 John M'Cord, s. l. w., Hall's, Butts.*
245 Jemima Lovejoy, w. r. s., Madden's, Pike.
246 William Mullins, Jr., Stanfield's, Campbell.*
247 John Morgan, Phillips's, Jasper.
248 Samuel Watts, 101st, Hancock.
249 William Downs, r. s., 10th, Effingham.*
250 Benjamin F. Parker, M'Culler's, Newton.*
251 Wallis Brown, r. s., Wilson's, Pike.*
252 Joshua Burroughs, Mobley's, De Kalb.*
253 Joshua Grace, sol., Crow's, Pike.
254 Mary Ann M'Dowell, w., 366th, Jasper.
255 Crawford Norton, Gittens's, Fayette.*
256 Willise Maynor, 72d, Burke.*
257 Benjamin G. Webb, Hardman's, Oglethorpe.
258 Peter A. P. Carre, 600th, Richmond.
259 Leacy Hardy, w., Salem, Baldwin.*
260 Thomas B. Wilson, Foote's, De Kalb.*
261 Jane M'Minn, w. r. s., Stephens's, Habersham.
262 Philemon Forster, Givins's, De Kalb.
263 John Norman, Jr., Hinton's, Wilkes.
264 Ulysses Lewis, Few's, Muscogee.*
265 Charles Jordan, Young's, Jefferson.
266 Elizabeth Holland, w., Murphy's, Columbia.
267 Moses W. Young (by mother), Wood's, Morgan.
268 David Felts, Grier's, Warren.
269 James Jones, Barron's, Houston.
270 Elbert Brown, Thomason's, Elbert.
271 George Bradshaw, Wolfskin's, Oglethorpe.*
272 James Coley, Coxe's, Talbot.
273 James Jamison, sol., Barnett's, Lowndes.
274 Thomas Beavers's ors., Phillips's, Jasper.
275 Jonathan Hart's ors., Peacock's, Washington.
276 James Comer, Sen., r. s., Comer's, Jones.

277 William Wells (Ft. Perry), Watson's, Marion.*
278 Michael O'Barr, Sen., Griffin's, Hall.
279 Elizabeth C. West, w., 120th, Richmond.
280 William Tedder, Dobbs's, Hall.
281 John Conner, M'Euin's, Monroe.*
282 Thomas Fambrough's ors., 147th, Greene.*
283 Owen Owens, Brock's, Habersham.
284 Washington Jones, Hart's, Jones.
285 John Mass's ors., Benson's, Lincoln.
286 Thomas A. Hay, Fulk's, Wilkes.*
287 Elizabeth Smith, w., Seay's, Hall.
288 Guy W. Smith, Peurifoy's, Henry.*
289 John Speakman's ors., Cleland's, Chatham.
290 Thomas Dickson's ors., Johnson's, Bibb.
291 James M. Daniel, Hill's, Monroe.
292 Susan Parker, blind, Camp's, Warren.*
293 Henry Stokes, Peurifoy's, Henry.*
294 Mortimore R. Wallis, Candler's, Bibb.
295 Simeon W. Stallings, 494th, Upson.
296 David B. Squires, Flynn's, Muscogee.
297 John K. Stell, Wynn's, Gwinnett.
298 Stephen O. Quinn, Hand's, Appling.
299 William Arnold, Bridges's, Gwinnett.
300 John Dunn, r. s., Lamberth's, Fayette.
301 Robert Jeter, Perryman's, Warren.*
302 Agnes K. Scott, w., Alexander's, Jefferson.
303 George Stewart O'Dorherty, or., Say's, De Kalb.
304 John Wofford, Brown's, Habersham.
305 Edward Sharr, Orr's, Jackson.
306 Lewis Smith, Mason's, Washington.*
307 John Floyd, Jr., 510th, Early.
308 Robert M. Radney, 116th, Hancock.
309 Thomas C. Horton, Collier's, Monroe.
310 James Poage, Davis's, Clarke.*
311 Stern Moreman, 177th, Wilkes.
312 John James Almonds, Roe's, Burke.
313 A. H. Stephens, Athens, Clarke.
314 John C. Griffin, Parham's, Warren.
315 P. A. J. D. Vanlandingham, or., Grice's, Oglethorpe
316 William Heard, Robinson's, Harris.
317 Williamson M. Bracewell, Mullen's, Carroll.
318 James Harrell's ors., Bridges's, Gwinnett.
319 George Allen, 602d, Taliaferro.
320 James T. Simmons, Bradley's, Jones.*
321 Samuel Carter, Coward's, Lowndes.
322 John M. Bond, 2d section, Cherokee.
323 Seth Hunter, sol., Coxe's, Talbot.*
324 Henry Wolf, Gillis's, De Kalb.

1 Riley Allen, Martin's, Newton.
2 Henry Brewer, sol., Brewer's, Monroe.
3 William H. Wood, Curry's, Merriwether.
4 Alexander Herrington, 37th, Scriven.*
5 Henry Long, 114th, Hancock.*
6 Colin A. Hall, Dixon's, Irwin.
7 John M. Copeland, Carswell's, Jefferson.*
8 Thomas Pinchard's ors., 466th, Monroe.*
9 James Wheeler, Sen., Lay's, Jackson.*
10 James Hadaway, 293d, Jasper.
11 Robert Houston, Tower's, Gwinnett.*
12 Samuel May, Adams's, Columbia.
13 John Norris, Miller's, Jackson.
14 James M. Howze, 761st, Heard.
15 John Lamb, Groce's, Bibb.
16 Gregory Singleton, Gorley's, Putnam.
17 Ananias M'Dugal, Griffin's, Merriwether.*
18 John Stewart, Valleau's, Chatham.*
19 John Hedgecock's ors., Vining's, Putnam.
20 Churchwell's seven orphans, 124th, Richmond.
21 Sampson Gibbs, Stone's, Irwin.
22 Felix D. Woodyard, 279th, Morgan.
23 Wellborn Davis, Graves's, Lincoln.
24 Smith Crandall, Miller's, Jackson.
25 Wiley E. Wood, Whelchel's, Hall.*
26 William M. Penn, Hodges's, Newton.*
27 John S. Raiford, sol., 57th, Emanuel.
28 Jeremiah Baker, Morris's, Crawford.
29 James G. Dobbs, 1st section, Cherokee.
30 Samuel Loggins, Jr., Hamilton's, Hall.
31 John Thomas, r. s., Stewart's, Troup.
32 Isaac Evans, Covington's, Pike.*
33 Thomas Howard, sol., Jordan's, Bibb.
34 Daniel Goodman, Whitaker's, Crawford.*
35 Margaret Welbourn, w., Derick's, Henry.*
36 Robert H. Woolfolk, Grubbs's, Columbia.*
37 John Blackburn, 177th, Wilkes.*
38 Robert Douglass, Culbreath's, Columbia.*
39 Rutha Stewart, w., Bush's, Burke.*
40 Henry B. Rhodes, Streetman's, Twiggs.
41 Solomon W. Otwell, Barker's, Gwinnett.

42 John Pickens, Say's, De Kalb.
43 John Stephens, Curry's, Wilkinson.
44 Isaac Ramsay, Grubbs's, Columbia.
45 Moriah Payton, w., Morgan's, Madison.*
46 Moses Heath, sol., Griffin's, Burke.
47 Martin K. Calloway, 373d, Jasper.
48 William Bryant, 687th, Sumter.*
49 James N. Putnam, Kendrick's, Monroe.*
50 Lewis Ivey, Buck's, Houston.
51 James Perry, Herndon's, Carroll.
52 Andrew H. Beall, 295th, Jasper.
53 Willis J. Smith, Swiney's, Laurens.*
54 Andrew Robertson, Sutton's, Habersham.*
55 Jesse M'Murran, Nesbit's, Newton.*
56 John Easco, Colley's, Oglethorpe.*
57 P. Whittemore's four orphans, Brown's, Camden.
58 William Worley, mi., Hughes's, Habersham.*
59 Samuel Crow's ors., 470th, Upson.
60 Mary Ward, w., Deavour's, Habersham.*
61 Raba Roundtree, Compton's, Fayette.
62 Thomas Brooks, 142d, Greene.
63 Isaac A. Haiston, Griffin's, Fayette.
64 Sarah Simmons, w. r. s., 555th, Upson.
65 Anny Kilcrease, w., Hearn's, Butts.
66 Joel B. Mabry, Hampton's, Newton.
67 Thomas Lovelady, M'Clure's, Rabun.
68 Abel A. Tumblin, Harris's, De Kalb.*
69 Joseph Parmer, id., 510th, Early.*
70 Thomas Hudman, Mizell's, Talbot.*
71 Robert Harris's ors., a sol., 174th, Wilkes.
72 Vines H. Owens, House's, Henry.
73 Ann E. Wilson, w., 7th, Chatham.
74 Etheldred Silas, Pate's, Warren.
75 David R. Barlow, Perry's, Habersham.*
76 Martha Braziel, w., 245th, Jackson.*
77 Isaac Lamb, sen., 494th, Upson.
78 John W. Scott, Vining's, Putnam.*
79 Elizabeth Cobb, w., Tower's, Gwinnett.
80 William Morris, Covington's, Pike.
81 John M'Bryde, Jr., 398th, Richmond.
82 Henry Campbell, Tower's, Gwinnett.
83 John R. Moore, Wells's, Twiggs.
84 Matthew H. Heath, Parham's, Warren.
85 Joseph Turner, Thompson's, Henry.
86 Gabnel Morgan, Smith's, Liberty.*
87 Elias Thomas, Harrison's, Decatur.
88 Edmund Hancock, Blount's, Wilkinson.

89 Dawson B. Lane, Lane's, Morgan.
90 Leonard Wills, Chambers's, Gwinnett.*
91 Zacheus Exley, 11th, Effingham.*
92 Timothy Robey's ors., Phillips's, Jasper.
93 Thomas Barnett, Seay's, Hall.
94 Elijah Ragsdale, Hutson's, Newton.
95 Zadock Jackson, of Wilkes, Stokes's, Lincoln.
96 William Saye, s. d., Seay's, Hall.
97 Giles Webb's ors., Mason's, Washington.
98 Joseph Lyndsey, Harralson's, Troup.*
99 Frederic Huntington, Cleland's, Chatham.*
100 William Brown, s. i. w., Thomason's, Elbert.*
101 Samuel H. Beman, 138th, Greene.
102 John W. Watson, Royster's, Franklin.*
103 Jonathan Tate, Hughes's, Habersham.*
104 Wesley Bacchus, Johnson's, De Kalb.*
105 Joseph Osborn, Cleland's, Chatham.
106 Needham Parker, 633d, Dooly.*
107 Brice M'Ever, Cleghorn's, Madison.
108 William Barley, Butts's, Monroe.*
109 Benjamin T. Russell, Grider's, Morgan.
110 Lucy Crawford, w., Taylor's, Elbert.
111 Solomon Walker, 123d, Richmond.
112 Lewis J. Ramsey, Iverson's, Houston.*
113 Elizabeth Hennan, w., Jordan's, Harris.
114 Matilda A. Harden, w. s. l. w., 20th, Bryan.
115 Samuel Sturges's ors., Roe's, Burke.
116 Andrew M'Cullers, Stewart's, Troup.*
117 Margarett M'Daniel, h. a., Killen's, Decatur.
118 Joseph Henry's ors., 106th, Hancock.
119 John Taylor's minors, f. a., Sparks's, Washington.
120 William H. Howard, 122d, Richmond.*
121 Francis Miras's ors., 3d, Chatham.
122 Mary Keepers, w., Gray's, Henry.
123 Elizabeth Lowery, w., Jones's, Thomas.
124 Henry Culpepper's ors., Martin's, Laurens.
125 John Gammill, Alsobrook's, Jones.
126 Edmund Collins, r. s., Ross's, Monroe.*
127 James M'Cleland, sol., 142d, Greene.
128 Seaborn Bradford, Blair's, Lowndes.
129 James Vann, Mason's, Washington.*
130 Pearce Ogletree, Griffin's, Fayette.
131 John Bankley, s. l. w., 588th, Upson.
132 Matthew Hall, Buck-branch, Clarke.
133 David A. Barmoill, Burgess's, Carroll.*
134 Thomas Heery, 3d, Chatham.*
135 Samuel Tranum, Allen's, Campbell.

136 Andrew Flowers, Griffin's, De Kalb.*
137 Doctor Bird, 177th, Wilkes.*
138 Henry Darnell, s. i. w., 320th, Baldwin.
139 John L. Cope, Sanderlin's, Chatham.*
140 Presley Jones, Hampton's, Newton.
141 Samuel Tallant, Baley's, Butts.
142 James B. Norris, 7th, Chatham.*
143 Thomas Perdue, s. l. w., Graves's, Putnam.
144 James Waters, Sen., Price's, Hall.
145 Archibald Robertson, Burgess's, Carroll.*
146 Payton Partridge, Williams's, Washington.
147 John A. Farrar, Loven's, Henry.
148 Claborn Vaughn, Loveless's, Gwinnett.
149 Sarah Commins, w. r. s., 143d, Greene.*
150 James Spires, Marshall's, Crawford.
151 Lucinda & Henry Miller, ors., Green's, Oglethorpe
152 Lewis Wilhite, r. s., Wilhite's, Elbert.
153 William K. Osburn, Gittens's, Fayette.*
154 Wiley Phillips, Edwards's, Franklin.
155 Jesse Land, of Twiggs, Groce's, Bibb.
156 William Q. Anderson, Anderson's, Wilkes.
157 James H. Duke, Harralson's, Troup.
158 Jubal E. Waters, sol., Curry's, Merriwether.*
159 Margaret Crew, w., Sapp's, Muscogee.
160 James Armstrong, Hobbs's, Laurens.
161 Ann Densler, w., Valleau's, Chatham.
162 Mitchell C. Wallis, 417th, Walton.*
163 James W. Seals, Stewart's, Warren.
164 Richard Yarbrough, Harris's, Crawford.
165 Theophilus Hill, Barwick's, Washington.
166 Oliver Crawford, Smith's, Elbert.*
167 Seaborn Cowart, 49th, Emanuel.
168 Dawson Heath, Dearing's, Butts.*
169 William Snellgrove, Rutland's, Bibb.
170 John Baker, Cleland's, Chatham.*
171 John R. Greene, Johnson's, Jasper.
172 Kinchen Carr, Hughes's, Habersham.
173 George Slaten, Hughes's, Habersham.
174 Thomas S. P. Jones, Bell's, Columbia.*
175 Reuben Stapleton, 3d section, Cherokee.
176 Thomas Childress, Sen., Alberson's, Walton.
177 William Powell, id., Wright's, Tatnall.
178 Robert Jackson, Whipple's, Wilkinson.*
179 Owen Cook, Jones's, Thomas.
180 Anthony Metcalf's ors., 608th, Taliaferro.
181 James D. Jeffers, or., Peterson's, Burke.*
182 Elder's seven orphans, Robinson's, Fayette.

183 Joshua Barnes, Thames, Crawford.*
184 George Y. Lowe, Groce's, Bibb.
185 George Powell, 588th, Upson.*
186 Samuel Wilson, Mashburn's, Pulaski.*
187 James M. Crow, Barker's, Gwinnett.
188 Thomas Maddox, Hatton's, Baker.
189 Anderson Sturdevant, 454th, Walton.
190 Nancy Lewis, w. r. s., Hines's, Coweta.*
191 Beverly Justice, Burk's, Stewart.
192 Hugh Crooks, Price's, Hall.
193 David Proctor, sol., Phillips's, Monroe.
194 Middleton Brawner, Canning's, Elbert.
195 Pierce B. Pendergrast, Cleland's, Chatham
196 Ephraim S. Hopping, 168th, Wilkes.
197 John Murray, sol., Dearing's, Henry.*
198 Eli Bradley, sol., Baker's, Liberty.*
199 Nathaniel J. Patterson, Ogden's, Camden.*
200 John Westbrook, Allen's, Henry.
201 Thomas Johnston's ors., Hodges's, Newton.
202 James Alford, Gittens's, Fayette.
203 Catharine Meredith, w., Blount's, Wilkinson.
204 Allen Craige, 600th, Richmond.*
205 Elisha Harwell, Curry's, Merriwether.
206 William H. Huff, Tompkins's, Putnam.
207 Jordan R. Smith, Whitfield's, Washington.
208 Matthew Turner, 27th, Glynn.*
209 Thomas Guest's ors., 604th, Taliaferro.
210 Buckner Griffin, s. l. w., 559th, Walton.
211 Robert Hill, sol., 672d, Harris.*
212 Levi Wilkinson, Garner's, Coweta.
213 Aurelius Franklin, Athens, Clarke.
214 John J. Glover, Wilson's, Jasper.
215 Ezechael Daniel, s. l. w., Wood's, Morgan.
216 Leroy K. Crawford, Taylor's, Elbert.
217 M. A. & Julia Stephens, ors., Dilman's, Pulaski.
218 John Harris's ors., Wolfskin's, Oglethorpe.
219 Obediah Copeland, 162d, Greene.
220 Thomas H. Lary, Ball's, Monroe.
221 James B. Morris, Foote's, De Kalb.
222 Benjamin G. M'Cleskey, Daniel's, Hall.
223 Jane Streetman, w., Streetman's, Twiggs.
224 James Modesett, Bivins's, Jones.
225 Uriah Maxwell, Bostick's, Twiggs.
226 Hugh Brown, Deavours's, Habersham.
227 John Snider, Wooten's, Telfair.*
228 William Worthy, Jr., Rhodes's, De Kalb.
229 Sugars Bynam, r. s., Chambers's, Houston.*

230 Benjamin Pope, Ellsworth's, Bibb.
231 William Donaldson, 2d, Chatham.
232 Sarah Cheshire, w. r. s., Brewer's, Monroe.
233 James Bryan, 162d, Greene.
234 Archibald Perkins's ors., Night's, Morgan.
235 Joseph J. Dean, 279th, Morgan.
236 James Sapp, Hicks's, Decatur.
237 Wiley Clark, Chandler's, Franklin.
238 John Smith, Chambers's, Gwinnett.
239 William White's ors., Collier's, Monroe.
240 James Higginbotham, 334th, Wayne.*
241 Reddick Arrant, 561st, Upson.*
242 Aaron White, 373d, Jasper.
243 Louis N. Falligant, Sanderlin's, Chatham.
244 Matthew Jackson, Chiles's, Marion.*
245 Celia Austin, h. a., 1st section, Cherokee.*
246 Daniel Lynch, 2d, Chatham.*
247 Griffin Smith, Walker's, Harris.
248 Henry V. Vanbibber, Wilson's, Pike.*
249 Obadiah Adams, Rainey's, Twiggs.
250 Benjamin Tidwell, Hines's, Coweta.
251 James F. Shepperd, Blount's, Wilkinson.*
252 William Donaldson, Henson's, Rabun.
253 Garland Jenks's ors., Woodruff's, Campbell.
254 Michael H. Rudulph, sol., Hobkerk's, Camden.*
255 Isaac Horton, r. s., Barker's, Gwinnett.*
256 George W. Culpepper, Adams's, Columbia.
257 Thomas Pace's ors., 120th, Richmond.
258 George G. Tankersley, Huchinson's, Columbia.
259 Jain Joiner, w., Walker's, Houston.*
260 Ulysses Crutchfield, Dilman's, Pulaski.
261 Edwin T. Mitchell, Edwards's, Talbot,
262 Amos Bullard, 120th, Richmond.
263 Alexander Smith, Payne's, Merriwether.
264 James Crow, 1st section, Cherokee.*
265 William Hamby Smith, Mullen's, Carroll.*
266 Patrick Smith, 248th, Jackson.
267 James Cotney, 672d, Harris.*
268 Thomas Cureton's ors., Hampton's, Newton.
269 Thomas Bachellor's ors., 374th, Putnam.*
270 Kenneth M'Lennan, Morrison's, Montgomery.
271 Richard M. Park's ors., Dyer's, Habersham.
272 Brittain S. Osburn, Allen's, Henry.
273 Harrison M'Coy, or., Trout's, Hall.
274 George C. Dunham, s. l. w., Ogden's, Camden.*
275 Mary Rooks, w., 335th, Wayne.
276 Edward A. Denney, sol., Nellum's, Elbert.

277 David H. Wood, Pound's, Twiggs.*
278 James Bradshaw, Mashburn's, Pulaski.*
279 Kirby Goolsby, 362d, Jasper.
280 Solomon Barnes, Chastain's, Habersham.
281 Jeremiah Miller, Braddey's, Jones.
282 Robert Lightfoot, Williams's, Washington.*
283 Bennett Youngblood, Lamberth's, Fayette.
284 James R. Kenny, Wynn's, Gwinnett.
285 Ambrose Brown, Sen., Jones's, Habersham.
286 Merrada Mobley, Hardman's, Oglethorpe.
287 Anderson Hicks, Mullen's, Carroll.*
288 Jefferson Smith, 249th, Walton.
289 Richard Jones, 167th, Wilkes.
290 Ely H. Brinkley, Camp's, Warren.
291 John Conn, Hamilton's, Hall.
292 Joseph Prince, Walker's, Columbia.
293 Joseph C. Harris, 112th, Hancock.
294 William Meneeley, Curry's, Merriwether.
295 James L. Manning, Candler's, Bibb.*
296 Jane E. Wells's ors., Lamp's, Jefferson.
297 Hugh Gren, Hearn's, Butts.
298 Jane M'Gaha, w., 373d, Jasper.
299 Samuel Johnson, sol., Howell's, Troup.
300 Jesse Horn, Hamilton's, Gwinnett.
301 William Payne's ors., Bailey's, Butts.
302 Burgess Jester, Allen's, Henry.*
303 Francis Bates, Smith's, Habersham.
304 Richard Anderson, Givins's, De Kalb.
305 James H. Bellew, Royster's, Franklin.
306 Archibald Shelley, Walker's, Houston.*
307 Milner Echols, s. i. w., Park's, Walton.
308 Elijah Sisk, Dyer's, Habersham.*
309 David Mann's ors., Smith's, Wilkinson.
310 Henry Cammel's ors., Higginbotham's, Rabun.
311 Sarah Felt, w., Mizell's, Talbot.*
312 Wiley Tison, M'Cleland's, Irwin.*
313 Joel King, s. l. w., Williams's, Washington.
314 Zachariah Thompson, Allison's, Pike.
315 Elias Davis, Seay's, Hall.
316 George G. Smith, Newsom's, Warren.
317 Matthew Merit, Dixon's, Irwin.*
318 Zachariah White, r. s., 10th, Effingham.*
319 John Allen, Clark's, Morgan.
320 John R. Stanford, Perryman's, Warren.*
321 Thomas Bell's ors., Hart's, Jones.
322 John Turner, 734th, Lee.*
323 Aseania Twitty, w., Lay's, Jackson.*
324 Calvin Hagan's ors., Hand's, Appling.

1 James Wood, Sen., Mayo's, Wilkinson.*
2 Aug. & Nancy Richardson, ors., Britt's, Randolph.
3 Archibald Nicholson, Hill's, Stewart.*
4 James Lawson's ors., Smith's, Wilkinson.
5 John Phillips, Hodges's, Newton.
6 Henry Varnadore, r. s., 535th, Dooly.*
7 Hardy Johnson, sol., 55th, Emanuel.
8 Virginia M. F. Dousset, w., Valleau's, Chatham.
9 Carter Allen, Stephens's, Habersham.
10 Brooks Sparks, Shattoxe's, Coweta.
11 Selah Culpepper, Show's, Muscogee.
12 Jenkins's six orphans, 404th, Gwinnett.
13 James Kiren, Hitchcock's, Muscogee.*
14 Major E. Robbins, Newsom's, Warren.*
15 James Shearn, Pounds's, Twiggs.
16 Andrew Edwards's ors., Groce's, Bibb.
17 Henry Holcombe, sol., 2d section, Cherokee.
18 James Whittle, Morris's, Crawford.*
19 Benjamin D. Pittman, Moore's, Randolph.
20 Lard Burnes's ors., Wynn's, Gwinnett.
21 Margaret Chancey, w., Sinclair's, Houston
22 Mary Camp, 243d, Jackson.
23 Isaac Screws, 430th, Early.
24 Richard Garner, 249th, Walton.
25 John Collatt's ors., Allen's, Henry.
26 Mary Jones, or., 430th, Early.
27 Mary Buchannan, w. r. s., Wilson's, Jasper.
28 Henry Rape, Sen., Hood's, Henry.
29 John Rogers, Gunn's, Henry.
30 Archibald Warren's ors., 161st, Greene.
31 James M'Millon, M'Millon's, Lincoln.
32 James Leggett, Candler's, Bibb.
33 Peter Hutson, Nesbit's, Newton.*
34 David Bray, Bower's, Elbert.*
35 Owen Reed, Merck's, Hall.
36 Riley Tidwell, Calhoun's, Harris.*
37 James P. M. Murray, Jenkins's, Oglethorpe.*
38 Sarah M. Garrison, or., 406th, Gwinnett.*
39 William Tyson, Perryman's, Warren.
40 James Arnold, Ware's, Coweta.
41 Lewis Price, Smith's, Liberty.*

42 John M. C. Smith, Mullen's, Carroll.
43 Joab W. E. Horn, Chambers's, Houston.
44 John M'Cormack's or., 607th, Taliaferro.
45 Thomas Banks, Herndon's, Hall.
46 Balaam Clayton, Smith's, Habersham.
47 Lewis Knight, Sinquefield's, Washington.
48 Joseph Power, Rhodes's, De Kalb.
49 James Reynolds, Bryant's, Burke.*
50 Joseph Kersey, Peterson's, Burke.*
51 James Kinan, Bryan's, Pulaski.
52 Almond Duckworth, 117th, Hancock.*
53 John W. Gray, Miller's, Camden.
54 William Russell, 7th Peurifoy's, Henry.
55 John G. Bassett, Ellsworth's, Bibb.
56 Green B. Williams, 512th, Lee.*
57 Thomas H. Griffies, Seay's, Hall.*
58 Charles Jordan, Jr., 561st, Upson.
59 Nathaniel H. Collier, Howard's, Oglethorpe.
60 Elizabeth M. Whitehead, w., Roe's, Burke.
61 Isaac M. Adderhold, Royster's, Franklin.
62 Elijah Mixon, Hargrove's, Newton.
63 James Harviston, Newman's, Thomas.
64 Judith Sanford, w., 138th, Greene.
65 Benjamin Harrison, sol., Royster's, Franklin.
66 Thomas S. Tondee, 7th, Chatham.*
67 Blanset Sutton, w., M'Craney's, Lowndes.
68 James Farmer, sol., 69th, Burke.
69 Berry Wells, Smith's, Houston.
70 John Finley, 735th, Troup.
71 William Perry, Streetman's, Twiggs.
72 Eliza Bennett, w., 20th, Bryan.
73 Michael M. Channell, 307th, Putnam.*
74 George W. Wright's ors., Williams's, Jasper.
75 William Meeler, Welche's, Habersham.*
76 John Whitesides, Winter's, Jones.
77 Thomas R. Johnson, Orr's, Jackson.*
78 Temperance Cliborn, w., 720th, Decatur.
79 Robert Davis, Smith's, Henry.*
80 Sarah Christmas, w., Walker's, Houston.*
81 William S. Maddux, Hill's, Monroe.*
82 Stephen Copeland, Rhodes's, De Kalb.
83 Joseph Benton, Garner's, Coweta.
84 Jonathan Lea, sol., Jennings's, Clarke.
85 John H. Gray, Killen's, Decatur.
86 Daniel Phillips, Sanderlin's, Chatham.
87 John Hitchcock, 37th, Scriven.
88 Sally Rhodes, w., Downs's, Warren.

89 Robert A. Hardwick, Sinquefield's, Washington.
90 Jacob C. Butts, Grider's, Morgan.
91 Mark Sims, Allison's, Pike.*
92 Richmond L. Cegraves, Davis's, Gwinnett.
93 Jackson Grizzard, Camp's, Warren.
94 William Hawkins, Martin's, Jones.
95 Lazarus B. Anderson, 318th, Baldwin.
96 Hannah Christie, w., 11th, Effingham.
97 Fleming Pointer, Davis's, Clarke.*
98 Robt. Thompson, Sen., sol., Tuggle's, Merriwether
99 Hugh Boothe, George's, Appling.*
100 Maston Roland, Bowers's, Elbert.
101 W. A. David, of Cherokee, Latimer's, De Kalb.*
102 Peter J. Harris, 588th, Upson.
103 George Cotton, Sen., r. s., Lynn's, Warren.
104 Charles Haynie, s. i. w., Colley's, Oglethorpe.
105 John Whitlow, Morgan's, Clarke.
106 Mary Marcom, w., Bailey's, Camden.
107 William R. M'Gruder, r. s., 119th, Richmond.
108 Samuel Harper, or., Moseley's, Coweta.
109 Sarah Tatum, w., Brooks's, Muscogee.
110 Enoch J. Moore, Reid's, Gwinnett.
111 Hyram Mercer, Young's, Wilkinson.
112 James F. Buckelew, Derrick's, Henry.
113 John W. Hughes, Hughes's, Habersham.
114 Solomon M. Laney, Colquhoun's, Henry.
115 Isaiah Savell, Baugh's, Jackson.*
116 Benjamin Yarbrough, blind, Douglass's, Telfair.*
117 James R. Lane, Taylor's, Putnam.*
118 Nathan W. Haines, Sinquefield's, Washington.
119 James Dickeson, Liddell's, Jackson.*
120 James G. Hall, Ball's, Monroe.*
121 Thomas Lee, M'Millon's, Lincoln.*
122 Vines Daily, Mason's, Washington.*
123 Robert Jackson's ors., Lane's, Morgan.
124 Jared Tomlinson, Rainey's, Twiggs.
125 Oliver Hancock, Laurence's, Pike.
126 Hillery Allegood, Jr., Evans's, Laurens.
127 Angless Scarborough, w., Oliver's, Twiggs.
128 John S. Allen, 123d, Richmond.*
129 John R. Tucker, Dupree's, Washington.*
130 Daniel M. Luke, Stone's, Irwin.*
131 Mary A. Bostick, w., Ellis's, Pulaski.
132 Swan H. Skelton, Stower's, Elbert.*
133 David Smith, r. s., Bush's, Burke.
134 Hezekiah Wood, Dilman's, Pulaski.*
135 Ransom Griffin, Mobley's, De Kalb.*

136 William Hughes, Herndon's, Hall.
137 Cain Evans, Price's, Hall.*
138 Ann Studdard, w., Cleggs's, Walton.
139 James M. Potts, Riden's, Jackson.
140 John Varner, sol., Stanfield's, Campbell.*
141 Jesse Kitley, 779th, Heard.*
142 John Miars's ors., Hill's, Monroe.
143 Rhody Harris, w., Compton's, Fayette.*
144 Jonathan Lewelling, 250th, Walton.
145 James Denmer, r. s., Welche's, Habersham.
146 James M'Leod, Burnett's, Lowndes.
147 Malachi W. Davis, Barron's, Houston.*
148 James B. Morgan, Jr., Ross's, Monroe.
149 Absalom T. Davis, Herndon's, Hall.
150 Charles Sanford, Lester's, Monroe.*
151 Wyatt R. Parks, Rainey's, Twiggs.
152 Mordecai Sheftall, Sen., sol., 2d, Chatham.*
153 Thomas J. Rivers, Newsom's, Warren.
154 Elias Dilda, Ellis's, Rabun.
155 Aaron Wooten, Griffin's, Hall.
156 Joel Coffee, Sen., Coffee's, Rabun.
157 Thomas Simpson, Jordan's, Bibb.*
158 James M'Korkle, 574th, Early.
159 Charles Kn'oles, Gittens's, Fayette.
160 Ann Beals, w., 2d, Chatham.
161 Philip L. Albriton, Hendon's, Carroll.
162 William Walker's ors., Martin's, Stewart.
163 George Freeland, Sanderlin's, Chatham.
164 Roden Tant, 120th, Richmond.
165 Adolphus Sabal, 120th, Richmond.*
166 John Jones, Say's, De Kalb.
167 Henry Ball, miller, 510th, Early.
168 Buford Bird, s. l. w., 604th, Taliaferro.*
169 Richard Sisson, Smith's, Habersham.
170 David N. Buckhalter, Watson's, Marion.
171 Joseph P. Hackney, sol., Pollard's, Wilkes.
172 John Moore's ors., Sen., Campbell's, Wilkes.
173 Daniel Reed, 2d section, Cherokee.*
174 William Taylor, Mitchell's, Marion.*
175 William Haslett, Griffin's, De Kalb.
176 Joshua Smith, Sen., r. s., Dobbs's, Hall.
177 John Gregory, Marsh's, Thomas.
178 Charles B. Jordan, sol., Crow's, Merriwether.
179 James Lambert, Gibson's, Decatur.
180 John Christian, Frasier's, Monroe.
181 Elizabeth Mathews, w. r. s., Gunn's, Jefferson.
182 Bennett Tuck, Buck-branch, Clarke.

183 William Sallett, 22d, M'Intosh.*
184 John Hawkins, Underwood's, Putnam.
185 Mary Massey, w., Chandler's, Gwinnett.
186 Solomon Bridges, 466th, Monroe.*
187 William Johnson, Bishop's, Henry.
188 John Starkey Wilson, Ellsworth's, Bibb.
189 James P. Ellis, 466th, Monroe.
190 Marshall Covington, Covington's, Pike.
191 Wyley Parish, Harrison's, Decatur.
192 Lewis Smith, Mason's, Washington.*
193 Hilary H. Argo, Givins's, De Kalb.
194 Zachariah Jewell, sol., 56th, Emanuel.*
195 John Garrett, or., Wood's, Morgan.
196 Sarah Davis w., Gunn's, Jefferson.
197 John B. Maloney, Wynn's, Gwinnett.*
198 William Veal, Jr., Say's, De Kalb.
199 John Flowers, Groce's, Bibb.
200 Marion Cape, Coxe's, Franklin.
201 John Oliver, Dupree's, Washington.*
202 Sarah Riley, w., Watson's, Marion.
203 Jacob Bateman's ors., 600th, Richmond.
204 Augustus H. Palmer, 419th, Walton.
205 Elizabeth Keen, w. r. s., Blackshears's, Laurens.
206 Benjamin F. Shumate, Cher., Latimer's, De Kalb.
207 Henry Wilson, Marshall's, Crawford.
208 William M'Glawn, Thaxton's, Butts.
209 William H. Tisdell, 69th, Burke.*
210 Joseph M'Kinney, Sen., sol., Rutland's, Bibb.
211 Celia Morris, w. r. s., Sims's, Troup.
212 William Griffin, Killen's, Decatur.*
213 Samuel Owens, Mashburn's Pulaski.*
214 Joseph W. Hardy, 242d, Jackson.
215 James Holzendorf, Hall's, Camden.
216 John Houston, 672d, Harris.*
217 Riley Burnett, Burgess's, Carroll.*
218 Young Vickers, Hanner's, Campbell.
219 James Wright, Hendon's, Carroll.
220 William Hornsby, 271st, M'Intosh.*
221 Dillard Burgess, 585th, Dooly.*
222 Warren Taylor, Grier's, Warren.*
223 Samuel R. Weems, Dearing's, Henry.*
224 Richmond Howell, Hatton's, Baker.*
225 Bailey Pippin, 470th, Upson.
226 William B. Stallings, Lane's, Morgan.
227 English Pepper, Kendrick's, Monroe.
228 William M. C. Jepson, Flynn's, Muscogee.
229 William Hood, Stephens's, Habersham.

230 William Waters, 1st, Chatham.*
231 John M'Vay, s. l. w., 535th, Dooly.
232 Ashley Nelson, Lane's, Morgan.
233 Andrew Truluck, Marsh's, Thomas.
234 John H. Dent, Stanfield's, Campbell.
235 Reuben Jordan, Deavours's, Habersham.
236 George W. Clack, 249th, Walton.
237 George B. M'Collum, Wheeler's, Pulaski.
238 Jacob Stanley, Robinson's, Fayette.
239 William E. Dubose, M'Dowell's, Lincoln.*
240 Ann Fretwell, w., Crow's, Pike.
241 Cornelius Gibbs, Jr., Henson's, Rabun.*
242 James C. Sullivan, Parham's, Harris.*
243 Amy Brumbelow, w., Phillips's, Monroe.
244 John Bleach, Newman's, Thomas.
245 Dempsey Simmons's ors., Candler's, Bibb.
246 Larkin C. Dempsey, 406th, Gwinnett.
247 Ashur Jackson, Watson's, Marion.*
248 Howell Sasser, 80th, Scriven.
249 Elbert Barnton, Hampton's, Newton.
250 Absalom Bidell, 672d, Harris.*
251 Rebecca Hewell, w., 168th, Wilkes.*
252 John S. Perkins, 75th, Burke.
253 Chaney Wooten, Tilley's, Rabun.
254 Robert Birdsong, Candler's, Bibb.
255 Sampson Massey's or., Williams's, Washington.
256 David W. Culpepper, Martin's, Laurens.
257 Enoch Groover, Peavy's, Bulloch.*
258 Simeon M'Clendon, Britt's, Randolph.*
259 John M. Holladay, Hart's, Jones.
260 Shepherd G. Lane, Kelly's, Jasper.
261 Zachariah Harlin's ors., Derrick's, Henry.*
262 Hezekiah W. Pharr, Miller's, Jackson.
263 William J. Pullen, 141st, Greene.*
264 James Love, 293d, Jasper.*
265 Underhill H. More, Whitfield's, Washington.
266 John Wise's ors., Barwick's, Washington.
267 Robert D. Moon, Howard's, Oglethorpe.*
268 Nimrod E. Ducker, Smith's, Houston.*
269 David D. Foldes, 362d, Jasper.*
270 Duncan Lockbar, Gittens's, Fayette.*
271 Martin Palmer, 27th, Glynn.*
272 Benjamin Gachett's ors., Covington's, Pike.
273 John Harkins, Dyer's, Habersham.*
274 Hiram Hamilton, Berry's, Butts.*
275 Andrew M'Math, Newman's, Thomas.*
276 Henry H. Moseley, Gray's, Henry.*
277 James E. Wincey, 334th, Wayne.*

278 Thomas Slaughter, Pace's, Putnam.*
279 Sarah Sullivan, w., 600th, Richmond.
280 Thompson Eperson, Field's, Habersham.
281 Solomon Barefield, sol., 108th, Hancock.
282 James Eubank, Lamberth's, Fayette.
283 Martha Johnson, w., 118th, Hancock.
284 Margaret Lindsey, or., 72d, Burke.
285 Palmer A. Higgins, Hall's, Butts.
286 Sheriff Bruister, sol., Calhoun's, Harris.*
287 Martin Crow, Mackleroy's, Clarke.
288 Henry G. Hing, Wynn's, Gwinnett.
289 John Barr, Candler's, Bibb.*
290 Elizabeth Tabor, w. r. s., White's, Franklin.*
291 James Hunton's ors., Griffin's, Merriwether.
292 Allen Wigley, Hamilton's, Gwinnett.
293 Willis R. Ivie, M. Brown's, Habersham.
294 Ripley's three orphans, Hobkerk's, Camden.
295 Nancy L. Collier, w., Morgan's, Clarke.
296 Willis Hurst, Griffin's, Burke.
297 William Hodges, sol., Southwell's, Tatnall.
298 John C. Digby, Varner's, Merriwether.*
299 George W. Cannon's ors., Collier's, Monroe.*
300 Henry Anderson, Groover's, Thomas.*
301 Henry Vincent, Jr., Rooks's, Putnam.*
302 John Brock, M'Daniel's, Pulaski.
303 James Brown, Peavy's, Bulloch.*
304 Richardson Booker, Jr., 559th, Walton.
305 Mary Ramsay, w., Willis's, Franklin.
306 John D. Prater, 470th, Upson.*
307 Henry Carver, Whitehead's, Habersham.
308 Milley Tatum, w. r. s., Kendrick's, Monroe.*
309 Obadiah Smith, Bush's, Pulaski.
310 Joshua Whitaker, sol., Culbreath's, Columbia.*
311 William L. Astin, sol., 142d, Greene.*
312 William Roberson, Morrison's, Appling.
313 Josiah Burgess, r. s., 373d, Jasper.*
314 Dolison Prichard, Marshall's, Putnam.
315 John Andrews, Hearn's, Butts.*
316 John N. Harris, 693d, Harris.*
317 David Edingfield, Jr., 53d, Emanuel.
318 Sarah Tate, w., Williams's, Decatur.
319 Oliver W. Stephens, 15th, Liberty.
320 James A. Everett, Marshall's, Crawford.
321 William Harrison, Head's, Butts.
322 Silas Wray, Griffin's, Merriwether.
323 Clement T. Kennedy, May's, Monroe.*
324 James H. Sandridge, Lunsford's, Elbert.

1 Henry Tillman, 394th, Montgomery.
2 Jesse Ricketson, Jr., Stewart's, Warren.*
3 Lavisa Bags, w., Gunn's, Jefferson.*
4 Thomas Jerman, 600th, Richmond.
5 Sarah Terrell, w., Chambers's, Gwinnett.
6 Jesse Watson, Sinclair's, Houston.
7 Tucker Malding, George's, Appling.
8 Charles Hammond, Thaxton's, Butts.*
9 Jonathan Prewit, Smith's, Madison.
10 George F. Geyer, 9th, Effingham.*
11 Ishmael Broome, Lynn's, Warren.*
12 Robert Hamilton, Hamilton's, Hall.*
13 Uriah Sparks, M'Culler's, Newton.*
14 Edmond Raines, r. s., Jones's, Morgan.*
15 William Griffin, Camp's, Baker.*
16 Joseph Foshee, Arrington's, Merriwether.*
17 Robert Caldwell, Taylor's, Jones.
18 John W. Stozer, Curry's, Merriwether.
19 William L. Burke, Talley's, Troup.*
20 Frances Martin, w., 242d, Jackson.
21 John Goodman, Justice's, Bibb.
22 Benjamin Coxwell, Downs's, Warren.
23 Lawrence Holt, Baismore's, Jones.
24 Ransom Tedder, Dobbs's, Hall.
25 Nelson Garnett, Huchinson's, Columbia.*
26 William Hyman, Lynn's, Warren.*
27 John M'Vay, 535th, Dooly.
28 Mary M'Duffee, w., Blackstock's, Hall.
29 Charles Dames's ors., 122d, Richmond.
30 Lovett L. Brown, Wood's, Jefferson.
31 Harvey M. Mays, Fleming's, Franklin.
32 Winnifred Carter, w., 175th, Wilkes.
33 James Jordan, Higginbotham's, Madison.*
34 John Leftwick's ors., Thaxton's, Butts.*
35 David V. T. Pool, Martin's, Newton.*
36 John S. Thompson, Newman's, Thomas.*
37 Abraham Houseworth, Morton's, De Kalb.*
38 Jones Wynn's ors., Vining's, Putnam.
39 Baker's three orphans, 406th, Gwinnett.
40 William Henson, Jr., Roberts's, Hall.
41 Jesse Mobbs, Thomas's, Clarke.

42 William Pearson's ors., Butts's, Monroe.
43 Thomas Bryan, Sen., r. s., Sewell's, Franklin.*
44 George W. Nicholson, Howard's, Oglethorpe.
45 Goodwin Miller, 454th, Walton.*
46 John M'Kinne Cooper, or., Fitzpatrick's, Chatham
47 Hiram Mill Irons, Jordan's, Bibb.*
48 William Howard, Young's, Jefferson.*
49 James Sharpe, Candler's, Bibb.*
50 Jacob Kitchens, s. l. w., Kendrick's, Putnam.
51 Edmund May, Jr., Sparks's, Washington.*
52 Betsey Ann Evans, w., 278th, Morgan.
53 Joshua Horn, M'Gehee's, Troup.*
54 George W. Odams's ors., Monk's, Crawford.
55 Landoni Hamwick, Brown's, Habersham.*
56 Isaac Butler, Newman's, Thomas.
57 Thomas E. Baker, or., 15th, Liberty.
58 James H. M'Ewen, Jones's, Madison.
59 Henry D. Pane, s., Griffin's, Fayette.
60 John N. Fry, Sanderlin's, Chatham.*
61 Leonard Steed, Sen., Bell's, Columbia.*
62 Eason Lee, Hannah's, Jefferson.
63 Reuben Edwards, sol., Phillips's, Jasper.
64 John Seay, sol., Lay's, Jackson.
65 Harriet King, w., Fitzpatrick's, Chatham.
66 Peter Y. Crow, Higginbotham's, Rabun.
67 Joseph Tucker, 640th, Dooly.*
68 John Holladay's ors., Hart's, Jones.
69 George W. Stewart, 574th, Early.*
70 Peterson G. Brogden, Dearing's, Butts.*
71 Mary King, w., Rook's, Putnam.
72 Peggy Garner, w., Barnett's, Clarke.*
73 Robert Maxwell, 166th, Wilkes.*
74 George Duren, Sen., Martin's, Pike.
75 Absalom Gulliatt, 175th, Wilkes.
76 Ebenezer Folsom, Lester's, Pulaski.*
77 John J. Howell, Sinclair's, Houston.
78 Margarett Barnett, w. r. s., Orr's, Jackson.
79 William Crafton, Robison's, Washington.*
80 Willis Youngblood, Liddell's, Jackson.
81 Joseph Thigpen, Mashburn's, Pulaski.
82 Robert A. Steele, Crawford's, Morgan.*
83 James Perkins, Thompson's, Henry.
84 John Grubbs, Bridges's, Gwinnett.
85 Rachael Akeridge, w., 633d, Dooly.*
86 Thomas Hobbs, Newsom's, Warren.
87 Alexander Scott, M'Gill's, Lincoln.*
88 Jacob Prewett, Taylor's, Elbert.

89 David A. Barnwell, Burgess's, Carroll.
90 James Middleton, Cleland's, Chatham.*
91 Ursula Harvey, w. r. s., Kendrick's, Putnam.
92 William Mitchell, sol., Walker's, Harris.
93 Martha S. Davis, 168th, Wilkes.
94 Wyley F. Bishop, Dyer's, Habersham.
95 John Thompson, sol., 249th, Walton.*
96 Zealous Miller, Perry's, Baldwin.
97 William Norris, Reid's, Gwinnett.
98 John King, sol., Dilman's, Pulaski.*
99 Nancy Harvey, or., Kendrick's, Putnam.*
100 Burwell Batterell, 702d, Heard.
101 Ignitius Ward, Young's, Wilkinson.
102 Henry Spratlus's ors., 166th, Wilkes.
103 Mastin Pruiett, Reid's, Gwinnett.
104 Thomas Hairston, Foote's, De Kalb.
105 Lewis Gibson, 398th, Richmond.*
106 Ambrose Witcher, Smith's, Madison.
107 John Nash, Sen., Wynn's, Gwinnett.
108 William H. Mallory, Whisenhunt's, Carroll.
109 Wm. K. Williams, f. a., Haygood's, Washington.
110 Daniel M. Lloyd, 289th, Jasper.
111 William W. Taylor, Maguire's, Gwinnett.*
112 Hiram Scott, M'Dowell's, Lincoln.*
113 Seaborn H. Peaterson, 75th, Burke.*
114 William Warthen, or., Garner's, Washington.
115 Matthias M'Cormick, sol., Dilman's, Pulaski.
116 John Henry Stibbs, Valleau's, Chatham.
117 Alfred Butler, M'Ginnis's, Jackson.
118 Reuben Warren, Hamilton's, Gwinnett.
119 Stephen Jinnins, Eller's, Rabun.
120 William B. Hicks, Hood's, Henry.
121 Edmund B. Hattaway, Allen's, Clarke.
122 Milton B. Fluker, Martin's, Washington.
123 David Stephens, Martin's, Newton.
124 Benjamin Robertson, Jr., Daniel's, Hall.
125 William S. Jones, Smith's, Elbert.*
126 Robert Walker, Foote's, De Kalb.
127 Asa Musslewhite, M'Daniel's, Pulaski.*
128 Nancy Slaten, w., Seay's, Hall.
129 John Hardaway, Perryman's, Warren.
130 Thomas P. Dingler, Prophett's, Newton.
131 Solomon Lee, s. l. w., Garner's, Coweta.
132 Matthew M. Pinder, id., Barker's, Gwinnett.
133 Stephen B. Hester, Jr., Rick's, Laurens.
134 Wilson Dawson, Lynn's, Warren.
135 James Gilbert, Barker's, Gwinnett.
136 Stephen Treddwell, r. s., 702d, Heard.

137 Solomon Barefield, 108th, Hancock.
138 Elizabeth Dent, w., Taylor's, Putnam.
139 Rebecca Odam, w , Barwick's, Washington.
140 William Daniel, Smith's, Houston.
141 Christain Cope's ors., 9th, Effingham.
142 John O. Jordin, Smith's, Habersham.
143 Joel Estes, Jr., Reid's, Gwinnett.
144 Edmund Herring, sol., Killen's, Decatur.
145 Archibald Polk, Hargrove's, Newton.*
146 Durant Foskey, 56th, Emanuel.*
147 Edmund Liles, 333d, Wayne.*
148 Henry B. Horton, Bivins's, Jones.
149 James M. Everett, Goodwin's, Houston.
150 Susan Denby, w., 103d, Hancock.*
151 Jonathan Shochley, r. s., Ross's, Monroe.
152 John H. Brodnax, sol., Coker's, Troup.*
153 John Hudgins, Dyer's, Habersham.
154 Marcus L. Bunn, Calhoun's, Harris.*
155 Joannah Harris, w., Taylor's, Elbert.
156 Sarah Taylor, w., Wood's, Morgan.
157 Jesse Matthews, Morris's, Crawford.*
158 Joseph Ford, Stewart's, Warren.*
159 John G. Tankersley, Murphy's, Columbia.
160 Tolbert Arthur, Hall's, Oglethorpe.
161 Benjamin Samuil, Jr., Jones's, Lincoln.*
162 Matthew Amberson, Jones's, Morgan.
163 John Yarber, Morris's, Crawford.
164 William Terrill, s. i. w., Taylor's, Elbert.
165 Moses Watkins, sol. in '92, Espy's, Clarke.
166 Philip Matthews's ors., Cleland's, Chatham.*
167 John Williams, Hand's, Appling.
168 Charles F. Rapp, Valleau's, Chatham.
169 William Chavers, 777th, Randolph.
170 William Tynan, Sanderlin's, Chatham.*
171 Mary C. Bergan, or., 9th, Effingham.
172 George Blitch, 10th, Effingham.*
173 William S. Whitten, Willis's, Franklin.
174 Robert Malone, sol., Williams's, Decatur.
175 John Reddick, or., Paris, Burke.
176 James Anderson, sol., Seally's, Talbot.
177 John Dean, Kelly's, Elbert.*
178 Abraham S. Coriell, 398th, Richmond.*
179 Joseph Janson, 34th, Scriven.
180 Anderson's six orphans, 121st, Richmond.
181 William Thomas Delegat, 22d, M'Intosh.
182 Arthur Johns, 293d, Jasper.
183 Christian Broadwell, w. r. s., Liddell's, Jackson.*

184 Hannah Terry, w. r. s., Newsom's, Warren.
185 Charles Womack, sol., Norris's, Monroe.
186 James Peay, 600th, Richmond.*
187 James Upton, Whisenhunt's, Carroll.
188 Randolph Edes, sol., Orr's Jackson.
189 John G. Smith, Blount's, Wilkinson.
190 Solomon Baker, Winter's, Jones.
191 Elizabeth Prior, w., Wood's, Morgan.
192 James Davis, Evans's, Fayette.
193 William Fason, r. s., 117th, Hancock.
194 William Arnold, Sen., r. s., Scroggins's, Oglethorpe
195 John M. Beavers, 295th, Jasper.
196 Amelia Horn, or., 145th, Greene.
197 John Owen, Polhill's, Burke.
198 David Patrick, r. s., Hall's, Oglethorpe.
199 Henry H. Hand, sol., Iverson's, Houston.
200 Abijah Catlin, 143d, Greene.
201 William Smith, Kelly's, Elbert.
202 Thomas H. Persons, Norris's, Monroe.
203 Moses V. Ellison, Givens's, De Kalb.
204 Joseph R. Turnbull, 561st, Upson.
205 Mary S. Mathis, Rooks's, Putnam.
206 David Sutley, Moore's, Randolph.
207 William Keele, Welche's, Habersham.
208 Thomas Parnell's ors., 2d section, Cherokee.
209 John L. Shelby, 535th, Dooly.
210 John Freeman, 34th, Scriven.
211 Davis Whitehead, M'Coy's, Houston.*
212 Caroline N. Pepper, w., 271st, M'Intosh.
213 Ephraigm Pennington, sol., Lamberth's, Fayette.
214 Henry Smith, Gunn's, Jones.*
215 Francis Darrence, Brewton's, Tatnall.
216 Abraham Holder, 589th, Upson.
217 Ira Wood, Hobkerk's, Camden.*
218 Ingram Parr's or., Mangum's, Franklin.
219 Mitchell Jordan, Wilcox's, Telfair.
220 Jeremiah B. Hancock, Morris's, Crawford.
221 James M'Guffey, Say's, De Kalb.
222 Johnston M'Elroy, Gittens's, Fayette.
223 Jethrew Arline, Martin's, Laurens.
224 Jacob Crotwell, 404th, Gwinnett.
225 Jemima Blair, w., Walker's, Columbia.
226 Elhanan Wells, Price's, Hall.*
227 William E. Mann, Vining's, Putnam.
228 Aner Owen, w., Hamilton's, Hall.
229 John Sappington, r. s., House's, Henry.*
230 David L. Wilkins, Duke's, Carroll.

6

231 Henry Mitchell, sol., Gittens's, Fayette.
232 Frances Howell, w., Howard's, Oglethorpe.
233 Davi H. Jones, Brewer's, Walton.
234 James Awood, Harris's, De Kalb.
235 Rubin Favours, Phillips's, Talbot.
236 Elijah M'Coy, 3d section, Cherokee.
237 Martha Hemphill, w., 279th, Morgan.
238 Nathan Roberts, sol., 49th, Emanuel.*
239 James Smith, Higginbotham's, Madison.*
240 James Anderson, Studstill's, Lowndes.
241 Stephens Powell, 535th, Dooly.*
242 William Callaway, Lester's, Monroe.
243 James S. Jones, Butts's, Monroe.*
244 Charles Hunter, sol., Rainey's, Twiggs.*
245 John Goodson, Kendrick's, Putnam.
246 Abraham Perkins, 141st, Greene.
247 William Wilde, Justice's, Bibb.
248 William Arnold, Sen., Jenkins's, Oglethorpe.
249 Jesse Thompson, Reid's, Gwinnett.
250 Jane Clark, w. r. s., Burnett's, Lowndes.
251 Michael Peacock, Walden's, Pulaski.*
252 William Godfrey, 14th, Hancock.
253 James Almand, Howell's, Elbert.
254 Francis Foster, 419th, Walton.*
255 Nathaniel Griggs, sol., Higginbotham's, Carroll.
256 John Love, sol., Stanfield's, Campbell.*
257 John Magner, Groce's, Bibb.*
258 Benjamin H. Emmerson, Winter's, Jones.
259 John P. Henry, Shearer's, Coweta.
260 Robert K. Thompson, Wynn's, Gwinnett.
261 Francis Mayfield, or., Butts's, Monroe.
262 Allison Caison, Green's, Ware.
263 Thomas Redding, sol., Ross's, Monroe.
264 Elisha C. Barnett, Price's, Hall.
265 Patrick O'Reiley, Valleau's, Chatham.*
266 Charles Rieleey, 119th, Richmond.*
267 Middleton Thompson, Morgan's, Clark.
268 Gideon Holsey, sol., 116th, Hancock.
269 Nancy Spradley, w., Chill's, Marion.
270 Thompson M. Henson, Keener's, Rabun.
271 Henly Snow, Nesbit's, Newton.*
272 William Clements, s. l. w., 761st, Heard.*
273 Mark Russell, Howard's, Oglethorpe.
274 Minor of Daniel M'Kinzie, f. a., 555th, Upson.
275 Joshua H. Newberry, sol., 1st section, Cherokee.
276 David Aughtry, 120th, Richmond.*
277 Samuel Norwood, Coxe's, Franklin.

278 James W. Frazier, Parham's, Harris.
279 Noah Red, Bush's, Burke.
280 Neill M'Leran, Mashburn's, Pulaski.
281 Andrew M. Norris, Dyer's, Habersham.
282 Hosea W. Henderson, Mashburn's, Pulaski.
283 Richard M'Duff, Williams's, Jasper.*
284 Ambrose K. Blackwell, Price's, Hall.
285 Benjamin P. Shepherd, Jordan's, Harris.
286 Epps Maulden, Fleming's, Franklin.
287 William Falkner, s. i. w., Wilhite's, Elbert.*
288 Margaret Ingram, w., Evans's, Laurens.*
289 James R. Donnan, Rooks's, Putman.
290 Benjamin Franklin, Robinson's, Harris.
291 Alfred B. Reese, of Morgan, Canning's, Elbert.*
292 William Guy, Sweat's, Ware.
293 John Perrion, Herndon's, Carroll.
294 Roland Skinner, Nesbit's, Newton.*
295 William Vaughan, Colley's, Oglethorpe.
296 John Glenn, Neal's, Campbell.
297 James R. Gilbert, Crow's, Pike.
298 Edward Miles, Bell's, Columbia.
299 Frederic Cherry, Chambers's, Houston.
300 Washington G. Atkinson, Berry's, Butts.
301 Sampson Smith, Harris's, Crawford.
302 Thomas Rusk, 559th, Walton.
303 Rebecca Heeth, w., Johnson's, Warren.
304 Sarah M. Clements, w., Smith's, Madison.*
305 William Kees's ors., Bell's, Burke.
306 John Barge, Neal's, Campbell.
307 William L. Edmundson, Howell's, Troup.
308 Willis Whitaker, Williams's, Washington.
309 G. Palmer's minors, f. a., Streetman's, Twiggs.
310 Benjamin Borum's ors., Morgan's, Madison.
311 Wylie J. Garrard, Blackstock's, Hall.
312 Mark Castleberry, Jr., 2d section, Cherokee.
313 William M. Jones, Prescott's, Twiggs.
314 Charlotte M'Leod, w., Heard's, De Kalb.
315 John F. Simmons's ors., Peace's, Wilkinson.
316 Shadrack Traywick, 118th, Hancock.
317 James Helton, sol., York's, Stewart.
318 William Venable, sol., Robinson's, Fayette.
319 Henry Gaither, Capt. Prophett's, Newton.
320 Robert M. Stell, Tuggle's, Merriwether.*
321 Theophilus Holcomb, mi., Stephens's, Habersham
322 Reuben S. Hatcher, Smith's, Wilkinson.*
323 Austin A. Bryant, sol., Stanfield's, Campbell.*
324 Lewis Sholars, Willingham's, Harris.

1 Jesse Adams, Derrick's, Henry.
2 William M. Perry, Bryan's, Monroe.
3 John W. Robinson, Craven's, Coweta.
4 John M'Colester's ors., Stower's, Elbert.
5 Joel C. Turman, 124th, Richmond.*
6 John C. Allen, 145th, Greene.*
7 Mary Goolsby, w. r. s., Green's, Oglethorpe.*
8 Spire A. Langston, Johnson's, De Kalb.
9 John Harris, Reid's, Gwinnett.
10 Elizabeth Grant, or., Ellsworth's, Bibb.
11 Sterling S. Snellgrove, Johnson's, Bibb.*
12 Elijah Graham, Hand's, Appling.
13 James Miller, Daniel's, Hall.
14 Prior L. Davis, Grice's, Oglethorpe.*
15 Anderson Abercrombie, sol., 102d, Hancock.*
16 Charles Bradford's ors., Bridges's, Gwinnett.
17 Joshua Gunter, Hudson's, Marion.*
18 Benjamin Avent, Edwards's, Talbot.*
19 Bud Lee, Mimmes's, Fayette.
20 Andrew M'Elroy, sol., Butts's, Monroe.*
21 Nancy Orr, w., Miller's, Jackson.
22 Henry Barrow, Gittens's, Fayette.
23 James Bell, Hines's, Coweta.*
24 Bryant Parker, 419th, Walton.
25 Nancy Zachry, or., Martin's, Newton.
26 Ludwell E. Malone, Martin's, Pike.
27 William Ward, Taylor's, Elbert.
28 George W. Barnes, 4th, Chatham.
29 William Sawyer, Morris's, Crawford.
30 William L. Nance, Ross's, Monroe.
31 Burrell M'Cullers, sol., Kelly's, Jasper.
32 Arnold B. Fussell, Sweat's, Ware.*
33 William Gilpin, Taylor's, Putnam.*
34 William Seals, Roberts's, Hall.
35 John R. Watkins, Peek's, Columbia.
36 William Jones's ors., Sullivan's, Jones.
37 (fr.) James Johnson, Camp's, Baker.
38 Barbara Merritt, w. r. s., 364th, Jasper.
39 Anna Moody, w. r. s., Hatchett's, Oglethorpe.
40 John Wright, r. s., M'Linn's, Butts.
41 Thomas Nichells, Dyer's, Habersham.

42 Charles R. Cosby, Cleggs's, Walton.
43 Abraham Gorden, House's, Henry.*
44 James W. Freeman, Athens, Clarke.
45 John S. C. M'Donald, 430th, Early.*
46 Littleton P. Hairston, Shearer's, Coweta.*
47 Alexander Hall, Kendrick's, Monroe.
48 John G. Pullin, Derrick's, Henry.*
49 Abel O. Embry, Heard's, De Kalb.*
50 Josiah Smith, Moffett's, Muscogee.*
51 Edward Meador, 249th, Walton.
52 John M'Lean, Nichols's, Fayette.
53 James J. Walker, 165th, Wilkes.
54 Jesse Herring, Jr., Reid's, Gwinnett.*
55 John Clark, Sanderlin's, Chatham.*
56 Anderson Nawlin, Jones's, Morgan.*
57 Solomon Jones, Hobbs's, Laurens.*
58 Burrell Pope, Holt's, Talbot.
59 Moses Ham, 20th, Bryan.*
60 Isaac Morrison, Alexander's, Jefferson.*
61 Dawson Weaver, Blount's, Wilkinson.*
62 Leroy Hammond, 406th, Gwinnett.*
63 Drewry Jeffreys, Brown's, Habersham.*
64 Matthew Bones's ors., Higginbotham's, Madison.
65 William Thornton, Gay's, Harris.
66 Darling P. Keadle, Hutson's, Newton.*
67 Elizabeth Reese, w., Harris's, Columbia.
68 S. H. Gilmore's ors., Talley's, Troup.
69 Francis Farrar, sol., Thomas's, Clarke.*
70 Reuben Hembree, Herndon's, Hall.
71 James H. Gaines, Brewer's, Monroe.
72 Thomas H. Parks, Scroggins's, Oglethorpe.*
73 Daniel Walling, Sen., Seay's, Hall.
74 Matthew J. Pass, s. l. w., Green's, Oglethorpe.
75 William H. Farmer, Willis's, Franklin.
76 Noah Lambert, sol., Killen's, Decatur.
77 Martha Akins, w., Folsom's, Lowndes.*
78 Thomas Florence, Levritt's, Lincoln.*
79 Demp. Wheddons's ors., Barwick's, Washington.
80 David Madden, Sen., Madden's, Pike.*
81 John T. Cox, Norris's, Monroe.*
82 Reason Burnett, Bower's, Elbert.*
83 Noel Crawford, 145th, Greene.*
84 Benjamin Cobb, Riden's, Jackson.*
85 James Greene, Mitchell's, Marion.
86 William H. Herrin, Head's, Butts.*
87 William Bond's ors., Reid's, Gwinnett.
88 John R. Allen, Kendrick's, Monroe.*

89 Conrod Augley, r. s., Hicks's, Decatur.
90 James Stephens, 417th, Walton.*
91 Hartwell Adams, 454th, Walton.*
92 Isaac B. Williamson, Bustin's, Pike.
93 John Hitchcock, Alberson's, Walton.
94 Zachariah Bailey, Morton's, De Kalb.*
95 Frances N. Taylor, w., 364th, Jasper.*
96 John Groover, Peavy's, Bulloch.*
97 William Clark, Jr., Park's, Walton.*
98 Martha Robuck, w., Bryan's, Pulaski.*
99 James Whitten, Price's, Hall.*
100 Jesse Daniel, s. l. w., 600th, Richmond.
101 James Smith, Sanderlin's, Chatham.*
102 Silas Yarbrough, 362d, Jasper.
103 Mary Ann Turner, w., 1st, Chatham.
104 George W. Wigley, Mullen's, Carroll.
105 William Goff, Curry's, Wilkinson.
106 (fr.) Benjamin B. Hardin, Dozier's, Columbia.
107 John A. Fleming, Huey's, Harris.
108 John S. Harris, Butts's, Monroe.
109 Augustus Lamkin, Levritt's, Lincoln.*
110 Philip C. Gieu, 320th, Baldwin.*
111 Alice Deadwylder, w. r. s., Wilhite's, Elbert.
112 James H. Couper, 26th, Glynn.
113 Daniel Wilson, Walker's, Harris.*
114 John Anderson, 656th, Troup.*
115 Thomas Hopper, s. i. w., Guice's, Oglethorpe.*
116 Enoch B. Hudson, Evans's, Laurens.*
117 Nancy Farnall, w., Hicks's, Decatur.*
118 John Barton, r. s., Martin's, Hall.*
119 John T. Bryan, Justice's, Bibb.*
120 John Crumby, Sutton's, Habersham.
121 Kinchen Martin, Wells's, Twiggs.
122 William Lynn, Jones's, Lincoln.*
123 Joseph Anderson, Anderson's, Rabun.
124 John Lightner, Baismore's, Jones.
125 Robert B. Cook, Ballard's, Morgan.
126 Nancy Williamson, w. r. s., Newman's, Thomas.*
127 Strous Melton, Park's, Walton.*
128 Joseph T. Dismuke's or., 104th, Hancock.
129 Stephen H. Neal, Ross's, Monroe.
130 Jeremiah Winter, 124th, Richmond.*
131 John R. Jones, Kendrick's, Monroe.*
132 William Muckleroy, Williams's, Jasper.
133 John Pressley, Jr., 555th, Upson.
134 William P. Price, Price's, Hall.*
135 Seaborn J. Austin, Sapp's, Muscogee.

136 Elizabeth Smith, w., 537th, Upson.*
137 Thomas Garner, r. s., Dobbs's, Hall.
138 Isaac W. Raiford's ors., Carswell's, Jefferson.
139 (fr.) Council B. Wolf, Wright's, Laurens.
140 (fr.) William Jones, sol., 103d, Hancock.
141 (fr.) Miller's four orphans, 458th, Early.
142 Hannah Edmundson, w., Bostick's, Twiggs.
143 Joshua Bedenbock, 12th, Effingham.
144 Syrus Callahan, Keener's, Rabun.
145 Charles Black, Smith's, Campbell.
146 Willis Beavers, Allen's, Henry.
147 Robert W. Dukes, 289th, Jasper.
148 Isham Pitman, Thomas's, Crawford.*
149 James Chandler's ors., David's, Franklin.
150 Thomas Pinkard's ors., 466th, Monroe.*
151 Joseph Bryan's ors., Hick's, Decatur.
152 William Glasson, Neal's, Campbell.*
153 John Autrey, sol. 1784–97, House's, Henry.*
154 James Kennedy, Fitzpatrick's, Chatham.
155 Abner F. Taylor, Welche's, Habersham.
156 Jason Johnson, Mason's, Washington.*
157 Mary Bolton, w. r. s., Parham's, Warren.
158 Ransom Shiver, 640th, Dooly.
159 Andrew Wages, 245th, Jackson.*
160 Austin R. Pierce, Hampton's, Newton.*
161 John M'Clain, M'Clure's, Rabun.*
162 Israel Martin, Martin's, Pike.*
163 John Kendrick, 121st, Richmond.*
164 Lucretia Wilkins, id., Woodruff's, Campbell.*
165 Robert E. M'Carthy, Sullivan's, Jones.
166 James Murray, Cutlett's, Franklin.
167 Charles Trippe, Linam's, Pulaski.
168 Thompson Eperson, r. s., Mangum's, Franklin.
169 (fr.) Nancy Taylor, w., Bush's, Pulaski.
170 (fr.) William Riley Naron, Ware's, Coweta.
171 Wilie R. Bell, Hart's, Jones.
172 William Thompson, sol., 466th, Monroe.
173 Joshua Mercer, Buck's, Houston.
174 John Keen, House's, Henry.
175 Thomas Childress, Sen., Alberson's, Walton.
176 Almond B. Alford, Vining's, Putnam.
177 Daniel Martin's ors., Reid's, Gwinnett.
178 James J. Russell, Whitehead's, Habersham.*
179 John F. Taber, Hall's, Oglethorpe.
180 Martin Kendrick, 174th, Wilkes.*
181 Josiah Murphy, Pounds's, Twiggs.
182 John Bowman, Lawrence's, Pike.

183 Charles L. Mathews, 146th, Greene.
184 Louis Hogue, 466th, Monroe.*
185 James Cater, Wynn's, Gwinnett.
186 Isacc Scott, Groce's, Bibb.
187 Samson M'Carty, Candler's, Bibb.
188 Richard Manning, Jr., Maguire's, Gwinnett.
189 Samuel Hopper, Anderson's, Rabun.
190 Robert Byers, Stephens's, Habersham.
191 Samuel Roach, r. s., 510th, Early.
192 Thomas Watson, Mullen's, Carroll.*
193 Mark S. Anthony, Benson's, Lincoln.*
194 Thomas J. Gray, Martin's, Newton.
195 John H. Johnson, Hines's, Coweta.
196 (fr.) William Murphrey, Lightfoot's, Washington.
197 Wootson Roberts, Rhodes's, De Kalb.
198 Abner Horn, 561st, Upson.
199 Henry W. Tindall, Peurifoy's, Henry.*
200 John C. Saunders, Welche's, Habersham.*
201 John Williamson, George's, Appling.*
202 John E. Bacon, 398th, Richmond.*
203 Labron Dees, Linam's, Pulaski.*
204 Charles S. Sherby, Smith's, Habersham.
205 Uriah Owens, Tompkins's, Putnam.
206 William Pullin, Derrick's, Henry.
207 Miles H. M'Gehee, Greene's, Oglethorpe.
208 Charles Ferguson, Park's, Walton.
209 Wade Love, 788th, Heard.
210 Winn Lear, Curry's, Wilkinson.*
211 John Johnson, sol., Hill's, Harris.
212 Richard Lawrence, sol., Bustin's, Pike.
213 Elbert Roundtree, 34th, Scriven.
214 David Hudgens, Sims's, Troup.
215 George W. Huckabay, 687th, Lee.
216 John C. Wilkinson, Lunceford's, Wilkes.
217 John Ryle, Young's, Wilkinson.
218 (fr.) Anderton Stafford, 588th, Upson.
219 William W. Smith, Deavours's, Habersham.
220 Mary Backley, w., 11th, Effingham.*
221 Mark Desabye, 71st, Burke.
222 Isaac Higgs, Southell's, Tatnall.*
223 Moses Pitman, Martin's, Pike.
224 Jesse Brown, r. s., 430th, Early.
225 Francis H. Combs, 398th, Richmond.*
226 Hugh M'Lin, Ellsworth's, Bibb.*
227 Samuel G. Snow's ors., Fenn's, Clarke.
228 Biven Booles, 148th, Greene.
229 John Cantrell, Chastain's, Habersham.

230 Samuel Wright, s., Jones's, Lincoln.
231 Simeon W. Yancy, Edwards's, Talbot.
232 Jane S. Harden, or., Newman's, Thomas.
233 James Whaley, 555th, Upson.
234 William Thompson, Sen., 30th, Scriven.*
335 John Smith, sol., Brown's, Camden.
236 Oswell Langley, Loveless's, Gwinnett.
237 Thomas Knight's ors., Herring's, Twiggs.*
238 (fr.) Tobias Holland, 608th, Taliaferro.
239 (fr.) James Ellis, Jr., Dawson's, Jasper.
240 Rebecca Raines, w., Night's, Morgan.
241 Allen Banks, Whelchel's, Hall.
242 William E. Prickett, Roberts's, Hall.
243 Allen Wood's ors., Martin's, Newton.
244 Henry Waters, Seay's, Hall.
245 Thomas B. Bullard, Smith's, Elbert.*
246 John Fowler, Roberts's, Hall.*
247 Willis C. Jenkins, Fulks's, Wilkes.
248 Elijah Garner's ors., Jack's, Clarke.
249 M. L. & E. J. Williams's ors., 777th, Randolph.*
250 Richard Purser, Loven's, Henry.
251 Moses Thompson, Smith's, Houston.
252 James Hall Bridges, Bridges's, Gwinnett.
253 James Moore, Vining's, Putnam.
254 Timothy T. Gnann, 9th, Effingham.*
255 Aaron Silghman, sol., Lamberth's, Fayette.
256 Alfred Johnson, 373d, Jasper.*
257 Joseph Messer, Brady's, Jones.

SEVENTEENTH DISTRICT, FIRST SECTION, CHEROKEE.

1 Reuben Taylor, Tuggle's, Merriwether.
2 Bressie O'Brien, 601st, Taliaferro.
3 William Davis, Higginbotham's, Rabun.*
4 Gabriel G. Coley, Daniel's, Hall.*
5 John Dial, Jr., 2d section, Cherokee.*
6 John King, Jr., Baismore's, Jones.
7 Richard W. Davis's ors., Downs's, Warren.
8 James H. Stedham, Duke's, Carroll.*
9 Meshack Maddox, Bustin's, Pike.
10 Elias Crews, Brown's, Camden.*
11 William Moore, sol., Fenn's, Clarke.*
12 George Brown, Ball's, Monroe.
13 William Nix, Mizell's, Talbot.*

14 William S. Booth, Parham's, Harris.*
15 James N. Fuller, or., Greer's, Merriwether.*
16 William Ray, Thompson's, Henry.*
17 William W. Russell, 105th, Baldwin.*
18 Joseph Floyd Mulvey, or., 22d, M'Intosh.
19 Wilborn Parks, Kelly's, Elbert.*
20 Joseph Davis, Stone's, Irwin.*
21 James A. Nunnely, 415th, Walton.*
22 Pleasant C. Jenkins, 148th, Greene.*
23 Paschal H. Sandford, 415th, Walton.*
24 William G. Thornton, 466th, Monroe.*
25 Henry Holland, Oliver's, Twiggs.*
26 Mary Fitts, w. r. s., Nellum's, Elbert.
27 John W. Haynes, Baugh's, Jackson.
28 John Pike, Payne's, Merriwether.
29 William Edes, Barker's, Gwinnett.*
30 Henry Pratt, Hargrove's, Oglethorpe.*
31 Elisha Hodge, M'Daniel's, Pulaski.*
32 John Guise, r. s., M'Dowell's, Lincoln.
33 Elisha Free, Sutton's, Habersham.
34 Joseph Marshall, Wood's, Jefferson.*
35 Alexander P. Crawford, Boynton's, Twiggs.*
36 Joseph B. Andrews, Sam Streetman's, Twiggs.
37 John Peuce, Welche's, Habersham.
38 Nicey Chambers, w., 117th, Hancock.*
39 John G. Edwards, Head's, Butts.*
40 Thomas W. Pearce, Stanton's, Newton.*
41 Drewry M. Allen, 147th, Greene.*
42 Richard C. Spann, sol., 430th, Early.
43 Isaiah Kelly, Strickland's, Merriwether.*
44 Jesse Fincher, Barker's, Gwinnett.*
45 Alexander Baley, 734th, Lee.
46 George H. Bryan, 672d, Harris.*
47 Benjamin Selman's ors., Garner's, Coweta.
48 Hugh M. D. King, Mays's, Monroe.
49 Meredith Honeycut's ors., Bostick's, Twiggs.
50 Mary Thomas, w., Harralson's, Troup.
51 Jeremiah Wofford, Woodruff's, Campbell.
52 Moses Lewis, Jones's, Morgan.*
53 John Chavers, 777th, Randolph.*
54 Bryan Beddingfield, Burk's, Stewart.*
55 John T. Acre, 601st, Taliaferro.
56 George Wolf, 175th, Wilkes.
57 Thomas Stone, Higginbotham's, Rabun.
58 J. Cartledge, Sen., r. s., Hutchinson's, Columbia.*
59 Riley Johnson, 789th, Sumter.
60 Jane Evans, w. r. s., Evans's, Fayette.

61 William A. Hicks, Clinton's, Campbell.
62 Margaret A. Brown, w., Crawford's, Franklin.
63 Alsa Mullens, id., 104th, Hancock.
64 Bennet H. M'Lane, Hatchett's, Oglethorpe.*
65 William Estes, Hines's, Coweta.*
66 Chil. of M. Benson, f. a., Underwood's, Putnam.
67 Abner Bishop, Daniel's, Hall.*
68 Robert Higginbotham, Nichols's, Fayette.
69 Elbert Harris, Craven's, Coweta.
70 John B. Blount, Capt. Prophett's, Newton.*
71 Philip Kennedy, 271st, M'Intosh.
72 Elizabeth Lindsey, Smith's, Houston.
73 Jesse Whitley, Alberson's, Walton.*
74 Susan L. Stacy, or., 15th, Liberty.
75 Ira Britt, Hitchcock's, Muscogee.*
76 Naome Prewett, w., Durrence's, Tatnall.*
77 Stephen H. Renfroe, r. s., Comer's, Jones.*
78 Daniel Powell, 559th, Walton.*
79 Charles R. Glazier, David's, Franklin.
80 Peter Caster, Kellum's, Talbot.
81 Aaron Herritt, Slater's, Bulloch.*
82 Levi Polk, Higginbotham's, Madison.*
83 Marquis Ambrose, Chambers's, Gwinnett.*
84 John S. Higdon's ors., Stewart's, Warren.
85 Robert Barrow, 72d, Burke.
86 Jesse Clements, Price's, Hall.
87 T. J. Williamson, Harralson's, Troup.*
88 Rial Griffin, Justice's, Bibb.
89 Robert Carter, Wynn's, Gwinnett.
90 John Joiner, or., Watson's, Marion.
91 James B. Smith, 122d, Richmond.*
92 George W. Nelson, Morrison's, Appling.*
93 Levi M'Ginnis, 404th, Gwinnett.
94 Jacob Brazelton, Jr., sol., 248th, Jackson.
95 Andrew J. Hitchcock, Few's, Muscogee.
96 Zadock Bonner, Higginbotham's, Carroll.
97 Jane Baker, w. r. s., Valleau's, Chatham.
98 Dominick O'Byrne, Sanderlin's, Chatham.
99 John Sheffield, 430th, Early.*
100 Alexander Wilson, Wilcox's, Telfair.
101 Joseph W. Quill, 320th, Baldwin.*
102 Henry Jemison's ors., Justice's, Bibb.
103 Joseph Mercier, 458th, Early.*
104 Jesse Hunter, 36th, Scriven.
105 William Frank's ors., 602d, Taliaferro.
106 John T. Goldsmith, Parham's, Harris.
107 Jeremiah White, Brock's, Habersham.

108 Milley Griggs, w., 102d, Hancock.
109 Larkin Pane, Tower's, Gwinnett.
110 Sylvester Narrimore, Gay's, Harris.
111 Edward Daniel, Daniel's, Hall.
112 Samuel Williams, M'Daniel's, Pulaski.*
113 Peter Flowers, Hughes's, Habersham.
114 Sterling G. Davis, Miller's, Jackson.
115 Abner Glanton, Sims's, Troup.
116 John G. Williams, Jones's, Bulloch.
117 Joshua Mires, Young's, Wilkinson.
118 Milton Reviere, 494th, Upson.*
119 William Dillard, 249th, Walton.*
120 James Ethridge, Peace's, Wilkinson.*
121 Samuel Jones, 335th, Wayne.
122 Thomas Sanford, Latimer's, De Kalb.
123 Madison Avory, Peek's, Columbia.*
124 Simeon G. Glenn, 289th, Jasper.
125 Ebenezer Jackson, Sen., r. s., Valleau's, Chatham*
126 Rhoda Reeves, w. of sol., 168th, Wilkes.
127 Thompson Epperson, r. s., Mangum's, Franklin.
128 Archibald Davis, Hand's, Appling.
129 Thomas Kitley, 779th, Heard.*
130 Levi C. Bohannon, Hendon's, Carroll.
131 William M'Celvale, Smith's, Campbell.*
132 Hart C. Peek, 142d, Greene.*
133 Zacheus Hudgins, Merck's, Hall.*
134 Turner H. Mann, sol., Rutland's, Bibb.*
135 Luke White, Hughes's, Habersham.
136 Andrew Hunter, Reid's, Gwinnett.*
137 William L. Starks, Peurifoy's, Henry.*
138 Hiram Wright, Hendon's, Carroll.
139 Thomas & Jinsey Nelson, ors., Hearn's, Butts.
140 Richard Dean, r. s., Chambers's, Houston.
141 William H. Bowen's ors., Shearer's, Coweta.
142 Reuben B. Edmunds, Hatchett's, Oglethorpe.
143 Thomas P. Jackson, Pace's, Putnam.
144 James Kenly, Anderson's, Rabun.
145 Andrew Nicholas's ors., 72d, Burke.
146 Matthew Harrell, Barron's, Houston.
147 John Webb, 406th, Gwinnett.
148 James Van Ness, Flynn's, Muscogee.
149 Harris Brantley, Sparks's, Washington.
150 Dial Peavy, r. s., Lamberth's, Fayette.
151 James Prince, Perry's, Habersham.
152 Matthew Norton, Huey's, Harris.*
153 James Adams, Robinson's, Fayette.*
154 Abel Vaughan, Colley's, Oglethorpe.

155 Ausbon Estes, Bridges's, Gwinnett.
156 Thomas H. Conner, Houston's, Chatham.*
157 Burwell Eaves, Stanfield's, Campbell.*
158 Usrey Almand's ors., Canning's, Elbert.
159 Frederic & Martha Palmer, f. a., Wilson's, Pike.
160 Jefferson H. Jones, Ball's, Monroe.
161 Henry Barton, Boynton's, Twiggs.
162 Milton Cooper, Higginbotham's, Carroll.*
163 Ezekiel Strickland, Sen., Stanton's, Newton.*
164 Hollis Cooley, 295th, Jasper.
165 John Craft's ors., Haygood's, Washington.
166 Mary Arnett, h. a., Royster's, Franklin.*
167 Elijah Poss, 177th, Wilkes.*
168 Sarah Payne, d. sol. l. w., 26th, Glynn.*
169 Thomas Young, sol., 271st, M'Intosh.*
170 Stephen B. Westbrook, Barker's, Gwinnett.
171 William J. Garrard, 176th, Wilkes.
172 James Lawless, Seas's, Madison.
173 Malacha Mercer, Summerlin's, Bulloch.*
174 Thomas C. Murrah, Wood's, Morgan.*
175 John S. Bradley, Baker's, Liberty.*
176 John R. Greenlee, Dean's, De Kalb.
177 James A. Parker, Gunn's, Jefferson.
178 Agnes Lawless, w. r. s., Seas's, Madison.
179 Robert Cagle, Gray's, Henry.
180 Elisha Mathis, s. l. w., Rooks's, Putnam.*
181 William R. Brown, Candler's, Bibb.
182 Calvin Hamilton's ors., Martin's, Washington.
183 Samuel Barefield, Bustin's, Pike.
184 John Brown, 334th, Wayne.*
185 Nathaniel Handy, r. s., Stephens's, Habersham.
186 Matthew Cofer, Loveless's, Gwinnett.
187 Benjamin F. Cleveland, Calhoun's, Harris.*
188 Jeptha Robinson, Jr., Griffin's, Fayette.*
189 Hanson Highfill, Jr., M. Brown's, Habersham.*
190 Sarah Aaron, w., M'Korkle's, Jasper.
191 James Roberts, Simmons's, Crawford.*
192 Elizabeth Talbot, w. r. s., Morgan's, Clarke.*
193 Michael Dickinson, Liddell's, Jackson.
194 Mary Shehee, w., Silman's, Pike.
195 Edward Barnard, Edwards's, Talbot.
196 William H. Rhodes, Lunceford's, Wilkes.
197 W. Allen Slaughter, s. l. w., Rooks's, Putnam.*
198 Abner B. Pollard, 1st, Chatham.
199 Jacob Lindsey, Jones's, Hall.
200 Rebecca Johnson, w., Peacock's, Washington.*
201 Armstead Hancock, Corley's, Putnam.

202 Joseph Wainwright, Ellsworth's, Bibb.
203 Andrew Millican, Johnson's, De Kalb.
204 James Gray, r. s., Madden's, Pike.
205 John S. Taiter, Hatton's, Baker.
206 Stephen Fennell, Goodwin's, Houston.
207 Dexter N. Gibson, Walker's, Columbia.*
208 William Cook, 118th, Hancock.*
209 John H. Beddingfield, Williams's, Washington.*
210 Elijah Smith, Nellum's, Elbert.*
211 Isaac Hayrgroves, Candler's, Bibb.
212 Thomas L. Lurry, Hargrove's, Newton.
213 Joseph Tynar, Britt's, Randolph.
214 William M'Farlan, Sutton's, Habersham.
215 Edward Harp, Gittens's, Fayette.
216 Joseph W. Walker, Dean's, De Kalb.
217 John Connell, r. s., Peterson's, Montgomery.*
218 Mary Kensey, w., Jones's, Habersham.
219 Zachariah Leatherwood, Smith's, Campbell.*
220 Jacob Smith, Crawford's, Franklin.
221 George Slatin, r. s., Lay's, Jackson.
222 George L. Hudgins, Blackstock's, Hall.
223 John M. Lambert, 72d, Burke.*
224 William Kennedy's ors., White's, Franklin.
225 Silas Cross, Roberts's, Hall.
226 Edmund Palmer, Price's, Hall.
227 Thomas H. D. Vanlandingham, 320th, Baldwin.*
228 John S. Jackson, 470th, Upson.*
229 Jason H. Mackey, Smith's, Henry.
230 John J. Miller, Braddey's, Jones.
231 Peril Smar, r. s., 121st, Richmond.*
232 Charles F. Humphreys, Holley's, Franklin.
233 Abraham Greeson, sol., 419th, Walton.
234 Moses Davis, Bower's, Elbert.
235 Zachariah H. Farmer, Silman's, Pike.*
236 Edward Hughes, Roe's, Burke.
237 Thomas Hairston, Foote's, De Kalb.
238 John Popham, Dyer's, Habersham.
239 Abner Lovelady, Burnett's, Habersham.
240 Martha Segraves, w., Seas's, Madison.*
241 Samuel Holton, Jr., Barron's, Houston.*
242 James Shannon, Athens, Clarke.*
243 Morning Mitchell, h. a., Say's, De Kalb.*
244 John M'Daniel, Gibson's, Decatur.
245 John Butler, Sen., 20th, Bryan.*
246 Littleberry Jackson, Daniel's, Hall.
247 Hartwill Murry's ors., Curry's, Wilkinson.
248 Seaborn Downs, 10th, Effingham.*

249 Elijah Bentley, 415th, Walton.*
250 Bealle Yarbrough's ors., Walker's, Columbia.
251 John Woods, Ellis's, Rabun.
252 Azariah Bradley, Nesbit's, Newton.
253 Benjamin B. Hodges, Slater's, Bulloch.*
254 Samuel G. Jones, 190th, Elbert.*
255 Simeon Russell, ———, Lee.
256 James Bigham, Gunn's, Jefferson.
257 S. and N. Jane Chasten, ors., 320th, Baldwin.*
258 John M. James, lun., 123d, Richmond.
259 Eliza Funderburk's ors., Hitchcock's, Muscogee.
260 John B. Barley, Griffin's, Burke.*
261 Noel Kennedy, Show's, Muscogee.*
262 Delilah Raper, h. a., Stephens's, Habersham.
263 Olivia Axon, or., 15th, Liberty.
264 Susan Ann Beall, w., M'Millon's, Lincoln.
265 Deskin Holcombe, Park's, Walton.*
266 George Perdee, Salem, Baldwin.*
267 Ledford Mobley, 249th, Walton.
268 Michael B. Isler, Camp's, Baker.
269 Mehena Todd, w., 4th, Chatham.
270 Austin Kilpatrick, Everett's, Washington.*
271 George W. Clarke, 600th, Richmond.
272 Algernoon S. Grier, Hall's, Butts.*
273 William Baldy, Newman's, Thomas.
274 Israel Clements, Robinson's, Fayette.
275 Elkanah Carroll, Turner's, Crawford.
276 Charles Spiller, Dean's, Clarke.
277 Williamson Terry, Shearer's, Coweta.*
278 Benjamin Harris, 279th, Morgan.
279 Elisha Betts, s. l. w., 419th, Walton.
280 Elizabeth Harper, w., Bishop's, Henry.
281 Thomas Rogers, Alberson's, Walton.
282 Littleton Tedder, Wright's, Laurens.
283 Edmund Jackson, Pace's, Putnam.
284 Hamilton Sharp, Blair's, Lowndes.
285 Elias Mimms, Martin's, Jones.
286 Gibson Slatin, Lay's, Jackson.
287 William Atchinson, Moseley's, Coweta.
288 Billy W. Hodges, Boynton's, Twiggs.
289 John Graham, Rick's, Laurens.
290 John Cook, Daniel's, Hall.
291 Gilbert Gay, Moseley's, Coweta.
292 Richard Card, Taylor's, Jones.
293 William Stringfellow, 119th, Richmond.
294 Rosannah Jemmison, w., 494th, Upson.
295 Reuben Hatcher, Sen., Justice's, Bibb.

296 George W. Collier, Gillis's, De Kalb.
297 Margaret Smith, Hampton's, Newton.
298 Evin Asbel, Hand's, Appling.
299 William Dean, sol., Smith's, Campbell.
300 Aaron Tucker, Strickland's, Merriwether.
301 William White, Davis's, Gwinnett.
302 David M. Smith, Crawford's, Franklin.
303 John Beggs, sol., Allen's, Bibb.
304 Isaiah Hand, Thompson's, Henry.
305 Judge E. Mattox, Coxe's, Morgan.
306 Samuel Price, Smith's, Henry.
307 Samuel Wellborns, sol. 1784–97, 167th, Wilkes.
308 Brinkley Cape, sol., Hood's, Henry.
309 John Thomasson, Seay's, Hall.
310 William Stephens, ———, Monroe.
311 John Smith's ors., Pearce's, Houston.
312 William Basley, Sweat's, Ware.*
313 Levi Masters, Kelly's, Elbert.
314 George Broach, Baismore's, Jones.*
315 John J. North, Thomas's, Ware.
316 John Evans, sol., Hodges's, Newton.
317 Robert Henry, Sen., r. s., Show's, Muscogee.
318 Julius Holmes, Groce's, Bibb.
319 Isaac Philips, Roberts's, Hall.*
320 Ashley A. M'Michael, 373d, Jasper.
321 Jesse Brundage, sol., 104th, Hancock.*
322 John Thomas, Southell's, Tatnall.
323 William A. Stephenson, Athens, Clarke.*
324 John Dorety, Coxe's, Talbot.

EIGHTEENTH DISTRICT, FIRST SECTION, CHEROKEE.

1 James Murray, Loven's, Henry.*
2 Hester Branch, w. r. s., Southwell's, Tatnall.*
3 John Mills, Park's, Walton.*
4 Seaborn Jones, Covington's, Pike.*
5 John A. Byrd, Athens, Clarke.*
6 Michael James's ors., 1st, Chatham.
7 Kinchen Harrison, sol., Newsom's, Warren.*
8 James Harrell, 561st, Upson.
9 Isaac Laroche's ors., 122d, Richmond.
10 William Savage, Hill's, Baldwin.*
11 William Bacon, Harris's, Columbia.
12 Felix H. Greene, Lunceford's, Wilkes.

13 Henry Guess, Gillis's, De Kalb.
14 Lorenzo D. Bowen, Hand's, Appling.*
15 Robert W. Lee, Howell's, Elbert.*
16 James Yarbrough, Gray's, Henry.*
17 John T. Spillers, 108th, Hancock.
18 John Hall, Head's, Butts.
19 William East, 735th, Troup.
20 Gilbert Blailock's ors., Hendon's, Carroll.
21 Philip Graham, Dearing's, Henry.
22 Andrew J. Morrow, Barker's, Gwinnett.
23 Nancy Duke, w. r. s., Night's, Morgan.
24 Daniel Martin, Young's, Carroll.
25 William Dison, Howell's, Troup.
26 Stephen Chatham's ors., Edwards's, Franklin.
27 Armstead Hardy, M'Ginnis's, Jackson.
28 Margaret Lovelady, w., Keener's, Rabun.
29 William H. Powell, Compton's, Fayette.
30 Isham Oliver, Adams's, Columbia.
31 Wilie Wright, Hodges's, Newton.
32 Emanuel Parris, 333d, Wayne.*
33 James Hatcher, or., Lamp's, Jefferson.*
34 Andrew Boyd, George's, Appling.
35 Caswell D. Morris's ors., Baismore's, Jones.
36 Francis N. Fordham, Buck's, Houston.
37 Robert M. Steger, Loven's, Henry.
38 John Marchman, Tompkins's, Putnam.*
39 John M'Cray's ors., Ellis's, Pulaski.*
40 John H. Hogan, Bostick's, Twiggs.*
41 Matthias Hoggle, Henton's, Wilkes.
42 Jacob C. Dyer, r. s., Tompkins's, Putnam.
43 Daniel M. G. Wilkinson, George's, Appling.*
44 John Wade, Hood's, Henry.
45 Jonathan Hicks, Sutton's, Habersham.
46 Richard Ward's ors., Thomason's, Elbert.
47 Arden Evan's ors., 278th, Morgan.
48 Elizabeth Roberts, w. r. s., 417th, Walton.
49 Francis Lewis, Wilson's, Pike.
50 Richard Blackstock, Daniel's, Hall.
51 Samuel P. Gragg, Pounds's, Twiggs.
52 Randol Willoughby, Elder's, Clarke.
53 Michael Barnwell, Chambers's, Houston.
54 Alexander Stewart, Grider's, Morgan.
55 Silas Mercer, 604th, Taliaferro.
56 Caleb Hillman, Parham's, Warren.
57 Washington Nelson, Clark's, Morgan.
58 Benjamin Dorton, Martin's, Pike.
59 Martha M'Intosh, w., Butts's, Monroe.*
8

60 Irwin Ewing, 112th, Hancock.*
61 Mary Swinney, lun., Morton's, De Kalb.
62 Delila M'Garrety, w., Bower's, Elbert.
63 Elisha Prickett, 121st, Richmond.*
64 Anderson Clements, 148th, Greene.
65 John Bruce, Dobbs's, Hall.
66 Alexander M'Carthy, 271st, M'Intosh.*
67 Littlebery M'Millon, 143d, Greene.
68 James Hunt, Chastain's, Habersham,
69 Isaac V. Cheek, Crawford's, Franklin.
70 Thomas C. Porter, 176th, Wilkes.
71 William Taylor, Mitchell's, Marion.*
72 Edny Ann Fears, or., 147th, Greene.
73 Daniel Jenkins, s., 406th, Gwinnett.*
74 John L. Rice, Hines's, Coweta.
75 John P. Burch, Ellis's, Rabun.*
76 Henry Buckannon, 295th, Jasper.*
77 Jacob Johnson, Camp's, Baker.*
78 Curlfriley Nelson, Dean's, De Kalb.*
79 William Mitchell, sol., Edwards's, Franklin.*
80 Dempsey Griffin, sol., Baker's, Liberty.
81 Joseph G. Boon, Blount's, Wilkinson.
82 Thomas L. Densler, 318th, Baldwin.*
83 Winship S. Page, Butts's, Monroe.
84 Joel Mann, 245th, Jackson.
85 Daniel Stanford, Culbreath's, Columbia.
86 Susannah Allen, w., Bustin's, Pike.
87 Mitchell Story, Norris's, Monroe.
88 Samuel Leathers, Jr., Duke's, Carroll.
89 Howard Robertson, Bridges's, Gwinnett.
90 Joseph Omans, Whipple's, Wilkinson.
91 John Ray, Sen., r. s., Hill's, Harris.
92 John Kendrick, 121st, Richmond.*
93 Ralegh Capp, 693d, Heard.*
94 John Ivins, Sutton's, Habersham.
95 Edward Morgan, Dobbs's, Hall.
96 Leroy Callaway, Kelly's, Jasper.
97 Prior Lewis, Jones's, Thomas.
98 Nancy Harvell, w., Flynn's, Muscogee.*
99 Jesse Hanson, Hines's, Coweta.
100 Eli Cox, Brock's, Habersham.
101 James Allen, Sen., sol., Arrington's, Merriwether.
102 James M. Houze, 761st, Heard.*
103 Perryman Bramblett, Reid's, Gwinnett.
104 Daniel Collins, Blackstock's, Hall.
105 Jeremiah Skelton's ors., Royster's, Franklin.
106 Daniel Shaptrine, Martin's, Pike.

107 Samuel L. Martin, Durrence's, Tatnall.*
108 Dempsey Murray, Paris, Burke.
109 Stephen Jackson, Edwards's, Talbot.
110 William E. Wellborn, Barker's, Gwinnett.*
111 James Tinsley's ors., 124th, Richmond.
112 Aulston Bunche's four orphans, 137th, Greene.
113 Archibald Woods, 71st, Burke.*
114 Bonatte C. Johnson, w., Edwards's, Talbot.
115 Ezekiel Strickland, Sen., sol., Stanton's, Newton.*
116 Anderson H. & J. J. Bryant, f. a., Seal's, Elbert.
117 George W. Hunter, Cleland's, Chatham.*
118 Jesse Coleman, r. s., 73d, Burke.*
119 James Ward, Roe's, Burke.
120 Hannah J. Brinson, w., Young's, Jefferson.
121 Berry T. Digby, Dawson's, Jasper.
122 Jefferson Roberts, 70th, Burke.
123 William S. Penn, Beaseley's, Oglethorpe.*
124 Mary Grady, w. r. s., Willis's, Franklin.
125 Ann Everidge, w., Blount's, Wilkinson.
126 Thomas M. White, Allen's, Campbell.
127 John Crews, 74th, Burke.*
128 William M. Rogers, Chandler's, Franklin.
129 Alexander Robinson, or., Mobley's, De Kalb.
130 John W. Tomme, Allen's, Henry.*
131 Alexander Bryan, sol., Ellsworth's, Bibb.
132 Norman W. M'Leod, Bourquin's, Chatham.
133 William Lowrey, Seay's, Hall.
134 Frederic Weaver, Higginbotham's, Rabun.
135 Leanah Stedham, w., Hill's, Harris.
136 Edward Lampkin, Athens, Clarke.
137 Samuel M. Perry, Perry's, Baldwin.*
138 Gause Jordan, Stewart's, Jones.
139 James Satterwhite, Hill's, Harris.
140 John Turner, Strickland's, Merriwether.
141 Jacob Klutts, Echols's, Clarke.
142 Samuel Tennison, sol., 735th, Troup.
143 Sarah Beck, w., Smith's, Campbell.
144 Robert C. Mays, Hall's, Butts.
145 Jehu Marsh's ors., Carswell's, Jefferson.
146 Middleton F. Nall, Thompson's, Henry.*
147 Dalegall Campbell, Allen's, Henry.*
148 Lewis Whitley, 537th, Upson.*
149 John J. Oberry, 24th, M'Intosh.
150 Stephen Moseley, 163d, Greene.*
151 Robert Boman, Stanfield's, Campbell.
152 Nancy Marchman, w., 160th, Greene.*
153 William Brady, sol., Goodwin's, Houston.

154 Thomas Stroud's ors., 55th, Emanuel.
155 Thomas J. Sanders, Hall's, Butts.
156 James Brewster, Sutton's, Habersham.
157 John Parks, Johnson's, Bibb.*
158 James C. Pemberton, Hill's, Baldwin.*
159 Thomas Presley, Allison's, Pike.
160 Armsted Atkinson, 606th, Taliaferro.*
161 Robert Lines, sol. 1784–97, Mackleroy's, Clarke.*
162 Richard J. Snelling, Yorks's, Stewart.
163 Thomas J. Grant, M. Brown's, Habersham.
164 David Smith's ors., Martin's, Newton.
165 John Smith, Thomas's, Ware.
166 Susannah Wheeler, w. r. s., 249th, Walton.*
167 Leonard Morrow, Atkinson's, Coweta.
168 William Wilkins, Jr., Robinson's, Putnam.*
169 Sol. Williams, Sen., Whitehead's, Habersham.
170 William Harry, sol., Allen's, Henry.*
171 John Scott, Sen., sol., Cleghorn's, Madison.
172 Samuel T. Pharr, 250th, Walton.
173 William Strickland, Loveless's, Gwinnett.
174 Henry Smith, Candler's, Bibb.
175 Wiatt A. Hunt, Hudson's, Marion.
176 Micajah Andrews, 15th, Liberty.
177 Robert Barron, 656th, Troup.
178 William Nunlee's ors., Smith's, Elbert.
179 Sidwell Kelley, Baismore's, Jones.
180 James, Barbary, & C. Ashley, ors., 458th, Early.
181 Jesse Dickinson, 406th, Gwinnett.*
182 William Mitchell, Sen., Willis's, Franklin.*
183 Jane Cook, w., Flynn's, Muscogee.
184 Thomas S. N. King, Wood's, Morgan.*
185 Dollerson Day, Clark's, Morgan.
186 Abram Coxe's ors., Nichols's, Fayette.
187 William Dowdy, Blackstock's, Hall.
188 Edward Houston, 11th, Effingham.*
189 George Boswell's ors., 605th, Taliaferro.
190 William Norman's ors., 166th, Wilkes.
191 William M. Craig, Effingham County, Chatham.
192 Thomas M. Cardin, Moore's, Randolph.*
193 William Hare, Watson's, Marion.
194 Isaac Wood, Will's, Twiggs.
195 Lucretia Bryan, w., Lockhart's, Bulloch.*
196 Thomas Keys, s. i. w., Clark's, Elbert.
197 Jeremiah G. Watson, Alsobrook's, Jones.*
198 Milledge Sapp, 777th, Randolph.
199 John Ingram, Sen., Vining's, Putnam.
200 Alfred Watkins, Bostick's, Twiggs.

201 Thomas Hudgeon, 395th, Emanuel.
202 John Worthy, Allen's, Bibb.
203 Absalom B. Bandy, Crawford's, Morgan.
204 John D. Buchannon, s. s., Alberson's, Walton.
205 Hilliard J. Jackson, Payne's, Merriwether.
206 Philip Coleman, Roberts's, Hall.
207 Elizabeth Alexander, w., Jennings's, Clarke.
208 (fr.) Elias Braden, Herndon's, Hall.
209 (fr.) John Hudgins, Dyer's, Habersham.
210 (fr.) John Thompson, Tuggle's, Merriwether.
211 Richard P. Massey, Moseley's, Wilkes.
212 William M. Thomas, or., Valleau's, Chatham.*
213 George Yarbrough, Mimm's, Fayette.
214 Henry W. Knowles, 365th, Jasper.
215 Charles Sharley, Camp's, Warren.
216 Philander O. Paris's ors., Stewart's, Warren.
217 Matthew Driggors, 24th, M'Intosh.
218 Elias Watson, 142d, Greene.
219 Jesse Davis, Rhodes's, De Kalb.*
220 Joshua Pemberton, sol., Harralson's, Troup.
221 Richard Hudson, Fleming's, Jefferson.*
222 Thomas Howell, David's, Franklin.*
223 Agnes Kelly, w., Maguire's, Morgan.
224 James Murphree's ors., 74th, Burke.
225 Warren Mize, Fleming's, Franklin.*
226 Edmund Coffey, Barker's, Gwinnett.
227 Charles J. Sorrells, 415th, Walton.
228 Elizabeth Bennett, w., 49th, Emanuel.
229 Willis Peacock, Peacock's, Washington.*
230 William H. Langford, 279th, Morgan.
231 Eleanor Coldwell, w., 144th, Greene.
232 Ruse Watkins, s. l. w., Guice's, Oglethorpe.
233 David Wright, Hodges's, Newton.
234 Alexander Langston, Holley's, Franklin.*
235 Elizabeth Freeman, w. r. s., Wilson's, Jasper.
236 James Terrell Goode, M'Clain's, Newton.*
237 John Dennard, Jr., Pounds's, Twiggs.
238 Harris W. Freeman, M'Clain's, Newton.
239 Robert Sanderlin, 600th, Richmond.
240 John Prestage's ors., Lamberth's, Fayette.
241 John Sharley, Smith's, Habersham.
242 James O. Smith, Jenkins's, Oglethorpe.
243 Samuel Berry, 734th, Lee.*
244 (fr.) John Baggett, 756th, Sumter.
245 (fr.) William A. Wilkison, Foote's, De Kalb.
246 William Fisher, Martin's, Washington.*
247 Samuel Smith, r. s., Sanderlin's, Chatham.

248 John J. Jackson, Valleau's, Chatham.*
249 Eli Morgan, 122d, Richmond.
250 John Musgrove, 537th, Upson.
251 Shadrack Smith, 271st, M'Intosh.
252 James English, Newman's, Thomas.
253 George Robinson, Pounds's, Twiggs.*
254 Alexander Johnson, Maguire's, Gwinnett.*
255 George D. Combs, 120th, Richmond.*
256 Starkey J. Sharpe, Peterson's, Burke.*
257 James P. Dozier's ors., Norris's, Monroe.
258 Abner Lowe, or., Dyer's, Habersham.
259 William King, r. s., Sweat's, Ware.*
260 Abner Groover, Groover's, Thomas.
261 William Dooley, Smith's, Habersham.
262 Green Brantley, Lightfoot's, Washington.
263 Daniel M'Dugall, M'Clure's, Rabun.*
264 Robert Stripling, M'Cleland's, Irwin.
265 Isham Williams, Higginbotham's, Madison.
266 Hester Beverly, i. t., Miller's, Ware.
267 Samuel Brown, 245th, Jackson.*
268 Green B. Holbrook, Hammond's, Franklin.
269 Martha Rowe, w., Say's, De Kalb.
270 John R. M'Millian, Smith's, Franklin.
271 Asa A. Turner's ors., Hammond's, Franklin.
272 William L. Burke, Jones's, Morgan.
273 Daniel G. Grantham, Jr., M'Cleland's, Irwin.
274 James G. Perryman, Thompson's, Henry.
275 (fr.) Isham Farmer, Allison's, Pike.
276 Armond Lefiles, sol., ———, M'Intosh.*
277 James R. Simmons, Loveless's, Henry.
278 Pleasant A. Cotes, Loven's, Henry.
279 Charles M. Vinson, 319th, Baldwin.
280 Solomon Thomas, Justice's, Bibb.*
281 Hannah Thomas, w., Whitehead's, Habersham.
282 Archibald R. S. Hunter, sol., 106th, Hancock.*
283 James E. Cosby, Pollard's, Wilkes.*
284 Charles Epperson, Mangum's, Franklin.*
285 Elizabeth Arrant, w. r. s., 561st, Upson.
286 Sarah T. Adams, w., Sanderlin's, Chatham.
287 Presley Garner, Barnett's, Clarke.
288 Waters Dunn, Tankersley's, Columbia.
289 Garratt Morris, sol., Morgan's, Clarke.
290 William Jackson, Reid's, Gwinnett.
291 Richard Jones Kolb, or., Barefield's, Jones.
292 Daniel Gordman, Whitaker's, Crawford.*
293 Arthur C. Perry's ors., Streetman's, Twiggs.
294 William Methvin, Oliver's, Twiggs.

295 William M. Henly, 1st, Chatham.*
296 David Harmon, 7th, Chatham.*
297 William H. Mallory, Whisenhunt's, Carroll.*
298 Nathan C. Munroe, Ellsworth's, Bibb.*
299 Alfred Bwich, Wooten's, Telfair.*
300 Henry Wood, Bryan's, Monroe.
301 Joseph F. Roper, Reid's, Gwinnett.
302 Clabourn A. Mann, Candler's, Bibb.
303 James Combs, Herring's, Twiggs.
304 (fr.) James A. Beard, Sen., Hughes's, Habersham.
305 William Stewart, 702d, Heard.*
306 Nicholas Brown, Royster's, Franklin.
307 Levi Hadaway, s. l. w., Coxe's, Morgan.
308 Isaac M'Ginty, sol., Martin's, Pike.*
309 Eleanor Gray, w., Willis's, Franklin.
310 Silvanus Pittman, Candler's, Bibb.
311 John F. Findley, Smith's, Campbell.*
312 Jacob D. Yonks, M'Daniel's, Pulaski.
313 Sarah Lambert, w. r. s., Lay's, Jackson.
314 Thomas G. Stewart, Candler's, Bibb.
315 John Butler, id., 789th, Sumter.
316 David Bell, Mattox's, Lowndes.
317 John Glover, Boynton's, Twiggs.

NINETEENTH DISTRICT, FIRST SECTION, CHEROKEE.

1 Robert R. Gilbert, Graves's, Putnam.
2 Lecenday Floid, or., Edwards's, Talbot.
3 Jesse Carter, Jr., Coward's, Lowndes.
4 William A. Guardner, Dearing's, Butts.
5 Fleming Davis, Rooks's, Putnam.
6 James Hutchins, Loveless's, Gwinnett.
7 Alexander Stringer, Roe's, Burke.
8 Lucy Walling, w., Merck's, Hall.*
9 James Livermon, Mizell's, Talbot.*
10 Starling Carroll, Hampton's, Newton.
11 David Mann's ors., Smith's, Wilkinson.
12 Nancy Lamar, w., Martin's, Jones.
13 William Smith, Groce's, Bibb.
14 John F. Johnson, Dozier's, Columbia.
15 Edwin H. Kennebrew, Hatchett's, Oglethorpe.
16 James Mathews, sol., 373d, Jasper.
17 Alexander Irwin, 537th, Upson.
18 Sarah Alexander, w. r. s., Chambers's, Gwinnett
19 Lewis D. Yancy, Jr., M'Korkle's, Jasper.

20 Russell Whaley, 249th, Walton.
21 Covington Brooks, Tankersley's, Columbia.
22 Martin D. Wheelus, Wood's, Morgan.
23 Benjamin Gheesling, Jr., Pate's, Warren.*
24 James and Jared Bull, ors., Williams's, Decatur.
25 Sabra Smith, w., Strickland's, Merriwether.*
26 Henry L. Wells, Dixon's, Irwin.*
27 Green P. Cozart, Moseley's, Wilkes.
28 Sarah Weaver, w., Blount's, Wilkinson.*
29 Squire Navels, Butts's, Monroe.*
30 John M'Crary, Jr., ———, Talbot.
31 Mark Ragan, s. i. w., Park's, Walton.
32 Stafford Williams, s. l. w., Gunn's, Jones.
33 Abslum Ogletree, sol., Griffin's, Fayette.
34 Susan Beeman, h. a., 63d, Taliaferro.
35 Miles Robinson, 319th, Baldwin.
36 William Stovall, Royster's, Franklin.
37 Tilmon Brooks, 735th, Troup.
38 Susannah Langbridge, w., Willis's, Franklin.
39 Ephraim P. Hill, Streetman's, Twiggs.
40 Henry Herrington, Copeland's, Houston.
41 John B. Whitaker, Martin's, Washington.
42 John Dixon, Mitchell's, Marion.
43 John Marshall's ors., 289th, Jasper.
44 Bryan Whitfield, M'Gehee's, Troup.
45 Thomas Bachellor's ors., 374th, Putnam.
46 John S. Bell, Price's, Hall.
47 Thomas Ray, 603d, Taliaferro.
48 Joab Clark, Jr., s. l. w., Hall's, Camden.*
49 Bethel Haines, Whitfield's, Washington.*
50 Thomas Tipton, Swain's, Thomas.*
51 Barnett Hawes, Baismore's, Jones.
52 Martin Chester, Harrison's, Decatur.*
53 Ephraim Wilson, Chambers's, Gwinnett.
54 Mabrey Lovejoy, Young's, Carroll.
55 Levi Pendley, Barker's, Gwinnett.
56 James T. Findley, 147th, Greene.
57 John Cartledge, 124th, Richmond.*
58 Ebenezer Deloach, Durrence's, Tatnall.*
59 Evan T. Davis, Dozier's, Columbia.
60 William Mattox, Baismore's, Jones.
61 Ashley Blackstock, Hines's, Coweta.
62 Isaac Collins, Sims's, Troup.
63 William Payne, Roberts's, Hall.
64 Paul Patrick, Sen., 249th, Walton.
65 M'Grewder Bryan, 162d, Greene.
66 Stephen E. Etchison, 415th, Walton.

67 John Anderson, Brewton's, Tatnall.
68 John Rutherford, Will's, Twiggs.
69 Alexander Harris, Dearing's, Henry.
70 Timothy Jackson, Mann's, Crawford.
71 (fr.) Wilson Palmer, Mizell's, Talbot.
72 William Dickson, Johnson's, Bibb.*
73 (fr.) Elias House, Hood's, Henry.
74 John W. West, Hughes's, Habersham.
75 Jesse Murphey, Chambers's, Gwinnett.
76 Ephroditus Bond, Lunceford's, Elbert.
77 George T. Jameson, Chambers's, Houston.*
78 Shadrick Moore, sol., Whitfield's, Washington.
79 Thomas Jeffers, 72d, Burke.*
80 Gillis Ivey Adams, sol., Higginbotham's, Carroll.
81 William Gillis, Morrison's, Montgomery.
82 John H. Willingham, 735th, Troup.
83 William M. Chiney, Stanton's, Newton.
84 Samuel Butler's ors., Bryan's, Monroe.
85 Morris M'Gill, sol., M'Gill's, Lincoln.
86 Anderson Sanderford's ors., Morgan's, Appling.
87 Mary Graybill, w., 101st, Hancock.
88 Henry C. Phelps, Flynn's, Muscogee.*
89 James Altman, of Crawford, Candler's, Bibb.
90 John Ledbetter, Roberts's, Hall.
91 William F. Mitchell, Barker's, Gwinnett.
92 James Stanford, Walker's, Columbia.*
93 John Manley, or., 1st, Chatham.
94 Alfred Hinsley, Dearing's, Henry.*
95 Robert W. P. Moore, Field's, Habersham.
96 John Roberts, Reid's, Gwinnett.
97 William Lowe, Sen., Arrington's, Merriwether.
98 Benjamin Scroggins, Sen., Miller's, Jackson.
99 Noah Bui's ors., Sanders's, Jones.
100 Meshack Johnson, 249th, Walton.
101 (fr.) William H. Harford, 15th, Liberty.
102 (fr.) E. Hotton, w., Haygood's, Washington.
103 (fr.) Iccabud Hood, 295th, Jasper.
104 William G. Wright, Davis's, Clarke.*
105 John Brownin, Groover's, Thomas.*
106 Stephen W. Stephens, Allen's, Henry.
107 William Stewart, Curry's, Wilkinson.
108 Aaron Cock's ors., f. a., s. l. w., Lester's, Pulaski.
109 Moses Blake, Chambers's, Gwinnett.
110 Thomas G. Glaze, M'Dowell's, Lincoln.
111 James Rash, Burnett's, Habersham.*
112 John Zellars, Stokes's, Lincoln.*
113 John Henderson, Baugh's, Jackson.
9

114 Samuel Pruett's ors., Neal's, Campbell.
115 (fr.) John Collins, 589th, Upson.*
116 (fr.) Riley Medlin, sol., Tower's, Gwinnett.
117 (fr.) Hezekiah Adams, Dean's, De Kalb.
118 (fr.) Archibald Boggs, 398th, Richmond.
119 Mathew Parham, Camp's, Warren.
120 Philips Crawford, r. s., Nesbit's, Newton.
121 Charles A. Haynie, Colley's, Oglethorpe.
122 (fr.) James Danely, or., Jordan's, Bibb.
123 (fr.) Jane S. Marks, w., Flynn's, Muscogee.
124 (fr.) Edward Crossley, 144th, Greene.
125 (fr.) Mary Badolet, w., Fitzpatrick's, Chatham.

FOURTH DISTRICT, SECOND SECTION, CHEROKEE

1 John L. Eubank, Jr., 242d, Jackson.*
2 Bolton Thurmond, M'Gehee's, Troup.
3 William Perrett, Winter's, Jones.
4 Lemuel Wilkerson, 454th, Walton.*
5 Elizabeth Martin, w., Gillis's, De Kalb.
6 Green Cowfield, 735th, Troup.
7 Edward Weaver, Durham's, Talbot.
8 Stephen Bodeford, 789th, Sumter.
9 Phereby Gaylord, w., 588th, Upson.
10 Newel Tullis, Sims's, Troup.
11 William B. Heath, sol., Frasier's, Monroe.*
12 Jeremiah Trout, 242d, Jackson.
13 John Coleman, Roberts's, Hall.
14 Mary Ann Jeannevette, or., 271st, M'Intosh.
15 Abram Weldon, 365th, Jasper.
16 William M. Wimbush, 466th, Monroe.
17 Cooper M'Ellhannon, Robinson's, Fayette.
18 Josiah Jarrard, Brock's, Habersham.*
19 (fr.) William Moon, Stewart's, Troup.
20 (fr.) James Townsend, Harp's, Stewart.
21 Charles Kaple, 603d, Taliaferro.*
22 Abner C. Dozier, 656th, Troup.
23 William Barnes's ors., Covington's, Pike.
24 Peter Dennis, sol., Coxe's, Talbot.
25 Richard Conier, Sen., 307th, Putnam.
26 Elijah B. Riden, Seas's, Madison.
27 John Woolf's ors., 10th, Effingham.
28 John Morgan, Hargrove's, Newton.
29 James Nobles, Newman's, Thomas.*

30 Alexander Forester, 250th, Walton.
31 Freeman Walker, Stewart's, Warren.
32 James Echols, Ware's, Coweta.
33 William Jackson, Sen., 162d, Greene.
34 William J. Young, Morton's, De Kalb.*
35 Sherod Boman, 3d section, Cherokee.
36 Charles Henry, sol., Bower's, Elbert.*
37 Rich. W. Habersham, Jr., Fitzpatrick's, Chatham.
38 Johnson W. Denman, Welche's, Habersham.
39 James Mikell, r. s., Slater's, Bulloch.
40 Asburn B. Bell, Clark's, Elbert.
41 Aramanors Anderson, Smith's, Habersham.
42 Samuel Stilman, Coker's, Troup.
43 Rebecca Cook, h. a., Dixon's, Irwin.
44 Wiley Bagley, sol., Barker's, Gwinnett.
45 Thomas Jones, 458th, Early.
46 R. Johnson (son of Edmund), Johnson's, Warren.
47 Seaborn Ivey, Alberson's, Walton.
48 Charles T. Hart (Sunbury), Baker's, Liberty.*
49 James Fiveash, Morrison's, Appling.*
50 Benjamin Harper, sol., 104th, Hancock.
51 Robert Augustus Holt, Park's, Walton.
52 Clemmew Jones, 735th, Troup.
53 Abner N. Bristow, 608th, Taliaferro.
54 Martin Hines, sol., Barnett's, Clarke.*
55 Eleanor Buckner, w., 404th, Gwinnett.*
56 Oliver Higginbotham, s. i. w., Alberson's, Walton.
57 (fr.) M'Gilbrey Barber, Dilman's, Pulaski.
58 (fr.) John Coley, Burnett's, Habersham.
59 Wilson Edwards, Latimer's, De Kalb.
60 John Magnan, Davis's, Jones.
61 John F. Wasson, Chambers's, Gwinnett.
62 Averilla Dopson, w., Chiles's, Marion.*
63 John A. Took, or., Peacock's, Washington.
64 Elijah Miller, sol., Burk's, Stewart.
65 Samuel G. Wheatley, Fulks's, Wilkes.*
66 George Moseley, Evans's, Fayette.
67 Thomas Wilson, Lynn's, Warren.*
68 Joseph Studdard, Cleggs's, Walton.*
69 Nancy Russell, w., Royster's, Franklin.
70 James S. Carruthers, Wheeler's, Pulaski.
71 Ashley G. Parker, Martin's, Laurens.
72 Samuel W. Skidmore, 279th, Morgan.
73 Willise Magnor, 72d, Burke.*
74 John Martin's ors., 494th, Upson.
75 Elijah Smallwood, Hamilton's, Hall.*
76 James H. Fielder, Clark's, Morgan.

77 Peterson G. Brogden, Dearing's, Butts.*
78 Duncan Cameron, Cook's, Telfair.
79 Robert Fennell's ors., Sam Streetman's, Twiggs.
80 William Wyatt, Ross's, Monroe.
81 Dudley Groce, 537th, Upson.*
82 William Garratt, Curry's, Wilkinson.*
83 Thomas S. Walton, Benson's, Lincoln.
84 Thomas J. M'Mullan, 494th, Upson.*
85 Hosea Bailey, Pearce's, Houston.*
86 Calvin Hayes, Miller's, Camden.*
87 Hilson W. Ivey, Kellum's, Talbot.
88 Dillard Norris, Pate's, Warren.*
89 Ebenezer W. Smith, Summerlin's, Bulloch.
90 Elizabeth Reid, w., 398th, Richmond.*
91 William W. Smith, Willis's, Franklin.
92 John Camron, Chambers's, Gwinnett.*
93 Mashack V. Crawford, Belcher's, Jasper.
94 Robert Castleberry, 777th, Randolph.
95 (fr.) Josiah Langley, Bryan's, Monroe.
96 (fr.) David Moses, 734th, Lee.
97 Thomas Hicks, Woodruff's, Campbell.
98 Edmund Cody, Sen., Pate's, Warren.
99 Lucinda Findley, w., 148th, Greene.
100 Hollis Boynton, Boynton's, Twiggs.
101 Martin Cornwall, Hughes's, Habersham.*
102 Thomas H. Connell, Thomas's, Clarke.*
103 John Bland, Bustin's, Pike.
104 Micajah W. Davis, Nichols's, Fayette.*
105 Benjamin E. Alford, Show's, Muscogee.*
106 Coleman Watkins, Miller's, Jackson.
107 Whitfield Gainus, Goodwin's, Houston.
108 Pryent E. Jackson, Gunn's, Henry.
109 William Townsend, Blackstock's, Hall.*
110 Allen A. Andrews, Coxe's, Talbot.*
111 John C. Henderson, Vining's, Putnam.
112 Fontain Formby, 735th, Troup.*
113 Donald M'Donald, Jr., Fleming's, Franklin.
114 Michael H. Goss, Hutson's, Newton.*
115 William H. Smith, 494th, Upson.*
116 James L. Wozencroft, Thomas's, Clarke.*
117 Edmund Ferguson, Price's, Hall.
118 Matthew Nelson, 600th, Richmond.*
119 James Maxwell, s. i. w., Brown's, Habersham.*
120 Morgan Sparks, or., Sparks's, Washington.*
121 Silas Kendrick, Grubbs's, Columbia.*
122 William Hughes, Hammond's, Franklin.*
123 Thomas B. Thompson, Jack's, Clarke.

124 Henry Oliver, Oliver's, Decatur.
125 Isaac Frasier, Williams's, Walton.
126 Rukin Tompkins, s. l. w.,Williams's,Washington.
127 Clark Martin, Hargrove's, Oglethorpe.
128 Josiah Prator, Daniel's, Hall.
129 John Burch, Sen., Ellis's, Rabun.
130 Clement A. Hogue, Arrington's, Merriwether.*
131 Martin Kenard, sol., Phillips's, Monroe.*
132 Charles M'Kenney, sol., Baugh's, Jackson.
133 (fr.) Elijah Gorday, 49th, Emanuel.*
134 (fr.) Howard Smith, sol., Harris's, De Kalb.*
135 James Parker, s. l. w., Williams's, Walton.
136 Hosea Cole, Gittens's, Fayette.*
137 James W. Evans, Chesnut's, Newton.
138 Elizabeth Tison, w. s. l. w., 512th, Lee.
139 Henry Thornton's ors., Jordin's, Harris.
140 Samuel Greenway, s. l. w., 55th, Emanuel.
141 Ann Bayer, w., 118th, Hancock.
142 Hilliard J. Askew, Bragaw's, Oglethorpe.
143 Francis M'Waters, M'Culler's, Newton.*
144 Benjamin Griffin, M'Cleland's, Irwin.*
145 Charles F. Capp, Valleau's, Chatham.
146 Thomas Millican, r. s., Johnson's, De Kalb.*
147 James A. Fawns, Valleau's, Chatham.*
148 Barbary Thomas, Marsh's, Thomas.
149 Elkanah Wilson, 1st, Chatham.*
150 Polly Jones, w., 600th, Richmond.
151 Winney Hill, id., 249th, Walton.
152 Lydia M. Baldwin, w., Valleau's, Chatham.
153 Daniel Alderman, Newman's, Thomas.*
154 Robert Howard, Colley's, Oglethorpe.*
155 Hugh Wise, M'Linn's, Butts.
156 James Hatchcox, Payne's, Merriwether.
157 Celia Giles, w., Everett's, Washington.
158 Sarah Wamack, w., Mason's, Washington.*
159 John Eperson, Mangum's, Franklin.*
160 William Bolin, 720th, Decatur.
161 Richardson Booker, Jr., 559th, Walton.*
162 Stephen T. Burgess, 585th, Dooly.*
163 James P. Askew, 107th, Hancock.
164 John Dean, Moseley's, Coweta.*
165 James Yeates's ors., Garner's, Washington.*
166 Thomas Jennings, M'Millon's, Lincoln.
167 Colmon W. Crow, Edwards's, Franklin.
168 Permelia Combs, w., Robinson's, Putman.
169 David Wilkins, Grubbs's, Columbia.
170 Silas Cross, Roberts's, Hall.

171 (fr.) William Liles, Lamberth's, Fayette.
172 (fr.) Burrell Bottoms, Allison's, Pike.
173 Patience Poarch, w., 374th, Putnam.
174 Hezekiah Stephens, Bryant's, Burke.
175 Augustus B. Longstreet, 119th, Richmond.*
176 Hartwill Bass, Underwood's, Putnam.
177 Orphans of William Carithers, Seas's, Madison.*
178 Grabella Coldwell, w., 22d, M'Intosh.*
179 Spencer Crawley's ors., Smith's, Henry.
180 Jeremiah A. Tharp, Sam Streetman's, Twiggs.*
181 Sanders Vann, sol., Harralson's, Troup.
182 Hugh Norton, or. of L. Norton, Bailey's, Camden.
183 Sarah Chain, w., Stewart's, Jones.*
184 Sarah Stone, w., Leveritt's, Lincoln.*
185 William Askew, sol., M'Korkle's, Jasper.
186 John Whitesett's ors., Baismore's, Jones.
187 William Whitlow, Thomas's, Clarke.
188 Edward B. Moxon, Wilcox's, Telfair.*
189 Edward M. Story, Shearer's, Coweta.
190 Nathan Eldridge's ors., Moore's, Randolph.
191 Jonathan M'Kay, Smith's, Henry.
192 John Green, Summerlin's, Bulloch.
193 Joseph Rogers, Alberson's, Walto n
194 Seaborn A. Smith, 785th, Sumter.*
195 Henry Bonner, 307th, Putnam.
196 Baty W. Thompson, Lester's, Pulaski.
197 Henry Weatherby, Bivins's, Jones.
198 Theophilus Blackwell, Michell's, Pulaski.
199 John Prewit, Taylor's, Elbert.
200 John Jenkins's ors., Winter's, Jones.
201 Richard Benett, 271st, M'Intosh.*
202 David Payne, Jr., Smith's, Franklin.*
203 Samuel Newell, Willis's, Franklin.
204 Edmund Greer, Crawford's, Morgan.*
205 Margaret Martin, w., Merck's, Hall.
206 Joshua H. Randolph, 248th, Jackson.
207 William P. Rogers, Ballard's, Morgan.
208 Green P. Haygood, Echols's, Clarke.*
209 (fr.) Ira E. Smith, Ware's, Coweta.
210 (fr.) James Nocks's ors., Sanderlin's, Chatham.
211 John D. Coates, Thompson's, Henry.
212 Thomas Bonner, Higginbotham's, Carroll.
213 David M'Vey, sol., Dilman's, Pulaski.
214 Nathaniel R. Lawson, Hammock's, Jasper.*
215 Joseph Trimble, Crawford's, Morgan.
216 Silas Grase, 111th, Hancock.*
217 Kinchen Worrell, 124th, Richmond.

218 Carvin Sawyer's ors., Morris's, Crawford.
219 Smelia Seabrook, Hart's, Jones.*
220 Samuel J. Martin, Williams's, Decatur.*
221 Dicy Carden, w., 415th, Walton.*
222 Joseph Waldrup, Sutton's, Habersham.*
223 Zachariah Smith, Allen's, Bibb.
224 Matthew Lufbarrow, sol., Valleau's, Chatham.*
225 Duncan Bohannon, M'Clain's, Newton.*
226 Wiley A. Roberts, 144th, Greene.*
227 Johnson Tucker, Edwards's, Franklin.
228 Edward R. Akin, sol., Athens, Clarke.*
229 William Smith, Sen., Hearn's, Butts.
230 Thomas H. Marler, 175th, Wilkes.*
231 Patrick O'Connell, Sanderlin's, Chatham.*
232 Charity Pile, w., Allen's, Henry.
233 Nathaniel R. Word, Kelly's, Jasper.*
234 David G. Clements, Wooten's, Telfair.
235 Naaman A. Little, Johnson's, De Kalb.
236 Robert B. Russell, Russell's, Henry.
237 Nancy Howard, w., Sinquefield's, Washington.*
238 Priscilla Evans, or., 756th, Sumter.*
239 John Register, s. l. w., Hobbs's, Laurens.
240 Moses Eastman, Valleau's, Chatham.
241 Walker R. Thornton, Fleming's, Franklin.
242 Edmund Pearce, sol., Whisenhunt's, Carroll.*
243 Henry D. Mitchell, Wooten's, Telfair.*
244 Abraham Johnson, Baismore's, Jones.
245 Robert Pryor, 73d, Burke.*
246 Matthew Anderson, sol., Bishop's, Henry.*
247 (fr.) Mary M. Clemman's, w., Prescott's, Twiggs.
248 (fr.) James Slaughter, Davis's, Jones.
249 Silas Crawford, Jack's, Clarke.*
250 Joshua Bussey, Leveritt's, Lincoln.*
251 James T. Carslarphen, Mann's, Crawford.
252 James H. M'Carter, Edwards's, Franklin.
253 Mary Burgess, w., Sewell's, Franklin.
254 John Draper, Thaxton's, Butts.
255 Henry Sharp, sol., 1st section, Cherokee.
256 John Nevill, Jones's, Bulloch.
257 Benjamin J. Barnett's ors., Seas's, Madison.
258 John M. Stroud, Stanfield's, Campbell.
259 Solomon Barber, Lamp's, Jefferson.
260 Sol. Williams, Sen., Whitehead's, Habersham.
261 Thomas H. Harden, 20th, Bryan.*
262 Alexander Robertson, Whelchel's, Hall.
263 Richard Cullins, Reid's, Gwinnett.*
264 David J. Porch, or., Bryan's, Monroe.

265 Elijah Ray's ors., Griffin's, Merriwether.
266 Payton Baughan, Strickland's, Merriwether.
267 William M. Johnson, Watson's, Marion.
268 Reuben Mullins, Griffin's, Hall.
269 James O. Lunders, Wynn's, Gwinnett.*
270 Joseph Coleman, 605th, Taliaferro.*
271 Charles Cantrill, Higginbotham's, Rabun.*
272 Jephthah Brantley, Peacock's, Washington.
273 Edward H. Campbell, or., Williams's, Washington
274 Martha Hinds, w. r. s., 3d, Chatham.
275 Wiley Jones's three orphans, Dean's, De Kalb.
276 Hiram Brady, Brown's, Habersham.
277 Tundy H. Greene, Mobley's, De Kalb.
278 Thomas King's ors., Bridges's, Gwinnett.
279 James Hall's ors., Hicks's, Decatur.
280 Citizen Sparks, Lamberth's, Fayette.
281 Robert Henderson, sol., M'Gills's, Lincoln.*
282 Richard Ramsay, Willis's, Franklin.
283 Robert Shepard, Barron's, Houston.
284 James Merrill's ors., Allen's, Monroe.
285 (fr.) Samuel Walder, Swiney's, Laurens.
286 (fr.) Larkin M. Elliott's ors., Brock's, Habersham.
287 Alfred Walker's or., Bustin's, Pike.
288 Richard Chitwood, sol., Brown's, Habersham.
289 James Chalmers, Ware's, Coweta.
290 Richard Herndon, Rick's, Laurens.
291 Ruth Ingram, w., Seay's, Hall.*
292 John Dempsey, s. i. w., Aderhold's, Campbell.
293 Thomas P. House, Coxe's, Franklin.*
294 James Shed, Higginbotham's, Rabun.
295 John Robinson, sol., Robinson's, Fayette.*
296 Solomon Newsom, Sen., Newsom's, Warren.*
297 Jacob Clark, Jr., Hall's, Camden.*
298 Elias Alread. Sen., Griffin's, Hall.*
299 Daniel Redwine, Rider's, Jackson.
300 Benjamin Nicholson, Watson's, Marion.*
301 Richard Bennett's ors., Sims's, Troup.
302 Ingram Bass, 101st, Hancock.
303 Elias Barlow, Morrison's, Montgomery.
304 William Hall, Miller's, Jackson.
305 James Wade, Walker's, Harris.
306 Jacob Wilcox, Cleland's, Chatham.
307 James N. Hodgen, Perryman's, Warren.
308 James Arnold's ors., Robinson's, Washington.
309 Thomas Willis, Sanders's, Jones.
310 Stephen Woodall, 177th, Wilkes.
311 James White, 561st, Upson.*

312 Clemeth Cavender, Seay's, Hall.*
313 Joseph A. Sturdevant, 366th, Jasper.
314 James M. Renfroe, Haygood's Washington.
315 Isaac N. Moreland, Talley's, Troup.*
316 Frances B. Golden, w. r. s., Anderson's, Wilkes.
317 Alexander Shaw, 745th, Sumter.
318 Thomas Valentine, Talley's, Troup.
319 George Tilley's ors., Roe's, Burke.
320 William Nobles's ors., 417th, Walton.
321 John Griffin, Watson's, Marion.
322 William W. Oates, Valleau's, Chatham.*

Note—For the balance of this district, see Appendix.

FIFTH DISTRICT, SECOND SECTION, CHEROKEE.

1 William W. Howard, Mashburn's, Pulaski.
2 Josiah Meeks, Mimm's, Fayette.
3 William Flarry, Lunceford's, Wilkes.
4 Samuel B. Wylie, Nesbit's, Newton.*
5 George Bolen, Harrison's, Decatur.
6 Reuben Duke, Rogers's, Burke.
7 Hilliard W. Perkins, Miller's, Jackson.
8 William Gaulding, or., Howell's, Elbert.
9 Robert Gillam, Allen's, Henry.
10 John Richardson, Merck's, Hall.
11 George W. Hammond, Madden's, Pike.*
12 Donoho Orran, sol., Sanderlin's, Chatham.*
13 Jesse Fulford, Folsom's, Lowndes.*
14 Warner P. Kennan, Head's, Butts.* ·
15 Noah W. Meadows, Hardman's, Oglethorpe.
16 Bray Warren's ors., Peurifoy's, Henry.
17 Jarkin & Tab. Forbes, ors., Smith's, Habersham.
18 William Roberts, sol., Brewer's, Monroe.
19 Andrew Valentine, Young's, Wilkinson.
20 Benjamin Evans, Seay's, Hall.
21 Gafen Johnson, Givens's, De Kalb.
22 John Haynes, sol., Baugh's, Jackson.*
23 Henry Passmore, Douglass's, Telfair.*
24 William Miller, sol., Merck's, Hall.
25 John M. Winbush, 364th, Jasper.
26 William Williamson, Price's, Hall.
27 Ephraim Driggors, Peavy's, Bulloch.
28 Wilson Roberts, 2d section, Cherokee.
29 Middleton G. Davis, Crawford's, Morgan.

30 Edward Kinnington, Jr., Gittens's, Fayette.*
31 James S. Meek, Perry's, Butts.
32 Joseph H. Ledbetter, Athens, Clarke.*
33 Henry Mann, Johnson's, De Kalb.*
34 Moses B. Dobbins, Peurifoy's, Henry.
35 William Mitchell, Jr., Willis's, Franklin.
36 Jesse Hearn, Streetman's, Twiggs.
37 Francis A. Wheat, 470th, Upson.
38 Elijah Sullivan, 320th, Baldwin.
39 John Robinson, Burgess's, Carroll.
40 Samuel Swilly's ors., Walker's, Houston.
41 David Griffin, Bishop's, Henry.
42 Burrell M'Cullers, sol. 1784–97, Kelly's, Jasper.
43 James W. Pearre, Tankersley's, Columbia.
44 Samuel Hadden, Hannah's, Jefferson.
45 Isaac Johnson's ors., Peacock's, Washington.
46 William B. Snead, 320th, Baldwin.
47 Henry Dobson, r. s., Price's, Hall.
48 Stephen H. Cash, Latimer's, De Kalb.*
49 Joseph Park, Curry's, Merriwether.
50 Owen Wood, Barnett's, Clarke.
51 Caleb Faircloth, Jr., Hatton's, Baker.
52 Paul Fitzsimmons, Alexander's, Jefferson.
53 William Carmichael, 788th, Heard.
54 George Turner, sol., 108th, Hancock.
55 P. Watkins, Sen., s. l. w., Guice's, Oglethorpe.*
56 Edward Kennington, Sen., Gittens's, Fayette.
57 Thomas P. Faine, Killen's, Decatur.
58 Alexander Leard, Covington's, Pike.*
59 Loxley Walker's ors., 561st, Upson.
60 Jesse Jackson, s. l. w., 470th, Upson.
61 Saml. L. Carithers's ors., Hardman's, Oglethorpe.
62 Martha Baun, 15th, Liberty.
63 David M. Satterwhite, Hill's, Harris.
64 James Deal, 49th, Emanuel.
65 James Moore, Bush's, Burke.
66 Thomas House, Seay's, Hall.
67 Seaborn Moseley, Peterson's, Montgomery.
68 Ann Cooke, w., Daniel's, Hall.
69 John Bryant, sol., Maguire's, Gwinnett.*
70 John W. Raines, Nellum's, Elbert.
71 John Silvey, 175th, Wilkes.*
72 Henry M. Duke, 294th, Jasper.
73 Ailcy Miller, w., Green's, Oglethorpe.
74 William Hines, sol., 75th, Burke.*
75 Allen Meeks, 56th, Emanuel.*
76 Silas Rooks, Walker's, Houston.
77 John Wester, 702d, Heard.*

78 John Prince, r. s., Dyer's, Habersham.
79 John S. Ingram, Berry's, Butts.
80 William Sowell, 36th, Scriven.
81 Abram Leathers, Duke's, Carroll.*
82 Robert Field, Smith's, Campbell.
83 Ansel Terrell, Marsh's, Thomas.*
84 F., Wm., & J. Rozier, f. a., Newsom's, Warren.
85 John Sparrow, Wheelus's, Pulaski.
86 William Godfrey, or., Griffin's, Burke.
87 Ezra Stacy, 15th, Liberty.
88 Eppes Tucker, Sen., Hampton's, Newton.*
89 Thomas Jones, Esq., s., 406th, Gwinnett.
90 Thomas Cape, Coxe's, Franklin.
91 Wiley Shurbutt, 735th, Troup.*
92 William Levins, Thomas's, Ware.
93 Mary Linzey, w., 395th, Emanuel.
94 Green Bailey, s. l. w., 470th, Upson.*
95 Henry Cabaness, r. s., Wilhite's, Elbert.
96 Wyton Clary, George's, Appling.*
97 Jesse Rambo, Chambers's, Gwinnett.*
98 Isaac N. Craven, Brock's, Habersham.
99 Johnston C. Rogers, Candler's, Bibb.
100 William B. Norman, Hinton's, Wilkes.
101 Elijah G. Hearn, Edwards's, Talbot.
102 Isaac Minis, sol., 3d, Chatham.*
103 Abraham Sherley, Smith's, Habersham.
104 Susannah Register, or., 585th, Dooly.
105 George Cook, M'Culler's, Newton.
106 Samuel P. Walker, or., Dean's, De Kalb.
107 Josua Keebler, 9th, Effingham.*
108 William Ragland, r. s., Peurifoy's, Henry.
109 Hamilton Reid, 789th, Sumter.
110 Elizabeth Tankersley, w., Frasier's, Monroe.
111 John Lamb, sol., 26th, Glynn.*
112 Newman Wilson, Roberts's, Hall.
113 Maria Williams, w., 4th, Chatham.
114 George Northern, Groce's, Bibb.
115 Francis Wilson, or., Cleland's, Chatham.
116 Martha Copeland, w. r. s., Rutland's, Bibb.
117 Jerusha Thomas, w., Varner's, Merriwether.
118 Arthur M'Affee, Peacock's, Washington.
119 Woodward's four children, f. a., Pate's, Warren.
120 Nancy Heath, w., Campbell's, Wilkes.
121 Alanson Clifton, 161st, Greene.
122 Martin Conner, M'Gill's, Lincoln.
123 Sophia Marsh, w., Carswell's, Jefferson.
124 Asa Ayres's ors., Smith's, Franklin.

125 Joseph Truchalett's ors., Valleau's, Chatham.
126 James Haddock, Bivins's, Jones.*
127 Catharine Lewis, w. r. s., Russell's, Henry.*
128 Oren D. Carstarphen, Mann's, Crawford.
129 T. Wilcox, Jr. (son of Thomas), Fryer's, Telfair.*
130 Robert Wood, Heard's, De Kalb.
131 George W. Houston, Willingham's, Harris.
132 Nathan Brewer's ors., M'Ewin's, Monroe.
133 John D. Delannoy, or., Valleau's, Chatham.
134 Lanson Young, Whitehead's, Habersham.
135 Thomas E. Buchannon, 295th, Jasper.
136 John Howell, Reid's, Gwinnett.
137 James Slater, Jordan's, Bibb.
138 William Goodwin, 124th, Richmond.
139 Abraham M'Collum's ors., Roberts's, Hall.
140 Elizabeth Raines, h. a., Mann's, Crawford.
141 Peter Richardson, Hill's, Stewart.
142 William E. Jones, 123d, Richmond.*
143 Tarpley T. P. Holt, 588th, Upson.
144 Wm. G. Springer, sol., Higginbotham's, Carroll.
145 Thomas B. Johnson, 373d, Jasper.
146 Samuel White, White's, Franklin.*
147 David W. Adrian, Coxe's, Franklin.
148 Daniel Shiver, sol., Dilman's, Pulaski.
149 James Kinan, Bryan's, Pulaski.
150 Elias Dunkin, Shearer's, Coweta.
151 Charles Saxton, Young's, Wilkinson.
152 Benjamin Martin's ors., Martin's, Jones.*
153 Calvin Stewart, Howell's, Troup.
154 Charles Crawford, sol., Mullen's, Carroll.
155 Zachariah Goolsby, 470th, Upson.
156 John W. Phillips, sol., Phillips's, Monroe.
157 Hugh M'Clendon, s. l. w., 734th, Lee.
158 John Armsted, Jr., Cleggs's, Walton.
159 Gideon Cummin's ors., Griffin's, Fayette.
160 William F. Barrett, Cleggs's, Walton.*
161 Nathan Shepherd, Herndon's, Hall.
162 Alfred Johnson, Cobb's, Muscogee.*
163 Charles J. Merriwether, Green's, Oglethorpe.*
164 James J. Herrington, 404th, Gwinnett.
165 Horace A. Latimer, Flynn's, Muscogee.*
166 Elijah V. Shore, sol., Peurifoy's, Henry.*
167 Thomas Head, sol., Coxe's, Morgan.
168 Thomas P. Grimes, 120th, Richmond.
169 Salome Cooper, w., Fitzpatrick's, Chatham.
170 Levi Martin, sol., Martin's, Pike.*
171 Mary Johns, wid., 57th, Emanuel.

172 Edward Jones, Cleland's, Chatham.
173 William Caston, Peacock's, Washington.
174 Mary Watson, wid., Collier's, Monroe.
175 Young Jessup, Monk's, Crawford.
176 Vann Davis's or., Willis's, Franklin.
177 John J. Cohen, 600th, Richmond.
178 Henry E. White, Barker's, Gwinnett.
179 Ely Stevens, M'Clain's, Newton.
180 Peter Sealy, Wilson's, Pike.
181 John L. Kelly, Jr., Anderson's, Rabun.
182 John Griffith, 672d, Harris.*
183 Gabriel Sisk, Jr., Dyer's, Habersham.
184 James H. Ransey, sol., Gunn's, Henry.
185 William Clark, 71st, Burke.*
186 John Garrett, sol., Curry's, Wilkinson.
187 Daniel M'Millon, 106th, Hancock.*
188 Mary Mizell, w., Brown's, Camden.*
189 Mary Irwin, w., 1st, Chatham.*
190 Willis Anthony, M'Ginnis's, Jackson.
191 Thomas P. Bond, Fitzpatrick's, Chatham.*
192 Absalum Joiner, r. s., Rutland's, Bibb.
193 Abner Hanson, Fleming's, Jefferson.
194 Ezekiel L. Tackett, Kendrick's, Monroe.
195 Mills Woodward's ors., Griffin's, Emanuel.
196 James Pullium, Gunn's, Jones.*
197 Benajah Smith, Arrington's, Merriwether.
198 William Mobley, Jordan's, Bibb.
199 Benjamin Fowler, s. s., Cleggs's, Walton.
200 Allen Brewer, 406th, Gwinnett.*
201 Alexander Martin, Harp's, Stewart.
202 Martin Dickson, Whitehead's, Habersham.
203 James Rowe, Collins's, Monroe.*
204 George W. Strong, Alberson's, Walton.*
205 Othneil Weaver, s. l. w., Moore's, Randolph.*
206 Elizabeth Farmer, w., Davis's, Jones.*
207 Sheldon Swift, Hitchcock's, Muscogee.
208 Alexander Hanna, Strahorn's, Heard.*
209 Henson S. Estes, Chambers's, Gwinnett.
210 John Gardner, sol., Dean's, Clarke.
211 John C. Stephens, Hines's, Coweta.
212 Tunison Cornell, Neal's, Campbell.
213 Samuel C. Head, Moseley's, Wilkes.
214 Andrew J. Berry, Shearer's, Coweta.
215 Gabriel Sizemore, 119th, Richmond.*
216 John Holder, Reid's, Gwinnett.*
217 David Mann's ors., O'Neal's, Laurens.
218 Sarah Leggett, w., George's, Appling.

219 Henry Clark, Hamilton's, Hall.
220 Thomas Abbott, Covington's, Pike.
221 Mitchell B. Hopper, Green's, Oglethorpe.*
222 Philip Burrow, Jr., Madden's, Pike.
223 Robert T. D. Todham, Cannon's, Wilkinson.
224 Alexander R. Buchannon, Kellum's, Talbot.
225 Moses Pinson, r. s., Whelchel's, Hall.
226 James Upshaw, Lunceford's, Elbert.*
227 John Dean, sol., Gaulding's, Lowndes.
228 John Wilcox, Jr., son of John, Wilcox's, Telfair.
229 John C. Williamson, Martin's, Jones.*
230 John W. Scroggin, Stewart's, Troup.
231 Allen Moon, Talley's, Troup.
232 Green M'Donald, Folsom's, Lowndes.
233 William Archer, Jr., 118th, Hancock.*
234 William R. Leister, Griffin's, De Kalb.
235 Jesse Herring, Sr., Reid's, Gwinnett.
236 Moses Griffin, Griffin's, Burke.
237 Elias C. Segraves, Davis's, Gwinnett.
238 R. R. Tenbroeck, Cleland's, Chatham.*
239 John Fleming, Craven's, Coweta.
240 Allen L. Hodge, Seas's, Madison.
241 John W. Betts, Mobley's, De Kalb.*
242 James E. May, Nichols's, Fayette.
243 Russel Thompson, Curry's, Wilkinson.
244 Lazarus Tilly, Keener's, Rabun.
245 Nathan Wright, 175th, Wilkes.
246 Moses S. Turner, Gillis's, De Kalb.
247 Isaac Brooks, Walker's, Houston.
248 Charles Finch, Howard's, Oglethorpe.
249 Robert Marlow, 35th, Scriven.
250 Obadiah Irwin, Whitaker's, Crawford.
251 Viney Chancey, dumb, Morgan's, Appling.
252 Henry Hamilton, or., Curry's, Merriwether.
253 George Berry, Perry's, Habersham.
254 Frederic Tillar's ors., David's, Franklin.
255 Thomas Forester, Henson's, Rabun.
256 John Dismukes, Bryan's, Monroe.*
257 William Williford, Jones's, Thomas.*
258 Joseph Walker, M. Brown's, Habersham.
259 Joseph B. Moore, Campbell's, Wilkes.
260 Robert Wilson, Jr., Anderson's, Rabun.
261 Absalem Irven, Coxe's, Talbot.
262 John H. Berry, Cleland's, Chatham.*
263 Hugh Boyd, Varner's, Merriwether.
264 Henry D. Hicks, Lester's, Monroe.
265 John Bustin, 374th, Putnam.

266 James Philips, sol., Bush's, Pulaski.
267 William Robertson's ors., Peterson's, Burke.
268 Green Hollifield, 294th, Jasper.
269 Joshua Stone's minors, 38th, Scriven.
270 Asa T. Edmonds, 419th, Walton.
271 Bennett Cooper, Chambers's, Gwinnett.*
272 James Merritt, Hughes's, Habersham.
273 Henry Champion, Young's, Jefferson.*
274 Nathan Land, Boynton's, Twiggs.
275 Stephen Pike, 417th, Walton.*
276 Robert Cowen, Nesbit's, Newton.
277 Jacob Mills, Comer's, Jones.
278 Wade Parker, Blackstock's, Hall.
279 Joshua R. Hutchinson, Collier's, Monroe.*
280 Elizabeth Sutton, f. a., Downs's, Warren.
281 John Manning, 320th, Baldwin.
282 Thomas Waters, m. s., Slater's, Bulloch.*
283 John Tebow's ors., M'Millon's, Lincoln.
284 Jesse Johnson, r. s., Say's, Jackson.*
285 William Sims, Herndon's, Hall.
286 Clemeth Cavender, Seay's, Hall.
287 Hiram Howell, of Prescott's, Boynton's, Twiggs.
288 James Rawls, Peavy's, Bulloch.*
289 John Burgamy, Kendrick's, Putnam.
290 Thomas J. Garrett, Harp's, Stewart.
291 T. Ward's 6 orphans, of Cher., Latimer's, De Kalb.
292 Richard L. Garner, or., Crawford's, Morgan.
293 John Adams, 693d, Heard.
294 John Cobb, Sen., s. l. w., Wolfskin's, Oglethorpe.*
295 John Tingle, Phillips's, Monroe.
296 Davis Saxon, 604th, Taliaferro.
297 Green B. Williamson, Sanders's, Jones.
298 John Wamack, 36th, Scriven.
299 Jeremiah Harrison, 419th, Walton.
300 Richard Willis, Canning's, Elbert.
301 James Lane, Crow's, Merriwether.
302 John Tant, 600th, Richmond.*
303 Lucien R. Wheeler, Jones's, Morgan.
304 James Gray's ors., Levritt's, Lincoln.
305 Sims's four orphans, 406th, Gwinnett.
306 John G. Burns, Nesbit's, Newton.
307 Celia Culbertson, w. r. s., Talley's, Troup.
308 George Gilman Smith, Ellsworth's, Bibb.*
309 Isaac Carr, Hamilton's, Gwinnett.
310 William Alexander, Echols's, Clarke.
311 John F. Hillyer, 419th, Walton.
312 John Cunningham, Watson's, Marion.*

313 Jesse Jenkins, Covington's, Pike.
314 William Self, 160th, Greene.
315 Hosea Young, Covington's, Pike.
316 Moses Murphey, Say's, De Kalb.*
317 Jacob Sellers, Swain's, Thomas.
318 Nimrod Patterson, Thomason's, Elbert.
319 William M. Hill, 466th, Monroe.*
320 James H. Carroll, Crawford's, Franklin.
321 Ira Camp, 417th, Walton.*
322 John Ward, Compton's, Fayette.*
323 Samuel H. Hulling, Robinson's, Putnam.*
324 William J. Downs, 672d, Harris.

SIXTH DISTRICT, SECOND SECTION, CHEROKEE.

1 Robert Arnett's ors., 34th, Scriven.*
2 Jonathan Miller, 364th, Jasper.*
3 John Dunkin, Shearer's, Coweta.
4 Sterling Haynes, Lawrence's, Pike.*
5 Peter Mickler, Bailey's, Camden.*
6 Stephen Merritt, Smith's, Wilkinson.*
7 Robert Brown, Oliver's, Twiggs.*
8 Allen Smith, Edwards's, Franklin.*
9 Anny Ansley, w., M'Dowell's, Lincoln.
10 Bryant Keen, Cook's, Telfair.
11 Joab Trull's ors., Bryan's, Pulaski.
12 John Chastain, Perry's, Habersham.
13 Henry K. Quillian, Brock's, Habersham.
14 Elias O. Hawthorn, Harrison's, Decatur.*
15 Josiah Carruth, Jones's, Madison.
16 Martha Chambers, w. r. s., Griffin's, Fayette.
17 Sally Carroll, w., Jones's, Hall.
18 James Hoyet, Sinclair's, Houston.
19 Elias Pollard, Show's, Muscogee.*
20 William Gibson, 167th, Wilkes.
21 Henry Killian, Chambers's, Gwinnett.*
22 Mary Hallman, or., Jones's, Bulloch.
23 Martin Hathaway, Valleau's, Chatham.
24 Elizabeth Cain, w., Field's, Habersham.
25 Charles F. Walthall, sol., Williams's, Jasper.
26 Young Carr, or., Taylor's, Putnam.
27 John Peck, Ballard's, Morgan.
28 William Thrower, 2d, Chatham.*
29 Enoch Cobb, 406th, Gwinnett.

30 William Autrey, Cleggs's, Walton.*
31 Thomas Bartlett, Robinson's, Washington.*
32 Benjamin Barron, Alsobrook's, Jones.
33 Eliz. Farechild, w. r. s., Whipple's, Wilkinson.*
34 Samuel B. Baldwin, Hill's, Monroe.
35 James Cockram, Field's, Habersham.
36 John B. and Mary F. Coley, ors., 574th, Early.
37 Edward Wilson, 510th, Early.
38 A. E. Holladay, Lockhart's, Bulloch.
39 Thomas Sweet Lather's ors., Valleau's, Chatham.
40 Larkin Wilson, sol., M'Ewin's, Monroe.
41 Wiley B. Jones, Fulks's, Wilkes.
42 Isaac Potts, Jones's, Habersham.*
43 George S. Reed, Sewell's, Franklin.
44 Burrell Raboy's ors., Winter's, Jones.
45 Napoleon B. Thompson, Jordan's, Bibb.
46 John S. Bobo, Mullen's, Carroll.
47 John Starnes, Griffin's, Hall.
48 William Flynt's ors., Brewer's, Walton.
49 Jacob Cochron, Sen., Herndon's, Hall.*
50 Gilmer's orphans, Allison's, Pike.
51 William Lewis, Hendon's, Carroll.*
52 Gilbert Sweat, 415th, Walton.*
53 Robert G. Brown, Morgan's, Madison.
54 Anna Bragg, w., Young's, Wilkinson.*
55 Daniel Parrott, 27th, Glynn.*
56 John Paples, Chambers's, Gwinnett.*
57 Perry Bowen, Miller's, Jackson.
58 Charles Moore, Jr., Wolfskin's, Oglethorpe.
59 Joseph King's orphans, Hall's, Monroe.
60 William Patterson, Stewart's, Troup.
61 John Whiteacre, Jr., Culbreath's, Columbia.*
62 Austin Gibson, or., Whitehead's, Habersham.
63 Shadrach Greene, 417th, Walton.*
64 William S. Rockwell, 320th, Baldwin.
65 William Y. Ethridge's ors., Robinson's, Putnam.
66 Thomas J. Barnes, Givens's, De Kalb.
67 William G. Porter's ors., 11th, Effingham.*
68 Hezekiah J. Parish, 49th, Emanuel.
69 John M'Graw, 470th, Upson.*
70 Stephen Folsome's ors., Swinney's, Laurens.
71 Robert R. Turner, Thompson's, Henry.*
72 Nathan Jordan, Camp's, Baker.*
73 Martha Barnett, w., Seas's, Madison.
74 Susan Smith, w. r. s., Morrison's, Montgomery.
75 Thomas Matthews, j. j., Wynn's, Gwinnett.
76 Stephen Kitchen's ors., Coxe's, Franklin.
11

77 Thomas Nelson, Mobley's, De Kalb.*
78 Thomas Qualls, Hamilton's, Hall.
79 James M. Hamley, Harrison's, Decatur.
80 T. Wylly, Sen., of Effingham County, Chatham.*
81 Joseph Y. Gardner, M'Millen's, Lincoln.
82 Charles D. Davis, 419th, Walton.*
83 Elizabeth M'Ewin, h. a., 243d, Jackson.*
84 Alfred Shivers, Dilman's, Pulaski.
85 John Mason, Dobbs's, Hall.
86 Joseph Heard, Miller's, Jackson.
87 Benjamin Garner, sol., Nesbit's, Newton.
88 James Wimberley, Winter's, Jones.*
89 Joseph Callahan, Robinson's, Fayette.
90 Graer Bishop, Rooks's, Putnam.
91 Peter Boyle, Liddell's, Jackson.*
92 Nancy M'Gough, w., Norris's, Monroe.
93 Henry M. Stevens, 15th, Liberty.
94 Elijah W. Couch, Crawford's, Franklin.*
95 John Lamb's ors., Camp's, Baker.
96 Mary Myers, w., 271st, M'Intosh.
97 Robert C. Hines, 15th, Liberty.*
98 Peter Johnson, Cleland's, Chatham.
99 Hope Brannon, sol., 37th, Scriven.*
100 John Robert Kittles, 37th, Scriven.
101 Absalom Stitchcomb, s. i. w., Lunceford's, Elbert.*
102 Hopson Dewberry, Phillips's, Monroe.*
103 Lewis M. Vining, Smith's, Campbell.
104 Daniel Scott, s. l. w., M'Clain's, Newton.
105 Lemuel Dorsey, 604th, Taliaferro.
106 Alexander Johnson, Groce's, Bibb.
107 Pinkney Yarber's ors., Smith's, Houston.
108 Gideon Watson, Taylor's, Houston.
109 Benjamin Faircloth, Hatton's, Baker.*
110 Katharine Hill., w., Wilson's, Jasper.*
111 Jordan C. Brooks, Tompkins's, Putnam.*
112 William Freeny, Groce's, Bibb.
113 Sarah Stallings, w., Ross's, Monroe.
114 Thomas F. Bethel, 561st, Upson.
115 George W. Turrentine, 693d, Heard.
116 Alfred Jonson, Martin's, Pike.*
117 John A. Allen, M'Gehee's, Troup.*
118 William Griffith, Liddell's, Jackson.*
119 James M. Nettles, 406th, Gwinnett.*
120 James Curry, Carpenter's, Tatnall.*
121 Alfred M. Horton, 102d, Hancock.*
122 Jesse Watson, Adams's, Columbia.*
123 Quintin Everett, 245th, Jackson.

124 Jeremiah Dean's ors., Maguire's, Gwinnett.
125 Austin Winzer, Gibson's, Decatur.
126 B. Smith, sol. 1784–97, Tompkins's, Putnam.*
127 Everett Paramore, Groover's, Thomas.
128 Mires's orphans, Young's, Wilkinson.
129 Mary Cannon, w. r. s., Jones's, Bulloch.*
130 Isaac Durham, r. s., Latimer's, De Kalb.
131 Gelford Pritchett, Polhill's, Burke.*
132 John S. Buckner, Frasier's, Monroe.
133 Jonathan A. Polk, Liddell's, Jackson.
134 John Vinson, Jr., Howell's, Troup.*
135 Bennett R. Hillman, Jones's, Morgan.*
136 Joseph Hill, Kendrick's, Monroe.*
137 William Jackson, Reid's, Gwinnett.*
138 William Morrell, Johnson's, Bibb.*
139 Nathaniel Nicholson, sol., Aderhold's, Campbell.*
140 Sydney Forbus, Dobbs's, Hall.*
141 Stephen M. Williams, Allison's, Pike.*
142 William Matthews, Parham's, Harris.*
143 Joseph Wilson, Jordan's, Bibb.*
144 Baty Beaver, Brock's, Habersham.*
145 Simeon Bishop, Mitchell's, Pulaski.*
146 Peter Avent, Edwards's, Talbot.
147 Wiley Murphy, Edwards's, Talbot.*
148 George Hurst, Griffin's, Burke.*
149 Malekiah R. Owens, 761st, Heard.*
150 Samuel Newell, Willis's, Franklin.
151 George Elliot, sol., M'Ginnis's, Jackson.
152 Thomas Edwards, Swain's, Thomas.
153 Samuel Pedier, 404th, Gwinnett.*
154 Thomas J. Williams, 470th, Upson.
155 Cornelius Kitchens, Gunn's, Jones.
156 John D. Moss, Hargrove's, Oglethorpe.
157 William H. Watson, Watson's, Marion.
158 James W. Latimer, Scroggins's, Oglethorpe.
159 James Mackleroy, Mackleroy's, Clarke.
160 Pleasant Lemmons, Harralson's, Troup.
161 Lewis Goodwin, r. s., Bostick's, Twiggs.*
162 John A. Boon, Barker's, Gwinnett.
163 Alvan Dean, Hammond's, Franklin.
164 William C. Oliver, Martin's, Pike.*
165 John M'Coy, Talley's, Troup.
166 Howell Moseley, Evans's, Fayette.
167 James Bradshaw, Jordan's, Harris.
168 Matthew F. Moseley, 167th, Wilkes.
169 Jesse K. Sumner, 55th, Emanuel.*
170 Elijah Tarver's ors., 589th, Upson.

171 Thomas Preast, Seay's, Hall.*
172 Gilfred G. Thompson, Whelchel's, Hall.
173 William Pittard, Buck-branch, Clarke.
174 John Timmons, 2d section, Cherokee.
175 Matthew H. Wright, Shattox's, Coweta.
176 Hellen M'Donald, w., Dawson's, Jasper.*
177 John S. Smith, 242d, Jackson.*
178 Thomas Haley, id., Taylor's, Elbert.*
179 Hanibal Allen, Espy's, Clarke.*
180 William Bastian's ors., Grubbs's, Columbia.
181 Martin Preast, Seay's, Hall.*
182 Albert Simonton, 144th, Greene.*
183 Alexander Bean, 250th, Walton.*
184 Mary Mapp, w., 160th, Greene.*
185 Elijah E. Jones, Christie's, Jefferson.
186 Kennedy Dennard, sol., Martin's, Stewart.*
187 Barbery Ray, w., Griffin's, Merriwether.
188 Littleberry Hutchens, 1st section, Cherokee.
189 John C. Harris, Johnson's, De Kalb.*
190 James Sturdevant, 589th, Upson.*
191 Susannah Johnson, w., Pounds's, Twiggs.
192 Thomas Sharp, Nesbit's, Newton.
193 Jared Kennington, Bush's, Pulaski.*
194 Moses Holcomb, r. s., 3d section, Cherokee.
195 Silas Plunkett, 108th, Hancock.
196 Ephraim Lee, Loveless's Gwinnett.
197 Jesse Mills's ors., Whitaker's, Crawford.
198 Robert W. Skipp, Shearer's, Coweta.
199 James Abney, Tuggle's, Merriwether.*
200 Neal Barnes, 720th, Decatur.
201 Elizabeth Gardner, w., 122d, Richmond.
202 John Nobles, Kellum's, Talbot.*
203 Leonard Haines, Barwick's, Washington.
204 John Underwood, sol., Pounds's, Twiggs.
205 William Gentry, Phillips's, Talbot.*
206 Cutdon Roundtree, Evans's, Fayette.*
207 Louisa Durkee, or., Cleland's, Chatham.*
208 Thornton Mead, Maguire's, Gwinnett.
209 William Roughton, Sinquefield's, Washington.*
210 Hardy Bennefield, Martin's, Newton.
211 Winney D. Davis, Loveless's, Gwinnett.*
212 Charles Muggridge, 38th, Scriven.*
213 Daniel Mobley, Hicks's, Decatur.
214 Alfred M. Echols, Shearer's, Coweta.*
215 Jones's four orphans, Bryant's, Burke.
216 John Clayton, Heard's, De Kalb.
217 Pleasant Shipp, 417th, Walton.

218 Margaret Crawford, w., Keener's, Rabun.
219 John and Eliza Hornsby, ors., 24th, M'Intosh.
220 Jesse Key Kendall, Sen., Stephens's, Habersham*
221 William M'Murrain, sol., Peace's, Wilkinson.*
222 Margaret Ann Coutteau, or., Griffin's, Burke.*
223 Thomas Coker, Blackstock's, Hall.
224 Elias Bagget, Jones's, Thomas.
225 John J. Boillat, 271st, M'Intosh.
226 Daniel H. Williams, Jordon's, Bibb.*
227 Allen Shivers, Sinclair's, Houston.
228 Alfred E. Wadsworth, Covington's, Pike.*
229 Mary S. Pledger, or., Lunceford's, Elbert.
230 Robert Palmer's ors., Stewart's, Warren.
231 William H. Shuman, 19th, Bryan.
232 James Thompson, M'Millon's, Lincoln.*
233 Luke T. Clark's ors., Murphey's, Columbia.
234 Jeremiah Brown, Smith's, Wilkinson.
235 George Danner, Stokes's, Lincoln.*
236 Edward A. Soullard, Jr., 120th, Richmond.
237 Pleasant Drake, s. l. w., Hall's, Butts.*
238 Mary Bostwick, w. r. s., Jones's, Morgan.*
239 John S. Blalock, Curry's, Merriwether.*
240 William Bulloch, 516th, Dooly.*
241 John White, sol., Espy's, Clarke.
242 Wiley Belcher's ors., Bishop's, Henry.*
243 William S. Talley's ors., 163d, Greene.*
244 Tyri S. Harris, Stanton's, Newton.
245 Arthur Peacock, Taylor's, Houston.
246 James Brown, Loveless's, Gwinnett.
247 Abel Stephens, Rainey's, Twiggs.
248 Solomon Brown, s. l. w., 603d, Taliaferro.*
249 William M. Morton, sol., Barnett's, Clarke.
250 Jeremiah C. Smith, s. l. w., Mashburn's, Pulaski.
251 Manning's four orphans, Fryer's, Telfair.
252 James Walker, 122d, Richmond.*
253 James M. Shepperd, Peterson's, Burke.*
254 Uriah Dumas, 466th, Monroe.*
255 John S. Davis, Merck's, Hall.*
256 Parks Hardman, of Cherokee, Latimer's, De Kalb
257 James T. Wright, Jenkins's, Oglethorpe.
258 Dennis M'Clendon, M'Coy's, Houston.*
259 John G. Smith, or., Cleghorn's, Madison.
260 David P. Brown, Stewart's, Jones.
261 Robert P. Barton, Hopkins's, Camden.
262 Hiram Meadows, Peace's, Wilkinson.
263 Jones Douglass, sol., Barker's, Gwinnett.*
264 Eliz. Jenkins, h. a. 3 years, Walker's, Putnam.*

265 George Hullman, Southell's, Tatnall.
266 Richard H. Caldwell, Athens, Clarke.
267 John Lee, Prescott's, Twiggs.
268 Craddock Gober, David's, Franklin.
269 Madison Baker, Canning's, Elbert.
270 William Stacks, Allen's, Campbell.
271 James Jackson, Catlett's, Franklin.
272 Jones's five orphans, 119th, Richmond.
273 Levi Jester, r. s., Thaxton's, Butts.
274 Levi C. Bostick, Killen's, Decatur.
275 Alexander G. Tylor, 366th, Jasper.*
276 Sarah Dubose, w. r. s., 69th, Burke.
277 Joseph Anderson, Herndon's, Hall.*
278 John Blount's ors., Arrington's, Merriwether.
279 Whitfield W. Bond, Hughes's, Habersham.
280 Hezekiah Walker, Wilcox's, Telfair.*
281 Rachel Heard, w., Miller's, Jackson.*
282 Bryant S. Rutledge, Say's, De Kalb.*
283 Isaac Turner, Summerlin's, Bulloch.*
284 John Karr, Roberts's, Hall.
285 William Wilson, Walker's, Houston.*
286 John H. Kennedy, sol., Hart's, Jones.
287 Joseph Griffin, r. s., Harralson's, Troup.
288 John Hardegree, Jack's, Clarke.
289 Marlin T. Crow, Echols's, Clarke.
290 Liberty Matthews, Wynn's, Gwinnett.*
291 Benjamin H. Rice, Pollard's, Wilkes.*
292 William Ware, Nesbit's, Newton.
293 Amos Lewis, 406th, Gwinnett.*
294 Wilson Tanner, s. l. w., Morrison's, Appling.
295 William Wallis, s. i. w., Stanton's, Newton.
296 James B. Phillips, s. l. w., Atkinson's, Coweta.*
297 Sarah Bennett, 734th, Lee.*
298 Clark J. Cook, 120th, Richmond.
299 William T. Tomnee, 589th, Upson.*
300 James Eaton, Winter's, Jones.
301 William K. Hawkins, Ballard's, Morgan.
302 Charles Wheelan, Shearer's, Coweta.
303 Daniel Pratt, Sullivan's, Jones.
304 John Harris, Estes's, Putnam.*
305 Thomas Coalson, Bryan's, Pulaski.
306 Samuel Croft, Coker's, Troup.
307 Benjamin Avent, Edwards's, Talbot.
308 Stephen Williams, Hannah's, Jefferson.
309 William Hortman, Whitaker's, Crawford.*
310 Ruth Williams, w., Perry's, Habersham.
311 Rebecca Coleman, or., Hatton's, Baker.

312 Gilbert Clarke, 466th, Monroe.
313 Alexander Johnson's ors., Baismore's, Jones.
314 Hezekiah Jones, Martin's, Laurens.*
315 Jackson Stone, Wilcox's, Telfair.*
316 William Anderson, Dawson's, Jasper.*
317 Elizabeth Rye, w. r. s., Huey's, Harris.
318 Samuel Garrard, Price's, Hall.
319 William Crane, 102d, Hancock.
320 Absalom Wofford, 248th, Jackson.*
321 Edmund M. Butler, m. s., 160th, Greene.*
322 Bryant Broome, Lynn's, Warren.
323 Elizabeth O'Neal, w., Underwood's, Putnam.
324 William Heflin, Allison's, Pike.

SEVENTH DISTRICT, SECOND SECTION, CHEROKEE.

1 John Gurley, Hughes's, Habersham.*
2 Sirass B. Oliver, Martin's, Washington.*
3 Ward Hudson, Guice's, Oglethorpe.*
4 John Laton, s. l. w., Peacock's, Washington.*
5 Simon C. Vick, George's, Appling.
6 William Pentecost, r. s., Lay's, Jackson.*
7 Kenneth Gillis, Gillis's, De Kalb.
8 Charles W. Nixon, Gunn's, Henry.*
9 Williamson Phipps, Rainey's, Twiggs.
10 Stephen Meritt, sol., Smith's, Wilkinson.*
11 Benjamin Boyt, Bryan's, Burke.*
12 Jeremiah Blangett's ors., Nellum's, Elbert.
13 Sarah Coleman, w., 119th, Richmond.
14 Rowland A. Tolbert, Higginbotham's, Madison.
15 John L. D. Ward, Thomas's, Clarke.
16 Joshua Westbrook's or., Mangum's, Franklin.
17 James Statham, sol., Jennings's, Clarke.
18 Elijah Henderson, Sanderlin's, Chatham.
19 Miles G. Dobbins, Peurifoy's, Henry.*
20 Osburn R. O'Neal, 366th, Jasper.
21 Noah Adams, Wood's, Jefferson.
22 Seaborn Ethridge, Young's, Wilkinson.
23 Edmund Smithwick, s. l. w., Hines's, Coweta.
24 John Nichols, Nichols's, Fayette.*
25 Kintchen Carr, Hughes's, Habersham.
26 Richard S. Flake, 36th, Scriven.*
27 Thomas H. Jones, 406th, Gwinnett.
28 James Owen, 404th, Gwinnett.

29 William P. Merriman, 120th, Richmond.
30 Jeremiah Gentry, Edwards's, Franklin.*
31 William Williamson, or., Taylor's, Houston.
32 Ezekiel Miller, Hill's, Baldwin.*
33 Thomas H. Turner, Martin's, Pike.
34 Samuel Studdard, Cleggs's, Walton.*
35 M'Alister's orphans, 406th, Gwinnett.
36 Pleasant Moreman, Bustin's, Pike.*
37 George W. Young, House's, Henry.*
38 Washington Williams, Slater's, Bulloch.
39 Stephen Garner, 364th, Jasper.*
40 Judkins Hunt, sol., Bustin's, Pike.
41 Robert Chandler, Wynn's, Gwinnett.
42 Mary H. Cobb, w., 601st, Taliaferro.*
43 William Jones, Mitchell's, Marion.*
44 William D. Murphy, Alexander's, Jefferson.
45 Benjamin S. Vickers, Folsom's, Lowndes.
46 Isham Nelson, Hearn's, Butts.
47 John Neely, 537th, Upson.*
48 William M'Millen, 161st, Greene.
49 John Newby, sol. 1784–97, 373d, Jasper.*
50 Nancy Tiller, w., Colley's, Oglethorpe.
51 William Hambz, Sen., Henson's, Rabun.
52 Chapman Barefield, Ross's, Monroe.*
53 Michael Albright, Rhodes's, De Kalb.
54 Charles A. Marlin, Price's, Hall.
55 John D. Kerr's orphans, 141st, Greene.
56 Joshua Milner, Park's, Walton.
57 William Edwards's ors., Herring's, Twiggs.*
58 Benjamin Tackwell, Espy's, Clark.
59 Green M'Donald, Rutland's, Bibb.*
60 Jesse Whitley, Alberson's, Walton.
61 Henry Glover, Candler's, Bibb.
62 Edward Pharr, 415th, Walton.
63 John Williamson, s. i.w., Peterson's, Montgomery.*
64 John Brown, Bush's, Pulaski.
65 Martha Hugins, w., Hitchcock's, Muscogee.
66 John Casner, 119th, Richmond.*
67 Jesse Elebee, Peavy's, Bulloch.*
68 Henry Peppers, 249th, Walton.
69 Sanford Higgins, Reid's, Gwinnett.*
70 James Welch, Will's, Twiggs.
71 David Garrison, Latimer's, De Kalb.
72 Daniel Barringer, 320th, Baldwin.*
73 Seaborn M'Hargue, 555th, Upson.
74 William Nichols, Morton's, De Kalb.*
75 James Crews, 605th, Taliaferro.

76 Philip Prichard, sol., Woodruff's, Campbell.*
77 John C. Terry, Gittens's, Fayette.
78 Thomas Smith, Gunn's, Henry.
79 Absalom Martin, Chastain's, Habersham.
80 Benjamin Rice, sol., Hutson's, Newton.
81 John C. Helverston, sol., Ellsworth's, Bibb.
82 Thomas Gardner's ors., Bostick's, Twiggs.
83 Cornelius Gordan, Nesbit's, Newton.
84 Ezekiel Strickland, Sen., Stanton's, Newton.*
85 Elizabeth F. Hampton, w., Dozier's, Columbia.
86 Sarah Parker, w., 103d, Hancock.
87 Benjamin Cain, Hughes's, Habersham.
88 Godfrey Luther, Blackstock's, Hall.
89 David Thompson, Nesbit's, Newton.
90 Mary H. Whitworth, w., Reid's, Gwinnett.
91 Isam Hancock, r. s., Welche's, Habersham.
92 Benjamin James, Davis's, Jones.
93 John H. Stone, Bell's, Columbia.
94 Eli Hendrick, Nellum's, Elbert.
95 John Neeves, 458th, Early.
96 Elizabeth Lee, w., Harrison's, Decatur.
97 Daniel D. Baker, Johnson's, De Kalb.
98 James Huckaby, sol., 687th, Lee.
99 Charles Knoles, sol., Gittens's, Fayette.
100 Joseph Coe, Wright's, Tatnall.
101 Abram Smith, blind, 1st section, Cherokee.
102 William Wood, Johnson's, De Kalb.
103 Waters Dunn, Tankersley's, Columbia.
104 Alexander Berryhill, sol., Wheeler's, Pulaski.
105 Lepsey Deadwilde's ors., Bustin's, Pike.
106 Robert Church, Miller's, Camden.
107 William A. Hendon, Stanfield's, Campbell.
108 John Skinner, Sen., sol., 119th, Richmond.*
109 Thomas Wills, Athens, Clarke.
110 Moses Caraker, 537th, Upson.*
111 Joseph Nobles, 785th, Sumter.
112 Alfred L. Boren, Moseley's, Wilkes.
113 Isham Huskette, Nesbit's, Newton.
114 James Leak, Sen., Belcher's, Jasper.*
115 Z. L. Zachry, Martin's, Newton.
116 Young Gresham's or., Echols's, Clarke.*
117 Barshaba White, w., Williams's, Jasper.*
118 William H. Deupree, Bragaw's, Oglethorpe.*
119 Wiliam A. Dawson, Hendon's, Rabun.
120 Ahashaby Johnston, Blackstock's, Hall.*
121 Hiram Sharp, sol., Hendon's, Carroll.
122 Benjamin W. Blasengane, 788th, Heard.
12

123 Henry S. Mozley, Keener's, Rabun.*
124 Martha E. Anderson, w., Alexander's, Jefferson.
125 James H. Fenny, Stewart's, Jones.
126 Hugh Goen, Hearn's, Butts.
127 Adam Spooner, Killen's, Decatur.
128 Charles Bradley, Williams's, Washington.
129 James J. Smith, Moore's, Randolph.*
130 David Johnson, Watson's, Marion.*
131 Seth Arms, 295th, Jasper.*
132 Mary Haye's, w., Whitehead's, Habersham.*
133 James Killgore, 248th, Jackson.
134 Rebecca Mann, w., Gittens's, Fayette.
135 John Chalmers, sol., Coxe's, Franklin.
136 Charles T. Hart (Sunbury), Baker's, Liberty.*
137 William Mitchell, 119th, Richmond.
138 William J. Smith, Jones's, Morgan.
139 Sentus Bernard, Wellington Island, Chatham.
140 Donaldson Coley, Herring's, Twiggs.
141 Daniel Boatwright, Kelly's, Elbert.*
142 William C. Hudson, Loveless's, Gwinnett.*
143 James Hayman, Bryant's, Burke.*
144 Levin H. Ellis, 102d, Hancock.
145 Elizabeth, Moore, w., Campbell's, Wilkes.
146 Mary Sanders, w., Fleming's, Jefferson.
147 Elisha Landrum,, Say's, De Kalb.
148 Albert P. Torrence, Brooks's, Muscogee.
149 Kenneth Daniel, Everett's, Washington.
150 Willis Thurmond's ors., Trout's, Hall.
151 William Thomas, 559th, Walton.
152 John Molesbee, Candler's, Bibb.
153 James E. Todd, sol., 672d, Harris.
154 Juda Garlick, w., Roe's, Burke.
155 Thomas Brady, s. i. w., Mayo's, Wilkinson.
156 William Fielder, of Cherokee, Harris's, De Kalb.
157 Henry Irby, Dean's, De Kalb.*
158 Joseph L. Heargroves, 8th, Chatham.*
159 Pleasant Baugh, sol., 144th, Greene.
160 John Landrum, r. s., Hinton's, Wilkes.
161 Thomas Hicks, Walker's, Harris.
162 Henry Martin, Robinson's, Washington.
163 Daniel E. Cornwell, Taylor's, Elbert.*
164 Josiah M'Cully, House's, Henry.
165 James Rahn, 9th, Effingham.
166 Edward T. Terrell, or., Pace's, Putnam.
167 Thomas Rutherford, Jr., Loveless's, Gwinnett.
168 Jane Kinneyhorn, w., Brooks's, Muscogee.
169 Matthew Mizell, Wilcox's, Telfair.

170 David Howell, Martin's, Pike.*
171 Jackson Ingram, Williams's, Decatur.
172 Amy Castleton, w., 364th, Jasper.
173 John Williams, Garner's, Coweta.
174 Burwell Pope, s. l. w., Wolfskin's, Oglethorpe.*
175 John Adams Meigs, blind or., 600th, Richmond.
176 Nathaniel Renfroe, Everett's, Washington.*
177 Henry Davis, Mimm's, Fayette.*
178 Leonard Peek, id., 148th, Greene.
179 Lewis Jenkins, Loveless's, Gwinnett.
180 James Duncan, 555th, Upson.*
181 David Crane, Shattox's, Coweta.
182 Mary Williams, h. a., 34th, Scriven.
183 Clia Williams, w., Crow's, Merriwether.*
184 William T. Cain, or., Dupree's, Washington.
185 Joel English, Pate's, Warren.
186 John Bickers, sol., 143d, Greene.*
187 Daniel W. Webb, Mitchell's, Pulaski.
188 Henry Watkin's four orphans, Givins's, De Kalb.
189 Martin S. Watkins's ors., 165th, Wilkes.
190 John Thomas, Harrison's, Decatur.*
191 James B. Johnson, Jordan's, Bibb.
192 John Pearson, Butts's, Monroe.*
193 Martha Mitchell, h. a. 3 years, Gorley's, Putnam.
194 Thomas Nevil, Jones's, Bulloch.*
195 James Kivlin, Few's, Muscogee.
196 Thomas M. Foster, Frasier's, Monroe.
197 Elijah P. Allen, Compton's, Fayette.*
198 Madderson Veeles, Jordan's, Bibb.
199 William M. Parsons, mi., f. a., 105th, Baldwin.
200 William J. Owen, Loven's, Henry.
201 Elizabeth Long, w., Griffin's, Burke.*
202 William Thomas, sol., Adams's, Columbia.*
203 John Dailey, Jr., Peurifoy's, Henry.
204 Robert Armour, Hamilton's, Hall.
205 James Jones's ors., Jones's, Thomas.
206 William Walker, Seay's, Hall.
207 William M. Jones, Prescott's, Twiggs.
208 John L. Burke, Coxe's, Morgan.
209 Drury Boatwright, Edwards's, Franklin.*
210 Francis W. King, Canning's, Elbert.
211 John Moore's ors., Jr., Campbell's, Wilkes.
212 David Barnett, Hardman's, Oglethorpe.
213 Miles Fowler, Loveless's, Gwinnett.
214 William Hughes, Hamilton's, Gwinnett.
215 Elizabeth Temples, w., Dearing's, Henry.
216 Miles's orphans, Young's, Wilkinson.

217 John E. Farmer, Dearing's, Henry.
218 Henry Mitchell, Royster's, Franklin.
219 Mary Cook, w., 294th, Jasper.
220 William T. Gurley, Smith's, Campbell.
221 Wiley Hales, sol., Buck-branch, Clarke.
222 Frendy S. Peers, Hamilton's, Hall.
223 Thomas Griggs, sol., 109th, Hancock.
224 Thomas W. Gilbert, Liddell's, Jackson.
225 William R. King, Williams's, Washington.*
226 Edmund Lucas, Rhodes's, De Kalb.
227 George Ward, Laurence's, Pike.
228 Benjamin Couger, Barker's, Gwinnett.
229 Benjamin Sheftall, sol., 2d district, Chatham.
230 James B. Ellis, 114th, Hancock.
231 John Franklin, Moffett's, Muscogee.*
232 Vincent Nayell, Valleau's, Chatham.
233 Charity Weatherford, w., Morton's, De Kalb.*
234 Roger M'Grath, Moffett's, Muscogee.
235 Levi Jester, Head's, Butts.
236 William Tillman, or., 113th, Hancock.
237 Elijah Garrett, Stanfield's, Campbell.
238 Jane Holder, w., Brown's, Camden.
239 Isaac Downs, Harralson's, Troup.
240 John Farrar, Royster's, Franklin.
241 Batson Bulluke, sol., Jordan's, Bibb.
242 Cornelius G. Martin, Green's, Oglethorpe.
243 Jacob Pool, 119th, Richmond.*
244 Milton Rose, 561st, Upson.*
245 James Studdard's ors., Cleggs's, Walton.
246 Horace B. Gould, 25th, Glynn.
247 James Norris, Jr., Pate's, Warren.
248 Daniel M'Nal, Lamberth's, Fayette.
249 Michael Kinkham, 248th, Jackson.
250 Simeon Hedgecock, Mashburn's, Pulaski.*
251 Ezekiel C. Kirkpatrick, Hodges's, Newton.
252 John Cheeves's ors., Vining's, Putnam.
253 William Tankersley, Huchinson's, Columbia.
254 William Brown, Selman's, Pike.
255 Louis Williams, Morrison's, Appling.
256 Jane Boyd, w., Newsom's, Warren.
257 Wilson P. Williford, Robinson's, Fayette.
258 Hamilton Barge, Hampton's, Newton.
259 Orphans of Alexander Smith, Pearce's, Houston.
260 Forres Green, s. l. w., 417th, Walton.
261 William Williams, Hand's, Appling.
262 Hezekiah Wheeler, Kendrick's, Monroe.
263 James Jones, Pace's, Putnam.

264 Thomas H. Harup, Kendrick's, Monroe.*
265 Elizabeth Cannon, w. r. s., 373d, Jasper.*
266 John Chapman, Sutton's, Habersham.
267 Benajah A. Moye, Sinquefield's, Washington.
268 Bartholomew Furney, Bryan's, Pulaski.
269 Henry C. Smith, Fryer's, Telfair.*
270 William H. Brown, 788th, Heard.*
271 Thomas Dunman, Merck's, Hall.
272 Johnathan Johnson, Jr., Wynn's, Gwinnett.
273 Jacob Shuffield, sol., Waltze's, Morgan.
274 Moses Harris, Newby's, Jones.*
275 David Chapman, Stower's, Elbert.
276 James T. Jones, Clifton's, Tatnall.
277 Newsom Owen, Kendrick's, Monroe.*
278 William Bailey, M'Gehee's, Troup.*
279 Reuben Cumbo, Tuggle's, Merriwether.
280 Hezekiah Walker, Wilcox's, Telfair.*
281 Mary Footman, w., 15th, Liberty.
282 Hannah Ewing, w., M'Culler's, Newton.
283 John M. Cooper's ors., Cleland's, Chatham.
284 Dennis Cason, Robison's, Washington.
285 Alexander M'Iver, 120th, Richmond.
286 Matthew Melton, Pearce's, Houston.
287 Edmund Dismuke's or., Gunn's, Jones.
288 Robert Northcutt's ors., Hannah's, Jefferson.
289 Hiram B. Perkins, Dyer's, Habersham.
290 Cuthbert S. Hollier, Howard's, Oglethorpe.
291 Nathan Cook, 102d, Hancock.
292 Samuel Pruitt, Sewell's, Franklin.
293 Jehu King, Young's, Wilkinson.
294 John G. Clark, Smith's, Houston.
295 Harmon Sanders, Arrington's, Merriwether.*
296 Benjamin F. Land, Williams's, Decatur.
297 James George, Hicks's, Decatur.
298 Elijah P. Allen, Compton's, Fayette.
299 Harriet H. Hannon, or., 120th, Richmond.
300 Charles Jenkins, sol., 117th, Hancock.*
301 William Gardner, Parham's, Harris.*
302 James Duncan, 608th, Taliaferro.*
303 David Walson, Howell's, Troup.
304 Alexander Martin's ors., 15th, Liberty.
305 Crawford B. Williams, Perry's, Habersham.
306 Aaron Smith, Carpenter's, Tatnall.*
307 Thomas Horne, Butts's, Monroe.*
308 Etheldred M'Clendon's ors., 295th, Jasper.
309 Richmond Sanders, 470th, Upson.
310 James H. Gaines, Brewer's, Monroe.

311 Burton H. Wright, Fulks's, Wilkes.
312 Henry Holmes, Boynton's, Twiggs.*
313 Rebecca Evans, w., 458th, Early.
314 Enoch Young, Latimer's, De Kalb.*
315 Thomas Speights, 105th, Baldwin.
316 Betsey Leyrs, lun., 6th, Chatham.
317 Freeman Biggs, Barnett's, Clarke.
318 Absolum Montgomery, b. m., Griden's, Morgan.
319 Little B. Bowles, 141st, Greene.
320 Bazil Miller, Stone's, Irwin.
321 Jacob Moore, Hart's, Jones.*
322 William Harris, Britt's, Randolph.*
323 Robert Miller, Nesbit's, Newton.
324 Mat. Thompson, s. l. w., Underwood's, Putnam.

EIGHTH DISTRICT, SECOND SECTION, CHEROKEE.

1 James T. Phillips, M'Gehee's, Troup.
2 Thomas Jones, Will's, Twiggs.*
3 James Anderson, Herndon's, Hall.*
4 Thomas Hurst, 12th, Effingham.
5 John Boswell, sol., Lunceford's, Wilkes.
6 George W. Johnson, Talley's, Troup.
7 Thomas Cawley, Dearing's, Henry.*
8 Silas Turner, Gittens's, Fayette.
9 Samuel Smith, Price's, Hall.
10 Vines H. Owen, House's, Henry.
11 Jesse Bateman, Rainey's, Twiggs.
12 Archibald Dougherty, Tankersley's, Columbia.*
13 Nathan Philips, sol., Kelly's, Jasper.
14 David A. Crockett, 278th, Morgan.
15 James Moore, Harp's, Stewart.*
16 Thomas Barron, sol., Jordan's, Harris.
17 Jacob Carter, Coward's, Lowndes.*
18 James Blassingame, s. s., Cleggs's, Walton.
19 George Brock, 2d section, Cherokee.
20 Robert Laseter, sol., Mays's, Monroe.*
21 Simeon Ellington, s. l. w., Blackshear's, Laurens.
22 John Harris, Stower's, Elbert.
23 Needham Waters's ors., Prescott's, Twiggs.
24 Jacob Brock, Hicks's, Decatur.*
25 Oswell E. Caspin, or., 121st, Richmond.
26 Henry Smith, sol., Higginbotham's, Madison.
27 Elijah Cloud, Hudson's, Marion.*

28 Josiah Crain, Head's, Butts.
29 James Thurman, M'Linn's, Butts.*
30 Edmund C. Beard, sol., York's, Stewart.
31 Rushing Lane, Vining's, Putnam.
32 Philip Thornton, 175th, Wilkes.
33 John Saunders, 732d, Dooly.
34 Charles Gates, Sen., r. s., 406th, Gwinnett.*
35 Ann Morriss, w., Stewart's, Jones.
36 Reuben G. Lake, Peek's, Columbia.
37 George Crowder, Allen's, Henry.
38 Charles Cox, 588th, Upson.
39 Elizabeth Wood, w., Martin's, Newton.
40 Thomas M. Caters, or., Rainey's, Twiggs.
41 James Stinson, 119th, Richmond.*
42 Horace Rhodes, Rainey's, Twiggs.
43 James G. Park's ors., Hitchcock's, Muscogee.
44 William Y. Moore, 415th, Walton.*
45 James Hoopugh, Mackleroy's, Clarke.*
46 Joshua Teasley, sol., Clark's, Elbert.*
47 Henry Vincent, Jr., Rooks's, Putnam.
48 Tilman Leak, Wilson's, Pike.*
49 Robert Avary, Seay's, Hall.*
50 Arthur S. Nevitts, Valleau's, Chatham.*
51 Charles Hudson's ors., M'Clain's, Newton.
52 Hiram M. Harper, M. Brown's, Habersham.*
53 William P. Bailey, M'Culler's, Newton.*
54 George Millen, Fitzpatrick's, Chatham.*
55 Griffin Watson, Stewart's, Troup.
56 John O. Baker, 15th, Liberty.
57 Woodward Moore, 537th, Upson.
58 Reuben W. Gamblin, Seay's, Hall.*
59 Isaac Moore, r. s., Collins's, Henry.*
60 Elizabeth Weeks, w., 600th, Richmond.
61 Samuel Sikes, Smith's, Houston.*
62 Augustus Pless, 735th, Troup.
63 James Nash, Jr., Smith's, Elbert.*
64 David Pensell, Bragaw's, Oglethorpe.
65 Wiley Meeks, Garner's, Washington.*
66 James B. Smith, 122d, Richmond.*
67 Jeremiah Durham, 138th, Greene
68 Andy Poss's ors., Guice's, Oglethorpe.
69 James Underwood, Carpenter's, Tatnall.
70 Daniel M'Rae, Whisenhunt's, Carroll.
71 Joel Reid, Dean's, De Kalb.
72 William Black, Colley's, Oglethorpe.
73 Sarah Head, w. r. s., Lunceford's, Elbert.
74 Moses Foose, Martin's, Washington.*

75 Eli Daniel, Martin's, Newton.*
76 Lemuel Laseter, Stanton's, Newton.
77 Dennis Fowler, Whisenhunt's, Carroll.
78 John M. Donnelly, or., 271st, M'Intosh.
79 Ruffin Hendley, or., Harp's, Stewart.
80 Dicy Page, w., Mitchell's, Marion.*
81 George Merck, Sen., Price's, Hall.
82 Edith Ryals, w., Edwards's, Montgomery.
83 Samuel Lathers, Jr., Mullen's, Carroll.
84 John M'Elwreath, Clinton's, Campbell.
85 Ira Christian, Howell's, Elbert.*
86 Peter Smith's ors., Alsobrook's, Jones.
87 Henry Shelton Oliver, Thomason's, Elbert.
88 Campbell Renfroe, Mann's, Crawford.*
89 James F. Gibson, Derrick's, Henry.*
90 M. W. Warren, 279th, Morgan.
91 Samuel Hillhouse, Jones's, Hall.
92 William Powill, Jr., Gittens's, Fayette.
93 William Colwell, Newby's, Jones.
94 Edmund Reid's 7 orphans, Gillis's, De Kalb.
95 Willis Rabun, Whisenhunt's, Carroll.
96 John Conner, M'Ewin's, Monroe.*
97 James N. Taylor, Taylor's, Houston.
98 Edmund Tabb, Bush's, Burke.
99 Miles Paty, Gillis's, De Kalb.
100 Alexander H. M'Donald, Valleau's, Chatham.
101 James W. Powell, 535th, Dooly.
102 William M'Clain, Royster's, Franklin.*
103 William W. Puckett, Chesnut's, Newton.
104 James M'Call, 406th, Gwinnett.
105 Rebecca Northern, w., Turner's, Crawford.
106 Solomon Snellgrove, 759th, Sumter.
107 James Willoughby, Elder's, Clarke.
108 Benajah Williams, Welche's, Habersham.
109 Henry C. Laughter, Anderson's, Wilkes.
110 Larkin Turner, Crawford's, Morgan.
111 James M'Whorter, Price's, Hall.
112 Rebecca Williams, w., Griffin's, Hall.
113 Larkin Hegason, sol., Crow's, Pike.
114 Martha J. Abbott's ors., Harris's, Crawford.
115 Abraham Horton, Jones's, Habersham.*
116 Joseph Ware, 124th, Richmond.
117 Samuel Couch, Stower's, Elbert.
118 James Be Ville's ors., 12th, Effingham.
119 John Dickin, Sen., Baley's, Butts.*
120 Samuel B. M'Clure, sol., Wagnon's, Carroll.
121 Joseph Lopez, 1st, Chatham.

122 William Shannon's ors., M'Gill's, Lincoln.
123 John Albright, 2d section, Cherokee.
124 Clarissa Aslin, f. a., Silman's, Pike.
125 Joseph Dean, 1st, Chatham.
126 Edward Rodgers, sol., Ellsworth's, Bibb.*
127 George Donaldson, Newman's, Thomas.*
128 Gabriel M'Clendon, 512th, Lee.
129 Willie B. Chappell, Gunn's, Jones.
130 John Newson, Jr., Newsom's, Warren.
131 Griffin Mathis, 373d, Jasper.*
132 George Creel, Smith's, Henry.
133 Levy Johnson, Tuggle's, Merriwether.
134 Charles A. Campbell, 293d, Jasper.
135 Anderson Harwell, s. l. w., 374th, Putnam.*
136 John Kimbrough, s. l. w., Baley's, Butts.
137 Thomas Pierce, Jr., 73d, Burke.
138 Thomas J. Webb, 687th, Lee.
139 Charles P. North, 561st, Upson.
140 Woody Jackson, Martin's, Pike.
141 John Jackson, Kelly's, Elbert.*
142 Nathan M'Leroy, 672d, Harris.
143 Wm. Parish, 9th, Effingham county, Chatham.*
144 Silas Hollis, m. s., Valleau's, Chatham.
145 Gabriel Jones, r. s., Groce's, Bibb.
146 Burnett Stephens, Dilman's, Pulaski.*
147 Hugh Fergurson, Brock's, Habersham.
148 James Dismukes, Whipple's, Wilkinson.
149 Hail Maxey, Hall's, Oglethorpe.
150 Milley Lee, w., Mason's, Washington.
151 Samuel Jackson, sol., Salem, Baldwin.
152 Thomas Bell, Chesnut's, Newton.
153 John R. Medlock, 406th, Gwinnett.*
154 John Glaze, Chastain's, Habersham.
155 Solomon Lacks, Griffin's, Merriwether.
156 James E. Hardeman, Shearer's, Coweta.*
157 Southerlin Cane, 537th, Upson.
158 John Weeks, 319th, Baldwin.
159 Andrew M. Park, Riden's, Jackson.
160 John Robertson, 277th, Morgan.
161 Thomas Riddle, Jr., Griffin's, Merriwether.*
162 James Ammons, 242d, Jackson.
163 John Richardson's or., Allen's, Bibb.
164 Biggars J. Sparrow, Wheeler's, Pulaski.*
165 Bryant Ivy, Parham's, Warren.
166 Henry P. Garrison, Flynn's, Muscogee.
167 Benjamin Merritt, s. l. w., Alsobrook's, Jones.*
168 George W. Young, 600th, Richmond.*

169 Jane Bostwick, w., M'Dowell's, Lincoln.
170 William Manson, Fleming's, Jefferson.
171 William Furgerson, M'Gehee's, Troup.*
172 Samuel Noles, White's, Franklin.
173 Dempsey Johnson, Hardman's, Oglethorpe.
174 Myrack Ivey, Collier's, Monroe.*
175 William Arnold's ors., Wheeler's, Pulaski.
176 Young Hall, Howell's, Troup.
177 Stephen Fitshaw, 417th, Walton.*
178 Martha Andrews, w., Hargrove's, Oglethorpe.
179 William Webb, Martin's, Hall.*
180 Wm. H. H. Massengale, Dozier's, Columbia.*
181 Elizabeth Hudman, w., Allen's, Henry.*
182 James L. Huchinson, Shearer's, Coweta.*
183 John N. Simpson's ors., 175th, Wilkes.
184 John Hendrick, r. s., Bustin's, Pike.
185 Ezekiel Mason, Latimer's, De Kalb.
186 Howell Peoples, Newsom's, Warren.
187 David R. Anderson, Orr's, Jackson.*
188 Bartley Tucker, Compton's, Fayette.
189 John Irvin Hodges, Linam's, Pulaski.
190 Bushrod Pettit, Dozier's, Columbia.*
191 Joshua Johnson, 406th, Gwinnett.*
192 Charles Mason, 243d, Jackson.*
193 John Slack, Fulks's, Wilkes.*
194 Joshua Gay, Jr., 574th, Early.
195 Richard Stokes, 7th, Chatham.*
196 James Hartley, Walker's, Houston.*
197 Mary Warren, w. r. s., Herndon's, Hall.*
198 Philip Chesher, Holt's, Talbot.
199 John Eberhart's ors., Merck's, Hall.
200 Nancy Sammons, w., Lamp's, Jefferson.
201 John Jones, Say's, De Kalb.
202 Thomas L. Pope, Ross's, Monroe.
203 Wiley Patterson, sol., Hart's, Jones.*
204 Hannah Swindell, w., 415th, Walton.*
205 Barton Rice's ors., Jones's, Hall.
206 Jesse Wiggins, M'Culler's, Newton.
207 Wm. R. Cowen, Ware's, Coweta.
208 Ninian Barrett, sol., Crawford's, Morgan.
209 William Orr, Williams's, Washington.
210 Charles Williford, sol., Robinson's, Fayette.
211 John Smith, Evans's, Fayette.*
212 Stafford Gipson, Griffin's, Fayette.
213 Gilbird Smith, Moore's, Randolph.
214 Ephraim M. Poole, Mobley's, De Kalb.
215 Absalom W. Rhodes, 121st, Richmond.

216 James Gordon, Edwards's, Talbot.*
217 Wiley S. Clements, Phillips's, Monroe.*
218 James Powell, Shattox's, Coweta.*
219 William Jackson, Jr., 160th, Greene.*
220 Clabourn Alsobrook, of Lee, Mashburn's, Pulaski.
221 Thomas J. Laughren, Davis's, Jones.
222 Franklin P. Hall, Hand's, Appling.*
223 John Cadenhead, Calhoun's, Harris.
224 John M. Jourdan, Lester's, Monroe.*
225 William R. Miers, Blackstock's, Hall.
226 John Hanna, Strahorn's, Heard.
227 John Marlow, 320th, Baldwin.*
228 William Housley, Jr., 600th, Richmond.
229 James G. Swain, sol., Lynn's, Warren.*
230 Jeremiah Perryman, Perryman's, Warren.
231 John S. Reeves, 36th, Scriven.
232 Owen Tomlin, sol., Mitchell's, Marion.*
233 Theodosius E. Massengale, Dozier's, Columbia.
234 Gren B. Hill, sol., Belcher's, Jasper.*
235 Hillery Beall, Dawson's, Jasper.
236 William Ellis, 319th, Baldwin.
237 Nancy Ragland, w., Kendrick's, Putnam.
238 Laurence Baggett, Moseley's, Coweta.*
239 James Driggers, Nesbit's, Newton.*
240 Slaughter Hill, Mizell's, Talbot.*
241 William Pirtle, Trout's, Hall.
242 James Nichols, Foote's, De Kalb.
243 Archibald York, sol., Howell's, Troup.
244 Levi Watts, Deavours's, Habersham.
245 Silas Rawls, Chambers's, Houston.
246 Charles Stewart's ors., Linam's, Pulaski.
247 Dorothy Mabry, lun., Valleau's, Chatham.
248 Jesse S. Coffey, Barker's, Gwinnett.
249 Richard Philpot, 4th section, Cherokee.*
250 James N. Bogle, Griffin's, Hall.
251 Randolph Holland, Allison's, Pike.*
252 Francis D. Mathis, Rooks's, Putnam.*
253 Eli M'Croan, Peterson's, Burke.
254 Walter Wadsworth, Latimer's, De Kalb.
255 John Boland, Maguire's, Gwinnett.
256 Edwin B. Weed, Valleau's, Chatham.
257 Stith H. Wright, Wagnon's, Carroll.
258 Nehemiah Payne, Sen., Price's, Hall.
259 Richard Parker, sol., Chesnut's, Newton.
260 Charles Coppedge, Allison's, Pike.
261 David Watson's ors., Perryman's, Warren.
262 Gideon Kirksey, Hearn's, Butts.

263 Mary B. Comer, w., 289th, Jasper.
264 Marshal P. Clark, Smith's, Elbert.
265 Stokely M. Brown, Brown's, Habersham.*
266 John Bennett, 49th, Emanuel.
267 John Youngblood, Strickland's, Merriwether.*
268 David Spencer, Hall's, Butts.
269 Hugh M. Reynolds, or., Hamilton's, Gwinnett.
270 Drusilly Posey, w., Ellis's, Pulaski.*
271 Albert W. Monk, Watson's, Marion.
272 John Porl, Herring's, Twiggs.
273 John A. Smith, Sims's, Troup.
274 Isaiah Warren, Lamberth's, Fayette.
275 John G. Roberts, Loveless's, Gwinnett.*
276 William Walraven, Gillis's, De Kalb.
277 Burril Jordan, M'Clain's, Newton.
278 Godfrey Purris, Wallis's, Irwin.
279 Horatio C. Bailey, Say's, De Kalb.
280 Thomas Norton, sol., Griffin's, De Kalb.
281 John O. Carter, Edwards's, Franklin.
282 Miall Wall, Hall's, Oglethorpe.
283 Zachariah Johnson, Sanders's, Jones.
284 Jesse Lee, M'Coy's, Houston.
285 Elijah W. Christian, Jr., Coker's, Troup.
286 William Lambert, Jr., Hanner's, Campbell.
287 Samuel Rowland, Mullen's, Carroll.*
288 Noah Ellis, Lawrence's, Pike.
289 Lucinda Turman, w., Brewer's, Walton.*
290 Shaderick M'Ginty, sol., Brewer's, Monroe.*
291 Henry Darnald, Johnson's, Bibb.
292 William M'Donald, 417th, Walton.
293 Williamson Brooks, Brooks's, Muscogee.*
294 Sarah Stephens, w., Bryant's, Burke.*
295 Reynolds's three ors., 111th, Hancock.
296 John P. Thiess, Levritt's, Lincoln.
297 John Maginty, r. s., Bustin's, Pike.
298 Teasdale's four orphans, Hobkerk's, Camden.
299 Thomas Gilbert, sol., Buck's, Houston.
300 Andrew Chisholm's ors., Canning's, Elbert.
301 George W. Swetman, or., Newman's, Thomas.*
302 Benjamin Bowers, sol., Perry's, Baldwin.
303 Hazlewood Hardwick, M'Ewin's, Monroe.
304 Arthur Harrup, r. s., Barefield's, Jones.
305 John A Casey's ors., Fleming's, Jefferson.
306 William Williford, Jones's, Thomas.*
307 John G. Tyas, Derrick's, Henry.
308 David M'Coy, Sen., sol., Grier's, Warren.
309 Horatio Brewer's ors., 190th, Elbert.

310 Abel M. Barnett, Hardman's, Oglethorpe.*
311 Felix Bouysson, Valleau's, Chatham.
312 Lovett Ethridge, Liddell's, Jackson.
313 James Rabb's ors., Harp's, Stewart.
314 John V. Brown, M. Brown's, Habersham.
315 Britton Johnson, Park's, Walton.
316 Jarit Burch, Sen., Ellis's, Rabun.
317 Nathan Collins, Burnett's, Habersham.
318 John Williams, Bustin's, Pike.*
319 Agrippa Scott, 406th, Gwinnett.
320 Nicholas A. Peurifoy, Phillips's, Monroe.
321 William Brown, Hamilton's, Gwinnett.
322 Hugh L. Irwin, Barron's, Houston.
323 Nathan G. Christie, Carswell's, Jefferson.*
324 John P. Durham, Butts's, Monroe.

NINTH DISTRICT, SECOND SECTION, CHEROKEE.

1 William Cray, Sanderlin's, Chatham.
2 Peter Brown, s. i. w., Peterson's, Montgomery.
3 Sarah Johnson, w. s. i. w., 693d, Heard.
4 Sarah Smith, w. r. s., 277th, Morgan.
5 Jason Brinson, 75th, Burke.*
6 Benjamin M'Donald, Culbreath's, Columbia.
7 William Burgamy, Jr., Garner's, Washington.*
8 David Moody, George's, Appling.
9 Benjamin Akins, 602d, Taliaferro.
10 John N. Hightower, Gittens's, Fayette.
11 Geo. Goodgame, or., Sinquefield's, Washington.
12 John Lyle, sol., Orr's, Jackson.*
13 Thomas W. Jones, Chisholm's, Morgan.*
14 Henry Rousseau, Kendricks's, Putnam.*
15 Enoch Bramlet, Jr., Chastain's, Habersham.
16 Parnell Vines, Moseley's, Coweta.*
17 Elizabeth Miller, id., 1st, Chatham.*
18 James M. Street, Riden's, Jackson.*
19 Joseph H. Hudson, Gunn's, Jefferson.
20 Henry Curbow, Smith's, Campbell.
21 John Wood's ors., Brock's, Habersham.
22 William Mitchell, Sen., r. s., Willis's, Franklin.
23 Sarah M'Dugall, M'Clure's, Rabun.
24 Henry J. Myddleton, sol., Houston's, Chatham.*
25 Martin G. Ledbetter, Espy's, Clarke.
26 Selina Elkins, w., 10th, Effingham.
27 Jacob Smith, Butts's, Monroe.

28 Jacob Leavens, Wilson's, Pike.*
29 Elijah Clark, M'Culler's, Newton.*
30 Thomas Wilson, Cobb's, Muscogee.*
31 James Driggers, Nesbit's, Newton.
32 Randolph Kent's ors., Jennings's, Clarke.
33 Joseph Robertson, Dobbs's, Hall.
34 Nancy Meeks, Coxe's, Franklin.
35 Henry Dickerson, r. s., Everett's, Washington.*
36 John Morris, Field's, Habersham.
37 William P. Moore, Jr., Anderson's, Rabun.*
38 Giddien Smith, sol., Dyer's, Habersham.
39 Lucy Drinkard, w., Capt. Prophett's, Newton.
40 Jane Wiley, w. r. s., Crow's, Pike.*
41 Matthew G. Ellis, 141st, Greene.
42 William Harris, Lynn's, Warren.
43 Philip A. M'Daniel, Foote's, De Kalb.
44 Littleberry Clark, 640th, Dooly.
45 Willis S. Breazeal, O'Neal's, Laurens.
46 David P. Simmons, Smith's, Madison.
47 Isaac Foster, M'Clure's, Rabun.*
48 Elisha Cloud, Hudson's, Marion.*
49 William B. Dennis, Craven's, Coweta.
50 Harison Anthony, Baugh's, Jackson.*
51 William C. Jolly, Holley's, Franklin.
52 John M'Graw, 470th, Upson.*
53 Mary Higginbotham, mi., f. a., Morgan's, Madison
54 Robert Right's or., M'Clendon's, Putnam.
55 John H. Baynes, Phillips's, Jasper.
56 Elizabeth Pattershall, w., Young's, Wilkinson.
57 John Cato's ors., Walker's, Houston.
58 John Landers, Griffin's, De Kalb.
59 William Jeter's ors., Few's, Muscogee.
60 Zachariah Adkinson, 121st, Richmond.*
61 John P. Carr, sol., Griffin's, De Kalb.
62 Sally Wells, h. a., Brown's, Habersham.
63 Henry W. Bruce, 102d, Hancock.*
64 Mary Barkesdale, w., Brown's, Habersham.
65 Thomas B. Shaw, sol., Cleland's, Chatham.*
66 Dolphin Floyd, sol., Frasier's, Monroe.
67 Henry Raper, Stephens's, Habersham.
68 John Ivens, Sutton's, Habersham.
69 Joseph J. Cotton's ors., Norris's, Monroe.*
70 Benton Walton, Shearer's, Coweta.*
71 Hezekiah Finley, Hughes's, Habersham.*
72 George A. Thrash, sol., Howell's, Troup.*
73 James M. Harris, 607th, Taliaferro.*
74 Allen B. Denton, 113th, Hancock.*

75 Benjamin Phillips, r. s., Brown's, Camden.
76 Henry K. Carter, Groce's, Bibb.*
77 Joseph C. Arnow, Hobkerk's, Camden.
78 Francis H. Wellman, sol., Valleau's, Chatham.
79 Andrew Galey, Dyer's, Habersham.
80 Garland Moseley, Whitehead's, Habersham.
81 Sumner's seven orphans, Bryant's, Burke.
82 Kilby Brown, s. l. w., Simmons's, Crawford.
83 Aaron Merritt's ors., Thames's, Crawford.
84 Joseph W. Slaughter, 294th, Jasper.
85 William W. Tilley, Carswell's, Jefferson.*
86 William Hamet, 600th, Richmond.*
87 William B. Tendall, Peterson's, Burke.*
88 John C. Gray, Griffith's, Harris.*
89 Littleberry Champion's ors., Hill's, Monroe.
90 John Humphries, Swain's, Thomas.
91 Elizabeth Wammock, w., Bryan's, Pulaski.
92 William H. Joyner's ors., Valleau's, Chatham.
93 Jane Willingham, w. r. s., Colley's, Oglethorpe.
94 Woodson P. Allen, 419th, Walton.
95 John T. Penn, s. l. w., Beasley's, Oglethorpe.*
96 John M'Vicker, r. s., Smith's, Henry.
97 Sarah Bachelor, w., 454th, Walton.*
98 James C. M'Ginty, Campbell's, Wilkes.
99 John Raper's ors., Whisenhunt's, Carroll.
100 James Cody, Tilley's, Rabun.
101 William Rankin, Cleland's, Chatham.
102 Turner Drake, Griffin's, De Kalb.*
103 Reuben Boatright, 57th, Emanuel.
104 Seth D. Threadcraft, sol., 4th, Chatham.*
105 Thomas Bowman, Sen., 249th, Walton.
106 John G. Mingledorff, sol., 11th, Effingham.
107 Needham Chesnut, Pearce's, Houston.
108 Warthen's four children, f. a., Hood's, Henry.
109 Emily Hill, w., Guice's, Oglethorpe.
110 Richard M. Burt, 374th, Putnam.
111 William Haddon, Carswell's, Jefferson.*
112 John C. Henderson, Allen's, Henry.
113 William L. Greene, 320th, Baldwin.*
114 Green Bell, Howell's, Elbert.*
115 Sarah Bradford, w., Bridges's, Gwinnett.
116 Green Clay, Sutton's, Habersham.
117 Allen Estes, Dearing's, Henry.
118 Susannah Hicks, w. r. s., 589th, Upson.
119 Frances Hearndon, w., 788th, Heard.*
120 Washington Thomas, M'Korkles, Jasper.
121 Caswell Burke, 3d section, Cherokee.

122 Mordecai M'Kinney, 417th, Walton.*
123 Corod Augley, blind, Hicks's, Decatur.
124 Henry Martin, Flynn's, Muscogee.
125 Jesse Bledsoe's ors., Robinson's, Putnam.
126 Edmund Baxley, 364th, Jasper.*
127 Ann E. Stewart, w., Cleland's, Chatham.
128 John H. Witherspoon, 243d, Jackson.*
129 Isaac Buzbin, Hargrove's, Oglethorpe.*
130 Willis Pitts, Justice's, Bibb.*
131 Joseph James's ors., 122d, Richmond.
132 Lawrence W. Hilton, Butts's, Monroe.*
133 Alexander H. Cooper, Few's, Muscogee.
134 George W. Evans, 606th, Taliaferro.*
135 Robert Carithers, r. s., Seas's, Madison.*
136 Robert Wilder's ors., Chambers's, Gwinnett.
137 Robert Glasgow, Brackett's, Newton.*
138 John D. Copeland, 160th, Greene.
139 John Wiley, s. i. w., Higginbotham's, Madison.*
140 James M. Strength, 373d, Jasper.
141 Bright Baker Harris, 22d, M'Intosh.*
142 Absalom Perkins, 601st, Taliaferro.
143 Joseph P. Beauford, Hammock's, Jasper.
144 Silas Ray, Brewer's, Walton.
145 Tilman Hawk, Allen's, Monroe.*
146 Amelia Mixen, h. a., 24th, M'Intosh.
147 George Morgan, s. l. w., Rooks's, Putnam.
148 John M. Morgan, Clinton's, Campbell.
149 John Reikman, 120th, Richmond.*
150 John Pelpy, Sutton's, Habersham.
151 Alburn Norman, or., Fleming's, Franklin.
152 Lewis Wilcox, Wilcox's, Telfair.*
153 John Slaughter, Edwards's, Talbot.
154 Thomas Gordon, Taylor's, Jones.
155 John Rigdon, Morrison's, Appling.*
156 J. Turner, Sen., widower, Carpenter's, Tatnall.
157 Josiah Hickman, sol., Blackstock's, Hall.
158 Malica Murphree, id., 74th, Burke.
159 James B. Smith, Swiney's, Laurens.
160 James L. Willis, Coxe's, Talbot.
161 Edward Johnson, s. l. w., 454th, Walton.
162 Thomas Pollard, Lamberth's, Fayette.
163 Margaret M'Collum, w. r. s., Crawford's, Franklin.
164 Jane Vern, w., 3d, Chatham.
165 Daniel Bowen, Wilcox's, Telfair.
166 Benjamin F. High, 279th, Morgan.
167 William Bacon, Ellsworth's, Bibb.
168 Smith Deen, Morrison's, Appling.

169 Isaiah C. Wallis, Liddell's, Jackson.*
170 James Singleton, sol., Allen's, Campbell.*
171 Wilson B. Clark, Barron's, Houston.*
172 Angus Johnson, Seal's, Elbert.
173 Alfred Howell, Newsom's, Warren.
174 Susan Winkler, w., 1st, Chatham.
175 Charles W. Brown, Bragaw's, Oglethorpe.*
176 Stephen T. Debusk, or., 271st, M'Intosh.
177 Nancy Watkins, w., Givins's, De Kalb.
178 William H. Malden, sol., Collins's, Henry.*
179 Jordan Spivey, 417th, Walton.
180 David Holley, Tower's, Gwinnett.
181 William A. Hunter, 140th, Greene.
182 James Y. Thompson, Nesbit's, Newton.
183 Cannay Burnam, Folsom's, Lowndes.
184 Eurick Johnson, Jr., Morgan's, Appling.
185 Allen M'Donald's ors., George's, Appling.
186 Samuel A. Breedlove, Shearer's, Coweta.*
187 Hillary Smith, Wilcox's, Telfair.
188 Lemuel Dodd, M. Brown's, Habersham.
189 George Grumbles, r. s., Bush's, Burke.*
190 Lydia Eislands, w., 271st, M'Intosh.*
191 Tillman Kelly, Newsom's, Warren.*
192 Elisha Harrell, Hicks's, Decatur.
193 Zedekiah Pope, Mitchell's, Pulaski.
194 Crispin Davis, Sen., Thaxton's, Butts.
195 William Collins, 108th, Hancock.*
196 Arthur J. Butts, 104th, Hancock.*
197 Friend O. Shockley, Ross's, Monroe.
198 Cyan L. Boykin, 36th, Scriven.
199 Kimmy Smith, 120th, Richmond.*
200 James Stafford, M'Craney's, Wayne.*
201 George W. Jennings, 320th, Baldwin.*
202 Elizabeth Wilcher, w. r. s., Chesnut's, Newton.
203 William Vaughn, Roberts's, Hall.
204 Robert Smith, Jr., Hall's, Butts.
205 John C. Phillips, Wynn's, Gwinnett.
206 Jane and Wm. Bryant, ors., Bryant's, Burke.
207 Bryan W. Collier, Mashburn's, Pulaski.
208 Elijah Boswell, Tompkins's, Putnam.
209 James M. Strong, Jack's, Clarke.
210 Sherwood Strand, Hall's, Oglethorpe.*
211 Jefferson Bazemore, Comer's, Jones.
212 Tatum Menefee, Robinson's, Fayette.
213 Albert B. Harris, M'Millon's, Lincoln.*
214 Bryan J. Roberts, Folsom's, Lowndes.*
215 William Driskill, Dawson's, Jasper.

216 Elizabeth Pence, w., Smith's, Habersham.
217 James Akridge, Swain's, Thomas.
218 Nathan Thompson, 146th, Greene.
219 Martin T. Cash, Taylor's, Elbert.
220 William A. Hammond, 279th, Morgan.
221 Charles Richardson, 561st, Upson.
222 Ephraim D. Spinks, Lynn's, Warren.
223 Peleg R. M'Crary, 319th, Baldwin.
224 Henry Childs, 364th, Jasper.
225 Hardy Johnson, r. s., 55th, Emanuel.
226 Ruth Weaver, w., Henson's, Rabun.
227 Joseph Pools, or., Crow's, Pike.*
228 Thomas N. Heard, 600th, Richmond.
229 William Bates, 143d, Greene.
230 Mary Cannady, w., 19th, Bryan.*
231 Waldrup Warren, Martin's, Pike.*
232 Henry Ball, miller, 510th, Early.*
233 Elizabeth Higgins, w., Reid's, Gwinnett.
234 Samuel Burdine, Gillis's, De Kalb.
235 William Graham, Russell's, Henry.*
236 Jesse M. Simmons, 604th, Taliaferro.
237 James E. Paul, Rainey's, Twiggs.
238 Thomas M. Turner, 1st, Chatham.*
239 William D. Scoggin, 318th, Baldwin.
240 Jacob Dreggors, 24th, M'Intosh.*
241 Anna J. C. Jones, or., of Claiborn, 419th, Walton.
242 John Wilder, Campbell's, Wilkes.*
243 Chesley B. Moore, Hart's, Jones.*
244 Peter Blois's ors., 4th, Chatham.
245 Collin Wood, Salem, Baldwin.
246 John Callaham, r. s., Jenkins's, Oglethorpe.*
247 Joseph Gouge, Sen., Barker's, Gwinnett.*
248 Hugh M'Linn, Ellsworth's, Bibb.*
249 William Blount, Herring's, Twiggs.
250 William Yates, Swain's, Thomas.
251 William Nash, Wynn's, Gwinnett.*
252 Dudley Bonds, Reid's, Gwinnett.
253 John Alliston, Guice's, Oglethorpe.
254 William White, Rhodes's, De Kalb.
255 Dawson Davis's ors., Loveless's, Gwinnett.
256 Joseph Crumpton, 404th, Gwinnett.
257 Charles Staples, Brackett's, Newton.
258 Thomas J. Smith, Park's, Walton.
259 Stephen Hayman, r. s., Bryant's, Burke.*
260 Jesse E. Smith, Camp's, Warren.*
261 Daniel Morrison, Morrison's, Montgomery.*
262 David Holeman, Davis's, Gwinnett.

263 William M. Ross, Young's, Wilkinson.
264 William Hudson's ors., Lunceford's, Elbert.
265 William F. Hendon, Mobley's, De Kalb.
266 Forgus Russell, Gray's, Henry.*
267 Tillman Harrison, sol., Liddell's, Jackson.
268 William Jones, Taylor's, Jones.
269 Carlton Nun, Justice's, Bibb.
270 Charlotte Robinson, w., Bostick's, Twiggs.
271 Baylis Donaldson, 404th, Gwinnett.
272 Peter Free, Payne's, Merriwether.
273 Thomas Black, Sutton's, Habersham.
274 Henry S. Autry, Coxe's, Morgan.*
275 Toliver Saxon Madding's ors., Gillis's, De Kalb.
276 Francis S. Taylor, Graves's, Lincoln.*
277 Elizabeth Walton, w., Vining's, Putnam.*
278 Ezekiel Sikes, Wright's, Tatnall.*
279 Felicia Felane, or., Cleland's, Chatham.
280 Walter A. Jenkins, Fulks's, Wilkes.
281 William W. Davis, Roe's, Burke.
282 James W. M'Cleskey, Orr's, Jackson.
283 Benjamin Little, Mobley's, De Kalb.
284 Green Cambron, Griffin's, De Kalb.
285 John L. Phillips, Cleland's, Chatham.
286 William G. Tyus, 108th, Hancock.*
287 Caroline L. Mordecai, w., 1st, Chatham.*
288 George W. Jones, Peek's, Columbia.
289 Mary Robbins, h. a., 34th, Scriven.*
290 James Willingham, Tankersley's, Columbia.
291 John W. Taylor, Thomason's, Elbert.
292 Moses Wiley, s. i. w., 102d, Hancock.*
293 John Brown, sol., Willis's, Franklin.
294 Cornelius Geiger, sol., 333d, Wayne.*
295 James W. Cato, Calhoun's, Harris.*
296 Whitfield Lindsey, Gunn's, Jones.
297 John G. Bethune, Greer's, Merriwether.
298 Ralph Bozeman, r. s., Swain's, Thomas.
299 Samuel S. D. Burdett, Sanders's, Jones.*
300 John Brown, Sinquefield's, Washington.*
301 Mary Nash, w., Sanders's, Jones.*
302 George Thomas, Mashburn's, Pulaski.
303 Mark P. Davis, Harris's, Columbia.
304 Thomas Chesser, Smith's, Liberty.*
305 Rosanna Jenkins, w. r. s., Bragaw's, Oglethorpe.
306 Nancy Tye, w., Wolfskin's, Oglethorpe.*
307 Lazarus Jones, Wynn's, Gwinnett.
308 Jonathan Thompson, M'Clure's, Rabun.
309 James Smith, sol., Salem, Baldwin.

310 John Ellis, Fryer's, Telfair.*
311 Edmund T. Penn, Hodges's, Newton.
312 Steward M'Elhannon, Say's, Jackson.
313 Jacob Tarver's ors., 117th, Hancock.
314 Patsey Vernon, w. r. s., Collins's, Oglethorpe.
315 William Hook's ors., 516th, Dooly.
316 Robert Wood, Monk's, Crawford.*
317 Nancy M'Duffee, h. a., 406th, Gwinnett.
318 Nancy Moore, w., Frasier's, Monroe.
319 Berry Nobles, Nichols's, Fayette.
320 Peter Gill, Taylor's, Jones.
321 Basdel Pratt, s. l. w., 605th, Taliaferro.*
322 James M. Turman, 559th, Walton.
323 Edison Reeves, Nichols's, Fayette.
324 David Weaver, Wood's, Morgan.*

TENTH DISTRICT, SECOND SECTION, CHEROKEE.

1 Robert Scott, Bustin's, Pike.
2 Joseph J. Williams, 656th, Troup.*
3 Alexander Modesett, Bivins's, Jones.*
4 Warren J. Phillips, Payne's, Merriwether.
5 John G. Barnett, Loveless's, Gwinnett.
6 Jackson M'Donald, Southwell's, Tatnall.
7 Benjamin Tillery, Allison's, Pike.*
8 Jonathan Powell, Hutson's, Newton.
9 Ibby Hurst, w., Roberts's, Hall.
10 Duncan Ray, Williams's, Decatur.*
11 Thomas Arnett, Downs's, Warren.
12 Daniel Young, Whitehead's, Habersham.
13 William Camp, Gray's, Henry.
14 Arba Washburn, 1st, Chatham.   [laski.
15 J. Rawlins, Sen., of G. Swamp, Mashburn's, Pu-
16 Simeon O'Neal, Underwood's, Putnam.
17 William T. Bell, 406th, Gwinnett.*
18 Richard W. Wood, Sen., Martin's, Newton.
19 Balas Carr's ors., Smith's, Wilkinson.
20 David Dyer, Wood's, Morgan.
21 Washington Brady, Groce's, Bibb.
22 Nathan W. Peters, Peurifoy's, Henry.*
23 Benjamin Gardner, Ellsworth's, Bibb.
24 James Kennedy's ors, Sewell's, Franklin.-
25 Ann Cowsert, h. d. l. w., Taylor's, Putnam.
26 Eusebius J. M'Cleskey, Orr's, Jackson.

27 Joseph Crenshaw, sol., Martin's, Pike.*
28 James Williams, 174th, Wilkes.
29 William Parker, Payne's, Merriwether.
30 Peter Renfroe's ors., Sparks's, Washington.*
31 Eli Donaldson, Kellum's, Talbot.*
32 Leander Wilson, Strahorn's, Heard.
33 Jonathan Stone, 404th, Gwinnett.*
34 Thomas Hingson, Phillips's, Jasper.*
35 Lydia Cook, w. r. s., 12th, Effingham.
36 Henry Myers, Sinclair's, Houston.
37 Elias Morgan's ors., Allen's, Henry.
38 Charles J. Malone, Williams's, Washington.
39 Zacheus Hudgins, Merck's, Hall.
40 Elijah Strawbridge, 242d, Jackson.
41 Eli Collins, Willingham's, Harris.
42 William B. Chandler, Curry's, Wilkinson.*
43 Isham West, sol., Streetman's, Twiggs.
44 William D. Ray, sol., 319th, Baldwin.
45 Daniel Brockwell, Tompkins's, Putnam.
46 William Shepherd, sol., Jordan's, Harris.
47 Archibald Matthews, Frasier's, Monroe.
48 Eldridge Whitehead, 242d, Jackson.
49 Sarah M'Kean, w., 398th, Richmond.*
50 Andrew Stewart, 600th, Richmond.
51 Ferdinan Smith, Hearn's, Butts.*
52 Benjamin E. Alford, Show's, Muscogee.
53 Thomas Bennett's ors., Sen., M'Ginnis's, Jackson
54 Stephen Nash, 394th, Montgomery.*
55 Robert Kirbon, Groce's, Bibb.
56 Tillman R. Denson, Prescott's, Twiggs.*
57 Martin H. Brown, Justice's, Bibb.*
58 David Rannals, Say's, De Kalb.
59 George Patterson, Ellis's, Rabun.
60 Jacob Young, Young's, Jefferson.
61 William Kirksey, Newman's, Thomas.
62 Erastus Stone, Whitaker's, Crawford.
63 William Alexander, Echols's, Clarke.
64 Adam Huchinson, s. l. w., 600th, Richmond.
65 Roley S. Edwards, Comer's, Jones.
66 John L. B. Harper, M'Cleland's, Irwin.
67 Andrew Gailey, Cleghorn's, Madison.
68 David Waggoner, Say's, De Kalb.
69 Reuben Brock, M. Brown's, Habersham.
70 John G. Maxey, Barnett's, Clarke.*
71 George W. Parker, sol., Peace's, Wilkinson.*
72 Thomas Stinson, Bryan's, Monroe.
73 Nancy Solomon, or., Latimer's, De Kalb.

74 Spencer Bruce, Parham's, Harris.
75 Milton Cooper, Higginbotham's, Carroll.*
76 James H. Jones, Jr., 102d, Hancock.
77 Lewis Brackett, Dobbs's, Hall.*
78 John Nunlee, sol., 190th, Elbert.
79 Moses Keys, 419th, Walton.*
80 John Grover, 19th, Bryan.*
81 Benjamin Bond, Bostick's, Twiggs.
82 William F. Greene, 318th, Baldwin.
83 James O. Smith, s. l. w., Jenkins's, Oglethorpe.
84 Henry P. Lewis, Bruce's, Greene.
85 Dicy Washington, or., 119th, Richmond.
86 John Adnan, Coxe's, Franklin.
87 Robert A. Long, Hendon's, Carroll.
88 Leonard Wills, r. s., Chambers's, Gwinnett.*
89 Tabitha Weekes, h. a., Comer's, Jones.
90 Barbara Whittimore, w., Brown's, Camden.
91 John Lee, Sen., 34th, Scriven.
92 Paschal Smith's ors., Wolfskin's, Oglethorpe.
93 Thomas Edge, Whitehead's, Habersham.*
94 Benjamin W. Woods, Smith's, Madison.
95 Hiram Hague, 119th, Richmond.*
96 Isaiah Doane, Hobkerk's, Camden.*
97 James Wilson, 35th, Scriven.
98 John Bowls, Hatton's, Baker.*
99 Lavina Harris, w. r. s., Guice's, Oglethorpe.*
100 James C. Walker, Graves's, Lincoln.
101 Maty Wynce, w., 374th, Putnam.
102 Calliway Williams, Higginbotham's, Rabun.
103 Elizabeth Seale, w. s. i. w., Green's, Oglethorpe.
104 Hartwell L. Odom, Garner's, Coweta.*
105 William Coats, 168th, Wilkes.
106 Edmund Abercrombie, s. i. w., 101st, Hancock.
107 Robert Crutchfield, s. i. w., 140th, Greene.
108 Thomas Hauks, Tower's, Gwinnett.
109 John W. Allen, s. i. w., Bostick's, Twiggs.*
110 George W. Willingham, Colley's, Oglethorpe.
111 Paschal H. Wood, Jones's, Morgan.*
112 John Bagley, Brooks's, Muscogee.
113 James S. Hatchett, Wills's, Franklin.*
114 Joseph Nichols, Young's, Wilkinson.*
115 Abraham Wood, Royster's, Franklin.
116 William J. Johnston, Lamp's, Jefferson.
117 Elijah Chandler, Sullivan's, Jones.
118 George Porter, House's, Henry.
119 Joseph H. C. Gindrat, 318th, Baldwin.
120 Perry G. Garman, Herndon's, Hall.

121 James Cumbert, Young's, Wilkinson.*
122 William P. Berry, Hampton's, Newton.
123 Isham Harris, Moseley's, Coweta.
124 John W. Jones, Ellis's, Pulaski.
125 Lemuel Clayton, Price's, Hall.
126 John Aron's ors., M'Korkle's, Jasper.
127 Agnes Wright, w., Hearn's, Butts.*
128 Randolph Helviston, Hopkins's, Camden.
129 John Kingery, Blount's, Wilkinson.
130 Elizabeth Mason, w., Bower's, Elbert.
131 John Tate, Jr., 2d section, Cherokee.
132 James M. Dickson, 113th, Hancock.
133 John R. Light, Roberts's, Hall.
134 James Turner, Gittens's, Fayette.
135 Harriet & N. W. Liverman, ors., 510th, Early.
136 John James Almond, Roe's, Burke.
137 Jane Porter, or., Smith's, Wilkinson.
138 William Bishop, Mullen's, Carroll.
139 Uriah Minter's minors, f. a., Brown's, Habersham.
140 Asa A. Ernest, sol., Justice's, Bibb.
141 Robert Knowles, Howell's, Troup.*
142 John P. Ryan, Shearer's, Coweta.
143 Dempsey White's ors., Blackstock's, Hall.
144 Alpheus Beall, ———, Wilkinson.
145 Charles Andrew, Jones's, Madison.
146 Henry Rogers, Talley's, Troup.
147 John Fuller, Jr., Hill's, Baldwin.
148 Lovick Baring, 735th, Troup.
149 William M'Intosh, 144th, Greene.*
150 Duke Williams, m. s., 160th, Greene.
151 Nancy Lewis, w., Hines's, Coweta.*
152 Benjamin Mayo's ors., 245th, Jackson.
153 Mary Lockett, w., 603d, Taliaferro.
154 Thomas Hursey, Fryer's, Telfair.
155 John Sappington, r. s., House's, Henry.*
156 William Howell, sol., Edwards's, Talbot.
157 James Mangum, Mobley's, De Kalb.
158 Gresham Bryan, Goodwin's, Houston.
159 James M. Collins, Whipple's, Wilkinson.
160 Sarah Brack, w. r. s., Cannon's, Wilkinson.
161 Mashack Biddy, 1st section, Cherokee.
162 Joshua Lazenby, sol., Perryman's, Warren.
163 James M'Walters, M'Cullers, Newton.*
164 Sikes Sanders's ors., 535th, Dooly.
165 Thomas P. Wilkins, Hendon's, Carroll.*
166 Thomas W. Brandon, 404th, Gwinnett.
167 Gilbert May, Sanderlin's, Chatham.*

168 Isaac A. M'Ewin, sol., Jones's, Madison.
169 Hugh A. Smith, Smith's, Houston.*
170 John S. Wosham, Whitehead's, Habersham.
171 Robert Love, Barwick's, Washington.*
172 Henry Strickland, Miller's, Jackson.
173 Allen Porterfield, Morgan's, Madison.
174 William Baker, sol., Heard's, De Kalb.
175 Green Bingham, Harralson's, Troup.
176 James Gallagher, Sanderlin's, Chatham.
177 Richard Hingson, Walker's, Harris.
178 Emeriah Popham, Dyer's, Habersham.
179 Satley Rogers, Varner's, Merriwether.*
180 Orren S. Woodward, Lester's, Monroe.
181 Jane Reynolds, h. a., Hart's, Jones.
182 Jesse Hart, Ball's, Monroe.
183 Elizabeth Eastwood, w., Walker's, Houston.
184 Francis Fickling, Hart's, Jones.*
185 Daniel C. Rowell, Harris's, Crawford.
186 James M'Coy, 588th, Upson.*
187 A. W. Ellington, Underwood's, Putnam.*
188 William H. Cassells, Gibson's, Decatur.
189 David T. White, Brackett's, Newton.
190 William Cummins, 147th, Greene.
191 Jacob Bowers, Bridges's, Gwinnett.
192 Bennett Crafton, 124th, Richmond.
193 Bailey Goddard's ors., Ellsworth's, Bibb.
194 Henry Lundy, Moore's, Randolph.
195 Teany Chapman, h. a., Seay's, Hall.
196 William F. Peoples, 494th, Upson.
197 Moses Strawhon, Wynn's, Gwinnett.
198 Nicholas Minor's ors., Tower's, Gwinnett.
199 John Edwards, s. i. w., Talley's, Troup.*
200 Robert H. Sledge, Graves's, Putnam.*
201 Jeremiah Mouldin, Dyer's, Habersham.
202 John Clefton, Mackleroy's, Clarke.
203 Elizabeth Matthews, w. r. s., Silman's, Pike.*
204 Septimus W. Slatter, Harp's, Stewart.
205 Edwin Irvin, or., Sanderlin's, Chatham.
206 Pleasant Moon's ors., Nellum's, Elbert.
207 George W. Carter, Ball's, Monroe.*
208 William Holley, Jr., Smith's, Houston.
209 Henry Hodges, Williams's, Washington.
210 Thomas J. Curtis, Harris's, Crawford.
211 Henry Bailey's ors., Coxe's, Talbot.
212 William A. Wenn, 454th, Walton.*
213 John Wheeler, M. Brown's, Habersham.
214 Asa C. S. Alexander, 510th, Early.

215 Joshua Saxon, Roe's, Burke.
216 John C. Carter, Brock's, Habersham.
217 Curtis Pinson, or., Ellis's, Rabun.
218 James Kitchens, sol., Morton's, De Kalb.
219 John M'Gee's ors., Lay's, Jackson.
220 Henry Singleton, Coffee's, Rabun.
221 Richard Iley, Sewell's, Franklin.*
222 Millicent Wright, w. of sol., Parham's, Warren.
223 Jesse B. Knight, Whitfield's, Washington.*
224 Frederic Lamb, Barker's, Gwinnett.
225 David Tallant, Dobbs's, Hall.
226 Trussey Jarman, Dean's, De Kalb.*
227 Daniel C. Howell, or., 34th, Scriven.
228 Levin Spark's ors., Martin's, Newton.
229 William A. Davis, Wolfskin's, Oglethorpe.
230 Henry W. Beauford, Wilson's, Jasper.
231 George W. Crawford, Stephens's, Habersham.*
232 John M'Donald, Sanderlin's, Chatham.*
233 William Clubb, s. l. w., Hall's, Camden.*
234 Richard Gunn., Jr., s. l. w., 602d, Taliaferro.
235 James Payne, Williams's, Washington.*
236 James L. Heard, Anderson's, Wilkes.
237 Jacob Wolfe, sol. 1784–97, Heard's, De Kalb.*
238 James Ponge, Davis's, Clarke.*
239 James Smylie, Jr., sol., Baker's, Liberty.*
240 Daniel M'Nair, Newsom's, Warren.*
241 Elizabeth Gideons, w. r. s., Phillips's, Talbot.
242 Sanford W. Moore, Mobley's, De Kalb.
243 Thomas Pledger, r. s., Lunceford's, Elbert.
244 Millicent Roberts, w., White's, Franklin.
245 Isaac D. Newton, Mashburn's, Pulaski.*
246 Henry Whisenhunt, Whisenhunt's, Carroll.
247 Richard W. Statum, Fulks's, Wilkes.*
248 Joel Hancock, Tuggle's, Merriwether.
249 James Davis, Jr., Nichols's, Fayette.
250 Jeremiah Lary's ors., Turner's, Crawford.
251 Alexander Dennard, Mashburn's, Pulaski.*
252 Starling T. Austin, Chandler's, Gwinnett.
253 John Poulks's ors., Whipple's, Wilkinson.
254 Hozea Holtzclaw, 175th, Wilkes.
255 James Hawkins, Price's, Hall.
256 William C. Carter, Blackshear's, Laurens.
257 John Sutton's ors., M'Craney's, Lowndes.
258 Sterling G. Smith, Allen's, Bibb.*
259 Sarah Thrower, w. r. s., Martin's, Newton.
260 Jonathan Peel, Robinson's, Harris.
261 John W. Yarbrough, Lynn's, Warren.

262 Gadwell J. Pearce, Daniel's, Hall.
263 Young P. Poole, Barker's, Gwinnett.
264 William Jackson, Collins's, Henry.*
265 Margaret Ard, or., Mason's, Washington.
266 Joel Dean's ors., Robison's, Washington.
267 Jesse Gidions, Oliver's, Decatur.
268 Burrell Cannon, sol., 373d, Jasper.*
269 John W. Graham, M'Clain's, Newton.
270 Michael C. Moore, Hines's, Coweta.
271 Daniel Killian, Chambers's, Gwinnett.
272 John Lovet, Thaxton's, Butts.
273 Richard Fortson, Walker's, Harris.
274 John Connell, Camp's, Warren.*
275 Henry K. Burroughs, Milledgeville, Baldwin.
276 Barney West, Dobb's, Hall.
277 Jesse Ballard, Lawrence's, Pike.*
278 Henry T. Barnley, Newsom's, Warren.
279 Sarah Preston, w., Hearn's, Butts.
280 Mark A. Candler's ors., Dozier's, Columbia.
281 William Nimmons, Shearer's, Coweta.
282 James Joines, Sinquefield's, Washington.
283 Josiah Sterlings's ors., Hardman's, Oglethorpe.
284 Martha Woods, w., Carpenter's, Tatnall.
285 Alfred M. Light, Roberts's, Hall.
286 Frances Langley, Hudson's, Marion.*
287 William F. Deen, 494th, Upson.
288 John Smith, Craven's, Coweta.
289 Mary Holiman, w. of sol., Williams's, Jasper.*
290 John Irby's three orphans, Dean's, De Kalb.
291 Samuel Bell, s. l. w., Jenkins's, Oglethorpe.
292 Joseph Jackson, 15th, Liberty.*
293 Rhoda Reeves, w., 168th, Wilkes.
294 Dickerson Raynalds, Grubbs's, Columbia.*
295 Littleton Gipson, Jones's, Lincoln.
296 John Cofer, Loveless's, Gwinnett.
297 Susannah Hewell, w. r. s., Fenn's, Clarke.
298 David Askew, Hammock's, Jasper.
299 Jesse Moore, m. s., Lockhart's, Bulloch.*
300 Elijah Smallwood, Hart's, Jones.*
301 Mary Ann Sharp, w. of sol., 75th, Burke.*
302 Lewis Day, 559th, Walton.*
303 Berry Simms, Martin's, Stewart.*
304 Lindsey Killibrew, Camp's, Warren.*
305 Margaret Chaplain, w., Riden's, Jackson.*
306 John Wood Cowan, Latimer's, De Kalb.
307 James Cook, Evans's, Fayette.
308 Harrison Harris, Tower's, Gwinnett.

309 Alfred J. Baynes, Phillips's, Jasper.*
310 Hartwell J. Lawrence, 142d, Greene.*
311 Thomas Hatchett, Hatchett's, Oglethorpe.
312 Berkley Perry, sol., Ball's, Monroe.
313 John Wilson, 450th, Early.*
314 William Watson, Swain's, Thomas.
315 Daniel Slade, Waller's, Putnam.
316 Perry Carroll, Whipple's, Wilkinson.
317 Stephen G. Cotton, Morris's, Crawford.
318 John Peoples, Ogden's, Camden.*
319 Richard D. Myers, Lane's, Morgan.
320 Nathaniel Legg's ors., Orre's, Jackson.
321 Robert A. Smith, Bragaw's, Oglethorpe.
322 James Hammett, Edwards's, Franklin.
323 Spear's three orphans, 271st, M'Intosh.
324 James Martin, Martin's, Jones.

ELEVENTH DISTRICT, SECOND SECTION, CHEROKEE.

1 Milton Davis, Brock's, Habersham.
2 Robert Avary, Seay's, Hall.
3 Henry S. Ray, Johnson's, Bibb.
4 Mary C. Butler, w. r. s., Bridges's, Gwinnett.*
5 Joseph Omans, Whipple's, Wilkinson.*
6 Henry Brooker, Pollard's, Wilkes.
7 William J. Head, 294th, Jasper.
8 James Pool, sol., Dearing's, Henry.*
9 John C. Griffin, 25th, Scriven.*
10 Edmund Camp's ors., 249th, Walton.
11 John S. Storey, Shearer's, Coweta.*
12 Daniel D. Born, Barker's, Gwinnett.*
13 Daniel Mills, Haygood's, Washington.*
14 T. Wilcox, Jr. (son of Thomas), Fryer's, Telfair.*
15 Howell Elliott, Taylor's, Jones.
16 George Doggett, s. i. w., ———, Oglethorpe.
17 Benjamin T. Harris, Wright's, Laurens.
18 Hugh Sparlin, Jones's, Habersham.
19 Green Johnson, Stewart's, Warren.
20 Lewis Chandler, 245th, Jackson.
21 John Godfrey, 574th, Early.
22 William Knowles, Cook's, Telfair.
23 Alexr. Caruthers, or. of John, Smith's, Houston.
24 John Buffington, Lawrence's, Pike.
25 Nesbitt P. J. Taylor, or., Cleland's, Chatham.

26 James Bemmington, Dobbs's, Hall.*
27 Amos Osborn, Coxe's, Franklin.*
28 David Barnett, Hardman's, Oglethorpe.
29 Jane M'Kenney, w. s. i. w., Brewer's, Monroe.
30 Catharine Burnside, w., Walker's, Columbia.
31 James L. Compton, 294th, Jasper.
32 Thomas Williams, Coffee's, Rabun.
33 William Wilson, Gunn's, Jefferson.*
34 Macklin Sells, sol., Harris's, Columbia.
35 William Little, Sen., r. s., 307th, Putnam.
36 Elizabeth Ball, or., Maguire's, Morgan.*
37 Philip Boss, 415th, Walton.
38 Alexander Malcom, 559th, Walton.
39 Joseph Rasberry's ors., Brewer's, Walton.
40 William Wood's ors., Martin's, Newton.
41 William B. Murphy, 320th, Baldwin.
42 Henry Wade, M. Brown's, Habersham.
43 Thomas M'Clure, Jennings's, Clarke.
44 Benjamin Young's ors., Gunn's, Jefferson.
45 J. S. Porter's ors., Baker county, 124th, Richmond.
46 Roger D. Barr, Rainey's, Twiggs.*
47 John Huff, Young's, Carroll.*
48 James D. Perdeu, Chambers's, Gwinnett.*
49 Charles Jordan, Thompson's, Henry.*
50 Alfred Royal, 535th, Dooly.*
51 Thomas Leak, s. i. w., Crow's, Pike.
52 Robert R. Hardin, s. l. w., Ballard's, Morgan.
53 John L. B. Duskin, Harp's, Stewart.
54 James Riley's minors, ———, Greene.
55 Thomas J. Bragg, Hatchett's, Oglethorpe.
56 Etheldred W. Cody, Lay's, Jackson.
57 Samuel Moseley, r. s., White's, Franklin.
58 John Brand, Loveless's, Gwinnett.
59 Wilson Folkner, Rhodes's, De Kalb.
60 John Puckett, Brackett's, Newton.
61 Susan D. Habersham, w., Fitzpatrick's, Chatham.*
62 Martin Scalf, M. Brown's, Habersham.*
63 Josephas Roads, Dyer's, Habersham.*
64 John Dyson's ors., sol., Moseley's, Wilkes.
65 James M. L. Peek, Tompkins's, Putnam.
66 Ann Archer, w., 259th, Scriven.
67 Josiah Vann, sol., Allen's, Campbell.*
68 David Barefield, 102d, Hancock.
69 Ezekiel Mathis, Wynn's, Gwinnett.
70 Benjamin W. Cash, Higginbotham's, Madison.
71 John S. Stony, Shearer's, Coweta.
72 Joel T. Goodwin, Cannon's, Wilkinson.

73 Elizabeth Boyd, w., Houston's, Chatham.
74 Alexander Farley's ors., Kendrick's, Monroe.
75 Thomas J. Willis, Burk's, Stewart.*
76 Barnett Haws, Baismore's, Jones.
77 John Keith, Will's, Twiggs.
78 Shadrach Hogan, Jr., Baugh's, Jackson.
79 Lewis Lively, Griffin's, Burke.
80 Richard Thurmond, 167th, Wilkes.
81 Allen Cleveland, Hall's, Butts.
82 Walker Duncan, 320th, Baldwin.*
83 Adam Carson, r. s., Alsobrook's, Jones.*
84 David D. Mimms, Mimms's, Fayette.*
85 Mary Bennett, w. r. s., Morgan's, Appling.*
86 Howell Vaughan, sol., Collier's, Monroe.*
87 Archibald W. Gentry, 162d, Greene.
88 Jesse Shepard, Coxe's, Talbot.
89 David Phillips, 333d, Wayne.*
90 Thomas W. Cain, 333d, Wayne.*
91 Elizabeth Ann Martin, 574th, Early.
92 George Wilcox (son of Thos.), Fryer's, Telfair.
93 Sarah Higginbotham, w., 27th, Glynn.
94 Moses Hunter, r. s., Whitehead's, Habersham.
95 Frederic Ashfield, 374th, Putnam.*
96 Feitrell Hall, Pace's, Putnam.*
97 William Worthy, Sen., Rhodes's, De Kalb.*
98 Edward Miles, Bell's, Columbia.
99 Samuel Barksdale, sol., Johnson's, Warren.*
100 Rena Fitzpatrick, Edwards's, Talbot.
101 James P. Kendrick, Kendrick's, Monroe.*
102 Joseph Walker, M. Brown's, Habersham.*
103 Joshua Jordan, Johnson's, Bibb.*
104 James Durance, Peavy's, Bulloch.
105 Samuel P. Aldridge, Crawford's, Morgan.
106 Richard T. Turner, Valleau's, Chatham.
107 Jonathan Winstell, 374th, Putnam.
108 Littleberry Eubank, Daring's, Butts.
109 Elias Harrell, Tower's, Gwinnett.
110 Richard Farrow, Dobbs's, Hall.*
111 John Wiggins, s. l. w., Lamberth's, Fayette.*
112 Joseph James's ors., 122d, Richmond.
113 Mary Maddux, w., Loveless's, Gwinnett.*
114 John Moore, sol., Bragaw's, Oglethorpe.
115 Gideon S. Carroll, 22d, M'Intosh.*
116 Henry S. Cook, Groce's, Bibb.*
117 Abi Bradford, w., 293d, Jasper.*
118 Mary Nash, w. r. s., Sanders's, Jones.*
119 Thomas Davis, Mimms's, Fayette.*

120 George Gambell, Kendrick's, Monroe.*
121 Joel Bruce, 160th, Greene.
122 Aaron Jones, Jr., Hendon's, Carroll.*
123 Jeremiah Sailors, House's, Henry.
124 Green Walden, Gray's, Henry.*
125 Elizabeth G. Colsom, w., Marsh's, Thomas.
126 Lard Little, Perry's, Habersham.*
127 John William Spain, or., Studstill's, Lowndes.
128 Rebecker Nix, w. r. s., Mizell's, Talbot.*
129 Thomas Dawson, sol., 295th, Jasper.*
130 John Barlow, Whipple's, Wilkinson.*
131 Robert Baldwin's ors., s. i. w., Mays's, Monroe.
132 John C. Bates, Whelchel's, Hall.*
133 John Kelly, Craven's, Coweta.*
134 John Williamson, George's, Appling.*
135 Joel Haines, Shattox's, Coweta.*
136 Isham Caswell, sol., Hitchcock's, Muscogee.*
137 R. N. Hicklin's ors., Everett's, Washington.
138 John Peterson's ors., Douglass's, Telfair.
139 John Screws, M'Korkle's, Jasper.*
140 Charles Clements, Jr., Robinson's, Fayette.*
141 William P. Pool, Herndon's, Hall.
142 James Boatright, Moseley's, Coweta.*
143 James Jackson's ors., 69th, Burke.
144 Edmund Duncan's ors., Davis's, Jones.
145 Daniel Blue, Sen., 27th, Glynn.
146 Rachel Smith, w. s. i. w., ———, Sumter.
147 Zachariah Harlin's ors., Derrick's, Henry.
148 Jefferson Wollis, Phillips's, Talbot.
149 Frances Peurifoy, or., Rooks's, Putnam.
150 Haley Shaw, 2d section, Cherokee.
151 Jesse Harris, Huey's, Harris.
152 H. V. Johnson, Athens, Clarke.*
153 John Perry, Monk's, Crawford.*
154 Charles M. Pratt, Hopkins's, Camden.*
155 James Clary, Williams's, Decatur.
156 Daniel Higdon, Flynn's, Muscogee.*
157 Joseph J. Henderson, Belcher's, Jasper.
158 Henry A. David, Colley's, Madison.
159 Butler Abney, Newby's, Jones.*
160 James Beasley, Ogden's, Camden.
161 Joseph T. Bradford, Turner's, Crawford.
162 Benjamin F. Lyons, Polhill's, Burke.
163 Randall Ramsay, sol., Hall's, Oglethorpe.
164 James Ramey, Coffee's, Rabun.
165 Lewis Wheelis, sol., Chambers's, Gwinnett.
166 Elias Brown, Barron's, Houston.

167 Reuben Smith, Anderson's, Wilkes.
168 George W. Ray, 470th, Upson.*
169 James Billingsleas's ors., Sullivan's, Jones.
170 Wilson Furr, Dobbs's, Hall.*
171 Ezekel Edge, Whitehead's, Habersham.
172 William Vermillion, Trout's, Hall.*
173 Mary Young, w., 398th, Richmond.*
174 William B. Rittenberry, 103d, Hancock.
175 William Merritt, s. l. w., Taylor's, Putnam.
176 John Fuller, sol., 242d, Jackson.
177 James Bassett, Ellsworth's, Bibb.
178 Mary Ann Douglass, or., Williams's, Decatur.*
179 Dilmus J. Lyle, Jr., 243d, Jackson.
180 John Carmichael, 245th, Jackson.
181 Oswell B. Jones's ors., Chandler's, Franklin.
182 Abraham Keener, Ellis's, Rabun.
183 Henry W. Todd, 161st, Greene.
184 Thomas Thrower, Martin's, Pike.*
185 Enoch Brown, Wilcox's, Telfair.
186 William Word, Hammond's, Franklin.
187 Lloyd Betts's ors., Carswell's, Jefferson.
188 Joshua Drake, or., 756th, Sumter.
189 Isaac Harrell, sol., Williams's, Decatur.*
190 William Jones, Thomason's, Elbert.
191 Alexander Clark, Pounds's, Twiggs.
192 William B. Dudley, Hargrove's, Oglethorpe.
193 James F. Nelson, 249th, Walton.
194 Wiley Smith, sol., Sims's, Troup.
195 Cosom Emer Bartlett, Lynn's, Muscogee.
196 John A. Stephens, Chambers's, Gwinnett.
197 Pleiades O. Lumpkin, 419th, Walton.
198 Jesse M. White, M'Clain's, Newton.*
199 Robert Stevens, 535th, Dooly.
200 Davidpert Corley, s. l. w., Craven's, Coweta.
201 P. Combic, of Camp's, Warren, 111th, Hancock.
202 Simon Ward, 119th, Richmond.*
203 Bryant Wasden, Lamp's, Jefferson.*
204 William Nelson, or., Grider's, Morgan.
205 William Grady, 248th, Jackson.*
206 Susannah Smead, w., Norris's, Monroe.
207 Jesse Edenfield, Griffin's, Emanuel.
208 Benajah Smith, Arrington's, Merriwether.
209 Henry P. Smith, Smith's, Madison.
210 Michael Everett, Cook's, Telfair.*
211 David Allison, 143d, Greene.
212 Stephen Gibbons, Jr., 121st, Richmond.*
213 Bozeman Adare, s. i. w., Mullen's, Carroll.*

214 Charles J. P. Averett, 124th, Richmond.*
215 Johnson Clark's ors., 162d, Greene.
216 Henry D. Mitchell, Wooten's, Telfair.
217 Zachariah Quick, Martin's, Washington.*
218 William Mitchell, Sen., r. s., Willis's, Franklin.
219 Jane Fincher, or., Davis's, Gwinnett.
220 Margaret Holmes, or., 26th, Glynn.
221 Charles Cato, 174th, Wilkes.
222 Ephraim Hancock, 417th, Walton.*
223 James Buchanan, sol., M'Korkle's, Jasper.
224 Barksdale Pickard, 114th, Hancock.
225 Green Young, Mason's, Washington.*
226 Henry Jennings, Dean's, Clarke.*
227 Richard Respass, Sen., 589th, Upson.*
228 Thomas Noble's ors., 335th, Wayne.
229 Angus Makal, Morrison's, Montgomery.*
230 Sarah Lacy, w. r .s., Hargrove's, Newton.
231 Anderson B. Dabney, Johnson's, De Kalb.
232 Elizabeth Harbour, w., Edwards's, Franklin.*
233 Hannah Culver, w., Chambers's, Gwinnett.
234 John Bowen, Martin's, Newton.
235 Prosser Parish, Gunn's, Jefferson.*
236 Henry K. Quillion, Brock's, Habersham.
237 James O. Scriven, 15th, Liberty.
238 Wiley Ballard, Streetman's, Twiggs.
239 Abraham Elton, s. l. w., Morris's, Crawford.
240 John Bird, M'Gehee's, Troup.*
241 Stephen Potts's ors., Belcher's, Jasper.
242 Frederic Duke, 756th, Sumter.*
243 Tully Choice, r. s., 101st, Hancock.
244 Joseph Catching, 145th, Greene.
245 Joseph Phillips, Ellis's, Pulaski.
246 Samuel Hefner, Higginbotham's, Rabun.
247 Hugh M. Comer, r. s., Stewart's, Jones.
248 James A. Chapman, Lynn's, Warren.
249 Levi Turner, Johnson's, Bibb.*
250 David Carnes, Mullen's, Carroll.
251 William H. Tait, s. i. w., Rhodes's, De Kalb.*
252 Thomas W. King, Bishop's, Henry.*
253 Robert Henry, Jr., Show's, Muscogee.
254 Robert L. Malone, M'Linn's, Butts.
255 William Mott, Brock's, Habersham.
256 Philip Hancock, Grice's, Oglethorpe.*
257 Edward Pate's ors., 279th, Morgan.
258 George W. Brantley, 510th, Early.
259 Henry W. Griffith, Newby's, Jones.
260 Samuel Deloach, Justice's, Bibb.

261 William Davis, M'Ewin's, Monroe.*
262 Thomas M. Harris, Moseley's, Coweta.*
263 Henry C. Sills, Wilson's, Pike.*
264 Washington D. Funderburk, Stewart's, Troup.
265 Sarah Ammons, w., Wood's, Morgan.
266 Martha Adams, w., 243d, Jackson.
267 Lolsey Currey, w., Sinquefield's, Washington.
268 John Garrett, 113th, Hancock.*
269 David Welsh, Adams's, Columbia.*
270 Jesse Mullins, Dobbs's, Hall.*
271 Wiley W. Gaither, Hall's, Butts.
272 James Hancock, Brock's, Habersham.*
273 Jesse H. Atchison, 415th, Walton.
274 Johannon Ricks, Bivins's, Jones.
275 David Sears, Williams's, Ware.
276 Eady Oliver, w., Martin's, Washington.*
277 Charles G. Murdock, 470th, Upson.
278 Daniel D. Copp, sol., Fitzpatrick's, Chatham.
279 John M'Millan, Morrison's, Montgomery.
280 Elias P. Butts, Cleland's, Chatham.
281 Abdias P. Webb, Sullivan's, Jones.*
282 Robert Moon's ors., Orr's, Jackson.
283 Thomas Martin, 59th, Emanuel.
284 John Chambless, 574th, Early.
285 Michael Barnwell, Chambers's, Houston.
286 Mary Hendrick, w., Hall's, Butts.
287 Solomon Smith's ors., Cannon's, Wilkinson.*
288 Marmaduke N. Kellebrew, Camp's, Warren.
289 Richard J. Holliday, sol., 177th, Wilkes.*
290 Joshua B. Bateman, 561st, Upson.
291 Leonard H. Clark, Edwards's, Talbot.*
292 John Patterson, Ellis's, Rabun.
293 Alexander G. Tyler, 366th, Jasper.*
294 Anna Tucker, Dupree's, Washington.
295 Charles F. Presley, Dearing's, Butts.
296 John Avrea, Jr., Vining's, Putnam.
297 Clement Y. Allen, Bustin's, Pike.
298 Martha Lightfoot, w., Williams's, Washington.*
299 Augustine G. Bryant, Blackstock's, Hall.
300 John L. Davis, Davis's, Clark.
301 Bennett Rylee, Martin's, Hall.
302 Daniel Wigley, Dobbs's, Hall.
303 Stephen S. M'Kenney, Rutland's, Bibb.
304 Isaac A. Langston's ors., Moore's, Randolph.
305 Eliza E. Dick, or., Sanderlin's, Chatham.
306 Moses M. Haynes, Bower's, Elbert.
307 Ella Warnock, Peterson's, Burke.

308 James V. White, Mobley's, De Kalb.
309 James Hudson, Jr., Clinton's, Campbell.
310 Frances Godden, w., Lamberth's, Fayette.
311 John F. Findley, Smith's, Campbell.*
312 Benjamin Newton, 49th, Emanuel.*
313 William Hunt, Miller's, Jackson.
314 Robert Gay, Wright's, Laurens.
315 David Ennis, Jordan's, Bibb.
316 Bozzal Freeman, Sen., sol., Ross's, Monroe.
317 Douglas H. Brown, 756th, Sumter.
318 David R. Huestin, Grider's, Morgan.
319 Robert R. Waller, Waller's, Putnam.
320 Solomon Farmer, Hutson's, Newton.*
321 Francis Pierson, s. i. w., Russell's, Henry.*
322 William P. Edwards, 12th, Effingham.
323 Thomas Hemphill, Cleghorn's, Madison.*
324 George Eberhart, s. i. w., Colley's, Madison.*

TWELFTH DISTRICT, SECOND SECTION, CHEROKEE.

1 Henry H. Hicks, 111th, Hancock.*
2 James R. Skinner, Reid's, Gwinnett.
3 James Fountain, sol., 1st, Chatham.*
4 Christopher Taylor, 466th, Monroe.
5 Richard Meador, 249th, Walton.
6 Rachel Magbee, w. r. s., Hall's, Butts.
7 James H. Bostwick, Carswell's, Jefferson.
8 Joel Hunt, Jr., Holley's, Franklin.*
9 John Ranew, Young's, Wilkinson.
10 Miles Bramblett, Reid's, Gwinnett.
11 Crawford H. Grier, 365th, Jasper.
12 Samuel Thames, Smith's, Houston.*
13 William Coxe's ors., 70th, Burke.
14 John Dupree's ors., 374th, Putnam.*
15 John Rankins, Gibson's, Decatur.
16 David D. Smith, sol., 458th, Early.
17 Peter Cooper, Valleau's, Chatham.*
18 John S. Littlefield's ors., Barron's, Houston.
19 Elizabeth Darris, w. r. s., 245th, Jackson.
20 Hurst's three orphans, Griffin's, Burke.
21 William D. Roe, 22d, M'Intosh.*
22 Simon Weldon, 373d, Jasper.*
23 David E. Blount, Hart's, Jones.
24 Alexander Wytcher, Dawson's, Jasper.

25 Allis Bell, w., Hargrove's, Oglethorpe.
26 William Urquhart, Roe's, Burke.*
27 James Spillers, 365th, Jasper.
28 John S. Mitchell, Peterson's, Burke.*
29 Henry M. Gunter, 454th, Walton.
30 Stephen M'Pherson, Reid's, Gwinnett.
31 Henry Lee, 672d, Harris.
32 John Shannon, Hopson's, Monroe.
33 Allen Partin, 250th, Walton.
34 Adam Ager's ors., M'Gill's, Lincoln.
35 Waller D. Whaley, Allen's, Monroe.*
36 Henry Jordan, Bragaw's, Oglethorpe.
37 James M. Richardson's ors., Smith's, Henry.
38 Harris Toney, Jr., Fleming's, Franklin.
39 John Swanson, 295th, Jasper.*
40 John Sturdevant, 101st, Hancock.
41 Leonard V. Griffin, Perry's, Habersham.
42 Allen Tooke, Smith's, Houston.
43 George B. Wood, Lay's, Jackson.
44 Jeremiah Chance, Roe's, Burke.
45 Caroline Hopkins, or., 271st, M'Intosh.
46 Randall Killingsworth, Robison's, Washington.*
47 Elsbury Yearty, Walden's, Pulaski.
48 Harrison Hammock, Watson's, Marion.
49 William M. Riley, Comer's, Jones.*
50 John Parham, Walker's, Harris.*
51 Samuel B. Williams, Johnson's, De Kalb.*
52 James Davis, s. l. w., Lamp's, Jefferson.*
53 Sarah Lacy, w., Hargrove's, Newton.*
54 Willis Cason, Sen., r. s., Lester's, Pulaski.
55 Anna Russell, h. a., Seay's, Hall.
56 John Gilbert, Adderhold's, Campbell.
57 William Blackman, Calhoun's, Harris.
58 Freeland Thornton, Roberts's, Hall.
59 Josiah Keen, M'Daniel's, Pulaski.*
60 Orpha Wilson, w., Roberts's, Hall.*
61 Baton Hattaway, sol., Down's, Warren.*
62 Daniel Garrard, Liddell's, Jackson.*
63 John H. Lowe, Groce's, Bibb.
64 Johnson Haynes, Whisenhunt's, Carroll.
65 George R. Edwards, Reid's, Gwinnett.
66 William Burford, r. s., Berry's, Butts.*
67 Joseph Davidson, Candler's, Bibb.*
68 Doct. John H. Hardee, 15th, Liberty.
69 John Simmons, Robinson's, Harris.
70 Daniel Thomas, Bridges's, Gwinnett.
71 Robert P. Moon, Smith's, Madison.*

72 William J. Howard, 120th, Richmond.
73 Joseph Patrick, 27th, Glynn.*
74 Amos Ellard, 1st section, Cherokee.*
75 Stephan Bryant, sol., Blackstock's, Hall.*
76 John A. Mullins, Kendrick's, Putnam.
77 Marcus B. Swinney, Coker's, Troup.
78 Moses & William Ogle, ors., Nesbit's, Newton.
79 James S. Jones, Peurifoy's, Henry.
80 George Thomas's ors., Hughes's, Habersham.*
81 William Perry, Coxe's, Franklin.
82 Elisha Horn's ors., 122d, Richmond.
83 Jesse Lewis, Young's, Jefferson.*
84 James R. Brock, Brock's, Habersham.*
85 Walter Smith, Cleland's, Chatham.
86 John B. Calef, Hart's, Jones.
87 Elizabeth Gentry, deaf, Evans's, Fayette.
88 Bettey Humphries, w., 318th, Baldwin.
89 Briton C. Tyler, Gorley's, Putnam.
90 Daniel D. Wall, 394th, Montgomery.
91 Silvester Murray, M'Millon's, Lincoln.*
92 Dennis W. Hall, Jones's, Hall.
93 Thomas Askew, sol., Cleveland's, Chatham.
94 Thomas Woods, Blair's, Lowndes.*
95 Britton J. Franks, 295th, Jasper.
96 Daniel E. Phillips, sol., 574th, Early.
97 Hillard Emanuel, Gibson's, Decatur.
98 Anslem L. Anthony, Hamilton's, Gwinnett.*
99 William Flewellin, sol., Sullivan's, Jones.
100 William Fulton, Cold Rain, Chatham.*
101 John P. Woolbright, Lunceford's, Wilkes.*
102 Jesse Benton, Coxe's, Talbot.
103 Chemhel Delamar, Head's, Butts.
104 Martin Andrews, sol., 167th, Wilkes.*
105 John Collins, or., 34th, Scriven.
106 Lucretia Miller, w. r. s., 458th, Early.
107 Timothy J. Russell, Peurifoy's, Henry.
108 James Watson, Barrow's, Houston.*
109 John Knight, 417th, Walton.*
110 James Ham, sol., Smith's, Elbert.
111 Henry Harding, Alberson's, Walton.
112 Elisha Anderson's ors., 75th, Burke.
113 John Bonds, Griffin's, Hall.
114 James Eaton, Riden's, Jackson.
115 John M'Donald, 15th, Liberty.
116 John Lassiter, Greer's, Merriwether.
117 Peter Parker, sol., Hatton's, Baker.*
118 Shrod Jones, Perryman's, Warren.

119 William M. Myhand, 279th, Morgan.*
120 Garland Jones, sol., Brooks's, Muscogee.*
121 Aven Scarborough, sol., Frasier's, Monroe.
122 Mary Almstead, w., Sanderlin's, Chatham.
123 Ann Reid, w., Smith's, Houston.
124 Francis E. R. Miller, Hobkerk's, Camden.*
125 Jacob Curry, s. l. w., 588th, Upson.*
126 Giles B. Taylor, Candler's, Bibb.
127 Henry Bunn, Rainey's, Twiggs.*
128 Jesse H. Watson, 140th, Greene.
129 David B. M. Shepherd, 36th, Scriven.
130 Eliza Wofford, or., 245th, Jackson.
131 John H. Cinibron, Ellsworth's, Bibb.
132 Ann Bennett, h. a., Cliett's, Columbia.*
133 William Allen, r. s., Smith's, Franklin.
134 Blakely Bagwell, Kellum's, Talbot.
135 Alfred Dokens, Smith's, Habersham.
136 Ransom Gentry, Peurifoy's, Henry.*
137 Francis M. Durrence, Brewton's, Tatnall.*
138 Elizabeth Evans, id., Harralson's, Troup.
139 Milas N. Cartwright, 141st, Greene.
140 John N. Alexander, Roberts's, Hall.*
141 Nancy M. Cox, w., Bell's, Columbia.*
142 Allen B. Chastain, Iverson's, Houston.
143 Isam Watson, r. s., Folsom's, Lowndes.*
144 Cornelius Goble, Henson's, Rabun.
145 Edwin Willis, Allen's, Monroe.*
146 Phebe Sutton, w., Curry's, Wilkinson.*
147 Milton Worthy, 404th, Gwinnett.*
148 Martin B. Daniel, 366th, Jasper.
149 Rebecca Brown, w. r. s., Bishop's, Henry.
150 John J. Jones, sol., Mizell's, Talbot.*
151 Allen Spears, Sen., Jones's, Thomas.
152 Robert Habersham, Jr., Fitzpatrick's, Chatham.
153 Mark Phillips, Strickland's, Merriwether.*
154 Wiley Lewis, Williams's, Decatur.
155 James S. Simms, Bragaw's, Oglethorpe.
156 John Garven, sol., Taylor's, Elbert.*
157 John Moreland, Jr., Underwood's, Putnam.*
158 Aaron Fowler, Higginbotham's, Rabun.*
159 Charles S. Hammon, 1st section, Cherokee.
160 Jonathan Willis's ors., Belcher's, Jasper.
161 Dulson Irwin, Allen's, Bibb.
162 Crawford Long, 114th, Hancock.
163 Lewis Black's ors., Baismore's, Jones.
164 Jethro H. Barnes, Collins's, Henry.
165 Jefferson Harris, Hutson's, Newton.*

166 Rachel Evenson, w. s. i. w., Seal's, Elbert.
167 John M'Canless, Burnett's, Habersham.*
168 David Sanders, Latimer's, De Kalb.*
169 Buckner M'Daniel, Oliver's, Decatur.*
170 Luke Turner, sol., 168th, Wilkes.*
171 Thomas A. Billups's ors., 143d, Greene.
172 Gideon Broxon, Cannon's, Wilkinson.*
173 Patience Echols, w., Mason's, Washington.*
174 John H. Landing, Peterson's, Burke.*
175 Armstead Roberts, 702d, Heard.
176 Joseph Ashfield, 374th, Putnam.
177 James Brock, M. Brown's, Habersham.
178 Joseph Dean, 1st, Chatham.*
179 Nathan Hoyt, Athens, Clarke.
180 Edward Hughes, sol., Sanderlin's, Chatham.
181 Gideon Strange, s. l. w., Dupree's, Washington.
182 John Giddens, 248th, Jackson.
183 Elizabeth Ingram, w., 608th, Taliaferro.
184 Abraham Herren, Gay's, Harris.
185 John Nutt, or., Maguire's, Morgan.
186 Jackson Kenny, 756th, Sumter.
187 John Holly, Mashburn's, Pulaski.
188 Lauchlin M'Currey, Kelly's, Elbert.
189 Travis Thigpen, or., Douglass's, Telfair.
190 George Wilson, Jones's, Habersham.*
191 John Harris, Say's, De Kalb.
192 Nathaniel Baker, 693d, Heard.*
193 Thomas S. Marshall, Newby's, Jones.
194 Abner Rainwater, 106th, Hancock.*
195 Enna Chandler, Stanfield's, Campbell.
196 Baker Wiggins, M'Culler's, Newton.*
197 Benjamin B. Clark, Dyer's, Habersham.
198 Peter P. Butler, Sen., Howell's, Elbert.*
199 Jacob T. Linder, Blackshear's, Laurens.
200 Elizabeth Mimms, or., Whipple's, Wilkinson.
201 William Ward's ors., 245th, Jackson.
202 Mark Turner, Gittens's, Fayette.*
203 Robert B. Houghton, Athens, Clarke.
204 Edward Lumpkin, Athens, Clarke.
205 William Davis, 417th, Walton.*
206 Solomon Segraves, Lawrence's, Pike.*
207 Thomas King, Hammond's, Franklin.
208 Stephen Swain, Swain's, Thomas.
209 William H. J. Chapman, Streetman's, Twiggs.
210 James Huey, Mobley's, De Kalb.
211 Theaford Satterfield, Jones's, Habersham.
212 John M'Dow, Rhodes's, De Kalb.

213 Benjamin Burden, 735th, Troup.
214 Lemuel P. Hoskins, Winter's, Jones.
215 Jared J. Moore, 116th, Hancock.
216 Larkin Hancock, sol., Allison's, Pike.
217 John W. D. Bowling, 735th, Troup.
218 Carlile Black, Hutson's, Newton.
219 Reuben Windham, Mitchell's, Marion.
220 Jesse Prosser's ors., Marshall's, Crawford.
221 Richard Panlette, Neal's, Campbell.
222 Nicholas Silovick (widower), Cleland's,Chatham.*
223 Absalom Auldridge, r. s., Walker's, Houston.
224 James Jordan's ors., Robinson's, Putnam.
225 William C. Rye, 470th, Upson.
226 William N. Stapler, Riden's, Jackson.
227 James Price, Mattox's, Lowndes.
228 George W. Ashburn, 589th, Upson.*
229 Thomas M. Smith, Willingham's, Harris.*
230 Thomas Hadley, Huey's, Harris.
231 William H. Potter, 243d, Jackson.*
232 Mary M'Mullen, w., 248th, Jackson.
233 Moses G. Anderson, Coffee's, Rabun.
234 Hardy Royall, Harp's, Stewart.
235 William Ayres, sol., Few's, Muscogee.
236 David W. Trantham, Woodruff's, Campbell.
237 Henry Allegood, Evans's, Laurens.*
238 Moses Young, Jr., 22d, M'Intosh.*
239 George Crotwell, 404th, Gwinnett.
240 Henry Thompson's ors., Silman's, Pike.
241 Jett T. Skidmore, Williams's, Walton.
242 Jeremiah M'Cormack's ors., Smith's, Houston.
243 James Ford, Hatton's, Baker.*
244 Rebecca Thornton, w., Vining's, Putnam.
245 Thomas W. Dwight, Jordan's, Bibb.*
246 Jane Oliver, w. r. s., Lunceford's, Elbert.
247 James Graham, Stephens's, Habersham.
248 Zipporah Tammons, w. r. s., 2d section, Cherokee.
249 Jeremiah R. Burkhalter, sol., Hill's, Harris.
250 James Henderson, 2d section, Cherokee.*
251 Jeremiah Walters, Jones's, Hall.
252 Nathan Haines, Jr., Barwick's, Washington.
253 Jesse Hays, Whipple's, Wilkinson.
254 Frederic Thompson, Mackleroy's, Clarke.*
255 Archibald Moon, Riden's, Jackson.
256 William Vickers, r. s., Griffin's, Merriwether.
257 John H. Parker, Talley's, Troup.
258 Creed T. Woodson, Sam Streetman's, Twiggs.*
259 Daniel M'Coy, Jones's, Hall.

260 John Wilson, Williams's, Washington.
261 James Arkins, r. s., Lamberth's, Fayette.
262 Richard Y. Loffton, Camp's, Baker.*
263 James Ferguson, 419th, Walton.
264 George H. Washington, Candler's, Bibb.
265 Eunice Horsey, w., 35th, Scriven.
266 William Kee, Loveless's, Gwinnett.
267 Montillion Ivey, Downs's, Warren.
268 Thomas Stephens, Coxe's, Talbot.
269 Joseph B. Christie, Christie's, Jefferson.
270 Joseph Denson, Sen., r. s., Underwood's, Putnam.
271 Robert Gillam, Allen's, Henry.
272 Reuben W. Bradford, Parham's, Harris.
273 James H. Durham, Stone's, Irwin.*
274 Lemuel Church, Hobkerk's, Camden.
275 Hozea Holtzclaw's ors., 174th, Wilkes.
276 Joshua M'Connell, Allen's, Henry.
277 Jesse W. Morriss, Bell's, Columbia.
278 Thomas T. Langley, Loveless's, Gwinnett.*
279 Champin Butler, of Twiggs, Groce's, Bibb.
280 Thomas Robison, Camp's, Warren.
281 Abner Anglin, Will's, Twiggs.
282 David Zarraw, Welche's, Habersham.
283 Benjaman H. Booth, sol., Echols's, Clarke.*
284 Sihon Wheelis, Griffin's, Merriwether.
285 Walter A. Mangham, Griffin's, Fayette.
286 James Grizzell, Dearing's, Henry.
287 Joseph W. George's ors., Brewer's, Monroe.
288 Gilbert D. Greer, sol., Gillis's, De Kalb.
289 Elizabeth Lane, w., Williams's, Jasper.
290 T. Hollingsworth, sol., Chambers's, Gwinnett.
291 Roland Mitchell, Royster's, Franklin.
292 John Fullwood, Sweat's, Ware.
293 James Moon, sol., 109th, Hancock.*
294 John Erwin, Crow's, Pike.
295 William Deason, Bustin's, Pike.
296 Susannah Hix, w., 555th, Upson.
297 Jacob B. Nash, Lunceford's, Wilkes.
298 Willis Caison, r. s., Green's, Ware.*
299 Nathan Butler, Green's, Oglethorpe.*
300 John M. Hancock, Higginbotham's, Madison.
301 William Foster, Willingham's, Harris.*
302 Reddick Grant, M'Ewin's, Monroe.*
303 Harrison Austin, Stanton's, Newton.
304 John Hutchins, Bridges's, Gwinnett.
305 Larkin Vincent, York's, Stewart.*
306 Samuel Darnall, sol., Belcher's, Jasper.

307 John P. Bryant, Cleghorn's, Madison.
308 Jason Collins, Wright's, Tatnall.*
309 James Hoopugh, Mackleroy's, Clarke.*
310 George W. Mill Irons, Kendrick's, Putnam.*
311 Josiah M'Gaher, Barnett's, Habersham.
312 William Harrell, Leveritt's, Lincoln.
313 James H. Burnett, 102d, Hancock.*
314 Duncan Leverett, Curry's, Merriwether.
315 John Parham, Walker's, Harris.*
316 Jeremiah Freeman, Kelly's, Jasper.*
317 Littleton Whitten, 277th, Morgan.
318 Dennis Pacetty, Hobkerk's, Camden.
319 James St. John's, Sen., r. s., M'Culler's, Newton.
320 Margaret Caroline Discomb, or., 2d, Chatham.
321 Robert Findley's five ors., 148th, Greene.
322 David B. Butler, Candler's, Bibb.
323 Edward Williams, 693d, Heard.
324 Susannah Yates, w., Lamberth's, Fayette.*

13th DISTRICT, SECOND SECTION, CHEROKEE.

1 Coflens Spevoy, Strickland's, Merriwether.*
2 John A. Boutwell, 320th, Baldwin.
3 Henry Bohannon, Mizell's, Talbot.
4 Jeremiah Pittman, Allen's, Henry.
5 David J. Berry, Jr., Evans's, Fayette.
6 Elizabeth Trainum, w., 278th, Morgan.*
7 John J. Ford, s. l. w., 512th, Lee.
8 John Turner, r. s., Colley's, Oglethorpe.
9 James House, Benson's, Lincoln.
10 Warren B. Massey, Taylor's, Houston.
11 Axiom S. Allford, Camp's, Warren.
12 Rhoda Hardin, mi., f. a., Bower's, Elbert.
13 Margaret Combs, w., Lunceford's, Wilkes.
14 Arthur Mangum, Liddell's, Jackson.*
15 William Smith, Sen., Craven's, Coweta.
16 Rhoda Davis, w., Polhill's, Burke.*
17 Allen Wicker's ors., Streetman's, Twiggs.
18 Benjamin Regester, Barwick's, Washington.
19 William E. Weaver, Colley's, Oglethorpe.*
20 Isaac Tomlin, Brock's, Habersham.
21 Richardson Mayo, M'Linn's, Butts.
22 Edward Fair, Hatton's, Baker.
23 Brittian Gant's ors., Rooks's, Putnam.

17

24 George Bragg, sol., Wilson's, Madison.
25 Zachariah W. Hall, Rooks's, Putnam.*
26 Knotley W. Cone, 318th, Baldwin.*
27 Benjamin Spraberry, Foote's, De Kalb.
28 Lemuel J. Hillburn, Latimer's, De Kalb.
29 Thomas Grier, Grier's, Warren.
30 Lemuel B. Hendrick, Groce's, Bibb.
31 Wesley Pitts, Sanders's, Jones.
32 Francis C. D. Bouchelle, Athens, Clarke.*
33 John Brack, Lockhart's, Bulloch.
34 Burwell Bartlett, 113th, Hancock.*
35 Elijah Smith, Peterson's, Montgomery.*
36 Sarah Youngblood, w., 278th, Morgan.*
37 Jesse Waldrip, Mullen's, Carroll.*
38 Burrell Veal, Prescott's, Twiggs.
39 Enoch W. Womble, s. l. w., 561st, Upson.
40 Simeon Warnock, Peterson's, Burke.*
41 Angus G. Gunnells, 588th, Upson.
42 Thomas D. Hanley, or., Groover's, Thomas.
43 Nathan Breedlove's ors., Edwards's, Talbot.
44 Robert Holmes's ors., Wolfskin's, Oglethorpe.
45 John A. Coursey, Hampton's, Newton.
46 Elizabeth Morgan, f. a., Allen's, Henry.
47 Evan Pearson, Jones's, Habersham.
48 Gilliard Barns, Silman's, Pike.
49 Robert E. Gilkeyson, Bishop's, Henry.
50 Martha Ann Waller, or., Miller's, Jackson.
51 Jacob Greathouse, sol., M'Clain's, Newton.
52 George Glover, Ellsworth's, Bibb.*
53 Thomas H. Wilson, Riden's, Jackson.*
54 Henry Thompson, Hampton's, Newton.*
55 Winney Huff, w., Green's, Oglethorpe.
56 Jane M'Cutchen, w. r. s., Griffin's, Hall.*
57 Mulford Marsh, Roe's, Burke.*
58 Andrew J. Davis, Gunn's, Jefferson.
59 Wiley Radin, 148th, Greene.
60 Pyent E. Jackson, Gunn's, Henry.
61 Elias Beall, Kellum's, Talbot.
62 Robert R. Arrington, Boynton's, Twiggs.
63 William Garner's ors., Mackleroy's, Clarke.
64 Richard Eubanks, sol., Tankersley's, Columbia.
65 John Hutson, Colquhoun's, Henry.
66 Francis Jones, Whisenhunt's, Carroll.
67 Jane Gammill, w. r. s., Calhoun's, Harris.
68 Alexander Irwin, s. l. w., Robinson's, Washington
69 William O'Neal, Varner's, Merriwether.
70 William Griffin, 37th, Scriven.*

71 Robert Applewhite, sol., Waltze's, Morgan.
72 Edward Thomas, Hampton's, Newton.
73 Joseph Hood, Thompson's, Henry.
74 Joseph Bridger, Whipple's, Wilkinson.*
75 Francis Bradford, Bridges's, Gwinnett.
76 Joseph Little's ors., 250th, Walton.
77 John B. Ryal's, Edwards's, Montgomery.
78 Lovick Green, Johnson's, Lowndes.
79 John Gray, Reid's, Gwinnett.*
80 Henry J. Miller, Morrison's, Montgomery.
81 William Donaldson, Kellum's, Talbot.
82 John Hancock, Newman's, Thomas.
83 John Hare, sol., Pounds's, Twiggs.*
84 Edwin Dyer, 404th, Gwinnett.
85 Abraham F. Powell, Wooten's, Telfair.*
86 William Cash, Johnson's, De Kalb.*
87 Benjamin Gatchett's ors., Covington's, Pike.
88 William Hopkins, Ellis's, Rabun.
89 Ralph Croft, Griffith's, Harris.
90 John Rever's ors., 289th, Jasper.
91 Hardy Hall, s. l. w., Douglass's, Telfair.
92 David C. Butler, Whipple's, Wilkinson.
93 George W. Glore, Givens's, De Kalb.
94 George F. Shepherd, Thompson's, Henry.
95 Royston Pollard, 559th, Walton.*
96 Elias Godman, or., 123d, Richmond.
97 Hardy E. Hunter, 25th, Scriven.
98 William Slade, s. l. w., Dupree's, Washington.
99 Thomas Matthews, Lane's, Morgan.
100 Owen Bryan, Oliver's, Twiggs.*
101 Carleton Whitney, Parham's, Harris.
102 Riley M. Willingham, Shearer's, Coweta.*
103 Henderson Highfield, Johnson's, Warren.
104 William L. Jeter, Candler's, Bibb.
105 Dolford H. Silvey, Lunceford's, Wilkes.
106 Nancy M'Clure, w., Williams's, Jasper.
107 John Cannon, s. l. w., Hobbs's, Laurens.
108 Mary Crows, w., Ogden's, Camden.
109 Eli Wood, Edwards's, Franklin.
110 Milton Paxton, Whitehead's, Habersham.
111 Rucker Mauldin, 406th, Gwinnett.
112 David Holloman, 307th, Putnam.
113 John White, Keener's, Rabun.
114 Mary Malone, w., Bustin's, Pike.
115 Samson Pugh, Baugh's, Jackson.
116 Henry Ingerville, Hall's, Camden.*
117 Sam. Robinson, s. l. w., Robison's, Washington.*

118 Tinsley Upshaw, Alberson's, Walton.
119 William Christian, sol., Coker's, Troup.
120 William R. Polk, Liddell's, Jackson.
121 John Stephens, M'Linn's, Butts.*
122 Benjamin Cason, Park's, Walton.*
123 Samson Stallings, Walker's, Harris.
124 Micajah F. M'Cune, Harris's, Butts.*
125 Nathaniel Holton, Jones's, Thomas.
126 Daniel Heidt, 3d, Chatham.
127 Samuel Hammons, 147th, Greene.
128 Jacob Herndon, Dyer's, Habersham.*
129 Gen. David Adams, Sen., sol., 364th, Jasper.*
130 William D. Baldwin, Burk's, Stewart.
131 Nelson Gray, Peurifoy's, Henry.*
132 John Thrash, sol., Howell's, Troup.*
133 James Reid, Peek's, Columbia.
134 Thomas Winston, 149th, Greene.*
135 Pickins H. Gillespie, Mangum's, Franklin.
136 John B. Post, Stewart's, Troup.
137 William Robertson, 537th, Upson.*
138 Philip Levar's ors., Will's, Twiggs.
139 Jesse Seaborn, Hill's, Baldwin.
140 Thornton Gibson's ors., Murphy's, Columbia.
141 William Cason, 333d, Wayne.*
142 Walker's orphans, Calhoun's, Harris.
143 John S. Lavender, Peace's, Wilkinson.
144 William R. Moss, 111th, Hancock.
145 Robert Henderson, r. s., Miller's, Jackson.
146 Drury M'Millian, Jones's, Habersham.*
147 Marshall Christian, 245th, Jackson.
148 Byren Shell, 734th, Lee.
149 Joel Rees, Graves's, Putnam.
150 Mary Ann O'Neal, w. s. i. w., 22d, M'Intosh.*
151 Simeon Williams, Latimer's, De Kalb.
152 William L. Johnson, Phillips's, Talbot.
153 Mary Zellner, w., Gay's, Harris.
154 Benjamin M. Powell, of Gwinnett, Park's, Walton
155 William Dillard, 249th, Walton.
156 Redeick Fannin, Phillips's, Talbot.
157 David Lyons, 672d, Harris.*
158 Anson Goolsby, Edwards's, Talbot.
159 Wm. A. David, of Cherokee, Latimer's, De Kalb.
160 William H. Tanner, Hearn's, Butts.
161 Benjamin Mashburn, id., 756th, Sumter.*
162 Thomas E. Neisbit, Harp's, Stewart.
163 Bartley Thompson, Liddell's, Jackson.*
164 John Graham, Hand's, Appling.

165 Gideon Smith, Robison's, Washington.*
166 Joab Dudley, Trout's, Hall.*
167 Robert Rivers, 365th, Jasper.*
168 Junius Hillger, Athens, Clarke.
169 John B. Smith, Smith's, Campbell.
170 John Huston, Blount's, Wilkinson.
171 Anthony Peeter, s. i. w., 294th, Jasper.
172 George Adams, 364th, Jasper.*
173 John Jones, Green's, Oglethorpe.
174 Andrew Dorsey, Brock's, Habersham.
175 Lemuel Coats, Burgess's, Carroll.*
176 Thomas M. Jones, Blackstock's, Hall.
177 Lewis G. Chiles, 190th, Elbert.
178 Moses Stallings, Hatchett's, Oglethorpe.
179 Robert J. Goza, Johnson's, De Kalb.
180 William Glozier, Hampton's, Newton.
181 Truman Barber, Price's, Hall.
182 John Radford, Will's, Twiggs.
183 Alexander G. Fryer, Roe's, Burke.
184 Williamson Forester, Chastain's, Habersham.
185 William Davis, Nichols's, Fayette.
186 Aaron Underwood, sol., 406th, Gwinnett.
187 Lewis Pitchford, Brock's, Habersham.
188 James A. Reeves, Fenn's, Clarke.
189 Samuel Newman, Este's, Putnam.
190 John Thompson's ors., 146th, Greene.
191 Thos. W. Johnson's ors., Hargrove's, Oglethorpe.
192 John Gentry, Moore's, Randolph.
193 Tabman A. Culver, 111th, Hancock.*
194 Charles Dean, Edwards's, Franklin.
195 James S. Williams, Shearer's, Coweta.
196 Elijah Wiggins, Night's, Morgan.*
197 Stephen Davis, Beasley's, Oglethorpe.
198 Lucy J. Capps, or., Marshall's, Putnam.
199 David Wood, 789th, Sumter.
200 John Belcher, Carswell's, Jefferson.
201 Wm. F. Smith's ors., Sinquefield's, Washington.
202 Thomas J. Daggett, 561st, Upson.
203 John T. Young, 2d section, Cherokee.
204 William Merritt, 537th, Upson.*
205 Joel Embry, 672d, Harris.
206 John Raines, Willis's, Twiggs.
207 Margaret Colwell, w., Aderhold's, Campbell.
208 William Ellison's five ors., Givens's, De Kalb.
209 Marshall Martin, sol., Grier's, Merriwether.
210 William Cooper's ors., 600th, Richmond.
211 James Parkes, Kelly's, Elbert.*

212 Joseph H. Jones, Stower's, Elbert.
213 Alexander Williamson, Moseley's, Coweta.
214 Matthew Bishop, Goodwin's, Houston.*
215 William Mallinax, Sewell's, Franklin.
216 William Tomberlin, Justice's, Bibb.
217 Mary E. Blome, w., 320th, Baldwin.
218 Abner Darden, 601st, Taliaferro.
219 Frederic Metts, r. s., Martin's, Washington.
220 William H. Harris, Grider's, Morgan.
221 James Glenn, Esq., sol., M'Gehee's, Troup.*
222 Martin Graham, Houstoun's, Chatham.
223 William H. Thompson, Valleau's, Chatham.
224 William Vangters, Chandler's, Franklin.
225 John B. Jones, Covington's, Pike.*
226 John Morris, or., Perryman's, Warren.
227 Miles Gibbs's ors., Coxe's, Morgan.
228 Thomas Thedford, Calhoun's, Harris.
229 Abial Pearce, Ellsworth's, Bibb.*
230 Jesse Ballard, s. l. w., Hines's, Coweta.
231 William H. Askew, Bryan's, Monroe.
232 Thomas Akins, sol., Wilson's, Jasper.
233 John M'Invale, Harp's, Stewart.
234 William Lindsey, Strickland's, Merriwether.
235 Malachi Pittman, Lightfoot's, Washington.
236 John A. Minshew, Burgess's, Carroll.
237 Jonathan Burks, Dearing's, Henry.*
238 Willaby Brunt's ors., 162d, Greene.
239 Bryant Ingram, Johnson's, De Kalb.
240 John H. Pool, Catlett's, Franklin.
241 Harrison Hooper, Gillis's, De Kalb.*
242 Aaron Smith, sol., Carpenter's, Tatnall.*
243 John Smith's ors., Perryman's, Warren.
244 William P. Hall, Mullen's, Carroll.*
245 Joab Larrance, Jones's, Madison.
246 Rebecca Williams, w., Whelchel's, Hall.
247 William Faircloth, Bryan's, Pulaski.
248 William J. Gillstrap, Dilman's, Pulaski.
249 Jesse M. Davis, 167th, Wilkes.
250 Elizabeth Dupree, w., 374th, Putnam.
251 Solomon Watkins, Say's, De Kalb.
252 James Johnson, 404th, Gwinnett.
253 Radford Browning, Jr., Mashe's, Thomas.
254 Julia Williams, Strickland's, Merriwether.
255 Young B. Olive, Adams's, Columbia.
256 Miens Yancy, Daniel's, Hall.
257 William Zeigler, Morris's, Crawford.
258 Seaborn Mikell, Peavy's, Bulloch.

259 Moses D. White, 672d, Harris.
260 Caleb Parker, Dilman's, Pulaski.
261 Joseph M. Dent, Jr., 167th, Wilkes.
262 Claiborn Upchurch, 103d, Hancock.*
263 Archibald G. M'Neal, Hargrove's, Newton.*
264 Wylie Curry, Huston's, Wilkes.
265 Jordan Goodson, s., Griffin's, Fayette.*
266 William Hancock, Blount's, Wilkinson.
267 William Simmons, Maguire's, Gwinnett.*
268 Lemuel R. Tankersley, Daniel's, Hall.
269 Godfrey M. Hartsfield, Allen's, Monroe.
270 William Kerlin, 242d, Jackson.
271 William C. Watson, Gittens's, Fayette.
272 David Coleman, Garner's, Washington.
273 Joseph Kiser, Jr., Merck's, Hall.
274 John King's ors., Whitfield's, Washington.
275 Asa Rowe, s. l. w., Taylor's, Putnam.
276 Burrel House, Seas's, Madison.*
277 George Pitts, Mashburn's, Pulaski.
278 Thomas K. Forester, Henson's, Rabun.
279 James Stratton, Baley's, Butts.*
280 Thomas M. Jones, Candler's, Bibb.
281 James Grice, Rainey's, Twiggs.
282 David F. Riley, Johnson's, Bibb.
283 Elizabeth Bradshaw, w., Mashburn's, Pulaski.
284 Comfort Magee, w., Crawford's, Morgan.*
285 John Carder, 1st section, Cherokee.
286 Barnes T. Dixon, Collier's, Monroe.
287 Alfrederic Ming, Swiney's, Laurens.
288 James Jones, Anderson's, Wilkes.
289 George W. Teel, Smith's, Campbell.
290 David Cannup, minor, Hughes's, Habersham.
291 Charles Jordan, Sen., Crow's, Merriwether.*
292 Patrick Gray, 1st, Chatham.*
293 David C. Geer, 138th, Greene.
294 Isaac Benton's ors., Evans's, Laurens.
295 Ephraim Liles, r. s., Bostick's, Twiggs.
296 Eleanor A. Wells, w., Wilson's, Jasper.*
297 Benj. B. Smith, s. i. w., Bostick's, Twiggs.
298 William Tindall, Barnett's, Clarke.
299 Solomon Townsend, Heard's, De Kalb.*
300 William Clark, 75th, Burke.*
301 Robert Dearing, 165th, Wilkes.
302 William Dye, Polhill's, Burke.
303 Jephty Langston, Mullen's, Carroll.
304 Aron J. Benton, Griffin's, Merriwether.*
305 Matthew Murphy, Sen., Allen's, Campbell.*

306 Elizabeth Yellowby, w., Hobkerk's, Camden.
307 (fr.) John M. Watson, sol., Hanner's, Campbell.*
308 (fr.) John Ingram, or., 633d, Dooly.
309 (fr.) Rilant Watts, 56th, Emanuel.*
310 (fr.) Bedford Hopkins, Robinson's, Harris.
311 (fr.) Simeon Wooten, Bryan's, Pulaski.
312 (fr.) Lewis J. Sharp, Riden's, Jackson.*
313 (fr.) Henry Maury, Brewer's, Monroe.*
314 (fr.) Dudley Lawson, Durham's, Talbot.
315 (fr.) Rebecca Creemmy, w. r. s., Hand's, Appling.
316 (fr.) Rezin Darsey, Harris's, Columbia.*
317 (fr.) Christopher Lynch, Candler's, Bibb.
318 Robert Augustus Holt, Park's, Walton.*
319 Eli Hughes, Colquhoun's, Henry.
320 Mary Watts, w., Newby's, Jones.
321 William B. Hopkins, 494th, Upson.*
322 John Adams, Atkinson's, Coweta.*
323 Bazzel Rowlin, Talley's, Troup.*
324 Thomas Gaines, sol., Allen's, Monroe.

14th DISTRICT, SECOND SECTION, CHEROKEE.

1 Asia Garrett, Jones's, Hall.
2 William W. Wash, Cleland's, Chatham.*
3 Alfred Quinn, Candler's, Bibb.
4 Ephraim Shelton, Brock's, Habersham.*
5 John Carroll, r. s., 393d, Jasper.*
6 William Smith, Ellis's, Rabun.
7 Charles Magrada, Dean's, De Kalb.*
8 John Buchannon's ors,, 295th, Jasper.
9 Asa J. Bishop, 101st, Hancock.
10 Hiram Turner, Hughes's, Habersham.
11 Averitt Holton, 789th, Sumter.*
12 Henry Stone, r. s., Sweat's, Ware.*
13 Ezekiel Brown, Jr., Walker's, Harris.
14 Allen C. Ramsey, 119th, Richmond.
15 Elijah B. Moseley, Smith's, Campbell.
16 James Rutland, Frasier's, Monroe.*
17 Jared Dennard, sol., Jordan's, Harris.*
18 George N. Graves, Chesnut's, Newton.*
19 Rachel Smith, w., 318th, Baldwin.
20 John G. Raines, sol., Justice's, Bibb.*
21 Jackson Kennedy, or., 119th, Richmond.*
22 John B. Wallace, Pollard's, Wilkes.*

23 James Farris, Alberson's, Walton.*
24 Sarah Ann M'Call, or., Valleau's, Chatham.
25 Elijah Moore, Tower's, Gwinnett.
26 Memucan Horton, Neal's, Campbell.
27 Warren Merryfield, Pearce's, Houston.
28 William H. Hobbs, Collier's, Monroe.
29 Robert Hide, 788th, Heard.
30 John Biddell, 140th, Greene.*
31 Thomas Merriwether, r. s., M'Korkles, Jasper.
32 George Duncan, 417th, Walton.*
33 David M. Keith, Curry's, Merriwether.
34 William Pugh, Roberts's, Hall.*
35 William P. Johnson, Maguire's, Morgan.
36 John J. Dufour, Hobkerk's, Camden.
37 Matthew Wicker, Peace's, Wilkinson.*
38 Aaron Mattox, Southell's, Tatnall.*
39 Sarah Kite, w., Compton's, Fayette.
40 John Durham, Killen's, Decatur.
41 William N. Davis, Whisenhunt's, Carroll.
42 Mary Combs, w., Lunceford's, Wilkes.
43 Abigail Purcell, deaf, White's, Franklin.
44 John Boozer, Sen., 404th, Gwinnett.
45 William Thompson, r. s., Smith's, Habersham.
46 Daniel D. Copp, Fitzpatrick's, Chatham.
47 Joel Godard, Stewart's, Jones.*
48 John Williamson, Harralson's, Troup.*
49 John L. Simms, 406th, Gwinnett.*
50 Asa Walker, Clark's, Morgan.*
51 Jesse Wiggins, Roe's, Burke.
52 George W. Jones, 373d, Jasper.*
53 William Reynolds, 113th, Hancock.*
54 Elijah Corley, Moffett's, Muscogee.
55 Leonidus W. Hill, Hill's, Stewart.*
56 James Adair, Herndon's, Hall.*
57 Robert M. Gilbert, 756th, Sumter.*
58 James R. Oberry, 24th, M'Intosh.*
59 William L. Crayton, Peurifoy's, Henry.
60 John West, Winter's, Jones.
61 James R. Hanham, 2d, Chatham.
62 John S. Irbey, Berry's, Butts.*
63 John Jones's ors., Groce's, Bibb.
64 Susannah Wyche, w., Braddy's, Jones.
65 James C. Aaron, Jones's, Madison.*
66 John Pope Evans, Chisolm's, Morgan.
67 Archibald H. Coplin, Dearing's, Henry.*
68 Joseph White, 588th, Upson.*
69 Jane Tool, w. r. s., Baismore's, Jones.

70 Hannah Longstreet, w., 398th, Richmond.*
71 David Glaze's ors., M'Dowell's, Lincoln.*
72 Henry Smith, Killen's, Decatur.
73 Thomas J. Perryman, Bostick's, Twiggs.*
74 Reuben Wilkison, sol., Calhoun's, Harris.*
75 Benjamin Keaton, Mason's, Washington.*
76 William Buckelow, Barker's, Gwinnett.
77 Aulston Bunch's four orphans, 137th, Greene.
78 John Halliday's ors., Moseley's, Wilkes.
79 James Caswell, Gittens's, Fayette.
80 Nancy Slaughter, w., Pace's, Putnam.
81 John Powell's ors., Bragaw's, Oglethorpe.
82 William Hall's ors., Hamilton's, Gwinnett.
83 Thomas R. Mills, Valleau's, Chatham.
84 John Denmark, Peavy's, Bulloch.*
85 Diana Hester, w., Bivins's, Jones.*
86 Littleton Joy, sol., 34th, Scriven.
87 Elijah Miles, Gay's, Harris.*
88 James Terrell, 190th, Elbert.
89 David Brumbelow, Jordan's, Bibb.*
90 Ansel B. Prewett, Dean's, De Kalb.
91 Ribeas Westmoreland, mi., Barnett's, Habersham
92 Daniel M. Clark, Jordan's, Harris.
93 Sarah Ushee, w., 25th, Scriven.
94 Josiah N. Wilson, 106th, Hancock.*
95 William M. Conn, 2d section, Cherokee.*
96 Henry Hall, 56th, Emanuel.*
97 William B. Kimbough, Givens's, De Kalb.*
98 Susannah M'Bee, w., Dean's, De Kalb.
99 Frederic Daniel, r. s., Wilson's, Pike.*
100 David Harris's ors., Stanton's, Newton.
101 Joseph Osborn, 243d, Jackson.
102 Robert S. Hardman, Green's, Oglethorpe.
103 Isaac C. Griggs, Roe's, Burke.*
104 Matthew Ingram, 561st, Upson.
105 John Richards, House's, Henry.*
106 Wiley L. Clements, Phillips's, Monroe.
107 William W. Wash, Cleland's, Chatham.*
108 Elisha Butler, 720th, Decatur.*
109 Rachel Herd, w. of sol., Miller's, Jackson.
110 Chandler's seven orphans, Bryant's, Burke.
111 Isom Thomas, 5th, Chatham.
112 Joseph Robinson, 672d, Harris.*
113 Berry J. Bridges, s. i. w., Hardman's, Oglethorpe*
114 Nancy Holland, w., Trout's, Hall.*
115 Johnson Burks, Dearing's, Henry.*
116 George W. Danull, s. l. w., Rick's, Laurens.

117 John White, sol., Killen's, Decatur.
118 John Allison, Allison's, Pike.
119 Joseph Stinson, Edwards's, Talbot.
120 Mary Archer, w., 259th, Scriven.
121 William Gholston, or., Smith's, Madison.
122 William A. Crombie, Allen's, Henry.
123 George Foster, Tilley's, Rabun.*
124 Sarah Canter, w., Garner's, Washington.*
125 Thomas Haynes, Bishop's, Henry.*
126 Richard Ragsdale, Sutton's, Habersham.
127 Char. Hearndon, w. s. i. w., Martin's, Washington*
128 John Copeland, s. l. w., Este's, Putnam.*
129 Charles A. Harden, 20th, Bryan.
130 Eleazer Hamilton, Lay's, Jackson.*
131 Jesse Hodges, Williams's, Jasper.*
132 Erben C. Heath, 788th, Heard.
133 Moses Mulkey, sol., Whitehead's, Habersham.
134 Luke J. Barefield, Lamp's, Jefferson.*
135 Lodowick M. Thompson, 137th, Greene.*
136 Randolph H. Ramsey, 119th, Richmond.
137 Abraham S. Allen, Bustin's, Pike.*
138 James H. Fielder, Clark's, Morgan.
139 John Martin's ors., Seay's, Hall.
140 Thomas Truitt, s. l. w., 604th, Taliaferro.
141 Joseph Smith, Craven's, Coweta.*
142 Claiborn Gunter, Miller's, Jackson.
143 Jane F. Taylor, w., Cleland's, Chatham.
144 James M. Millener, Harp's, Stewart.
145 Elizabeth Wyatt, w., Russell's, Henry.
146 Nancy P. Brimberry, w., Monk's, Crawford.*
147 Jesse Edenfield, sol., Griffin's, Emanuel.
148 John B. Marable, s. l. w., Baley's, Butts.
149 John H. Russell, Whitehead's, Habersham.*
150 James Parker, 672d, Harris.*
151 Peter Rawlins, Loveless's, Gwinnett.*
152 John Kelly, Marshall's, Putnam.
153 Martin W. Armstrong, Roberts's, Hall.
154 John M. Settle, Kendrick's, Monroe.
155 J. Yarborough's 3 orphans, Brock's, Habersham.
156 Abner Reeves, 166th, Wilkes.
157 Michael Howard, Martin's, Pike.*
158 Elizabeth Kenebrew, w., Jones's, Lincoln.*
159 Bryant Keen, Cook's, Telfair.*
160 Mary Brown, w. r. s., Woodruff's, Campbell.*
161 John Harrell, Bostick's, Twiggs.*
162 Matilda P. Weisley, or., Martin's, Newton.
163 Aaron Gordman, Payne's, Merriwether.

164 Madison Williams, 656th, Troup.*
165 James Veal, Tompkins's, Putnam.*
166 Thomas Miles's ors., Phillips's, Monroe.*
167 Milton M. Ham, Iverson's, Houston.*
168 Lewis R. Barnes, 108th, Hancock.*
169 William A. Magouirk, M'Culler's, Newton.*
170 John Slatter, Jones's, Thomas.*
171 David Lasley, 163d, Greene.*
172 Samuel Sipperer, Peace's, Wilkinson.
173 Joseph Smith, Durrence's, Tatnall.
174 Nancy Thompson, w., 362d, Jasper.
175 William H. Smith, 494th, Upson.*
176 Turner Harris, Stewart's, Warren.
177 Zephaniah T. Conner, Ellsworth's, Bibb.*
178 William H. Johnston, Moseley's, Wilkes.
179 Ashley Cox, 362d, Jasper.*
180 Charles D. Fenley, 365th, Jasper.*
181 William B. Wallace, Peterson's, Burke.
182 Alexander M'Donald, Ellsworth's, Bibb.
183 James G. Clifton, Bourguin's, Chatham.*
184 Robert Lindsey's or., M'Craney's, Lowndes.
185 Daniel Haynes, Silman's, Pike.
186 Ann Greer, w., Fenn's, Clark.
187 James W. Haynes, Bower's, Elbert.
188 Jason Rigil, Rainey's, Twiggs.
189 Joseph Henderson, sol., Martin's, Newton.
190 James M'Call Smith, Smith's, Campbell.*
191 Neddy Pennington, r. s., Sullivan's, Jones.*
192 Solomon Lasiter, Bustin's, Pike.
193 John Roberts, r. s., Tower's, Gwinnett.*
194 Charles Dean, Edwards's, Franklin.*
195 Thomas Gorham's or., Crawford's, Franklin.*
196 William T. Pike, Town, Baldwin.*
197 Rainey Eads, Colley's, Oglethorpe.*
198 James M. Rush, Stephens's, Habersham.*
199 Doctor A. Childers, 510th, Early.*
200 Hezekiah Harden, Hill's, Stewart.*
201 Andrew Ult, Hicks's, Decatur.*
202 John White, Peterson's, Montgomery.*
203 Sherwood Stroud, 249th, Walton.*
204 Rebecca Brock, w., Brock's, Habersham.*
205 Drury Clark, Walker's, Houston.*
206 John D. Spruce, Barker's, Gwinnett.*
207 Mary Crawford, w. r. s., Mullen's, Carroll.
208 Amos Wingate's ors., Dilman's, Pulaski.
209 William Williams, Bostick's, Twiggs.
210 Nancy M'Cullers, w., Stewart's, Warren.

211 Jemima Cole, w., Perry's, Habersham.
212 Bythum Deese, Bush's, Pulaski.
213 Daniel Palmer, 103d, Hancock.
214 John Gay, Lockhart's, Bulloch.*
215 Nicholas Hernandes, Cleland's, Chatham.
216 Jackson Ballard, or., Bridges's, Gwinnett.
217 Joseph W. Wortham, Harralson's, Troup.
218 S. W. Harris's ors., Athens, Clarke.
219 Thomas J. Wheeler, Lynn's, Warren.
220 Thomas Carlton, Newman's, Thomas.
221 John M'Mahan, Coxe's, Morgan.
222 John M. Lucas, sol., 12th, Effingham.
223 George Prothro, Kelly's, Elbert.
224 Phillip Iseley, Loveless's, Gwinnett.
225 William Moore, or., Night's, Morgan.
226 Wythel Rigil, sol., Rainey's, Twiggs.*
227 Edward Drinchard, 693d, Heard.
228 Seaborn Woodcock, Jones's, Bulloch.*
229 William D. Lightfoot, Williams's, Washington.*
230 Mary Goolsby, w., Green's, Oglethorpe.*
231 Sarah Hodges, w., Williams's, Washington.
232 Ezekiel S. Miller, Miller's, Ware.
233 James Wadkins, 162d, Greene.
234 Charles W. Griffin, Griffin's, De Kalb.
235 Thomas S. Beck, 174th, Wilkes.
236 George Cashaw, or., Henson's, Rabun.
237 Martha Dickson, w., Edwards's, Talbot.
238 Peyton H. Colbert, Seas's, Madison.*
239 Sarah Wright, w., Huchinson's, Columbia.
240 John Bowman, Whitaker's, Crawford.*
241 Vincent Hamilton, Dyer's, Habersham.*
242 John D. Peden, Chambers's, Gwinnett.
243 Thomas J. Bowen, Chastain's, Habersham.*
244 William Robertson, 537th, Upson.*
245 George Osbourn, Moseley's, Coweta.
246 John H. Lowe, Jr., Elder's, Clarke.*
247 Alexander Autry, Jr., Coxe's, Morgan.
248 Mathias Turner, Heard's, De Kalb.*
249 Benjamin Hudgens, Woodruff's, Campbell.*
250 Joseph A. Langford, Justice's, Bibb.*
251 Caleb George, Sims's, Troup.
252 William D. Pogue, Jones's, Hall.
253 William Bryce, Latimer's, De Kalb.
254 Paschal H. Sanford, 415th, Walton.
255 Christopher Freeman, 289th, Jasper.
256 Richard Nolen, Baley's, Butts.
257 Jeremiah A. M'Clung, Loveless's, Gwinnett.

258　Alexander Patterson, M'Craney's, Lowndes.
259　Sarah Brown, or., Williams's, Washington.
260　Henry Carter, Candler's, Bibb.*
261　William A. Rhymes, sol., 656th, Troup.*
262　Mary Lewis, w., 2d, Chatham.
263　Daniel Avera, Moore's, Randolph.*
264　Hannah & James Beard, ors., 119th, Richmond.*
265　Joseph Leonard, Salem, Baldwin.*
266　Patrick Froley, 35th, Scriven.*
267　Thomas B. M'Crary, Hitchcock's, Muscogee.*
268　Philander O. Parris's ors., Stewart's, Warren.
269　Alldridge Jackson, 277th, Morgan.
270　James Blount's ors., Sullivan's, Jones.
271　Charles Walsingham, 9th, Effingham.*
272　James Gray, Brewer's, Monroe.*
273　Samuel Elrod, Sen., r. s., Jones's, Habersham.*
274　Sarah G. Haig, w., Fitzpatrick's, Chatham.
275　Bartimeus Williams, Blair's, Lowndes.*
276　James Lesueur's ors., Ross's, Monroe.
277　Antoni P. Dilliac, M. Brown's, Habersham.*
278　Davis Lovelady, Bishop's, Henry.*
279　Samuel Spillards, 111th, Hancock.*
280　William Frazier, Sparks's, Washington.*
281　Spencer Martin, Merck's, Hall.*
282　Joseph Hightower, M'Coy's, Houston.
283　William Jack, Robinson's, Fayette.*
284　James Mappen's ors., Brackett's, Newton.
285　William H. Tumlin, Dobbs's, Hall.
286　Reason Davis, Davis's, Gwinnett.
287　John Black, Sen., Hutson's, Newton.*
288　Michael Brannon, r. s., Chambers's, Gwinnett.
289　James D. Tucker, Jenkins's, Oglethorpe.*
290　Francis Culpepper, w., Lynn's, Warren.*
291　Wiley Alford, 140th, Greene.
292　David Lawson's ors., Hammock's, Jasper.
293　Edwin R. Anderson, 102d, Hancock.
294　Henry Simms, Williams's, Walton.
295　George Wilkie, Jones's, Hall.*
296　William Hare, Watson's, Marion.*
297　George W. Tisinger, 561st, Upson.
298　Samuel Hemphill, Hitchcock's, Muscogee.*
299　Thomas Laseter, 735th, Troup.*
300　Adam Simmon's ors., Hardman's, Oglethorpe.
301　Silas Shirey, Robinson's, Washington.
302　Peter Adams, 759th, Sumter.
303　Elizabeth Gideons, w., Phillips's, Talbot.
304　James H. Gilmore, Robinson's, Harris.

305 Daniel Holtzclaw, Flynn's, Muscogee.*
306 Edward Mansell, Williams's, Ware.*
307 David Branch, Wallis's, Irwin.*
308 Sarah Harvey, w. r. s., Bostick's, Twiggs.*
309 John H. Jones, sol., Tuggle's, Merriwether.*
310 Pleasant Ousley, Collier's, Monroe.*
311 William Terry, 404th, Gwinnett.
312 James Hall, Smith's, Wilkinson.*
313 Drury Clark, Walker's, Houston.
314 Ivey Smith, r. s., George's, Appling.*
315 Benjamin Newberry, or., Jordan's, Bibb.
316 Neill Wilkinson, George's, Appling.*
317 Mark M. Shipp, 417th, Walton.*
318 Peterson Heeth, Parham's, Warren.
319 Josiah Reynold's ors., Maguire's, Gwinnett.
320 Samuel W. Griffith, Jordan's, Bibb.*
321 Smith Turner, Wallis's, Irwin.
322 Alexander B. Stephens, Hargrove's, Oglethorpe.*
323 John H. Dickerson's ors., Jones's, Hall.
324 Winefred Payne, w., Morris's, Crawford.

20th DISTRICT, SECOND SECTION, CHEROKEE.

1 Unity Willoughby, w. r. s., Rutland's, Bibb.*
2 Lucy Gill, w., Smith's, Liberty.*
3 Jesse Locklear, Gittens's, Fayette.*
4 Susannah M'Arty, w., Compton's, Fayette.*
5 Nancy Christian, w., Jones's, Madison.*
6 James M. Anthony, Compton's, Fayette.*
7 Pryor Thornton's ors., M'Ginnis's, Jackson.
8 Calvin Wilkinson, Garner's, Coweta.
9 Dennis Cason, Robison's, Washington.
10 John Wilkinson, Ballard's, Morgan.*
11 Robert Tuggle, sol., Hammock's, Jasper.
12 Nancy Branon, or., 759th, Sumter.*
13 Arthur Rice, Hutson's, Newton.
14 Henry Partan, Hampton's, Newton.*
15 Jacob Herndon, Dyer's, Habersham.*
16 James Johnson's or., Herring's, Twiggs.
17 John Brown, 334th, Wayne.*
18 Samuel T. Curry, Smith's, Madison.
19 (fr.) James Morris, Edwards's, Talbot.*
20 (fr.) Henry Herrington, Copelin's, Houston.*
21 James Head, Jr., 277th, Morgan.

22 William Beesley, Lockhart's, Bulloch.*
23 John B. Martin, Ballard's, Morgan.
24 John Beaseley, Jr., Hughes's, Habersham.
25 Abslom Weaver, Moore's, Randolph.*
26 John M'Corcle, Jr., Graves's, Lincoln.*
27 Thomas Dowell, m. s., Sanderlin's, Chatham.*
28 James Shannon, Athens, Clarke.*
29 Edward M. Lovejoy, Dearing's, Henry.
30 Joseph H. Bradford, 2d section, Cherokee.*
31 James Blackstock, Jr., sol., Heard's, De Kalb.
32 Berry Jones's ors., Peavy's, Bulloch.
33 Enoch Knight's ors., 120th, Richmond.
34 John Ayres, Salem, Baldwin.*
35 Andrew S. Wilson, Jones's, Hall.*
36 John B. Lenard's ors., Moseley's, Wilkes.
37 Pitmilner Rainey, Gillis's, De Kalb.
38 Dottson Harvill, s. i. w., Russell's, Henry.
39 James Miller, Hart's, Jones.
40 James Cox, Williams's, Washington.
41 Denson Crow, Crow's, Pike.*
42 William White, Davis's, Gwinnett.*
43 Jeremiah Farr, Hines's, Coweta.*
44 Solomon Baker, Winter's, Jones.
45 Yearly Martin, Freeman's, Jasper.*
46 Michael Cody's ors., s. i. w., Perryman's, Warren.
47 Jeptha Robinson, Jr., Gittens's, Fayette.
48 Sion Gamblin, Seay's, Hall.*
49 Major Hilliard, 535th, Dooly.*
50 Moses Watts, Stewart's, Troup.*
51 John G. Mitchell, 140th, Greene.
52 Laban Moore, Carswell's, Jefferson.
53 Abner Taylor, M. Brown's, Habersham.*
54 Jesse Padget, Dobbs's, Hall.
55 Dennis N. Touchstone, Bustin's, Pike.
56 Jesse G. Carr, 250th, Walton.*
57 (fr.) Margaret Browning, w. r. s., Morgan's, Clarke.
58 (fr.) Elbert E. Craig, Cleland's, Chatham.*
59 Benjamin Morris, Sparks's, Washington.
60 George S. Bradford, 2d section, Cherokee.*
61 James Adams, blind, Seal's, Elbert.*
62 William Goble, Henson's, Rabun.
63 Edy Carroll, w., 1st section, Cherokee.
64 Enoch Spinks, Night's, Morgan.*
65 Nancy Cunningham, w. r. s., 192d, Elbert.*
66 Joseph Gartrell, 177th, Wilkes.*
67 James P. Pinson, Hargrove's, Oglethorpe.*
68 George Harris, s. i. w., Craven's, Coweta.*

69 James Spratlin, 166th, Wilkes.*
70 Henry Watkins's four ors., Givin's, De Kalb.
71 Absalom Payne's ors., O'Neal's, Laurens.
72 Joshua R. Hays, Phillips's, Talbot.*
73 Peny Pruitt, w. r. s., Martin's, Newton.*
74 James J. Summerlin, Jones's, Morgan.
75 Thomas Arundale, Higginbotham's, Rabun.
76 William Bryan, Bryan's, Monroe.*
77 Lewis M. Matthews, Martin's, Newton.*
78 George Menefee, Atkinson's, Coweta.
79 William Bentley, Brewer's, Walton.*
80 John C. Aderhold, Jr., Royster's, Franklin.*
81 Thomas Cannup, r. s., Hughes's, Habersham.
82 Benjamin Bond, Bostick's, Twiggs.*
83 Seaborn Jones, Ware's, Coweta.*
84 Pleasant Roberts, 374th, Putnam.*
85 Louiza S. Hays, w., Campbell's, Wilkes.
86 Thornton Burke, sol., Allison's, Pike.*
87 John M'Celvy, Holly's, Franklin.*
88 John Sander, Cobb's, Muscogee.
89 Henry Hardy, sol., Royster's, Franklin.
90 James Beard, Davis's, Jones.*
91 William Devaux, sol., Moseley's, Wilkes.*
92 Elias Davis, Swain's, Thomas.
93 Washington Randolph, 248th, Jackson.
94 James V. Hogg, Hall's, Butts.*
95 (fr.) Starling Gardner, Jr., Stewart's, Warren.
96 (fr.) William M. Beard, Athens, Clarke.
97 James Blair, r. s., Whitehead's, Habersham.
98 Benjamin Coxwell, Jordan's, Bibb.
99 John Hawes, Levritt's, Lincoln.
100 Abraham Heath, Arrington's, Merriwether.
101 Benjamin Dorton, r. s., Martin's, Pike.*
102 Rebecca Herd, w., Henson's, Rabun.*
103 Peterson Sanders, Hudson's, Marion.
104 Allen M'Kaskill, Ballard's, Morgan.
105 William J. Ogilvie, Jenkins's, Oglethorpe.*
106 James Bradford, Strickland's, Merriwether.*
107 Silas Turner, Gittens's, Fayette.*
108 Thomas Harvell, Miller's, Jackson.
109 Martha Maddox, w., 149th, Greene.
110 Mary Vincent, w., M'Linn's, Butts.
111 Jeremiah Spivey, Christie's, Jefferson.*
112 Willis Spear, sol., 735th, Troup.
113 Ivey Fountain, Carswell's, Jefferson.*
114 James White, 1st section, Cherokee.
115 Mary Price, or., Park's, Walton.*

116 Martha Heath, w., Stewart's, Warren.*
117 Barrabas Kelly, Bower's, Elbert.*
118 William Watson, Hutson's, Newton.*
119 William Drew, id., 57th, Emanuel.*
120 Robert W. Tuck, Buck-branch, Clarke.
121 Elizabeth Brown, w. r. s., 73d, Burke.*
122 Timothy M'Graw, Perryman's, Warren.*
123 Eli Frost, Justice's, Bibb.*
124 Jacob Lee, 19th, Bryan.*
125 Samuel Allen's ors., 121st, Richmond.
126 James Beasley, sol., Foote's, De Kalb.*
127 Jefferson Hamby, Henson's, Rabun.*
128 Elijah Bowen, r. s., Clifton's, Tatnall.*
129 Allen Malone, Jones's, Hall.*
130 John R. Richardson, 588th, Upson.
131 Thomas Jackson, Whipple's, Wilkinson.
132 William M'Callum, Barnett's, Clarke.*
133 (fr.) Augustus G. W. Hodges, Salem, Baldwin.
134 (fr.) Henry Vaughan, Collier's, Monroe.*
135 Burkett Jeffries, Kelly's, Jasper.*
136 Christopher C. Huntington, or., 119th, Richmond.
137 Thomas G. Wood, 419th, Walton.*
138 Preston Bailey's ors., 176th, Wilkes.
139 Joseph R. Craal, Candler's, Bibb.
140 William Waters, 1st, Chatham.*
141 Littleton Whitten, 277th, Morgan.*
142 Moses Royal, Griffin's, Burke.
143 Frederic H. Williams's 3 orphans, 137th, Greene.*
144 Samuel Gillispie's ors., Hargrove's, Oglethorpe.
145 S. Stewart (son of John), Brackett's, Newton.
146 Daniel Harley, Ellsworth's, Bibb.*
147 Samuel Belflower, Bailey's, Laurens.*
148 Isaac Hill, Curry's, Merriwether.*
149 Murdock Gillis's ors., Sen., 395th, Emanuel.*
150 Joseph Vardaman, sol., Greer's, Merriwether.*
151 Allen Waters, 633d, Dooly.*
152 Abner Stanley, 588th, Upson.*
153 John M'Call, Stone's, Irwin.*
154 M. H. Guest, of Cherokee, Latimer's, De Kalb.*
155 Vincent Davis, Downs's, Warren.*
156 William Glozier, Hampton's, Newton.*
157 Mary Levar, w. r. s., Will's, Twiggs.*
158 Thomas P. Reynolds, Britt's, Randolph.*
159 John Sturges's ors., Cliett's, Columbia.*
160 Simon Roberts's ors., Dozier's, Columbia.
161 Allen Castleberry, Belcher's, Jasper.*
162 John Cook, Gunn's, Jefferson.

163 Patsey Durham, w., 138th, Greene.
164 M'Calvis Spence, Tower's, Gwinnett.
165 James Godwin's ors., 320th, Baldwin.
166 David Burk, Jr., 80th, Scriven.*
167 Larkin Bagwell, 406th, Gwinnett.*
168 Duncan C. M'Lauchlin, Green's, Oglethorpe.*
169 John Chapman, sol., Watson's, Marion.*
170 John M'Daniel, Hill's, Monroe.*
171 (fr.) Catharine Stubblefield, w., Norris's, Monroe.*
172 (fr.) John Brooks, Adams's, Columbia.*
173 J. Pendley, w., of Cher., Latimer's, De Kalb.*
174 Benjamin Williams, 672d, Harris.*
175 John Porter, 430th, Early.*
176 Ezekiel Calhoun, Baismore's, Jones.*
177 George H. Wallis, Dobbs's, Hall.*
178 David Kellum, Hollon's, Emanuel.
179 Hyram Merritt, Coxe's, Talbot.
180 Lawson B. Hamright, Smith's, Habersham.*
181 Samuel J. Nicholson's or., 143d, Greene.
182 C. S. M. Payne, Athens, Clarke.*
183 John Balinger, Jr., Bower's, Elbert.
184 Manderson's orphans, Mayo's, Wilkinson.
185 Phineas L. Moore, Dean's, Clarke.*
186 Pleasant B. Patterson, Newby's, Jones.*
187 Robert D. Smith, Morris's, Crawford.*
188 Thomas M. Chandler, 6th, Chatham.
189 Solomon Land, Neal's, Campbell.*
190 John Hammock, Hampton's, Newton.*
191 Robert Jerkins, Whipple's, Wilkinson.*
192 David M. Stewart's ors., House's, Henry.
193 Edward Hawkins, 374th, Putnam.
194 Osburn Peek, 144th, Greene.*
195 Abraham M. Woolsey, 398th, Richmond.*
196 Newby Connell's ors., 107th, Hancock.
197 Henry Deloach, Davis's, Jones.
198 Ellison Cobb, Hamilton's, Gwinnett.
199 Shadrick Meaks, Robinson's, Harris.
200 William Green, 417th, Walton.*
201 James Murray, Mullen's, Carroll.*
202 William Herm's or., 2d, Chatham.
203 Turner Harris, Stewart's, Warren.
204 John Bass, 73d, Burke.
205 John Willis, Rainey's, Twiggs.*
206 Major W. Lord, Higginbotham's, Madison.*
207 Charles Davenport, Barker's, Gwinnett.*
208 William Jeffries, sol., Phillips's, Jasper.*
209 (fr.) Sarah Bayles, w. r. s., Downs's, Warren.

210 (fr.) Patrick M'Gee, Sanderlin's, Chatham.
211 Samuel Gray, Jr., Greer's, Merriwether.
212 Larkin Brantley, Jordan's, Harris.*
213 Thomas Holder, sol., Curry's, Wilkinson.*
214 Thomas W. Bledsoe, Stanton's, Newton.*
215 Shadrack Rice, Brooks's, Muscogee.
216 Thomas Ewing, Dean's, De Kalb.*
217 Elizabeth Lawrence, w., Bell's, Columbia.
218 Frederic H. Herring, 295th, Jasper.*
219 Jonathan West, sol., Bostick's, Twiggs.
220 Patrick Froley, 35th, Scriven.*
221 Berry Jones, Johnson's, Bibb.*
222 Luke P. Lanair, Lockhart's, Bulloch.*
223 John Collins, Sen., sol., Blackstock's, Hall.*
224 John Cox, 633d, Dooly.*
225 James H. Culberson, Stewart's, Troup.
226 Thomas H. Bray, 672d, Harris.
227 James Glasson, sol., Fenn's, Clarke.*
228 David Godwin, Moore's, Randolph.
229 David Blackwell, 404th, Gwinnett.
230 John S. Davis, Smith's, Franklin.*
231 Lydia Bohannon, w. r. s., Morgan's, Appling.*
232 Peter Tatom's ors., 656th, Troup.
233 Samuel Dunn, 406th, Gwinnett.*
234 James King, Cleland's, Chatham.*
235 Cargel Drake, 117th, Hancock.*
236 Theophilus Flowers, Howell's, Troup.
237 M. L. Barron, Athens, Clarke.
238 Edward T. Howard, 406th, Gwinnett.*
239 John Crossley, 144th, Greene.
240 Jacob Early, sol., Grice's, Oglethorpe.*
241 Thomas J. Hines, 373d, Jasper.*
242 Joshua Nicholson, Perry's, Habersham.
243 William Randle, Clark's, Morgan.*
244 Johnson Mathis, Barrow's, Houston.*
245 Sarah Ann Thompson, or., 374th, Putnam.
246 Elizabeth Lord, w., Mayo's, Wilkinson.*
247 (fr.) John Martin, 494th, Upson.
248 (fr.) Hezekiah Bailey, 600th, Richmond.
249 Humphrey Bearden, r. s., Barnett's, Clarke.*
250 Morgan Brown, Wood's, Morgan.*
251 Ann Rose, w., Houston's, Chatham.
252 Julius R. Bates, Martin's, Hall.*
253 Allen C. Daniel, Morgan's, Madison.*
254 Tim. C. Goldin, of Carroll, Johnson's, De Kalb.*
255 George W. Amos, 101st, Hancock.
256 Millington S. Johnson, 118th, Hancock.*

257 Richard Harris, of Cherokee, Harris's, De Kalb.*
258 Jacob A. Dove, 4th, Chatham.
259 Needham Stevens, Bryan's, Pulaski.
260 James Hudgens, Bridges's, Gwinnett.
261 Enoch Wood Spofford, 398th, Richmond.*
262 John H. Thomas, Ross's, Monroe.
263 Stephen Stovall, 245th, Jackson.
264 James Russell, Sen., Peurifoy's, Henry.
265 Jonathan Lasseter, Smith's, Campbell.
266 Joseph T. Saxon, Rainey's, Twiggs.
267 Benajer Goss, Hodges's, Newton.*
268 James Beasley, 395th, Emanuel.*
269 Martha Alexander, w., 293d, Jasper.
270 Thomas Bonner, Jr., Night's, Morgan.
271 Samuel H. Blackwell, Hammock's, Jasper.
272 Anthony B. Lovett, 34th, Scriven.
273 William R. B. Russell, Cleland's, Chatham.*
274 Warren R. Andrews, 602d, Taliaferro.
275 William H. Wyatt, Wilson's, Jasper.
276 Richmond Ansley, Perryman's, Warren.
277 Aaron White, 373d, Jasper.*
278 William Turner, 59th, Emanuel.*
279 Alexander Wells, 374th, Putnam.
280 Henry Morris, Phillips's, Monroe.
281 Abel Brooks, Aderhold's, Campbell.*
282 Baker Ayres, r. s., Whitehead's, Habersham.
283 David Cason, Green's, Ware.
284 Matthew Heath, 162d, Greene.*
285 (fr.) Youngsett Dindy, Lawrence's, Pike.*
286 (fr.) Bright W. Hargrave, Mullen's, Carroll.*
287 Thomas Hanney, Griffin's, De Kalb.*
288 Thomas F. Leggett, Moore's, Randolph.*
289 Robert Foster, 163d, Greene.*
290 John T. Leftwich, 788th, Heard.
291 Sarah Clensey, w., 22d, M'Intosh.*
292 Williamson Phillips, sol., Crawford's, Franklin.*
293 Elijah Hogan, Martin's, Hall.*
294 Hiram Proctor, 2d section, Cherokee.*
295 Neal M'Donnell, Nesbit's, Newton.
296 Alfred Powell, Martin's, Hall.*
297 Mark A. Turner's ors., Griffin's, Fayette.
298 Henry Barlow, Whipple's, Wilkinson.*
299 Chloe C. Collier, w., 143d, Greene.
300 Cealey Leverett, w. r. s., Griffin's, De Kalb.
301 Ann Owen, w., Griffin's, De Kalb.*
302 James Leak, Sen., r. s., Belcher's, Jasper.
303 T. B. Pinson, son of Boyd, Hargrove's, Oglethorpe*

304 James Jordan, Higginbotham's, Madison.*
305 Nimrod Dean, Martin's, Hall.
306 Reuben Thornton, Fleming's, Franklin.*
307 James S. Cronan, Field's, Habersham.
308 James K. Cowan, Givins's, De Kalb.*
309 Edward Harris, White's, Franklin.*
310 John Sanders, 470th, Upson.*
311 Abraham Register, Thomas's, Ware.
312 William Shaw, Higginbotham's, Rabun.*
313 Thomas J. Trammell, Williams's, Walton.*
314 Nancy England, w., Park's, Walton.*
315 Benjamin Fanning, sol., Thomason's, Elbert.*
316 Joseph J. Pinson, Hargrove's, Oglethorpe.*
317 John M. Mason, sol., 112th, Hancock.*
318 John Davies, 102d, Hancock.
319 Thomas Harbin, Brock's, Habersham.*
320 James L. Mitchell, Hall's, Oglethorpe.*
321 Amis Wright, w. r. s., Hearn's, Butts.*
322 George W. Barnes, 4th, Chatham.*
323 (fr.) Levin Walker, Atkinson's, Coweta.
324 (fr.) Gilford E. Hendrick, Wilson's, Madison.*
325 Lewis Phillips, Kelly's, Jasper.*
326 John Thompson, Whelchel's, Hall.
327 Mordica B. Pittman, Allen's, Bibb.*
328 William C. Hope, Jones's, Hall.*
329 George Kinkle, Chastain's, Habersham.
330 Thomas P. Fielder, of Newton, Park's, Walton.*
331 Nathaniel Vincent, Rooks's, Putnam.*
332 Jarrell Malone, Hancock's, Jasper.*
333 Thomas Glenn, r. s., Baismore's, Jones.
334 Elbert Rutherford, 4th section, Cherokee.
335 John Mills's ors., Smith's, Franklin.
336 Elijah Davis, sol., Hamilton's, Hall.*
337 Burgis Tilley's ors., Whitehead's, Habersham.
338 James Milton, Groover's, Thomas.*
339 Richard Dozier, Sen., Parham's, Warren.*
340 John T. Watts, Taylor's, Jones.
341 Jacob Edwards, sol., 415th, Walton.
342 William Jeffers, 72d, Burke.*

22d DISTRICT, SECOND SECTION, CHEROKEE.

1 Osborn Arrant, 561st, Upson.
2 Jeremiah F. Horton, Bower's, Elbert.*
3 Reuben Fassett, Jr., Dobbs's, Hall.
4 Evander Quick, Gittens's, Fayette.*
5 James Prather, Collins's, Henry.
6 Melyer Bumgarner, 406th, Gwinnett.*
7 Reuben Kemp's ors., Martin's, Washington.*
8 Allen Arrant, 561st, Upson.*
9 Ann Martin, w., Anderson's, Rabun.*
10 James Griffith, Jordan's, Bibb.*
11 John A. Beasley, Hendon's, Carroll.*
12 Tilman Pullen, M'Clain's, Newton.*
13 George Dudley's ors., 37th, Scriven.*
14 Elizabeth Clinch, w., Hobbs's, Laurens.*
15 William M'Waters, 777th, Randolph.
16 William Lawless's ors., Hargrove's, Oglethorpe.*
17 William Beck, Gunn's, Henry.
18 Elisha Holt, Gittens's, Fayette.*
19 Meshack Joiner, Crow's, Pike.*
20 John T. Chapman, Winter's, Jones.
21 Burrell White, Royster's, Franklin.
22 John K. C. Waller, Phillips's, Monroe.
23 M. Brown, Turner's son, Garner's, Washington.*
24 John Taylor, 466th, Monroe.
25 George Mitchell, Harris's, De Kalb.
26 Abram Leathers, Duke's, Carroll.*
27 William M. W. Maxwell, 15th, Liberty.
28 Eliza Josaphine Coppedge, or., Taylor's, Putnam.
29 Henry Pope's ors., Justice's, Bibb.
30 Vincent Bowden, Sam Streetman's, Twiggs.*
31 Nancy D. Lewis, w., Perry's, Baldwin.*
32 Robert Kennedy, Robison's, Washington.
33 Samuel Raney, Blair's, Lowndes.*
34 David Argo, Givens's, De Kalb.*
35 Clinton Alford, Mizell's, Talbot.
36 Lawson Wright, Parham's, Warren.
37 Esau Davis, sol., Martin's, Jones.*
38 John G. Gallaspy, 419th, Walton.
39 James Howard, Herndon's, Hall.
40 William Hubbard, Daniel's, Hall.*
41 Solomon Sheftall, Jr., 7th, Chatham.

42 Ezekiel Bonds, Griffin's, Hall.*
43 Benjamin Milton Sweat's, Ware.*
44 Dempsey J. Carr, Justice's, Bibb.*
45 John H. Strange, 73d, Burke.*
46 Thomas Story's ors., Orr's, Jackson.
47 Beverly Christopher, Will's, Twiggs.*
48 William H. Morrow's ors., Stanton's, Newton.
49 Benjamin Thomas, 735th, Troup.
50 Arthur C. Foil, Alexander's, Jefferson.*
51 Solomon Williams, 735th, Troup.*
52 Anna M. Colton, or., Hill's, Harris.
53 Elizabeth L. Jordan, M'Clendon's, Putnam.
54 Isham Spaulding, Miller's, Camden.*
55 John Willis, 3d section, Cherokee.
56 Sampson Vickry, Jr., Field's, Habersham.*
57 James P. Allen, 120th, Richmond.
58 James Osburn, Nesbit's, Newton.
59 Solomon Collum, Neal's, Campbell.
60 Sarah Smith, w., Will's, Twiggs.
61 William Brooker, Hand's, Appling.
62 Mary E. Berthelot, or., Fitzpatrick's, Chatham.
63 Zachariah K. Hamilton, Mann's, Crawford.*
64 William Willis, Jr., s. l. w., 588th, Upson.
65 Samuel Etris, Field's, Habersham.
66 Kitching's four orphans, Hargrove's, Newton.*
67 William Robbins, 120th, Richmond.
68 William A. Johnson, Ross's, Monroe.
69 James Peavy, Grier's, Warren.
70 John Thornton's ors., M'Ginnis's, Jackson.
71 Jacob B. Shropshire, Britt's, Randolph.*
72 Archibald Bulloch, 4th, Chatham.
73 William W. Cooksey, 417th, Walton.
74 Clark Brewer, Clark's, Morgan.
75 John Moses, Allen's, Campbell.
76 John W. R. Thomason, Chandler's, Franklin.
77 Samuel Kite, Gittens's, Fayette.*
78 Jacob Setzer, r. s., Edwards's, Franklin.
79 Simpson Fulton's ors., Shattox's, Coweta.
80 Abijah Wilbanks, M'Ginnis's, Jackson.*
81 William Fraley, 113th, Hancock.
82 Polly Butler, minor, f. a., Colley's, Oglethorpe.
83 Richard Speak, Sen., M'Linn's, Butts.
84 D. Taylor, Sen., s. i. w., Higginbotham's, Madison.
85 David Gray, Killen's, Decatur.
86 Zaccheus Pate, Jones's, Thomas.*
87 Ellison H. Flaherty, Simmons's, Crawford.
88 Anderson Moseley, White's, Franklin.

89 Joseph Huie, Jr., Evans's, Fayette.
90 Reese Barber, Buck-branch, Clarke.*
91 William H. Neyland, Roe's, Burke.
92 John Mack, Cleggs's, Walton.*
93 Rebecca Moore, id., Coker's, Troup.
94 William Evens, Jones's, Morgan.*
95 Mary Ann Buchannon, f. a., Phillips's, Jasper.*
96 Starling Tarver's ors., Robison's, Washington.
97 John Potts, r. s., Jones's, Habersham.
98 Edward Franklin's ors., Lockhart's, Bulloch.
99 John Arnett, r. s., Groover's, Thomas.*
100 Archibald Hagan, M'Clain's, Newton.*
101 Asa Harper, Garner's, Coweta.
102 Caleb Stephens, Hannah's, Jefferson.*
103 Jonathan Jones, Higginbotham's, Rabun.*
104 John P. Tiller, Colley's, Oglethorpe.
105 James Britton, Baley's, Butts.
106 Hope Hall Waller, Waller's, Putnam.
107 Robert Mitchell, r. s., Rutland's, Bibb.*
108 Stephen G. M'Cray, Phillips's, Jasper.
109 Josiah Nobles, Walker's, Houston.
110 George Clewis, Hicks's, Decatur.
111 Majempsey Moore, Mashburn's, Pulaski.
112 Littleberry Huff, Barnett's, Clarke.
113 George C. Branch, Perry's, Habersham.*
114 Isaac D. Braswell, 417th, Walton.*
115 Edward Walthall's ors., Williams's, Jasper.
116 Granville White, 633d, Dooly.
117 Mary Tombs, w., 374th, Putnam.*
118 John G. Shelnut, Park's, Walton.
119 Ezekiel Haynes, sol., Silman's, Pike.*
120 Hugh Donaldson, Newman's, Thomas.
121 Henry Freeman, Hammond's, Franklin.
122 Sarah Wagnon, w., Payne's, Merriwether.
123 Dickson W. Darnell, Hodges's, Newton.
124 Thomas Story, sol., Huey's, Harris.
125 Asa Adams, 398th, Richmond.
126 Richard Wages, 119th, Richmond.
127 Jesse Choice, 101st, Hancock.*
128 Hillary Hooks, Whipple's, Wilkinson.
129 Daniel Chandler, Chandler's, Franklin.
130 John B. Dudley, Barker's, Gwinnett.*
131 Wm. and Anna Keaton, ors., Smith's, Liberty.
132 Joseph M'Mullin, citizen, Bostick's, Twiggs.*
133 Nancy Carroll, w., 242d, Jackson.
134 Robert Black, sol., Hutson's, Newton.
135 John Brown, Jr., Bower's, Elbert.

136 Isaac Langston, Russell's, Henry.
137 William Hopkins, Ellis's, Rabun.
138 Thomas Reynolds, Brewer's, Walton.*
139 Charity Varnedoe, 15th, Liberty.
140 William Gibson's ors., 588th, Upson.
141 Charles A. Heard, Smith's, Campbell.
142 Tabitha Fouche, w., 175th, Wilkes.
143 Robert Shurley, Dean's, Clarke.*
144 Jefferson G. Reynolds, Alberson's, Walton.
145 Joseph Bryan's ors., Cook's, Telfair.
146 William W. Grice, Payne's, Merriwether.
147 Henry P. Thomas, Athens, Clarke.*
148 Ephraim Bailey, Moseley's, Wilkes.
149 Archibald Wilkins, Jr., 15th, Liberty.*
150 William C. Hancock, Brock's, Habersham.*
151 Solomon Welch, 494th, Upson.
152 Milicart Wright, w., Parham's, Warren.
153 James M. Sanford, sol., Walker's, Harris.
154 Benjamin Baker, Sen., sol., 404th, Gwinnett.
155 Henry B. Mearse, 38th, Scriven.
156 John Hardman, s. l. w., Johnson's, De Kalb.
157 Young H. Greer, 148th, Greene.
158 Calvin Penny, Rainey's, Twiggs.
159 Jones T. Douglass, Barker's, Gwinnett.
160 Joseph D. Brooks, Tompkins's, Putnam.*
161 William Beard, 34th, Scriven.
162 William Lee, Gray's, Henry.
163 Charles Roper, Reid's, Gwinnett.
164 Allen Williamson, Barker's, Gwinnett.
165 Jane Stewart, w. r. s., Bryan's, Monroe.
166 Martha W. Johnson, w., Compton's, Fayette.
167 George Williams, Walker's, Harris.
168 Tryon Smith, 415th, Walton.
169 Benjamin Phillips, r. s., Brown's, Camden.
170 John J. Hussey, Tuggle's, Merriwether.
171 Chapley W. Dempsey, Aderhold's, Campbell.
172 Jacob Blocker's ors., Durrence's, Tatnall.
173 Rachel Burk, w., Hendon's, Carroll.
174 Samuel Garrard, Price's, Hall.
175 Mark S. Elam, Sapp's, Muscogee.*
176 Abner Horn, 561st, Upson.
177 George D. Stansell, Martin's, Newton.
178 Isaac Alger, Jordan's, Bibb.
179 Matthew Lasitor, sol., Ball's, Monroe.*
180 Redding R. Lewis, Garner's, Washington.*
181 William J. Orr, Martin's, Washington.*
182 John Dougherty, Shearer's, Coweta.

183 William Childress, Cobb's, Muscogee.
184 Needham Chesnut, r. s., Pearce's, Houston.*
185 Barnard Murry, 603d, Taliaferro.
186 Alexander M'Larty, Foote's, De Kalb.*
187 Benjamin Warner, Jordan's, Bibb.*
188 Mary M'Mullin, w., Simmons's, Crawford.
189 Lewis Kent, Griffin's, Merriwether.*
190 Beverly A. Freeman, Peurifoy's, Henry.
191 Ephraim M'Clain, M'Clure's, Rabun.
192 Matthew Nelson, 600th, Richmond.
193 Joseph Hodges, Echols's, Clarke.
194 Robert F. Henderson, 3d section, Cherokee.
195 William Weeks, Gunn's, Jefferson.
196 John L. Brock, Brock's, Habersham.*
197 Elisha Sterling, Groce's, Bibb.*
198 James Rylee, Sen., r. s., Blackstock's, Hall.
199 Elisha Holland, Jack's, Clarke.*
200 Daniel Loyd, Blount's, Wilkinson.*
201 James Stevens, Sanderlin's, Chatham.
202 William Brown, Hatton's, Baker.
203 Martha Stephens, w., Berry's, Butts.*
204 Philip Ware, s. l. w., Ware's, Coweta.
205 Solomon Manning, Bridges's, Gwinnett.
206 Sarah Ann Miller, f. a., Johnson's, Bibb.
207 Jonathan Humphrey, Crawford's, Franklin.
208 Isaac Smith, Lamberth's, Fayette.*
209 Mary Dowdy, w., 36th, Scriven.
210 H. W. Hagerman, Graves's, Lincoln.*
211 William Ezzeel's ors., Hamilton's, Gwinnett.
212 Richard W. Roffe, Burk's, Stewart.
213 Samuel E. Buckler, Flynn's, Muscogee.
214 Richard W. Oates, r. s., 672d, Harris.
215 Benjamin Thompson's ors., Gum Swamp, Pulaski
216 William M. Bird's ors., 374th, Putnam.
217 Elisha Douglass, 510th, Early.*
218 Jesse M. Skinner, or., Head's, Butts.
219 Jessy H. Lively, Griffin's, Burke.
220 Nathan Cook, 102d, Hancock.
221 Arthur Warren, Seay's, Hall.
222 Wilson F. Blackstock, Heard's, De Kalb.
223 Thomas Potts, Orr's, Jackson.
224 Reuben Trainum's ors., 278th, Morgan.
225 Thomas Smith, Norman's, Wilkes.*
226 Thomas F. Mickle, 779th, Heard.
227 Ann Sager, w. r. s., 163d, Greene.*
228 Alexander Jarratt, 318th, Baldwin.
229 David Wright's 7 orphans, Gillis's, De Kalb.

230 Terrell Harrison, Royster's, Franklin.
231 Benjamin B. White, Canning's, Elbert.
232 James H. Killian, Iverson's, Houston.*
233 Miles Estes, Reid's, Gwinnett.
234 Jesse Strickland, Gunn's, Henry.
235 Henry F. Hudson, or., Williams's, Washington.*
236 Osborn Eley, Moffett's, Muscogee.
237 Willis Douglass's ors., Frasier's, Monroe.
238 Laurence Richardson's ors., Adams's, Columbia.
239 Joseph Jones, Cliett's, Columbia.
240 John B. Wells, 20th, Bryan.*
241 Benjamin Talbert, 319th, Baldwin.
242 Ellison Groce, Anderson's, Wilkes.
243 Richard M. Faulk, Hill's, Stewart.
244 Isaiah M'Elhannon, Aderhold's, Campbell.
245 John Conner, Sutton's, Habersham.
246 Thomas Jones, Lynn's, Warren.
247 Francis Gilmore, Nichols's, Fayette.
248 William Freeman, Jones's, Hall.*
249 Ann Killgore, w., Blackstock's, Hall.
250 Granderson Greenwood, Latimer's, De Kalb.
251 Bartholomew Porter, Jones's, Madison.*
252 Henry Shiry, 250th, Walton.*
253 Joseph M'Kindley, Harris's, Crawford.*
254 Elias Skipper, Johnson's, Lowndes.
255 James W. Richards, 735th, Troup.
256 Benjamin Odell, Keener's, Rabun.
257 James Register, s. l. w., Hobbs's, Laurens.
258 George N. Legg, Baugh's, Jackson.
259 James Miller's or., Catlett's, Franklin.
260 Isaac Hendrick, s. l. w., Dearing's, Butts.
261 Charles Strozier, Ross's, Monroe.
262 John E. Scott, 38th, Scriven.
263 Robert Wood, Monk's, Crawford.*
264 Thomas Greene, s. l. w., Barwick's, Washington.*
265 James M. Ware, Morgan's, Madison.
266 Elias Hendrick, r. s.. Wilson's, Madison.*
267 Alexander Williams, Stephens's, Habersham.
268 William Watts, Calhoun's, Harris.
269 Elizabeth Sumner, w., Bryant's, Burke.
270 Hardage Walker, M. Brown's, Habersham.*
271 William Harris, Robinson's, Fayette.
272 Jared Jefferson Taylor, Robison's, Washington.
273 James Quintin, Barker's, Gwinnett.
274 James M. Woodyard, or., 279th, Morgan.
275 Alfred M'Duff, Wilson's, Madison.*
276 Jonathan Reeves, sol., Hodges's, Newton.

277 Aspasia Carruth, Dobbs's, Hall.
278 Henry R. Rodgers, Ellsworth's, Bibb.*
279 John Culpepper, Miller's, Jackson.
280 Joel Henry, Seal's, Elbert.
281 Aaron Mattox, Mattox's, Lowndes.*
282 Lydia Bohannon, w. r. s., Morgan's, Appling.*
283 Drury Dunn, 406th, Gwinnett.
284 Eubank's three orphans, 112th, Hancock.
285 Parker Bird, Summerlin's, Bulloch.
286 David W. Calhoun, Few's, Muscogee.*
287 Thomas R. Porter, Beasley's, Oglethorpe.*
288 Jordan Jones, sol., 190th, Elbert.*
289 William R. King, Herndon's, Hall.*
290 James Bedingfield, Wright's, Laurens.*
291 Margaret Jones, w., M'Clendon's, Putnam.*
292 Thomas H. Wynn, 672d, Harris.*
293 Elisha Sterling, Groce's, Bibb.*
294 Elijah W. Matthews, Martin's, Newton.*
295 Donald Fraser's ors., 15th, Liberty.
296 Daniel Stagner's ors., 373d, Jasper.
297 Eleven S. Tomlinson, 419th, Walton.
298 Lavinia and Jane Porter, ors., House's, Henry.
299 Larkin Barton, sol., Greer's, Merriwether.
300 Jerry Yearwood, Smith's, Habersham.
301 Thomas Lake, Brewer's, Walton.
302 Moses Davidson, Streetman's, Twiggs.
303 James Martin, 59th, Emanuel.*
304 Judge B. Loper, 10th, Effingham.
305 John Floyd, s. i. w., Wood's, Morgan.*
306 Hugh M'Ginley, 123d, Richmond.*
307 Lewis Shiflet, Jr., Stower's, Elbert.
308 John Smith, 143d, Greene.
309 James Gillespie, 454th, Walton.
310 Fleming Davis, Rooks's, Putnam.
311 Lewis Brantley, s. i. w., Givens's, De Kalb.
312 William Bass, Brackett's, Newton.*
313 Elias Barnett, Willis's, Franklin.
314 Jacob A. Moore, Tower's, Gwinnett.
315 Reuben Weed, Chambers's, Gwinnett.
316 William W. Holt, M'Daniel's, Pulaski.*
317 Gabriel P. R. Faircloth's ors., Lyman's, Pulaski.
318 James Hagins, Slater's, Bulloch.*
319 Elbert Herren's 3 orphans, Mobley's, De Kalb.
320 James Bottoms, Bustin's, Pike.*
321 Mary Lamb, w., Roe's, Burke.*
322 Anna Davis, or., Coward's, Lowndes.*
323 William M. Carr, Hughes's, Habersham.*
324 John Hughes, sol., Mashburn's, Pulaski.*

23d DISTRICT, SECOND SECTION, CHEROKEE.

1 Precious C. Edwards, w., 603d, Taliaferro.*
2 Josiah Jerril, 141st, Greene.*
3 Cain Evans, Price's, Hall.*
4 Mark George, Coxe's, Talbot.*
5 Albert Pittman, Ellsworth's, Bibb.*
6 Aley Hughes, Oliver's, Twiggs.
7 James D. Head, 294th, Jasper.
8 John Heidleberg, s. l. w., 633d, Dooly.
9 Ezra Stacy, 15th, Liberty.
10 Hugh Matthews, 120th, Richmond.*
11 Benjamin Camp, Sen., 249th, Walton.
12 Glidwell Killebrew, 271st, M'Intosh.*
13 Jesse Lovil, M'Clure's, Rabun.
14 Samuel Lee, Woodruff's, Campbell.*
15 Levi H. Turner, Collins's, Henry.
16 Isaac Daniel, sol., Mackleroy's, Clarke.*
17 David Bolton, 406th, Gwinnett.
18 Peter M. Curry, Johnson's, Bibb.*
19 Charles Dowdy, 1st section, Cherokee.
20 Wiley Tiner, Young's, Carroll.
21 Rowland Williams, M'Daniel's, Pulaski.
22 William C. Crawford, ———, Baker.
23 James M'Gill, Chambers's, Gwinnett.
24 Thomas M. White, Allen's, Campbell.*
25 Robert W. Richardson, 147th, Greene.*
26 Robert Hemphill's ors., Liddell's, Jackson.
27 John Webb, sol., Wilson's, Jasper.*
28 Tabitha Watson, w., Sullivan's, Jones.*
29 David Fulsom, Morris's, Crawford.
30 Robert G. M'Afee, Crow's, Pike.*
31 David Smith, sol., Willis's, Franklin.
32 William E. Haney, Payne's, Merriwether.
33 Hugh Mills, Loveless's, Gwinnett.*
34 John Payne, Royster's, Franklin.*
35 John S. Walker, sol., Benson's, Lincoln.*
36 William Spears, r. s., Edwards's, Franklin.*
37 Jesse Mixon, 260th, Scriven.*
38 Matthew C. Rodgers, Seay's, Hall.*
39 Harris Sanders, Baugh's, Jackson.*
40 Jonathan B. M'Crary, Edwards's, Talbot.*
41 N. and E. Chambers, ors., Dean's, De Kalb.

42 William Toty's ors., 143d, Greene.*
43 Archibald Smith, Gittens's, Fayette.
44 Joseph Boyd, Varner's, Merriwether.
45 John K. M. Charlton's ors., Moseley's, Wilkes.*
46 Smith Cook, s. i. w., Smith's, Elbert.
47 Jeremiah Perry, Givens's, De Kalb.
48 Hiram Johnson, Hendon's, Carroll.
49 Wade Wheeler, Ball's, Monroe.
50 Dianna Pearson, w., Hearn's, Butts.
51 Christopher Whitman, Evans's, Fayette.*
52 Robert J. Goza, Johnson's, De Kalb.
53 Abijah Shiver, Dilman's, Pulaski.*
54 Levicy Dunn, w., 600th, Richmond.*
55 Lewis Suddeth, 419th, Walton.
56 Hezekiah C. M'Elhenney, 373d, Jasper.*
57 William Pickett's ors., M'Millon's, Lincoln.
58 William H. Dill, 120th, Richmond.
59 Thomas Wilson, sol., Mays's, Monroe.
60 Sarah Dubose, w., 69th, Burke.
61 Archibald L. Polk, Hargrove's, Newton.*
62 Nathaniel Higgason, Hitchcock's, Muscogee.*
63 Benjamin Hudgens, Woodruff's, Campbell.
64 John S. Worsham, Whitehead's, Habersham.
65 James Rice, Willis's, Franklin.
66 Baker Ayers, r. s., Whitehead's, Habersham.
67 William Martin, M'Ginnis's, Jackson.
68 Jesse Hobby, Wallis's, Irwin.*
69 Robert Brooks, r. s.. Taylor's, Houston.*
70 Thomas Taylor's or., Maguire's, Gwinnett.
71 Jonathan Howard, Sen., 1st section, Cherokee.*
72 James C. Scott, Say's, De Kalb.*
73 Caleb Ever's ors., Harris's, Crawford.
74 John Worthy, Edwards's, Franklin.*
75 Asa Brown's ors., Wood's, Jefferson.
76 Julian Thompson, or., Young's, Jefferson.*
77 James M. Mangham, s. l. w., Thaxton's, Butts.*
78 Charles Culverhouse, s. l. w., 601st, Taliaferro.*
79 William O. Bowman, Chastain's, Habersham.*
80 Robert Little, Colquhoun's, Henry.*
81 John Cook, Curry's, Wilkinson.*
82 Thomas Bond's ors., Stokes's, Lincoln.
83 John Whitlock, Dean's, De Kalb.
84 William Wilson, 510th, Early.
85 James Odam, 417th, Walton.
86 John Brown, sol., 334th, Wayne.
87 David A. Clark, 561st, Upson.
88 John W. H. Rice, Harp's, Stewart.

89 George W. Sillavent, 734th, Lee.
90 Thomas Simpson, Jordan's, Bibb.*
91 Lewis Bullard, Peacock's, Washington.*
92 William M. Leigh, Cleland's, Chatham.
93 Joseph W. Hamilton, 406th, Gwinnett.
94 William Robertson, David's, Franklin.
95 William D. Tucker, Thames, Crawford.
96 Thomas M'Gough, s. l. w., Hall's, Butts.
97 Seaborn Jones, 319th, Baldwin.
98 Margaret Holland, w., 295th, Jasper.*
99 Henry Rhodes, 162d, Greene.
100 Benjamin E. Spencer, 143d, Greene.
101 Mary Harper, w., Harris's, Crawford.
102 Biddy Proctor, w. r. s., 406th, Gwinnett.*
103 Starling Glover, Hudson's, Marion.*
104 Robert W. Trimble, Wood's, Morgan.*
105 William Neely, Merck's, Hall.*
106 James Mathies, Hatton's, Baker.*
107 William Eaton, Aderhold's, Campbell.
108 Kinbird Strickling, Mashburn's, Pulaski.
109 Rhoda Kemp, w., 333d, Wayne.
110 Micajah Garvin, Wilson's, Madison.*
111 Edmund Niblett, Crow's, Merriwether.*
112 Mary O. Andrew, w., Barnett's, Clarke.*
113 Richard L. Pindarvis, 27th, Glynn.*
114 George W. Langford, 672d, Harris.
115 Benjamin H. Jones, Clifton's, Tatnall.*
116 Penneywill Folsom, Burnett's, Lowndes.*
117 Daniel M'Daniel, farmer, Liddell's, Jackson.*
118 Tabitha Reins, w., Peace's, Wilkinson.*
119 Fielding Lewis, sol., Hill's, Baldwin.*
120 F. & Clarissa Barnes, f. a., Hampton's, Newton.
121 Leonard Wosham, Salem, Baldwin.*
122 Hezekiah Trotter, 470th, Upson.
123 William Barnwell, sol., Allen's, Henry.
124 Barnabas Hart, s. l. w., Peacock's, Washington.
125 Jephtha P. Hill, 466th, Monroe.
126 Henry Skipper, 788th, Heard.
127 Elizabeth Flewellen, w., Candler's, Bibb.
128 James Hall, Marsh's, Thomas.*
129 Solomon Johnson, sol., Strickland's, Merriwether.*
130 Isaac H. Parker, Waltze's, Morgan.
131 William H. Crane, 295th, Jasper.*
132 Daniel Butler, 2d section, Cherokee.
133 Samuel Roberson, Taylor's, Elbert.
134 Elsey A. Rowan, d. & d., Peurifoy's, Henry.
135 Peter W. Smith, Thompson's, Henry.*

136 James S. Bryant, Beasley's, Oglethorpe.*
137 Eden Dudley, s. l. w., Barwick's, Washington.
138 Luke Merritt, Dixon's, Irwin.
139 Jordan Jackson, Lamberth's, Fayette.*
140 John Wood, Butts's, Monroe.*
141 John Harrell, 20th, Decatur.*
142 Wiley B. Brown, Bower's, Elbert.*
143 Silas S. Starr, Hodges's, Newton.*
144 Hawkins Howard, s. l. w., Mobley's, De Kalb.*
145 James Rice, Jr., Hanner's, Campbell.*
146 Reuben Westmoreland, s. i. w., Allison's, Pike.*
147 Silas Moseley, Gray's, Henry.*
148 Elias Drake's ors., 73d, Burke.
149 Georgianna Wolf, or., Cleland's, Chatham.
150 Bolin Radford, sol., Candler's, Bibb.*
151 Willis Wright, 144th, Greene.
152 Silas M'Cleland, M'Cleland's, Irwin.*
153 William Emerson's ors., Winter's, Jones.
154 Abel Lewise, sol., 69th, Burke.*
155 Hiram King, 574th, Early.*
156 Fletcher's four orphans, Hill's, Stewart.
157 James Hightower, s. l. w., 588th, Upson.
158 John Moore, r. s., 116th, Hancock.*
159 Rufus K. Watters, Royster's, Franklin.
160 Drury Christian's or., David's, Franklin.
161 Zabud Little, Derrick's, Henry.*
162 Shellman Fulford, Swain's, Thomas.
163 Joseph Hodges, Echols's, Clarke.
164 Abel Eberhart, Colley's, Oglethorpe.
165 John Chancey, Sinclair's, Houston.*
166 William Holliway, Hill's, Monroe.*
167 Lewis Morgan Barnes, 101st, Hancock.
168 Rebecca Wilson, w. r. s., 138th, Greene.*
169 William Donaldson, Kellum's, Talbot.
170 Jeremiah Ivey, Williams's, Walton.*
171 Samuel Holliman, r. s., Dozier's, Columbia.*
172 Sarah Jones, w., of Chatham, 124th, Richmond.*
173 Abraham B. Ragan, Curry's, Merriwether.*
174 William H. Edwards, Clark's, Elbert.
175 Allen Dinmons, sol., Wilson's, Pike.
176 Francis Darsey, Harris's, Columbia.
177 Martha Russell, w., Grider's, Morgan.
178 Willis Thrower, 80th, Scriven.*
179 Hiram Vaughters, Chandler's, Franklin.
180 Thomas S. Twiss, 120th, Richmond.*
181 Mordecai Brown's ors., r. s., Bishop's, Henry.
182 Tabitha Milton, w. of sol., Echols's, Walton.

21

183 James Patillo, sol., House's, Henry.*
184 Silas Worley, M'Clure's, Rabun.*
185 Micajah Martin, Mobley's, De Kalb.
186 Samuel D. Durham, 138th, Greene.
187 Charles Hook's ors., Vining's, Putnam.*
188 James R. Bluster, f. a., Butts's, Monroe.
189 Solomon Lockett, or., Mays's, Monroe.
190 John Arnold, Jr., 116th, Hancock.*
191 John S. Littlefield's ors., Barron's, Houston.
192 Hiram Potts, Jones's, Habersham.
193 Michael Hincle, 761st, Heard.*
194 John Shaddox, Silman's, Pike.*
195 Isaac Dixon, Sanders's, Jones.*
196 Jonathan Jewett, 398th, Richmond.*
197 Thomas Lasley, 672d, Harris.
198 Voilet Reed, w., Dobbs's, Hall.
199 Lovick P. Clements, Hines's, Coweta.*
200 Henry Mills, 122d, Richmond.*
201 Thomas Cook, Sen., sol., Gray's, Henry.
202 Norman J. Sinquilliat, 271st, M'Intosh.*
203 James Holmes, sol., Johnson's, Bibb.
204 Jesse Crummey, Hand's, Appling.
205 James H. Shic, Clark's, Morgan.
206 William H. Campbell, Ballard's, Morgan.
207 William Bridges, Harris's, Butts.
208 Charles W. Boyce, 454th, Walton.*
209 Tobias Burgamy, Garner's, Washington.*
210 Wesley King, Whipple's, Wilkinson.
211 James Davis, sol., Roberts's, Hall.*
212 James Wadsworth, r. s., Davis's, Jones.*
213 Noah H. Griffin, Blair's, Lowndes.*
214 Edmund Brown, Allen's, Henry.*
215 William M'Burnett, Greer's, Merriwether.
216 John Bledsoe, 146th, Greene.*
217 Mary Daniel, w. r. s., Mason's, Washington.*
218 Martin Owens, 588th, Upson.
219 John Griffiths's ors., 53d, Emanuel.*
220 James Pace, sol., Harp's, Stewart.
221 Joshua Davis, Coward's, Lowndes.
222 Elisha Wells, Maguire's, Gwinnett.
223 James Morrison's ors., Valleau's, Chatham.
224 James S. Tison, sol., 735th, Troup.
225 George W. Dunham, 15th, Liberty.
226 William D. King, 176th, Wilkes.
227 Bartemas Jaseph, 600th, Richmond.
228 John B. Harkness, Berry's, Butts.*
229 James Bevil, 192d, Elbert.

230 Wilson Collins, Hudson's, Marion.
231 Helena M'Whorter, w., Howard's, Oglethorpe.
232 David S. Files, Whitaker's, Crawford.*
233 Wyatt Whatley, sol., M'Korkle's, Jasper.
234 David Laughren, Winter's, Jones.*
235 Thomas Jones, 365th, Jasper.
236 Nimrod Roberts, Shattox's, Coweta.
237 James Fitzgerald, Harp's, Stewart.
238 Daniel Southerland, Sen., Welche's, Habersham.
239 George W. Varner, Frasier's, Monroe.
240 John S. Reeves, 36th, Scriven.
241 Calvin Stricklin, Allen's, Campbell.
242 John M'Lelion, Southwell's, Tatnall.
243 Edward Burch, r. s., Dilmon's, Pulaski.
244 Robert Creamer, Crow's, Pike.
245 Woody B. Smith, 406th, Gwinnett.
246 Joseph Miller, Peterson's, Montgomery.
247 Washington White, Strickland's, Merriwether.
248 Ezekiel S. Candler, or., 588th, Upson.*
249 Ashley W. Street, Edwards's, Talbot.*
250 Robert Adams's ors., Robinson's, Putnam.*
251 Jesse Bullard, Lawrence's, Pike.*
252 Moses Roberts, 243d, Jackson.
253 John Cupps, or., Chambers's, Gwinnett.
254 Elijah Edwards, Dobbs's, Hall.
255 John W. Almand, Howell's, Elbert.*
256 James Brown, Walker's, Houston.*
257 George K. Chatham, Robinson's, Harris.*
258 John G. Fry, s. l. w., Atkinson's, Coweta.*
259 William L. Caldwell, Wynn's, Gwinnett.
260 Robert Nelson Adams, Wilcox's, Telfair.
261 Timothy Alderman, Summerlin's, Bulloch.
262 Eli B. W. Spivy, Moffett's, Muscogee.
263 Nancy Leyon, or., Jones's, Thomas.
264 Isaac N. Young, Chambers's, Gwinnett.*
265 Cluff Martin's ors., Colley's, Oglethorpe.
266 Eliza and H. Boswell, ors., Tompkins's, Putnam.
267 Henry Mitchell, 3d section, Cherokee.
268 Samuel Densmore, Brock's, Habersham.*
269 Charlotte A. Wright, w., Marshall's, Putnam.*
270 James M. Putnam, Kendrick's, Monroe.
271 Amon Cobb, 601st, Taliaferro.
272 Wiley Dudley, Smith's, Madison.
273 Hezekiah Cockran, Chastain's, Habersham.
274 Jesse Hyott, 588th, Upson.*
275 Roscoe Edmunds, Hargrove's, Newton.*
276 Stephen D. Mayo, M'Linn's, Butts.

277 James Hinton, Strickland's, Merriwether.
278 George Patterson, Whelchel's, Hall.ᵌ
279 Sarah Davidson, w., Allison's, Pike.
280 Joseph Moles, 6th, Chatham.
281 Richard C. Bowen, sol., Chastain's, Habersham.
282 Archibald T. Moss, Stanton's, Newton.*
283 William Handley, Jr., Mitchell's, Pulaski.*
284 John A. Mattox, Brewton's, Tatnall.*
285 Joseph Scott, Allison's, Pike.*
286 Thomas Farrow, M'Ewin's, Monroe.*
287 Grey Harrell, Rutland's, Bibb.
288 John G. Barnett, Derrick's, Henry.
289 Orlando Sheppard's ors., Brown's, Walton.
290 Francis Nunn, Newsom's, Warren.*
291 John Bates, Sen., Whelchel's, Hall.*
292 David H. Culberson, Stewart's, Troup.*
293 Jordan Adams, Howard's, Oglethorpe.*
294 William Freeman, Alsobrook's, Jones.*
295 Tabithy Stewart, w. r. s., 34th, Scriven.*
296 Zebulon Howard, Graves's, Lincoln.*
297 William Cleveland, Hughes's, Habersham.
298 Solomon Crider, deaf, Edwards's, Franklin.
299 William Hawkins, Martin's, Jones.
300 William Jones's ors., Greer's, Warren.
301 Thomas B. Martin, Robinson's, Harris.*
302 John Spann, Williams's, Decatur.
303 Johnathan Seckenger, 10th, Effingham.*
304 Frances Huggens, w., 122d, Richmond.*
305 Henry Wimberly, Rutland's, Bibb.*
306 Samuel Brady, r. s., Watson's, Marion.*
307 Daniel Freeman, sol., 289th, Jasper.*
308 John R. Green, Gray's, Henry.*
309 William C. Gilham, Howard's, Oglethorpe.
310 James Haston, Blount's, Wilkinson.*
311 John A. Wallis, Maguire's, Gwinnett.*
312 Gilliam Preston's ors., Hearn's, Butts.
313 D. H. Reid, orphan of A. Reid, Estes's, Putnam.*
314 Littleton P. Mackey's ors., Hampton's, Newton.
315 William Turner, Sen., Collins's, Henry.
316 John Strickland, Barker's, Gwinnett.*
317 Elizabeth Shropshire, w., Coxe's, Talbot.*
318 Edmund Franklin, Moffett's, Muscogee.*
319 Jones Kendrick, sol., 174th, Wilkes.*
320 Joseph Allen, Chandler's, Franklin.
321 Hillery Atkins, Chambers's, Gwinnett.*
322 Samuel Nunn, Walker's, Harris.*
323 Alvis Stafford, 588th, Upson.*
324 John W. Griffin, Cleggs's, Walton.*

24th DISTRICT, SECOND SECTION, CHEROKEE.

1 Reason A. Bell, Hill's, Stewart.*
2 Martin Wells's ors., Newman's, Thomas.*
3 Frederic E. Brooking, 118th, Hancock.
4 Lucy and Eliz. Goulding, ors., Howell's, Elbert.*
5 Owen W. Owen, 307th, Putnam.
6 Thomas Denny, sol., Smith's, Madison.*
7 Fauntleroy Lewis, sol., 117th, Hancock.*
8 Clara Harris, w. r. s., Talley's, Troup.*
9 William Webb, Martin's, Hall.*
10 Moses Smith's ors., 693d, Heard.
11 John M'Right, Allen's, Henry.
12 John Henderson, Atkinson's, Coweta.
13 Joshua Hall, Bridges's, Gwinnett.
14 Isaac Highsmith, Jr., 335th, Wayne.*
15 William Bird, 9th, Effingham.
16 James King, Hammond's, Franklin.
17 Susannah Gray, w. r. s., Clark's, Elbert.
18 William M. Harper, Head's, Butts.
19 Elijah Wallis, 177th, Randolph.
20 Daniel J. Amos, 101st, Hancock.
21 David Carr, Parham's, Warren.*
22 John Burk, Jr., Whisenhunt's, Carroll.
23 Robert Jenkins, Stewart's, Troup.
24 Francis Foster, sol., Harralson's, Troup.
25 Erasmus G. Marable, Baley's, Butts.
26 Etheldred Harrel, Sen., r. s., M'Daniel's, Pulaski.
27 James Wilcox, Candler's, Bibb.*
28 Jesse Locke, 271st, M'Intosh.
29 Archibald Kendrick, Gorley's, Putnam.
30 Ira Neal, Camp's, Warren.
31 Thomas J. Floyd, Walden's, Pulaski.
32 John Buckner's ors., Bryan's, Monroe.
33 Jeptha V. Reynolds, Kendrick's, Monroe.*
34 James W. Coleman, Hatton's, Baker.
35 Thomas Maxwell, Seas's, Madison.*
36 Evenezer S. Rees, 271st, M'Intosh.*
37 Francis M. Evans, Hodges's, Newton.
38 Asa Linch, Parham's, Harris.
39 Thomas Sinson, sol., Wallis's, Irwin.*
40 Mary Carroll, w. r. s., 167th, Wilkes.*
41 Emanuel H. Moomaugh, 245th, Jackson.

42 Jesse Hurst, 260th, Scriven.*
43 Benjamin Lowry, 415th, Walton.
44 Elijah Kent, Hatchett's, Oglethorpe.*
45 Jeremiah Wallis, White's, Franklin.
46 Thomas Scoggins, s. i. w., Coker's, Troup.
47 Isaac Williams, Perry's, Habersham.
48 Moses Presley, Nichols's, Fayette.
49 Mayor Ellis, Williams's, Washington.
50 Cary Greenwood, w., Brown's, Habersham.
51 Jesse M'Minn, Stephens's, Habersham.
52 Joshua Fincher, Howell's, Troup.
53 Isaac T. Moreland, Gunn's, Jones.
54 Benjamin Vaughan, Hanner's, Campbell.
55 S. Kenneday, s. l. w., Robison's, Washington.*
56 Beniah King, Bishop's, Henry.
57 John M. W. Peel, Hannah's, Jefferson.*
58 Valentine Colton, Candler's, Bibb.
59 Isaiah Depew, Herndon's, Hall.
60 Jesse Williams, Say's, De Kalb.
61 Fleet Hall, Will's, Twiggs.
62 Henry Lamb, Oliver's, Twiggs.*
63 Priscilla Nottage, w., Summerlin's, Bulloch.*
64 Henry H. Redding's ors., 80th, Scriven.
65 Henry Brewer's ors., Bailey's, Laurens.
66 Thomas Heath's ors., Williams's, Jasper.
67 Rebecca Derracott, w. r. s., Canning's, Elbert.*
68 Joshua Griffin, Chiles's, Marion.
69 James Griffith, Jordan's, Bibb.*
70 John Y. Allgood, 3d section, Cherokee.*
71 Margaret Wooley, w., Daniel's, Hall.
72 Sarah Fleming, w. s. i. w., Seal's, Elbert.
73 Merida Kendrick, s. l. w., Kendrick's, Putnam.*
74 Jesse Fowler, Wood's, Jefferson.*
75 John M. Secrest, or., Maguire's, Morgan.*
76 William Roberts, Madden's, Pike.*
77 Sampson Wilder, sol., Parham's, Warren.*
78 Arthur M. Taylor, Barrow's, Houston.
79 Abner Temples, Hudson's, Marion.*
80 William Pearre's ors., Harris's, Columbia.
81 Simeon Hammock, 177th, Wilkes.*
82 William M'G. Williams, Stewart's, Troup.
83 Andrew L. Smith, M'Culler's, Newton.
84 Frederic Ward, 307th, Putnam.
85 Loami Powell, mi., 633d, Dooly.*
86 John M'Duffee, Griffin's, Merriwether.
87 James G. Smith, 320th, Baldwin.
88 John Saxon, 3d section, Cherokee.

89 William H. Bush, Curry's, Wilkinson.
90 James Head, Sen., sol., 277th, Morgan.
91 James Isbell, Royster's, Franklin.
92 William R. Walker, 163d, Greene.*
93 Andrew Hancock, Allen's, Campbell.
94 William Campbell, Hall's, Oglethorpe.
95 Joseph Jones's ors., Blount's, Wilkinson.
96 Robert Seal's ors., M'Dowell's, Lincoln.
97 James Wimberly, sol., Pounds's, Twiggs.
98 James Johnson's ors., O'Neal's, Laurens.
99 John Speights, 117th, Hancock.
100 Jesse Patridge, Braddy's, Jones.
101 Charles Horton, Jr., Hughes's, Habersham.
102 John A. Gisert, Candler's, Bibb.
103 John Willf, Sen., Henson's, Rabun.
104 Richard Kenon, Sen., Hampton's, Newton.*
105 Johannah Sheerhouse, w., 9th, Effingham.*
106 Sherrod Brown, Evans's, Fayette.*
107 Hugh Porter, Daniel's, Hall.
108 William W. Davenport, Green's, Oglethorpe.
109 James Fiveash, Morrison's, Appling.*
110 Henry Hammock, Sullivan's, Jones.*
111 Archibald M'Eachin, Candler's, Bibb.*
112 Rebecca Ingram, w., Jones's, Madison.*
113 Jane Gant, w., Hobkerk's, Camden.
114 Joseph Buchannon, Morrison's, Montgomery.
115 Hayle Cronick, 417th, Walton.
116 Michael Spann, sol., Fitzpatrick's, Chatham.
117 Howell Frales, M'Gehee's, Troup.
118 John Abney, Miller's, Jackson.*
119 James Fleming's ors., 320th, Baldwin.
120 William S. Johnston, 279th, Morgan.
121 John T. Roper, Reid's, Gwinnett.
122 Colby R. Jackson, Tuggle's, Merriwether.
123 George Gorton, 600th, Richmond.
124 Benjamin B. Crawford, Kelly's, Jasper.
125 William Spears, 702d, Heard.
126 Jacob Stillwell, r. s., 735th, Troup.
127 Millington Musgrove, Jones's, Lincoln.
128 Angus Shaw, Cook's, Telfair.
129 George J. Bogan, Mitchell's, Marion.
130 Thomas M'Gullion's ors., Herndon's, Hall.
131 Tarrence Bryan, sol., Edwards's, Franklin.
132 William Morris, Coker's, Troup.
133 Absalom T. Tatom, Talley's, Troup.
134 Charles Warden, s. l. w., Coxe's, Franklin.
135 Richard Strickland, Jr., Higginbotham's, Madison

136 William Bennefield, Martin's, Newton.*
137 John Sanders, r. s., Griffin's, De Kalb.
138 William L. Justiss, 419th, Walton.*
139 Phillips Laney, Colquhoun's, Henry.
140 George Wyche, sol., Peterson's, Montgomery.
141 Daniel Grant, 73d, Burke.*
142 William Holly, Park's, Walton.*
143 John M'Gilvary, Shearer's, Coweta.
144 Janders Stallings, sol., Moffett's, Muscogee.
145 John Tate, Jr., 2d section, Cherokee.
146 Elisha K. Davis, Stephens's, Habersham.
147 Jane Cannon, f. a., Davis's, Gwinnett.
148 Leonard Walker, 123d, Richmond.*
149 David Crumpton's ors., Boynton's, Twiggs.
150 James Hodges, Burnett's, Habersham.
151 James A. Head, Martin's, Hall.
152 John M. Boggs, Smith's, Campbell.
153 Thomas Howard, Givens's, De Kalb.
154 Randol M'Donald, 2d section, Cherokee.
155 Nancy Grice, w., Rainey's, Twiggs.
156 William Green, 271st, M'Intosh.*
157 Addison's five children, f. a., Alberson's, Walton.
158 Rachel L. Conner, w., 25th, Scriven.
159 Benjamin F. Harris, Mays's, Monroe.
160 William Spradley, 271st, M'Intosh.*
161 Andrew Tucker's or., Burnett's, Lowndes.*
162 Francis Jones, Cliett's, Columbia.*
163 Hiram Davis, Peavy's, Bulloch.*
164 Rachel Adrian, w., Coxe's, Franklin.
165 Robert Brown, sol., 373d, Jasper.
166 John Rutherford, Will's, Twiggs.
167 Archibald Buye, 35th, Scriven.
168 Jeptha Strickland, sol., 116th, Hancock.
169 James Hodnett, Talley's, Troup.
170 William C. Parks, M'Gill's, Lincoln.*
171 John Hodgekirk's ors., Ogeechee, Chatham.
172 Jacob Hersman, 3d, Chatham.
173 John Young, Merck's, Hall.
174 John Haupt, Jr., Cleland's, Chatham.
175 Henry H. Watterson, 243d, Jackson.*
176 Edmund Heard, 600th, Richmond.*
177 Clarissa C. Boyd, w., 365th, Jasper.*
178 William Scogen, 140th, Greene.*
179 Matilda Cannon, h. a., Davis's, Gwinnett.
180 Oliver Johnson, Dean's, De Kalb.
181 Ezekiel P. Ware, 406th, Gwinnett.*
182 Stephen Hammock, Hampton's, Newton.

183 George S. Butler, Smith's, Elbert.*
184 Elizabeth Jourdan, w. r. s., Camp's, Warren.
185 William Magourick, sol., Crow's, Merriwether.
186 Mary Callahand, w., 535th, Dooly.
187 Mason Chambler, Miller's, Jackson.*
188 George Stephens, sol., Stanfield's, Campbell.
189 Andrew Hammel, t., Ellsworth's, Bibb.
190 Shadrack Ellis, r. s., Coxe's, Talbot.*
191 Edmund Camp's ors., 249th, Walton.
192 Leroy W. Hicks, Mann's, Crawford.
193 David Lawson's ors., Gorley's, Putnam.
194 Martin Shuman, 19th, Bryan.*
195 Asa Holloway's ors., Bragaw's, Oglethorpe.
196 John M. Norris, Calhoun's, Harris.
197 James S. Thompson, Tuggle's, Merriwether
198 John H. Smith, Edwards's, Talbot.
199 James Gamage, Taylor's, Jones.
200 Jamima Alderman, w., Summerlin's, Bulloch.
201 James King, 398th, Richmond.*
202 Hampton H. Howard, Walker's, Houston.
203 Amos Wagoner, s. l. w., Taylor's, Putnam.*
204 Needham Freeman, Jones's, Habersham.
205 Vinson Jones, Taylor's, Putnam.
206 Mary Horne, 57th, Emanuel.*
207 James S. Bishop's ors., Bishop's, Henry.
208 William H. Stone, Dearing's, Butts.
209 Enoch Roe, 510th, Early.
210 Spencer Taylor, Welche's, Habersham.
211 James Shaw, Peurifoy's, Henry.
212 Thomas Hudnett, Hodges's, Newton.*
213 Drewry Glover, Hicks's, Decatur.*
214 Nancy Gilbert, w., 374th, Putnam.
215 Martin F. Fordham, Hobbs's, Laurens.
216 John Watson's ors., Atkinson's, Coweta.
217 William B. Woodruff, 406th, Gwinnett.*
218 George Elrod, Whelchel's, Hall.*
219 Esau Brooks, Tower's, Gwinnett.*
220 William Tucker, Hutson's, Newton.*
221 Benjamin F. Liles, Grubbs's, Columbia.*
222 William Crawford, sol., Mays's, Monroe.*
223 David M'Intosh's ors., Wood's, Morgan.*
224 Joseph Eller, Anderson's, Rabun.
225 Elisha Norris, sol., Hamilton's, Hall.
226 John Barnett, 404th, Gwinnett.
227 James Bowdon, r. s., Hill's, Monroe.
228 Riley Collins, Willingham's, Harris.
229 Benjamin H. Lamkin, Chambers's, Gwinnett.

230 William H. Coe's ors., Cleland's, Chatham.
231 Fanny Gafford, w., Campbell's, Wilkes.*
232 Daniel Redenhour, Few's, Muscogee.
233 Philip Roots Thompson, 398th, Richmond.*
234 William Taynor, Stower's, Elbert.
235 Eldridge Kenney, Athens, Clarke.
236 Frederic Hicks, sol., Walker's, Harris.
237 Joshua P. Shopshire, Ware's, Coweta.
238 Jesse J. Hayden, or., 245th, Jackson.
239 John Mingledorf, sol., 72d, Burke.
240 Anderson Covington, Covington's, Pike.
241 Elam C. Bardich, Blackshear's, Laurens.
242 John Ogle, Atkinson's, Coweta.
243 Daniel Carroll, Newman's, Thomas.
244 Benjamin P. Rouse, Hutson's, Marion.
245 John Henderson, Jones's, Hall.
246 Daniel Lee, M'Culler's, Newton.*
247 George P. Fellows, Athens, Clarke.
248 Thomas Adcock, Foote's, De Kalb.*
249 Cornelius Collins, sol., Grubbs's, Columbia.
250 John Bledsoe, 146th, Greene.*
251 Hardy Jurnagin, Hatton's, Baker.
252 Madison Humphries, Gridon's, Morgan.*
253 William T. Burnes, 37th, Scriven.
254 Elijah Bradshaw, Wolfskin's, Oglethorpe.*
255 Sarah Jackson, w., Collins's, Henry.*
256 William P. Beasley, 368th, Jasper.
257 William Aikin, Baley's, Butts.
258 Kinchen Rambo, Chambers's, Gwinnett.*
259 Josiah Beall, 561st, Upson.
260 William G. Sims, Hargrove's, Oglethorpe.
261 Thomas Heath, Collier's, Monroe.*
262 John Evans, Sen., 606th, Taliaferro.
263 Elijah Shaw's ors., Lay's, Jackson.
264 Willis Wilder, Chambers's, Gwinnett.
265 Lingsey's 6 children, f. a., Smith's, Houston.
266 John H. Fuller, Harralson's, Troup.*
267 Eben T. Elliott, Hughes's, Habersham.
268 James A. Clifford, wid'r., Valleau's, Chatham.*
269 Edward Curd, 788th, Heard.
270 George W. Blair, Ellis's, Rabun.*
271 James Dougherty, Tankersley's, Columbia.*
272 Caswell Haddock, 319th, Baldwin.
273 Isam Hancock, r. s., Welche's, Habersham.
274 Edward O. Sheffield, 535th, Dooly.*
275 William Whitehead, 242d, Jackson.
276 John William Young, sol., Chiles's, Marion.

277 Harriet D. Conyers, or., Craven's, Coweta.
278 Francis Hester, Jack's, Clark.
279 Duncan G. Camron, Sewell's, Franklin.
280 Spirus Stanley, 118th, Hancock.*
281 Albin Ryland, Downs's, Warren.
282 Micajah L. Hines, Marshall's, Putnam.
283 John J. Higgins, Brock's, Habersham.
284 Andrew Mirick, Newman's, Thomas.*
285 David Wright's seven ors., Gillis's, De Kalb.
286 Cordy Bachellor, 162d, Greene.*
287 Anselm Bridges, Shearer's, Coweta.
288 Enoch Beesley, Lockhart's, Bulloch.*
289 Henry Skipper, 788th, Heard.
290 Atheldred Newburn, sol., Mattox's, Lowndes.*
291 John Lewis's ors., Parham's, Warren.
292 Cowart's five orphans, Hargrove's, Newton.
293 Benjamin Haile, Elder's, Clarke.*
294 Rebecca Leftwick, w., Maguire's, Morgan.
295 Jane Maloy, h. a., Brown's, Habersham.*
296 Jane E. Postell, w., Valleau's, Chatham.*
297 Sinah Williams, w., Barker's, Gwinnett.
298 Thomas Faver, 166th, Wilkes.
299 James S. Harvey, Durham's, Talbot.
300 Henry W. Stewart, Allen's, Henry.
301 Thomas Hill, Lawrence's, Pike.
302 Samuel Hillhouse, Jones's, Hall.
303 Mary Cone, w., 318th, Baldwin.*
304 Aaron Robinson's ors., Bostick's, Twiggs.
305 Braxton P. Smith, Mimms's, Fayette.
306 Henry Burnes, Wynn's, Gwinnett.
307 Joshua Agee, 177th, Wilkes.*
308 Moses Beesley, Burnett's, Lowndes.
309 John M. Legrand, r. s., Nellum's, Elbert.*
310 John Sanders, 1st section, Cherokee.
311 Mary Moore, w., 105th, Baldwin.
312 Luraney Luker, w. r. s., Arrington's, Merriwether.
313 Martha Lawson, w. r. s., Whipple's, Wilkinson.
314 Augustin Reed, Lay's, Jackson.
315 Henry M'Millian, Jones's, Habersham.*
316 George Stewart, 2d section, Cherokee.
317 J. G. & B. A. Hardin, ors., Crow's, Merriwether.
318 John Lawrence's ors., Barwick's, Washington.
319 Joshua Broughton, Dearing's, Henry.
320 Mary F. Scott, or., 27th, Glynn.*
321 Thomas J. Payne, Trout's, Hall.
322 Michael O. Barr, Sen., Griffin's, Hall.
323 William Holder, Wood's, Jefferson.
324 Henry Freeman, sol., Hammond's, Franklin.

25th DISTRICT, SECOND SECTION, CHEROKEE.

1 Neal Harkins, Candler's, Bibb.
2 Robert Rushton's ors., 788th, Heard.
3 Susan Osmer, w., Chisholm's, Morgan.*
4 Loami Brown, r. s., 535th, Dooly.*
5 Richard Woodruff, Norman's, Wilkes.
6 Andrew Lott, Trout's, Hall.
7 John Gillis, Peterson's, Montgomery.*
8 Lewis D. W. Smith, Hearn's, Butts.
9 James Austin, 250th, Walton.
10 Jesse Williams, Say's, De Kalb.
11 Lovick P. M'Donald, Harralson's, Troup.
12 Henry John Tallis, Fitzpatrick's, Chatham.*
13 Joseph Higgins, Hearn's, Butts.
14 John Gilbert, Seas's, Madison.*
15 Alexander W. Willey, 271st, M'Intosh.*
16 Peter Adams, Hill's, Stewart.
17 Thomas Hickson, 362d, Jasper.
18 Benoni T. Harrison, Parham's, Warren.
19 William Poore's or., 466th, Monroe.
20 Margaret England, w. r. s., Brock's, Habersham.
21 Ebenezer Nelson, Brooks's, Muscogee.
22 Hilliard J. Perkin's or., Atkinson's, Coweta.
23 Jesse Richardson, r. s., Barnett's, Habersham.*
24 Henry Coon, sol., Griffin's, Merriwether.*
25 John H. Dyson, Moseley's, Wilkes.
26 John M'Dermed, M'Craney's, Lowndes.*
27 Jesse Veasey, Jr., 142d, Greene.*
28 Madison C. Davis, Hines's, Coweta.*
29 John H. Howard, Hinton's, Wilkes.*
30 Robert Colquitt, r. s., ———, Oglethorpe.*
31 William Kent, Ballard's, Morgan.*
32 Silas Grubbs, 373d, Jasper.
33 Jordan Webb, Dean's, De Kalb.*
34 John Webb, s. l. w., Mason's, Washington.*
35 John Wisenbaker, 9th, Effingham.*
36 John M. Godley, Hammock's, Jasper.
37 George W. Stamps, Bridges's, Gwinnett.
38 David Chesnut, Chesnut's, Newton.*
39 Parker Slay, Smith's, Elbert.*
40 Philip H. Wyatt, Tuggle's, Merriwether.*
41 Merphy Jump, Mitchell's, Pulaski.*

42 Abda White, Thompson's, Henry.*
43 James Dowdell, sol., Willingham's, Harris.*
44 Uriah Ammons's ors., Wood's, Morgan.*
45 Sarah Bosworth, w., Few's, Muscogee.*
46 Nathan Singletery, Wilcox's, Telfair.*
47 Margaret Herms, w., 2d, Chatham.*
48 John T. Akins, Jones's, Morgan.*
49 John P. Floyd, Morgan's, Madison.*
50 James Harrison, Hall's, Butts.*
51 James Henderson, Thomason's, Elbert.*
52 Thomas Orr, Roberts's, Hall.
53 Isaac Stanford, Whitaker's, Crawford.*
54 John Linsey, Whitfield's, Washington.*
55 John F. Stewart, Hargrove's, Newton.*
56 Allen N. Lightfoot, Perryman's, Warren.
57 Edwin Mercer, Linam's, Pulaski.*
58 Benjamin Brantley's ors., Hobbs's, Laurens.*
59 Anselm Evans, sol., Flynn's, Muscogee.*
60 Joseph Glover, sol., Candler's, Bibb.
61 Gabriel Childs, Sanders's, Jones.*
62 John Keith, Will's, Twiggs.
63 Nancy G. Doggett, id., 293d, Jasper.
64 Azariah Pogue, Walker's, Harris.
65 John M'Konky, White's, Franklin.
66 Christopher Smith, Higginbotham's, Rabun.
67 Peter J. Thiess, Young's, Carroll.*
68 Jesse M'Clendon, 734th, Lee.
69 Azariah Cowart, 72d, Burke.
70 Isaac Campbell, sol., 335th, Wayne.*
71 John Barton, r. s., Martin's, Hall.
72 David Lasseter, Peace's, Wilkinson.
73 David M'Daniel, Hargrove's, Newton.
74 Edward W. Gill, 458th, Early.
75 William Jenkins, Willingham's, Harris.
76 Samuel White, Perry's, Baldwin.*
77 Isaac Brown, Butts's, Monroe.
78 William Hall, Thompson's, Henry.*
79 Aaron Roper, Herndon's, Hall.
80 John Smith, Night's, Morgan.
81 Henry West, Will's, Twiggs.
82 Reuben Blalock, 588th, Upson.
83 Isum Reese, 466th, Monroe.*
84 Lewis W. Rosser, Underwood's, Putnam.*
85 Samuel Foster, Anderson's, Rabun.*
86 Moses Link, Field's, Habersham.*
87 Jesse Brown, Thames, Crawford.*
88 William W. Young, 756th, Sumter.*

89 Newberry Elrod, Jones's, Habersham.*
90 John Jones's ors., Mays's, Monroe.
91 Alexander Cabeen, 537th, Upson.*
92 Matthew Duncan, Shattox's, Coweta.*
93 David Langston, Harris's, Columbia.*
94 Edmund Bagg's ors., Few's, Muscogee.
95 Nancy Culver, w. r. s., 111th Hancock.*
96 William L. Connally, Jones's, Madison.
97 Isham Ethridge, Davis's, Jones.*
98 Hays Bowdre, s. l. w., 398th, Richmond.*
99 James Chapman. Wilson's, Pike.*
100 John Lawless, Chastain's, Habersham.
101 Drius Burns, Silman's, Pike.*
102 James Wilson, 142d, Greene.
103 William W. Johns, Wright's, Tatnall.
104 David Woodruff, Norman's, Wilkes.
105 William H. Underwood, sol., Price's, Hall.
106 Mary Mappin, w. r. s., Dozier's, Columbia.*
107 Thomas Carlton, Newman's, Thomas.*
108 Hiram Carter, Perry's, Baldwin.*
109 Samuel Desheroon, sol., R. Brown's, Habersham.
110 Solomon Ray, Griffin's, Merriwether.
111 James Reddew, Burnett's, Habersham.
112 Lucandes Jackson, w., Grier's, Warren.
113 John Harrell, s. i. w., Hicks's, Decatur.*
114 William Daniell, sol. 1784–97, 55th, Emanuel.
115 Mary Smith, w., Will's, Twiggs.
116 Barbara M'Daniel, w., Nichols's, Fayette.
117 Isaac M'Bee's five ors., Dean's, De Kalb.
118 John May, 756th, Sumter.*
119 James B. Darracatt, 601st, Taliaferro.*
120 John Churchwell, Streetman's, Twiggs.
121 Mary Gullett, w., Burnett's, Habersham.*
122 Joel P. Sayers, Greer's, Merriwether.
123 Asa C. Hardin, 404th, Gwinnett.*
124 Joshua Lee, Blount's, Wilkinson.*
125. David Walker, 103d, Hancock.*
126 James G. Park's ors., Hitchcock's, Muscogee.
127 Thomas Simmons, William's, Ware.
128 Miner Mead, r. s., Whisenhunt's, Carroll.
129 Richard King, Kendrick's, Monroe.
130 Washington Thompson, Braddy's, Jones.*
131 Champ Mariable, sol., Belcher's, Jasper.
132 Luke Hendrix, Whelchel's, Hall.
133 John Jackson's ors., Covington's, Pike.
134 Nancy Wilson, w., Rutland's, Bibb.
135 William F. Young, Morris's, Crawford.

136 Martha Whaley, w., Pate's, Warren.
137 Thomas Macklin, Perry's, Baldwin.*
138 Henry C. Smith, Fryer's, Telfair.*
139 Nehemiah Guthrie, 417th, Walton.
140 Susannah Monk, w. r. s., Kendrick's, Putnam.*
141 William Streatman, Sen., Newman's, Thomas.*
142 Mager Night, Loveless's, Gwinnett.
143 Joseph Ganahl, Valleau's, Chatham.
144 Andrew M. Reeks, M'Culler's, Newton.
145 Peter Yates, Lamberth's, Fayette.
146 Allen Glover, Robinson's, Harris.
147 William A. Muncreef, 146th, Greene.*
148 Sarah Jones, w., Foote's, De Kalb.
149 Noah Scarborough, sol., Goodwin's, Houston
150 William Randle's ors., Clark's, Morgan.
151 Joseph S. M'Guire, Orr's, Jackson.
152 James Wilson, 34th, Scriven.*
153 Elizabeth Farris, d. & d., M'Clain's, Newton.
154 Green Whiddon, Barwick's, Washington.*
155 James Buckelew, s. l. w., 512th, Lee.*
156 Thomas G. Frazier, 307th, Putnam.
157 Thomas Turner, Jr., Gittens's, Fayette.
158 Barnett Slatham, M'Dowell's, Lincoln.*
159 Henry Strickland, Hobbs's, Laurens.
160 John P. Keaton, Smith's, Liberty.
161 John W. Roundtree, 34th, Scriven.*
162 Eli Tollison, Johnson's, De Kalb.
163 John Dugger, Groover's, Thomas.
164 A. and S. Dillard, ors., 70th, Burke.
165 John Cockerell, Hargrove's, Newton.*
166 Wilson Shipman, Stephens's, Habersham.
167 William R. Sayre's ors., Sanders's, Jones.
168 Thomas A. Latham, Smith's, Campbell.
169 Drury Dunn, Bragaw's, Oglethorpe.
170 Andrew Doming, Cannon's, Wilkinson.
171 Charlotte Lockhart, w. r. s., Brewer's, Monroe.
172 Allen Martin, Davis's, Gwinnett.
173 Philemon Hodges, r. s., Few's, Muscogee.
174 William Burton, 192d, Elbert.*
175 Elizabeth Page, h. a., Stower's, Elbert.*
176 Susannah Simpson, w., Young's, Wilkinson.
177 Frances Colston, w., M'Gillis's, Lincoln.*
178 Elizabeth Thorp, w., 101st, Hancock.
179 Blanton F. Thornton, Guice's, Oglethorpe.
180 John Grubbs, Bridges's, Gwinnett.
181 Mary Williams, w., Sam Streetman's, Twiggs.
182 Jacob Gilder, s. i. w., Bustin's, Pike.*

183 James Fould, r. s., Smith's, Wilkinson.
184 Benjamin Odell, Keener's, Rabun.
185 Benjamin F. Land, Williams's, Decatur.
186 Solloman Wethers, M'Gill's, Lincoln.
187 William Clines, Walker's, Houston.*
188 Obadiah Miller, 404th, Gwinnett.
189 John Bitterton, sol., House's, Henry.
190 James C. Hoy, Perry's, Baldwin.
191 William Scott, Atkinson's, Coweta.*
192 Samuel Weldon, 118th, Hancock.*
193 Youngsett Dindy, Lawrence's, Pike.*
194 Haley Butler, sol., Lunceford's, Elbert.
195 William Jackson, Sen., Hughes's, Habersham.*
196 Peter Verdell, sol., Liberty Island, Chatham.*
197 Frederic B. Proctor, Curry's, Merriwether.*
198 James Reddew, sol., Burnett's, Habersham.
199 Colsbey Smith, r. s., Peacock's, Washington.
200 Daniel Cline, Ellis's, Rabun.
201 William Daniell, s. l. w., 55th, Emanuel.
202 Martha Boling, Perry's, Habersham.
203 William Binion's ors., Bell's, Columbia.
204 Jane Ray, w. r. s., Durham's, Talbot.
205 Hiram Hemphill, 245th, Jackson.
206 Ezekiel Thomas, Douglass's, Telfair.*
207 George H. Purdon, Brock's, Habersham.
208 Howell Mathis, 732d, Dooly.
209 Mary Mophfitt, w. r. s., Tuggle's, Merriwether.*
210 William H. Garnett, Reid's, Gwinnett.*
211 John R. Hunt, sol., Rainey's, Twiggs.*
212 Jeremiah Hammock, 177th, Wilkes.
213 James A. Wiggins, Dupree's, Washington.
214 Nathaniel W. A. Harris, Baismore's, Jones.*
215 Richard T. Sankey, 143d, Greene.*
216 Nancy Brown, w., Lane's, Morgan.
217 Andrew Havens, sol., Marsh's, Thomas.*
218 Thomas J. King, Underwood's, Putnam.
219 William Foster, Sen., s. i. w., Thaxton's, Butts.
220 Dempsey Baker, Jr., Jordan's, Bibb.*
221 Nancy Wiggins, Dean's, Clarke.*
222 Elijah Meadows, 602d, Taliaferro.
223 Lemuel G. Dawson, 588th, Upson.
224 Joseph Watson, Candler's, Bibb.*
225 Ezekiel Ratchford, 245th, Jackson.*
226 Timothy Sanders, Harrison's, Decatur.*
227 Thomas Hornsby, Heard's, De Kalb.
228 J. Cartledge, Sen., r. s., Huchinson's, Columbia.*
229 Jesse Brazeel's ors., 168th, Wilkes.

230 John Fulton's ors., 15th, Liberty.*
231 William E. Tucker, Hall's, Butts.
232 Jesse Bell, Davis's, Jones.
233 Zion Pike, Williams's, Jasper.
234 Daniel Parker, Sen., r. s., 555th, Upson.
235 Joseph Chastain, Field's, Habersham.
236 Sikes Collins, Wright's, Tatnall.
237 Erastes Paine, or., 294th, Jasper.
238 Trustin Phillips, Hodges's, Newton.
239 Andrew Charro, Mullen's, Carroll.*
240 Greenlee Holly, Berry's, Butts.
241 William Hancock, Newman's, Thomas.
242 Wilkes E. Chappell, 249th, Walton.
243 David Sparks, sol., Stanfield's, Campbell.
244 Hiram Hubbert, sol., Allison's, Pike.
245 Felix Collins, Blackstock's, Hall.
246 John Bee Robinson, 1st, Chatham.
247 Benjamin Dye's ors., 119th, Richmond.
248 Sampson Ikener, Dupree's, Washington.
249 Elizabeth Hood, w., Groce's, Bibb.*
250 Elisha Trice's or., Sullivan's, Jones.
251 Elijah Smith, Hobbs's, Laurens.
252 James Howell, Walker's, Houston.
253 Obadiah Edwards, Jr., 10th, Effingham.
254 Daniel S. M'Coy, Hughes's, Habersham.
255 Henry Howze's ors., Morgan's, Clarke.
256 Martha Fincher, w., Davis's, Gwinnett.
257 Joseph Thomas, 119th, Richmond.
258 Firney Holliday, s. i. w., 75th, Burke.*
259 Sarah L. Heath, id., Frasier's, Monroe.*
260 William Stoker, Neal's, Campbell.
261 Washington Barentine, Thompson's, Henry.
262 Jarett Glover, 248th, Jackson.
263 Stephen Johnson, 640th, Dooly.*
264 John Dorsey, Daniel's, Hall.
265 James Noel, 404th, Gwinnett.
266 Samuel Beall, Camp's, Warren.*
267 Josephus Eastes, 307th, Putnam.
268 Ezekiel Arnold, Colquhoun's, Henry.
269 Zachariah Ethridge, Stewart's, Troup.
270 Smith Horsley, 470th, Upson.*
271 James Carter, s. l. w., 589th, Upson.
272 Abiel Campfield's ors., 398th, Richmond.
273 Rachel Way, h. a., Goodwin's, Houston.
274 Willis Newman, dumb, Mashburn's, Pulaski.
275 John West, r. s., Kellum's, Talbot.
276 Ninian B. Sims, sol., 277th, Morgan.

277 Sarah Curry, w. of sol., Graves's, Lincoln.
278 Susannah Dorsett, w., Lawrence's, Pike.
279 David J. Lyle, Lay's, Jackson.
280 Jeptha H. Ward, Taylor's, Elbert.
281 John Cobb's, Jr., Wolfskin's, Oglethorpe.
282 Lucy Duffil, w. r. s., Colley's, Oglethorpe.
283 Robert Walker, Bustin's, Pike.*
284 Benjamin P. Mercier, 318th, Baldwin.*
285 Richard Collier's ors., Robinson's, Harris.*
286 Cooper B. Fuller, White's, Franklin.
287 Charles Samples, Barker's, Gwinnett.
288 Edwin Adams, Payne's, Merriwether.
289 Thomas May, 143d, Greene.*
290 John Johnston, Coxe's, Franklin.*
291 Nancy Ramey, w., Smith's, Wilkinson.*
292 Sebiah Chatfield, w., Allen's, Bibb.
293 Nancy Watts, w., 140th, Greene.*
294 Mary Mercer, w., Linam's, Pulaski.
295 Richard N. Rhodes, Hutson's, Newton.*
296 William Craddock, Tower's, Gwinnett.
297 Rhoda Bishop, w., Liddell's, Jackson.*
298 Wiley Gilder, Herndon's, Hall.
299 Gideon Prigett, or., Watson's, Marion.
300 Thomas Hardy, Sims's, Troup.
301 James Hodge's ors., 277th, Morgan.*
302 Thomas Martin, Justice's, Bibb.
303 Levi Bowen, 318th, Baldwin.
304 Maruim Eastwood, w., Everett's, Washington.
305 Stokeley T. Nelson, Maguire's, Gwinnett.
306 Mary Williams, w. r. s., Slater's, Bulloch.
307 Noble Anderson, Coffee's, Rabun.
308 Joanna Gilder, or., Herndon's, Hall.
309 George Rousseau, sol., Durham's, Talbot.
310 Martin H. Joyce, Gibson's, Decatur.
311 Bethan Ivey, Parham's, Warren.
312 David Ross, Butt's, Monroe.
313 Sarah Gill, w., Smith's, Liberty.
314 John Nix, Sen., r. s., Herndon's, Hall.
315 John Cowper, Sen., 25th, Glynn.
316 William Varner's ors., Stewart's, Warren.
317 William Hopkins, Huey's, Harris.*
318 Daniel Jones, Jones's, Lincoln.
319 John Garret, 113th, Hancock.*
320 James Dorsett, Gunn's, Jones.
321 Isaac N. Heggie, Grubbs's, Columbia.
322 George Garess, Whitfield's, Washington.
323 Alfred M. Horton, sol., 102d, Hancock.*
324 James Swords, r. s., Park's, Walton.*

26th DISTRICT, SECOND SECTION, CHEROKEE.

1 Thoms Hunt, Chastain's, Habersham.
2 John W. A. Sanford, 320th, Baldwin.
3 Alexander S. Greene, 604th, Taliaferro.*
4 Thomas H. Marler, 175th, Wilkes.*
5 David Colley, s. l. w., Colley's, Oglethorpe.*
6 Fortunatus Dobbs, 248th, Jackson.
7 John C. Ragsdale, Hutson's, Newton.*
8 Presby R. Clarke, House's, Henry.*
9 James Turner, Heard's, De Kalb.
10 Samson V. Cain, M'Dowell's, Lincoln.
11 Isaiah Taylor, Sparks's, Washington.*
12 Richard Powell, 516th, Dooly.
13 Ansel Godfrey, Coffee's, Rabun.
14 Robert S. Norton, Hampton's, Newton.
15 Kernealus Norton, Griffin's, Fayette.*
16 William Jerkins's ors., Blair's, Lowndes.
17 Charles Ferguson, Park's, Walton.
18 Isaac W. Chesnut, or., Marshall's, Putnam.
19 Margaret Wilkinson, w., Talley's, Troup.
20 Robert C. Barnes, Dawson's, Jasper.
21 John Milton, Talley's, Troup.
22 Mary M'Coy, w., Price's, Hall.
23 Jesse Bentley, 417th, Walton.
24 Jacob Barentine, Thompson's, Henry.
25 John M'Govern, Athens, Clarke.
26 Isaac Jones's ors., Covington's, Pike.
27 Garland Moseley, Whitehead's, Habersham.
28 James M. Hill, Coker's, Troup.
29 Samuel Farriss, Keener's, Rabun.
30 Arthur A. Morgan, Iverson's, Houston.
31 William H. Raiford, Derrick's, Henry.
32 Larken Pane, Tower's, Gwinnett.
33 Joseph Stanford, Rooks's, Putnam.
34 Ladson's seven orphans, Cleland's, Chatham.
35 Rebecca Echols, Willis's, Franklin.
36 James Cash, sol., Bustin's, Pike.
37 Jesse G. Christian, Lunceford's, Elbert.
38 John Arnold's ors., Guice's, Oglethorpe.*
39 Thomas Rice, Jr., Maguire's, Gwinnett.*
40 Stephen Harris, 404th, Gwinnett.
41 Carter Hill, 249th, Walton.

42 Benjamin F. Owen, Bragaw's, Oglethorpe.
43 John J. Glover, Baker's, Gwinnett.*
44 Richard Freeman, Marsh's, Thomas.
45 Julian R. Proctor, Kellum's, Talbot.*
46 Margaret H. Alexander, w., 293d, Jasper.
47 Robert Williamson's ors., Craven's, Coweta.
48 Moses M. Brown, Allen's, Bibb.
49 Isaac Hand, Jr., Smith's, Henry.
50 Isham Ponder, Herndon's, Hall.*
51 Thomas Jones, 458th, Early.
52 John W. Mott, Lawrence's, Pike.
53 Cassander Mallow, w., Whisenhunt's, Carroll.*
54 Thomas Walker, M'Clain's, Newton.
55 Vilinda Anderson, w., Jones's, Habersham.
56 John Underwood, Mitchell's, Marion.
57 Adam C. Brenson, 86th, Scriven.
58 Willis Rabun, Whisenhunt's, Carroll.
59 Joel Norriss, Norriss's, Monroe.
60 Dolford H. Silvey, Lunceford's, Wilkes.
61 Elizabeth Ward, w., Lawrence's, Pike.
62 John Jennings, 334th, Wayne.*
63 Simeon Bowse, Curry's, Wilkinson.*
64 Henry Conner, s. s., Cleggs's, Walton.*
65 Vincent Gordon, Jones's, Madison.*
66 Joseph Farris, 6th, Chatham.
67 Ann Ohern, lu., 271st, M'Intosh.
68 Amos Chunn, Jr., Tuggle's, Merriwether.
69 William Kidd, s. l. w., Jenkins's, Oglethorpe.*
70 Jesse Hammack, Nesbit's, Newton.
71 Jesse Doles, Sapp's, Muscogee.
72 William Jones, Woodruff's, Campbell.
73 O. E. Taylor, Wilham's, Walton.
74 Bedy Sharp, w., 70th, Burke.
75 John Williams, r. s., Welche's, Habersham.
76 James Lewis, Jones's, Morgan.*
77 Alexander Brannen, m. s., Sanderlin's, Bulloch.*
78 Jonathan Webb, Jones's, Habersham.
79 Jedethani Porter's ors., Martin's, Pike.
80 William Moore, Peace's, Wilkinson.
81 Susannah W. H. Walton, f. a., Mays's, Monroe.
82 Alfred Beaty, Williams's, Walton.
83 Susannah Tillory, w., Grider's, Morgan.
84 Bazil Haman, Colley's, Madison.
85 Benjamin Salter, Curry's, Wilkinson.
86 Charles Mills, Wheeler's, Pulaski.*
87 John Armstrong, 1st section, Cherokee.
88 Nathan Harris, Guice's, Oglethorpe.

89 Joel Blackwell, David's, Franklin.
90 Solomon Palmore, Jr., Field's, Habersham.
91 Bud C. Wall, 190th, Elbert.
92 Abner Wadson, Nellum's, Elbert.
93 John R. Kain, 398th, Richmond.
94 Ephraim P. Hill, Streetman's, Twiggs.
95 James Boalt, Griffin's, Fayette.
96 William Holladay, r. s., Prescott's, Twiggs.*
97 Thomas J. Booker, Jones's, Lincoln.*
98 Rachel Cronick, w. r. s., 417th, Walton.
99 Alfred Ansley, Perryman's, Warren.
100 Jean Davis, w., 693d, Heard.
101 Mary Brown, w. r. s., Mobley's, De Kalb.
102 Thomas S. Lee, Whitaker's, Crawford.*
103 William A. Mabry, 147th, Greene.*
104 John P. Claxton, 608th, Taliaferro.
105 James Gray, Heard's, De Kalb.*
106 Willis Whitaker, Williams's, Washington.
107 William Dixon, Riden's, Jackson.*
108 Samuel Coxe, Gittens's, Fayette.
109 Ann Poullere, w., Cleland's, Chatham.
110 Hannah Pate, w., Carswell's, Jefferson.
111 Asa Holston, Strickland's, Merriwether.
112 Lewis Livingston, 398th, Richmond.*
113 John Garess, Whitfield's, Washington.*
114 Aaron B. Puckett's ors., Tower's, Gwinnett.
115 John Stillwell, sol., 735th, Troup.*
116 Elizabeth S. Doyall, h. a., Reid's, Gwinnett.*
117 Jesse Low, 454th, Walton.
118 John Warren, Talley's, Troup.
119 James Wade, sol., M'Craney's, Lowndes.*
120 Thomas Conner, Tompkins's, Putnam.
121 Elisha Howell, Boynton's, Twiggs.
122 Peter Beavers's four ors., Foote's, De Kalb.
123 Arthur Barden, 535th, Dooly.
124 Stephen Garrett, Willis's, Franklin.
125 Martin Brown, Dearing's, Henry.
126 Henry Wood, Robison's, Washington.
127 John R. Gahagan, 600th, Richmond.
128 David Stewart, or., Wynn's, Gwinnett.
129 James Morgan, Will's, Twiggs.
130 Jasper Bankston, Hutson's, Newton.
131 Elizabeth M'Michael, w., 295th, Jasper.
132 John Hackney, sol., 149th, Greene.*
133 Gales Jinks, Berry's, Butts.
134 Michael Cawley, s. l. w., Bailey's, Laurens.
135 Hiram Trammell, Tower's, Gwinnett.

136 Stephen P. Bailey, Baley's, Butts.*
137 Nathaniel H. Smith's ors., Ware's, Coweta.*
138 Silas Worley, Jones's, Habersham.
139 William Quinton, 3d section, Cherokee.
140 Samuel S. Nesbit, Burk's, Stewart.
141 Jesse J. Jones, Latimer's, De Kalb.
142 W. Jordan, w. r. s., Sinquefield's, Washington.
143 Galphin Harvey's ors., Peterson's, Burke.
144 Nancy Brady, w., 537th, Upson.
145 Wilson H. White, Sam Streetman's, Twiggs.
146 John B. Post, Stewart's, Troup.
147 Ann H. Dunn, w., Bell's, Burke.
148 Mary Pinson, w., Hargrove's, Oglethorpe.
149 Stephen A. Gamell, Smith's, Habersham.
150 Anna Hall, w., 785th, Sumter.
151 John M. Trippe, 101st, Hancock.
152 Archibald Smith, 35th, Scriven.
153 John F. Whaley, Compton's, Fayette.*
154 James Branch, r. s., Rick's, Laurens.
155 Benjamin F. Collier, Head's, Butts.
156 William Newton, Griffin's, Fayette.
157 Timothy Ranew, Rutland's, Bibb.
158 George J. Bulkley, Cleland's, Chatham.
159 Abraham Elrod, Sen., Dobbs's, Hall.
160 William Brown, Peace's, Wilkinson.
161 Thomas Eden, sol., 2d, Chatham.*
162 William May, Jr., Sparks's, Washington.*
163 Daniel M'Collum, r. s., Jones's, Habersham.
164 Selah Spears, w., Hines's, Coweta.
165 Benjamin Jourdan, r. s., Tuggle's, Merriwether.
166 John E. Lewis, 105th, Baldwin.*
167 William Wright, Peace's, Wilkinson.
168 William E. Pert, Moore's, Randolph.
169 David Shepperd, Barwick's, Washington.*
170 Elijah Jones, Clark's, Elbert.
171 Morton Dobbs, Smith's, Franklin.
172 John Warren, f. a., Lawrence's, Pike.
173 Tilman Cook, Vining's, Putnam.
174 William Terrell, Foote's, De Kalb.
175 James Haywood, Sen., sol., Camp's, Warren.
176 William Kemp, s. i. w., Harrison's, Decatur.
177 John Hill, sol., Allen's, Henry.
178 John B. Lennard, Moseley's, Wilkes.
179 Hugh Brown, Ogden's, Camden.
180 Benjamin Durden, Sam Streetman's, Twiggs.
181 John N. Davis, Phillips's, Monroe.
182 Timothy White, Parham's, Warren.

183 Elizabeth Hutson, w., M'Ginnis's, Jackson.
184 John Suddeth, sol., 404th, Gwinnett.
185 Jacob A. Clements, Edwards's, Talbot.
186 Rhody Miller, w., Silman's, Pike.
187 John B. James, 466th, Monroe.
188 John Brooks, Thames, Crawford.
189 James Hacrow, Wagnon's, Carroll.
190 William York, Whisenhunt's, Carroll.
191 Stephen Johnson, Sen., sol., 166th, Wilkes.
192 Phillip Howell, M'Gehee's, Troup.
193 Ezekiel Cothron, Morrison's, Appling.
194 Elijah Smith, M. Brown's, Habersham.
195 Benjamin Green, 271st, M'Intosh.
196 Roger L. Fulton, Boynton's, Twiggs.
197 Samuel Brewton, Brewton's, Tatnall.
198 John Mabrey's ors., ———, Greene.
199 Aristarcus Wood, sol., Allen's, Monroe.
200 Jacob Parker, Royster's, Franklin.
201 John Wilson, Mason's, Washington.*
202 John A. Barnes, 119th, Richmond.
203 Charles Wilt, 245th, Jackson.
204 Henry Hines, 535th, Dooly.*
205 James Darbey, or., Lester's, Monroe.
206 Reuben Nunley, Brown's, Habersham.
207 Joshua Williams, Walden's, Pulaski.
208 Elisha Harrel, Alexander's, Jefferson.
209 Samuel Leathers, Jr., Mullen's, Carroll.
210 Isaac B. Lawrence, Catlett's, Franklin.
211 James Shepperd, Blount's, Wilkinson.*
212 John W. Talley, 406th, Gwinnett.
213 James Holden, Brock's, Habersham.
214 Allen Page's ors., Barron's, Houston.
215 Elisha Winn, sol., Chambers's, Gwinnett.
216 Augustin L. Grant, Athens, Clarke.
217 Isaac Yarbrough, Dyer's, Habersham.
218 J—— Wilkinson's ors., Dean's, Clarke.
219 Benjamin B. Sturges, Cleland's, Chatham.
220 Laban Pitts, 735th, Troup.
221 Jonathan Watson, Stewart's, Jones.
222 Eleazer Brack's ors., Cannon's, Wilkinson.
223 William Barefoot, Jr., Walden's, Pulaski.
224 Patience Raiford, w., 320th Baldwin.
225 Payton R. Martin, Walker's, Columbia.*
226 Amos Daniel, s. l. w., Martin's, Washington.
227 Solomon Sweat, Gillis's, De Kalb.
228 Allison Kent, sol., Ballard's, Morgan.
229 Eli Wood, Edwards's, Franklin.*

230 James Farris, Latimer's, De Kalb.
231 William Rhodes's ors., Thaxton's, Butts.
232 Mary Weaver, w. r. s., Moore's, Randolph.
233 Jacob Kirkland, f. a., 516th, Dooly.
234 John Daniel, Daniel's, Hall.
235 Radford Runnels, 602d, Taliaferro.
236 John W. Cox, Rainey's, Twiggs.*
237 John T. M'Uin, or., Hearn's, Butts.*
238 Hiram Henigan, Phillips's, Monroe.
239 Nancy Gresham, w. s. i. w., 146th, Greene.*
240 William Lunceford, M'Clure's, Rabun.*
241 Thomas Hawkins, Gorley's, Putnam.
242 Parham H. Heeth's ors., Parham's, Warren.
243 Stephen H. Willis, 166th, Wilkes.*
244 Mary C. W. M'Rae, Valleau's, Chatham.
245 James R. Jones's ors., Shearer's, Coweta.
246 Armstead Smith, Higginbotham's, Carroll.
247 Archibald Short, Talley's, Troup.
248 David Garrin, Herndon's, Hall.
249 Elkanah Talley, sol., Talley's, Troup.
250 Joshua F. Hodges, Slater's, Bulloch.
251 John J. Pasmore, Blount's, Wilkinson.*
252 Elias Fulsum, Moffett's, Muscogee.*
253 Jesse Watters, Herring's, Twiggs.
254 Lott N. Ridgedell, Gittens's, Fayette.
255 Howell Horn, Moore's, Randolph.
256 Elias Willmaker, 175th, Wilkes.
257 Joel W. Perry, 510th, Early.
258 Cash Willingham, s. l. w., 417th, Walton.
259 Aaron Cohen, Valleau's, Chatham.
260 John Johnson, Athens, Clarke.
261 John Hanes, Sen., Daniel's, Hall.*
262 Jacob Beck, M'Gehee's, Troup.
263 Hardy Lasseter, Kendrick's, Monroe.*
264 John Hollingsworth, Candler's, Bibb.*
265 William Tucker, 190th, Elbert.*
266 Thomas Davis, Mimms's, Fayette.
267 Richard Smith, s. i. w., 162d, Greene.
268 Barnabas Barron, Jr., M'Ginnis's, Jackson.
269 Charlotte Rowell, w., Robertson's, Telfair.
270 Pleasant H. Rogers, Robinson's, Putnam.
271 Joseph Mark, Sims's, Troup.
272 Jeremiah Messick, sol., Edwards's, Talbot.
273 Jacob Funderburk, sol., Brooks's, Muscogee.
274 Thomas Higgs, Sen., r. s., Daniel's, Hall.
275 Robert Grant, 190th, Elbert.
276 Marg. M'Whorter, w. r. s., Beasley's, Oglethorpe*
277 Green Wood, s. l. w., Shearer's, Coweta.*

278 John Tillary, Sen., r. s., Hearn's, Butts.*
279 Thomas W. Rawlins, Mashburn's, Pulaski.
280 Elijah Sapp, Jr., Carpenter's, Tatnall.
281 Elijah Dodd, Allen's, Campbell.*
282 Henry Peck, Hargrove's, Newton.
283 John Barnett, s. l. w., Haygood's, Washington.
284 Joseph Eason, sol., Lane's, Morgan.
285 Nancy Teat, w., Collier's, Monroe.*
286 John Hill, Mitchell's, Marion.
287 Alexander Raines, Mann's, Crawford.*
288 Nehemiah Hadder, Barker's, Gwinnett.
289 James Tanner, Mann's, Crawford.*
290 William Justice, Jr., Ellis's, Rabun.
291 John N. M'Intosh, 22d, M'Intosh.
292 Arthur P. Watson, Watson's, Marion.
293 James Pate's ors., Griffin's, Fayette.
294 William Strickland, Loveless's, Gwinnett.
295 Thomas Flannigin, Brown's, Habersham.
296 John Campbell's ors., Morrison's, Appling.
297 Seth Lee Allen, Woodruff's, Campbell.
298 Jesse D. Tatom, Watson's, Marion.*
299 Lewis Tary, Chastain's, Habersham.*
300 David Argo, Givins's, De Kalb.*
301 Joseph Roe, sol., Roe's, Burke.
302 John Kowls, Cook's, Telfair.
303 Stephen H. Neal, Ross's, Monroe.
304 Benjamin Tidwell, Hines's, Coweta.
305 James C. Rawls, 242d, Jackson.*
306 William W. Mixon, 38th, Scriven.
307 Charles Groover, or., Peavy's, Bulloch.
308 Tolbert Woodall, Scroggins's, Oglethorpe.
309 William H. Boswell, Grubbs's, Columbia.
310 Talmon Harbour, Edwards's, Franklin.
311 Russell B. Sorrells, 415th, Walton.
312 Edward H. Sturdevant, Martin's, Stewart.*
313 Allen Jones, Camp's, Warren.*
314 Simeon Free, Sutton's, Habersham.*
315 William Shaw's ors., 600th, Richmond.
316 John A. Jacobs, 248th, Jackson.
317 Elizabeth Coleman, w. r. s., Ellsworth's, Bibb.
318 Thomas Tomberton, Stone's, Irwin.
319 Comfort Bowen, w., 535th, Dooly.
320 Abner Beverly, 561st, Upson.
321 George Harrison, Johnson's, Warren.
322 William Ginn, Seal's, Elbert.
323 Littleberry A. Williams, 162d, Greene.
324 Bartley Greene, Johnson's, Lowndes.*

27th DISTRICT, SECOND SECTION, CHEROKEE.

1 Robert J. Castens, Ellsworth's, Bibb.
2 Thomas Hemphill, Cleghorn's, Madison.*
3 Thomas Welch, Burgess's, Carroll.
4 William Tait, 245th, Jackson.
5 Wiley Hall, Frasier's, Monroe.*
6 Robert Finley, M'Culler's, Newton.*
7 Eliza Boyles, or., Wooten's, Telfair.
8 Thomas Parkins, Hitchcock's, Muscogee.
9 Joseph Dawson, r. s., Baley's, Butts.*
10 Henry H. Porter, sol., Groce's, Bibb.
11 David Turner, of Jones, Groce's, Bibb.
12 Baxter Adams, Lane's, Morgan.
13 William Dickerson, Brackett's, Newton.
14 Willis Barrington, Martin's, Stewart.*
15 John M. Langham, 537th, Upson.*
16 Mary Wingate, w. r. s., 600th, Richmond.
17 Foster Blodgett, 600th, Richmond.*
18 Hensley Blackwell, Edwards's, Franklin.
19 Toliver Reed, Chastain's, Habersham.
20 Thomas Luke's ors., Peek's, Columbia.
21 Elijah Evans, 605th, Taliaferro.*
22 Ann Ganes, w. r. s., Jones's, Thomas.
23 John M. Strand, Stanfield's, Campbell.
24 Richard T. Lingo, 319th, Baldwin.
25 Jesse Wilkinson, 759th, Sumter.*
26 Tuscan H. Ball, Few's, Muscogee.
27 Thomas H. Gordon, Carswell's, Jefferson.
28 Elizabeth Parks, w., Johnson's, Bibb.
29 Middleton Witt, 245th, Jackson.
30 Elizabeth Sturges, w., Cleland's, Chatham.
31 Vines Drake, 103d, Hancock.
32 Henry Futch, Jones's, Bulloch.*
33 Jesse Fincher, Barker's, Gwinnett.
34 James F. Scroggin, Neal's, Campbell.
35 Jesse Mannor, Mann's, Crawford.
36 William Daniel, Daniel's, Hall.
37 Robert Moon's ors., Orr's, Jackson.
38 Eleazer Simpson, Cobb's, Muscogee.
39 Matthew Smith, 320th, Baldwin.*
40 Garland Grogan, Dean's, De Kalb.
41 Samuel Jamison, Blount's, Wilkinson.

42 Elijah Twilley, sol., Salem, Baldwin.*
43 Daniel W. Howell, Howell's, Troup.*
44 William R. Nelms, Seal's, Elbert.
45 Bailey Welden, Gunn's, Henry.
46 Andrew Browning, Johnson's, De Kalb.
47 Thomas Dickson's ors., Riden's, Jackson.
48 John F. Jeffers, or., Walker's, Columbia.*
49 John Pounds, Wynn's, Gwinnett.
50 James Haggins, Whitehead's, Habersham.
51 Joseph L. Key, Williams's, Jasper.
52 Elisha Knight, M'Korkle's, Jasper.
53 Jacob B. Nash, Lunceford's, Wilkes.
54 Biram Eaton, Martin's, Hall.*
55 Moses Daniel, Williams's, Washington.
56 Richard T. Sappington, House's, Henry.
57 David H. Starling, 494th, Upson.
58 James Smith, sol., Coxe's, Talbot.
59 Susannah Johnson, w., 190th, Elbert.
60 William Bowden's ors., Bragaw's, Oglethorpe.
61 Thomas H. Flint, Candler's, Bibb.
62 Jesse Pugh, Seay's, Hall.
63 John Veal, sol., Griffin's, De Kalb.
64 John H. Canant, Dawson's, Jasper.
65 Jordan M'Collum, Bush's, Burke.
66 David Johnson, Sutton's, Habersham.
67 Robert Johnson's or., Johnson's, Warren.
68 William Pierson, Mizell's, Talbot.
69 Mary Ann Danman, or., Mann's, Crawford.
70 A. D. and E. W. Rucks, ors., 404th, Gwinnett.
71 David Maddux, Chesnut's, Newton.
72 John Watson's ors., Atkinson's, Coweta.
73 Elizabeth Doles, w. r. s., 318th, Baldwin.
74 Nicholas Ware's ors., 120th, Richmond.
75 Humphrey Cooper, Jr., Stanton's, Newton.
76 Henry Ivey, Perryman's, Warren.
77 William Medford, sol., 111th, Hancock.*
78 Presley Holly's ors., Bailey's, Laurens.
79 Westley Puckett, Maguire's, Gwinnett.*
80 William Rumbley, Leverett's, Lincoln.
81 Robert N. Fleming, Peurifoy's, Henry.
82 Benjamin F. Patello, House's, Henry.
83 Henry Wright, Taylor's, Elbert.
84 Alfred Hicks, Sutton's, Habersham.
85 William Chambless, sol., Talley's, Troup.*
86 David M. Scarborough, Bailey's, Laurens.
87 Mary A. Kelly, w., Valleau's, Chatham.
88 Robert A. Huchinson, 398th, Richmond.

89 Jeptha V. Smith, sol., Strickland's, Merriwether.
90 Perryman Mackey Tate, Smith's, Habersham.
91 John G. Owen, Crow's, Merriwether.*
92 James L. Ingram, sol., Buck's, Houston.
93 Benjamin C. Allefriend, Slaughter's, Greene.
94 John Lee, Allen's, Henry.
95 William Griffin's ors., Pounds's, Twiggs.
96 Robert W. Alston, sol., 320th, Baldwin.
97 Thomas Miles, Jones's, Habersham.
98 Joel Kelly, Sewell's, Franklin.
99 Larkin Smith, Sen., r. s., Jenkins's, Oglethorpe.
100 Alfred M. Steger, Loven's, Henry.
101 James Turrentine, Allison's, Pike.
102 John W. G. Smith, Alsobrook's, Jones.
103 Amos Wingate, Sen., Dilman's, Pulaski.
104 Monclaiborn Andrews, Stewart's, Warren.
105 Wiley Milam, M'Korkle's, Jasper.*
106 Caleb Hillman, Parham's, Warren.
107 David R. Cook, Gunn's, Jones.*
108 William Newborn, Johnson's, Lowndes.*
109 James O. Kees, Edwards's, Franklin.*
110 James Hutchins's ors., 600th, Richmond.
111 Murphey's minors, f. a., Chesnut's, Newton.
112 Eli Blankenship, Downs's, Warren.*
113 John L. Haines, Sutton's, Habersham.
114 Mary Salter, w., 687th, Sumter.
115 James M. Barefield, Ballard's, Morgan.
116 Moses Jones, Robinson's, Harris.
117 Thomas Slay, r. s., Johnson's, De Kalb.
118 David Jefferson Brasier, Strayhorn's, Heard.
119 James O. Kelly, sol., Smith's, Madison.
120 Josiah Williams, Williams's, Ware.*
121 Philip Galahan, 398th, Richmond.*
122 William Bird's ors., 59th, Emanuel.
123 Enoch Biles, Mobley's, De Kalb.
124 Jesse Jones, Smith's, Elbert.*
125 James S. Miller, Ware's, Coweta.
126 Robert W. Lee, Howell's, Elbert.*
127 James A. Robertson, Seas's, Madison.
128 George W. L. Twiggs, 123d, Richmond.*
129 Reuben Weed, Chambers's, Gwinnett.
130 Mark Harwell, 374th, Putnam.
131 Hugh C. Bruce, Dobbs's, Hall.
132 James N. Harper, M'Dowell's, Lincoln.*
133 John Caps, Derrick's, Henry.*
134 James M. Reaves, Williams's, Jasper.
135 Oliver Sewell, Sewell's, Franklin.

136 George W. Grisham, 494th, Upson.*
137 Archibald M'Elvy, Givins's, De Kalb.*
138 Jesse Lott, Sen., Blackstock's, Hall.*
139 James L. Lewis, 101st, Hancock.
140 William Cooper, Walden's, Pulaski.
141 Alford Evas, Bower's, Elbert.
142 Newell Tullis, Sims's, Troup.*
143 Kenneth Daniel, Everett's, Washington.*
144 William A. Camron, 250th, Walton.
145 George W. Reynolds, 102d, Hancock.*
146 Hollinger Brown, sol., Hart's, Jones.
147 Robert, A. Evans, Candler's, Bibb.*
148 James P. Stedley, Nellum's, Elbert.
149 John Hamilton, sol., Newman's, Thomas.*
150 Shadrach Bivins, sol., Hill's, Baldwin.
151 Henry Jewell, 56th, Emanuel.*
152 Eliz. Whatley, w. s. i. w., Hargrove's, Newton.
153 Eleanor Jones, or., of Telfair county, Pulaski.
154 William T. Jones, Wilson's, Pike.*
155 Alfred Shaw, Ballard's, Morgan.
156 David M'Fadding's ors., Robinson's, Putnam.
157 Jacob M'Cullough, 454th, Walton.
158 Isaac Goggins, Mizell's, Talbot.*
159 Wyatt Yarbrough, Coxe's, Morgan.
160 Joseph Gault, Rhodes's, De Kalb.*
161 Neill Wilkinson, George's, Appling.*
162 David D. Anderson, Say's, De Kalb.*
163 Uel Harper, Russell's, Henry.
164 William Daniel, Daniel's, Hall.*
165 Martin S. Davenport, Thomas's, Clarke.*
166 Burton Ferrell, Marsh's, Thomas.
167 Samuel R. Barber, Morton's, De Kalb.
168 William H. Pierson, Burk's, Stewart.*
169 Wright Permenter, Winter's, Jones.*
170 John W. Allen, Walden's, Pulaski.
171 Elizabeth Fairchild, w., Whipple's, Wilkinson.
172 Joseph Youn, M'Daniel's, Pulaski.*
173 Martin Witt, Young's, Wilkinson.
174 Thomas Buffington's ors., Martin's, Hall.
175 Henry Zinn, r. s., 122d, Richmond.*
176 William P. Simmons, Lester's, Monroe.
177 Thomas Pass, Whelchel's, Hall.
178 Ezekiel Causey, Alexander's, Jefferson.
179 Robert Hamilton, Phillip's, Monroe.
180 James A. Mock, or., 34th, Scriven.*
181 Thomas Bennett, Seay's, Hall.
182 Silva Reese, w. r. s., Seay's, Hall.*

183 Seborn Taylor, Stone's, Irwin.
184 J. Kirkpatrick, of Cherokee, Latimer's, De Kalb.
185 Thomas R. Woodall, 588th, Upson.
186 Hanford Buris, Peacock's, Washington.*
187 Francis C. Armstrong, Anderson's, Wilkes.
188 John M. Beland, Phillip's, Jasper.
189 Henry Sikes, or., Culbreath's, Columbia.
190 Lydia Bennett, w. s. i. w., 19th, Bryan.
191 Richard J. Manley, Moffett's, Muscogee.
192 Robert H. Taylor, Bush's, Burke.
193 William S. Taylor, 34th, Scriven.
194 William Prothro, Kelly's, Elbert.*
195 Bennett Williams, Hill's, Harris.*
196 Garrett Hudman, Gunn's, Henry.*
197 Randolph B. Fell, Cleland's, Chatham.*
198 Robert Lemmond, Lane's, Morgan.*
199 Dilly Owens, w., Marshall's, Crawford.
200 John Tuhett, r. s., Silman's, Pike.
201 Henry Turner, Watson's, Marion.
202 Mary Daniel, w., Hobbs's, Laurens.*
203 John J. Harper, M. Brown's, Habersham.
204 William Beavers, sol., Espy's, Clarke.
205 Thomas Downs, Smith's, Madison.
206 James M. Alexander, 672d, Harris.
207 George Habersham, r. s., Thames, Crawford.
208 Jefferson Roberts, 260th, Scriven.
209 Tarlton Johns, Brown's, Camden.*
210 Fred. K. Horton's ors., Robison's, Washington.
211 William Joines, Williams's, Washington.*
212 William F. Smith, Phillips's, Talbot.
213 Samuel C. Harrison, Mitchell's, Pulaski.
214 Jacob Surrency, Sen., Southell's, Tatnall.
215 Anna Hardman, w., Colley's, Oglethorpe.*
216 Bennet Lynus, Henson's, Rabun.
217 William Bridges, Green's, Oglethorpe.
218 Alfred Allen, Brackett's, Newton.
219 George Martin, Mason's, Washington.
220 Charles B. Hitt, 398th, Richmond.
221 Sarah Williams, w., Oliver's, Twiggs.*
222 David Rees's ors., Marshall's, Putnam,
223 James Ewing's ors., Brackett's, Newton.
224 Arthur Jones, Jr., 190th, Elbert.*
225 John Farrar, Royster's, Franklin.*
226 Richard Hooper, r. s., Chandler's, Franklin.
227 Richard Thomas, Wright's, Laurens.
228 Olive Payne, w., Baley's, Butts.
229 Shadrick Gaither, sol., Hanner's, Campbell.

230 Thomas Brigman, Candler's, Bibb.
231 Samuel Douglass's ors., 561st, Upson.
232 Nancy Burger, w., Barnett's, Clarke.
233 Sarah S. Logan, w., Wynn's, Gwinnett.
234 Lunsford Long, 454th, Walton.
235 Henry Brown, 319th, Baldwin.
236 Henry H. Williams, Say's, De Kalb.
237 Thomas Atwood, Say's, De Kalb.
238 Mary Dame, w., Taylor's, Jones.
239 Mary Wood, w., Coker's, Troup.*
240 Richard & Franklin Cox, ors., 11th, Effingham.
241 Joseph E. Silveird, Cleland's, Chatham.*
242 Robert M'Cutchen, Griffin's, Hall.
243 Mary Cryer, w., Wood's, Morgan.
244 Sarah Miller, w., Morton's, De Kalb.
245 John Gay, Lockhart's, Bulloch.*
246 Matthew Knight, M'Korkle's, Jasper.
247 Elizabeth Bell, w. s. i. w., 419th, Walton.
248 Stephen Stephens, s. l. w., 601st, Taliaferro.
249 George W. Cannon, Stewart's, Jones.
250 Bryan W. Jones, Mitchell's, Marion.*
251 Amos Richardson, r. s., Stewart's, Elbert.*
252 Charles A. Greiner, Williams's, Washington.*
253 Robert Paul, Prescott's, Twiggs.
254 Gabriel Capers, Ellsworth's, Bibb.
255 James Starrell, r. s., Dyer's, Habersham.
256 John Greenway, Polhill's, Burke.
257 John B. Reeves, Hall's, Butts.
258 William Terrill, r. s., Foote's, De Kalb.
259 William A. Sangster, Walker's, Houston.*
260 William Tollison, Maguire's, Gwinnett.
261 William B. Loveliless, Stanfield's, Campbell.
262 John Conden, r. s., Howard's, Oglethorpe.*
263 Henry Haas, Hobbs's, Laurens.
264 William Hurst, s. l. w., Hand's, Appling.
265 Nathan Chancey, Sinclair's, Houston.
266 Thomas Campbell, sol., Thomas's, Clarke.*
267 William H. Wood, Curry's, Merriwether.
268 Thomas Hopkins, Chambers's, Houston.
269 James B. Smith, 70th, Burke.*
270 James H. Webb, sol., Oliver's, Twiggs.
271 Joseph Henderson, sol., Miller's, Jackson.
272 William S. Dixon, Whipple's, Wilkinson.
273 Josiah Townsend, 334th, Wayne.*
274 James D. Huguenin, Valleau's, Chatham.
275 Simeon Moore, Moore's, Randolph.
276 Benjamin Rhodes, Coker's, Troup.

277 Jesse Willingham's ors., Durham's, Talbot.
278 Larkin Dodgen, Johnson's, De Kalb.
279 Jesse D. Tatom, Watson's, Marion.*
280 David Abbott, Loveless's, Gwinnett.
281 Talbot Woodall, Scroggins's, Oglethorpe.
282 Reuben Bramblet, Sen., Tilly's, Rabun.
283 Cuyler Sapp, 19th, Bryan.*
284 Randolph Smith's ors., Martin's, Newton.
285 Emildred Edwards, w., Britt's, Randolph.
286 Walton Whatley, Allen's, Monroe.*
287 Ezekiel Wilder, 788th, Heard.
288 William M'Daniel, Swain's, Thomas.*
289 James Boyet, Lester's, Pulaski.
290 James Diamond, sol., Griffin's, De Kalb.
291 Delaney Mask, Coker's, Troup.
292 Daniel Jackson's ors., Collins's, Henry.
293 William Parker, Cook's, Telfair.
294 Arthur Satterfield, Brock's, Habersham.
295 Jonathan Fountain, Hannah's, Jefferson.
296 Nancy Harden, w., Carpenter's, Tatnall.
297 Rebecca Dourville, w., Valleau's, Chatham.
298 Elizabeth Dexter, or., 4th, Chatham.
299 William O. Price, Valleau's, Chatham.*
300 Mary Smith, w. r. s., Strickland's, Merriwether.
301 John W. Brantley, Dillon's, Jasper.
302 James Lock, sol., Butts's, Monroe.
303 James Chambless's ors., Davis's, Jones.
304 Lorenzo D. Monroe, Maguire's, Gwinnett.
305 John Bell's ors., 720th, Decatur.
306 Elizabeth Magee, w. r. s., Rooks's, Putnam.*
307 William Amis, Wolfskin's, Oglethorpe.*
308 John G. Smith's ors., 761st, Heard.
309 John Terrell, Martin's, Pike.
310 William W. Clayton, Dean's, Clarke.
311 John Bryant, Beasely's, Oglethorpe.
312 John P. Markey, Groover's, Thomas.
313 Oliver C. Cleveland, Hearn's, Butts.*
314 Josiah Seay, Seay's, Hall.
315 Lucinda Page, or., 4th section, Cherokee.
316 John J. Duncan, Payne's, Merriwether.
317 John W. Austin, Chambers's, Gwinnett.*
318 Strawther Gaines, Tailor's, Elbert.
319 Jonathan Thomas, sol., Vining's, Putnam.*
320 Thomas Clark, Perry's, Habersham.*
321 James Jones's ors., Groce's, Bibb.
322 Gaines Harris, Clark's, Elbert.
323 John Jones, O'Neal's, Laurens.
324 Charles P. Payne, Griffin's, Hall.

FIFTH DISTRICT, THIRD SECTION, CHEROKEE.

1 John Holcombe, s. i. w., White's, Franklin.
2 John Silas, Stewart's, Warren.
3 William A. Swift, Hampton's, Newton.
4 William Peddy, s. l. w., 693d, Heard.
5 William Blair, Jr., Phillips's, Monroe.
6 James Butler, 20th, Bryan.*
7 Thomas B. Hawes, Show's, Muscogee.*
8 Mary M'Clain, w. r. s., Tower's, Gwinnett.
9 Jesse Brown, Young's, Wilkinson.
10 William Faris, 404th, Gwinnett.*
11 Portick Gray, Butts's, Monroe.*
12 William Combs, Bryan's, Monroe.
13 Rebecca Huskey, w., Campbell's, Wilkes.
14 Nathan S. Dorough, Simmons's, Crawford.*
15 Benjamin Tison, Newman's, Thomas.*
16 Micajah Simmons, Silman's, Pike.*
17 Allen J. Rigsby, Watson's, Marion.*
18 William A. Fuller, Mobley's, De Kalb.
19 Mary Indson, w., Martin's, Hall.
20 Billington S. Worthy, 2d section, Cherokee.*
21 C. Hamilton, w. r. s., Peterson's, Montgomery.*
22 William T. Howard, Bragaw's, Oglethorpe.*
23 Thomas Higgins, sol., Reid's, Gwinnett.
24 Nancy Morris, w., Hart's, Jones.*
25 Ambrose Day, 320th, Baldwin.*
26 Drury Towns's two orphans, 140th, Greene.
27 William Russell, 7th Peurifoy's, Henry.*
28 Stephen Ford, Bailey's, Laurens.
29 Hezekiah Anderson's ors., 36th, Scriven.
30 William Blankinship, Sewell's, Franklin.
31 Thomas B. Lyons, Hood's, Henry.
32 Isom Harris's ors., Dawson's, Jasper.
33 Garrett Oglesby, Hinton's, Wilkes.
34 John Shaddix, Evans's, Fayette.
35 Samuel Jenkins's ors., Peterson's, Burke.
36 William Head, Sen., Hopson's, Monroe.*
37 Thomas J. Clark, Canning's, Elbert.*
38 Joel Holcombe, s. l. w., Martin's, Newton.
39 Thomas Dick, sol., Whipple's, Wilkinson.
40 John Rainwater, 142d, Greene.
41 Elizabeth Gilmore, or., Martin's, Hall.

42 George W. Haley, Dearing's, Henry.
43 M'Allister Williamson, Sanders's, Jones.
44 Nancy Hallman, w., Southwell's, Tatnall.*
45 Thomas Matthew, j. j., Wynn's, Gwinnett.*
46 Bryan Wadsworth, Griffin's, Merriwether.*
47 William Clements, Alexander's, Jefferson.*
48 Moses C. Fondren, Groce's, Bibb.*
49 Levi Tolbert, Morgan's, Madison.*
50 Erasmus Riddlespurger, Maguire's, Gwinnett.*
51 Joseph Ellett, 603d, Taliaferro.*
52 William Pierce, 2d section, Cherokee.*
53 Henry Matthews's ors., Wynn's, Gwinnett.*
54 William Ward, Brown's, Habersham.
55 Gabriel M'Cleland, Wallis's, Irwin.*
56 Nancy D. Gernett, w., ———, Harris.*
57 Absalom Fleming, M'Gill's, Lincoln.*
58 Francis J. Hobby, sol., Ellis's, Pulaski.*
59 Anthony Story, s. l. w., Shearer's, Coweta.*
60 Bentley Cutlaw's ors., Iverson's, Houston.
61 William Price, Tilley's, Rabun.*
62 Edward Plummer, Maguire's, Gwinnett.*
63 Alexander B. Thomas, Hitchcock's, Muscogee.*
64 Solomon Groce, sol., Groce's, Bibb.
65 William Broadnax's ors., Davis's, Clarke.*
66 Elijah Garner's, ors., Jack's, Clarke.
67 Balding Fitzjarald, Mashburn's, Pulaski.
68 Thomas Stowers, s. l. w., Stowers's, Elbert.
69 James Owins, Winter's, Jones.
70 William H. Finny, Silman's, Pike.
71 Jeremiah Murphy, Clinton's, Campbell.
72 Benjamin J. Sigars, 250th, Walton.
73 William A. Pollard, 605th, Taliaferro.
74 Daniel R. Mitchell, Price's, Hall.
75 Francis L. Upson, Bragaw's, Oglethorpe.
76 Lewis Bobo, Sen., Stowers's, Elbert.
77 William Turner, Latimer's, De Kalb.
78 Duncan G. Camron, Sewell's, Franklin.*
79 Milley Middlebrooks, Stanton's, Newton.*
80 John Duncan, Loven's, Henry.*
81 Jonathan Nutt, Shattox's, Coweta.*
82 Edward Bass's ors., Jordan's, Harris.*
83 Isaac Woodall, 318th, Baldwin.*
84 John M'Lelion, Southwell's, Tatnall.
85 Julius Robuck, Wheeler's, Pulaski.*
86 James M'Bride, 260th, Scriven.
87 Caraway Taylor, 122d, Richmond.
88 John L. Norman, Anderson's, Wilkes.*

89 William Bird's ors., 59th, Emanuel.*
90 William S. Hungerford, Bragaw's, Oglethorpe.*
91 James Harris, sol., 735th, Troup.*
92 Nancy Bachelder, w. r. s., Young's, Wilkinson.*
93 Moses Nelson, 559th, Walton.*
94 Stephen Ellis, Buck's, Houston.
95 David Smith, Mullen's, Carroll.*
96 E. Edwards, w. s. i. w., Wolfskin's, Oglethorpe.*
97 David G. Rogers, York's, Stewart.*
98 Lewis Greene, 4th section, Cherokee.*
99 Edward H. Parish, Allen's, Campbell.*
100 Jane Norton, w., Brackett's, Newton.*
101 Nancy Bentley, w. of sol., Graves's, Lincoln.
102 James L. Campton, 294th, Jasper.*
103 William Emerson's ors., Winter's, Jones.
104 Nathan B. Barnett, Head's, Butts.*
105 Jesse Beam, Bridges's, Gwinnett.*
106 Daniel Lott, Douglass's, Telfair.
107 Samuel Smith, Morgan's, Appling.
108 James S. Morgan, Peurifoy's, Henry.*
109 John W. Dean, Mizell's, Talbot.
110 Sharp R. Spights, Winter's, Jones.
111 Sophia Wallace, w., M'Gill's, Lincoln.
112 Lewise Wiett, 71st, Burke.*
113 John Turner, Polhill's, Burke.*
114 Wilie Vinson, Davis's, Jones.*
115 William H. Threlkeld, Sen., Howell's, Elbert.*
116 John Tamplin, Hart's, Jones.
117 Littleberry Thompson, Riden's, Jackson.*
118 William H. Palmer, Orr's, Jackson.*
119 Thomas Francis, Griffin's, Burke. *
120 Sarah S. Molear, f. a., M'Korkle's, Jasper.*
121 Rachel Yarbrough, w. r. s., Moffett's, Muscogee.*
122 John H. Wallace, Norris's, Monroe.*
123 John Hay, 687th, Lee.*
124 Harriet Taff, or. of W. B., ———, Houston.
125 Thomas Hatton, Robinson's, Putnam.*
126 John P. Atchison, 404th, Gwinnett.*
127 Ann Pitt, w., 2d, Chatham.*
128 Nathan Lofton, Camp's, Baker.*
129 Zimry W. Tate, Hinton's, Wilkes.*
130 Matthew M. Moxley, 71st, Burke.*
131 Jesse M. Wilson, Barnett's, Clarke.*
132 John N. Wilson, Colley's, Oglethorpe.*
133 Brinkley Jackson, Hughes's, Habersham.*
134 William J. Wright, Sanders's, Jones.*
135 Sarah Quinnd, or., Carswell's, Jefferson.*

136 Dago Hernandez's ors., Cleland's, Chatham.
137 William Anderson's ors., Alexander's, Jefferson.
138 Thomas Hightower, Talley's, Troup.*
139 Sarah Lindsey, w., Peace's, Wilkinson.
140 Nancy Smith, w., Sanders's, Jones.
141 John Hendricks, 788th, Heard.*
142 William Roberts's ors., Smith's, Wilkinson.
143 Lucretia Stephens, or., Lamp's, Jefferson.
144 Nathan Eckley's ors., 168th, Wilkes.
145 Reynolds's four orphans, 121st, Richmond.
146 Benjamin J. Morell, 11th, Effingham.
147 Levi Jester, Thaxton's, Butts.
148 Elijah Dicken, sol., Downs's, Warren.
149 Susan Buie, w., Taylor's, Houston.
150 Wm. W. Montgomery, s. l. w., 398th, Richmond*
151 David Lowry, sol., 3d section, Cherokee.*
152 Amos Subers, Candler's, Bibb.*
153 George Hardin, Colley's, Oglethorpe.*
154 Ann M'Daniel, w., Royster's, Franklin.
155 George W. Wood, Craven's, Coweta.*
156 Boland Boon, 333d, Wayne.*
157 John J. Murphey, sol., Sims's, Troup.*
158 James Ewing, 118th, Hancock.
159 Josiah Burgess, r. s., 373d, Jasper.*
160 John R. Skinner, sol., Bell's, Burke.*
161 Berrien Griffin, 12th, Effingham.*
162 Elisha Harris, sol., Watson's, Marion.
163 Catharine Kill, w., Bishop's, Henry.*
164 Burwell Aycock, Sen., Wolfskin's, Oglethorpe.*
165 Tersas Shaw, or., 307th, Putnam.
166 Alexander Summer, 56th, Emanuel.*
167 Elizabeth Carter, h. a., 55th, Emanuel.*
168 George Grimes, 104th, Hancock.*
169 Shadrick Greene, Barker's, Gwinnett.
170 Mark Black, Jones's, Habersham.*
171 John Cook, Sen., Harp's, Stewart.*
172 John Burnett's ors., Justice's, Bibb.*
173 John Boman, Justice's, Bibb.*
174 John Barber, Slater's, Bulloch.*
175 Baley Swearingen, 585th, Dooly.*
176 Adam Jones, s. i. w., Young's, Wilkinson.*
177 Joshua Inman's ors., Espy's, Clarke.
178 George Young, Nichols's, Fayette.*
179 James Floyd, Merck's, Hall.*
180 William O. Davis, Gunn's, Jones.
181 Evin Rice, Iverson's, Houston.
182 William G. Hatcher, Blount's, Wilkinson.

183 Lazarus Hinson, r. s., Smith's, Franklin.
184 Exa Raper, w., Whisenhunt's, Carroll.
185 Samuel Stewart, 245th, Jackson.*
186 Hannah Holbrook, w., Tower's, Gwinnett.*
187 Benjamin Jean, 104th, Hancock.*
188 Jeremiah Griffin, sol., Murphey's, Columbia.*
189 Blewford Sanders, Gum Swamp, Pulaski.
190 Crawford Hopper, Green's, Oglethorpe.*
191 John Lawson, Coxe's, Talbot.*
192 Calvin Brannan, Nesbit's, Newton.*
193 David Richardson's ors., 57th, Emanuel.
194 Zadoc Barnett, Say's, De Kalb.*
195 Zachariah Hopson, sol., Marsh's, Thomas.*
196 Thomas J. Sheppard, Maguire's, Morgan.*
197 James Sprayberry, Givens's, De Kalb.*
198 John Keatongue's ors., Brooks's, Muscogee.*
199 Green H. Martin, Frasier's, Monroe.*
200 Edward Montgomery, Streetman's, Twiggs.*
201 William H. Calhune, Justice's, Bibb.*
202 Aaron Knight, Mobley's, De Kalb.*
203 William T. Pike, Town, Baldwin.*
204 George W. Culpepper, Arrington's, Merriwether*
205 Edmund Barker, 656th, Troup.*
206 Hardin Roberts, Jr., Roberts's, Hall.*
207 John Howell, Whipple's, Wilkinson.*
208 Flora M'Innis, w., Dixon's, Irwin.*
209 Silas Watson, s. l. w., Bailey's, Laurens.*
210 Absalom Abney, Groce's, Bibb.*
211 Aaron Strickland's ors., 333d, Wayne.*
212 James Tulley, Aderhold's, Campbell.*
213 William T. Thomason, Catlett's, Franklin.*
214 William M'Kenzie, Chambers's, Houston.
215 Ellington Creddille, Russell's, Henry.
216 A. Brown, Jr., mi., Jones's, Habersham.
217 William Gassett, Mann's, Crawford.*
218 Denatius Hidle, Bryan's, Monroe.*
219 John H. Wallace, Norris's, Monroe.*
220 Russell Baker, Crawford's, Franklin.*
221 Michael Densler, sol., Island, Chatham.*
222 David Palmer, 243d, Jackson.*
223 Jared Miles, M'Dowell's, Lincoln.*
224 William Drummond, Sen., 415th, Walton.*
225 Joseph Barker, sol., 10th, Houston.*
226 William Ammond's ors., 335th, Wayne.
227 James Parker, 17th dist. of Liberty, Chatham.*
228 John Owens, Swiney's, Laurens.*
229 James Johnson, or., Jordan's, Bibb.*

230 Elisha Hill, Gittens's, Fayette.*
231 John Adcock, sol., Gay's, Harris.*
232 Alexander Martin's ors., 15th, Liberty.*
233 John Hagins, 22d, M'Intosh.*
234 William N. Davis, Whisenhunt's, Carroll.
235 T. B. Teat, Sen., s. l. w., Underwood's, Putnam.*
236 Wright Kersey, 59th, Emanuel.
237 Dennis Wirthington, Coward's, Lowndes.
238 Stephen Holton's ors., Haygood's, Washington.
239 Gibson West, Bell's, Burke.
240 Sarah Dobbs, w. r. s., Dobbs's, Hall.*
241 Azariah Tomlin, Martin's, Newton.*
242 Sarah Harris, wid. of sol., 607th, Taliaferro.*
243 David Freeman, 38th, Scriven.*
244 Thomas Mattox, Wood's, Morgan.
245 William Jackson, Daniel's, Hall.
246 James Clayton, Sen., Head's, Butts.*
247 David S. Green, Orr's, Jackson.*
248 James Baggs, Hatton's, Baker.*
249 Jason Tomlin, Shattox's, Coweta.*
250 Berry Hendrick, Prescott's, Twiggs.
251 John E. Loyd, Jr., Coxe's, Talbot.
252 William E. Wilson, Graves's, Putnam.*
253 William R. Brantley, 250th, Walton.*
254 Mark M'Elwreath, Clinton's, Campbell.*
255 Edward & J. Wilson, ors., ———, Chatham.*
256 Robert Taylor, Ellis's, Rabun.*
257 James Turvaville, Loven's, Henry.*
258 William Tayler, Candler's, Bibb.*
259 Thomas S. Martin, Flynn's, Muscogee.*
260 John F. Stewart, Silman's, Pike.
261 Abraham Williams, Riden's, Jackson.
262 Thomas Watson, Jr., Adison's, Columbia.
263 Rebecca Onsley, w., Coxe's, Talbot.
264 John Balinger, Sen., Bower's, Elbert.
265 Elizabeth Patterson, w., Price's, Hall.*
266 Harmond Hurst, sol., 124th, Richmond.*
267 James Finney, sol., Newby's, Jones.
268 Jeremiah Tate, Williams's, Decatur.
269 Thomas Colbert, Clark's, Elbert.*
270 Byrd Cannon, Jones's, Habersham.*
271 Patience Thomas, h. a., Ellsworth's, Bibb.*
272 Smith Wells, 415th, Walton.*
273 John Meador's six orphans, Givens's, De Kalb.
274 Thomas J. Beck, 174th, Wilkes.*
275 Anne M. Bradley, or., Colley's, Oglethorpe.
276 Horace N. Harrison, 271st, M'Intosh.*

277 John W. Black, Canning's, Elbert.*
278 Angus M'Ennis, Wooten's, Telfair.*
279 Edmund Harrison, 602d, Taliaferro.*
280 James Richardson, Brackett's, Newton.*
281 John W. Parks, M'Gill's, Lincoln.*
282 Joseph Stone, Sen., Heard's, De Kalb.
283 Greenberry Whaley, Harralson's, Troup.
284 Benjamin Ledbetter's or., Stewart's, Jones.*
285 Jehu J. Glenn, Nesbit's, Newton.
286 Lunsford Upchurch, 103d, Hancock.*
287 Francis Sheils, 120th, Richmond.*
288 Henry H. Greer, 147th, Greene.*
289 Robert Barber, citizen, Athens, Clarke.*
290 Joseph R. Shipp, Jr., 417th, Walton.*
291 Aaron Jones, Sen., Hendon's, Carroll.
292 Priscilla Whitney, w., Sanderlin's, Chatham.*
293 Stephen Holton's ors., Haygood's, Washington.
294 Young W. White, Hill's, Baldwin.
295 James M. Wellborn, Tankersley's, Columbia.
296 Gordan M. Cumbaa, or., 71st, Burke.
297 Henry Moffett, Moffett's, Muscogee.*
298 William Vaughn, Allen's, Henry.
299 Joseph Bornett, Roe's, Burke.
300 William Oliver, 320th, Baldwin.
301 Temple Morris, Deavours's, Habersham.
302 James H. Sherrod, Wood's, Jefferson.*
303 Howell Billingsby, 702d, Heard.
304 Elisha Asbell, Prescott's, Twiggs.
305 John Underwood, judge, Ware's, Coweta.*
306 Zenus Hubbard, Orr's, Jackson.
307 James Horton, s. l. w., Moore's, Crawford.
308 John Gordon, Bryant's, Burke.*
309 Lucy Bellamy, w., Edwards's, Franklin.*
310 John Gill, sol., 319th, Baldwin.
311 Samuel Forbes, Neal's, Campbell.*
312 Betsey Buckhannon, Sparks's, Washington.
313 Thomas Edge, Whitehead's, Habersham.*
314 Elijah Moore, sol., Tower's, Gwinnett.*
315 Joel Inman, Rooks's, Putnam.*
316 John T. Howard, Few's, Muscogee.*
317 William Morris, Foote's, De Kalb.
318 James Houston, Atkinson's, Coweta.
319 Lewis Sealf, Perry's, Habersham.
320 William B. Elliot's ors., Hammock's, Jasper.*
321 Mark Ward, 35th, Scriven.*
322 William Anglin, Moseley's, Coweta.*
323 Asa Douglass, Tompkins's, Putnam.*
324 Lewis Borders, Bustin's, Pike.*

SIXTH DISTRICT, THIRD SECTION, CHEROKEE.

1 Levi Deaton, Trout's, Hall.
2 Mary Burnes, w., Talley's, Troup.
3 Ivey F. Stegall, Smith's, Henry.
4 William J. Perryman, Kendrick's, Monroe.*
5 John Miller's ors., 415th, Walton.
6 Madison Carnes, Keener's, Rabun.
7 William M. Watts, 761st, Heard.
8 Amalia Ramy, w., Chambers's, Gwinnett.*
9 John M'Manus, Walker's, Harris.*
10 Roger Bell, 559th, Walton.
11 Joseph B. Williams, Wilcox's, Telfair.
12 Abner F. Taylor, Welche's, Habersham.*
13 George W. Waller, Waller's, Putnam.*
14 William Thompson, r. s., Smith's, Habersham.*
15 Jonas Conger, Sen., Barker's, Gwinnett.
16 (fr.) William B. Cheek, Crawford's, Franklin.
17 (fr.) John Sorels, Walker's, Houston.
18 Benjamin Jones's ors., Jones's, Lincoln.
19 R. N. Hicklin's ors., Everett's, Washington.
20 John Sanders, Baugh's, Jackson.
21 Caleb Wood, M'Ginnis's, Jackson.
22 Lewis D. Ford, 398th, Richmond.
23 William Hays, Barker's, Gwinnett.*
24 Mathias Perrin, Smith's, Elbert.*
25 John R. Wooten, 320th, Baldwin.*
26 John L. Graves, Stanton's, Newton.
27 Randol Winslet, Collier's, Monroe.
28 Lewis Gregory, Britt's, Randolph.*
29 John Hatcher, Will's, Twiggs.*
30 William R. Robins, Mizell's, Talbot.
31 Gideon Greene, Sparks's, Washington.*
32 John Brady, Sen., Groce's, Bibb.
33 Jesse Low, 454th, Walton.
34 Joseph Tary, Chambers's, Gwinnett.
35 Jennett Wooten, w., Heard's, De Kalb.
36 John Cook, M'Culler's, Newton.
37 Jessey Skinner, 71st, Burke.
38 Ashley P. Weeks, Cook's, Telfair.
39 Thomas J. M'Cliskey, sol., Candler's, Bibb.*
40 Benjamin Thomas, 745th, Sumter.
41 Citizen Sparks, Lamberth's, Fayette.*

42 Joseph Thompson, Latimer's, De Kalb.*
43 Benajah Hughes, Shattox's, Coweta.
44 Spencer Phillips, M'Ewin's, Monroe.
45 Charles Milton, Bryant's, Burke.
46 Abner F. Upchurch, Peurifoy's, Henry.
47 Amelia Foster, f. a., Wilson's, Pike.
48 (fr.) Josiah Bowdoin, 365th, Jasper.
49 (fr.) Amos Wingate, sol., Dilman's, Pulaski.
50 Robert Wilson's ors., Jones's, Hall.
51 Thomas W. Daughtry, Evans's, Fayette.*
52 William Trammell, Peek's, Columbia.
53 Barnard C. Heard's ors., 190th, Elbert.
54 James Jones, 111th, Hancock.*
55 Henry Atwood, 22d, M'Intosh.*
56 Thomas Franklin, Hendon's, Carroll.
57 William Harkins, s. l. w., Craven's, Coweta.*
58 Thomas H. Jeffres, 168th, Wilkes.
59 Canida P. Lee, 788th, Heard.*
60 Tandy H. Greene, Mobley's, De Kalb.
61 Daniel Adams, Bostick's, Twiggs.*
62 Sylvanus Bell, Jr., Hines's, Coweta.
63 Francis Fickling, Hart's, Jones.*
64 William Martin, Bush's, Burke.*
65 Anderson W. Adcock, Walker's, Harris.*
66 Mary Ann Holton, or., 120th, Richmond.
67 Thomas S. Pace, Hanner's, Campbell.*
68 William Smith, Whelchel's, Hall.
69 Anderson White, Cleghorn's, Madison.
70 William J. Due, Justice's, Bibb.
71 Joshua Stewart, Calhoun's, Harris.*
72 T. Duke's ors., 70th, Burke.
73 Hardy Mitchell, Stewart's, Troup.*
74 Abraham Duncan, Sinclair's, Houston.
75 William Blow, Bivins's, Jones.*
76 Martha W. Johnson, w. r. s., Compton's, Fayette.
77 James H. Shorter, Flynn's, Muscogee.
78 Absalom Payne, Sen., sol., Smith's, Wilkinson.
79 Stephen Dunn, Collins's, Henry.*
80 (fr.) M'Carty's three orphans, 123d, Richmond.
81 (fr.) Leonard Bissell, 419th, Walton.
82 James W. Rice, Dean's, De Kalb.
83 John Yarber, Morris's, Crawford.*
84 Thomas A. Parsons, Roe's, Burke.
85 Obed Cook, 1st section, Cherokee.
86 James Ranson, Hall's, Butts.*
87 Asa Simmons, Arrington's, Merriwether.*
88 Silas W. Cash, Bustin's, Pike.*

89 Frederic Huntington, Cleland's, Chatham.*
90 William Graham, Hammond's, Franklin.
91 Malichi Williford, Camp's, Warren.*
92 George Ratliff, Few's, Muscogee.*
93 William Keadle, Brackett's, Newton.*
94 Alexander Gresling, Parham's, Warren.*
95 James Alford, Gittens's, Fayette.
96 Peter M'Keller, 334th, Wayne.*
97 Joseph Naylor, Gunn's, Henry.*
98 Lauchlin M'Curry, Seal's, Elbert.
99 Jeremiah Dean's ors., Maguire's, Gwinnett.
100 James Bowman, 249th, Walton.
101 James Coward, Brewton's, Tatnall.
102 John Colquitt, s: l. w., Jenkins's, Oglethorpe.*
103 Hiram Thomas, Bragaw's, Oglethorpe.*
104 Caull Coker's ors., Royster's, Franklin.*
105 John Maginty, r. s., Bustin's, Pike.*
106 Thomas Mathis, Espy's, Clarke.*
107 Nathaniel Miller, r. s., Perry's, Baldwin.
108 William T. Gibson, Wright's, Laurens.*
109 Josiah Walton, r. s., Hinton's, Wilkes.
110 Thomas B. Garrett, or., Wood's, Morgan.
111 Wm. H. & D. M. Gugle, ors., Cleland's, Chatham.
112 (fr.) S. M. Granberry, Sam Streetman's, Twiggs.
113 (fr.) James Kerby, Slater's, Bulloch.
114 Benj. Moreman, s. l. w., Blackshear's, Laurens.
115 Archibald Strickland, Goulding's, Lowndes.
116 Jane Pipkins, or., Hill's, Harris.*
117 Howell Mangum, r. s., Mangum's, Franklin.
118 James Miller, Hart's, Jones.*
119 Benjamin Scott, sol., Lawrence's, Pike.
120 James M. Butts, Maguire's, Morgan.*
121 Jordan W. Lee, Streetman's, Twiggs.
122 Williby Tillory, Alsobrook's, Jones.*
123 James M. Renfroe, Haygood's, Washington.
124 Simeon W. Stallings, 494th, Upson.
125 Lewis Jenkins, r. s., Loveless's, Gwinnett.
126 Henry Chappell, Arrington's, Merriwether.
127 Wiley Dobbs, Chandler's, Franklin.
128 Solomon Sellers, r. s., Hand's, Appling.
129 Peter Warrington, Coward's, Lowndes.
130 Clem Powers, sol., 10th, Effingham.*
131 James H. Davison, Say's, De Kalb.
132 Anderson Rosier, Cannon's, Wilkinson.
133 Joseph Dougless, Butts's, Monroe.
134 John Killgore, 175th, Wilkes.*
135 Richard H. Veal, Everett's, Washington.*

136 James Morris, Groce's, Bibb.*
137 John W. Strother, Brewer's, Monroe.*
138 Jesse Bowles, 605th, Taliaferro.*
139 John Saxon, 3d section, Cherokee.*
140 William S. Crafford, 734th, Lee.*
141 Rolin H. Dixon, Newman's, Thomas.*
142 Wilson Turner, Salem, Baldwin.*
143 Rachael Sturges, w., Roe's, Burke.
144 (fr.) John Roche, Fitzpatrick's, Chatham.*
145 (fr.) Jonathan Johns, 74th, Burke.
146 Elizabeth Hubbard, w. r. s., Guice's, Oglethorpe.*
147 Nancy Moseley, w., 175th, Wilkes.
148 Samuel M. Smith, sol., Anderson's, Wilkes.
149 Timothy Harris, Brown's, Camden.*
150 Amos Chancey, Sinclair's, Houston.*
151 Robert D. Inzer, Johnson's, De Kalb.*
152 Membrence Williams, Winter's, Jones.
153 Harriet T. Eubanks, w., Graves's, Lincoln.*
154 Ezekiel S. Miller, Miller's, Ware.
155 George W. M'Callister, s. l. w., 20th, Bryan.*
156 John Franklin, Jr., 26th, Glynn.*
157 Pierson Pettit, Dozier's, Columbia.*
158 Joshua Ginn, Hendon's, Carroll.*
159 Woodson Young, House's, Henry.*
160 William M'Kinney, Collins's, Henry.*
161 James Eastwood, Everett's, Washington.*
162 James Harris, 103d, Hancock.
163 Frances Wynne, w., Johnson's, Warren.*
164 Nathaniel Smith, Compton's, Fayette.*
165 Marvin H. Weisley, Martin's, Newton.*
166 Nathan Bowles, r. s., M'Ginnis's, Jackson.
167 Pendleton T. Beddell, 672d, Harris.*
168 Henry Boykin, Hendon's, Carroll.*
169 Thomas L. Densler, 318th, Baldwin.*
170 James R. Lamaster, Chastain's, Habersham.*
171 George W. Dunston, M'Ginnis's, Jackson.*
172 Reuben Butler, Night's, Morgan.*
173 Nancy Legan, w., Brackett's, Newton.
174 William Feaston, Sanderlin's, Chatham.
175 Adam H. Thompson, Hamilton's, Hall.
176 (fr.) Abel O. Embry, Heard's, De Kalb.*
177 (fr.) Elijah Floyd, Oliver's, Twiggs.
178 Ezekiel Ward, 588th, Upson.*
179 Alder Halsey, Jr., Hamilton's, Hall.
180 John L. Lewis, Sullivan's, Jones.*
181 Sarah Battle, w. r. s., 602d, Taliaferro.
182 William Dickson, 101st, Hancock.*

183 William Willis, Edwards's, Talbot.*
184 Joseph Ratchford, 245th, Jackson.*
185 William Davis, or., Compton's, Fayette.
186 Susannah Grant, w., Morris's, Crawford.
187 John Batchelor, Miller's, Jackson.*
188 Peter Twitty's ors., 417th, Walton.
189 I. Fuller's minors, f. a., Everett's, Washington.
190 William Mason, Fenn's, Clarke.*
191 William Ivey, Robinson's, Fayette.*
192 Canida P. Lee, 788th, Heard.*
193 Augustus Haywood, Few's, Muscogee.
194 Bridger Sanders, sol., Wood's, Morgan.*
195 William Wadsworth, Allen's, Bibb.
196 Sylvester A. Edwards, 12th, Effingham.*
197 William O'Neal's ors., Jones's, Lincoln.
198 James Hendley's ors., 34th, Scriven.
199 John Barefield, sol., Bustin's, Pike.
200 William Hilton, Craven's, Coweta.
201 James L. Sewell, Night's, Morgan.*
202 Archibald Y. Paul, Peurifoy's, Henry.
203 David G. Pugh, Newby's, Jones.*
204 Sarah E. Poytress, or., 34th, Scriven.
205 Henry P. Gribbon, 2d, Chatham.*
206 Joshua Echols, Willis's, Franklin.*
207 James Cheeves, s. s., Cleggs's, Walton.*
208 (fr.) Bright Skipper, Craven's, Coweta.
209 (fr.) Joseph D. Greaves, 602d, Taliaferro.*
210 Henry Colton, 138th, Greene.*
211 Guifford R. Otwell, Allen's, Henry.*
212 Mary Worsham, w. r. s., Park's, Walton.*
213 James Baird, s. l. w., Thaxton's, Butts.*
214 John Wede, Loveless's, Gwinnett.*
215 Tryon Patterson, M'Ginnis's, Jackson.
216 Wiley Lewis's ors., Groover's, Thomas.
217 Thomas Dickey, Loven's, Henry.*
218 Abraham Prim, Hill's, Stewart.
219 Simeon Turman, Sewell's, Franklin.
220 James Akins, sol., Wilson's, Jasper.
221 Jesse White, 656th, Troup.
222 Coonrod Weaver, Henson's, Rabun.*
223 Elizabeth Way, 15th, Liberty.*
224 James H. Bird, 516th, Dooly.*
225 Abel Butler, Coxe's, Talbot.*
226 Richard S. Mason, Head's, Butts.
227 Robert Brooks, Barker's, Gwinnett.*
228 Fanny Marks, w., 12th, Effingham.*
229 John Bray, Bower's, Elbert.*

230 Thomas E. Hardee, sol., Hopkins's, Camden.*
231 Aaron Dodd, Anderson's, Wilkes.
232 William Fowler, Chambers's, Gwinnett.
233 Levicey Lipsey, w., 35th, Scriven.
234 Lawson B. Hamright, Smith's, Habersham.*
235 James B. Lewis, 108th, Hancock.*
236 William James, Davis's, Gwinnett.*
237 Derrel Doby, M'Korkle's, Jasper.*
238 Cotmon Melvin, Nichols's, Fayette.
239 James H. Russell, M'Craney's, Wayne.*
240 (fr.) Frederic Cox, 416th, Gwinnett.*
241 (fr.) Bright Miller, Dupree's, Washington.*
242 John O'Bryant's ors., 243d, Jackson.*
243 Judge R. Hodges, 35th, Scriven.*
244 Charity Colclough, w., 607th, Taliaferro.*
245 John Roe, 22d, M'Intosh.*
246 Turner B. Godfrey, Tuggle's, Merriwether.*
247 John Rainey, 277th, Morgan.*
248 Redding Young, 19th, Bryan.
249 Lemuel Morgan, 789th, Sumter.
250 Mary Jones, w., 603d, Taliaferro.
251 Henry Cambron, Griffin's, De Kalb.*
252 Thomas Baker, Hood's, Henry.*
253 Samuel K. M'Kutchen, Griffin's, Hall.
254 Haley M'Clendon, s. l. w., Mann's, Crawford.
255 Alvah Steele, Hobkerk's, Camden.
256 Jordan Hopper, Green's, Oglethorpe.
257 Cathren Melton, w., Groce's, Bibb.*
258 Jacob Fogle, 320th, Baldwin.*
259 Jethro Norris, Sen., s. i. w., 419th, Walton.
260 William Whiddon, s. i. w., Harrison's, Decatur.
261 Jacob Sewell, Night's, Morgan.
262 Leah Jones, w., 259th, Scriven.
263 John Potts, r. s., Jones's, Habersham.*
264 Thomas Watson's ors., 672d, Harris.
265 Henry Sanders, Loven's, Henry.*
266 John Keen, Dilman's, Pulaski.*
267 Peter Roman's ors., Smith's, Habersham.
268 Charles A. Sudduth, 458th, Early.
269 Winnaford Jordan, w., Sinquefield's, Washington
270 David E. Garrison, Jones's, Hall.
271 Molly Ware, w., Morgan's, Madison.
272 (fr.) West Harris, Stewart's, Warren.
273 (fr.) John Crittenden, Coxe's, Talbot.
274 Harrison Strange, Mangum's, Franklin.
275 William Grigory, Williams's, Washington.*
276 James M. Vickers, id., M'Cleland's, Irwin.

277   John Hallman's ors., Southwell's, Tatnall.
278   Hiram Berry's ors., 3d section, Cherokee.
279   Martha Baxter, w., Dearing's, Henry.
280   Matthew Pearce, sol., 144th, Greene.*
281   Moses P. Belknap, Flynn's, Muscogee.*
282   Mary D. Kent, f. a., Hood's, Henry.
283   Mary Ross, w. r. s., Robinson's, Harris.
284   Samuel Goodbread, Hall's, Camden.
285   John Green, Chambers's, Gwinnett.
286   James W. Gunn, Gunn's, Henry.
287   Joseph Sanders, s. s., Seas's, Madison.
288   Jeam Higginbotham, w. r. s., Canning's, Elbert.
289   John W. Enfurgers, Taylor's, Jones.
290   (fr.) Andrew J. Owens, Baismore's, Jones.
291   (fr.) Michael Barnwell, r. s., Chambers's, Houston.
292   (fr.) Gideon H. Smith, Jr., Smith's, Habersham.*
293   (fr.) John H. Warwick, Mullen's, Carroll.
294   (fr.) G. M'Crinmon, Peterson's, Montgomery.*
295   (fr.) William Joiner, 121st, Richmond.
296   (fr.) Efford L. Jones's ors., Waltze's, Morgan.
297   (fr.) Henry M. Turner, Russell's, Henry.*
298   (fr.) Elizabeth Tyler, w. r. s., Prophett's, Newton.*
299   (fr.) Jewrystone Smith, Hill's, Stewart.*
300   (fr.) Levi Martin, 242d, Jackson.*
301   (fr.) Seaborn Bourger, Jones's, Morgan.
302   (fr.) Leonard C. Hunter, Valleau's, Chatham.*
303   (fr.) John W. Crow, Holley's, Franklin.
304   (fr.) Marvell Kelly, Strickland's, Merriwether.

SEVENTH DISTRICT, THIRD SECTION, CHEROKEE.

1   Enoch Dunlop, Heard's, De Kalb.
2   John Jones, Mitchell's, Marion.*
3   Robert Tucker, r. s., Stower's, Elbert.
4   Starling Cook, Williams's, Washington.
5   William O. Thompson, Salem, Baldwin.
6   John Blanks, Hutson's, Newton.
7   William Hendley, Coxe's, Talbot.
8   Jonathan Winslett, 374th, Putnam.
9   Isaac R. Porter, Whipple's, Wilkinson.
10   Elijah Lingo's ors., Will's, Twiggs.
11   Elmer Derby, 398th, Richmond.*
12   Hamilton W. Thomas, 271st, M'Intosh.*
13   Arthur Youngblood, 113th, Hancock.*

14 Willis Cofiela, 735th, Troup.
15 Elias H. Avary, Foote's, De Kalb.
16 Joan Davis, Shearer's, Coweta.
17 Elijah Goolsby, 537th, Upson.
18 Joel M. Weaver, Gittens's, Fayette.*
19 Abraham Huggins, 122d, Richmond.*
20 James M'Connell, sol., Derrick's, Henry.
21 Vincent Dye, Downs's, Warren.*
22 Julius King, Will's, Twiggs.
23 Andrew E. Greer, Foote's, De Kalb.
24 William Lashley, Covington's, Pike.*
25 Henry Smith, Moore's, Randolph.*
26 Allen Motes, Downs's, Warren.
27 Eleanor Motes, w., Bostick's, Twiggs.
28 James Culpepper, Grier's, Warren.
29 Matthew M. Petty, Wood's, Morgan.*
30 William Myers, Kelly's, Elbert.*
31 Spirnger W. Handley, Norris's, Monroe.*
32 James Seals, Young's, Wilkinson.
33 Bevil G. G. A. Lucas, Flynn's, Muscogee.*
34 John A. Barksdale, M. Brown's, Habersham.*
35 William Tims, Bridges's, Gwinnett.*
36 Samuel Mitchell, Wilson's, Pike.
37 William A. Taylor, Jordan's, Harris.*
38 Benjamin Williamson, s. i. w., 260th, Scriven.*
39 Marshall M. Runnells, Edwards's, Talbot.*
40 James H. Williamson, Nichols's, Fayette.
41 J. Furlow, sol. 1784–97, Tuggle's, Merriwether.
42 John Lord, Waltze's, Morgan.*
43 Amaziah Waddle, Griffin's, De Kalb.
44 Lewis L. C. Harper, M'Cleland's, Irwin.
45 Green C. Thaxton, of Butts, Allen's, Monroe.
46 Elizabeth Savage, or., 1st, Chatham.
47 Faith Bird, w., 59th, Emanuel.*
48 George M. Taylor, Jordan's, Harris.
49 John Walraven, sol., Baugh's, Jackson.*
50 Philip Lane, Dean's, Clarke.
51 John Mayo, sol., 271st, M'Intosh.*
52 George M'Lean, Martin's, Pike.*
53 James C. Rogers, Johnson's, Warren.*
54 Milus Nesbit, or., Ballard's, Morgan.
55 Oroondatus Whitaker, Kendrick's, Putnam.
56 Daniel Trussell, Williams's, Jasper.*
57 James B. Street, Cleland's, Chatham.*
58 Timothy D. Meagher's ors., Cleland's, Chatham.
59 George Wilkie, Jones's, Hall.*
60 William Campbell, Jr., Hall's, Oglethorpe.

61 Nathan Spence, Sen., Loveless's, Gwinnett.*
62 Eli Taunton, Mitchell's, Marion.*
63 John Knight, 398th, Richmond.*
64 Henry Dorch's ors., Wilcox's, Telfair.
65 Ambrose Sanders, Jr., Bostick's, Twiggs.*
66 Benjamin Burch, Canning's, Elbert.*
67 John Fountain, Davis's, Gwinnett.*
68 Sanuel Trainam's ors., Mann's, Crawford.*
69 William Martin, Belcher's, Jasper.
70 Charles W. Thompson, Lane's, Morgan.*
71 John M'Invale, Harp's, Stewart.
72 Wm. & Henry Byram, f. a., 779th, Heard.
73 John J. Carter, Rick's, Laurens.*
74 Giles Widner, Lay's, Jackson.*
75 Christopher Longcrier, 656th, Troup.*
76 Blake Denmon, Whitehead's, Habersham.
77 Willie Allen, 108th, Hancock.*
78 Silas M. Henry, Parham's, Warren.*
79 Benjamin E. Brown, Wood's, Jefferson.
80 Elisha Lowry, sol., Crawford's, Franklin.
81 Sapthey Cagle, House's, Henry.
82 Joseph Palmer's ors., Orr's, Jackson.*
83 Caleb Veazey, 142d, Greene.*
84 Levi Yancy, Hamilton's, Gwinnett.*
85 Joshua L. Mitchell, Peurifoy's, Henry.*
86 John P. O'Kelley, Chastain's, Habersham.*
87 Polly Culberson, w., Stewart's, Troup.
88 Mary Nelson, w., Grider's, Morgan.
89 John D. Brown, Garner's, Washington.*
90 Patilla Waldrip, Hearn's, Butts.
91 Jeremiah Ashmore, M'Millon's, Lincoln.*
92 Daniel Lofley, Sinquefield's, Washington.
93 Hezekiah Spears, Jones's, Habersham.
94 James J. Wall, Mashburn's, Pulaski.
95 Peter G. Morrow, Jr., 415th, Walton.
96 Richard Woodruff, r. s., Norman's, Wilkes.
97 Benjamin Gammill, Calhoun's, Harris.
98 James Midley, Hitchcock's, Muscogee.*
99 Lewis Coffey, Barker's, Gwinnett.
100 William Hardman's ors., Colley's, Oglethorpe.*
101 Obe Thomas, Winter's, Jones.*
102 John Preston, Whitaker's, Crawford.
103 William R. Weaver, sol., Gittens's, Fayette.*
104 Crawford Tucker, Dearing's, Henry.*
105 Archibald Beckham, or., Williams's, Washington.
106 Wilie Glover, Taylor's, Jones.*
107 John Wynne, Curry's, Wilkinson.*

108 David Durham, Griffin's, De Kalb.*
109 James Voyles, Jr., Martin's, Hall.*
110 John Baker, Cleland's, Chatham.*
111 Hardy Huse, Hatton's, Baker.*
112 Thomas Morris's ors., Stewart's, Jones.
113 William Verdin, s. l. w., 588th, Upson.*
114 Rachel Britt, w., 57th, Emanuel.
115 John Hairston, Few's, Muscogee.*
116 Benajah Williamson, Taylor's, Houston.*
117 Ebenezer Fain, Sen., r. s., Burnett's, Habersham.*
118 Robert Shipp, Sen., Shearer's, Coweta.*
119 William Blalock, 1st section, Cherokee.*
120 Nathaniel Reid, Rhodes's, De Kalb.*
121 Elisha Grubbs, Coxe's, Talbot.
122 Benoni Gray, 454th, Walton.*
123 William Patrick, r. s., 49th, Emanuel.*
124 Benjamin Merrell, Mullen's, Carroll.
125 Jeremiah Atwell, 124th, Richmond.*
126 John Allgood, s. i. w., Park's, Walton.*
127 Elizabeth Ann Stroud, or., Anderson's, Rabun.*
128 John Nichols, 417th, Walton.*
129 Job Baxley's ors., Walker's, Harris.
130 James Southall's ors., Bostick's, Twiggs.
131 Aaron Mincey, Sen., Chastain's, Habersham.
132 James A. Morrow, Higginbotham's, Rabun.
133 William W. Cotten, Jr., Moore's, Randolph.
134 Absalom Baker, Heard's, De Kalb.*
135 Jacob Rump, 26th, Glynn.
136 Charles Fletcher, 364th, Jasper.
137 Mournan Box, or., Bivins's, Jones.
138 Mary Vinzant, h. a., Brewton's, Tatnall.
139 James M'Mannus, Sanderlin's, Chatham.
140 Sands Stanley's ors., Southwell's, Tatnall.
141 James M. Hill, Ellsworth's, Bibb.*
142 Lewis Jones, M. Brown's, Habersham.
143 Samuel Cook's ors., Johnson's, Warren.
144 William Royalls, 702d, Heard.*
145 Wilson Bird, 102d, Hancock.
146 Hardin Chambers's ors., 117th, Hancock.
147 Avington Cleghorn, Trout's, Hall.*
148 William Myrick, Parham's, Harris.
149 Mark S. Elam, Sapp's, Muscogee.
150 Elizabeth Ward, w. r. s., Lawrence's, Pike.
151 Mary Craddock, h. a., Fryer's, Telfair.
152 James C. Sullivan, Parham's, Harris.
153 William W. Williams, Maguire's, Gwinnett.*
154 John M. O'Winslett, Arrington's, Merriwether.*

155 William Creddille, m. s., 162d, Greene.
156 Clara Bateman, w., 600th, Richmond.
157 Robert Fane, Kelly's, Elbert.*
158 William Flether, ———, Irwin.
159 John Harris, 589th, Upson.*
160 Robert F. Pendrey, Fleming's, Jefferson.*
161 William L. Caldwell, Gibson's, Decatur.
162 William M. Bird, Daniel's, Hall.*
163 Matthew Marshall, M'Coy's, Houston.
164 Elvilah Slatter, w. r. s., Will's, Twiggs.
165 John Chastain, 250th, Walton.
166 Murdock Chisholm, Ellsworth's, Bibb.*
167 Jeptha M. Stanford, Mann's, Crawford.
168 James W. Downey, 588th, Upson.
169 Giles C. Hays, Barker's, Gwinnett.
170 Jesse Lawrance, Madden's, Pike.*
171 Sarah Teasler, w., Seal's, Elbert.*
172 Dennis M'Clendon, Madden's, Pike.*
173 Benjamin Jones, Barnett's, Clarke.*
174 James H. Harrell, Sam Streetman's, Twiggs.
175 William Campbell, Belcher's, Jasper.*
176 John G. Austin, Roberts's, Hall.*
177 William Millican, Cleghorn's, Madison.
178 Zylphia Dyatt, w., 24th, M'Intosh.*
179 Howell Spell, 34th, Scriven.*
180 Elizabeth Norton, w., Bailey's, Camden.
181 James Johnston, Sen., M'Culler's, Newton.
182 James Sharmon, 289th, Jasper.
183 Elbridge J. Jones, Foote's, De Kalb.
184 William Loym, Haygood's, Washington.
185 Josiah Deardon, sol. 1797, Kellum's, Talbot.
186 Joshua Sorrows's ors., Smith's, Madison.
187 Henry B. Horton, Bivins's, Jones.*
188 David Garrison, Latimer's, De Kalb.
189 Thomas Crawford, Jr., 149th, Greene.
190 William Bowen, Dixon's, Irwin.
191 Thomas Carpenter, sol., Thompson's, Henry.*
192 T. G. C. Hampton's minors, f. a., 245th, Jackson.
193 Allen M. Tatum, Watson's, Marion.*
194 Edmund Stallworth, Colquhoun's, Henry.
195 Elijah Crittentun, Lunceford's, Elbert.*
196 Littleberry Womble, Peterson's, Montgomery.*
197 John B. Bullock, Curry's, Merriwether.
198 Wilkins J. Russell, Howell's, Troup.
199 Miles B. Russell, Brown's, Habersham.
200 John Jones, Jr., Mattox's, Lowndes.
201 James Thompson, sol., Jordan's, Bibb.

202 Sarah Dunn, or., Harris's, Crawford.
203 William Barlow, Whipple's, Wilkinson.
204 Daniel Clark's ors., Walker's, Houston.*
205 James Bryant, 243d, Jackson.*
206 Robert Welch, 295th, Jasper.*
207 Archibald Stokes, s. i. w., 192d, Elbert.*
208 Casper M. Amos, Baley's, Butts.*
209 Etheldridge Howell, Dilman's, Pulaski.
210 Daniel Gartman, Fryer's, Telfair.
211 William Spruill, Gittens's, Fayette.
212 John Oats, 72d, Burke.*
213 Joseph Lites, Derrick's, Henry.
214 John L. Hairston, Berry's, Butts.
215 John Bell's ors., Ellis's, Rabun.
216 Edward A. Elder, M'Ewin's, Monroe.
217 Frances Clenault, w., Benson's, Lincoln.*
218 Henry Shiry, 250th, Walton.
219 Aaron Baxley, Dearing's, Henry.
220 Stephen Pells, Jones's, Morgan.
221 Thomas Atkerson's ors., Gum Swamp, Pulaski.
222 William Studstill, s. l. w., Wilcox's, Telfair.*
223 Samuel G. Wheatley, Fulks's, Wilkes.*
224 Daniel Jones, Jones's, Lincoln.
225 Benjamin Chapman, sol., Givins's, De Kalb.*
226 Thomas Hickson, 362d, Jasper.
227 Nancy Farrar, w., Cliett's, Columbia.
228 Nathaniel Hines, Jr., 160th, Greene.
229 John R. Slaughter, 693d, Heard.
230 Robert Brower, Cleland's, Chatham.
231 Marler's three orphans, Hargrove's, Newton.
232 Daniel Walker, 419th, Walton.*
233 Samuel M'Junkin, 419th, Walton.
234 Perryman May, Harris's, Columbia.
235 John Anderson, Anderson's, Rabun.
236 Thomas Usery, r. s., Turner's, Crawford.*
237 Ambrose Powell, Mason's, Washington.
238 John Wiggins, Alberson's, Walton.*
239 Robert Bryant's or., Davis's, Jones.*
240 John Peek, sol., Hargrove's, Newton.
241 Sanford Babb, M'Korkle's, Jasper.
242 Henry B. Lane, Davis's, Clarke.
243 William Allen, Lockhart's, Bulloch.*
244 Joseph Lindsey, Jones's, Thomas.*
245 David Hicks, Jones's, Madison.
246 John M'Cans, 735th, Troup.*
247 Benjamin E. Harris, 147th, Greene.
248 James Newton, Newman's, Thomas.

249 James F. Godbey, Griffin's, Burke.
250 John Cross, Sen., r. s., Brook's, Muscogee.*
251 Anthony M. Elton, r. s., Riden's, Jackson.
252 William S. Thomas, 419th, Walton.
253 Stephen Weathers, or., Covington's, Pike.
254 Jesse Wright, Young's, Jefferson.
255 Seth Thompson, r. s., Curry's, Merriwether.
256 Barton Thrasher, Barnett's, Clarke.
257 William M'Cord, Hill's, Monroe.*
258 George Nowland Staley, Cleland's, Chatham.
259 Thomas Hanson, 454th, Walton.*
260 Amasa May, Collier's, Monroe.
261 John F. Comer, Stewart's, Jones.*
262 John Johnson, Colley's, Oglethorpe.*
263 Amos Cox, Riden's, Jackson.*
264 Daniel Fling, 165th, Wilkes.
265 William Kiersey, Moseley's, Coweta.
266 Benoni T. Harrison, Parham's, Warren.
267 John D. Kirkpatrick, Mays's, Monroe.
268 Sutton Young, Herndon's, Hall.*
269 Sion Pearce, sol., Bridges's, Gwinnett.*
270 Sarah Oglesby, w., Sanderlin's, Chatham.
271 G. Washington Garrett, or., Prophett's, Newton.
272 Lewis Cape, sol., Hood's, Henry.*
273 William J. Sailers, Jones's, Madison.
274 Douglass W. Odom, Linam's, Pulaski.*
275 Seaborn J. Collins, sol., Brooks's, Muscogee.
276 William Wetter, r. s., Athens, Clarke.
277 Jason G. Sears, Bragaw's, Oglethorpe.*
278 Holland's orphans, Griffin's, Burke.
279 Peter Messer, Nichols's, Fayette.*
280 Josiah Crosby, 11th, Effingham.*
281 William H. D. Page, 470th, Upson.
282 John Thompson, sol., Barnett's, Clarke.
283 Jesse Ingraham, Buck's, Houston.*
284 Ahel R. Freeman, Candler's, Bibb.
285 Canaday Morgan, or., Smith's, Liberty.
286 James L. Irwin, son of Kit, Hutson's, Newton.
287 James Goodman, 122d, Richmond.
288 Reuben Bramblett, Reid's, Gwinnett.
289 Sarah Kelly, h. a., 122d, Richmond.*
290 John D. Collins, Whitehead's, Habersham.*
291 William T. Royal, Griffin's, Burke.*
292 William G. Hall, r. s., Kendrick's, Putnam.
293 Crawford Downs, 672d, Harris.
294 Jesse Harrell, s. l. w., Williams's, Washington.*
295 Robert N. Young, Hall's, Butts.

296 Dorothy Randolph, w., Moseley's, Wilkes.*
297 John F. Vessels, Stewart's, Troup.
298 Robert Tedder, Dobbs's, Hall.
299 Nicholas Whitham, Cleveland's, Habersham.
300 Larkin Satterfield, Jones's, Habersham.*
301 William P. Hopkins, 22d, M'Intosh.*
302 Wiley Smith, Edwards's, Franklin.
303 Demere's five orphans, 25th, Glynn.
304 Joseph Wood's ors., ———, Houston.
305 Jesse H. Alsobrook, Gunn's, Jones.*
306 Horace Clark, 120th, Richmond.
307 William N. Dingler, Phillips's, Jasper.
308 Samuel Bivins, Dupree's, Washington.*
309 Allen Cleveland, Hall's, Butts.
310 Jonathan Gibson, Stanton's, Newton.
311 Isaac H. Myers, Lane's, Morgan.
312 William H. Boyal, Hamilton's, Gwinnett.*
313 Hugh B. Hairston, Berry's, Butts.*
314 Edward W. Delegat, 22d, M'Intosh.
315 Meredith Buckner, Watson's, Marion.*
316 Andrew G. Semmes, sol., Moseley's, Wilkes.
317 Berry Goyn, 588th, Upson.*
318 Hardy T. Sanders, Morgan's, Madison.*
319 Duncan Leverett, sol., Curry's, Merriwether.
320 John M. Piper, Talley's, Troup.
321 Morris Jacobs, 248th, Jackson.*
322 Samuel Paxon, Few's, Muscogee.*
323 Pleasant Watts, Anderson's, Rabun
324 Andrew Shelnut, Park's, Walton.

EIGHTH DISTRICT, THIRD SECTION, CHEROKEE.

1 Jediah Ayres,[a] Royster's, Franklin.*
2 William J. Wallace, Ogden's, Camden.*
3 West Lane, 633d, Dooly.*
4 Hardy Cowart, Chesnut's, Newton.*
5 Henry Bradshaw, Edwards's, Talbot.*
6 Thomas S. Burke, Roe's, Burke.
7 Ezekiel Boog's ors., Hill's, Baldwin.*
8 Lloud Betts's ors., Carswell's, Jefferson.
9 John M'Clendon, Harp's, Stewart.
10 Daniel Brown, sol., Streetman's, Twiggs.*

[a] See Executive Order of 3d June, 1836.

11 Winney Hambet, id., Dearing's, Butts.*
12 William Hide, M'Clain's, Newton.*
13 Denton Williams's ors., Trout's, Hall.
14 James Standley, Clifton's, Tatnall.
15 Claiborn Upchurch, 103d, Hancock.*
16 Little B. Jenkins's ors., 146th, Greene.
17 John Rowan, Madden's, Pike.*
18 John Wheeler, M. Brown's, Habersham.
19 Mary Ann Cook, or., Bush's, Burke.
20 John W. Heard, 122d, Richmond.
21 James O'Kelly, s. l. w., 417th, Walton.
22 Jacob Wiley, 510th, Early.
23 Lucibert Eason, w., Compton's, Fayette.*
24 Ira Richards, Few's, Muscogee.*
25 Andrew H. Thompson, Marsh's, Thomas.*
26 Thomas Wood's 3 orphans, Griffin's, De Kalb.
27 William Bryson, 398th, Richmond.
28 Presley G. Davenport, Thomas's, Clarke.*
29 Mary Hague, or. of sol., Gillis's, De Kalb.*
30 George H. Smith, 34th, Scriven.*
31 John Martin, Covington's, Pike.*
32 W. Williams, s. l. w., M'Clendon's, Putnam.
33 Everett Wells, Wood's, Jefferson.
34 Samuel Knox, Sen., Liddell's, Jackson.
35 John & R. A. Elliott, ors., 124th, Richmond.*
36 Alexander Wells's ors., 34th, Scriven.
37 Nathaniel D. Stanford, Rooks's, Putnam.*
38 Francis E. Thomas, d. & d., Athens, Clarke.*
39 Michael M'Elwreath, Clinton's, Campbell.
40 Henry Brett, s. l. w., Whitfield's, Washington.*
41 Hannah Tait, w., Rhodes's, De Kalb.
42 Allen Camron, Clifton's, Tatnall.*
43 Milly Middlebrooks, w. r. s., Stanton's, Newton.*
44 John W. Campbell, Johnson's, De Kalb.*
45 John W. Mattox, Smith's, Elbert.
46 Ashley Lindsey, Folsom's, Lowndes.*
47 Thomas Cannally's ors., Hammond's, Franklin.
48 Elijah Swan, sol., M'Gill's, Lincoln.*
49 Daniel Clary, M'Millon's, Lincoln.*
50 John Bankston, Smith's, Henry.*
51 Eli W. Boneman, sol., Frasier's, Monroe.
52 Archibald Smith, Chastain's, Habersham.*
53 Thomasell Hogan, Berry's, Butts.*
54 John T. Dunn, 605th, Taliaferro.*
55 William Chitwood, Brown's, Habersham.*
56 Jesse Cohron, Campbell's, Wilkes.
57 Stephen H. H. Mills, 789th, Sumter.*

58 John Strickland, Hudson's, Marion.*
59 Noah Walton's ors., M'Dowell's, Lincoln.
60 Frances Bruson, w. r. s., Sinclair's, Houston.*
61 Frederic Temple, Jr., 510th, Early.*
26 Elijah Holtzclaw, sol., 148th, Greene.
63 James Shadix, s. l. w., Shattox's, Coweta.*
64 Joel Phillips, Hampton's, Newton.*
65 Jonathan Crow's ors., Holley's, Franklin.*
66 George W. Jones, Boynton's, Twiggs.
67 Thomas Beasley, Jr., Lockhart's, Bulloch.
68 Young W. Lewis, Ballard's, Morgan.*
69 Amos Morgan's 5 orphans, Heard's, De Kalb.*
70 William R. Richey,Tayler's, Jones.
71 Robert Smith, Jr., Hearn's, Butts.*
72 Jeptha Robinson, Sen., Griffin's, Fayette.
73 Starling Howard, sol., Ballard's, Morgan.*
74 Wesley Griggs, Rooks's, Putnam.
75 George W. Right, Loveless's, Gwinnett.
76 Jett Wright's ors., Hall's, Oglethorpe.
77 Leonard Sparks, Shattox's, Coweta.*
78 Robert Cates, Loveless's, Gwinnett.*
79 Miles Hasset, Smith's, Houston.*
80 Martin Palmer, 27th, Glynn.*
81 Hiram Thompson, 277th, Morgan.*
82 David Attaway, Jr., Rogers's, Burke.*
83 James Huling, 167th, Wilkes.
84 John Evett, Stephens's, Habersham.*
85 Kindred Partin, Swiney's, Laurens.*
86 William Fisher, Martin's, Washington.*
87 John Mooney, Sen., Jones's, Hall.*
88 Elijah M. D. Vaughn, Robertson's, Fayette.*
89 Alexander Simpson, s. l. w., 585th, Dooly.*
90 Fountleroy F. Chain, Sinclair's, Houston.
91 Nicholas P. M'Donald, Newsom's, Warren.
92 Hardy Fulgem's ors., 75th, Burke.
93 Robert T. Banks, Chandler's, Franklin.
94 James Carson's ors., Moseley's, Coweta.
95 Nancy Newsom, w. r. s., Crawford's, Morgan.*
96 Kyeah Woodward, w., Lester's, Monroe.
97 Jonathan D. Parish, Collins's, Henry.*
98 Mary, Wm., & E. Dean, ors., 404th, Gwinnett.
99 Specey Rusheon, w. r. s., Sweat's, Ware.
100 Drury Gilbert, s. i. w., 555th, Upson.*
101 Francis Luck, Daniel's, Hall.*
102 Hiram Cape, Martin's, Hall.*
103 David Lee, 34th, Scriven.
104 Murdoc Cammel, Blackstock's, Hall.

105 James Maner, Mackleroy's, Clarke.*
106 James Philpot, Whisenhunt's, Carroll.
107 William Farmer, Kelly's, Elbert.*
108 Thomas M'Watley, s. l. w., Hannah's, Jefferson.*
109 Isham M. Shell, Loven's, Henry.*
110 Alexander Mars, 687th, Lee.
111 Anson Holcomb, Stephens's, Habersham.
112 Abner Coleman, Baismore's, Jones.*
113 William H. Crockett, 419th, Walton.*
114 William Gober, Hutson's, Newton.*
115 John Greer, Mays's, Monroe.
116 Jonathan Gunn, 602d, Taliaferro.*
117 Charles Powell, 417th, Walton.*
118 Thomas Colley's or., Echols's, Clarke.
119 George W. Leveritt, 162d, Greene.*
120 John Smith, Hatton's, Baker.*
121 Redman Rees's ors., Parham's, Warren.
122 Lewis Goodwin, r. s., Bostick's, Twiggs.
123 William Ham, r. s., Whitaker's, Crawford.
124 Edmon Parmer, sol., Bush's, Burke.*
125 William Bradford, Roberts's, Hall.*
126 Mary J. Rowland's or., Butts's, Monroe.
127 Benjamin R. Lee, 36th, Scriven.*
128 Sarah Beard, w., Cleggs's, Walton.
129 John Doby, r. s., M'Korkle's, Jasper.*
130 Joshua Smith, Sen., Dobbs's, Hall.
131 Matthew C. Farly, Taylor's, Putnam.
132 Andrew W. Spence, Mayo's, Wilkinson.*
133 Jourden Gilbert, Hill's, Harris.*
134 Robert F. Greene, Braddy's, Jones.*
135 Nancy Zachry, or., s. i. w., Martin's, Newton.
136 Turner W. Taylor, Taylor's, Elbert.*
137 Lewis B. Callaway, 168th, Wilkes.*
138 James J. Allen, Royster's, Franklin.*
139 John Molton, Mitchell's, Marion.
140 Thomas Garrett, Dixon's, Irwin.
141 Nathan Jones, Jones's, Hall.
142 James Plunkett, Brackett's, Newton.
143 James H. Wilson, 559th, Walton.
144 John Gresham, sol., 561st, Upson.*
145 Eli T. Smith, or., Gray's, Henry.
146 John Johnson, Jr., 250th, Walton.
147 Moses E. Whorter, Pierce's, Hall.
148 Eli Floyd, s. l. w., Hobbs's, Laurens.
149 Moses W. Simmons, Coxe's, Franklin.
150 John M. C. Smith, Mullen's, Carroll.*
151 Sarah Allen, w., 69th, Burke.*

152 Richard Chaney, 394th, Montgomery.*
153 William Mayes, sol., M'Ginnis's, Jackson.
154 Littleton Fitzgerald, Mashburn's, Pulaski.
155 Elizabeth Visage, w. r. s., Ellis's, Rabun.*
156 David V. Burton, Bryant's, Burke.*
157 Thomas Mulford, Paris, Burke.*
158 Nathan Beesley, Sweat's, Ware.
159 Alsay Sanders, Watson's, Marion.
160 Henry H. Stephens, Howell's, Elbert.*
161 John Hawkins, s. l. w., Waller's, Putnam.*
162 William Mellevee, Edwards's, Franklin.
163 William Lackey, s. l. w., Williams's, Walton.
164 Jonas Dawson, Keener's, Rabun.*
165 William J. Delk, Loveless's, Gwinnett.
166 George W. Jones, Wynn's, Gwinnett.
167 Matthew Gaston, s. l. w., Hall's, Butts.*
168 Nathaniel Olmstead's ors., Valleau's, Chatham.*
169 Robert Henry Lysle, Alberson's, Walton.
170 Jackson Hendrix, or., Jones's, Hall.
171 William Arrington, Higginbotham's, Carroll.
172 Rachael Cushman, w., Sanderlin's, Chatham.*
173 Thomas M'Clure, Mullen's, Carroll.
174 James Harrison, Hill's, Baldwin.*
175 William Thompson, r. s., Thomas's, Ware.*
176 Jacob Simmermon, Brock's, Habersham.
177 Reuben B. Pickett, Jones's, Madison.
178 Eleazar Russ, Hudson's, Marion.
179 William Crow, 1st section, Cherokee.
180 John R. Pettitbo, sol., Waltze's, Morgan.
181 Mary Warren, w., Griffin's, Emanuel.
182 Rebecca Condle, w., Win's, Twiggs.*
183 Joseph Martin, Will's, Twiggs.*
184 William Armstrong, Parham's, Warren.
185 Thomas Waters, Slater's, Bulloch.*
186 Sutherland W. Robertson, Perry's, Habersham.*
187 Asa Adams, Peterson's, Montgomery.*
188 Henry Briton, sol., Bragaw's, Oglethorpe.*
189 James W. Campbell, 36th, Scriven.*
190 George Hollaway, Mullen's, Carroll.
191 Henry Hyman, Grier's, Warren.*
192 William Blaloch, or., Smith's, Houston.
193 James W. Alsobrook, Gunn's, Jones.
194 Matthew J. Williams, Chambers's, Gwinnett.
195 Benjamin F. Williams, Perry's, Habersham.
196 Petsey Crews, or., Darrence's, Tatnall.
197 Polly Ann Spraggins, h. a., Davis's, Gwinnett.*
198 James D. Peders, Chambers's, Gwinnett.*

199 John F. Glatigny, 3d, Chatham.*
200 Benjamin Laprad, 466th, Monroe.*
201 Molly Burnett, w. r. s., Burnett's, Lowndes.*
202 George H. Washington, Candler's, Bibb.*
203 Robert Walker, Madden's, Pike.*
204 Thomas Jones, 59th, Emanuel.*
205 Eliza Toyl, or., Carswell's, Jefferson.*
206 Duke Thurmond, Trout's, Hall.*
207 Shannon's three orphans, 119th, Richmond.
208 James Yancey, sol., Loveless's, Gwinnett.*
209 James Hubanks, 535th, Dooly.*
210 Elizabeth Pharr, w., 250th, Walton.
211 Lawrence Gahagan, Bustin's, Pike.
212 Augustus C. Smith, Phillip's, Jasper.
213 Debitha Lee, w., Young's, Wilkinson.*
214 John D. Blair, Garner's, Washington.*
215 Joel Barnett, r. s., Hargrove's, Oglethorpe.*
216 Hugh Ingram, Jr., Williams's, Decatur.
217 Hiram Thigpen, Downs's, Warren.
218 Mary White, w., Kelly's, Elbert.*
219 Hiram Berry's ors., 3d section, Cherokee.
220 Josiah Cheatham, Dean's, Clarke.*
221 Robert Smith, Sen., r. s., Hearn's, Butts.
222 Joseph Wilson, Jordan's, Bibb.*
223 Hester Bell, d. & d., Whisenhunt's, Carroll.
224 Mary Farmer, w., 69th, Burke.*
225 William T. Willingham, Colley's, Oglethorpe.
226 Gilbert Malone, Arrington's, Merriwether.
227 Mary Nelson, or., Atkinson's, Coweta.*
228 Benjamin Cason, Park's, Walton.
229 Edmon O. Kerby, Clark's, Morgan.
230 Isaac Covert, 27th, Glynn.*
231 Benjamin C. Sims, 101st, Hancock.
232 Jacob Collins, Griffin's, Burke.
233 George P. Cooper, Rainey's, Twiggs.*
234 Charles H. Porter, sol., Coxe's, Talbot.*
235 David Hudgins's ors., Taylor's, Putnam.
236 John Morgan, Hill's, Harris.*
237 John Forrest, Harp's, Stewart.*
238 James A. Edwards, Derrick's, Henry.*
239 Jesse Hood, Garner's, Coweta.*
240 James Williams, Stephens's, Habersham.*
241 Mary Reynolds, w., Prescott's, Twiggs.
242 Samuel Smith, sol., Robinson's, Harris.*
243 Littlebery White Waldravin, 735th, Troup.
244 Stephen C. Turner, Walker's, Harris.
245 James Brown, Foote's, De Kalb.

246 Eli Walden, Lamp's, Jefferson.
247 Thomas Whooten, s. i. w., Griffin's, De Kalb.
248 Wherry Buck, Ellsworth's, Bibb.
249 Paschal C. Phillips, Givins's, De Kalb.
250 Benjamin Burgess, Willis's, Franklin.*
251 Jos. & H. Simpson, ors., Hobkerk's, Canden.
252 Hope Ogletree, Griffin's, Fayette.*
253 Henry J. B. Moore, Sullivan's, Jones.*
254 Joseph Fitzpatrick's ors., 140th, Greene.
255 Elizabeth Oliver, w., 38th, Scriven.
256 Richard F. Earnest, Valleau's, Chatham.
257 William Thompson, Wheeler's, Pulaski.
258 Manervy Ann Paris, or., Newman's, Thomas.
259 Robert B. Warren, Valleau's, Chatham.
260 Henry Huff, Herndon's, Hall.
261 Nancy Steelman, w., Young's, Jefferson.*
262 Peter Barbre, 537th, Upson.*
263 Bennett Noah, 454th, Walton.
264 Elizabeth Barr, w. r. s., Sinclair's, Houston.*
265 James Reddin, Barnett's, Habersham.*
266 Solomon Holmes, or., Coxe's, Franklin.
267 Reuben Wall, Watson's, Marion.*
268 John Yeales, 1st, Chatham.*
269 Moses S. Horriss, 333d, Wayne.*
270 Josiah Meeks, Mimms's, Fayette.
271 John K. Daniel, sol., 146th, Greene.
272 Noah Phillips, 510th, Earley.*
273 Malabet Davis, 22d, M'Intosh.
274 Easter Chesser, w. r. s., Jennings's, Clarke.
275 Richard Kidd, sol., York's, Stewart.*
276 Stephen H. Sanders, 119th, Richmond.*
277 William Hamson's ors., Adams's, Columbia.
278 Everett W. Spraberry, Givins's, De Kalb.*
279 David J. Miller, Miller's, Ware.
280 Thomas C. Clark, Elder's, Clarke.
281 Wilkins Hunt, sol., Mays's, Monroe.
282 John H. Fambrough, Wolfskin's, Oglethorpe.*
283 James Spivey, sol., Adams's, Columbia.*
284 James Bracewell, sol., Tower's, Gwinnett.
285 Andrew Stratton, 293d, Jasper.
286 Turner Evans, sol., Peurifoy's, Henry.*
287 Charles D. Williams, s. l. w., 600th, Richmond.*
288 Nicholas Albright, Foote's, De Kalb.
289 Shadrick Wheeler, Ball's, Monroe.
290 Nathan Youngblood, 117th, Hancock.
291 Joholm Spaw, Williams's, Decatur.
292 Ethenton Cooley, Taylor's, Jones.*

293 John M. Spradlin, Robinson's, Fayette.
294 William P. Maxwell, Seal's, Elbert.
295 Robert G. F. Donaldson, Lockhart's, Bulloch.
296 Thomas S. Hunt, Peurifoy's, Henry.*
297 Philip Lee's ors., 1st, Chatham.*
298 John Barker, Barker's, Gwinnett.*
299 John Fleming, Craven's, Coweta.
300 Moses Jones, Robinson's, Harris.*
301 Andrew Huff, Parham's, Harris.*
302 John Parker, Gunn's, Henry.*
303 John Green, Robinson's, Harris.
304 Simeon White, Edwards's, Montgomery.
305 Margaret Danely, Hand's, Appling.
306 William Farrow, Martin's, Hall.*
307 George Mullard, Lockhart's, Bulloch.*
308 John R. Dawson, Stewart's, Warren.
309 John G. Smith, or., 761st, Heard.
310 Willis Bonner's five orphans, Givins's, De Kalb.
311 James P. Ellis, 466th, Monroe.*
312 Charles Whiting, Ballard's, Morgan.*
313 Nancy Rivers, w., Estes's, Putnam.*
314 Jesse E. Northington, Williams's, Washington.
315 Elijah Crawford's 7 orphans, Latimer's, De Kalb.
316 Paschal P. Pye, Guice's, Oglethorpe.*
317 John H. Slurr, Bishop's, Henry.
318 Randolph Crow, Sen., Hammond's, Franklin.
319 Brice Martin, M'Ginnis's, Jackson.
320 William M'Cord, Jr., 559th, Walton.
321 Bell's four children, f. a., Moseley's, Coweta.
322 Zachariah Roquemore, Moore's, Randolph.
323 Francis Durden, Everett's, Washington.
324 John F. G. Davis, sol., Fitzpatrick's, Chatham.

NINTH DISTRICT, THIRD SECTION, CHEROKEE.

1 Malone Mullens, s. i. w. '84–97, 104th, Hancock.
2 Cary Mullican, Griffin's, Fayette.*
3 Benjamin Allday, Whipple's, Wilkinson.*
4 Sarah Shurat, w., 2d section, Cherokee.
5 Jacob V. Gooddown, Phillips's, Talbot.*
6 J. Luke, son of R. G. Luke, Peek's, Columbia.*
7 Nancy Chandler, w., Sewell's, Franklin.*
8 James J. Pearce, Perry's, Habersham.*
9 Spicey Hoyle, Wilson's, Pike.

10 Samuel T. Ridgway, Wilhite's, Elbert.
11 Andrew Young, Tuggle's, Merriwether.*
12 E. A. Buffington's ors., Brown's, Habersham.*
13 Benjamin Thurmon, 289th, Jasper.*
14 Lucretia Martin, w., 417th, Walton.*
15 Michael Stapleton, Sanderlin's, Chatham.*
16 Thomas Blackburn, 537th, Upson.*
17 James Simmons, 604th, Taliaferro.*
18 Martha M. Langston, or., Brooks's, Muscogee.*
19 John Goble, Henson's, Rabun.*
20 Joseph Wilson, 362d, Jasper.*
21 Joel P. Wiggins, Dean's, Clarke.*
22 David Young, Sam Streetman's, Twiggs.*
23 Duncan Buchannan, Morrison's, Montgomery.*
24 Thomas Davis, Jr., 561st, Upson.*
25 Elizabeth J. W. Tray, or., Tuggle's, Merriwether.
26 Henry Champion, or., 2d, Chatham.*
27 Griffin S. Jones, 417th, Walton.*
28 Dicey Pass, w., Arrington's, Merriwether.*
29 Joshua Anderson, mi., Jones's, Habersham.*
30 William Davis, s. l. w., Moseley's, Coweta.
31 Elbert Lewis, Roe's, Burke.*
32 Lary J. Simmons, Whipple's, Wilkinson.*
33 Glenn H. Sanson, 559th, Walton.
34 Alberbert O. Parmelee, 398th, Richmond.
35 Middleton Upshaw, Lunceford's, Elbert.*
36 William M. Strickland, 702d, Heard.*
37 David Hays, White's, Franklin.*
38 Pliny Wheeler, Dozier's, Columbia.
39 George Blythe, Dyer's, Habersham.*
40 Dugal Stuart, Blackshear's, Laurens.
41 Robert Warren, Justice's, Bibb.*
42 John Hammet, r. s., Newsom's, Warren.*
43 John J. Hendricks, M. Brown's, Habersham.
44 Archibald M'Craine, M'Craney's, Lowndes.*
45 Thomas N. Davis, s. l. w., Park's, Walton.*
46 Mark Thompson, Rainey's, Twiggs.*
47 Henry A. Burton's ors., 10th, Effingham.
48 John Evans, 318th, Baldwin.*
49 Sarah Ringgold, w., 26th, Glynn.
50 John Martin, Mason's, Washington.*
51 Jeremiah Clark, s. l. w., Robinson's, Putnam.*
52 Dennis Touchstone's ors., Bustin's, Pike.*
53 Jacob Helton, Field's, Habersham.*
54 John English, Pate's, Warren.
55 Archibald Nobles, Cobbs's, Muscogee.
56 Horace Holtzclaw, Coxe's, Talbot.

57 James A. Stoddard, Ellsworth's, Bibb.*
58 Joseph Quinton, 2d section, Cherokee.*
59 Shelbey Downs, sol., Nesbit's, Newton.*
60 Thomas Pearce, Bridges's, Gwinnett.*
61 Daniel A. Baas, sol., 10th, Effingham.*
62 Joseph Alexander, Espy's, Clarke.
63 Henry Buchannan, 295th, Jasper.*
64 Levi Hutchins, Mobley's, De Kalb.*
65 John M'Dade, Reed's, Gwinnett.*
66 Henry Dillon, 295th, Jasper.
67 Noah B. Knapp, Fitzpatrick's, Chatham.*
68 William S. Glaze, 406th, Gwinnett.*
69 James R. Carroll, Hampton's, Newton.*
70 William Foster's ors., Allen's, Henry.
71 Robert Byers, Baley's, Butts.*
72 John Heard's ors., Anderson's, Wilkes.
73 Thomas Hunt, Chastain's, Habersham.
74 John Key, Barefield's, Jones.
75 Wm. S. Smith, Talley's, Troup.
76 William South, Hardman's, Oglethorpe.*
77 Jesse M. Thornton, 140th, Geeene.
78 John Lay, 2d section, Cherokee.*
79 Hail Pruit, Daniel's, Hall.
80 James Smith, Griffin's, Merriwether.*
81 William Martin, 49th, Emanuel.*
82 Alexander W. Stephens, 20th, Bryan.*
83 Wright Welch, Greer's, Merriwether.*
84 Joseph Norman's ors., 15th, Liberty.
85 Charles Hulsy, Hamilton's, Hall.*
86 Joseph S. Lunsford, Burk's, Stewart.*
87 Valentine Horsley, 470th, Upson.*
88 George F. Sheppard, Peterson's, Burke.
89 William Faulks's ors., Prescott's, Twiggs.
90 Sarah & J. R. Anderson, ors., Seal's, Madison.
91 Squire Parker, Brown's, Habersham.*
92 James Wood, Jr., Mayo's, Wilkinson.*
93 George W. Gibson, sol., Campbell's, Wilkes.*
94 John Tillmon, s. l. w., 588th, Upson.*
95 Robert S. Hooks, Camp's, Baker.*
96 Ann Low, w. s. i. w., 22d, M'Intosh.*
97 Victoria Russell, h. a., Cleland's, Chatham.*
98 Lunsford Harris, Moseley's, Coweta.*
99 Aaron Smith, Lawrence's, Pike.*
100 Archibald Matthews, Durham's, Talbot.*
101 William Rhodes's ors., Hutson's, Newton.*
102 Rufus Knight, 57th, Emanuel.*
103 Wiley Jones, 243d, Jackson.*

104 Jesse Key Kendall, Sen., Stephens's, Habersham.
105 William Appleby, sol., Orr's, Jackson.
106 William Allen, Woodruff's, Campbell.*
107 Maria Tomme, 589th, Upson.*
108 Jefferson Falkner, 788th, Heard.*
109 John Swords, s. l. w., Park's, Walton.*
110 Embargo C. Lane, Seal's, Madison.
111 Sarah Boswell, w., Tompkins's, Putnam.
112 Absalom Hancock, Green's, Oglethorpe.*
113 Daniel Davis, Wood's, Jefferson.*
114 Samuel C. Atkinson, Baismore's, Jones.*
115 Ephraim Morgan, sol., 335th, Wayne.*
116 Charles E. Taylor, Bush's, Pulaski.*
117 Alexander Hogan, Whisenhunt's, Carroll.*
118 Charles R. Glazier, David's, Franklin.*
119 John Allwood, Sen., Park's, Walton.*
120 Daniel F. Sullivan's ors., Smith's, Liberty.
121 Doctor W. Dial, mi., f. a., Smith's, Madison.
122 William Patterson, Morrison's, Appling.*
123 Peter J. Goulding's ors., Peterson's, Burke.
124 Nancy Ray, w., Atkinson's, Coweta.*
125 Jackson Struion, Brackett's, Newton.
126 Thomas Dewberry, Frasier's, Monroe.*
127 Peter Dennis, Coxe's, Talbot.
128 George Hunt's three orphans, 138th, Greene.
129 Pleasant Worley, Sen., Hughes's, Habersham.
130 Walden Wise, Morgan's, Clarke.
131 James Ellis, Sen., sol., Dawson's, Jasper.*
132 James Donaldson, Jones's, Bulloch.*
133 Alexander Turner, Chiles's, Marion.*
134 Seaborn Cox, Bush's, Burke.*
135 Daniel M'Cook, Johnson's, Bibb.*
136 John T. Taylor, 398th, Richmond.*
137 George Wheeler, Lay's, Jackson.*
138 Daniel Kirkland, Buck's, Houston.*
139 Bridgar Webb, sol., Wilhite's, Elbert.*
140 Josiah Hatcher's ors., Pounds's, Twiggs.*
141 Calvin Stewart, Howell's, Troup.*
142 Levin Grumbles, Jordan's, Bibb.
143 John Roach, Stephens's, Habersham.*
144 David Watkins's ors., Culbreath's, Columbia.
145 Griffin G. L. D. Luke, Peek's, Columbia.
146 Jane Phillips, w., Robison's, Washington.*
147 Joseph Garrett, 114th, Hancock.
148 Milly Stewart, or., Welch's, Habersham.
149 Edward A. Broadus, 295th, Jasper.
150 Hosea W. Sellevant's ors., Morris's, Crawford.*

151 George W. Mill Irons, Kendrick's, Putnam.*
152 George M'Duffee, Dixon's, Irwin.*
153 John M. Forbes, Evans's, Fayette.*
154 William Rhodes, 732d, Dooly.*
155 Allen B. Strong, Candler's, Bibb.*
156 Brooks Harper, Mullen's, Carroll.*
157 James Farless, s. i. w., ———, Houston.*
158 John Plufer, Grany's, Henry.*
159 Simeon Sheffield, Peavy's, Bulloch.*
160 Benjamin Adams, r. s., Pate's, Warren.*
161 Anthony Crumbey, Loven's, Henry.*
162 John Miers, Seay's, Hall.
163 John Lee, s. l. w., Garner's, Coweta.
164 John Waits, 406th, Gwinnett.*
165 Mary Brantley, w. r. s., Gorley's, Putnam.*
166 Thomas Cardwell, Hendon's, Carroll.*
167 William S. Crafford, 734th, Lee.*
168 David W. Gregory, Tuggle's, Merriwether.*
169 Joel Buckelew, Bush's, Burke.*
170 D. Tompkins's three orphans, Bailey's, Camden.*
171 Colman Barnes, Robison's, Washington.*
172 Thomas Lepley, 250th, Walton.
173 John Luckalur, or., 260th, Scriven.*
174 Thomas Thaxton, or., Strickland's, Merriwether.*
175 Alfred B. Trammel, Allison's, Pike.*
176 Reuben Cloud, Sen., sol., Williams's, Decatur.
177 William B. Bruster, Harralson's, Troup.
178 James Carlton, Hines's, Coweta.*
179 David Seamore, Peterson's, Montgomery.*
180 William T. Willbanks, Edwards's, Franklin.*
181 Jemenia Greene, w., 245th, Jackson.
182 James C. Wood, Davis's, Jones.*
183 John H. Malphen, Brown's, Camden.*
184 William Arnold's ors., Scroggins's, Oglethorpe.
185 Wiley E. Mangham, Crow's, Pike.
186 James E. Head, Evans's, Fayette.*
187 Richard Glass, s. l. w., Compton's, Fayette.*
188 Chesley A. Yaun, 535th, Dooly.*
189 Robert M. Johnson, Davis's, Gwinnett.*
190 Jane Parks, w., Riden's, Jackson.*
191 Benjamin Grainger, 120th, Richmond.*
192 John L. Rice, Hines's, Coweta.*
193 George W. Martin, Moore's, Randolph.*
194 James Lockhart, r. s., Taylor's, Elbert.
195 Dorothy Randolph, w. r. s., Moseley's, Wilkes.*
196 John L. Evans, sol., Dean's, De Kalb.*
197 William Northern's ors., Turner's, Crawford.*

198 Manoah D. Robinson, Few's, Muscogee.*
199 John Buye, blind, 35th, Scriven.*
200 Jacob Deen, Cleghorn's, Madison.*
201 Bridger Haynie, s. i. w., Moseley's, Coweta.*
202 Jane Turner, w., 307th, Putnam.*
203 Mary Hendrix, w. r. s., 35th, Scriven.*
204 Uriah Carter, Robinson's, Fayette.*
205 Hillery Phillips, Collins's, Henry.
206 Leonard Musselwhite, Jr., Fryer's, Telfair.*
207 William Long, Edwards's, Talbot.*
208 James R. Russell, Daniel's, Hall.*
209 James Bell, Hines's, Coweta.*
210 James Jackson, s. l. w., 454th, Walton.*
211 Elizabeth Harnage, w. s. 1797, Baker's, Liberty.*
212 Augustus J. Davis, Fulks's, Wilkes.
213 Lewis Moore, Berry's, Butts.*
214 John Jones's ors., Groce's, Bibb.
215 William Blanchard, Rainey's, Twiggs.*
216 Thomas Jackson Charlton, 20th, Bryan.
217 Tillman Allen, 106th, Hancock.*
218 Sarah Sutton, w. r. s., Vinings's, Putnam.*
219 Nicholas Osburn, Barnett's, Clarke.*
220 David M'Cants, Gunn's, Henry.*
221 Benjamin King, Lay's, Jackson.
222 James Halstock, Shearer's, Coweta.*
223 Samuel Davis, Jr., Peavy's, Bulloch.*
224 Thomas Turley, Grier's, Warren.*
225 David S. Turvill, sol., 143d, Greene.*
226 James Grindle, Chastain's, Habersham.*
227 Green Atkinson, Grier's, Warren.
228 Jesse Farmer's three ors., Givins's, De Kalb.
229 Thomas B. I. Hill, Scroggins's, Oglethorpe.*
230 Joseph Cone, Hill's, Baldwin.*
231 Thomas Farmer, Barwick's, Washington.*
232 James Plunkett, Reed's, Gwinnett.*
233 John N. Simpson's ors., 175th, Wilkes.
234 Thomas Griffin, Griffin's, Fayette.
235 John Garnett's ors., Fitzpatrick's, Chatham.
236 Burrel Blackman, Calhoun's, Harris.*
237 Thomas Hill, Sen., Smith's, Campbell.*
238 Little Berry, Burnett's, Habersham.*
239 William D. Conyers, sol., Hampton's, Newton.*
240 Susannah Grizzard, w. r. s., Camp's, Warren.
241 John Gauting, sol., Durham's, Talbot.*
242 Jeremiah Freeman, Kelly's, Jasper.*
243 Clabourne Brown, Tower's, Gwinnett.*
244 James Nix, House's, Henry.*

245 Elizabeth Clark, w., 24th, M'Intosh.*
246 William J. Pierce, Martin's, Stewart.
247 William Holley, Park's, Walton.*
248 Eliza White, w., 4th, Chatham.*
249 William L. Connally, Jones's, Madison.*
250 Samuel Hodges, sol., 36th, Scriven.
251 John H. Starr, Brock's, Habersham.*
252 John B. Kendricks, 174th, Wilkes.*
253 Amster Denham, Robinson's, Fayette.*
254 John Driskill's ors., Thaxton's, Butts.
255 Matthew Calson's ors., 36th, Scriven.*
256 Catharine Garr, w. r. s., Wood's, Morgan.*
257 Moses Parker, 243d, Jackson.*
258 John P. Greiner, 122d, Richmond.*
259 Samuel Groves, sol., Smith's, Madison.
260 John Nicholson, Martin's, Pike.*
261 William Prewett, Allen's, Campbell.*
262 Andrew Rowland, Price's, Hall.*
263 Temperence Woodly, Smith's, Elbert.*
264 Jesse Castleberry, Edwards's, Talbot.*
265 John Jobell, Silman's, Pike.*
266 Wade H. Hall, Hudson's, Marion.*
267 Bedford Luck, Lawrence's, Pike.
268 Thomas Wadal, sol., Coxe's, Morgan.
269 Archibald Irwin, Hampton's, Newton.
270 Thomas W. Dutton, Few's, Muscogee.
271 Coleman Reeves, Flynn's, Muscogee.
272 Isam Watson, r. s., Folsom's, Lowndes.*
273 Michael Poncil, sol., 26th, Glynn.
274 Joel Gammon, sol., Lester's, Monroe.
275 Joseph Hill, Kendrick's, Monroe.*
276 Joseph M. Loyd, Curry's, Wilkinson.*
277 James A. Sissions, 735th, Troup.
278 Elder's eight orphans, Robinson's, Fayette.
279 John Stewart, Sen., Brackett's, Newton.*
280 Allen Loveless, Latimer's, De Kalb.*
281 Augustus M. Sanders, Murphy's, Columbia.*
282 Aaron Clements, Griffin's, Hall.*
283 David D. Tarvin, Iverson's, Houston.*
284 Noble Simmons, sol., 2d section, Cherokee.*
285 John M'Clain, r. s., Thomas's, Ware.
286 Abdallah Swanson, 295th, Jasper.*
287 Hudson H. Nash, Smith's, Elbert.*
288 A. H. Merdock's two ors., Hughes's, Habersham.*
289 Jeremiah Houghton, sol., Stewart's, Troup.
290 Vincent R. Tommey, Prophett's, Newton.*
291 Thomas Hannah, 25th, Scriven.*

292 L. Robertson's ors., of Macon, Richmond.*
293 William Barker, Sen., sol., Smith's, Houston.*
294 Zachariah Bevill, 36th, Scriven.*
295 John A. Miller, 143d, Greene.*
296 Colonel H. Boyd, Whelchel's, Hall.*
297 N. Hutcheson's ors., Loveless's, Gwinnett.
298 Benjamin R. M'Coy, sol., Crawford's, Morgan.
299 Edward Wade, Stewart's, Warren.*
300 Alexander R. M'Loughlin, Candler's, Bibb.*
301 John Nesbit, Jun., Athens, Clarke.
302 Littleberry M'Millen, 143d, Greene.
303 Joel Mitchell, s. l. w., Phillips's, Jasper.*
304 John T. Davis, sol., Arrington's, Merriwether.*
305 Gasaway Snelgrems, Whitehead's, Habersham.*
306 Stephen Swain, 55th, Emanuel.*
307 Andrew Harkins, 245th, Jackson.*
308 Shadrac Smith, Ogden's, Camden.*
309 William Laper, Ogden's, Camden.*
310 Moses Fellingine, s. l. w., Britt's, Randolph.*
311 Orray Tickner's ors., Sullivan's, Jones.*
312 Charlton Y. Perry, Streetman's, Twiggs.*
313 Peter Free, Payne's, Merriwether.*
314 Margaret Turke, w. r. s., Fleming's, Franklin.
315 John Humphrey, Williams's, Decatur.*
316 James Nolen, Hamilton's, Gwinnett.
317 William Kem, Cleland's, Chatham.*
318 David Hamilton's ors., Tuggle's, Merriwether.
319 Alexander Avria, M'Coy's, Houston.
320 Alfred Coseys, sol., Garner's, Washington.*
321 Eugenius A. Nesbit, Ballard's, Morgan.*
322 John R. Plummer, 417th, Walton.*
323 John Grimes, Martin's, Stewart.*
324 Payton's three orphans, Morgan's, Madison.

TENTH DISTRICT, THIRD SECTION, CHEROKEE.

1 Henry Dobson, Dyer's, Habersham.*
2 Jacob E. Smith, Phillips's, Jasper.
3 Fred. K. Horton's ors., Robison's, Washington.
4 Ann Higginbotham, w., Morgan's, Madison.*
5 James Parker, Bustin's, Pike.*
6 William Sugler, Whitaker's, Crawford.*
7 Sabrina Gardiner, w., 122d, Richmond.*
8 William Gilliland, Jr., Evans's, Fayette.*

9　William Harrison, Head's, Butts.
10　Joseph L. Ellis, Ellsworth's, Bibb.
11　Ephraim Smith, Wagnon's, Carroll.
12　John Bee Robinson, 1st, Chatham.*
13　Mossman Houstoun, lu., of M'Intosh, Chatham.*
14　Presley Holly's ors., Bailey's, Laurens.
15　Samuel Singleton, Allison's, Pike.*
16　Samuel M. Holloman, Camp's, Baker.*
17　J. Jones, Sen., sol. 1784–97, M'Clain's, Newton.*
18　William Burbee, Young's, Wilkinson.*
19　William H. Robertson, Seas's, Madison.*
20　Orsburn Wilkes, M'Gehee's, Troup.*
21　Jesse Evans, Adams's, Columbia.*
22　Anabella Barnett, or., Martin's, Washington.*
23　Elijah Fenn, sol., Gibson's, Decatur.
24　Silas Reeve, 119th, Richmond.*
25　Robert H. Whebell, Cleland's, Chatham.*
26　William Gassett, Mann's, Crawford.*
27　Robert Ivey, Hargrove's, Newton.
28　Harriett S. Vickers, w., 320th, Baldwin.
29　William M. Williams, Grubbs's, Columbia.
30　John Nelson, Norris's, Monroe.*
31　Thomas Jackson, Daniel's, Hall.
32　Smith Wells, 415th, Walton.*
33　Abraham Stow, 103d, Hancock.
34　William W. Johnston, 20th, Bryan.*
35　Thomas O. Atha, Park's, Walton.
36　Jesse J. Jones, Latimer's, De Kalb.*
37　Marshall Perdue, Bryan's, Monroe.*
38　William C. Davis, Huey's, Harris.
39　Eleazer Tracey's ors., Harris's, Columbia.
40　Francis Torrel, Cleland's, Chatham.*
41　Labun Watson, s. l. w., Bailey's, Laurens.
42　Joseph R. Sultar, sol., 334th, Wayne.*
43　M. Hendeson, sol. 1784–97, Moore's, Randolph.*
44　Jeptha P. Parker, Butts's, Monroe.*
45　Jarrett Thomas, Wilson's, Jasper.*
46　James Gilbert, sol., Barker's, Gwinnett.
47　James Green, 702d, Heard.*
48　William Giles, s. i. w., M'Linn's, Butts.*
49　Stephen Bird's ors., Martin's, Jones.
50　Beverly O. Downman, Buck's, Houston.
51　John C. Nichelson, 143d, Greene.*
52　Mustin R. White, Royster's, Franklin.*
53　James Leathers's ors., Mullen's, Carroll.
54　John Gideon, Linam's, Pulaski.*
55　William R. H. Moseley, 148th, Greene.*

56 Alexander Hewatt, Johnson's, De Kalb.*
57 Thomas M'Calhene, Harp's, Stewart.
58 John Rylee, Martin's, Hall.
59 Bradford M'Adams, Wolfskin's, Oglethorpe.
60 John Speers, Jones's, Habersham.*
61 Nathaniel Pridgeon, Atkinson's, Coweta.*
62 Edy Halbrooks, r. s., Crawford's, Franklin.*
63 William Duke, Sen., sol., Parham's, Harris.*
64 Philip Vanhorn, M. Brown's, Habersham.*
65 Henry Byne, 69th, Burke.
66 John Culbreath, 137th, Greene.*
67 James Perdue, Bryan's, Monroe.
68 Abel Champeon, Hill's, Monroe.*
69 Richard Bassett, Sen., r. s., Hill's, Harris.
70 William Nix's ors., White's, Franklin.
71 Benjamin O. Jones, doctor, Ware's, Coweta.
72 Adam T. Johnson, s. l. w., Lay's, Jackson.*
73 Jesse H. Nelms, Phillips's, Jasper.
74 Jesse Wiggins, M'Culler's, Newton.
75 Davis C. Gresham, 143d, Greene.*
76 Susannah Ashly, w., Whitehead's, Habersham.
77 Ittar Bryan, Loveless's, Gwinnett.
78 James M. Lesley, Curry's, Merriwether.
79 Jesse Jenkins, Chandler's, Franklin.*
80 Hardaway Collier, Collier's, Monroe.*
81 Albert Johnston, Rutland's, Bibb.*
82 Thomas Ray, White's, Franklin.*
83 William Taylor, Iverson's, Houston.*
84 John A. Wills, Neal's, Campbell.*
85 Daniel M'Clean, Groover's, Thomas.*
86 Susannah Redwin, w., Price's, Hall.*
87 Jesse Garrett, Edwards's, Franklin.*
88 Thomas Bell, Martin's, Hall.
89 William Blake, Hendon's, Carroll.
90 Thomas Miller, 143d, Greene.
91 Rhosedy Blackwell, or., Price's, Hall.*
92 Figures Newsom, Newsom's, Warren.*
93 David Higgins, Hearn's, Butts.*
94 John M'Carter, Givins's, De Kalb.*
95 Adam Denzimore, 2d section, Cherokee.*
96 James Stewart's ors., 141st, Greene.*
97 Thomas Reynolds, Brewer's, Walton.*
98 George W. Snow, Wagnon's, Carroll.
99 James Mikell, r. s., Slater's, Bulloch.*
100 William C. Hamilton, Tuggle's, Merriwether.
101 Willis Hall, Taylor's, Putnam.*
102 Robert B. Elder, s. l. w., Sparks's, Washington.*

103 Nathaniel Russell, Evans's, Laurens.*
104 Joseph H. Cunningham, Gittens's, Fayette.
105 G. B. Musselwhite, Sinquefield's, Washington.*
106 Cary James, 404th, Gwinnett.
107 David Crimm, Peurifoy's, Henry.*
108 William Turner, Strickland's, Merriwether.*
109 Sion Pitman, 687th, Sumter.*
110 Haywood Barrow, Huey's, Harris.*
111 Joseph Pottle, Hobkerk's, Camden.*
112 William B. Kimbrough, Graves's, Putnam.
113 J. Rousseau, Sen., s. l. w., Kendrick's, Putnam.*
114 James Wadsworth's, Bivins's, Jones.*
115 Mary Russell, w., 6th, Chatham.
116 Joseph Greer, Griffin's, Hall.
117 Michael Buff, sol., Smith's, Madison.*
118 Isaac Miller, 271st, M'Intosh.*
119 Haynes's four orphans, Latimer's, De Kalb.
120 Samuel Waits, r. s., M'Gehee's, Troup.
121 David Holloway, sol., Elder's, Clarke.*
122 Cornelius Bradley, Sen., Curry's, Wilkinson.*
123 P. & Wm. King, f. a., Collins's, Henry.*
124 John N. Champion, 2d, Chatham.
125 David W. Palman, Jenkins's, Oglethorpe.*
126 Samuel Kerlin, Howell's, Elbert.
127 Jepthah West, Stephens's, Habersham.*
128 Rebecca Tomlinson, w., Cowart's, Lowndes.*
129 Michael Barnwell, r. s., Chambers's, Houston.*
130 John Tompson, 417th, Walton.*
131 William Stewart, Mullen's, Carroll.*
132 Seaborn Newsom, Park's, Washington.*
133 James Moore, Harrison's, Decatur.*
134 Boswell Goyens, 555th, Upson.
135 John Morris, Jr., Coker's, Troup.*
136 Burgess Jester, Allen's, Henry.*
137 Simeon Pattello, Few's, Muscogee.*
138 William M'Elhenney, Jr., 373d, Jasper.*
139 John Head, Jr., Martin's, Hall.*
140 Francis Dancy's ors., Curry's, Wilkinson.
141 John Runnels, Edwards's, Talbot.
142 Isaac Hall, r. s., Payne's, Merriwether.*
143 John F. Wasson, Chambers's, Gwinnett.
144 James M. Feagan, Winter's, Jones.
145 Alfred Watkins, Bostick's, Twiggs.
146 William Langley, 404th, Gwinnett.
147 Hardy Lewis Fennel, 588th, Upson.*
148 Zachariah M'Clendon, Mann's, Crawford.*
149 John M'Clendon, Harp's, Stewart.

150 Alexander W. Snead, 108th, Hancock.*
151 Greenberry Gandy, Newman's, Thomas.*
152 Mary Ballard, w., 72d, Burke.*
153 Margaret Campbell, w., 406th, Gwinnett.
154 John T. Bryan, Justice's, Bibb.*
155 James Word, Aderhold's, Campbell.
156 John S. Holt, s. l. w., 120th, Richmond.
157 Wiley Adams, Peterson's, Montgomery.*
158 Nathaniel Moody, Baker's, Liberty.*
159 James Sowell, Hood's, Henry.*
160 William Spain, Ellis's, Pulaski.*
161 Joseph Payne, O'Neal's, Laurens.*
162 Wiley Muckelroy, Phillips's, Monroe.*
163 Allen M'Walker, 470th, Upson.
164 Henry C. Spier, 466th, Monroe.*
165 Matthew Smith, s. l. w., Martin's, Laurens.*
166 Nathaniel Venable's ors., 245th, Jackson.
167 Jacob Oxford, Hughes's, Habersham.*
168 William A. Thompson, Ellsworth's, Bibb.
169 Elizabeth Sanford, w., Morgan's, Appling.*
170 William B. Mann, M'Culler's, Newton.*
171 Stephen Palmer, Herndon's, Hall.*
172 Edward Miller, id., Martin's, Jones.
173 Thomas Wilson, Mays's, Monroe.
174 Curry Bennett Dickson, Monk's, Crawford.*
175 Charles Walden, Wright's, Laurens.
176 Elias Davis, Whitaker's, Crawford.
177 George B. Harris, or., 6th, Chatham.
178 William Wood, Davis's, Jones.*
179 William Hollaway's ors., M'Linn's, Butts.
180 Walker's orphans, Morrison's, Montgomery.
181 Littlebury B. Jackson, Loveless's, Gwinnett.*
182 Rachael Culpepper, w., Iverson's, Houston.
183 James Crowley, sol., Martin's, Pike.*
184 Christians Heights, Mullen's, Carroll.*
185 Elijah Twilly, Hudson's, Marion.
186 Travis Nichols, s. l. w., Nichols's, Fayette.
187 Ranson Dees, Davis's, Jones.*
188 Elizabeth Greene, w., Bailey's, Laurens.
189 Vincent Thompson, Dearing's, Henry.*
190 James Wilmoreland, 404th, Gwinnett.
191 Charles Walden, Wright's, Laurens.
192 Burwell Whalley, Alberson's, Walton.
193 James Garner, 761st, Heard.*
194 Hollis M. Pate, Compton's, Fayette.*
195 Daniel R. Sutley, Moore's, Randolph.*
196 Josiah Baismore, Baismore's, Jones.*

197 William Garrett, sol., Harp's, Stewart.*
198 Jesse Hammett, Mullen's, Carroll.*
199 James H. Dumas, 466th, Monroe.*
200 Sarah Taylor, w., Wood's, Morgan.*
201 David G. Rogers, York's, Stewart.*
202 William Kitchen, Collins's, Henry.*
203 George Long, 373d, Jasper.*
204 Gabriel Dix, sol., 26th, Glynn.*
205 Robert N. Brooking, sol., 113th, Hancock.*
206 Dempsey Fennel, Newman's, Thomas.*
207 David Hickox, Green's, Ware.*
208 James Bell, Coxe's, Franklin.*
209 George L. Alexander, 293d, Jasper.*
210 Mary Truluck, Hicks's, Decatur.*
211 William Legraird's or., Crawford's, Franklin.
212 Howard Cash, Johnson's, De Kalb.
213 William L. Tipton, Jones's, Habersham.
214 Thomas Arria, Vining's, Putnam.
215 William Scott, r. s., Atkinson's, Coweta.*
216 James H. Worly, Burnett's, Habersham.*
217 Henry Singleton, Ball's, Monroe.*
218 Henry Roser, Fitzpatrick's, Chatham.*
219 George Runnels, 320th, Baldwin.*
220 William Moore, Bishop's, Henry.
221 Proctor Williamson, Whitaker's, Crawford.
222 Andrew M'Neal, Rutland's, Bibb.
223 Pleasant A. Lawson, Robinson's, Putnam.*
224 William W. Perry, M'Ginnis's, Jackson.*
225 James Vogles, Sen., Martin's, Hall.
226 William Silton, Field's, Habersham.*
227 Francis C. Black, Holton's, Emanuel.*
228 Matthew Higginbotham, Morgan's, Madison.*
229 Whitsen Jarrett, Riden's, Jackson.*
230 David Blackwell, 404th, Gwinnett.*
231 John Daniel, Kendrick's, Putnam.*
232 Patrick Dailly Bond, Gittens's, Fayette.*
233 Green Tanner, Morrison's, Appling.*
234 Lewis Brunley, Wood's, Morgan.*
235 John Slaughter, Edwards's, Talbot.*
236 Bleoford Albright, Bridges's, Gwinnett.*
237 Elisha Walkins, Roe's, Burke.*
238 Jacob Lewis's ors., 38th, Scriven.*
239 Alfred Grogan, Wynn's, Gwinnett.*
240 Jesse Attaway, Rogers's, Burke.*
241 William Lundy, 113th, Hancock.*   .
242 Edward Black, sol., Campbell's, Wilkes.*
243 Thomas M. Berrien, sol., Roe's, Burke.*

244 Job Tye, Wolfskin's, Oglethorpe.*
245 Samuel Player, 122d, Richmond.*
246 Daniel Boatwright, Kelly's, Elbert.*
247 Mark Lott, Douglass's, Telfair.
248 Samuel M. White, 537th, Upson.*
249 Rebecca Slater, w., Whitaker's, Crawford.*
250 William Doughtee, Jr., Kendrick's, Monroe.*
251 Elijah White, Whitfield's, Washington.*
252 William Eubank's ors., Graves's, Lincoln.
253 Charles Grover, or., Peavy's, Bulloch.*
254 John B. Cartwright, 143d, Greene.
255 Beverly Daniel, Daniel's, Hall.
256 Robert Cade's ors., Jr., Bragaw's, Oglethorpe.
257 Arthur Bar's ors., Boynton's, Twiggs.
258 James Cody's ors., Pate's, Warren.
259 William T. Blackshear, Blackshear's, Laurens.*
260 Dexter F. Richards, Kendrick's, Putnam.*
261 William C. Alley, Dyer's, Habersham.
262 John Shiflet, Stower's, Elbert.*
263 William A. Cowan, sol., Will's, Twiggs.*
264 David M'Murran, r. s., Nesbit's, Newton.*
265 T. W. Baldwin's ors., Hargrove's, Oglethorpe.
266 Wade H. Anderson, Walden's, Pulaski.*
267 Albert G. Beaty, Miller's, Jackson.
268 Dabner Berry's ors., 600th, Richmond.*
269 John Cooksey, r. s., M'Culler's, Newton.*
270 Sanford Goodwin, Reid's, Gwinnett.
271 James N. Right, Mayo's, Wilkinson.
272 John Orr's ors., Miller's, Jackson.
273 Eliz. Snellgrove, or., Whitehead's, Habersham.*
274 Abner M'Durman, Lane's, Morgan.*
275 Powel P. Vincent, Rooks's, Putnam.
276 Alfred C. Mason, Estes's, Putnam.*
277 Natham Brewton, Brewton's, Tatnall.*
278 David Clark's ors., 600th, Richmond.
279 Reuben R. Darden, Kellum's, Talbot.*
280 James Cobb, Willis's, Franklin.*
281 Aaron Dodd, Anderson's, Wilkes.
282 Little B. Jackson, 147th, Greene.
283 Lee Lay, 4th, Chatham.*
284 James L. Pair, Johnson's, De Kalb.
285 Edwin A. Gallagher, 600th, Richmond.*
286 Daniel M'Daniel, Iverson's, Houston.*
287 Henry Cambron, Griffin's, De Kalb.*
288 Thomas M'Gran, 120th, Richmond.*
289 Turner Robertson, Peterson's, Burke.*
290 William P. Denison, Williams's, Ware.*

291 Johnathan P. Cordrey, Barwick's, Washington.*
292 Madison Carter, 589th, Upson.*
293 John Davis, r. s., M'Craney's, Lowndes.*
294 Mary Page, w., Barrow's, Houston.
295 William B. Roberts, 117th, Hancock.*
296 Nicholas Berry, 34th, Scriven.*
297 John Jackson, Jr., Morgan's, Clarke.*
298 Susan Deshields, w., Ballard's, Morgan.
299 Minton Shaw, Collins's, Henry.*
300 Thomas May, 143d, Greene.*
301 Francis Paris's ors., Paris, Burke.*
302 David Robertson, Sutton's, Habersham.
303 John Tillet, Miller's, Ware.*
304 William J. Coxe, or., Smith's, Madison.*
305 Andrew Defoor, Smith's, Habersham.*
306 John Carter, M'Linn's, Butts.*
307 James S. Walker, Hearn's, Butts.
308 Abel Butler, sol., Coxe's, Talbot.*
309 John Heatly, sol., Madden's, Pike.*
310 Joseph Phillips, Peterson's, Montgomery.
311 William Chapman, Martin's, Stewart.*
312 Brice C. M'Ever, Jones's, Hall.
313 James Hollimon's ors., Dozier's, Columbia.
314 William Williams, 49th, Emanuel.*
315 Jared Joines, Sinquefield's, Washington.*
316 Seth P. Pool, 1st section, Cherokee.*
317 Seaborn Gwyn, 250th, Walton.*
318 David Weaver, Wood's, Morgan.*
319 Isaac Gray, Levritt's, Lincoln.*
320 Thomas Holmes, r. s., David's, Franklin.
321 Triplett Shumate's ors., Cliett's, Columbia.*
322 William Gallaway, 419th, Walton.*
323 Josiah Pollard, Lunceford's, Wilkes.
324 Samuel Brasswell, sol., Thomas's, Clarke.*

ELEVENTH DISTRICT, THIRD SECTION, CHEROKEE.

1 George King, Hammond's, Franklin.
2 Jesse Smith, Sen., r. s., Edwards's, Franklin.
3 William Braddaway, Braddy's, Jones.
4 William W. Griffin, Griffin's, De Kalb.
5 James J. Smith, Herndon's, Hall.
6 James Askew's ors., 107th, Hancock.
7 Henry Matthews's ors., Wynn's, Gwinnett.

8 Mercer Rhodes, Martin's, Newton.*
9 Reuben Harris, 419th, Walton.
10 David O. Dye, Rogers's, Burke.*
11 Abraham Brooks, Strickland's, Merriwether.*
12 Richard Marrifee, Mizell's, Talbot.
13 James Baxter's ors., Allen's, Henry.
14 Stephen Collins, Swain's, Thomas.*
15 Abraham Wright, Curry's, Merriwether.
16 Zachariah Jordan, Bostick's, Twiggs.*
17 William Kieth, Whelchel's, Hall.
18 Robert Hodges, Prescott's, Twiggs.
19 Catharine Moulder, w., Gittens's, Fayette.
20 Joseph J. Collins, Gay's, Harris.*
21 William Leverett's ors., Whipple's, Wilkinson.*
22 Elizabeth Bladen, or., 121st, Richmond.*
23 Zachariah Kitchens, Morton's, De Kalb.*
24 Allen Gunter, Stower's, Elbert.*
25 Starling Willaford's ors., 687th, Lee.
26 Thomas M'Gehee, 293d, Jasper.*
27 William Jordan, Givins's, De Kalb.*
28 Mary Johnson, w., Seay's, Hall.
29 William M'Gehee, Taylor's, Jones.
30 George Crotwell, 404th, Gwinnett.*
31 John Cason, Park's, Walton.
32 Thomas M. Carden, s. l. w., Moore's, Randolph.*
33 Cooper B. Tate, Edwards's, Franklin.*
34 Elizabeth Yarbrough, w., Brock's, Habersham.
35 Robert Burke, Jr., sol., Collier's, Monroe.
36 Jesse Farr, Robinson's, Fayette.*
37 Ivey W. Gregory, Gunn's, Jefferson.*
38 Ambrose Jones, 116th, Hancock.
39 William Jones, Sen., r. s., Wilson's, Jasper.
40 John Allen, sol., Salem, Baldwin.*
41 Benjamin Tompkins, Martin's, Stewart.*
42 Ewin Brown, 295th, Jasper.*
43 Joshua Hennington, Bush's, Pulaski.*
44 John Conn, Hamilton's, Hall.
45 William Clayton, Young's, Carroll.*
46 John Lumpkin, 119th, Richmond.*
47 James E. Blan, Griffin's, Fayette.
48 James Prescott, Rogers's, Burke.
49 Abraham L. Venable's or., Robinson's, Harris
50 Mary Jeter, w., Parham's, Warren.*
51 Eve Boggs, w. r. s., 242d, Jackson.*
52 Bower's orphans, 271st, M'Intosh.
53 James D. Frierson, Candler's, Bibb.*
54 Franklin Taylor, Lay's, Jackson.*

55 Martin Mahuffey, Mullen's, Carroll.*
56 John Sutherland's ors., Field's, Habersham.
57 Joseph Stiles, s. i. w., 1st, Chatham.*
58 John Fitzpatrick, Will's, Twiggs.*
59 Hiram Evans, Dobbs's, Hall.*
60 Benj. Collins's two orphans, Martin's, De Kalb.*
61 John J. M. Smith, Newman's, Thomas.*
62 Joseph Guice, 419th, Walton.
63 Charles Atkins, Sen., r. s., 558th, Upson.*
64 John Campbell, Carswell's, Jefferson.*
65 James Kenedy, Fitzpatrick's, Chatham.*
66 James Logan's ors., Wynn's, Gwinnett.
67 William Harris, Heard's, De Kalb.*
68 Thomas R. Hanson, 693d, Heard.*
69 Richard Dowdey, Coxe's, Talbot.*
70 Lewis Hays, sol., Allen's, Henry.*
71 Berry Hobbs, 640th, Dooly.*
72 Sally Lynn, w. r. s., Williams's, Jasper.*
73 Charles F. Bugg, Bell's, Columbia.*
74 Samuel Smith, Mason's, Washington.*
75 George Varner, r. s., Smith's, Franklin.
76 Rebecca White, w., Hill's, Stewart.
77 Charles L. Holcomb, Deavours's, Habersham.
78 Angus M'Lead's ors., Peterson's, Montgomery.
79 James Chesnut, Hudson's, Marion.
80 John R. M'Mullians, r. s., Smith's, Franklin.*
81 John C. White, Brackett's, Newton.*
82 Reuben Bishop, sol., Griffin's, De Kalb.*
83 James Briggers, Peavy's, Bulloch.
84 Joseph Nixon's six orphans, Harris's, De Kalb.
85 Janis Daugley, Mizell's, Talbot.*
86 John J. Young, Washington's, Carroll.*
87 Clem Martin, 600th, Richmond.*
88 Josiah Pinder, Underwood's, Putnam.
89 Milley Martin, w., Seay's, Hall.
90 James Black, Sewell's, Franklin.
91 John C. Jordan, Jordan's, Harris.*
92 Erastus Young, Gunn's, Jefferson.
93 James S. Thompson, Tuggle's, Merriwether.*
94 Peter Haynie, 242d, Jackson.
95 Edmon O'Neal's ors., Underwood's, Putnam.*
96 Isaac Durham, Latimer's, De Kalb.*
97 Kinchen Curl, sol., Johnson's, Bibb.*
98 Sarah Dannally, w., M'Clendon's, Putnam.
99 Francis M. Stribling, Norman's, Wilkes.
100 William Smith, Jr., Hearn's, Butts.*
101 William Haukinsspruce, Baker's, Gwinnett.*

102 Samuel Crofton, Pace's, Putnam.
103 William W. Adams, sol., Mitchell's, Pulaski.*
104 Thomas H. Blair, Cook's, Telfair.*
105 James Turner, Jr., Kendrick's, Monroe.
106 Lewis H. Linch, s. l. w., Taylor's, Putnam.*
107 Stephen Lile, Jr., Lamberth's, Fayette.
108 Green Furgerson, 561st, Upson.
109 Seaborn Skinner, 119th, Richmond.*
110 Susan Golding, w., Hargrove's, Oglethorpe.*
111 Mary Jackson, w. r. s., Martin's, Washington.*
112 Susannah M. Furlow, w., Cleggs's, Walton.
113 Gilbert Austin, Chambers's, Gwinnett.
114 Elihu Woodall, Ellsworth's, Bibb.
115 Dicey Pool, w. r. s., Crow's, Pike.
116 Mary Ernest, w., Justice's, Bibb.
117 George Storey, Craven's, Coweta.*
118 Carter Steplerd, Maguire's, Morgan.*
119 Hamilton Bayles, Wootten's, Telfair.*
120 Wiley T. Hodges, Dupree's, Washington.*
121 Adam Wall, sol., M'Millon's, Lincoln.*
122 William Morris, Edwards's, Talbot.*
123 Lott Mercer, Bishop's, Henry.*
124 Ferdinan Vickers, sol., Griffin's, Merriwether.*
125 R. R. Browning, Sen., sol., Newman's, Thomas.*
126 James C. Humphreys, 36th, Scriven.*
127 Susy Jackson, Herndon's, Hall.
128 Lewis Green, 4th section, Cherokee.
129 Joseph Barnes's ors., Taylor's, Putnam.
130 David Harrell, Williams's, Washington.*
131 James Doster, Roberts's, Hall.
132 John H. Jones, Ball's, Monroe.*
133 William H. Alexander, Holley's, Franklin.*
134 James Garner, 761st, Heard.*
135 Thomas Matthews, Lane's, Morgan.
136 Elijah Chastain, Ellis's, Rabun.
137 William Piles, Whitaker's, Crawford.*
138 Ann Burton, w., M'Linn's, Butts.*
139 Thomas Garner, Lane's, Morgan.*
140 Reuben Kemp, Ball's, Monroe.*
141 Southey Littleton, Jr., Kendrick's, Monroe.*
142 James Stubbs, Chandler's, Franklin.*
143 John Kights, Curry's, Merriwether.*
144 Burrel Smith, sol., Griffin's, De Kalb.*
145 James M. Thomas, M'Coy's, Houston.
146 Anne Springer, w. r. s., Moseley's, Wilkes.*
147 Thomas H. Wamock, sol., 35th, Scriven.*
148 Sini Bell Smith, Craven's, Coweta.*

149 Henry W. Carter, Davis's, Clarke.*
150 James R. Cook, Clietts's, Columbia.*
151 Mary M'Neely, w., 248th, Jackson.*
152 Alexander Harris, Dearing's, Henry.
153 Benjamin Chastain, Sen., Dyer's, Habersham.
154 Apser Thompson, Crawford's, Morgan.
155 Joseph Roderick, 516th, Dooly.*
156 Hughy Hall, 735th, Troup.*
157 Zachariah Cowart, Sen., r. s., 510th, Early.*
158 Samuel Deloach, Justice's, Bibb.
159 Thomas Moris, Higginbotham's, Rabun.
160 Jemima Fincher, w., Smith's, Henry.
161 John Forsyth, Jr., 398th, Richmond.*
162 Allen M'Carty, Brewer's, Walton.
163 William Cobb, Cobb's, Muscogee.
164 Howell Horton, Everett's, Washington.*
165 Henry W. Bond, Lunceford's, Elbert.*
166 Francis Pierson, Russell's, Henry.*
167 John T. Blake, Candler's, Bibb.*
168 James S. Owens, M'Millon's, Lincoln.*
169 Richard Speak, Sen., r. s., M'Linn's, Butts.*
170 Michael Kerkcum, 248th, Jackson.
171 Peter Stewart, Rutland's, Bibb.
172 Elhum Brewer, Hargrove's, Newton.
173 Lydia Cooper, w., 3d, Chatham.
174 Allen Wheeler's ors., Wood's, Morgan.
175 Charles E. Mims, Few's, Muscogee.
176 Elizabeth Sheffield, w., Winter's, Jones.
177 John Smith's ors., Sanders's, Jones.
178 Alfred Shaw, Ballard's, Morgan.*
179 Ishmael Ayres, Lester's, Pulaski.*
180 Sarah Ann Langrooth, or., 1st, Chatham.
181 John Robertson, sol., Coxe's, Talbot.*
182 Charles Jordan, Sen., r. s., Crow's, Merriwether.*
183 William Ganer, or., 118th, Hancock.*
184 William Sheffield, Sen., s. l. w., 104th, Hancock.*
185 Absolum Bumgarner, 406th, Gwinnett.
186 Richmond Dozier, Sinclair's, Houston.
187 William J. Gober, sol., Wynn's, Gwinnett.
188 James K. Stokes, Dupree's, Washington.
189 William Craddock, Tower's, Gwinnett.*
190 Charles Harvey, Mashburn's, Pulaski.
191 Jonathan M. Peck, Peurifoy's, Henry.*
192 Jeremiah H. Moore, 143d, Greene.
193 Thomas Hogan, Clinton's, Campbell.*
194 Wiley Barber, Coxe's, Talbot.*
195 William Jones,ᵃ Edwards's, Franklin.

a See Executive Order of 11th July, 1833.

196 Samuel Woodruff, Woodruff's, Campbell.*
197 Charles H. Jackson, ———, Chatham.
198 Celia Barley, w., Griffin's, Burke.*
199 Simpson Newell, Madden's, Pike.
200 Harrison Westmoreland, Allison's, Pike.
201 William Barnett, Hardiman's, Oglethorpe.*
202 Samuel Brooks's ors., Madden's, Pike,
203 Samuel H. Fiske, Sanderlin's, Chatham.*
204 John W. Simmons, Hill's, Morgan.*
205 Samuel P. Yomans, Newman's, Thomas.*
206 Benjamin F. Lane, Johnson's, Bibb.*
207 Sarah Cook, w., Gray's, Henry.
208 Allen M'Daniel, sol., Covington's, Pike.*
209 Samuel Pearson, Bryan's, Monroe.
210 Mary G. Walker, w., 398th, Richmond.
211 William S. Sanders, Price's, Hall.*
212 John W. Satterhee, 113th, Hancock.
213 Harvy M. Mays, Fleming's, Franklin.*
214 John E. Leverett, Griffin's, De Kalb.
215 Henry Morgan, Sen., Hamilton's, Gwinnett.
216 Willis Curry, Hall's, Butts.
217 Levi M. Crawford, Dean's, Clarke.
218 Jonathan Studstill, 430th, Early.*
219 Matthew C. Dukes, Groover's, Thomas.*
220 John Todd's ors., Sullivan's, Jones.*
221 Thomas Beard, 34th, Scriven.
222 James T. Johnston, Hodges's, Newton.*
223 Ezekiel Hall, Kendrick's, Putnam.
224 Benjamin Barbee, Peace's, Wilkinson.
225 Charles G. Fletcher, Lockhart's, Bulloch
226 Simeon H. Weaver, Vining's, Putnam.
227 Thomas G. Phillip, 404th, Gwinnett.*
228 David Cook, Mackleroy's, Clarke.*
229 James Lanier, sol., Chambers's, Gwinnett.*
230 William F. Scott, sol., 320th, Baldwin.
231 Thomas Foster, 122d, Richmond.*
232 John Smith, 143d, Greene.
233 Bartholomew Westbrooks, Lamberth's, Fayette.
234 Richard M. Hackney, Nichols's, Fayette.
235 James Norris, sol. 1784–97, M'Culler's, Newton.
236 David G. Hutchinson, 417th, Walton.*
237 Patrick M'Callum, sol., Ball's, Monroe.
238 John Watson, Wilcox's, Telfair.
239 Spencer Thomas, sol., 466th, Monroe.*
240 Wm. O. Dabney, s. l. w., Hargrove's, Oglethorpe.*
241 David Hassard, Robison's, Washington.*
242 George M. Gresham, sol., Chambers's, Gwinnett.*

243 William T. Brawner, Morton's, De Kalb.*
244 Lovick P. M'Donald, Harralson's, Troup.*
245 David M. Fitts, 3d, Chatham.
246 James Kemp, Rhodes's, De Kalb.
247 Clemmon Lindsey, Strickland's, Merriwether.
248 James M. Mitchell, Mitchell's, Pulaski.
249 Dennis Fowler, Whisenhunt's, Carroll.*
250 Jesse C. Knight, Smith's, Henry.*
251 James Reynolds, 108th, Hancock.*
252 Henry Thompson, Holton's, Emanuel.
253 Dempsey Button, Norris's, Monroe.
254 Pascal H. Magourk, Coxe's, Talbot.
255 John B. Norrell, 122d, Richmond.*
256 Stephen K. Williams, Allison's, Pike.
257 Beal Edwards, 10th, Effingham.*
258 Mary Ann Richardson, w., Smith's, Henry.*
259 Martha Long, w. r. s., 114th, Hancock.
260 Barnett Jackson, Price's, Hall.
261 Jacob Cline, White's, Franklin.*
262 Morgan W. M'Afer, Willingham's, Harris.*
263 John Leathers, Mullen's, Carroll.*
264 Jonathan Burgess, sol., Howard's, Oglethorpe.*
265 Goodman Hughes, Hughes's, Habersham.
266 Pleasant R. Mayo, Watson's, Marion.*
267 Joel Dryden, Williams's, Ware.*
268 John Williams's ors., Edwards's, Franklin.*
269 Jacob Skinner, 72d, Burke.
270 Isaac Holland, Few's, Muscogee.
271 Neal F. Cochrane, 149th, Greene.
272 Samuel Finley, sol., Price's, Hall.
273 Edward Hopkins, Hopkins's, Camden.*
274 Patrick W. Flynn, Flynn's, Muscogee.
275 Alexander Crawford, Bishop's, Henry.*
276 John Giles, sol., Garner's, Washington.
277 James Walker, Sen., r. s., 470th, Upson.*
278 James Merrill's ors., Allen's, Monroe.
279 Joseph H. Watts, Chisholm's, Morgan.*
280 James L. Coleman, 119th, Richmond.
281 Hugh B. Greenwood's 3 ors., Latimer's, De Kalb*
282 Stephen Nolen, Hamilton's, Gwinnett.
283 Henry Harden, Hearn's, Butts.
284 Bryant Burnam, Folsom's, Lowndes.*
285 John Browning, sol., Morgan's, Clarke.
286 Robert Jennings, r. s., Hatchett's, Oglethorpe.
287 Penelepy Hadler, w., Nichols's, Fayette.
288 William Smith, Harp's, Stewart.*
289 Elizabeth Edwards, Wolfskin's, Oglethorpe.

290 John Waldron, Bourquin's, Chatham.
291 John Watkins, Roe's, Burke.*
292 James Gilmore, r. s., Sparks's, Washington.*
293 Bennet M. Stroger, Camp's, Merriwether.*
294 Beverly Watkins, Brown's, Habersham.
295 Allen Jones, Ballard's, Morgan.
296 John W. Stewart, House's, Henry.*
297 Hardy H. Jean, 779th, Heard.*
298 Henry M'Donnell, Sanderlin's, Chatham.*
299 John Speers, Morrison's, Montgomery.
300 James B. Bryant, Paris, Burke.*
301 Benjamin Kiker, Burnett's, Habersham.*
302 William Bramblet, Dobbs's, Hall.*
303 Enoch Rigby, Smith's, Houston.
304 Jeremiah Keadle, Bryan's, Monroe.*
305 Obedience Easterling, w., Wynn's, Gwinnett.
306 Ira E. Smith, Ware's, Coweta.
307 Isham Corley, Mizell's, Talbot.*
308 Charles W. Dehham, Tompkins's, Putnam.
309 Samuel W. Jones, Justice's, Bibb.
310 Anthony Lewis, s. i. w., 38th, Scriven.*
311 Eli R. Callaway's ors., Bragaw's, Oglethorpe.
312 Elizabeth Page, mi., f. a., Stower's, Elbert.
313 James Blanset, Williams's, Decatur.
314 Abel F. Nelson, Norris's, Monroe.*
315 Charles Horton, Sen., Hughes's, Habersham.
316 Martin Shaw, Folsom's, Lowndes.
317 Hezekiah Bailey, 600th, Richmond.*
318 William Gilbert, sol., 1st, Chatham.*
319 Elizabeth Hendrey, w., 259th, Scriven.
320 Thomas Fielder, sol., Clark's, Morgan.*
321 James B. Tally, Latimer's, De Kalb.*
322 James Halsey, sol., Dobbs's, Hall.*
323 Morris Ansly, Perryman's, Warren.*
324 Jesse J. Weaver, Bailey's, Laurens.

31

TWELFTH DISTRICT, THIRD SECTION, CHEROKEE.

1 William Selman, r. s., 555th, Upson.
2 M'Cullus Springer, Stewart's, Warren.
3 John Duke, Burnett's, Lowndes.*
4 Samuel Worthy, Rhodes's, De Kalb.*
5 Richard Smith, Sen., Lynn's, Warren.
6 Ely Holly, Polhill's, Burke.*
7 Theodore Brown, 122d, Richmond.
8 Joel D. Trammell, Williams's, Walton.
9 David Canley, Peterson's, Montgomery.
10 John Strayhorn, Davis's, Gwinnett.
11 Randal Cox, Bush's, Burke.*
12 David M. Fitts, 3d, Chatham.*
13 William E. Grady, Moore's, Randolph.
14 Stark Brown, s. i. w., 419th, Walton.*
15 Easley Dawson, Field's, Habersham.*
16 George Nolen, Russell's, Henry.*
17 James Beverly, Jr., 561st, Upson.
18 William Holloman, Taylor's, Houston.
19 (fr.) Elizabeth Brown, w., Mashburn's, Pulaski.*
20 (fr.) Lucy H. Johnson, or., Jordan's, Bibb.
21 Wm. A. Herring's ors., Howell's, Elbert.
22 Samuel B. Moore, Mashburn's, Pulaski.
23 Richard W. Wood, Jr., Martin's, Newton.
24 Nancy Martin, w., Rhodes's, De Kalb.*
25 James Cochran, 248th, Jackson.*
26 John Schley, Jr., Few's, Muscogee.*
27 Pascal Brooks, sol., Aderhold's, Campbell.
28 Tarpley Turvalyville, Duke's, Carroll.*
29 Patsey Vernon, w. r. s., Colley's, Oglethorpe.
30 Frederic Davidson, Brock's, Habersham.
31 Brigs W. Hopson, M'Ewin's, Monroe.*
32 Sarah D. Parks, w., Robinson's, Putnam.*
33 William Elliot, Lester's, Monroe.*
34 David Holder, Stewart's, Warren.
35 M. S. E. & N. M'Dill, ors., 404th, Gwinnett.
36 William Pace, Brooks's, Muscogee.
37 Obedience Bass, w. s.1784–97, Parham's, Warren*
38 Dixon Cureton, Coxe's, Talbot.*
39 Joseph S. Johnson, sol., Compton's, Fayette.*
40 William Brown, Sen., m. s., Peavy's, Bulloch.*
41 Henry F. Millink, sol., Cleland's, Chatham.*

42 James D. Randle, M'Clendon's, Putnam.
43 George Wilcox, Dixon's, Irwin.*
44 Paul Dupon, Cleland's, Chatham.*
45 Needham Dearn, Williams's, Decatur.*
46 John Chappell, 249th, Walton.
47 Elizabeth Cannon, w., Hughes's, Habersham.*
48 John Russell, 6th, Chatham.*
49 Mark A. Lane, Moseley's, Wilkes.*
50 Isaac Hathcock, Peace's, Wilkinson.*
51 Wyatt Foard's ors., Martin's, Jones.
52 Joseph Todd, sol., 537th, Upson.
53 John G. Fry, Atkinson's, Coweta.*
54 John P. Lloyds, Kellum's, Talbot.
55 Isham Tennell's ors., Evans's, Laurens.
56 Patrick G. Halloway, 588th, Upson.*
57 (fr.) David Akridge, sol., Thomas's, Clarke.
58 (fr.) William Guthrie, Atkinson's, Coweta.
59 Zuba Wells, h. a., Hall's, Oglethorpe.
60 William Jackson, Sen., 162d, Greene.
61 John Hays, Latimer's, De Kalb.*
62 Absolem Harris, Scroggins's, Oglethorpe.*
63 Nancy Gordron, w. r. s., Gunn's, Jones.
64 Isaaci Mobley, s. l. w., Hardman's, Oglethorpe.*
65 Benjamin Nipper, Douglass's, Telfair.*
66 Nathaniel Denham, Slone's, Irwin.*
67 Henry H. Mangham, Mizell's, Talbot.*
68 Carswell Hearn, Walker's, Houston.
69 John W. H. Mercer, Cleland's, Chatham.*
70 John Gentry, Burgess's, Carroll.
71 Simeon Freeman, 295th, Jasper.
72 John W. Lewis, 105th, Baldwin.
73 Jordan Hillard, Bailey's, Laurens.*
74 William Lowe, Sen., Arrington's, Merriwether.*
75 Jane Paris, w. r. s., Whitehead's, Habersham.*
76 George L. Douglass, Frasier's, Monroe.
77 James Brooks, Dyer's, Habersham.
78 Elijah Shaw, or., Lay's, Jackson.
79 Robert S. Wood, Berry's, Butts.*
80 Andrew S. Hamilton, Keener's, Rabun.*
81 Samuel Shearman, Maguire's, Morgan.
82 Joseph Camp, Jr., 249th, Walton.
83 Henry Nichols, 72d, Burke.*
84 John W. Osburn, 118th, Hancock.*
85 William D. Algiers, sol., Burk's, Stewart.
86 Daniel Aderhold, Aderhold's, Campbell.*
87 Joshua Hall, Griffin's, Burke.*
88 Hardy Brown, Herring's, Twiggs.

89   Eleary Delony, Morton's, De Kalb.*
90   Mary Edmondson, w., Lynn's, Warren.
91   Richard Hughes, Thomas's, Clarke.
92   Ambrose Baber, sol., Ellsworth's, Bibb.
93   Nathaniel Miller, Perry's, Baldwin.
94   Reuben R. Mobley, sol., Huey's, Harris.*
95   (fr.) John M'Quean, Peterson's, Montgomery.
96   (fr.) Jas. W. & A. F. Stubbs, ors., Bivins's, Jones.
97   Augustus G. Bryant, Blackstock's, Hall.*
98   John Barefield, Barefield's, Jones.
99   William Watkins, Sen., Flynn's, Muscogee.*
100 William Cochran, Sen., Chastain's, Habersham.
101 Rebecca Smith, w., 144th, Greene.*
102 Zachariah C. Kidd, Jenkins's, Oglethorpe.*
103 Thomas R. Blair, Garner's, Washington.*
104 Stephen Jackson, Hall's, Butts.
105 James Willis, Smith's, Henry.
106 William Touchstone, sol., Gray's, Henry.
107 George W. Johnson, Valleau's, Chatham.*
108 Benjamin Parr, idiot, Holley's, Franklin.*
109 James Henry Edenfield's ors., Tenyer's, Telfair.
110 Thomas M. Calhem, Harp's, Stewart.*
111 John Holt, Jones's, Hall.*
112 Jesse Mann, Gittens's, Fayette.*
113 Hilliard O'Neal, M'Ewin's, Monroe.
114 Jacob Rowe, 320th, Baldwin.
115 Levi Florence's ors., 600th, Richmond.
116 Josiah Bass, 735th, Troup.*
117 Rodey Gibbons, h. a., 34th, Scriven.
118 Joseph B. Byars, Baley's, Butts.*
119 Ephraim Turner's ors., 395th, Emanuel.
120 Samuel Howard, Howard's, Oglethorpe.*
121 Allen Strickland, Morrison's, Appling.
122 Cortis Hudspeth, Guice's, Oglethorpe.*
123 Margaret Patton, w., Jordan's, Bibb.
124 Joseph T. Talley, Holley's, Franklin.
125 Elijah Smith, Smith's, Habersham.
126 Edward W. Williams's ors., 36th, Scriven.*
127 John C. Henderson, Allen's, Henry.
128 James M. Bentley, Peurifoy's, Henry.*
129 William Seacalraun, Herndon's, Hall.*
130 Thomas Overton, 602d, Taliaferro.
131 William Peters's ors., Oliver's, Twiggs.
132 John Harris, sol., Adams's, Columbia.
133 (fr.) William Sikes, Brown's, Camden.*
134 (fr.) John Nix, Reid's, Gwinnett.
135 Griffin M'Mitchell, Hall's, Butts.*

136 J. Owdonis's ors., Dyer's, Habersham.
137 Isaiah Dodson, House's, Henry.
138 John Fenn, 398th, Richmond.
139 Philip Blanchett's ors., 243d, Jackson.*
140 Edwin Anderson, Lay's, Jackson.
141 Silus M'Cleland, M'Cleland's, Irwin.
142 James Kings's ors., Gibson's, Decatur.
143 John J. Davis, 600th, Richmond.*
144 James Collins, 733d, Dooly.
145 James Boyas, Cook's, Telfair.
146 Elizabeth Luckett, w., 603d, Taliaferro.*
147 Robert Meek, Hood's, Henry.*
148 Mary & Henry Prescott, ors., Griffin's, Burke.*
149 James W. M. Berrien, 102d, Hancock.*
150 William Gunn, Gunn's, Jones.*
151 George Holzendorf, or., Hopkins's, Camden.*
152 Theophilus Jones, Walker's, Houston.*
153 Willis C. Norris, Reed's, Gwinnett.*
154 Elizabeth Senerson, w., Lockhart's, Bulloch.*
155 Milley Coleman, w., Rooks's, Putnam.*
156 Richard Johnson, 559th, Walton.
157 Hugh A. Lawrence, Grider's, Morgan.*
158 William Smith, Allen's, Bibb.*
159 James Gamage, Taylor's, Jones.*
160 William Tedder, r. s., Morrison's, Montgomery.
161 Thomas Crumby, Sutton's, Habersham.*
162 Jonathan Hill, Cleland's, Chatham.*
163 David B. White, 588th, Upson.*
164 Hamilton M'Cook, Johnson's, Bibb.*
165 Milton Paxton, Whitehead's, Habersham.*
166 Starkey J. Sharp, Peterson's, Burke.*
167 Henry Moses, 430th, Early.
168 Robert Summers, Head's, Butts.
169 Girome Trihay, Cleland's, Chatham.*
170 Philip W. Hemphill, Liddell's, Jackson.
171 (fr.) Caleb Hall, Sen., Bridges's, Gwinnett.
172 (fr.) Eli Melton, Swiney's, Laurens.
173 Simeon L. Duncan, Payne's, Merriwether.*
174 Allen Night, Hutson's, Newton.*
175 John Bennett, 49th, Emanuel.
176 John Balinger, Jr., Bower's, Elbert.
177 Elisha Findly, Sinclair's, Houston.*
178 Mary Stokes, w., 373d, Jasper.*
179 Alex. R. M'Cant's ors., Whitaker's, Crawford.
180 Edmon Atwater, 470th, Upson.*
181 John Clark, Wallis's, Irwin.
182 William Ballard's ors., Braddy's, Jones.

183 Paschal Gresham, Hill's, Monroe.
184 William A. Coleman, Carswell's, Jefferson.
185 Michael Aderhold, Gittens's, Fayette.*
186 Samuel D. Button, Turner's, Crawford.
187 Allen G. Holley, Chandler's, Franklin.
188 Margaret Jarell, w., 320th, Baldwin.
189 John Curbon, Thaxton's, Butts.
190 Samuel Stewart, Hill's, Baldwin.
191 Thomas G. Cook, Winter's, Jones.
192 Benjamin Allen, 5th, Chatham.*
193 William C. Slatter, Few's, Muscogee.*
194 William A. Radney, Sims's, Troup.
195 Jonathan Sanderfur, Harris's, Crawford.*
196 Noah Goode, Perry's, Habersham.
197 Jacob Bird, 11th, Effingham.*
198 James B. Simmons, Talley's, Troup.*
199 Isaac Hughes, Mobley's, De Kalb.*
200 Benjamin F. Chastain, Dyer's, Habersham.*
201 John and Nancy Cullers, ors., 124th, Richmond.*
202 Richard Hill, 249th, Walton.*
203 John Cameron's ors., M'Clain's, Newton.
204 John Dillashow, Wilson's, Pike.*
205 Augustin H. Ferrel, Alsobrook's, Jones.*
206 Tippin's children, f. a., Durrence's, Tatnall.
207 Sarah R. Horton, w., 248th, Jackson.*
208 Jeremiah Fraser, 177th, Wilkes.*
209 (fr.) John Lock's or., Bailey's, Laurens.*
210 (fr.) William E. Jones, 245th, Jackson.
211 James Ruffin's ors., 537th, Upson.*
212 Starkey Baysmore, 34th, Scriven.*
213 Eli J. Martin, Bostick's, Twiggs.*
214 William G. Hall, Blair's, Lowndes.*
215 Burrel W. Edmonds,, 419th, Walton.
216 Henly Snow, Nesbit's, Newton.*
217 James H. Bell, Dean's, De Kalb.
218 Elias Nicks, Walden's, Pulaski.
219 Andrew Smith, Colley's, Oglethorpe.*
220 David Fudge, Adams's, Columbia.*
221 Andrew Clark, Smith's, Campbell.*
222 James Williamson, 589th, Upson.*
223 Joel Harrell, Rutland's, Bibb.*
224 Daniel B. Edes, 600th, Richmond.
225 Benjamin Manning, Daniel's, Hall.
226 George M. Finger, Justice's, Bibb.*
227 James Brown, Loveless's, Gwinnett.*
228 Jerusia Ray, w., Park's, Walton.*
229 Robert W. Price, Smith's, Henry.

230 Martha Hill, w., Ross's, Monroe.*
231 Malchel Johnson, Brooks's, Muscogee.*
232 Thomas A. Pool, M'Ewin's, Monroe.
233 Hugh M'Donald, sol., Hamilton's, Hall.
234 John L. Smith, Whitaker's, Crawford.*
235 Luke Ross, Candler's, Bibb.
236 Charles G. Turner, Covington's, Pike.*
237 Martha Simmons, w., Newby's, Jones.*
238 Nathaniel Smith, 417th, Walton.*
239 Edmund J. Foulds, 362d, Jasper.*
240 Johnston Ammons, 555th, Upson.*
241 David Hays, White's, Franklin.*
242 John Russell, Swiney's, Lowndes.
243 Thomas John's ors., Cleland's, Chatham.
244 Emesley Beels, Bird's, De Kalb.*
245 Frederic Buckley, 11th, Effingham.*
246 Thomas Mobley, Moore's, Randolph.*
247 (fr.) P. W. Patterson, Willingham's, Harris.*
248 (fr.) Joseph L. M'Ginnis, Foote's, De Kalb.*
249 Wyche M. J. Elders, Elders's, Clarke.
250 William E. Jones, 245th, Jackson.
251 Samuel Cartright, 161st, Greene.
252 Levi Rush, 785th, Sumter.
253 Wm. Lunsford, sol. 1784-97, M'Clure's, Rabun.*
254 George Metz, Allen's, Henry.*
255 Alfred C. Bacon, Durrence's, Tatnall.*
256 John Pattison, Dyer's, Habersham.*
257 Lewis Ivey, Perryman's, Warren.*
258 James Northcut, Mays's, Monroe.*
259 Frederic Lits, Derrick's, Henry.*
260 Martin Blackburn, 35th, Scriven.*
261 John Dixon, 192d, Elbert.*
262 Jesse Griffin, 406th, Gwinnett.
263 John Tracy, 1st, Chatham.
264 Enoch Dawson, Keener's, Rabun.*
265 Thomas Robinson, Sen., s. l. w., Hall's, Butts.*
266 Henry Yaun, 789th, Sumter.*
267 John Crawford, Smith's, Wilkinson.
268 John Hudgins, Martin's, Newton.*
269 William B. Stacky, 600th, Richmond.*
270 Nancy Smith, w., Cleghorn's, Madison.*
271 Benjamin Wootten's or., 166th, Wilkes.
272 George Douglass, Candler's, Bibb.
273 John T. Hurb, Valleau's, Chatham.
274 Andrew Valentine, Young's, Wilkinson.*
275 Stephen Godby, Griffin's, Burke.*
276 John P. Hardy, Brewer's, Monroe.*

277 Augustin Wilson, Williams's, Washington.*
278 Hamilton Snead, 398th, Richmond.
279 Peter Wylie, Smith's, Houston.*
280 Samuel Stiles, 20th, Bryan.
281 William Fitzpatrick, Barrow's, Houston.
282 Cleton D. Sperlock, Whitfield's, Washington.*
283 Nathan Lowrey, sol., Chastain's, Habersham.*
284 George Dolton, Brown's, Habersham.
285 (fr.) William Alby, Leverett's, Lincoln.*
286 (fr.) Joel P. Leverett, 162d, Greene.
287 Henry Haleley, Hall's, Butts.
288 Benajah Saxon, sol., Harralson's, Troup.*
289 Edward Short's ors., Mizell's, Talbot.
290 John Edwards, s. l. w., Pace's, Putnam.
291 Joseph M. White, Chambers's, Gwinnett.*
292 Ichabud Hudman, 466th, Monroe.
293 Elihu Woodall, Ellsworth's, Bibb.
294 Thomas Gardner's ors., Bostick's, Twiggs.
295 Ivin Strickland, Gunn's, Henry.*
296 Loyall Scranton, Valleau's, Chatham.*
297 Barnaby Goddin's ors., Lamberth's, Fayette.
298 John Meadows, M'Culler's, Newton.
299 Gen. David Adams, Sen., 364th, Jasper.*
300 William Walker, Burgess's, Carroll.
301 Ellis Berman, Barron's, Houston.*
302 Edmond W. Anderson, Fulks's, Wilkes.*
303 William G. Perdu, Graves's, Putnam.
304 John H. Stewart, Atkins's, Monroe.
305 James R. Blackburn, 35th, Scriven.*
306 John Moffett, Davis's, Gwinnett.*
307 Jesse Sanford, Dyer's, Habersham.*
308 William Southall, Candler's, Bibb.*
309 Willis Wright, 789th, Sumter.
310 Elizabeth Fuller, w. r. s., 148th, Greene.*
311 Caroline Barnett, w. r. s., Davis's, Clarke.*
312 Allen Tucker, r. s., 148th, Greene.
313 Thomas Greenway, Griffin's, Hall.*
314 Jesse Barnes, Smith's, Houston.*
315 Elijah B. Head, Lamberth's, Fayette.*
316 Susannah Millican, w., Dearing's, Henry.
317 Mitchell and D. Bennett, ors., 404th, Gwinnett.
318 Greene Moore, 143d, Greene.*
319 Anderson Ray, 470th, Upson.
320 Philip Hancock, Guice's, Oglethorpe.
321 Matthew Ellison, Baugh's, Jackson *
322 Joseph Roberts, 106th, Hancock.
323 (fr.) Giles Newton, Gittens's, Fayette.

324 (fr.) James M. Haynes, Mizell's, Talbot.
325 William Williford, sol., Smith's, Campbell.
326 Peyton Wade, Merck's, Hall.*
327 William J. Webb, Blackshear's, Laurens.*
328 Alexander Curry, Blackshear's, Laurens.*
329 Thompson Ashley, Kelly's, Elbert.
330 Joseph V. Warker, Wolfskin's, Oglethorpe.*
331 David Blaylock, Burgess's, Carroll.
332 John W. Selman, 559th, Walton.*
333 Green D. Barnett, 373d, Jasper.*
334 John Maison, Burk's, Stewart.
335 Daniel Walker, Jr., 119th, Richmond.*
336 John W. Gastin, or., 4th, Chatham.
337 Margaret Todd, w., Sullivan's, Jones.*
338 Benjamin M'Kinney, Jr., Rutland's, Bibb.
339 Alfred G. P. Blans, Braddy's, Jones.*
340 Daniel E. Bagnell's ors., Wynn's, Gwinnett.
341 Hezekiah Thorne, Huey's, Harris.*
342 Phineas M. Nightingale, Miller's, Camden.*
343 Enoch Herndon, Woodruff's, Campbell.
344 Isaac Wimberley's or., 74th, Burke.
345 Euriah C. Morris, Sims's, Troup.
346 Philip A. Clayton, Ellsworth's, Bibb.
347 Priscilla Strad, w. r. s., Bryan's, Monroe.*
348 Preston E .Bowdre, 561st, Upson.
349 Wm. M. Harper, r. s., Chastain's, Habersham.*
350 Elizabeth Hinesleay, w., Alsobrook's, Jones.
351 William Hinton, Newsom's, Warren.
352 Green Hill, sol., Studstill's, Lowndes.
353 Josiah Weakley, Downs's, Warren.*
354 Lorenzo D. Trout, Dobbs's, Hall.*
355 Elizabeth Childs, w. r. s., Sanders's, Jones.
356 Robert G. Johnson, Hardman's, Oglethorpe.
357 Richard G. Harben, Reed's, Gwinnett.*
358 David K. Collins, Wright's, Tatnall.*
359 Joab Trull's ors., Bryant's, Pulaski.
360 David R. Brown's ors., 271st, M'Intosh.*
361 (fr.) Amos Alsobrook, Jr., Sanders's, Jones.*

THIRTEENTH DISTRICT, THIRD SECTION, CHEROKEE.

1 Azeriah Bradley, Nesbit's, Newton.
2 Alexander M'Crackin, M'Clain's, Newton.*
3 Littleberry Hicks, Stewart's, Troup.*
4 Washington Warren, Martin's, Pike.*
5 John Wright, Reed's, Gwinnett.
6 Alexander Branden, 365th, Jasper.*
7 Alexander R. Ralston, s. l. w., 123d, Richmond.*
8 Elizabeth Lansford, w. r. s., Dawson's, Jasper.
9 John Sims, 406th, Gwinnett.
10 Samuel G. Jones, 190th, Elbert.*
11 George Davis, 119th, Richmond.*
12 Grovestine's three ors., Hobkerk's, Camden.
13 Joseph J. Kelburn, 600th, Richmond.
14 James Duncan, Sen., M. Brown's, Habersham.*
15 John Taylor's ors., Thomason's, Elbert.
16 John Moore, Vining's, Putnam.
17 Jordan Spivy, 417th, Walton.
18 Peter Graham, Walker's, Harris.
19 Mary E. Whilley, or., Bridges's, Gwinnett.*
20 Tompson Banks, Guice's, Oglethorpe.*
21 Nathaniel M. Crawford, Bragaw's, Oglethorpe.*
22 James Webb, Bush's, Stewart.
23 Perry G. Sinquefield, Hannah's, Jefferson.*
24 Joshua Stone's, minors, 38th, Scriven.
25 Jackson Hatcher, Jordan's, Bibb.*
26 Nimrod H. Penly, 1st section, Cherokee.
27 George Tyler, Russell's, Henry.*
28 William H. Kelly, Hines's, Coweta.
29 Angel D. La Pemere, sol., 248th, Jackson.
30 Valentine M'Kinne, Mitchell's, Marion.
31 Wyat Collins's ors., Fulks's, Wilkes.*
32 Mary T. Hines, 75th, Burke.
33 John Barnett, Johnson's, De Kalb.
34 Francis Riviere, 588th, Upson.*
35 James Wammock, Alsobrook's, Jones.*
36 George W. Justiss, Waltze's, Morgan.
37 David F. Riley, Johnson's, Bibb.
38 James Tuggs, Buck's, Houston.*
39 Simri Rose, Ellsworth's, Bibb.
40 Edmund Hand, Smith's, Henry.
41 John J. Starling, 494th, Upson.

42 Susannah Eubanks, w. r. s., Herndon's, Hall.
43 Thomas Christopher, Lunceford's, Wilkes.
44 William Furcron, Bragaw's, Oglethorpe.
45 Samuel M. Callaway, Alberson's, Walton.
46 John E. Wammock, Rooks's, Putnam.
47 Ebenezer C. Hatcher, 318th, Baldwin.*
48 William Crawley, Night's, Morgan.*
49 Elizabeth Arnold, w., Dupree's, Washington.*
50 Claiborn Dolton, Hatchett's, Oglethorpe.
51 Alexander Scott, Griffin's, De Kalb.*
52 George C. Shivers, Hitchcock's, Muscogee.*
53 David Mitzger, r. s., 11th, Effingham.*
54 Richard Horn, Curry's, Wilkinson.
55 Wright Sanders, Sen., Hatton's, Baker.
56 Caswell Hopson, sol., Tuggle's, Merriwether *
57 J. Cowart's ors., Hargrove's, Newton.*
58 Sarah M'Donald, w., Morrison's, Appling.*
59 Benjamin M'Clendon, Hand's, Appling.
60 John Jerman, Holt's, Talbot.*
61 Lewis Killgore, Varner's, Merriwether.
62 Jonathan Luther, Gillis's, De Kalb.*
63 Benjamin Conner, Downs's, Warren.
64 Pencint Tanner, 271st, M'Intosh.*
65 Nancy Reynolds, w., 121st, Richmond.*
66 Jeremiah Baggas, sol., Coxe's, Morgan.*
67 Major Griffin, Jones's, Thomas.*
68 Ezekiel Perry, Martin's, Stewart.*
69 James Wade, David's, Franklin.*
70 John Dean, Sen., Hughes's, Habersham.
71 Charles Duke, Sen., s. i. w., Coxe's, Morgan.*
72 Samuel Jeter, sol., Leverett's, Lincoln.*
73 Margaret Barnett, w., Orr's, Jackson.
74 Joseph A. Pelot, Valleau's, Chatham.
75 James Higgins, Reed's, Gwinnett.*
76 William W. S. Knight, 72d, Burke.
77 William Dougherty, Tankersley's, Columbia.*
78 Canpey Darbey, w., Lester's, Monroe.
79 Benjamin Scroggins, Sen., Miller's, Jackson.*
80 Eli Glaze, Bivins's, Jones.*
81 Andrew Bowen, Sen, Brock's, Habersham.*
82 Sarah Davis, w., Perry's, Baldwin.*
83 John H. Messer, or., 34th, Scriven.
84 Samuel J. Lazenby, Harris's, Columbia.
85 Alsa Kemp, Roberts's, Hall.
86 Berry Maxwell, 168th, Wilkes.*
87 John S. Colquette, Hanner's, Campbell.*
88 Tegnal H. Jones, Mangum's, Franklin.*

89 Aquelter A. Phelps, Sims's, Troup.
90 Joseph Speer, Nichols's, Fayette.
91 David Christopher, Barnett's, Clarke.*
92 Elizabeth Rhodes, w., Hatchett's, Oglethorpe.
93 Joseph Holland, Griffin's, Burke.*
94 Charles P. Huckabay, 687th, Lee.*
95 Robison's children, f. a., Robison's, Washington.
96 Moses Butts, Moffett's, Muscogee.
97 Joseph Collins, 120th, Richmond.*
98 Joseph Sensabaugh, Ellis's, Pulaski.*
99 Robert Allen, sol., Bustin's, Pike.
100 John K. M. Charlton's ors., Moseley's, Wilkes.*
101 Samuel Knox, Jr., sol., Liddell's, Jackson.*
102 Robert Lemmond, Lane's, Morgan.*
103 Kimbrough H. Vinant, Bush's, Stewart.*
104 Thomas Willis, sol., Bush's, Stewart.
105 John Blakely, Elder's, Clarke.
106 Martin Luker, s. i. w., 788th, Heard.
107 Allen Lawrence, Kendrick's, Putnam.
108 Michael Rogers, Groce's, Bibb.
109 Alexander Turner, Loven's, Henry.
110 William Rakestraw, Neal's, Campbell.
111 George Nobles, Edwards's, Talbot.
112 John A. Sanford, 470th, Upson.
113 Job Weston, sol., Canning's, Elbert.*
114 James M'Walters, M'Culler's, Newton.*
115 Harris Brantley, Peacock's, Washington.*
116 Edmund H. Worrill, Canning's, Elbert.*
117 Thomas Tuggle, 294th, Jasper.
118 John Adams, 249th, Walton.
119 Tilmon Douglass, 419th, Walton.
120 Benjamin T. Brown, Lester's, Monroe.
121 Reuben Wheelus, Wood's, Morgan.*
122 Stephen Swann, Allen's, Monroe.*
123 Samuel J. Bush, Peace's, Wilkinson.*
124 John Lindsay's ors., Dixon's, Irwin.
125 Abner Howard, Hatton's, Baker.
126 Elijah Langston, Holley's, Franklin.
127 James Martin, David's, Franklin.
128 David Thurman, Mobley's, De Kalb.
129 Ann Tuder, w., Edwards's, Talbot.*
130 William Shockley, Roberts's, Hall.*
131 Mansfield B. Stames, Griffin's, De Kalb.
132 Elijah Tippen, 404th, Gwinnett.*
133 Abraham Johnson, Latimer's, De Kalb.
134 John Slaley, or., 11th, Effingham.
135 Jesse Mill Irons, Kendrick's Putnam.

136 Benjamin Matthews, sol., Blount's, Wilkinson.*
137 Murdock M'Swain Wadsworth, Buck's, Stewart.*
138 Bryant Pace, sol., Iverson's, Houston.*
139 Richard Bush, Walden's, Pulaski.*
140 Thomas Rainy, Sen., Coffee's, Rabun.*
141 James C. Mulkey, Chastain's, Habersham.*
142 Ellis Willoughby, Elder's, Clarke.
143 John Herrin, Jr., M. Brown's, Habersham.
144 Ammon J. Forres, Johnson's, De Kalb.*
145 Heggins Orplis, 22d, M'Intosh.
146 Joseph Payne, O'Neal's, Laurens.*
147 Thomas Howell, r. s., Brown's, Camden.
148 William M. Bayer, 117th, Hancock.
149 John Bowman, 406th, Gwinnett.
150 John K. Slaughter, Pace's, Putnam.
151 John Holt's ors., Barwick's, Washington.
152 David Harmon, blind, 7th, Chatham.
153 Joseph Scott's ors., Wilson's, Pike.
154 Sarah Brown, w., Garner's, Washington.*
155 Thomas M. Cardin, Moore's, Randolph.*
156 John R. M'Millan, r. s., Smith's, Franklin.
157 Sarah Butts, w., Nichols's, Fayette.
158 Van Degary, Stower's, Elbert.
159 Charles Gates, Sen., r. s., 406th, Gwinnett.*
160 Thomas Conn's five orphans, Dean's, De Kalb.
161 Benjamin Hurst, 5th, Columbia.*
162 Nathaniel Booth, Howell's, Elbert.
163 Nehemiah Guthrey, 417th, Walton.
164 Harmon Runnels, sol., Johnson's, Warren.
165 Peter Albritton, Robison's, Washington.*
166 John Hawkins, s. l. w., Underwood's, Putnam.*
167 Mary Roberts, w., Woodruff's, Campbell.
168 James Story, Crow's, Pike.
169 John R. Patterson's ors., Martin's, Stewart.
170 Joseph Miller, Braddy's, Jones.
171 Wodson Worley, Higginbotham's, Rabun.*
172 William M. Starney, Shearer's, Coweta.*
173 Robert Moore, Night's, Morgan.*
174 William Powell, Davis's, Jones.*
175 A. Hollingsworth's ors., Stephens's, Habersham.
176 John Kill, sol., Latimer's, De Kalb.
177 Elizabeth Smith, Woodruff's, Campbell.
178 James A. Satterfield, Jones's, Habersham.*
179 Noel Nelson, sol., Lane's, Morgan.
180 Priscilla Good, w., Candler's, Bibb.
181 Henry Dregors, sol., 17th dis., Liberty, Chatham.*
182 Marian F. Thrilkeld, Lunceford's, Elbert.

183 Lizya Pitts, id. or lu., Sanders's, Jones.
184 Elizabeth A. Irwin, or., Polhill's, Burke.*
185 Amster Donham, Robinson's, Fayette.
186 Mary Pridgen, w., Summerlin's, Bulloch.
187 Joseph Waddall, Coffee's, Rabun.*
188 Robert Robison, Lightfoot's, Washington.*
189 Mary Nichols, w. r. s., Bostick's, Twiggs.
190 Katharine Abbot, w., Neal's, Campbell.*
191 Philip Perry, Perry's, Habersham.*
192 Matthew C. Goldsmith, Atkinson's, Coweta.*
193 Jesse Caps, 53d, Emanuel.*
194 Henry Calton, sol., 138th, Greene.*
195 Richard A. Rison, M'Gehee's, Troup.*
196 Martha Myrick, w., 318th, Baldwin.*
197 Robert Wetherington, Smith's, Houston.
198 James Beasley, Coxe's, Talbot.
199 Mitchell Bennett, sol., Chambers's, Gwinnett.
200 Reddick P. Sims, Mangum's, Franklin.*
201 David Hollomon, 307th, Putnam.*
202 Joshua Bradley, sol., Lawrence's, Pike.*
203 Ransom R. Bryant, M'Gehee's, Troup.*
204 Jeremiah Neal, 294th, Jasper.
205 J. W. D. Bohannan, Brackett's, Newton.
206 Peggy M'Crary, w., Camp's, Warren.
207 Lazaras Dempsey, Johnson's, De Kalb.*
208 John A. Wills, Bragaw's, Oglethorpe.*
209 Sarah Phillips, h. a., Swain's, Thomas.
210 Samuel Fowler, Lester's, Monroe.
211 John Lovil, M'Clure's, Rabun.
212 William M'Lochlin, Ellsworth's, Bibb.
213 Berry Belgew, Coxe's, Talbot.
214 Gains Nelson, Foote's, De Kalb.*
215 Reuben Nail, r. s., Carpenter's, Tatnall.
216 Amanda Whatley, or., Hampton's, Newton.
217 John Cannedy, Allen's, Campbell.
218 John P. Evans, 278th, Morgan.*
219 Henry Spivey, or., Christie's, Jefferson.*
220 Nathaniel Affut, r. s., Williams's, Washington.
221 Elijah Tucker, 56th, Emanuel.
222 Robert Rogers, 417th, Walton.
223 Henry Tullson, Head's, Butts.*
224 Isaiah Burton, Tuggle's, Merriwether.
225 Phinehas Oliver, sol., Iverson's, Houston.*
226 Berry Humphries, Hutson's, Newton.
227 Asahel Beach, 600th, Richmond.*
228 John M'Garrity, Mobley's, De Kalb.
229 Jesse Mayo, sol., Peace's, Wilkinson.

230 John Watkins, Dearing's, Henry.*
231 Robert Williams, sol., 35th, Scriven.
232 Larkin Loony, Royster's, Franklin.
233 James Smith, Edward's, Franklin.
234 Isaac Carter, Morrison's, Appling.
235 Barnabas Meadows, sol., Fleming's, Franklin.*
236 Hallasha Odom, Garner's, Coweta.
237 William J. Howard, Latimer's, De Kalb.
238 Jeremiah Files, Edwards's, Talbot.*
239 William Jordan, r. s., M'Clain's, Newton.*
240 Roland Kinsay, Jones's, Habersham.*
241 Wiley Sledge, Dean's, Clarke.*
242 John Fitzgerald, Harp's, Stewart.*
243 Thomas Blitch, Sen., 12th, Effingham.*
244 Elijah Hammon, Jr., Hammon's, Campbell.*
245 Martin Hasnuo, Cleland's, Chatham.*
246 Ambrose M. Haley, House's, Henry.
247 Nancy Laden, w., Dobbs's, Hall.
248 Nathaniel Connelley's ors., Barker's, Gwinnett.
249 Jemima Sandefer, w., Hampton's, Newton.
250 Collin J. Pope, Ross's, Monroe.*
251 John Gunter's ors., Thames, Crawford.
252 Jesse Williams, Martin's, Stewart.
253 William H. Bradberry, Morgan's, Madison.
254 John Tweedell's ors., Hargrove's, Oglethorpe.
255 Emily G. Blackshear, w., Marsh's, Thomas.*
256 Charles B. Beavers, Smith's, Campbell.
257 Manning Bouling's ors., Morton's, De Kalb.*
258 Warren Hawks, Hardman's, Oglethorpe.
259 Henry Oldham, 243d, Jackson.*
260 Jason Pluute, Dyer's, Habersham.
261 Sharad Edwards, Groover's, Thomas.
262 Isaac Justice, sol., Norris's, Monroe.
263 John Robert Kittles, 37th, Scriven.
264 David Statham, Fenn's, Clarke.*
265 George Hargraves, Few's, Muscogee.
266 James King, s. l. w., Hall's, Butts.
267 John Roberts, Sen., sol., Johnson's, Lowndes.*
268 L. D. Buckner, 320th, Baldwin.
269 Richard Johnson's ors., Pounds's, Twiggs.
270 Martin England, Burnett's, Habersham.*
271 James Barnett, Willis's, Franklin.*
272 James Gore, Jr., Hudson's, Marion.*
273 James P. Glaver, Wilson's, Jasper.*
274 Thomas Wood, 693d, Heard.
275 Green Posey, Harralson's, Troup.*
276 James M'Bride, Barker's, Gwinnett.*

277 Turner Everett's ors., 633d, Dooly.
278 Francis M. Patterson, or., Price's, Hall.*
279 James H. Barnett, 102d, Hancock.
280 Jonathan Peacock, Sen., Phillip's, Talbot.*
281 Stewart Lee, M'Linn's, Butts.*
282 Berry Stephens, or., 633d, Dooly.
283 Thomas W. Coxe, M'Gehee's, Troup.
284 Thomas C. Murrah, Wood's, Morgan.*
285 Richard Simmons, 404th, Gwinnett.
286 William Armor, Hamilton's, Hall.
287 Joseph Boggs's ors., Hendon's, Carroll.
288 Isaac Gibson, Walker's, Columbia.
289 William Ewing, Reid's, Gwinnett.*
290 Jeremiah Dean, Price's, Hall.*
291 Christopher Coleman, Davis's, Gwinnett.*
292 Ezariah Ennis, 34th, Scriven.*
293 Frances Scott, w. r. s., 143d, Greene.
294 John Mac Rea, Morrison's, Montgomery.*
295 Martin Rouse, Catlett's, Franklin.*
296 John Wynn's ors., Marshall's, Putnam.
297 Charles Wheeler, sol., Smith's, Habersham.*
298 Fleming A. Alexander, Clark's, Elbert.*
299 Wm. Brossell, Sen., s. l. w., Nichols's, Fayette.*
300 Newsom Taunton, Sen., sol., Mitchell's, Marion.*
301 John Cooper, Cliett's, Columbia.*
302 Thomas Tibbs, sol., Thomason's, Elbert.*
303 William R. S. Canter, Garner's, Washington.*
304 Anon Wills, Sanders's, Jones.*
305 William M. Heaslet, Flynn's, Muscogee.*
306 Thomas S. Middlebrooks, Hill's, Monroe.
307 Frederic F. Doney, Gittens's, Fayette.*
308 Asa Griffin, Blair's, Lowndes.*
309 William Griffin, Killen's, Decatur.*
310 John M'Intire, Sen., Dyer's, Habersham.*
311 William D. Shockley, 537th, Upson.
312 David Monroe, Sen., r. s., 73d, Burke.*
313 Drury Corken, Peterson's, Burke.*
314 John Sutherland, or., Walker's, Columbia.*
315 Andrew Holliday, Bourquin's, Chatham.
316 Temperance Brady, w., Iverson's, Houston.
317 Orphans of Peter Sangster, Buck's, Houston.
318 Joseph P. M'Cullock, 104th, Hancock.*
319 Ebenezer Smith, sol., Anderson's, Wilkes.
320 James K. Lewis, 105th, Baldwin.*
321 Augustus C. M'Clane, Newby's, Jones.
322 Richard Hetton, s. l. w., Sharp's, Washington.*
323 Levi Bush, Bush's, Pulaski.*
324 William Hennard, s. l. w., Nichols's, Fayette.*

FOURTEENTH DISTRICT, THIRD SECTION, CHEROKEE.

1 Enoch M. Fincher, Ellsworth's, Bibb.
2. Alfred G. Pogue, Parham's, Warren.
3 Edmund Butts, s. l. w., 374th, Putnam.*
4 Rachael Martin, w., 145th, Greene.
5 Jacob Davis, sol., Brewton's, Tatnall.
6 William H. Wiley, Alberson's, Walton.*
7 Edward W. Solomon, Sanderlin's, Chatham.*
8 Luke Williams, 430th, Early.*
9 Daniel Drummond, Wynn's, Gwinnett.*
10 Thomas Huson, s. l. w., M'Clain's, Newton.
11 John Slappey, 687th, Lee.*
12 Joshua R. Bowing, Crawford's, Morgan.
13 John Huff, sol., Young's, Carroll.*
14 Alford Sarmon, Herndon's, Hall.*
15 Henry Tulley, Sen., r. s., M'Culler's, Newton.
16 Neadham Bryant, Durham's, Talbot.*
17 John S. Heard, s. l. w., 761st, Heard.*
18 Phillips's three orphans, Brewton's, Tatnall.
19 Shem Bulter's ors., 15th, Liberty.
20 Robert Shankland, Harris's, Columbia.*
21 Rucker Mouldin, 406th, Gwinnett.*
22 Thomas W. Strickland, Hudson's, Marion.*
23 Henry Wyche, sol., Hart's, Jones.*
24 Thomas J. Sanford, 470th, Upson.*
25 Jesse Butler, Wolfskin's, Oglethorpe.*
26 John W. Pruitt, 785th, Sumter.*
27 Thomas Johnson, Dearing's, Butts.*
28 John Turner, Groce's, Bibb.*
29 Cornelius Gentry, Brown's, Habersham.*
30 William Davis, r. s., Nichols's, Fayette.*
31 Bailey Harris's ors., Jordan's, Bibb.
32 William L. Conner, 36th, Scriven.*
33 Elias Hawkins, Wheeler's, Pulaski.*
34 Martin Defurr, White's, Franklin.*
35 Elizabeth Trainum, w. r. s., 278th, Morgan.*
36 David Holland, Smith's, Houston.*
37 Murdock M'Kaskill, 417th, Walton.*
38 William Simmons, Mizell's, Talbot.*
39 Henry Turner, Harp's, Habersham.*
40 John Mattox, r. s., 404th, Gwinnett.*
41 William Hanson, Peek's, Columbia.*

42 John R. Hearne, Hines's, Coweta.
43 Silas Brown, Dearing's, Henry.*
44 Thomas Cobb, 732d, Dooly.
45 Osburn Manning, Daniel's, Hall.*
46 Mary Harden, h. a., Bower's, Elbert.
47 Joseph Wall, s. i. w., Sam Streetman's, Twiggs.*
48 William Guynn, sol., Martin's, Pike.*
49 Josiah Spivey, Harris's, Columbia.*
50 John Tillman, Cliett's, Columbia.
51 William Brantley, Sen., Peacock's, Washington.*
52 James Dean, Iverson's, Houston.*
53 William Whiddon, Barwick's, Washington.*
54 Marcus Smallwood, Collins's, Henry.*
55 Howel Horn, s. l. w., Barefield's, Jones.*
56 George Wilson, r. s., 454th, Walton.
57 Isaiah Kennett, Johnson's, De Kalb.*
58 William S. Freeman, Davis's, Franklin.*
59 John B. Crumpler, 585th, Dooly.
60 Fabyan Moody, 307th, Putnam.*
61 Mary Horn, w., 122d, Richmond.*
62 Jonathan Walker, Athens, Clarke.*
63 Hillary Anderson, Young's, Jefferson.
64 Thomas Murray, r. s., Murphy's, Columbia.*
65 William W. Elliott, Dyer's, Habersham.*
66 Seaborn Jackson, Lunceford's, Wilkes.
67 Jasper M'Crary, Camp's, Warren.*
68 Griffin Messer, Griffin's, Emanuel.*
69 Garret M. Beasley, Jones's, Morgan.*
70 William Johnsor.'s ors., Morris's, Crawford.
71 James Robinson, Payne's, Merriwether.*
72 Thomas Durham, Latimer's, De Kalb.*
73 Elijah Mills, Bailey's, Laurens.*
74 William Garrott, Alberson's, Walton.
75 Nancy Betts, w., Sanders's, Jones.
76 Joshua C. Weeks, Evans's, Laurens.
77 Henry E. W. Clarke, Hobkerk's, Camden.*
78 Nancy Humphries, w., Winter's, Jones.*
79 Alfred Hursley, Dearing's, Henry.*
80 John Bowden, sol., 466th, Monroe.*
81 Samuel G. Lightbourn, Cleland's, Chatham.
82 Thomas Hatchett, Hatchett's, Oglethorpe.*
83 Solomon Jennings, s. i. w., Green's, Oglethorpe.*
84 Lewis Davis's ors., Barwick's, Washington.*
85 Jacob Reed, sol., Hatton's, Baker.*
86 Albert Tatum, Allens's, Henry.
87 William S. Mitchell, sol., 117th, Hancock.
88 George Raden, 148th, Greene.*

89 John Wilson's ors., Roberts's, Hall.
90 Isham Fielding, Dobbs's, Hall.*
91 Henry S. Turner, 293d, Jasper.*
92 Richard B. Coleman, Huey's, Harris.*
93 John Layle, Dearing's, Henry.*
94 Charles B. Hurst's ors., Griffin's, Burke.
95 Hezekiah Singleton's ors., Smith's, Henry.
96 Edwin O'Neal, Wood's, Morgan.
97 Christopher Brack's ors., Givins's, De Kalb.*
98 Thomas J. Bowen, 779th, Heard.*
99 Bird Martin, Robison's, Washington.
100 William Williard, d. & d., Lane's, Morgan.
101 Crawford Haste, Prescott's, Twiggs.*
102 John H. Garrett, Wood's, Morgan.*
103 Thomas W. Rowlins, Mashburn's, Pulaski.*
104 John Askey, Smith's, Henry.
105 Alfred Titman, Lightfoot's, Washington.
106 Ezra M'Crary, Camp's, Warren.
107 John Worthy, Allen's, Bibb.*
108 John Morris, sol., Harralson's, Troup.
109 Abraham Dunner, 175th, Wilkes.*
110 James Leverick, 120th, Richmond.*
111 John Willis, Baugh's, Jackson.*
112 Thomas Jackson, Russell's, Henry.*
113 Alpheus Beal, ———, Wilkinson.
114 Benjamin Morris, sol., Higginbotham's, Madison.*
115 John Sinnard, Jr., Nichols's, Fayette.*
116 Francis Wilson, 35th, Scriven.*
117 Woody Bailey, Phillips's, Jasper.
118 William Browning, Blackshear's, Thomas.*
119 Samuel Black's ors., Colley's, Oglethorpe.*
120 Joseph Manning, sol., 334th, Wayne.*
121 Charles R. Greene, Cleggs's, Walton.
122 William Hinton, 454th, Walton.
123 Isaac Matthews, sol. 1784–97, Riden's, Jackson.*
124 John Meadows, M'Culler's, Newton.*
125 Westley Yarbraw's ors., Groce's, Bibb.*
126 William Shaw, Johnson's, De Kalb.*
127 James Neal, sol., Wilson's, Pike.*
128 Warren Aken, Clark's, Elbert.*
129 Abner Hammond, 320th, Baldwin.*
130 Foster Rowsey, sol., Howell's, Elbert.*
131 John A. Fry, Sanderlin's, Chatham.*
132 Patrick Cunningham, Groce's, Bibb.*
133 William Smith, Wynn's, Gwinnett.
134 Ann M'Coy, w. r. s., 603d, Taliaferro.*
135 Champion Allen, 175th, Wilkes.*

136 John W. Carlton, 138th, Greene.*
137 Henry Turner's ors., Peterson's, Montgomery.*
138 Leverett's orphans, Griffin's, Burke.
139 James Rogers, Hamilton's, Gwinnett.*
140 John Tire, s. l. w., Morgan's, Appling.*
141 Pierce Costly, M'Culler's, Newton.*
142 Shadrick Floyd, Rick's, Laurens.
143 Luke Gibson, sol., Bishop's, Henry.*
144 William J. Willis, 588th, Upson.
145 Elisha Blissel's ors., Berry's, Butts.
146 John P. Sykes, sol., 102d, Hancock.
147 Penelopy Finch, w., Allen's, Bibb.*
148 Marcus Smallwood, Collins's, Henry.*
149 James F. Montgomery, Gillis's, De Kalb.*
150 Archibald Willingham, Willingham's, Harris.*
151 Nancy Vaughan, w., 404th, Gwinnett.*
152 Archibald M'Pherson, Hudson's, Marion.*
153 Moses Thompson, or., 245th, Jackson.*
154 Alexander Smith, Smith's, Houston.*
155 Joseph H. M'Bryer, Mullen's, Carroll.*
156 Robert Farrar's ors., Gunn's, Jones.
157 Martin Tomlin, Atkinson's, Coweta.*
158 William White, Sen., Brackett's, Newton.
159 George Dawson, sol., 143d, Greene.
160 William Elliot, sol., Covington's, Pike.
161 Henry G. Turner, 293d, Jasper.*
162 Aaron Mattox, Mattox's, Lowndes.*
163 William Bohler, 119th, Richmond.*
164 James Carrington, 745th, Sumter.*
165 John Dryden, Baker's, Liberty.*
166 John Taylor, Winter's, Jones.*
167 Milly Foard, h. a., Baismore's, Jones.*
168 John S. Wilson, sol., Hammock's, Jasper.*
169 Mark Morgan, Garner's, Coweta.
170 Tabitha Bateman, w. r. s., Smith's, Houston.*
171 William J. Wynne, Marshall's, Putnam.*
172 Thomas Jordan, Crow's, Merriwether.*
173 Robert Lyons, M'Gehee's, Troup.
174 Neal M'Leod, Martin's, Stewart.*
175 John Collins, Summerlin's, Bulloch.*
176 William Vincent, Rooks's, Putnam.
177 Perry G. Russell, Deavours's, Habersham.*
178 William Fooley's ors., Stewart's, Jones.
179 Thomas Robinson, Chambers's, Gwinnett.*
180 James N. Calhoun, Martin's, Washington.*
181 Ira Walden, Stewart's, Warren.
182 Sarah Cash, w. r. s., Orr's, Jackson.

183 Demsy C. Bennett, Pollard's, Wilkes.*
184 William Davis, Braddy's, Jones.*
185 John A. Moores, Strickland's, Merriwether.*
186 T. Ware, sol. 1784–97, Tuggle's, Merriwether.*
187 Michael W. Youngblood, Liddell's, Jackson.*
188 Thomas Hodnett, Hodges's, Newton.*
189 Frederic L. Howell, Martin's, Pike.*
190 Samuel J. Power, Howard's, Oglethorpe.*
191 James P. Coxe, Kendrick's, Monroe.*
192 David Castleberry, f. a. 5 m., Rhodes's, De Kalb.
193 Abraham Garrett, Loveless's, Gwinnett.
194 Thomas Chapman, 603d, Taliaferro.
195 Matthew Marshall, Jr., Young's, Jefferson.*
196 James Blalock, s. l. w., 588th, Upson.
197 Allen G. Simmons, s. l. w., Simmons's, Crawford.
198 Edward Stony, sol., Liddell's, Jackson.
199 Vashti Meadow, w., Givins's, De Kalb.
200 Thomas G. M'Farland, Ballard's, Morgan.
201 Arthur Clark, Kendrick's, Monroe.
202 Sarah Morris, w., Foote's, De Kalb.*
203 John Barefield, s. l. w., Barefield's, Jones.
204 Oliver M. Porter, 137th, Greene.
205 Martin Ingram, 2d section, Cherokee.*
206 John T. Floyd, 143d, Greene.*
207 Martin Moss, Stower's, Elbert.*
208 William Wamack, Peacock's, Washington.*
209 George W. Parham, Wilhite's, Elbert.*
210 John R. Shad, Wilmington Island, Chatham.*
211 Thomas W. Thompson, Peavy's, Bulloch.*
212 Aaron Daniel's ors., Brewton's, Tatnall.*
213 Thomas Robinson, Jr., Hall's, Butts.*
214 Orasmus Camp, Camp's, Baker.*
215 John Turner's ors., Kelly's, Jasper.
216 Thomas Gill, or., 24th, M'Intosh.
217 Ebenezer Jenks, Jr., 19th, Bryant.*
218 Elizabeth Heds, w., 121st, Richmond.
219 Joshua Parham, Jr., Wilhite's, Elbert.*
220 Calef Simmons, Griffin's, Fayette.
221 Rolan Dixon, Sen., Newman's, Thomas.*
222 Gideon Smith, Robison's, Washington.*
223 Hamilton Garmany, 404th, Gwinnett.
224 Mary Day, h. a., Strickland's, Merriwether.*
225 William H. Lucas, 102d, Hancock.
226 Larkin Bayles, Allen's, Campbell.*
227 Sidney M. Pardue, Britt's, Randolph.*
228 Willmouth Fox, w., 362d, Jasper.
229 Legrands S. Wright, Night's, Morgan.*

230 Thomas L. Brown, Blair's, Lowndes.*
231 Benjamin Cochrane, Wynn's, Gwinnett.
232 John B. Jones, Davis's, Jones.
233 William S. Jones, Jr., Watkins's, Columbia.
234 Lewis Wooten, Frasier's, Monroe.*
235 William Willer, cit., Athens, Clarke.
236 Thomas Tanner, r. s., Griffin's, De Kalb.*
237 William Price, Martin's, Stewart.
238 James Smith, Sanderlin's, Chatham.*
239 William L. Todd's ors., Barefield's, Jones.*
240 John W. Hoskins, Mann's, Crawford.*
241 James Isham Bruce, id., 120th, Richmond.*
242 Lindsey Holland, Mimms's, Fayette.*
243 James Johnson, Jr., 118th, Hancock.*
244 George M. Head, Head's, Butts.*
245 Edmund Henderson, Augusta, Richmond.
246 William Bond, Phillips's, Talbot.*
247 Anthony Johnson, 293d, Jasper.*
248 Peter Ball, Rhodes's, De Kalb.*
249 Anderson Owens, 406th, Gwinnett.
250 John T. Candle, Will's, Twiggs.
251 Rhoda A. Moore, w., Collins's, Henry.
252 Dennis M'Lendon, Benson's, Lincoln.
253 Wilie Cherry, 604th, Taliaferro.*
254 Benjamin Gholston, sol., Tower's, Gwinnett.*
255 Edmond Clay, Durham's, Talbot.*
256 Kinchen Newson, s. l. w., Sparks's, Washington.*
257 Elijah D. Vaughn, Allen's, Henry.
258 Joel Dean's ors., Robison's, Washington.*
259 James V. Hogg, Hall's, Butts.*
260 Forana M. Oliver, Smith's, Elbert.*
261 James Roper, s. l. w., Graves's, Putnam.*
262 John Bolton, 406th, Gwinnett.
263 William M'Kenzie, Chambers's, Houston.*
264 William Jamison, Bostick's, Twiggs.*
265 John Y. Smith, 271st, M'Intosh.*
266 Henry Kight, Williams's, Jasper.*
267 James Jones, or., Groce's, Bibb.*
268 Jesse Thomas, sol., Wood's, Morgan.
269 James Everitt, Boynton's, Twiggs.
270 Thomas R. Chandler, Brewer's, Walton.
271 John M. Norman, Miller's, Ware.
272 John Richardson, Hudson's, Marion.*
273 John G. Brooker, Hand's, Appling.
274 Jesse Stephens, 588th, Upson.*
275 Joseph G. Booth, Wilhite's, Elbert.*
276 Richard H. Embry, Allison's, Pike.*

277 Isabella Estes, w., M'Clendon's, Putnam.*
278 John T. Morrow, 419th, Walton.*
279 Robert Henderson, Sen., r. s., Jones's, Hall.*
280 James Bryan, Martin's, Hall.*
281 Meshack M'Ginty, Martin's, Hall.
282 Asher Lane, Hinton's, Wilkes.*
283 Thomas G. Weatherington, Clinton's, Campbell.*
284 Milliton M. Blalock, 785th, Sumter.*
285 Alexander Camron, Clifton's Tatnall.*
286 Isham Oliver, Turner's, Crawford.*
287 Adam Thompson, Hamilton's, Hall.*
288 Curtis Williamson, 37th, Scriven.
289 Aldridge Bunn, 162d, Greene.*
290 William Scarfe, Jr., Mobley's, De Kalb.
291 Elizabeth Whitehead, w., 672d, Harris.*
292 Solomon Peek, Bower's, Elbert.
293 Charles Muggridge, 38th, Scriven.*
294 William Suttles, r. s., Mobley's, De Kalb.*
295 Nathan Harris's ors., Newsom's, Warren.
296 Thomas H. Capers, Ellsworth's, Bibb.*
297 James O. Wilkinson, Young's, Jefferson.*
298 William Brown, 4th, Chatham.
299 Nicey B. Bolds's ors., Cleggs's, Walton.*
300 Isabella Hamilton, w., Tuggle's, Merriwether.*
301 Joanna Graves, w., Stanton's, Newton.*
302 John Folsom, Folsom's, Lowndes.*
303 James Gunn, Jr., Jennings's, Clarke.*
304 Wellburn Hunt, Athens, Clarke.*
305 Jackson Cannon, Kellum's, Talbot.
306 Uriah C. Spraberry, Givins's, De Kalb.*
307 William W. Carlisle, 656th, Troup.
308 Davis B. Reid, Rhodes's, De Kalb.
309 Ansel Watson, Dobbs's, Hall.*
310 Ann Williams, h. a., Haygood's, Washington.*
311 George G. Tankersley, Huchinson's, Columbia.
312 Elizabeth Weaver, h. a., Pound's, Twiggs.*
313 Elijah Ogden, George's, Appling.*
314 John Dowd, r. s., Newsom's, Warren.*
315 (fr.) Antonio Lewis, Cliett's, Columbia.*
316 (fr.) David Biggars, Buck-branch, Clarke.*
317 (fr.) Sterling Wood, Jordan's, Bibb.*
318 (fr.) John Rabun, Bostick's, Twiggs.
319 (fr.) Floyd Jourdaine, Stone's, Irwin.
320 (fr.) Thornton Mead, Maguire's, Gwinnett.*
321 (fr.) John J. Holmes, Haygood's, Washington.*
322 (fr.) William Williams, Barker's, Gwinnett.*
323 (fr.) James J. Hendrick, Wilson's, Madison.*
324 (fr.) David Moncrief, Johnson's, Bibb.

FIFTEENTH DISTRICT, THIRD SECTION, CHEROKEE.

1 John D. Floyd, Merck's, Hall.*
2 Jeremiah H. Moore, 143d, Greene.*
3 Lacey Witcher, 4th section, Cherokee.*
4 Richard Winget, Smith's, Houston.*
5 Gabriel M. C. Clements, Wooten's, Telfair.*
6 Asa Adams, Peterson's, Montgomery.*
7 Elizabeth Popwell, w., 24th, M'Intosh.
8 Hiram Turner, Whisenhunt's, Carroll.*
9 Robert Creamer, Crow's, Pike.*
10 Wilkes T. Leonard, Burnett's, Habersham.*
11 George Loving, Ellsworth's, Bibb.*
12 Daniel Duncan, Anderson's, Rabun.*
13 Willis Hollis, 466th, Monroe.*
14 Stephen Whitmire, Jr., Liddell's, Jackson.*
15 Thomas Biggs, Stower's, Elbert.
16 Edwin Allen, 112th, Hancock.
17 Lewis Summons, s. l. w., Lamp's, Jefferson.*
18 Jonathan Herring, Morgan's, Madison.*
19 Nancy Miller's or., Hill's, Baldwin.*
20 Richard Pittman, 4th, Chatham.
21 Anderson W. Bell, Hamilton's, Hall.*
22 John Hames, Sen., r. s., Daniel's, Hall.
23 Hannah Ward, w., Dawson's, Jasper.
24 James Adams, r. s., Seal's, Elbert.*
25 William Grant, 106th, Hancock.*
26 James Tollison, Maguire's, Gwinnett.*
27 James S. Holmes, 174th, Wilkes.
28 Thomas Hardy, Neal's, Campbell.
29 Willis Hughs, M. Brown's, Habersham.
30 John Middleton, 404th, Gwinnett.
31 James Cocroft, 138th, Greene.
32 Mary Loyd, w. r. s., 404th, Gwinnett.*
33 Charles L. Hays, Brooks's, Muscogee.*
34 William Word, Newman's, Thomas.*
35 Thomas Douglass, sol., Fulks's, Wilkes.*
36 Briggs W. Hopson, 779th, Heard.*
37 William M'Kinnee, or., Field's, Habersham.*
38 Lazarus Telly, r. s., Keener's, Rabun.*
39 Jacob Buffington's ors., Allen's, Monroe.
40 Jesse Simpson, Young's, Wilkinson.*
41 John Clay, Haygood's, Washington.*

42 Ranson Powell's ors., Dyer's, Habersham.
43 David Wright's ors., M'Ewin's, Monroe.
44 Joel A. Dees, Smith's, Henry.*
45 Elizabeth M. Ray, w., Murphy's, Columbia.
46 Isaac C. Butterworth, Price's, Hall.*
47 Marshal Covington, Covington's, Pike.
48 William Fleming, Ware's, Coweta.
49 Etheldred Futral, Smith's, Henry.
50 Case Turner's or., Dobbs's, Hall.
51 Paschal Murphy's ors., Howard's, Oglethorpe.
52 Robert Champion, Burges's, Carroll.*
53 Sidney Barr, Dyer's, Habersham.*
54 Littleberry Matthews, Martin's, Pike.*
55 Josiah Hancock, Walker's, Columbia.*
56 Samuel Williams, Williams's, Decatur.*
57 Tennel H. Wilson, M'Ginnis's, Jackson.*
58 Sarah A. Carson, or., Cleland's, Chatham.
59 John Jordans, Harp's, Jones.*
60 Wiley Tyler, Strickland's, Merriwether.
61 James Lewis, 38th, Scriven.*
62 John Bruce, Belcher's, Jasper.*
63 Brinkley Gandy, Newman's, Thomas.*
64 Jane Ward, w. r. s., 190th, Elbert.*
65 James R. Morris, Morton's, De Kalb.*
66 Jordan D. Ranson, Lynn's, Warren.*
67 Smith M'Donald, Greer's, Merriwether.
68 John M. Russell's ors., Cleland's, Chatham.
69 Adaline M'Coe, w., Cleland's, Chatham.
70 Loftin Reeves, Griffin's, De Kalb.
71 John Hays, r. s., Latimer's, De Kalb.
72 Salisbury Garrison, Catlett's, Franklin.
73 George M'Dill, Nesbit's, Newton.*
74 Mary Ann Haslam, w., 9th, Effingham.*
75 Nathan C. Morgan, Norris's, Monroe.*
76 William Luckley, Jr., 144th, Greene.
77 Samson Vichey, Sen., Field's, Habersham.*
78 John Osburn Watson, M'Coy's, Houston.
79 Emery B. Hughs, 557th, Walton.
80 William M'Mullen, Liddell's, Jackson.
81 John Owens, sol., 70th, Burke.
82 Jonas Smith's ors., Talley's, Troup.
83 George G. B. Adams, Hughes's, Habersham.
84 William W. Kelebrew, Calhoun's, Harris.
85 Littleberry Adams, Pate's, Warren.
86 John T. Rudulph, Hobkerk's, Camden.*
87 Henry J. Glass, Flynn's, Muscogee.*
88 Robert N. M'Linn, M'Linn's, Butts.*

89 David Kennamore, Jones's, Habersham.*
90 Robert Curtis, s. l. w., Harris's, Crawford.*
91 Lewis Brown, Candler's, Bibb.*
92 Lemuel Canadee, Lamberth's, Fayette.*
93 Alexander Gunn, Covington's, Pike.*
94 Thomas Woods, George's, Appling.*
95 Nancy Smith, w., Lynn's, Warren.
96 James Russell, Sen., Peurifoy's, Henry.
97 William Forester, Chastain's, Habersham.
98 John Adams, Wood's, Jefferson.
99 Elisha Hindsman, Lunceford's, Wilkes.*
100 A. Mullinax's two orphans, Jones's, Habersham.*
101 James L. Newton, 600th, Richmond.
102 Simeon Mell, Kellum's, Talbot.*
103 Washington Allen, Chambers's, Gwinnett.*
104 John Pepper, Jr., 249th, Walton.*
105 Andrew Shepherd's ors., Moseley's, Wilkes.*
106 Green B. Parmer, Orr's, Jackson.
107 Joseph Buckhannon, 168th, Wilkes.*
108 Obadiah Smith, 640th, Dooly.*
109 Robert Henderson, Thaxton's, Butts.
110 William J. More, Wilhite's, Elbert.*
111 Elie Banks, sol., Sanders's, Jones.*
112 John Leverman's ors., 122d, Richmond.
113 Edmond W. Reynolds, 406th, Gwinnett.
114 William Tucker, 294th, Jasper.*
115 David S. Thomas, 293d, Jasper.
116 Nathan Lindsey, Blair's, Lowndes.*
117 Alsey Johnston, or., 735th, Troup.
118 Crisper Davis, Thaxton's, Butts.*
119 John Peddy, Barrow's, Houston.*
120 Mordica Alexander, sol., Hatton's, Baker.*
121 James M. White, Martin's, Newton.
122 Paschal Angle, Lamberth's, Fayette.*
123 James Massey's ors., 165th, Wilkes.
124 William Fayder, Jones's, Morgan.*
125 Sarah Mackin, w., Chambers's, Gwinnett.
126 Thomas J. Smith, Lunceford's, Elbert.*
127 Athijah Milloun, Taylor's, Jones.*
128 Tillman J. Turner, Collins's, Henry.*
129 John Anderson, Dilman's, Pulaski.*
130 John Brown, Sinquefield's, Washington.*
131 James Riley's minors, ———, Greene.*
132 William Ferrill, Say's, De Kalb.*
133 Robert S. Gordon, or., Echols's, Clarke
134 James W. Carter, Robinson's, Fayette.*
135 David Malcom, s. l. w., 559th, Walton.

136 Jared Renfroe's ors., Haygood's, Washington.
137 James Mathison, Bailey's, Laurens.
138 Washington Coleman, 102d, Hancock.*
139 Thomas Denson, 415th, Walton.*
140 A. F. Temples, Watson's, Marion.*
141 William H. Carter, Oliver's, Decatur.
142 Oswell B. Langley, Reid's, Gwinnett.*
143 Silas Monk's ors., Kendrick's, Putnam.*
144 Abraham Joiner's ors., Barwick's, Washington.
145 Sanford Ramey's ors., 279th, Morgan.*
146 Bird Puckett, Maguire's, Gwinnett.*
147 John S. Prather, Talley's, Troup.*
148 James G. Perryman, Thompson's, Henry.*
149 Samuel S. Johnson, York's, Stewart.*
150 John Brunt, 162d, Greene.*
151 Felix C. Catonnett, Valleau's, Chatham.*
152 Milton Hudson, Fleming's, Franklin.*
153 W. A. Tennell, s. l. w., Lightfoot's, Washington.*
154 Canly Taylor, Mayo's, Wilkinson.*
155 Littleton, G. Hilliard, Bailey's, Laurens.*
156 John Paine, 102d, Hancock.*
157 David Baldwin, sol., Sanders's, Jones.*
158 John W. Dubs, Houston's, Chatham.*
159 William Hulmes's ors., Thomason's, Elbert.*
160 Samuel Young, Loven's, Henry.*
161 George Greer, Jordan's, Bibb.*
162 Rice Mathis, Folsom's, Lowndes.*
163 James Gray, Hendon's, Carroll.*
164 William Tomalson, r. s., Everett's, Washington.
165 Willis P. Sanders, Watson's, Marion.*
166 David Rosser's ors., 307th, Putnam.*
167 Moses Benton, 49th Bryan's, Chatham.*
168 Hubbard Williams, Hearn's, Butts.*
169 Jane A. Breuse, 2d, Chatham.*
170 Samuel M'Crary, Daniel's, Hall.*
171 George Young, Sen., r. s., Howard's, Oglethorpe*
172 John Ingram, Lester's, Monroe.*
173 Elizabeth Hudson, h. a., Lamp's, Jefferson.*
174 Jeremiah Matthews, s. l. w., Martin's, Newton.*
175 Margaret Cummins, w. s., Griffin's, Fayette.*
176 Mountraville Corley, Griffin's, De Kalb.*
177 Ethel Tucker, Jr., 190th, Elbert.*
178 William Spines, Graves's, Lincoln.*
179 Frederic B. Brown, Pounds's, Twiggs.*
180 Berryan Henderson, Sweat's, Ware.*
181 Alfred Wyche, Braddy's, Jones.*
182 Hugh G. Johnson, sol., Wilson's, Pike.*

183 Patrick Butler, Sen., r. s., Smith's, Elbert.*
184 Nancy Gaulding, w., Howell's, Elbert.*
185 Young B. Jenkins, 146th, Greene.*
186 Willis Kirbee, 162d, Greene.*
187 William Williams, Bostick's, Twiggs.*
188 John Manders, Bridges's, Gwinnett.*
189 Abraham Mallet, M'Gill's, Lincoln.*
190 John Eubanks, Crow's, Pike.*
191 James D. Eubanks, Monk's, Crawford.*
192 Charles Hudson's ors., M'Clain's, Newton.*
193 William Russell's ors., Barker's, Gwinnett.
194 Thomas W. Poe, Smith's, Habersham.*
195 James M. Davison, Howard's, Oglethorpe.*
196 William F. Harrison, 419th, Walton.*
197 Richard W. Watson, Watson's, Marion.*
198 William B. Terrell, Taylor's, Elbert.*
199 James Stovall, Willis's, Franklin.*
200 Thomas I. Tengle, Griffin's, De Kalb.*
201 John D. Blair, Garner's, Washington.*
202 Henry T. Woodall, Silman's, Pike.*
203 Augustus M. Honeycut, Harris's, Columbia.*
204 Charles Buck, 129th, Richmond.*
205 John Hines, r. s., 73d, Burke.*
206 Charles R. Johns, Wilson's, Pike.*
207 Jesse Swinney, Morton's, De Kalb.*
208 Elias Thomas, M'Coy's, Houston.*
209 Thomas Crouch, Pace's, Putnam.*
210 Henry Howzi's ors., Morgan's, Clarke.*
211 Murdock M'Kinni, Groover's, Thomas.*
212 Sarah Terrell, w., 190th, Elbert.
213 Daniel P. Roger, Coxe's, Morgan.*
214 Shadrack Bullard, Hughes's, Habersham.*
215 David Williams, Payne's, Merriwether.*
216 Soloman Strickland, Cleghorn's, Marion.
217 Richard Procton, Stephens's, Habersham.*
218 George W. Griffin, Griffin's, Burke.
219 Thomas Mossey, Gray's, Thomas.*
220 Polly Watkins, w., Athens, Clarke.*
221 Asa Thompson's ors., Varner's, Merriwether.
222 Silas J. Worly, Field's, Habersham.*
223 Thomas Coats, Iverson's, Houston.*
224 Sanford Whitehead, Morgan's, Clarke.
225 Edward Hatchett, Hatchett's, Oglethorpe.*
  1 (fr.) Elemileck Sanderford, Moseley's, Wilkes.*
  2 (fr.) Harriet Hodge, mi., f. a., M'Daniel's, Pulaski
  3 (fr.) Jer. Taylor, Jr., Whitehead's, Habersham.
  4 (fr.) Alfred Spence, Night's, Morgan.*

5 (fr.) Thomas White, Morton's, De Kalb.
6 (fr.) Mary Napp, w. r. s., 160th, Greene.
7 (fr.) Sylvanus Gibson, Walker's, Harris.*
8 (fr.) John C. Parkerson, Hart's, Jones.
9 (fr.) Moses Huchison, Stower's, Elbert.*
10 (fr.) Job B. Gibson, Hicks's, Decatur.
11 (fr.) Reu. Brown, or., Arrington's, Merriwether.*
12 (fr.) David M'Glann, Hill's, Monroe.*
13 (fr.) Jeremiah Wilson, sol., Blair's, Lowndes.*
14 (fr.) M. Garner, Sen., sol., Garner's, Washington*
15 (fr.) John S. Fleman, Jenkins's, Oglethorpe.*
16 (fr.) James Hall, Robinson's, Harris.
17 (fr.) John B. Moran, Taylor's, Putnam.
18 (fr.) Isham Daniel, Sinclair's, Houston.*
19 (fr.) William Smith's ors., Fryer's, Telfair.*
20 (fr.) Aaron Crim, 175th, Wilkes.*
21 (fr.) Joshua Fowler, Winter's, Jones.*
22 (fr.) Joshua Brown, Barker's, Gwinnett.
23 (fr.) Sarah Campbell, w., 417th, Walton.*
24 (fr.) Robert Johnson, Smith's, Houston.
25 (fr.) Solomon Bennett, Wheeler's, Pulaski.
26 (fr.) Daniel Kent, Bostick's, Twiggs.*
27 (fr.) Thomas H. Moore, Tower's, Gwinnett.
28 (fr.) Eliz. Watson, w. r. s., Murphy's, Columbia.
29 (fr.) Tilman D. Peurifoy, Groover's, Thomas.
30 (fr.) Thomas Lundy's ors., Justice's, Bibb.
31 (fr.) Archibald L. W. Stroud, Smith's, Campbell.*

SIXTEENTH DISTRICT, THIRD SECTION, CHEROKEE.

1 George W. Findley, 148th, Greene.
2 Elisha Stevens, Shattox's, Coweta.*
3 Eldad M'Lendon's ors., Benson's, Lincoln.
4 Charles G. Johnson, Oliver's, Twiggs.*
5 Thomas Johnson, Griffin's, De Kalb.
6 John P. Floyd, Morgan's, Madison.
7 Gideon Cummens's ors., Griffin's, Fayette.
8 Nathan Holliday, Crow's, Pike.*
9 Ruffin L. Johnson, Bryan's, Pulaski.*
10 John Fellbright, Sewell's, Franklin.
11 Benjamin Lokey, Mizell's, Talbot.*
12 Samuel Wilks, Davis's, Clarke.*
13 William Lekyl Shurman, 19th, Bryan.*
14 William Barringtine, Barwick's, Washington.*
15 Christopher Rider, Jr., Chastain's, Habersham.*

16 Haly Shaw, 2d section, Cherokee.*
17 Jasper Jones, 279th, Morgan.*
18 Shadrack Doggeel, 561st, Upson.*
19 George R. Braziel, 245th, Jackson.*
20 John Chappell, 249th, Walton.*
21 Robert B. M'Cord, 559th, Walton.
22 William Jackson Craw, Woodruff's, Campbell.
23 James Hill's ors., Valleau's, Chatham.*
24 David Bishop, sol., Nesbit's, Newton.*
25 Westly Stone, 320th, Baldwin.*
26 Levi Jackson, Hughes's, Habersham.*
27 Miles Garret, Jr., 561st, Upson.
28 Nathan N. Lester, Lester's, Pulaski.*
29 Margaret M'Loughlin, w., Wooten's Telfair.*
30 Alex. St. C. Tennille, Williams's, Washington.
31 Benjamin Bryant, Jr., Sinclair's, Houston.*
32 James Johnson, s. l. w., 120th, Richmond.
33 Charles Stiller, Dean's, Clarke.*
34 James Bailey, Reid's, Gwinnett.
35 Rester T. Hines, sol., 466th, Monroe.
36 Mary E. Garkin, or., Merck's, Hall.
37 George Mansell, sol., Mashburn's, Pulaski.*
38 William Wyatt, Ross's, Monroe.
39 Elizabeth Gilstrop, h. a., ———, Pulaski.*
40 Middleton W. Brown, Brown's, Elbert.*
41 Henry H. Langford, s. l. w., Mann's, Crawford.
42 Wilkins Smith, 101st, Hancock.*
43 Dickson Thomas, Jones's, Bulloch.*
44 Thomas W. L. Lewis, Bruce's, Greene.*
45 Sarah Spears, w., Thames, Crawford.
46 John Barnes, Hampton's, Newton.
47 Zadock Moore, Underwood's, Putnam.*
48 Thomas M'Call, r. s., Hobbs's, Laurens.*
49 John R. Reins, Pace's, Wilkinson.*
50 Elijah G. Hearn, 561st, Upson.*
51 Elijah Cleckser, Compton's, Fayette.*
52 Daniel Brewer, Coxe's, Talbot.
53 John Adams, Derrick's, Henry.*
54 John Vining, Lamp's, Jefferson.
55 Michael Dunn, sol., Merck's, Hall.*
56 Person Duncan, Jr., Nellum's, Elbert.*
57 Francis J. Pinckard, 466th, Monroe.*
58 Daniel Rudling, Riden's, Jackson.
59 William Carroll, Newsom's, Warren.*
60 Luzer Howard, 687th, Lee.
61 Landem Jones, Taylor's, Jones.*
62 Stanford Meritt, Thomas's, Crawford.*

63 John Bowen, r. s., Barker's, Gwinnett.*
64 Zechariah Johns, Sen., 702d, Heard.
65 James Highsaw, Loveless's, Gwinnett.
66 John S. Randle, Robinson's, Putnam.
67 James Clayton, Burgess's, Carroll.*
68 Samuel G. Dawson, 588th, Upson.*
69 Seaborn Jones, Jones's, Lincoln.*
70 David Cooper, Allen's, Henry.
71 Harris Tomlinson, Williams's, Washington.*
72 John B. Wick, Candler's, Bibb.
73 William F. Bond, Mayo's, Wilkinson.*
74 Jesse Tomlin, Martin's, Newton.*
75 Jepthah Fannin, s. l. w., Ballard's, Morgan.
76 James W. Cook, r. s., 248th, Jackson.
77 John Farmer's ors., 277th, Morgan.
78 Jonathan Rhan, r. s., 11th, Effingham.*
79 Rebecca Drake, w., Nichols's, Fayette.*
80 Dorcas Carler, w., Fitzpatrick's, Chatham.*
81 Andrew M'Ever, s. i. w., Cleghorn's, Madison.*
82 Peyton Lawrence, Allison's, Pike.
83 Reuben Boyett, or., Allen's, Henry.
84 William R. Wright, Whisenhunt's, Carroll.
85 Ann Bryan, w. r. s., 73d, Burke.*
86 James Cochran, Wynn's, Gwinnett.
87 Silas Ramy, Vining's, Putnam.
88 Henry C. Morgan, Curry's, Merriwether.*
89 Jess Johnson, s. l. w., 693d, Heard.
90 Gilbert Pettes, Mann's, Crawford.
91 James Herndon, Rick's, Laurens.
92 Rebekah Kirk, w., Parham's, Harris.*
93 James Humbert, Young's, Wilkinson.*
94 William G. Robinson, Smith's, Liberty.*
95 James Johnson, Clinton's, Campbell.*
96 William G. M'Bride, or., Alexander's, Jefferson.*
97 Anny Blake, w., 11th, Effingham.
98 Adam Crotwell, 404th, Gwinnett.*
99 Owen Bryan, Oliver's, Twiggs.*
100 Benjamin P. Shepherd, Jordan's, Harris.*
101 Sally Ralls, w., 143d, Greene.
102 William Broadwell, Merck's, Hall.
103 Jesse C. Wall, Clark's, Elbert.
104 Rebecca Williams, w. r. s., Whelchel's, Hall.
105 Milton H. Haynie, Lane's, Morgan.
106 James M. Porter, Ballard's, Morgan.
107 Jesse W. Howell, sol., Hargrove's, Newton.
108 John M'Doffee, Griffin's, Merriwether.*
109 William M'Coy, Everett's, Washington.

110 Smith Lewis, Sanderlin's, Chatham.*
111 Leroy Pollard, Show's, Muscogee.*
112 Anslen Bugg, sol., Field's, Habersham.
113 Mekin Huff, Curry's, Merriwether.*
114 John R. Bostick, Alexander's, Jefferson.*
115 Alford Beates, Williams's, Walton.*
116 John Gilbert, r. s., 243d, Jackson.*
117 Nathan W. Isler, Cannon's, Wilkinson.*
118 Thomas Evans, Howell's, Troup.*
119 Thomas W. Jarrad, Brock's, Habersham.*
120 Robert Barnwell, r. s., Griffin's, Hall.
121 James Davis, 190th, Elbert.
122 Abel Barnes, sol., Tompkins's, Putnam.*
123 Alfred W. Ferguson, Hearn's, Butts.
124 Jonathan Bullard, Sutton's, Habersham.
125 Samuel H. Russell, 108th, Hancock.*
126 Ann Wilson, w. r. s., 12th, Effingham.*
127 Robert W. Smith, Jack's, Clarke.
128 Ladock Piper, sol., Hargrove's, Newton.*
129 John Thompson, or., Davis's, Jones.
130 John Taylor, Sparks's, Washington.*
131 Russel Fish, Hammock's, Jasper.*
132 Thomas Godfrey's ors., Reid's, Gwinnett.
133 T. R. Brown, s. l. w., Scroggins's, Oglethorpe.
134 Clark R. Coppedge, Allison's, Pike.
135 Jordan G. Watson, Phillips's, Talbot.
136 Margaret Wood, w., 419th, Walton.*
137 Martha M'Ever, blind, Morton's, De Kalb.
138 Sarah M'Clennon, w., 49th, Emanuel.*
139 John Gilliland, Compton's, Fayette.
140 William Buffington, Taylor's, Elbert.
141 Peter Clasedge, Moore's, Randolph.*
142 David W. Garrison, Dean's, Clarke.*
143 James Turner, Gittens's, Fayette.*
144 William Smith, sol., Higginbotham's, Madison.*
145 Anthony Oliver, Jenkins's, Oglethorpe.
146 Emenuly J. Edmondson, f. a., Morgan's, Clarke.
147 Henry Cobb's ors., Tower's, Gwinnett.
148 Hugh Harrison, Chandler's, Franklin.
149 Osburn Wiggins, sol., Smith's, Houston.
150 William Hollis, 466th, Monroe.*
151 John S. Ray, Thompson's, Henry.*
152 James Lambert, Gibson's, Decatur.*
153 John M'Daniel, Hargrove's, Newton.*
154 Archibald Bruce, 561st, Upson.
155 Hampton Montgomery, Streetman's, Twiggs.*
156 Henry N. Pope, Loven's, Henry.*

157 William Bridges, Green's, Oglethorpe.*
158 Vinson E. Vickers's ors., 320th, Baldwin.
159 Richard M. Head, Moseley's, Wilkes.*
160 John M. Smith, M'Clain's, Newton.
161 Samuel B. White, Nesbit's, Newton.
162 Ruth Obunion, w., Blount's, Wilkinson.*
163 James W. Lumpkin, Aderhold's, Campbell.
164 James A. Barthetoit, Flynn's, Muscogee.
165 Edwin J. L. Easter, 320th, Baldwin.
166 Elias J. Dixon, Frasier's, Monroe.
167 Henry Dake, Jr., Lay's, Jackson.
168 Robert Dean, Burnett's, Habersham.
169 Jordan Driver, Mays's, Monroe.
170 Godfrey Luther, Blackstock's, Hall. ·
171 Benjamin Folsom, sol., Crow's, Merriwether.
172 Micajah Dixon, s. l. w., Whitaker's, Crawford.
173 John Poullin's ors., Cleland's, Chatham.
174 William Miles, Bishop's, Henry.*
175 Joseph Tomme's ors., Allen's, Henry.*
176 Emeline Habzendorp, or., 24th, M'Intosh.
177 Allen M'Lean, Wootten's, Telfair.
178 Daniel Johnson, Latimer's, De Kalb.
179 John Harrist, M'Gehee's, Troup.
180 Wade Ward, Bryan's, Pulaski.*
181 Mary Salter, w., Butts's, Monroe.
182 David P. Robinson, Wright's, Laurens.
183 Elizabeth Mitchell, w., 466th, Monroe.*
184 John H. Smith, Howard's, Oglethorpe.
185 Milledge Ramy, Smith's, Campbell.
186 Moses Harshaw, Burnett's, Habersham.*
187 Robert Bledsoe, s. l. w., Robinson's, Putnam.
188 Johnston Sarter, Roberts's, Hall.*
189 John Clark, Curry's, Merriwether.
190 Archibald E. Lard, Martin's, Newton.*
191 James Perry's or., Martin's, Laurens.
192 Peter Ellis, Hall's, Oglethorpe.
193 Polly Coward, w., Martin's, Washington.*
194 Benjamin Warren Jackson, Braddy's, Jones.
195 Herman Elkin, or., 10th, Effingham.
196 Isaac Pippin's ors., Talley's, Troup.
197 James Smith's or., Smith's, Wilkinson.
198 Joseph Ecton, s. l. w., Strahorn's, Heard.*
199 Phebe Russell, w., Gunn's, Jones.
200 Holloway Saunders, Givins's, De Kalb.*
201 Samuel Tinsley, Ellsworth's, Bibb.*
202 Abraham D. Bennison, Say's, De Kalb.
203 Adam W. Y. Harvey, Mashburn's, Pulaski.*

204 William Ammons, 334th, Wayne.*
205 Benjamin Wheeler, Neal's, Campbell.*
206 Noah Ashworth, Taylor's, Elbert.*
207 Nathan N. Lester, Lester's, Pulaski.*
208 Mary Ann W. Shepherd, w., Gittens's, Fayette.
209 William Fraser, 271st, M'Intosh.*
210 Elias J. Brannin, Wilson's, Pike.*
211 Margaret Kilpatrick, w., Atkinson's, Coweta.*
212 Robert Crutchfield, sol., 140th, Greene.*
213 Andrew Morris, M'Linn's, Butts.*
214 William Goodman, 122d, Richmond.*
215 Nancy Ann Lester, Hicks's, Decatur.*
216 Willis A. Woods, Groover's, Thomas.
217 John Hendrix, Price's, Hall.
218 Abner Cherry, Justice's, Bibb.*
219 Peyton Holt, s. l. w., Rooks's, Putnam.*
220 William C. Germany, Madden's, Pike.*
221 Robert Neal, Allen's, Monroe.*
222 William M. Ware, Lane's, Morgan.
223 Hiram Weaver, 510th, Early.
224 Clement Waters, r. s., Welche's, Habersham.
225 Jacob Callaway, s. 1784-97, 165th, Wilkes.*
226 William Owenby's ors., Phillip's, Jasper.*
227 Andrew A. Howe, Mann's, Crawford.*
228 Justus Bradshaw, 148th, Greene.
229 John Hardy, Vining's, Putnam.*
230 John Hill, 109th, Hancock.*
231 Robert Smith, Jr., Hall's, Butts.*
232 Charles Stewart, s. i. w., 34th, Scriven.*
233 Samuel Brady, r. s., Watson's, Marion.*
234 George M. Williams, Linam's, Pulaski.*
235 James Canada's or., Dupree's, Washington.*
236 John Cooper; Cliett's, Columbia.*
237 William Clay, Haygood's, Washington.*
238 John Coleman, 73d, Burke.*
239 Mary Ann E. Ford, minor, Gray's, Henry.*
240 Thomas Butler, Fitzpatrick's, Chatham.*
241 Noah Slay, Johnson's, De Kalb.*
242 Stephen H. Tucker, Clark's, Elbert.*
243 William Lamb, 113th, Hancock.*
244 Isaac Hopkins, r. s., Norman's, Wilkes.*
245 William B. Bell, 589th, Upson.*
246 Joel Johnson, Jr., 249th, Walton.*
247 John P. Hutchins, Chambers's, Gwinnett.*
248 James Chambers, Lester's, Monroe.
249 William Jones, M. Brown's, Habersham.*
250 Wright M. Beasly, 56th, Emanuel.*
251 Jesse Pitts, Pearce's, Houston.

252 Thomas Phillips, sol., Wilhite's, Elbert.*
253 Jeroyal Blackwell, Say's, Hall.
254 Boyce Eidson, 415th, Walton.
255 Arthur Ginn, Butts's, Monroe.*
256 Abnery M. Zachry, 278th, Morgan.*
257 Vinzant Mount, Fitzpatrick's, Chatham.*
258 Seth Stone's, or., Bivins's, Jones.*
259 William Tucker, 190th, Elbert.
260 Grant B. Reeves, 3d, Chatham.*
261 John N. Smith, Williams's, Ware.*
262 David Hutchins, Mobley's, De Kalb.*
263 Leonard Cagle, House's, Henry.*
264 Robinson's or., Martin's, Pike.*
265 Charles M'Lemore, 656th, Troup.*
266 Josiah Warren's ors., Griffin's, Emanuel.*
267 Duncan Merkerson, Burgess's, Carroll.
268 Burrell White, Royster's, Franklin.*
269 Polly Snow, w., Fenn's, Clarke.*
270 Gracey Butler, w., Russell's, Henry.*

22d DISTRICT, THIRD SECTION, CHEROKEE.

1 John W. A. Pistell, Peurifoy's, Henry.*
2 Mark Ward, 35th, Scriven.*
3 Henry Thornton's ors., Jordan's, Harris.
4 Sarah Coleman, w., 174th, Wilkes.*
5 William K. Patton, Gittens's, Fayette.*
6 James W. Plummer, Loveless's, Gwinnett.*
7 Walter J. Wills, or., Phillip's, Talbot.*
8 Capal Garrison, Catletts, Franklin.*
9 Elizabeth Brown, h. a., ——, Upson.*
10 Alexander Craig, Hood's, Henry.
11 John Whelchel, Jr., Whelchel's, Hall.*
12 James J. Daniel, sol., Taylor's, Elbert.
13 Thomas Knowles, s. i. w., 160th, Greene.*
14 Simeon Ackridge, sol., Gillis's, De Kalb.*
15 Abner Henley's or., Pollard's, Wilkes.
16 Francis H. Cooke, 398th, Richmond.
17 Stephen Williamson, Kelly's, Elbert.*
18 Grant Tailer, Wood's, Morgan.
19 Pester Hinton, r. s., Tayler's, Elbert.
20 Benjamin F. Fuller, Bridges's, Gwinnett.
21 Pleasant Worley, Sen., Hughes's, Habersham.
22 John Dyass, Morgan's, Appling.*

23 Nancy Whorton, w., Coxe's, Franklin.
24 Pryor Crittenton, Smith's, Madison.
25 Samuel D. Vaughan, Robinson's, Fayette.
26 Gabriel Wallis, Martin's Newton.*
27 Rhoda Lawrence, w., Brock's, Habersham.*
28 Joel Brown, Mobley's, De Kalb.*
29 Robert Carter, r. s., M'Clain's, Newton.*
30 Reuben Adams, Jr., 454th, Walton.*
31 Joshua Clark, s. l. w., 734th, Lee.*
32 Matthew Sigler, M'Korkle's, Jasper.*
33 Wiley G. Marchman, Gittens's, Fayette.*
34 Martin White, Lunceford's, Elbert.*
35 Peter & Nancy Smith, ors., Williams's, Ware.*
36 Benjamin Moore, 320th, Baldwin.*
37 William B. Hardison, Edwards's, Talbot.*
38 Benjamin W. Hays, 294th, Jasper.
39 Richard Holmes, Hines's, Coweta.*
40 Elias Brown, Camp's, Warren.*
41 Williamson Bird's ors., Campbell's, Wilkes.*
42 Rebecca Totmon, w. s. i. w., Stower's, Elbert.*
43 Lewis Jenkins, Greer's, Merriwether.*
44 Nancy Wood, w., Brock's, Habersham.*
45 Jourdan Levritt's or., Levritt's, Lincoln.*
46 John Walton's or., Bragaw's, Oglethorpe.
47 David Altman, Walker's, Houston.*
48 James Jordan, Hill's, Stewart.*
49 Thomas L. Larry, Hargrove's, Newton.*
50 John Hudson, Crow's, Pike.*
51 John Grover, 19th, Bryan.*
52 Henry Dobson, r. s., Price's, Hall.
53 Elisha Bowen's ors., Summerlin's, Bulloch.
54 John B. Puckett, Maguire's, Gwinnett.
55 Benjamin Brantley's ors., Hobbs's, Laurens.*
56 Susannah Turner, h. a., Hobbs's, Laurens.*
57 John Robberson, Chastain's, Habersham.
58 Mary Kirklin, w. r. s., Stewart's, Troup.*
59 Moses Tilles, Sen., Watson's, Marion.*
60 William Culwell's or., Aderhold's, Campbell.
61 George Cook, Rutland's, Bibb.*
62 William M. Jones, Allen's, Bibb.
63 Francis Delamar, Hill's, Monroe.
64 Roger Lawson's ors., Boynton's, Twiggs.
65 Robert Reeves, sol., Dobbs's, Hall.
66 George Malcom, Jr., 559th, Walton.*
67 Lucretia M'Cool, w., 335th, Wayne.*
68 William Tindall's ors., Harris's, Columbia.*
69 Thomas Carlton, Newman's, Thomas.*

70 Thomas Ingram, 555th, Upson.*
71 William Culpepper's ors., Lynn's, Warren.*
72 Alexander Patterson, Kellum's, Talbot.*
73 Payton Sherman, Russell's, Henry.*
74 Jesse Moses, Robinson's, Fayette.*
75 Henry Varnadore, 535th, Dooly.*
76 Caleb Herndon, sol., Herndon's, Hall.*
77 John G. King, Hall's, Butts.
78 Harrison Harris, Tower's, Gwinnett.*
79 John Bird, 174th, Wilkes.*
80 Abigail M'Cullers, w., Mayo's, Wilkinson.
81 Anderson Roberts, 588th, Upson.
82 Loborn Manning, Martin's, Stewart.
83 William Ross, 589th, Upson.
84 Benjamin Martin's ors., Sullivan's, Jones.*
85 John S. Butler, Camp's, Baker.*
86 Echols Daniel, ———, Crawford.
87 Elizabeth Marshall, w., 289th, Jasper.
88 Peter M'Kellar, Covington's, Pike.*
89 Rely Wilson, 1st section, Cherokee.
90 Mary Mede, w., Mackleroy's, Clarke.
91 M. W. Tomlinson, w. r. s., Chustus's, Jefferson.
92 Joseph Huil, Sen., sol., Evans's, Fayette.
93 James M. Madden, Madden's, Pike.
94 James Henderson, Burnett's, Habersham.
95 David B. Bush, Sealy's, Talbot.
96 James Herasling, sol., M'Gehee's, Troup.*
97 Wm. M. Livingston, 535th, Dooly.*
98 William Dickson, 777th, Randolph.
99 Charles H. Norris, 118th, Hancock.*
100 James Caraway, 561st, Upson.*
101 Thomas Wadesworth, M'Gill's, Lincoln.
102 Larkin Wansloca, sol., Taylor's, Elbert.*
103 Edmond Jordan, s. i. w., Bragaw's, Oglethorpe.*
104 Ansalum S. Jackson, Lunceford's, Wilkes.*
105 Bedy Barnes, w., Taylor's, Putnam.*
106 Elijah Williams, 406th, Gwinnett.*
107 Abert M. Spalding, 192d, Elbert.*
108 Benjamin Fort, 374th, Putnam.*
109 John Loflin's ors., 555th, Upson.
110 William Brantley, Barwick's, Washington.*
111 Dempsey Johnson, Hardman's, Oglethorpe.
112 Susannah Sett, w. r. s., Johnson's, De Kalb.*
113 Beverly O. Downman, Buck's, Houston.
114 Telfair Posey, Lester's, Pulaski.
115 William Wilson, Jones's, Hall.
116 Unice Harris, w., Craven's, Coweta.

117 John R. M. Neil, Moore's, Randolph.*
118 William Sanford, Goodwin's, Houston.
119 George Grimsley, Oliver's, Twiggs.*
120 Henry Wheelus, Gunn's, Jones.*
121 George Merk, Miller's, Jackson.
122 Washington Bazemore, Simmons's, Crawford.*
123 William Spircey, Sen., Graves's, Putnam.*
124 Chrischana Mitchell, w., Lamberth's, Fayette.*
125 John Johns, s. s., Cleggs's, Walton.
126 Sally Hampton, h. a., 245th, Jackson.
127 William H. Boyd, Hamilton's, Gwinnett.*
128 Esther Jepson, w., Flynn's, Muscogee.*
129 M. Watkins, Sen., r. s., Garner's, Washington.*
130 Charles D. Vickers, 419th, Walton.*
131 Allen C. Sturdevant, Alberson's, Walton.*
132 Alfred T. Pittman, Ross's, Monroe.*
133 John R. Mann, Lunceford's, Elbert.*
134 John Willf, Jr., Henson's, Rabun.*
135 David C. Stovall, Sewell's, Franklin.*
136 John Parsons, Harris's, De Kalb.*
137 Tuscan H. Ball, Few's, Muscogee.
138 Charles Bradley, Williams's, Washington.
139 Martin H. Harris, or., Salem, Baldwin.
140 Charles Cox, 588th, Upson.
141 James Walker, Sen., Wallis's, Irwin.*
142 John F. M'Korkle, Murphy's, Columbia.*
143 Malcomb Lester, 588th, Upson.
144 George W. M'Donald, 271st, M'Intosh.*
145 Peter Young, Bridges's, Gwinnett.*
146 Robert Russell, Arrington's, Merriwether.
147 Adam Andrews, Hinton's, Wilkes.
148 George W. Carter, Moseley's, Wilkes.*
149 Charley B. Snipes, 470th, Upson.*
150 James Powell, Culbreath's, Columbia.*
151 Thomas J. Mann, Hill's, Monroe.*
152 Hazel Loveless, M'Clain's, Newton.*
153 John H. Holland, Baugh's, Jackson.
154 Samuel Shephard, r. s., Seal's, Elbert.*
155 Samuel Chambers, Griffin's, Fayette.*
156 William Reynolds, Jr., Peterson's, Burke.*
157 Jane Howard, w., Fitzpatrick's, Chatham.
158 John Hennington, Bush's, Pulaski.
159 Walter Button, 26th, Glynn.*
160 S. W. Harris's ors., Athens, Clarke.
161 Benjamin A. Denson, Prescott's, Twiggs.
162 Micajah Dyer, Colley's, Oglethorpe.*
163 Hiram Coothen, Parham's, Harris.*

164 Thomas Smith, sol., 118th, Hancock.
165 Willis C. Whigham, Fleming's, Jefferson.
166 Jasper Bryan, Bryan's, Monroe.*
167 Charles Thomas, Coxe's, Talbot.
168 Marthy Riddle, w., Sinquefield's, Washington.*
169 Burkette Wellborn, Night's, Morgan.*
170 John Torrence, sol., Smith's, Campbell.*
171 Abraham M. Paul, Newby's, Jones.
172 Charles Jennings, sol., Levritt's, Lincoln.*
173 Samuel Lewis, Morris's, Crawford.*
174 John Culpepper, Sen., Marshall's, Crawford.
175 Benjamin Davis, Hines's, Coweta.
176 Ephraim Kitchens, Fleming's, Franklin.
177 John C. Gallman, Allen's, Henry.
178 John Mathis's ors., Dupree's, Washington.
179 Ezekiel Perdu, Graves's, Putnam.*
180 Thomas Purdain, sol., 334th, Wayne.*
181 Benajah Prescotte, Griffin's, Burke.*
182 Sarah Rushing, w. r. s., Haygood's, Washington.
183 Starling Jenkins, Roe's, Burke.*
184 William Dodds, Tower's, Gwinnett.
185 Mason Morris, Hines's, Coweta.
186 Abraham Levrett, sol., Maguire's, Morgan.*
187 Alexander Morris, Hargrove's, Oglethorpe.
188 James J. Bently, s. l. w., Park's, Walton.
189 Haywood Jones's ors., sol., Dilman's, Pulaski.
190 Solomon R. Vickers, 124th, Richmond.
191 Martha Daniel, w., 603d, Taliaferro.
192 Daniel Redwine, Riden's, Jackson.
193 John C. Tyus, Greer's, Merriwether.
194 Eliza Richardson, w. r. s., 395th, Emanuel.
195 James High, 10th, Effingham.
196 Dolly Peterson, w., Hart's, Jones.
197 Jonathan Walker, sol., Mullen's, Carroll.
198 Stephen Haynee, Sutton's, Habersham.
199 Thomas Threlkela's ors., Lunceford's, Elbert.
200 Nancy Culver, w., 111th, Hancock.
201 Louis Tilly, Tilly's, Rabun.
202 John S. Folk, Oliver's, Twiggs.
203 William Hulmes's ors., Thomason's, Elbert.
204 Thomas J. Douthet, Mullen's, Carroll.*
205 John Iby's three ors., Dean's, De Kalb.
206 James Thomas, Hopkins's, Camden.
207 John Thompson, Russell's, Henry.
208 John Ballard, Ware's, Coweta.*
209 John Holland, Sen., Jones's, Hall.
210 Reuben Donalson, Williams's, Decatur.

211 Abraham Surcell, Smith's, Franklin.
212 Archibald Smith's ors., Peterson's, Montgomery.
213 John Howard, Jones's, Lincoln.
214 Sarah D. Eades, Canning's, Elbert.
215 John E. Leverett, Griffin's, De Kalb.
216 William K. Osburn, Gittens's, Fayette.*
217 John L. Sims, 406th, Gwinnett.*
218 Jeremiah Taylor, 466th, Monroe.
219 John Harper, Bustin's, Pike.*
220 Euphamy Thomas, w., Williams's, Washington.
221 Lewis Chandler, sol., David's, Franklin.
222 Jesse William, Bostick's, Twiggs.
223 Asa T. Meek, 36th, Scriven.*
224 Allen Hancock, Marsh's, Thomas.*
225 George B. Wright, Nichols's, Fayette.*
226 Clarissa Barnhill, w., Foote's, De Kalb.*
227 C. Stanley's ors., Harrison's, Decatur.*
228 Nathan F. Spark, Mays's, Monroe.
229 William Ray, 147th, Greene.
230 Mary Hair, w., Oliver's, Decatur.
231 Alexander Ivy, Parham's, Warren.
232 David Shepherd, s. l. w., Peacock's, Washington.*
233 Merdock M'Canley, Newman's, Thomas.*
234 William Lee, lun., Martin's, Washington.
235 Samuel C. Dunlap, Chambers's, Gwinnett.
236 Jarrett Percell, Smith's, Franklin.
237 Samuel G. Hunter, Lay's, Jackson.
238 Lovey Parker, h. a., Kendrick's, Putnam.
239 William Mizell, sol., Pearce's, Houston.
240 William Worsham, Lester's, Monroe.
241 Sarah Berry, w., 3d section, Cherokee.*
242 Henry Tillman, 394th, Montgomery.*
243 George W. Moore, Cleland's, Chatham.*
244 Susannah Bryan, w., Edwards's, Franklin.
245 Jesse Dotton, Hatchett's, Oglethorpe.*
246 Isaiah Carter, Bell's, Burke.
247 Henry Adams, Sen., Chastain's, Habersham.
248 John Hart, sol., Ball's, Monroe.*
249 Malaki Tillman, Lightfoot's, Washington.*
250 Jacob Wilf, Gittens's, Fayette.*
251 Leonard Carden, or., Martin's, Newton.
252 Homes Tupper, Fitzpatrick's, Chatham.*
253 James B. Walker, 120th, Richmond.
254 Uriah F. Case, Moseley's, Wilkes.*
255 Ica Atkins, Sen., r. s., Mitchell's, Pulaski.
256 Nathan Smith, Jr., Brown's, Camden.
257 Hopkins Daniel, Mizell's, Talbot.

258 M. Pepper's ors., 271st, M'Intosh.*
259 Abner H. Strickland, Taylor's, Elbert.*
260 Joseph L. Key, Williams's, Jasper.
261 James Wilf, Gittens's, Fayette.
262 William H. Powell, Compton's, Fayette.
263 Marjam B. Baisden, or., 318th, Baldwin.
264 John Harbison, Chesnut's, Newton.*
265 Presley B. Roberts, Bower's, Elbert.
266 John Ashly, Kelly's, Elbert.
267 David Howe's ors., Collier's, Monroe.*
268 William F. Barrett, Cleggs's, Walton.
269 Samson Warren, Martin's, Pike.*
270 Josiah W. Bachelder, 672d, Harris.
271 Presley Riddell, Phillips's, Monroe.*
272 Zealas East, 656th, Troup.*
273 Warren Shaw, Jr., White's, Franklin.
274 Dudley Red, Polhill's, Burke.
275 Wm. F. Smith's ors., Sinquefield's, Washington.
276 John A. James, Justice's, Bibb.
277 John Murphy, 177th, Wilkes.
278 John W. Walker, Ballard's, Morgan.
279 Wade H. Allison, Arrington's, Merriwether.*
280 Robert Williams, Martin's, Hall.
281 Joseph Gouge, Jr., Chambers's, Gwinnett.
282 Luther Goodrich, Moseley's, Wilkes.*
283 Ezra M'Crary, Camp's, Warren.
284 William Waldrip, Dean's, De Kalb.
285 William G. Reggins, Sweat's, Ware.*
286 Allen Gray, Head's, Butts.
287 Charles Hutchins, Heard's, De Kalb.*
288 William Weisley, Martin's, Newton.*
289 Solomon Page, Jr., Barwick's, Washington.*
290 James Lindsey, Jr., Fulks's, Wilkes.*
291 George W. Young, House's, Henry.
292 Thomas Ingraham, sol., Robinson's, Harris.
293 James M. Keath, Stewart's, Troup.
294 Joel M'Clendon, sol., Bush's, Stewart.
295 John Burch, Bell's, Burke.
296 John F. Smith, 334th, Wayne.*
297 Frederic Smith, M'Gillen's, Troup.
298 John H. Hatcher, Cliett's, Columbia.
299 John Perry, Sullivan's, Jones.*
300 Sarah Hogins, w., Lamberth's, Fayette.
301 John Harval's ors., Perryman's, Warren.
302 Frederic Robeson's ors., 334th, Wayne.
303 Thomas Bailey, sol., Pearce's, Houston.
304 John W. M'Callister, Ellis's, Pulaski.

305 Richard D. Hightower, Martin's, Laurens.*
306 Hillary Anderson, Young's, Jefferson.*
307 Wesly Turner, Gittens's, Fayette.
308 George W. Wren, Kendrick's, Putnam.
309 Adam Jones, Peavy's, Bulloch.*
310 James Herrington, Holton's, Emanuel.*
311 Stephen Gibbons, Sen., 121st, Richmond.*
312 John Brown, Whitaker's, Crawford.
313 Green Hartsfield, Hardman's, Oglethorpe.
314 Solomon Walker, 23d, Richmond.*
315 Isaac and Rebecca Sikes, ors., 19th, Bryan.
316 George Crawford, Collier's, Monroe.*
317 Ephraim Taylor, Mitchell's, Marion.
318 Michael S. Hammock, Hampton's, Newton.
319 Samuel Whitfield, Blackshear's, Lowndes.*
320 Samuel Ward, Edwards's, Talbot.*
321 Thomas O. Glascock, 120th, Richmond.*
322 Alexander Williamson, Moseley's, Coweta.*
323 James Wright, House's, Henry.
324 Christ. Deadwilder, sol. 1784–97, 373d, Jasper.*
325 M'Gillis's ors., 19th, Bryan.
326 Thomas Moreland, Stewart's, Warren.
327 Simri Rose, Ellsworth's, Bibb.
328 Robert James, s. l. w., Wolfskin's, Oglethorpe.
329 John Fetters, 119th, Richmond.*
330 John A. Powell, M'Clain's, Newton.
331 (fr.) Sarah Chestein, w., Hatton's, Baker.
332 (fr.) Nicholas Baker, Waller's, Irwin.
333 (fr.) Lewis Daniel, sol., Crow's, Pike.
334 (fr.) Allen Scarborough, Bailey's, Laurens.
335 (fr.) Elizabeth Porter, w. r. s., Dozier's, Columbia.
336 (fr.) Robert F. Sinclair's ors., Frasier's, Monroe.*
337 (fr.) John Anthony, Compton's, Fayette.
338 (fr.) Margarette M'Cibben, w. r. s., Hood's, Henry
339 (fr.) Silas N. Clay, Clinton's, Campbell.
340 (fr.) David Ogletree, Kendrick's, Monroe.
341 (fr.) Richard Goowin, Goodwin's, Houston.
342 (fr.) Daniél Groover, Sewell's, Franklin.*

23d DISTRICT, THIRD SECTION, CHEROKEE.

1 Neavil Bennett, Seay's, Hall.
2 Claiborn Gorman, Neal's, Campbell.
3 Nathaniel Harbon, Herndon's, Hall.*
4 Christopher Gillespie, Hargrove's, Oglethorpe.
5 James M. Butler, Bryan's, Monroe.*
6 Alexander Means, Sen., Lunceford's, Elbert.*
7 Thomas R. Slaughter, 119th, Richmond.*
8 Theophilus T. Horseley, Sutton's, Habersham.*
9 Henry Sillelton, Pearce's, Houston.
10 Alexander Thompson, Rainey's, Twiggs.*
11 Matthew E. Rylander, Ellsworth's, Bibb.*
12 Martin Norton, Sen., Griffin's, Fayette.*
13 John Timmons, Camp's, Baker.*
14 Michael Dougherty, sol., Walker's, Columbia.*
15 Jesse Wannack, Welche's, Habersham.*
16 John Fisher, Burnett's, Habersham.*
17 Josiah Horton, Ball's, Monroe.*
18 Jane Borsen, or., Wolfskin's, Oglethorpe.*
19 Abner Fuller, sol., Tuggle's, Merriwether.
20 William Bell, sol., Hampton's, Newton.
21 William Cox, Crawford's, Morgan.
22 Allison T. Herrick, Valleau's, Chatham.
23 James Hamilton, Morgan's, Clarke.*
24 John Hatcher, s. i. w., Blount's, Wilkinson.*
25 Reuben R. Derden, Kellum's, Talbot.*
26 Jesse Crawford, sol., 365th, Jasper.*
27 Benjamin Taylor, Kelly's, Jasper.*
28 Columbus M. Park, 161st, Greene.*
29 Helm Hunt, sol., Chastain's, Habersham.*
30 Sarah Stiles, w., Miller's, Jackson.*
31 William Waterer, Oliver's, Twiggs.*
32 Seymore Spencer Pool, or., Williams's, Walton.*
33 Dennis M'Carty, Thames, Crawford.*
34 Sarah Porter, w., Martin's, Pike.
35 James Wood, Cleland's, Chatham.*
36 Robert Scott, Johnson's, De Kalb.
37 Jefferson Trammell, Graves's, Lincoln.*
38 Jessea Dupree, sol., Walker's, Houston.*
39 Zilpha Pittman, or., Lightfoot's, Washington.*
40 Samuel Campbell, 122d, Richmond.*
41 John B. Elkins, 10th, Effingham.*

42 John Sanders, 470th, Upson.
43 Eli Harris, Kendrick's, Putnam.
44 John G. Campbell, Chesnut's, Newton.*
45 John Hayes, Martin's, Hall.*
46 Robert Kirbon, Groce's, Bibb.*
47 Damaris Jackson's or., Watson's, Marion.
48 Jane Mountain, w., Gunn's, Jefferson.*
49 Bethany Knight, w. r. s., 57th, Emanuel.*
50 William Holton, 57th, Emanuel.
51 John Gibbins, Robinson's, Harris.*
52 William C. Harris, 693d, Heard.
53 Josiah Hatcher, r. s., Allison's, Pike.*
54 William Duke, Alberson's, Walton.*
55 Nathan Johnson, 49th, Emanuel.*
56 Albert M. Spalding, 192d, Elbert.*
57 Samuel Moore, 687th, Lee.*
58 Nathan Sorrell, Ellis's, Pulaski.*
59 James L. Coleman, Woodruff's, Campbell.
60 Larkin Welcher, sol., Downs's, Warren.
61 James D. Indsor, Martin's, Hall.
62 Etheldred Tarver, Polhill's, Burke.
63 John Wyatt, Sen., Aderhold's, Campbell.*
64 Joseph Wood's ors., ———, Houston.
65 William Bone, Jr., f. a., Candler's, Bibb.*
66 Thomas Jones, sol., Willingham's, Harris.*
67 Griffin Mathis, 168th, Wilkes.*
68 Isaiah Cheek, sol., Stanton's, Newton.*
69 Joseph Bailey, Chandler's, Franklin.*
70 John Hussie's ors., Tuggle's, Merriwether.
71 Drury Flowers, 373d, Jasper.*
72 William Ezzell, Reid's, Gwinnett.*
73 Young G. Malone, 146th, Greene.
74 Enoch Meadows, Craven's, Coweta.
75 Benjamin S. Cannon, Stewart's, Jones.*
76 John Martin's or., Braddy's, Jones.
77 Henry Lunsford, 605th, Taliaferro.*
78 Allen G. Veal, Griffin's, De Kalb.
79 John Hornsby, Jr., Heard's, De Kalb.
80 Cornelius Hardy, sol., Williams's, Jasper.
81 James Early, Adams's, Columbia.*
82 William Bridges, Peterson's, Montgomery.*
83 Richard Keiffer, Houston's, Chatham.
84 Elijah Duncan, Baugh's, Jackson.*
85 George F. Adams, 245th, Jackson.
86 Sanford Hargroves, 141st, Greene.*
87 Elisha Wylly, Sanderlin's, Chatham.*
88 John B. Heard, Mann's, Crawford.

89 Hiram Mahaffy, Hendon's, Carroll.*
90 Dawson Satlewhite, sol., Williams's, Jasper.*
91 James J. Shockly, Seay's, Hall.*
92 James Gaston, Nesbit's, Newton.*
93 Joseph Sanson, 34th, Scriven.*
94 Mary Curlie, w., Alberson's, Walton.*
95 Robert Grier, Hall's, Butts.*
96 James Brannon, 1st section, Cherokee.*
97 Edwards Clerly, Peavy's, Bulloch.*
98 Joshua Humphries, m. s., Cleland's, Chatham.*
99 Ann Andrews, w., 608th, Taliaferro.
100 Hiram Reddingfield, Sullivan's, Jones.
101 William Yancey, Smith's, Campbell.
102 Frederic Ball's ors., Moseley's, Wilkes.
103 George Harper, r. s., Gunn's, Jones.
104 Jobe W. Smith, Smith's, Houston.
105 Rachel Webb, w., Baugh's, Jackson.*
106 William Rowls, sol., Walker's, Harris.*
107 William Goodwin, 124th, Richmond.*
108 Sidney S. Holland's ors., Murphy's, Columbia.*
109 Absolem Terrell, Hood's, Henry.*
110 Michael Kelly, Allison's, Pike.*
111 Barney West, Dobbs's, Hall.*
112 William Lawhorn, 470th, Upson.*
113 Cornelius Gibbs, r. s., Henson's, Rabun.*
114 Pleasent W. Short, Hargrove's, Oglethorpe.
115 Thomas Todd, Reid's, Gwinnett.*
116 Benjamin M. Witcher, 3d section, Cherokee.*
117 Cuthbert Reese, sol., 293d, Jasper.*
118 James B. Alexander, Taylor's, Elbert.
119 Edward Rhyner, 56th, Emanuel.*
120 Abijah Wise, Morgan's, Clarke.*
121 William R. Cunningham, Athens, Clarke.*
122 William H. Harrell, M'Daniel's, Pulaski.*
123 John H. Dicks, Ballard's, Morgan.*
124 James Wisenbaker, 9th, Effingham.
125 Sylvester B. J. Cratin, 601st, Taliaferro.
126 Theresa Famell, h. a., Peterson's, Burke.*
127 William Chesnut, Pearce's, Houston.*
128 Elizabeth Glenn, w. r. s., M'Gehee's, Troup.*
129 Aaron Hyman's ors., Lynn's, Warren.*
130 Richard J. Burrell, 168th, Wilkes.
131 John Dunn, Sen., Coffee's, Rabun.*
132 Mary Yeales, w., Garner's, Washington.*
133 John A. Howard, Norris's, Monroe.*
134 Ann Alman, w., Nellum's, Elbert.
135 Neel M'Duffee, Cook's, Telfair.*

136 Henry Morris, Groce's, Bibb.
137 Alexander Harrison, Culbreath's, Columbia.*
138 John Barrenton, M'Clendon's, Putnam.
139 Silas Cason, Folsom's, Lowndes.
140 William Furgeson, M'Gehee's, Troup.
141 James Chatham's ors., Heard's, De Kalb.
142 Oliver Salmons, Kelly's, Elbert.*
143 Edward Sturdevant, Martin's, Stewart.
144 John W. Runnels, 602d, Taliaferro.
145 Henry B. Lee, Harralson's, Troup.*
146 William B. Smith, Lahmen's, De Kalb.
147 Henry Crowell, s. l. w., Turner's, Crawford.
148 John Clark, Wallis's, Irwin.*
149 William Jones, Sen., Clark's, Elbert.*
150 Patch Pendergrast's ors., Sanderlin's, Chatham.
151 Charles J. Simmons, 307th, Putnam.
152 Hambleton Cole, 55th, Emanuel.*
153 William Overstreet's ors., 1st, Chatham.*
154 John G. Burdett, 175th, Wilkes.*
155 Anderson Robinson, Coxe's, Talbot.*
156 Fountain Wood, Hardman's, Oglethorpe.*
157 Isabella Bones, w., 398th, Richmond.
158 Zachariah Daniel, Martin's, Washington.*
159 William G. Norton, Compton's, Fayette.*
160 Jeremiah R. Brazeel, 168th, Wilkes.*
161 Rogers's children, f. a., Hampton's, Newton.
162 John Franklin, Crawford's, Morgan.*
163 Edward S. Rolston, Brown's, Habersham.*
164 Thomas Morgan, Smith's, Elbert.*
165 Joseph Wilder, Monk's, Crawford.*
166 John Hambleton, Sen., White's, Franklin.*
167 Elijah Watson, s. l. w., Mason's, Washington.*
168 Wiley Wamack, Whipple's, Wilkinson.*
169 Erastus Humphrey, 144th, Greene.*
170 William Carlisle, Candler's, P:hb.*
171 James M'Murphy, 320th, Baldwin.*
172 Nancy Newson, Crawford's, Morgan.*
173 John Hewe, of Cherokee, Latimer's, De Kalb.
174 Sterling M. Shackleford, Thomason's, Elbert.*
175 James Hodge, Burnett's, Habersham.*
176 Jacob Bruner, Burnett's, Habersham.
177 Charles Montgomery, Hamilton's, Gwinnett.
178 Robert C. Bryan, 104th, Hancock.*
179 Josiah D. Mercer, Linam's, Pulaski.
180 Sarah Allen, w., Belcher's, Jasper.
181 Sarah Wilkinson, w., Strickland's, Merriwether.*
182 John Cone's orphans, 318th, Baldwin.

183 Thomas Ellison, Davis's, Gwinnett.
184 Isham Ethridge, Davis's, Jones.*
185 Reuben Harris, Latimer's, De Kalb.
186 John Weems, Sen., Brock's, Habersham.
187 Enoch Andrews, sol., Smith's, Franklin.*
188 Diana Hester, w. r. s., Bivins's, Jones.*
189 Davis Arnold, Nellum's, Elbert.*
190 James Morris, Nichols's, Fayette.*
191 Alsey Leget, w., Thompson's, Henry.*
192 Diana Gray, w. r. s., Willis's, Franklin.*
193 John White, 248th, Jackson.
194 Joannah Andrews, w., Martin's, Pike.*
195 John Oustead, Chambers's, Gwinnett.*
196 Rachael Ferguson, w. of sol., 119th, Richmond.*
197 John Buckner's or., Bryan's, Monroe.*
198 James M. Roberts, Graves's, Putnam.*
199 John M. Jones, Silman's, Pike.*
200 Hugh Spurlin, Jones's, Habersham.
201 Reuben Bennett's three orphans, 137th, Greene.
202 Wilmoth T. Whatley, sol., Harp's, Stewart.*
203 Mitchell G. Hudson, Robinson's, Harris.
204 John Cox, Dyer's, Habersham.*
205 Samuel Hays, Chambers's, Houston.*
206 Benjamin Drane, Adams's, Columbia.*
207 Myrack Ivy, Collier's, Monroe.*
208 Henry B. Cabiness, s. l. w., Alsobrook's, Jones.
209 Lewis Dennis's ors., Bell's, Burke.
210 Frances Herndon, w. r. s., 788th, Heard.*
211 Benjamin Justice, or., Night's, Morgan.
212 Jacob Gunn, sol., 105th, Baldwin.
213 Nathaniel Lewis, r. s., Cleland's, Chatham.*
214 Hiram Meritt, Coxe's, Talbot.
215 George Grumbles, r. s., Bush's, Burke.*
216 Ann Ward, w. s. l. w., 20th, Bryan.
217 John Coggens, Marsh's, Thomas.*
218 Richard Derby's ors., Howard's, Oglethorpe.
219 Charles T. Culpepper, Buck's, Houston.*
220 Edmund Dorsey, M'Culler's, Newton.
221 James Morgan, Shattox's, Coweta.
222 Elizabeth Wicked, w., Lightfoot's, Washington.*
223 Asa Travis, Hicks's, Decatur.*
224 David Hadaway's ors., Gunn's, Jones.
225 John D. Bonn, 415th, Walton.
226 Hugh Lawson, Barron's, Houston.
227 John Alexander, f. a., Killen's, Decatur.
228 Jesse Carter, Sen., Morrison's, Appling.
229 William J. Durham, Orr's, Jackson.

230 William Askew, 161st, Greene.
231 Jacobus H. Watts, Wood's, Morgan.
232 Jacob Eberhart, s. i. w., Colley's, Oglethorpe.*
233 George W. Morgan, Hamilton's, Gwinnett.
234 William Gilliland, Miller's, Jackson.*
235 Walter Jones, s. s., 320th, Baldwin.
236 James Nelson Franklin, 147th, Greene.*
237 Hugh Brown, Deavours's, Habersham.*
238 Julia Swindell, id., 415th, Walton.*
239 Nathaniel G. Pace, Dupree's, Washington.*
240 Sarah M. Sheftall, w., 2d, Chatham.
241 William Eidson, 561st, Upson.*
242 Stephen Garrett, Willis's, Franklin.*
243 Deverew Luge, Campbell's, Wilkes.*
244 Stephen Carter, Robinson's, Fayette.*
245 Major Peace, sol., 113th, Hancock.*
246 John T. Ransom, Bishop's, Henry.*
247 Margaret Reid, w., Scroggins's, Oglethorpe.*
248 Hugh Walton, Bryant's, Burke.*
249 David M. Stewart, Morris's, Crawford.*
250 Thomas M. Kirkpatrick, Latimer's, De Kalb.
251 James Walker, Coward's, Lowndes.*
252 Andrew Lambert, 34th, Scriven.*
253 Matilda Fowler, or., Taylor's, Elbert.*
254 Absolem Harris, Scroggins's, Oglethorpe.*
255 Luel M. M'Clung, 243d, Jackson.*
256 James Jones, Groce's, Bibb.
257 William W. Smith, Jr., Bower's, Elbert.
258 Evan Davis, sol., Dozier's, Columbia.
259 Ann E. Williamson, w., Jack's, Clarke.
260 Jefferson Bond, 1st section, Cherokee.
261 William Tilley, 510th, Early.
262 Richard C. Head, Griffin's, Fayette.
263 Benjamin Jones, Jones's, Morgan.
264 Nathaniel Quick, Iverson's, Houston.*
265 Nicey Glenn, w., 141st, Greene.*
266 Hannah Baxter, Allen's, Henry.*
267 William Clements, Allen's, Bibb.*
268 Joseph Foster, Barker's, Gwinnett.
269 Thomas B. Martin, Robinson's, Harris.*
270 John M. Hammock, Humphries's, Newton.*
271 White's five orphans, Rhodes's, De Kalb.*
272 Daniel D. Barker, Johnson's, De Kalb.*
273 Garrett Hardman, Gunn's, Henry.*
274 Harris Dennard, Boynton's, Twiggs.*
275 Patrick M. Reynolds, f. a., Thomas's, Clarke.*
276 Ambrose Saunders, Jr., Bostick's, Twiggs.*

277 William R. Williamson, Craven's, Coweta.*
278 James Dillport, Holley's, Franklin.*
279 Adam Blair, Phillip's, Monroe.*
280 Solomon Davidson, Whitehead's, Habersham.
281 Tabitha Batemon, w., Smith's, Houston.*
282 Matthew C. Butts, 113th, Hancock.*
283 Feriby Freeman, w., 34th, Scriven.*
284 Stephen C. Browns, Jordan's, Bibb.*
285 Nancy Young, w., Latimer's, De Kalb.*
286 Nicholas Jenkins, Holton's, Emanuel.*
287 James Hunter, 106th, Hancock.
288 Elisha Turner, Dobbs's, Hall.*
289 Abram S. Greene, 656th, Troup.*
290 Joseph Brantley, Peacock's, Washington.*
291 Isham Huskett, Nesbit's, Newton.*
292 Easther Dyson, w. r. s., 734th, Lee.*
293 Allen Clark, Bridges's, Gwinnett.*
294 William Hamilton, Peacock's, Washington.
295 William Mitchell, 119th, Richmond.*
296 Mary Beavers, Foot's, De Kalb.*
297 Ezekiel Cloud, sol. 1784–97, Peurifoy's, Henry.*
298 Edward B. Stafford, Blair's, Lowndes.*
299 John Thomas, sol., 333d, Wayne.*
300 William W. Allen, 1st, Chatham.*
301 Alfred Wetherford, Pounds's, Twiggs.*
302 James Germany, Cliett's, Columbia.*
303 Sarah F. Hubbard, or., Stewart's, Troup.*
304 Robert Young's ors., 398th, Richmond.*
305 Mary Jones, w. r. s., Jones's, Hall.*
306 Stephen Burran, 756th, Sumter.*
307 Joshua R. Buckhalter, sol., Camp's, Warren.*
308 John Mooney, Wilcox's, Telfair.*
309 William M'Crary's ors., Edwards's, Talbot.*
310 Rees M. Braidies, 119th, Richmond.*
311 William A. Henderson, Belcher's, Jasper.*
312 Benjamin Jester, Thaxton's, Butts.*
313 Obedience Price, w., Blount's, Wilkinson.*
314 Richard H. Waters, Price's, Hall.
315 George Spann, 430th, Early.*
316 Drury Peeples, Chambers's, Gwinnett.*
317 Aenon Cross, 73d, Burke.*
318 Samuel Barker, 362d, Jasper.*
319 Robert Stafford, 334th, Wayne.*
320 Mary Bandy, w., 24th, M'Intosh.*
321 Winse Sheffield, 430th, Early.*
322 John Hill, Bush's, Burke.*
323 John Williams, Cook's, Telfair.*

324 James E. Gonder, 112th, Hancock.*
325 John Basse, Sinclair's, Houston.*
326 James P. Thompson, 36th, Scriven.*
327 John W. Anderson, Maguire's, Gwinnett.
328 James H. Callaway, Peurifoy's, Henry.*
329 Jesse Sandlin, 687th, Lee.
330 Joseph Garner, Willis's, Franklin.*
331 Joseph H. Bush, Hinton's, Wilkes.*
332 Thomas Terry, Taylor's, Elbert.*
333 Jacob Fulton, Estes's, Putnam.*
334 James Monk, Hitchcock's, Muscogee.*
335 William B. Curtis, 145th, Greene.*
336 Susannah Holt, w., Barwick's, Washington.*
337 William Leem, 561st, Upson.*
338 Isaac W. Mullen, s. l. w., Carswell's, Jefferson.*
339 Isaac Newberry, Jordan's, Bibb.*
340 Robert Webb, Hudson's, Newton.*
341 Hillyard B. Mabry, Mizell's, Talbot.*
342 William Hicks, Hicks's, Decatur.
343 Ann Glenn, w. r. s., Phillips's, Jasper.*
344 Benjamin Popup's ors., Lester's, Pulaski.
345 C. H. Garrison, Strickland's, Merriwether.*
346 Benjamin Smith, r. s., Craven's, Coweta.*
347 George Tucker, Justice's, Bibb.*
348 Duncan M'Millian, M'Craney's, Lowndes.
349 Thomas E. Buckannon, 295th, Jasper.
350 Mikel Pope, Compton's, Fayette.*
351 William S. Phillips's ors., Sanderlin's, Chatham.*
352 Harris Nosworthy, 73d, Burke.*
353 Robert M'Corkle, Graves's, Lincoln.*
354 William Park's ors., Kendrick's, Monroe.*
355 Timothy Free, Sutton's, Habersham.*
356 William Richardson, Griffin's, De Kalb.*
357 Joseph T. Simmons, Williams's, Washington.*
358 Joseph R. Nicks, 672d, Harris.*
359 Jerid S. Suddeth, Mackleroy's, Clarke.*
360 Thomas Edge, Thompson's, Henry.*

24th DISTRICT, THIRD SECTION, CHEROKEE.

1 Benjamin Raine, Wilcox's, Telfair.*
2 Thomas Ray, Whitt's, Franklin.*
3 Washington Speir, 319th, Baldwin.
4 William Vinson, Young's, Wilkinson.
5 Willis Gammon, sol., M'Ewin's, Monroe.
6 Henry Huey, r. s., Latimer's, De Kalb.
7 Robert Childress's ors., Davis's, Clarke.
8 James Smith, 101st, Hancock.
9 Benjamin W. Leach, 3d, Chatham.
10 William H. Puryear, sol., Davis's, Clarke.
11 Thomas Butler King, 25th, Glynn.
12 David Long, 114th, Hancock.
13 John Young, Herndon's, Hall.*
14 Moses Daniel, sol., Newman's, Thomas.*
15 Susan N. M'Call, w., Cleland's, Chatham.*
16 James M. Parmer, 118th, Hancock.*
17 Nancy Walthall, w., Williams's, Jasper.*
18 James Griffin's or., Head's, Butts.
19 Oliver S. Burt, Brock's, Habersham.
20 William J. Turk, 318th, Baldwin.
21 William Eester, 10th Effingham, Chatham.*
22 Elizabeth Thornton, w., M'Ginnis's, Jackson.*
23 William Stone, r. s., Phillips's, Jasper.
24 James L. Harrison, Campbell's, Wilkes.
25 William Barkesdale, Graves's, Putnam.*
26 Thomas Brigman, Candler's, Bibb.*
27 Levi Noble's ors., Hobbs's, Laurens.
28 William Riggins, Chambers's, Houston.
29 John Saxon, 245th, Jackson.*
30 George W. Martin, Hatchett's, Oglethorpe.
31 Gardner Willey, Hand's, Appling.
32 Joseph Hubbard, Whelchel's, Hall.*
33 Peter U. Groce, Smith's, Wilkinson.*
34 William Lard, r. s., Riden's, Jackson.
35 John Bentley, sol., Hart's, Jones.
36 James Brimer, Hamilton's, Gwinnett.
37 Alexander Powell's ors., Wootten's, Telfair.
38 Sidney M. Pegg, Compton's, Fayette.
39 Michael Oliver, Ellis's, Rabun.*
40 David M. Scott, Bryan's, Monroe.*
41 Elizabeth Smith, d. & d., Riden's, Jackson.*

42 Edward S. Hicks, 589th, Upson.
43 Harvey M'Collum, Jones's, Habersham.*
44 William Hudgins, 561st, Upson.
45 Charles Arnold, r. s., Carpenter's, Tatnall.*
46 James Love, Russell's, Henry.*
47 Preston Wise, Peavy's, Bulloch.*
48 Lemuel Martin, Martin's, Washington.*
49 Anthony Phillips, Peterson's, Montgomery.*
50 Hiram Scott, Robison's, Washington.*
51 Watson A. Crawford, Brooks's, Muscogee.*
52 William Griffin, Rutland's, Bibb.*
53 William Carroll, Parham's, Warren.*
54 Nathan Morris, Allen's, Campbell.*
55 Williams Spears, Edwards's, Franklin.*
56 Elijah Martin, Jr., Belcher's, Jasper.*
57 Sarah Johnson, w. r. s., 693d, Heard.
58 George Reid, sol., Whisenhunt's, Carroll.*
59 Wily Siner, Young's, Carroll.*
60 James Blount, Streetman's, Twiggs.*
61 Rapha Childs, Foot's, De Kalb.
62 John M. Dowdy, Merck's, Hall.*
63 Artemas W. Ogilvie, ———, Oglethorpe.*
64 Jesse Ivey's ors., 102d, Hancock.
65 John D. Jordan, Parham's, Harris.*
66 George W. M'Allister, 21st, Bryan.*
67 William Hicks, Walker's, Harris.*
68 Jethro Baker, Mobley's, De Kalb.*
69 Thomas Pope, Lester's, Pulaski.*
70 Duke H. Hodge, Hodges's, Newton.*
71 Rice Durrett, sol., Groce's, Bibb.*
72 Nancy Johnson, w., Martin's, Stewart.*
73 Samuel Ewing, r. s., 102d, Hancock.
74 Robert Cunningham, Holt's, Talbot.
75 James Simmons, sol., Crawford's, Morgan.
76 William R. Cansey, 334th, Wayne,*
77 Abraham Herren, Gay's, Harris.
78 Levi Marchman, 160th, Greene.
79 Adam Beasley, Phillips's, Monroe.*
80 Jacob Smith, sol., Oliver's, Twiggs.*
81 John Allen, 119th, Richmond.*
82 Bowling Hobbs, Hobbs's, Laurens.
83 Joseph Ganahl, Valleau's, Chatham.
84 Betsey Williams, w., Brewton's, Tatnall.*
85 Uriah Richard, sol., Madden's, Pike.*
86 Randol Chapman, m. s., 162d, Greene.
87 James Bruce, m. s., 162d, Greene.
88 Thomas Carroll, Bostick's, Twiggs,*

89 Richard S. Penn, Hines's, Coweta.
90 John Mizell, Sullivan's, Jones.
91 William Jones, Gunn's, Jones.*
92 Charles Bolton, 260th, Scriven.*
93 John B. Tindell, Culbreath's, Columbia.*
94 Millington Conner, Lester's, Pulaski.*
95 John W. Strother, Brewer's, Monroe.*
96 Joab M'Collum, Brock's, Habersham.*
97 Hogan Hadsworth, Graves's, Lincoln.*
98 David Chapman, Stower's, Elbert.*
99 Drewry Wilkins, Dawson's, Jasper.*
100 Pryor Thomton's ors., M'Ginnis's, Jackson.
101 E. Gaither, w. s. 1784–97, Robinson's, Putnam.*
102 John Whaley, Evans's, Fayette.*
103 David Anthony, r. s., David's, Franklin.
104 William Jackson, Brock's, Habersham.*
105 Benjamin Simmons, s. l. w., 207th, Putnam.
106 George Loftlin's ors., Graves's, Lincoln.
107 Samuel Tricit, Compton's, Fayette.*
108 John Cheshire, Justice's, Bibb.*
109 William Johnston, Groce's, Bibb.*
110 Elijah Bird, Givins's, De Kalb.
111 Abednago Turner, sol., Mays's, Monroe.
112 James L. Head, Griffin's, Fayette.
113 Amos Garnton's ors., Rick's, Laurens.
114 Nathaniel Hall, Bridges's, Gwinnett.
115 Larkin Jeiner, Mashburn's, Pulaski.*
116 William D. Tinsley, Greer's, Merriwether.
117 Charles Murphy, Latimer's, De Kalb.*
118 William M'Cay's ors., Phillips's, Monroe.
119 Reuben Y. Reynolds, Harris's, Columbia.*
120 William Mills, Mashburn's, Pulaski.*
121 Ester Kean, or., Dilman's, Pulaski.*
122 Archibald Wimpy, Willis's, Franklin.
123 William Harmon, Bryan's, Monroe.*
124 Elizabeth Watson, w., Whitehead's, Habersham.*
125 Thomas Brown, Loveless's, Gwinnett.*
126 Thomas Duren, Newman's, Thomas.*
127 William H. Tumlin, Dobbs's, Hall.
128 Beulah Leache, h. a., Rhode's, De Kalb.
129 Thomas J. Lawson, 109th, Hancock.
130 John Hubbard, Dobbs's, Hall.
131 William Baxly, Sen., Dearing's, Henry.
132 Jehu Crompton's ors., Mullen's, Carroll.
133 Joseph P. Manly, Gunn's, Henry.*
134 William Scott, Oliver's, Twiggs.
135 Elisha Cuslion, Britt's, Randolph.

136 Bryant Whitfield, sol., Bryant's, Burke.*
137 William Florence, 177th, Wilkes.
138 James F. Evans, Morrison's, Montgomery.
139 Joseph Holliday's ors., 74th, Burke.*
140 Deborah Simmons, Newsom's, Warren.
141 Joseph Howell, Perryman's, Warren.*
142 John Taylor's ors., M'Millon's, Lincoln.
143 Joseph Beadles, Ware's, Coweta.*
144 Joseph Miller, 404th, Gwinnett.*
145 Thomas J. Laseter, 470th, Upson.*
146 Whitington Moore, 105th, Baldwin.*
147 Thomas Lee, Hill's, Baldwin.
148 John Hill, Griffin's, Merriwether.*
149 William G. Gordon, 588th, Upson.*
150 Elizabeth Glenn, w. r. s., Liddell's, Jackson.
151 John Dixon, Mitchell's, Marion.
152 Thomas J. Collins, Sparks's, Washington.*
153 Thomas H. Yarbrough, Dean's, De Kalb.
154 Joseph Whaley, Waltze's, Morgan.
155 Thomas King, watchmaker, Rooks's, Putnam.*
156 Joseph E. Colquitt, Jenkins's, Oglethorpe.*
157 James Scott, Hill's, Harris.*
158 Charles Norman, Hendon's, Carroll.
159 Elijah Critenton, Lunceford's, Elbert.*
160 Allen Spears, Jones's, Thomas.*
161 Zelah Pullen, 141st, Greene.*
162 William Cash, Johnson's, De Kalb.
163 Lucinda Coxe, w., Smith's, Madison.*
164 William H. Howard, 122d, Richmond.
165 James W. Jackson, Pace's, Putnam.*
166 Dempsey B. Medford, Tower's, Gwinnett.
167 John D. Mullins, 2d section,Cherokee.
168 Martin Riley, Candler's, Bibb.*
169 Micager Bennett, Griffin's, Fayette.
170 Elender Hunt, w., Ross's, Monroe.
171 Brooks Sparks, Shattox's, Coweta.
172 Russell Mabury, Dobbs's, Hall.*
173 Benjamin Dunagan, Price's, Hall.*
174 Henry Godby, Sen., Griffin's, Burke.*
175 John B. Williams, Crow's, Merriwether.*
176 Wm. F. Vanlandingham, Ballard's, Morgan.*
177 Randel Johnson, Pate's, Warren.
178 John S. M'Gehee, sol., 167th, Wilkes.*
179 Felix G. Dinman, Willis's, Franklin.
180 William Thurman, Mobley's, De Kalb.
181 William Manning, sol., Price's, Hall.
182 Meredith Joiner, sol., Buck's, Houston.*

183 Henry Morningstar, 1st, Chatham.
184 Jonathan R. Davis, Neal's, Campbell.*
185 Franklin G. Brown, Groce's, Bibb.*
186 James S. Moore, 320th, Baldwin.
187 Eliza Hagins, or., Curry's, Merriwether.*
188 James Wood, r. s., Collier's, Monroe.*
189 William Scott, White's, Franklin.*
190 Mary Ford, w., Thomason's, Elbert.
191 John Perthe, Jr., Trout's, Hall.*
192 William S. Booth, Parham's, Harris.*
193 Willis Hodges, Brewton's, Tatnall.
194 William H. Davis's ors., 417th, Walton.
195 Josiah Spivey, Harris's, Columbia.*
196 William R. Perkins, Crawford's, Morgan.
197 John Taylor, M'Millon's, Lincoln.*
198 Reuben Phillips, Berry's, Butts.*
199 John M. C. Miller, Chesnut's, Newton.*
200 John A. White, 470th, Upson.*
201 Milsley L. Edwards, or., Britt's, Randolph.
202 Daniel Meadows, 73d, Burke.*
203 Jarrett P. Moody, Daniel's, Hall.
204 Lovvorn's ors., Nesbit's, Newton.
205 Robert Bessent, Hobkerk's, Camden.
206 Samuel Starke, 192d, Elbert.*
207 William C. Pitts, Salem, Baldwin.
208 Robert Dickerson, or., Sweat's, Ware.*
209 Shatteen C. Mitchell, M'Korkle's, Jasper.*
210 George Huie, Evans's, Fayette.*
211 James Vaughn, Oliver's, Twiggs.*
212 Mary Ann Kirk, or., 6th, Chatham.*
213 Theodore Turk, Fleming's, Franklin.*
214 Hudson H. Allen, Chambers's, Gwinnett.
215 William Sentell, Stanfield's, Campbell.
216 Matthew Lynam, Lynam's, Pulaski.
217 John M'Donald, sol., Durrence's, Tatnall.*
218 Alexander Hodges, Folsom's, Lowndes.*
219 Williamson Jones, Howell's, Troup.*
220 Martha Walker, w., Norman's, Wilkes.
221 John C. Austin, Cleland's, Chatham.*
222 Thomas Glenn, r. s., Baismore's, Jones.*
223 John Magruder's ors., Bell's, Columbia.*
224 William M. Coram, 777th, Randolph.*
225 John Turk, 319th, Baldwin.*
226 John C. Parkerson, Hart's, Jones.
227 Robert W. P. Moore, Field's, Habersham.*
228 Moses Littleton's ors., M'Gill's, Lincoln.
229 William Kerklin, 417th, Walton.*

230 Eli E. Harilson, 656th, Troup.*
231 Harman Thomasson, Seay's, Hall.*
232 John P. C. Richters, sol., 259th, Scriven.*
233 Elizabeth Ann Fuller, or., 248th, Jackson.*
234 Patrick Hart, Cleland's, Chatham.*
235 William G. Jones, dumb, Gunn's, Jefferson.*
236 William Morris, Smith's, Henry.*
237 Jourdan Tucker, 756th, Sumter *
238 Francis Bacon, Whitaker's, Crawford.*
239 William S. Richards, Whisenhunt's, Carroll.*
240 James Sutley, Hammond's, Franklin.*
241 Sarah Mires, w., Young's, Wilkinson.*
242 John H. Holdege, House's, Henry.
243 Polly Gibson, w., Phillip's, Jasper.
244 Absolem D. Smith, Hampton's, Newton.*
245 William Nash, Wynn's, Gwinnett.*
246 Andrew Floyd, Barker's, Liberty.*
247 Thomas Kinman's ors., Vining's, Putnam.*
248 Henry M'Connel, 2d section, Cherokee.
249 Margary Hobbs, w. r. s., Hughes's, Habersham.*
250 Wiloughby Caison, r. s., Green's, Ware.*
251 Elijah Fraser, M'Millon's, Lincoln.
252 James C. Roberts, 555th, Upson.*
253 John V. M'Intosh, Butts's, Monroe.*
254 Irvin Jackson, 166th, Wilkes.
255 Susan Wright, w. r. s., 104th, Hancock.*
256 John R. Jeter, sol., 144th, Greene.*
257 Joseph W. Drennan, Colley's, Madison.*
258 Elijah Yancy, 404th, Gwinnett.*
259 John Roberts, Reed's, Gwinnett.*
260 William H. Drummond, 404th, Gwinnett.*
261 Dunston Banks, sol. 1784–97, 373d, Jasper.*
262 Thomas R. Bond, Martin's, Pike.*
263 Elizabeth Cunningham, w., Liddell's, Jackson.*
264 Thomas Eason, s. l. w., Craven's, Coweta.*
265 Franklin Taylor, Lay's, Jackson.*
266 Jonathan Jeffers, 72d, Burke.*
267 John Moon's ors., Graves's, Lincoln.
268 Benajah S. Sheats, Morgan's, Clarke.*
269 Allen M'Call, Mashburn's, Pulaski.*
270 Michael D. Henigan, Phillip's, Monroe.*
271 Bronson Barden, Mitchell's, Marion.*
272 Thomas Mitchell, Dearing's, Henry.
273 Joshua Smith, Sen., Dobbs's, Hall.*
274 Jane Brazeel, w., 168th, Wilkes.*
275 William Carroll, Newsom's, Warren.*
276 Frederic Newton, Winter's, Jones.*

277 Elizabeth Emerees, w., Valleau's, Chatham.*
278 Heath's children, f. a., Harris's, De Kalb.
279 Benjamin White, s. l. w., Mann's, Crawford.
280 Watts Hancock, Clifton's, Tatnall.
281 Aaron Smith, sol., 104th, Hancock.*
282 Thomas Greer, sol., 365th, Jasper.
283 John Bryant, sol., Tompkins's, Putnam.*
284 John H. Davidson, Lamp's, Jefferson.*
285 Henry Pope, Gillis's, De Kalb.
286 Uriah Skinner, r. s., Roe's, Burke.
287 Micajah Posey, Mitchell's, Pulaski.*
288 Thomas W. Craven, Brock's, Habersham.*
289 Rebecca Russell, w., Grubbs's, Columbia.*
290 Elijah Rogers, Gunn's, Henry.*
291 Elizabeth Davis, blind, Stone's, Irwin.*
292 Allen Dennis's ors., M'Millon's, Lincoln.
293 M'Guder Wade, M'Daniel's, Pulaski.*
294 Benjamin Barton, 600th, Richmond.*
295 William J. Wightman, 398th, Richmond.*
296 Govy Black, Jones's, Habersham.*
297 Ichabod Davis, 589th, Upson.
298 William Kieslley, Moseley's, Coweta.*
299 Lemuel Coats, Burgess's, Carroll.*
300 Joshua James, sol., Sullivan's, Jones.*

25th DISTRICT, THIRD SECTION, CHEROKEE.

1 M'Guder Wade, M'Daniel's, Pulaski.*
2 Robert Castleberry, s. l. w., 177th, Randolph.
3 Littleton Story, Adams's, Columbia.
4 John P. Wiley, Seay's, Hall.*
5 Rebecca Mann, w., Loven's, Henry.*
6 Renslear Beesley, Lockhart's, Bulloch.*
7 Martin Deen, Morrison's, Appling.*
8 Terry's orphans, 406th, Gwinnett.
9 Philip Highnote, Smith's, Houston.*
10 John Smith, Peterson's, Burke.
11 Pleasant Burnett, Bower's, Elbert.*
12 Jehu F. Thompson, Lane's, Morgan.
13 Thomas J. Tanner, Barwick's, Washington.
14 John J. Hunt, Valleau's, Chatham.
15 Thomas Simmons, r. s., Williams's, Ware.
16 Harriett Schroder, or., Valleau's, Chatham.
17 Isaac Spence, Stewart's, Warren.

18 (fr.) Miles G. Buckner, Kendrick's, Putnam.
19 (fr.) John King, r. s., Liddell's, Jackson.
20 William A. Drake, 419th, Walton.
21 Charles Dodson, Belcher's, Jasper.
22 Stephens G. Reeves, Adams's, Columbia.
23 Asa Chandler, Thomason's, Elbert.*
24 Wm. Robinson, s. l. w., Sparks's, Washington.
25 James Prather, Culbreath's, Columbia.*
26 Moses Davidson, Smith's, Wilkinson.
27 John Swearingin, sol., Gum Swamp, Pulaski.
28 Martin Dobbs, Dobbs's, Hall.
29 John M. C. Evans, sol., 119th, Richmond.*
30 William Wallace, 248th, Jackson.
31 Talman W. Shepherd's ors., Maguire's, Morgan.
32 Nathan Hopson, Lynn's, Warren.
33 John Harvey, Barefield's, Jones.*
34 John W. Floyd, Arrington's, Merriwether.
35 Ellert Hodges, Martin's, Washington.*
36 Robert Brown, Hamilton's, Gwinnett.
37 Nancy Riunes Alston, h. a., Justice's, Bibb.
38 Anthony Burnett, Lester's, Monroe.
39 George W. Shoppey, 687th, Lee.
40 John T. Rolston, Herndon's, Hall.*
41 Alexander Morris, Hargrove's, Oglethorpe.*
42 John Jackson, Fenn's, Clarke.*
43 James M'Donald, Culbreath's, Columbia.
44 Martha Long, w., Seally's, Talbot.
45 N. Bridges's orphans, Candler's, Bibb.*
46 John N. Kile, sol., Blackstock's, Hall.
47 Manuel Furnandez, Barker's, Gwinnett.
48 Littleberry Hughs, Young's, Jefferson.
49 P. Brown's orphans, Brown's, Camden.
50 James Riley, sol., 789th, Sumter.*
51 James Hollis, sol., Walker's, Harris.*
52 William Wright, Hanner's, Campbell.
53 James Duke, Alberson's, Walton.
54 (fr.) John Dolton, r. s., Ellsworth's, Bibb.
55 (fr.) Noah Woodbott, 271st, M'Intosh.*
56 Burrel Tiller, Green's, Oglethorpe.
57 Wineyford Dyess, w., Miller's, Ware.
58 David Coleman, M'Culler's, Newton.*
59 Kendrell Carter's ors., Garner's, Washington.
60 Thomas Hiller, 271st, M'Intosh.
61 James Elder, Alberson's, Walton.
62 Franklin Cowan, Harp's, Stewart.*
63 Thomas Cook, Dearing's, Henry.
64 Ann M'Kinnon, w., 7th, Chatham.*

65 Thomas Caston, Williams's, Washington.*
66 N. W. Jones's ors., Chatham, 124th, Richmond.
67 William P. Lyle, Coker's, Troup.*
68 Gregory Singleton, Gorley's, Putnam.*
69 John Odlehill, Royster's, Franklin.*
70 Isaac Taylor, 600th, Richmond.*
71 Joseph Mimms, Martin's, Washington.*
72 William G. Lee, Garner's, Coweta.
73 Frances Youngblood, h. a., 112th, Hancock.
74 John Culpepper, Buck's, Houston.*
75 Samuel Cockrell, Gittens's, Fayette.
76 Nipper Adams, Coxe's, Morgan.*
77 William F. Deen, 494th, Upson.*
78 Robert C. Bryan, 104th, Hancock.
79 William R. Bowman, 9th, Effingham.*
80 Richard Colman, Jones's, Lincoln.*
81 Elijah Phillips, Atkinson's, Coweta.
82 Martin Golden, Flynn's, Muscogee.
83 Walter Thetford, sol., Wood's, Morgan.
84 Eldridge C. Butts, Gunn's, Jones.
85 George Waterson, Smith's, Habersham.
86 Paul Furr, sol., Griffin's, Hall.
87 Reuben Wilkes, 366th, Jasper.*
88 Moses Eason, Morgan's, Appling.*
89 James M'Gill, Chambers's, Gwinnett.
90 (fr.) Richard Singleton, Stanton's, Newton.
91 (fr.) Mary Billingsby, w., 702d, Heard.
92 John Smith, sol., 143d, Greene.
93 Charles Rogers, Chambers's, Gwinnett.
94 Isaac Beard, Jones's, Habersham.
95 Mary Stamper, w. r. s., Parham's, Warren.*
96 Toliver Kerr, Roberts's, Hall.*
97 Benjamin Lee, Slater's, Bulloch.
98 Fountain Wood, Hardman's, Oglethorpe.*
99 Norman Gillis, Peterson's, Montgomery.
100 Catharine Gaar, w., Wood's, Morgan.
101 Simeon Waters, Mason's, Washington.
102 L. Nathan Pearson, M'Culler's, Wilkinson.*
103 William F. Crew, Peurifoy's, Henry.*
104 Michael Whitmore, Jones's, Hall.*
105 John B. Moran, s. l. w., Taylor's, Putnam.
106 Tarver's children, f. a. 3 years, Oliver's, Decatur.
107 John Green, Whelchel's, Hall.*
108 Hiram Vaughter, Chandler's, Franklin.
109 Peter Guise, r. s., Stokes's, Lincoln.
110 M. Clendon's children, f. a., Whipple's, Wilkinson
111 Garner Crosby, Rhodes's, De Kalb.

112 Samuel Jones, Jones's, Lincoln.*
113 Samuel Watts, M'Clure's, Rabun.
114 Thomas C. Cleitte, Grubbs's, Columbia.*
115 William Chewning's ors., Sinclair's, Houston.
116 Lewis Davis, 55th, Emanuel.
117 James Bozeman's ors., Show's, Muscogee.
118 James Fare's ors., Hood's, Henry.
119 Nathaniel Bond, r. s., Seal's, Elbert.*
120 Ephraim Sizmore, Hamilton's, Gwinnett.
121 Elkin Todds, Downs's, Warren.
122 Jane Ferrel, w., 320th, Baldwin.
123 Judeth Peek, w., 608th, Taliaferro.*
124 Joseph Detoaches's ors., Davis's, Jones.
125 Elizabeth Smith, w., Crow's, Pike.   [wether.
126 (fr.) M. A. Douglass, w. r. s., Arrington's, Merri-
127 (fr.) Nathan Tucker, Blackshear's, Laurens.
128 David Miles, Evans's, Fayette.
129 William Leatherwood, Allen's, Campbell.*
130 John Deveregier, 22d, M'Intosh.*
131 Noah Pace, 12th, Effingham.
132 Job Jordan, r. s., Watson's, Marion.
133 William M. Dooly, Stower's, Elbert.*
134 Isaac Falkenberry, Culbreath's, Columbia.*
135 Meshack Joiner, Crow's, Pike.
136 Lemuel Leveritt, 118th, Hancock.
137 Daniel M'Cloud, 118th, Hancock.*
138 James B. Price, Coffee's, Rabun.
139 Littleberry Broach's ors., Colley's, Madison.
140 Henry Swanson, sol., 271st, M'Intosh.
141 John Massingil, 161st, Greene.
142 Nicholas Hardin, Robinson's, Fayette.
143 John Heath, Sutton's, Habersham.*
144 Lucretia Wamble, h. a., Haygood's, Washington.
145 Joseph F. Legur, Fitzpatrick's, Chatham.*
146 Mary Lucas, w. r. s., 102d, Hancock.
147 Richard Price, Martin's, Stewart.*
148 James Tompkins, Williams's, Washington.*
149 William Stubbs, Jr., Gittens's, Fayette.*
150 William Ham, r. s., Whitaker's, Crawford.
151 Allen J. Haile, Barnett's, Clarke.*
152 James A. Buck, Everett's, Washington.
153 William Barker, 734th, Lee.*
154 Thomas Key, Jr., Williams's, Jasper.
155 John Harris, r. s., Hargrove's, Newton.*
156 Emanuel Carpenter, Mullen's, Carroll.
157 Ambrose M'Ginnis, 406th, Gwinnett.
158 William H. Dyson, Moseley's, Wilkes.*

159 Martha J. Mason, f. a., Hammock's, Jasper.
160 Elijah Kent, Hatchett's, Oglethorpe.*
161 William Lesley, r. s., Bragaw's, Oglethorpe.
162 (fr.) John S. Thomas, Scott's, Baldwin.
163 (fr.) John Medlock, 406th, Gwinnett.*
164 Jesse Walters, Herring's, Twiggs.
165 Jesse Moon, 109th, Hancock.
166 William Hall's ors., Hamilton's, Gwinnett.
167 Brice C. M'Ever, Jones's, Hall.
168 Robert Harris's ors., Perryman's, Warren.
169 John Sansing, Sen., Smith's, Henry.*
170 William South, Hardman's, Oglethorpe.*
171 Solomon Meades, 260th, Scriven.*
172 A. Brown's ors., Nesbit's, Newton.
173 John H. Cone, Dean's, De Kalb.
174 William H. Alford, Mizell's, Talbot.
175 Isarel R. Bowen, Crawford's, Franklin.
176 Abraham Gimdains, Lynam's, Pulaski.*
177 Sarah A. Kirby, or., Mangum's, Morgan.
178 George W. Guest, Latimer's, De Kalb.*
179 David Watson, Sinclair's, Houston.
180 James Almond, sol., Wood's, Morgan.*
181 A. Y. J. Allen, 70th, Burke.*
182 Marquis Ambos, Chambers's, Gwinnett.
183 Brice Howard, 1st section, Cherokee.
184 Elisha Perryman, Jr., Perryman's, Warren.*
185 Zachariah W. Chace, Barefield's, Jones.*
186 Benjamin Horn, 57th, Emanuel.
187 Haness Spraberry, Givins's, De Kalb.
188 Nancy Daniel, w., 362d, Jasper.
189 John Hutchinson, 163d, Greene.
190 John C. Smith, Allen's, Monroe.*
191 Louisa M'Gowan, h. a., 120th, Richmond.*
192 William Bell, Hicks's, Decatur.
193 Charles Baker, Brown's, Habersham.
194 Mary Reedy, 2d, Chatham.
195 Holland Sumner, Bell's, Burke.
196 Willis B. Nall, Allison's, Pike.
197 Timothy C. Woods, 250th, Walton.
198 (fr.) John Hunt, Head's, Jones.
199 (fr.) Joseph H. Lee, Candler's, Bibb.
200 Jonathan Calloway, Thompson's, Henry.
201 Scott Gray, Candler's, Bibb.
202 Jacob Glaze, Chastain's, Habersham.
203 Fenn Peck, 271st, M'Intosh.
204 William Walker, s. i. w., 163d, Greene.
205 William Cross, Sen., Roberts's, Hall.

206 Asa Bishop, M'Gill's, Lincoln.*
207 William J. Minzies, 243d, Jackson.*
208 David Allen, or., Belcher's, Jasper.
209 John Gilliland, Compton's, Fayette.
210 Peter B. Allmond, Hood's, Henry.
211 James Tilly, s. l. w., 588th, Upson.
212 John Harris, Loveless's, Gwinnett.*
213 Hardy Pace, Collins's, Henry.*
214 Patrick Phillips, Peterson's, Montgomery.*
215 Seaborn Hawk, Phillips's, Jasper.
216 James Thornton, Covington's, Pike.*
217 Henry Martin, Rhodes's, De Kalb.*
218 Ruth Eiland, w. of sol., Davis's, Jones.*
219 William Nanlie's ors., Smith's, Elbert.*
220 Oliver P. Fears, Talley's, Troup.*
221 Elizabeth P. Ramey, Dean's, Clarke.*
222 L. C. Davis, 720th, Decatur.
223 Elias E. Bates, Daniel's, Hall.
224 John Taylor, Sen., 34th, Scriven.
225 Joseph Slade, Mayo's, Wilkinson.*
226 Colson Heath's ors., 307th, Putnam.
227 James Key Kendall, Stephens's, Habersham.*
228 Keziah Bailey, w. r. s., Martin's, Washington.*
229 William P. Phillips, Wynn's, Gwinnett.
230 James P. Dugger, Peavy's, Bulloch.*
231 Robert Daniell, Jennings's, Clarke.*
232 William H. Walker, Haygood's, Washington.
233 Mary W. Wills, w., Lamp's, Jefferson.*
234 (fr.) John Lasseter, Greer's, Merriwether.
235 (fr.) William Humphrey's ors., Rogers's, Burke.
236 Charles Tankesley, Perry's, Habersham.
237 Bennett H. Gates, sol., Arrington's, Merriwether.
238 Charles Lee, Groover's, Thomas.*
239 John W. Brawner, Allen's, Monroe.*
240 Asa V. Mann, Clark's, Elbert.
241 Frances Knight, w., Loveless's, Gwinnett.
242 John Meredith, Watson's, Marion.*
243 Robert Patten, Colley's, Madison.*
244 Dorothy Rhodes, w., Streetman's, Twiggs.*
245 Arthur Kilcrease, or., Hearn's, Butts.
246 Elijah Gordon, Crow's, Merriwether.
247 Leroy Hammond, 406th, Gwinnett.
248 John Cope, sol., 9th Effingham, Chatham.*
249 William P. Horton, 248th, Jackson.*
250 Wade H. Peevy, Reid's, Gwinnett.*
251 Joseph Fitzpatrick, Jones's, Madison.
252 Isaac Waters, sol., Will's, Twiggs.

253 William H. Murden, 606th, Taliaferro.*
254 Owen M'Dermott, Carswell's, Jefferson.
255 John Roberts, Tower's, Gwinnett.
256 Richard Shipp, 417th, Walton.
257 Amos A. Brood, 26th, Glynn.
258 Shadrack Reddick's ors., Newsom's, Warren.
259 Peter Dowell, sol., Houston's, Chatham.
260 Charles Emlin, Kelly's, Jasper.*
261 Ansil Ferril, Marsh's, Thomas.
262 William Smith's ors., Bragaw's, Oglethorpe.
263 Jonathan Mitchell, Price's, Hall.
264 Henry M. Wills, Maguire's, Gwinnett.
265 Laurence Horn's ors., 57th, Emanuel.
266 Harmon B. Carson, Moseley's, Coweta.
267 John Brewer's ors., 417th, Walton.
268 John Cunningham, sol., Watson's, Marion.*
269 Andrew Park, Curry's, Merriwether.
270 (fr.) Mary Dennis, w., 307th, Putnam.
271 (fr.) Robert Allen, Anderson's, Rabun.
272 Leister House, Benson's, Lincoln.*
273 Levi Woldrup, Mullen's, Carroll.
274 Abner Yeager, 404th, Gwinnett.*
275 Joseph Rogers's ors., Night's, Morgan.
276 Thomas William, Sen., sol., 1st, Chatham.
277 Nancy Jarroll's ors., Riden's, Jackson.
278 Ellias Wallace, Monk's, Crawford.*
279 Tucker Maulden, Oliver's, Twiggs.
280 Benton Storks, 559th, Walton.*
281 Thomas W. Dupree, Jr., Bailey's, Laurens.
282 Robert Grinsted's chil., f. a., Wright's, Laurens.
283 Rachael Biaz, w., 177th, Wilkes.*
284 Malinda Davis, w., Coward's, Lowndes.
285 Kinchen Farecloth, Hatton's, Baker.
286 John C. Fulder, s. l. w., Williams's, Walton.*
287 Green S. Traylor, Howell's, Troup.
288 William Sargent, Parham's, Harris.
289 Jane Churchwell, w., 124th, Richmond.*
290 Stephen Parker's ors., 101st, Hancock.
291 Martin Jones, Edwards's, Talbot.*
292 Solomon T. Thompson, 19th, Bryan.
293 Eli Buckner, s. l. w., Hall's, Butts.*
294 Zeachens Pate, Jones's, Thomas.*
295 Levi Cloud, Derrick's, Henry.
296 Rebecca Frederick, w., 12th, Effingham.*
297 Grissom Dekle, Newman's, Thomas.
298 David Woodall, M'Clure's, Rabun.
299 Thomas A. Dunn, Howard's, Oglethorpe.

300 Aaron Long, sol., 510th, Early.*
301 John G. Sapp, Hicks's, Decatur.
302 Jackson Smith, Smith's, Henry.
303 Jesse Goodwin, Phillip's, Jasper.*
304 James Temple, Jr., 510th, Early.*
305 Joseph Harris, Riden's, Jackson.
306 (fr.) Charles Gregory, sol., Silman's, Pike.
307 (fr.) William Permenter, sol., Allen's, Monroe.
308 (fr.) Septamus Thomas, 119th, Richmond.
309 (fr.) Nathan Thompson, 146th, Greene.
310 (fr.) Elizabeth Nolen, w., Baker's, Liberty.
311 (fr.) James Ferrill, 114th Hancock.*
312 (fr.) Aaron Lewis, Jones's, Morgan.
313 (fr.) Robert B. Binnion, 101st. Hancock.
314 (fr.) Charles D. Parr, Foote's, De Kalb.*
315 (fr.) Sarah Harrell, w., Alexander's, Jefferson.
316 (fr.) James English, Burnett's, Lowndes.
317 (fr.) Robert Douglass, Morrison's, Appling.*
318 (fr.) Silas M'Michael, Berry's, Butts.*
319 (fr.) Terry Runnels, Lunceford's, Wilkes.
320 (fr.) Charles G. Williams, Mashburn's, Pulaski.
321 (fr.) James Bridges's ors., Prescott's, Twiggs.
322 (fr.) Jesse Wallice, Johnson's, De Kalb.
323 (fr.) James Dupree, Peacock's, Washington.*
324 (fr.) Peter M. Oliver, Merck's, Hall.

26th DISTRICT, THIRD SECTION, CHEROKEE.

1 Philip Hening's or., Justice's, Bibb.
2 Elijah Needham, or., Comer's, Jones.*
3 William Raper, Price's, Hall.*
4 Pleasant J. Epperson, Coxe's, Franklin.*
5 William Wafford, Hamilton's, Hall.
6 B. Barratte, Hobkerk's, Camden.
7 Purnal Truitt, Lunceford's, Wilkes.*
8 Richard Draughon, sol., Baismore's, Jones.
9 Jordan Jones, 190th, Elbert.*
10 John F. Bowen, Foote's, De Kalb.*
11 Susannah Hubbard, w. r. s., Guice's, Oglethorpe.*
12 Richard M. Whitehead, Morgan's, Clarke.*
13 Thomas Wills, sol., Athens, Clarke.
14 Champain Marable, 555th, Upson.
15 Stephen Daniel's ors., 320th, Baldwin.*
16 Benjamin Dunaway, sol., Bush's, Stewart.*

17 John Peters, Curry's, Merriwether.*
18 Ebenezer Starnes's ors., 398th, Richmond.
19 Thomas Lindsey's ors., Boynton's, Twiggs.
20 John R. Cain, 687th, Lee.
21 Franklin M'Dade, Mullen's, Carroll.*
22 Sterling Coker, Hill's, Stewart.*
23 Mary Graham, w., Jenkins's, Oglethorpe.
24 James Kelly, Hatton's, Baker.*
25 John Cooper, Valleau's, Chatham.
26 Leroy Edwards, Williams's, Washington.*
27 Thomas Dickson, 192d, Elbert.*
28 Thomas Stubbs, sol., Rutland's, Bibb.
29 Edmond Shackleford, r. s., Taylor's, Elbert.
30 Jacob Hawk, sol., Hammond's, Jasper.
31 John Smith, Jr., Justice's, Bibb.
32 William Chapman, Smith's, Wilkinson.*
33 Thomas Harper, Jones's, Habersham.
34 Anguish Britt, Hatton's, Baker.
35 William Harrison, 470th, Upson.*
36 Richard Speak, Sen., r. s., M'Linn's, Butts.*
37 Richard Shipp, 417th, Walton.*
38 James E. Stewart, Stewart's, Troup.*
39 Elisha Delongs's ors., Reid's, Gwinnett.
40 Bershaba Jones, w., Sullivan's, Jones.
41 John Jones, 141st, Greene.
42 Winiford Dyess, w. r. s., Miller's, Ware.
43 John Rutherford, Jr., Perry's, Baldwin.*
44 Leroy Williams, Dyer's, Habersham.*
45 J. Loyd's ors., 404th, Gwinnett.
46 Isaac Callaway, or., 168th, Wilkes.*
47 Reuben K. Williams, Rutland's, Bibb.*
48 Nancy Keslerson, w. r. s., Rutland's, Bibb.*
49 Frances M. Galewood, w., 307th, Putnam.
50 Haden Malden, Thomason's, Elbert.
51 Harriet C. Wetherspoon's ors., 243d, Jackson.
52 Henry Wells, Goodwin's, Houston.*
53 David M'Gough, 144th, Greene.
54 William Wilson, r. s., Baugh's, Jackson.
55 John Wilson, Sen., r. s., 148th, Greene.*
56 Hardy Todd, Downs's, Warren.
57 Nernissis C. C. Gordon, h. a., Kellum's, Talbot.*
58 Smith Waller, Ball's, Monroe.
59 Absolem Maztin, Chastain's, Habersham.
60 William Clemmons, Marsh's, Thomas.*
61 Thomas Bell, Chesnut's, Newton.
62 John Newson, Monk's, Crawford.*
63 Solomon Seabolt, Hughes's, Habersham.*

64 John Lawrence, r. s., Taylor's, Putnam.
65 James Springle, 271st, M'Intosh.*
66 Gilbert Butler, Cleland's, Chatham.
67 Sarah Daniel, w. r. s., 121st, Richmond.*
68 James Branam, Dyer's, Habersham.
69 John Tomlinson, Jr., Coward's, Lowndes.
70 John Duke, Burnett's, Lowndes.*
71 Edwin Franklin, Collier's, Monroe.
72 Joshua Josey's ors., Smith's, Houston.*
73 Joseph Cook's ors., 320th, Baldwin.
74 Robertson Hill, Burnett's, Habersham.*
75 Edward F. Leavell, Johnson's, De Kalb.
76 Wm. Andrews, sol., Whisenhunt's, Carroll.
77 Glass's five orphans, 559th, Walton.
78 John C. Baldwin, 466th, Monroe.*
79 Charneck Sharp's children, Hobbs's, Laurens.
80 Louisa M. Kenne, id., f. in p., Mitchell's, Marion.
81 Matthew Rainey, sol., 373d, Jasper.*
82 James Golightly, Williams's, Washington.
83 John Waites, sol., 406th, Gwinnett.*
84 Christopher C. Lewis, Stewart's, Warren.
85 Charles A. Harden, 20th, Bryan.*
86 James Simmons, Stewart's, Jones.
87 Levicey Holloman, w. r. s., Mitchell's, Pulaski.*
88 Jarrett Thomas, Wilson's, Jasper.*
89 David Keptor's ors., Hamilton's, Hall.
90 Thomas Boyd, sol., Holt's, Pulaski.
91 William Epps, Will's, Twiggs.
92 Charles M'Coy, M'Coy's, Houston.*
93 Samuel Swilly's ors., Walker's, Houston.
94 Moses Martin, Flynn's, Muscogee.
95 Sansom W. Roberts, Coxe's, Morgan.
96 John A. Daniel's ors., Jordan's, Bibb.
97 Asa W. Harrison, Bishop's, Henry.*
98 John M'Lain, Iverson's, Houston.
99 James H. Reid, Shearer's, Coweta.*
100 John R. Grayson's ors., Cleland's, Chatham.*
101 Curtis Pye, Colley's, Oglethorpe.*
102 Cincinatus M. Lucas, Lester's, Monroe.
103 Richard Hazle, or., Curry's, Merriwether.
104 William Craig, Buck-branch, Clarke.
105 Samuel Pearson, Reid's, Gwinnett.*
106 Joseph Brambolow, id., Phillips's, Monroe.
107 Franklin Bowers, Walker's, Houston.
108 Henry S. Turner, Sinclair's, Houston.
109 John M'Kee's ors., Peurifoy's, Henry.
110 Joseph Turner, 119th, Richmond.*

111 James Rylee, Jr., sol., Martin's, Hall.*
112 Elisha Hunter, s. i. w., 140th, Greene.*
113 John Nales, sol., Curry's, Wilkinson.*
114 William B. Barington, Braddy's, Jones.
115 Pinckney Persons, 589th, Upson.*
116 Joel H. Bobb, Dean's, De Kalb.*
117 Henry Fulgham, Sapp's, Muscogee.*
118 Peter Roudham, Collins's, Henry.*
119 William Elisha Walker, or., 120th, Richmond.
120 David M'Culler, Curry's, Wilkinson.*
121 Allen Summerall, Carpenter's, Tatnall.*
122 Elijah Cash, Huchinson's, Columbia.*
123 Burwell Thompson, Price's, Hall.*
124 Archibald Perkins, r. s., 141st, Greene.
125 Caleb B. Elliott, Candler's, Bibb.
126 Susannah Castleberry, w., Morris's, Crawford.
127 Francis Powers, sol., Talley's, Troup.
128 Sarah Carswell, w., Whipple's, Wilkinson.
129 George L. Scott, 103d, Hancock.
130 Daniel Bough's ors., Espy's, Clarke.
131 John Holms, Candler's, Bibb.
132 William Brewer, Watson's, Marion.
133 Tyre Swift, sol., Edwards's, Franklin.*
134 Henry Darnald, Johnson's, Bibb.
135 Edward Kernel, 24th, M'Intosh.*
136 Abraham Simmons, sol., Cleghorn's, Madison.*
137 Jesse C. Bouchelle, sol., Athens, Clarke.*
138 Thomas D. Harris, Kendrick's, Putnam.
139 Mark Littleton, 1st section, Cherokee.
140 Daniel Walker, Jr., 119th, Richmond.*
141 John Prescott, Morgan's, Appling.*
142 Benjamin Stiles, 20th, Bryan.*
143 John Higgs, r. s., Edwards's, Montgomery.*
144 John Going, Merck's, Hall.*
145 Jesse Keyton's ors., Robinson's, Putnam.
146 Henry Lockhart, Stewart's, Warren.*
147 Hugh Abercrombie, Cleggs's, Walton.*
148 David T. White, Robinson's, Putnam.*
149 Ann Dyson, w. of sol. 1784–97, 175th, Wilkes.*
150 Thomas Kelly, black, Keener's, Rabun.*
151 Andrew B. Stephens's ors., 588th, Upson.
152 James M. Odum, 756th, Sumter.*
153 Matthew Rowlings, Cook's, Telfair.*
154 Providence L. Brock's ors., Edwards's, Talbot.*
155 Thomas Stroud's ors., 55th, Emanuel.
156 George S. Street, Jones's, Morgan.*
157 James Jones, Miller's, Ware.*

158 Catharine Sanders, w., Greer's, Merriwether.
159 Isaac W. Smith, s. l. w., Baley's, Butts.
160 Rabent Harkness, Barker's, Gwinnett.
161 Polly Northern, w., 604th, Taliaferro.
162 Ezekiel Brown, Jr., Walker's, Harris.*
163 James Bullock, mi.. f. a., Foote's, De Kalb.*
164 William Phillip, 395th, Emanuel.
165 William Hardman, Colley's, Oglethorpe.
166 Bennett Barron, Jones's, Bulloch.*
167 Austin Parker, Graves's, Putnam.*
168 Mary Ann Davis, w. r. s., Rhodes's, De Kalb.*
169 Absolem Scott's ors., Mays's, Monroe.
170 Martha Allison, w. r. s., 143d, Greene.
171 William Camp, Maguire's, Gwinnett.*
172 William Rooks, 260th, Scriven.*
173 Josiah Alford, 111th, Hancock.
174 Joseph Tilley's ors., Bell's, Burke.
175 Susannah Jane Thompson, 398th, Richmond.*
176 Jehit Jackson, Chastain's, Habersham.
177 David Thompson, s. l. w., Park's, Walton.
178 Elizabeth Blair, or., Garner's, Washington.*
179 Joshua Vickers, Mason's, Washington.*
180 Allen Martin, Davis's, Gwinnett.
181 Jessey Carlton, Swain's, Thomas.
182 Daniel H. Hunt, Huey's, Harris.*
183 Richard N. Wood, Bryan's, Pulaski.*
184 Moses P. Bailey, Evans's, Fayette.*
185 James Gallaher, Seas's, Madison.*
186 Elizabeth Parish, w. r. s., Lynn's, Warren.
187 David S. Deavenport, Allen's, Henry.
188 William H. Sanders's ors., Greer's, Merriwether.
189 Allen Eddins, Edwards's, Franklin.*
190 Alexander Smith, Sen., Smith's, Habersham.
191 Bethene Dismukes, w., Gunn's, Jones.
192 John Applewhite, 70th, Burke.*
193 Deberry C. Massengale, Dozier's, Columbia.
194 Josiah Walton, r. s., Hinton's, Wilkes.
195 Wiley Pope, sol., Brooks's, Muscogee.
196 Thomas Broom's ors., 122d, Richmond.
197 Nimrod Phillips, Oliver's, Twiggs.
198 Andrew Allen's ors., Graves's, Lincoln.
199 Malcom M'Daniel, 417th, Walton.*
200 Wiley A. Hanington, Martin's, Hall.
201 Robert L. Williams, Howard's, Oglethorpe.
202 Crawford B. Williams, Perry's, Habersham.
203 Benjamin P. Bussey, Kendrick's, Monroe.
204 Augustus G. Ormler, sol., 7th, Chatham.*

205 William Allen, Hatton's, Baker.
206 Joshua Seckenger, sol., 10th, Effingham.
207 John Floyd Raley, Iverson's, Houston.*
208 Edmund Edmundson, Robinson's, Putnam.
209 Samuel Chalmer, Deavours's, Habersham.
210 Charles Lyman, Martin's, Washington.*
211 John W. Daxley, 430th, Early.
212 Burton Haws's ors., Winter's, Jones.*
213 Mary Jackson, Bishop's, Henry.
214 Christian H. Dasher, sol., 9th, Effingham.*
215 Henry C. Bragg, 140th, Greene.*
216 Woodhurt Spurlock, 574th, Early.*
217 Stephen P. Bailey, Baley's, Butts.*
218 George Hall, 161st, Greene.*
219 Matthew Osburn, M'Korkle's, Jasper.*
220 William Henry Grimes, 398th, Richmond.
221 William Butler, Robinson's, Putnam.
222 Nathan Yarbrough, Says's, De Kalb.
223 Jessea Dennis's ors., M'Coy's, Houston.*
224 James Roberts, 69th, Burke.
225 Rosannah Carnes, w. r. s., Keener's, Rabun.
226 Thomas G. Lee, Valleau's, Chatham.*
227 Absolem Thompson, Whelchel's, Hall.*
228 Samuel Davis, 69th, Burke.*
229 Jemima Mays, w., Dupree's, Washington.*
230 Lewis Bird, Sanders's, Chatham.
231 Archibald J. Smith, 600th, Richmond.
232 Robert Ozmore, Dearing's, Henry.*
233 James Hearndon, Rick's, Laurens.
234 Greene Maddox, Head's, Butts.
235 William Brown, Allison's, Pike.
236 Fortune Burks, w., Norman's, Wilkes.
237 Leanah Miller, w., 112th, Hancock.
238 Daniel Pate's ors., Williams's, Decatur.
239 Edward D. Suttle, 167th, Wilkes.*
240 George Roberts, Huchinson's, Columbia.
241 James Perry's ors., Few's, Muscogee.
242 Isaac Spence, Stewart's, Warren.
243 Lewis L. Sexton, sol., 271st, M'Intosh.*
244 Elias D. J. Hines, Huey's, Harris.
245 Isaac White, Cannon's, Wilkinson.
246 Medrum Lesley, minor, 163d, Greene.
247 James B. Fambrough, Elder's, Clarke.
248 James Word, Hammond's, Franklin.*
249 James Colley, Jones's, Habersham.*
250 Hickman Dixon, Jr., Downs's, Warren.*
251 Gabriel Morris, Hughes's, Habersham.*

252 Alfred M'Daff, Wilson's, Madison.*
253 David Potts, Jones's, Habersham.*
254 Dugald M'Dugald, Williams's, Washington.*
255 Polly Robinson, w. r. s., Burgess's, Carroll.
256 William Thompson, Shattox's, Coweta.*
257 Parris Watson, 417th, Walton.*
258 Mary Vinson, w., Davis's, Jones.*
259 John Price, Lawrence's, Pike.*
260 David Keasler, Sen., Smith's, Franklin.
261 Mary Horasy, w., 600th, Richmond.
262 Nimrod E. Ducker, Smith's, Houston.*
263 James Finley, M'Culler's, Newton.*
264 David M'Dow, Rhodes's, De Kalb.
265 Mary Maddux, w., Head's, Butts.
266 William J. Biggs, Cleghorn's, Madison.*
267 Mary Rooks, w. r. s., 353d, Wayne.
268 Wily Hight, Jr., 249th, Walton.*
269 Henry Thomas, Wood's, Morgan.
270 John Sutton's ors., M'Craney's, Lowndes.
271 Aaron Hinson, Hendon's, Carroll.
272 Elijah Clark, Jr., Hutson's, Newton.
273 Peter Mac Gill, Peterson's, Montgomery.
274 James H. Grimmit, Coker's, Troup.
275 Henry Thompson, Holton's, Emanuel.*
276 Rebecca Ballinger, w., Dean's, De Kalb.
277 Edward Hood, 113th, Hancock.
278 Mary Harper, w. r. s., 101st, Hancock.
279 Burrell J. Carroll, 250th, Walton.
280 Elizabeth Conaway, w. r. s., Herndon's, Hall.*
281 Amy Peacock, w. r. s., 454th, Walton.
282 John Morris, r. s., Bush's, Pulaski.*
283 John W. Calhoun, Jordan's, Bibb.*
284 Miles's ors., Young's, Wilkinson.
285 James Deal, 49th, Emanuel.*
286 Samul Singleton, Allison's, Pike.*
287 Daniel Killian, Dobbs's, Hall.*
288 Stephen Coxe's ors., Coxe's, Morgan.
289 Adam Elrod's ors., Seay's, Hall.
290 William H. Williams, or., 320th, Baldwin.*
291 Daniel Oversheet's ors., 57th, Emanuel.
292 John Wiggins, 124th, Richmond.*
293 Jesse Coleman, r. s., 73d, Burke.
294 Hamblin Huff, 373d, Jasper.*
295 John Blaleck, Sen., Mobley's, De Kalb.*
296 Samuel R. Overbay, Jones's, Lincoln.
297 Stafford Long's ors., Hatton's, Baker.
298 John H. Holder, Barnett's, Clarke.*

299 Elias Watkins, Chastain's, Habersham.*
300 Wade Love, s. l. w., 788th, Heard.
301 Joel Evans, 756th, Sumter.*
302 John Mullens, sol., Edwards's, Talbot.*
303 Willis Argo, Maguire's, Gwinnett.*
304 John Sellers, Loven's, Henry.*
305 Felix Gresham, Mays's, Monroe.
306 Solomon Brown, 603d, Taliaferro.
307 John L. Weaver, Burnett's, Habersham.
308 Berry Pannell, Reid's, Gwinnett.
309 James Carter, Sen., sol., Perryman's, Warren.
310 Randel Sorrow, sol., Colley's, Oglethorpe.
311 E. W. King's orphans, Greer's, Merriwether.
312 John M'Dade, Reid's, Gwinnett.*
313 James O. Smith, Jenkins's, Oglethorpe.
314 James Leak, Sen., Belcher's, Jasper.
315 Adam Jones's ors., Hobbs's, Laurens.
316 Albin O. Haines, Sinquefield's, Washington.
317 Daniel Bird, Foote's, De Kalb.
318 John Richards, Whisenhunt's, Carroll.*
319 Victer E. Booth, Nellum's, Elbert.*
320 Mary Davis, w. r. s., Peterson's, Montgomery.
321 John Miller, Hart's, Jones.
322 Dennis Nolin, Southall's, Tatnall.*
323 Isaac Coker, r. s., Hood's, Henry.
324 John S. M. Curdy, Hodges's, Newton.

27th DISTRICT, THIRD SECTION, CHEROKEE.

1 James Ford, 72d, Burke.*
2 John L. Doyal, Reid's, Gwinnett.*
3 John Crumby, Sutton's, Habersham.
4 John Moore, Sen., r. s., Merck's, Hall.
5 Mary C. Ford, w., Martin's, Jones.*
6 Mary W. Tomlinson, Christie's, Jefferson.
7 S. Golightly, w. r. s., Williams's, Washington.*
8 Young F. Tigner, Payne's, Merriwether.*
9 William H. Cooper, Talley's, Troup.
10 Guilford Harris, Evans's, Fayette.
11 Thomas Kinsey, Jones's, Habersham.
12 William H. Guynn, 250th, Walton.
13 John Partin, Southwell's, Tatnall.*
14 William C. Todd, Pate's, Warren.*
15 Stephen Gibbons, Sen., 121st, Richmond.*

16 Wesley Camp, Stanfield's, Campbell.*
17 John Mobley, Dearing's, Henry.
18 (fr.) David Nolin, 242d, Jackson.*
19 (fr.) Nathaniel Bangor, Rhodes's, De Kalb.*
20 John Freel, Talley's, Troup.*
21 Thomas Smith, Canning's, Elbert.*
22 Godbay's ors., Griffin's, Burke.*
23 Thompson Mealer, Gunn's, Jones.
24 Matthew Averette, Harp's, Stewart.
25 George W. Foote, Mobley's, De Kalb.*
26 Uriah Bottle's or., 608th, Taliaferro.
27 James Stewart's ors., 141st, Greene.*
28 John T. Williams, 108th, Hancock.
29 Henry Etris, Field's, Habersham.*
30 William Wilson, Jones's, Hall.*
31 William Slater's ors., Peavy's, Bulloch.*
32 Henry E. White, Barker's, Gwinnett.
33 Alexander R. Ramsey, 4th section, Cherokee.
34 Rhasa Muslewhite, M'Craney's, Lowndes.
35 Daniel Mayo, Thomas's, Clarke.
36 Sarah Blaylock, w., Martin's, Hall.*
37 Thornton G. Kent, Bostick's, Twiggs.*
38 Micajah Phillips, Peterson's, Montgomery.
39 Edwin Adams, Payne's, Merriwether.
40 Sally Twitty, w. r. s., Lamberth's, Fayette.
41 William B. Weaver, s. l. w., Colley's, Oglethorpe.*
42 Edmond Lyon, Graves's, Lincoln.*
43 Theophilus A. Norwood, Hendon's, Carroll.
44 William Matthews, sol., Mayo's, Wilkinson.*
45 John Harris, Sen., s. l. w., 22d, M'Intosh.*
46 Andrew Y. Haynes, Hammond's, Franklin.*
47 A. Smith, sol. 1784–97, Curry's, Merriwether.
48 William Mitchell, Taylor's, Jones.*
49 Benjamin B. Kendrick, Coxe's, Talbot.*
50 John M'Kinzie, Trout's, Hall.*
51 Thomas M. Dillard, Howell's, Elbert.*
52 Solomon Ward, Perry's, Habersham.*
53 Jane Connolly, Justice's, Bibb.
54 (fr.) William Dollar, Nesbit's, Newton.
55 (fr.) Allen Perry, 574th, Early.
56 John W. Green, Wilson's, Jasper.*
57 William H. Boggs, Stower's, Elbert.*
58 Isaac Carter, Morrison's, Appling.
59 Nathaniel Cornally's ors., Barker's, Gwinnett.
60 Miles Nicks, M'Daniel's, Pulaski.*
61 Matthew Gentry, Willis's, Franklin.*
62 Elizabeth Hamilton, w., 22d, M'Intosh.

63 Joshua Burroughs, Mobley's, De Kalb.*
64 Shelman Durham, Brewer's, Monroe.
65 Micajah Crews, Brown's, Camden.*
66 Thomas J. Burdell, 175th, Wilkes.*
67 Martin Hathaway, Valleau's, Chatham.
68 Lewis J. Cooper, Jones's, Thomas.
69 Polly Jenkins, w., 146th, Greene.
70 Aaron Picken, Show's, Muscogee.
71 James Newton, Newman's, Thomas.
72 Wiley Phillip, Bower's, Elbert.*
73 Nancy Bailey, w., Talley's, Troup.
74 David Gillespy, Colquhoun's, Henry.*
75 John Rutherford, s. i. w., Perry's, Baldwin.*
76 Jacob Awtry, sol., Lane's, Monroe.*
77 Michael Carter, sol., Oliver's, Decatur.*
78 Stephens S. Phillips, Dozier's, Columbia.
79 Andrew Mitchell, Flynn's, Muscogee.*
80 John Moye, sol., 117th, Hancock.*
81 William Robertson, s. i. w., Taylor's, Elbert.*
82 John H. Hubbard, Johnson's, De Kalb.*
83 Mary Clark, w. r. s., Hannah's, Jefferson.*
84 James Scott, Vining's, Putnam.*
85 Orron Jarratt, Riden's, Jackson.*
86 John Barnes, Sen., s. i. w., Sparks's, Washington.*
87 William Dunn, Collins's, Henry.*
88 William A. Pittman, Mimms's, Fayette.*
89 James Southall's ors., Bostick's, Twiggs.
90 (fr.) John B. Garrison, 2d section, Cherokee.
91 (fr.) John B. Montree, 34th, Scriven.
92 Thomas Walker, s. i. w., M'Clain's, Newton.*
93 Henry Robinson's or., 242d, Jackson.
94 John E. Fowler, 1st, Chatham.*
95 Edmund Kelly, Moffet's, Muscogee.*
96 Archibald M'Millan's ors., 374th, Putnam.*
97 Alson M. Gratehouse, Mann's, Crawford.*
98 J. Castleberry, sol. 1784–97, 307th, Putnam.
99 Isaac Brown, Butts's, Monroe.
100 Josiah Whitehurts, Young's, Washington.
101 Thomas Parsons, Compton's, Fayette.*
102 Robert W. Tarpley, Hall's, Oglethorpe.*
103 James N. Mobley, Smith's, Liberty.*
104 Thomas W. Gilbert, Liddell's, Jackson.*
105 Duncan Gidden, Folsom's, Lowndes.
106 Peter Potts, Martin's, Newton.
107 Thomas Greene, Whelchel's, Hall.
108 John T. Stanfil, Edwards's, Montgomery.
109 Ezekiel Rutchford, Mimms's, Fayette.

110 Henry Cason, Park's, Walton.*
111 Elijah Wyatt, Neal's, Campbell.*
112 James Johnston, 8th, Chatham.
113 Richard Clark, Hall's, Camden.*
114 Drury Fowler, of Cherokee, Latimer's, De Kalb.*
115 William Webb, Hardman's, Oglethorpe.*
116 Henry T. Smartt, 293d, Jackson.*
117 Levi Brown, Dearing's, Henry.*
118 Benjamin Hasting, Brooks's, Muscogee.*
119 Robert Houston, Tower's, Gwinnett.*
120 Andrew G. Griffin, sol., Flynn's, Muscogee.*
121 J. and S. Spivy, ors., Payne's, Merriwether.
122 Isah Oliver, Martin's, Washington.*
123 John Coldwell, Hammock's, Jasper.*
124 Elkanah Lowyer, Morris's, Crawford.*
125 Mordecai Cox, Hughes's, Habersham.
126 (fr.) John Fling's or., Jones's, Wilkes.
127 (fr.) John J. Fielder, Allison's, Pike.
128 Gilson Chesnut, 640th, Dooly.
129 Harman Thomasson, Seay's, Hall.*
130 Noah Merideth, Williams's, Walton.*
131 Drury Smith, s. l. w., Nichols's, Fayette.*
132 Thomas U. Stephenson, Talley's, Troup.*
133 John L. Dorrough, Wood's, Morgan.*
134 Sarah Redding, w., 80th, Scriven.
135 Isaac Frazier, Whipple's, Wilkinson.*
136 John Sealy, Candler's, Bibb.*
137 Cornelius Connally, Head's, De Kalb.
138 Rebecca Shaw, w., Tower's, Gwinnett.*
139 John J. Geiger, Phillips's, Jasper.*
140 Lemuel Milligan, 4th section, Cherokee.*
141 Matthias Tenison, Mullen's, Carroll.*
142 William R. Thomas, Wood's, Morgan.*
143 Thomas L. Pope, Ross's, Monroe.
144 Henry Mercer, Moore's, Randolph.
145 Hugh M. Comer, r. s., Stewart's, Jones.
146 William Palery's two orphans, Gillis's, De Kalb.
147 James A. Abraham, Shearer's, Coweta.
148 Godbey's orphans, Griffin's, Burke.*
149 William Miller, sol., Prophett's, Newton.*
150 ªJohn Olive, Adams's, Columbia.
151 David Riddle, Bustin's, Pike.
152 William Lesley, r. s., Bragaw's, Oglethorpe.
153 Walter Been, r. s., Belcher's, Jasper.*
154 John Fears, 294th, Jasper.

a This lot was drawn, and then relinquished by the first drawer.

155 Ihom Herrin, Sen., A. Brown's, Habersham.
156 Jason Champeon, Hill's, Monroe.*
157 Sophia Ann Burnett, w., Justice's, Bibb.*
158 Philips Lumpkin, Rogers's, Burke.*
159 Edward H. Gresham, 148th, Greene.*
160 Catharine Hunter, w., 419th, Walton.*
161 Marry White, w., Roberts's, Hall.*
162 (fr.) William Shaw, Johnson's, De Kalb.
163 (fr.) Lanfair Whithart's ors., Coxe's, Talbot.
164 James V. Brown, Collier's, Monroe.*
165 Joseph L. Robinson, Carpenter's, Fayette.*
166 David Porterfield, Jr., Morgan's, Madison.*
167 Dickson Naylor, sol. 1784–97, 404th, Gwinnett.*
168 Byrum Howell, 278th, Morgan.
169 John F. Cannon, 271st, M'Intosh.*
170 Freeman D. Cardin's ors., Moore's, Randolph.
171 John Echols, Jr., Burnett's, Habersham.*
172 James H. Laing, Baker's, Liberty.
173 Richard Kobb, Harp's, Stewart.
174 Susannah Yates, w. r. s., Lamberth's, Fayette.*
175 Ralph Smith, sol., 1st section, Cherokee.*
176 M'Kinley Suggs, Bell's, Burke.*
177 John Boyd, Field's, Habersham.*
178 Burton E. Crawford, Stower's, Elbert.*
179 Samuel E. Silf, Kelly's, Elbert.*
180 Elisha Walden, Hodges's, Newton.
181 George Heard, Jr., Rhodes's, De Kalb.
182 Robert Smith, Sen., r. s., Hearn's, Butts.
183 Benjamin Dorton, r. s., Martin's, Pike.*
184 William Clarke, Dobbs's, Hall.
185 Cordy Bachellor, 162d, Greene.*
186 Matthew Arthur, sol., Hughes's, Habersham.*
187 Elizabeth Hail, or., Thomas's, Clarke.
188 James Walker, Atkinson's, Coweta.
189 Lee Swan, Williams's, Jasper.
190 Sarah Highsmith, w. r. s., 335th, Wayne.
191 Moses Brooks, id., 277th, Morgan.
192 William O. Bell, Dean's, De Kalb.*
193 Levi Herrin, Williams's, Ware.*
194 Thomas Grey, Fitzpatrick's, Chatham.*
195 Elender Golden, w. r. s., 417th, Walton.*
196 Kindred Boyd, Bryan's, Monroe.*
197 Elisha Clarke, Rooks's, Putnam.*
198 (fr.) Martin Deen, Morrison's, Appling.
199 (fr.) Elizabeth Herrin, lun., Head's, Butts.
200 Abraham Eason's ors., Compton's, Fayette.
201 John Babb, Dean's, De Kalb.*

202 William Hatten, s. l. w., Cook's, Telfair.*
203 Lucy Archer, id., 248th, Jackson.*
204 Callan Dorman's ors., Peacock's, Twiggs.
205 Samuel Pepper, Mullen's, Carroll.*
206 Thomas Jackson, 555th, Upson.*
207 Albert M. Berry, 101st, Hancock.
208 Sarah Terrell, id., Smith's, Liberty.
209 Willis House, Talley's, Troup.
210 John M'Ral, Robison's, Washington.*
211 Hugh Montgomery, Chastain's, Habersham.*
212 Martin R. Malone, Taylor's, Jones.*
213 Esau Brooks, Tower's, Gwinnett.*
214 William Cline, 419th, Walton.*
215 Nicholas Tompkins, Tompkins's, Putnam.
216 Samuel Broswell's ors., 415th, Walton.
217 Eldridge S. Cash, Johnson's, De Kalb.
218 Thomas H. Tuggle, Kelly's, Jasper.
219 Asahel Beach, 600th, Richmond.*
220 Lewis C. Simmons, Hatton's, Baker.*
221 George Iseley, 404th, Gwinnett.*
222 Thomas Childress, Jr., Martin's, Newton.*
223 James White, Rooks's, Putnam.
224 William Fountain, Barwick's, Washington.
225 Nathan Butler, s. l. w., Brewer's, Walton.
226 David Hunter, Miller's, Ware.
227 William F. Waters, Price's, Hall.*
228 Mark Maberry, Fleming's, Franklin.*
229 James Langham's ors., 537th, Upson.*
230 Benjamin Drane, Adams's, Columbia.*
231 Andrew J. Barron, 589th, Upson.*
232 Sarah Tabb, or., Bryant's, Burke.*
233 Esther Powers, w., Cleland's, Chatham.
234 (fr.) Leah Tillett, w., Miller's, Ware.
235 (fr.) Charles Furlow's or., Cleggs's, Walton.
236 Noah Hinton, sol., Norman's, Wilkes.*
237 Francis J. Rossenbury, Athens, Clarke.
238 Wiley Fowler, Talley's, Troup.
239 John Shaw, Stanfield's, Campbell.
240 Andrew Bird, Jr., 19th, Bryan.*
241 John B. Stewart, Ogden's, Camden.*
242 Milford Jones, Camp's, Warren.
243 Elizabeth Rudulph, w. r. s., Hobkerk's, Camden.
244 Robert Lang, Hendon's, Carroll.
245 Samuel Barrett, Moseley's, Coweta.*
246 Samuel Willeford, Jr., Smith's, Madison.*
247 Solomon R. Johnson, Jordan's, Bibb.
248 Michael Peterson Mattox's, Lowndes.*

249 Isaac Philips, or., Talley's, Troup.
250 Turner Floyd, Jenkins's, Oglethorpe.*
251 Abraham S. Smith, Hamilton's, Gwinnett.*
252 John P. Carter, Campbell's, Wilkes.*
253 George W. Hanson, Hines's, Coweta.
254 Jacob Dill, s. l. w., 120th, Richmond.*
255 Isaiah Dunnagan, Merck's, Hall.*
256 Hugh M. M'Cain, Hughes's, Harris.*
257 John W. Alexander, Alexander's, Jefferson.*
258 Randel Campbell, Peterson's, Montgomery.
259 William C. Hill, Jr., Newsom's, Warren.*
260 John Taylor, sol., Young's, Wilkinson.*
261 William Ragland, 295th, Jasper.*
262 Julias Cook, sol., Vining's, Putnam.*
263 Robert Collins, Sen., s. l. w., 589th, Upson.*
264 Jacob Alferd, sol., 107th, Hancock.*
265 William M. Russell, Whisenhunt's, Carroll.*
266 Jesse Bell, Goodwin's, Houston.
267 Wyatt Allen, Bush's, Pulaski.*
268 William Duke, sol., Belcher's, Jasper.*
269 John M. Wall, Lay's, Jackson.*
270 (fr.) W. Edmunds, w. r. s., Lunceford's, Wilkes.
271 (fr.) Edward W. Joines, Williams's, Washington.
272 James Jones, Williams's, Washington.
273 Joseph Lawrence, Crow's, Pike.
274 Jesse Ruark, Jones's, Morgan.
275 Abner Foster, 102d, Hancock.
276 Harbert H. Raney, Echols's, Clarke.*
277 John N. M'Intosh, 22d, M'Intosh.*
278 Warren B. S. Haile, Elder's, Clarke.
279 Thomas D. Marcus, Coxe's, Talbot.*
280 Bishop Wilkins, Clinton's, Campbell.*
281 William Tapley, Allen's, Bibb.*
282 James Fitzgerald, Gittens's, Fayette.*
283 Rachael Kent, w., 168th, Wilkes.
284 G. L. Barry, Decatur county, Swain's, Thomas.
285 William Roberts, Sen., sol., 71st, Burke.*
286 Washington G. Atkinson, Berry's, Butts.
287 Benjamin W. Lanier, 101st, Hancock.*
288 John Abbott, Reed's, Gwinnett.
289 Charity Davis's ors., Polhill's, Burke.
290 Thomas Whitehead, Newsom's, Warren.*
291 Abraham M. Matthews, 168th, Wilkes.
292 Silas Simmons, Wright's, Laurens.*
293 Nathaniel Beall, r. s., 124th, Richmond.
294 Uriah Wilcox, 15th, Liberty.*
295 Reuben A. Brantley, Hyrn's, Chatham.

296 William Buckin's ors., 124th, Richmond.
297 James Beasley, 395th, Emanuel.*
298 Zinn's three orphans, 119th, Richmond.
299 Fergus C. Lin, Hutson's, Newton.*
300 Joshua Elder, r. s., Robinson's, Fayette.*
301 Duncan Buchannan, Morrison's, Montgomery.
302 John Hubbard, 1st, Chatham.*
303 Moses Whelchel, Herndon's, Hall.*
304 Garland Dabney, Johnson's, De Kalb.
305 Francis Birdgman, Rainey's, Twiggs.
306 (fr.) Elijah Garrett, Norris's, Monroe.*
307 (fr.) Henry Curbow, Smith's, Campbell.
308 James Henry, Loven's, Henry.*
309 Shadrack Tutur, Dupree's, Washington.*
310 Chiles Root, Colley's, Oglethorpe.*
311 Nathan E. Biggars, Dean's, Clarke.
312 Samuel Wortham, Griffin's, Merriwether.*
313 Francis M. M'Junkin, Hammond's, Franklin.*
314 Joseph L. Roney, George's, Appling.*
315 Robert Butler, Candler's, Bibb.*
316 John Roundtree, 59th, Emanuel.
317 Washington Trammell, Hutson's, Newton.*
318 Isaac Fithean, 271st, M'Intosh.
319 Robert Cox, s. i. w., Green's, Oglethorpe.
320 Lewis Spears, Whipple's, Washington.*
321 William J. Rylander, Ellsworth's, Bibb.*
322 Elijah Griffin, Willis's, Franklin.*
323 Robert Tutte, Bell's, Burke.
324 John Lake, 454th, Walton.*
325 (fr.) Robert B. Camp, sol., Reid's, Gwinnett.*
326 (fr.) John F. Goggins, 466th, Monroe.*
327 (fr.) Richard Hannah, Hannah's, Jefferson.*
328 (fr.) Blake Fitzgerald, Newby's, Jones.
329 (fr.) William Miller, Harp's, Stewart.
330 (fr.) Jesse Mixon, 260th, Scriven.
331 (fr.) Abel Winningham, Hamilton's, Gwinnett.*
332 (fr.) Elizabeth Dorherty, w. r. s., Say's, De Kalb.
333 (fr.) Charles Sanford, Lester's, Monroe.*
334 (fr.) Gasper Rosy, Cleland's, Chatham.*
335 (fr.) Benjamin Harrison, Hearn's, Butts.*
336 (fr.) William Wilson, Hill's, Baldwin.
337 (fr.) William Babb, s. i. w., Dean's, De Kalb.
338 (fr.) William Griffith, Liddell's, Jackson.
339 (fr.) Joshua Zuber, Hall's, Oglethorpe.
340 (fr.) Aaron Haygood, Griffin's, De Kalb.
341 (fr.) Ann Bradford, w. r. s., Robinson's, Putnam.
342 (fr.) Branch P. Fulks, Anderson's, Wilkes.

28th DISTRICT, THIRD SECTION, CHEROKEE.

1 Matilda Hawkins, or., 510th, Early.
2 James Dennis, Covington's, Pike.
3 Charles Avera's ors., Griffin's, Fayette.*
4 Lucinda Cockram's ors., 4th section, Cherokee.
5 Thomas A. Hightower, Griffin's, Harris.*
6 Jacup Listrunk, M'Gill's, Lincoln.
7 William Collier's ors., Morgan's, Clarke.
8 Mary Taylor, w., 36th, Scriven.
9 John Green, Allen's, Bibb.*
10 Zachariah Gattin's ors., 278th, Morgan.
11 John Barr, Gunn's, Henry.*
12 James Tumble's ors., Young's, Jefferson.
13 David B. White, 588th, Upson.
14 Jehew Conyers, 73d, Burke.*
15 John Buie, Lockhart's, Bulloch.*
16 Nancy Shaw, w., Allen's, Campbell.*
17 Thomas W. Dwight, Jordan's, Bibb.*
18 (fr.) Mary M'Ree, w. r. s., Barnett's, Clarke.
19 (fr.) James Griffin, Crow's, Pike.*
20 Doctor A. Childers, 510th, Early.
21 Elizabeth Phillips, w., Mays's, Monroe.*
22 Elizabeth Houghton, w. r. s., Athens, Clarke.
23 James W. Walker, sol., Lane's, Morgan.*
24 Benjamin L. Greenwood, Hatton's, Baker.
25 Henry Harden, Hearn's, Butts.*
26 William Barker, Willingham's, Harris.
27 Alfred Mabry, 143d, Greene.*
28 James Bigham, Gunn's, Jefferson.*
29 James Hodge, 106th, Hancock.*
30 Charles T. Hulsay, Mullen's, Carroll.*
31 William Leatherwood, Allen's, Campbell.*
32 Andrew G. Watkins, Seay's, Hall.*
33 Dennis Ruarbe, Jr., Thomas's, Clarke.*
34 Older Neal, 149th, Greene.*
35 Spencer Cherry, Lightfoot's, Washington.
36 Jonathan Long, Tower's, Gwinnett.
37 Walton Molder, Gittens's, Fayette.*
38 Whitmill Williams, Edwards's, Talbot.*
39 Ann Wilson, w., 12th, Effingham.*
40 Rollen Osborn, Coker's, Troup.*
41 Edmund Carlisle, or., Night's, Morgan.

42 Jesse Lamberth, Lamberth's, Fayette.
43 David R. Anderson, Orr's, Jackson.*
44 Jeremiah Thompson, 138th, Greene.*
45 William M'Clenney's ors., Lamberth's, Fayette.*
46 Mary Chicoming, w. r. s., Lester's, Monroe.
47 Dickson Bruster, Coxe's, Morgan.*
48 Samuel Oliver, Hutson's, Newton.*
49 Henry Shepherd's ors., Wheeler's, Pulaski.
50 Wiley T. Hodges, Dupree's, Washington.
51 William S. Lawson, 735th, Troup.
52 Maford Cutts, sol., Goodwin's, Houston.
53 William Sanford, Goodwin's, Houston.
54 (fr.) James Espy, r. s., Buck-branch, Clarke.
55 (fr.) Hiram Mahaffee, Hendon's, Carroll.*
56 Thomas Reeves, Adams's, Columbia.
57 Frances Alson, h. a., Pounds's, Twiggs.
58 Green Sims, Stewart's, Jones.*
59 Robert Holiday, sol., Lay's, Jackson.
60 John T. Tribble, Seay's, Madison.*
61 Hilery Hooks, 734th, Lee.*
62 John W. Strozer, Curry's, Merriwether.*
63 Travis Johnson, Bishop's, Henry.
64 William M. Still, 415th, Walton.*
65 Wiley B. Jones, Fulks's, Wilkes.*
66 Joseph Thomas, Tuggle's, Merriwether.*
67 William Rouse, Blackstock's, Hall.*
68 George Graham, Mashburn's, Pulaski.*
69 Frederic L. Bowman, Williams's, Decatur.*
70 James H. Winchel, Tuggle's, Merriwether.*
71 Gibson S. Lanair, Lockhart's, Bulloch.
72 Henry Sanders, Athens, Clarke.
73 Abram Peavy, s. i. w., 603d, Taliaferro.*
74 Maria Merrill, w., Allen's, Monroe.
75 Jane Barkley, w., Hall's, Butts.*
76 George W. Holifield, 295th, Jasper.*
77 Peter Kensey, Sen., miller, Jones's, Habersham.
78 William Terry, Foote's, De Kalb.
79 Moses Johnson, Parham's, Warren.*
80 Adam Andrews, Hinton's, Wilkes.
81 Samuel Timmons, Wheeler's, Pulaski.*
82 Isaac Robertson, s. l. w., 561st, Upson.
83 Zachariah Cowart, Sen., r. s., 510th, Early.*
84 Abraham Greason's ors., Parham's, Warren.
85 Jane Duff, w., Nesbit's, Newton.
86 James Kendall, Griffin's, Fayette.
87 Martha Red, w., Davis's, Gwinnett.*
88 John Day, M'Clain's, Newton.

89 Newman Matthews, sol., M'Millon's, Lincoln.*
90 (fr.) John Vaughn, Jr., 72d, Burke.
91 (fr.) Hines Holt, s. s., Cleggs's, Walton.
92 Rebecca Breedlove, w., Gorley's, Putnam.
93 Samuel Jessop, Bostick's, Twiggs.*
94 James L. Brock, Hood's, Henry.
95 Hilliard J. Roe, Roe's, Burke.
96 Lovick W. Rasberry, Harralson's, Troup.
97 Robert Farrar's ors., Gunn's, Jones.
98 Reuben Herndern, 788th, Heard.*
99 William Palmer, r. s., Rhodes's, De Kalb.
100 Charles Staples, Brackett's, Newton.
101 Nancy Hatcher, w., 119th, Richmond.
102 Joshua Gay, Jr., 574th, Early.
103 Watson Sawyer, Morris's, Crawford.*
104 William Baldwin Harrison, Ellsworth's, Bibb.
105 William Pearsons, Pounds's, Twiggs.
106 Thomas Hamby's ors., Martin's, Newton.
107 William Bowers, M'Millon's, Lincoln.*
108 Dorotha Van Yevrin, w., Valleau's, Chatham.
109 Rhoda Bates, w., 142d, Greene.*
110 William Aikins, Walker's, Houston.*
111 Johnson Weems, Hammond's, Franklin.*
112 Ebenezer Weir, Nesbit's, Newton.
113 Leonard Sleed, Sen., Bell's, Columbia.
114 James Garganus, Justice's, Bibb.
115 William Allums, sol., Talley's, Troup.*
116 Jesse Page's ors., Mitchell's, Monroe.
117 Pierce Callahand, 535th, Dooly.*
118 Jonathan Vanwaggenen, Candler's, Bibb.*
119 Jesse Statham, sol. 1784-97, Jennings's, Clarke.*
120 John Bivins's ors., Perry's, Baldwin.
121 Nancy Bryant, w., Anderson's, Wilkes.
122 William Hulsay, Dobbs's, Hall.*
123 Anderson Barker, Smith's, Houston.
124 John F. Clements, Mattox's, Lowndes.
125 Jacob Diele, Dyer's, Habersham.*
126 (fr.) John T. Thompson, sol., Moseley's, Wilkes.
127 (fr.) John H. Bryan, 430th, Upson.
128 Richard Harvey, Whitaker's, Crawford.*
129 William Gilliam, Adams's, Columbia.*
130 Christ S. Baldwin, Burk's, Stewart.*
131 Enoch Brady, Jr., Chastain's, Habersham.*
132 John Tuhilt, Silman's, Pike.
133 Reuben Bishop, Griffin's, De Kalb.*
134 Lucinda Hunt, w., 177th, Wilkes.*
135 Renne Fitzpatrick, s. i. w., 779th, Heard.
41

136 William Fowler, Lester's, Monroe.*
137 William S. Mayo, Garner's, Coweta.
138 William Brooks, or., Smith's, Habersham.
139 Benjamin J. Russell, Whitehead's, Habersham.*
140 Dempsey Dison's ors., Cleggs's, Walton.
141 Winifred E. Hogan, w., 559th, Walton.
142 Benega Morris, 271st, M'Intosh.*
143 Reuben Sanders, 1st, Chatham.
144 Urbin C. Bailey, Allen's, Bibb.*
145 John Jones, Brewton's, Tatnall.
146 Prosser Parrish, Gunn's, Jefferson.*
147 Sarah Bird, w., 1st, Chatham.*
148 James Brewster, Heard's, De Kalb.
149 John R. Watson, M'Ewin's, Monroe.
150 Nathaniel G. Rice, sol., Pollard's, Wilkes.*
151 John Griggs, Jr., Taylor's, Putnam.
152 Henry Carlton, s. i. w., Givins's, De Kalb.*
153 J. D. M'Farland, sol., Talley's, Troup.
154 Lewis A. Dugas, 398th, Richmond.*
155 William Morgan, Seay's, Hall.*
156 Churchill Blakey, Huey's, Harris.*
157 Samuel Staton, Seay's, Hall.*
158 Alston S. Massey, r. s., Robinson's, Harris.*
159 Elizabeth Lewis, w., Parham's, Warren.*
160 Thomas Parson's ors., Gunn's, Jefferson.
161 Simeon Rogers, sol., 561st, Upson.*
162 (fr.) Robert Thomas, 466th, Monroe.
163 (fr.) William J. Lary, Chambers's, Gwinnett.
164 Littleton D. Glass, Jones's, Thomas.*
165 Alfred Brown, Whipple's, Wilkinson.*
166 James Irwin, Barnett's, Clarke.
167 David Patrick, r. s., Hall's, Oglethorpe.*
168 Jesse Jordan, Say's, De Kalb.*
169 William Henderson, 516th, Dooly.*
170 Adolphus Dauvergne, Price's, Hall.*
171 James Holmes, Canning's, Elbert.*
172 John Spradlie, Tower's, Gwinnett.*
173 T. W. Sweet, Candler's, Bibb.
174 Sarah A. Snell, or., Bryan's, Pulaski.
175 John Litton, r. s., Hughes's, Habersham.
176 James W. Jones, Howell's, Troup.*
177 Leonard Simpson, Say's, De Kalb.*
178 James Greer, 419th, Walton.*
179 Jordan Taply, Allen's, Bibb.*
180 Cornelius Gibbs, Sen., Henson's, Rabun.
181 John Crutchfield, 140th, Greene.*
182 Henry Mills, 122d, Richmond.*

183 Thomas Waller, Wilson's, Pike.*
184 James W. Bird, Jr., Morgan's, Madison.*
185 Daniel Wiggs, s. l. w., Moore's, Randolph.*
186 Lucy Hand, w., Hargrove's, Newton.
187 James Holland, 26th, Glynn.*
188 Henry Moffett, sol., Moffett's, Muscogee.*
189 Jesse George, Coffee's, Rabun.*
190 Matthew L. Hughs, Allen's, Bibb.*
191 Levi Mays, 138th, Greene.*
192 William Whitamore, or., 25th, Glynn.*
193 Joseph Session, Williams's, Washington.*
194 George W. Mercks, Jr., Price's, Hall.*
195 Julius Johnson, Canning's, Elbert.*
196 Darius Cox, sol., Brooks's, Muscogee.*
197 Robert N. Parrish, M'Craney's, Lowndes.*
198 (fr.) John Renfroe, Mann's, Crawford.
199 (fr.) Winefred Paine, w. r. s., Morris's, Crawford.
200 Isaac Holmes, Candler's, Bibb.
201 John Robinson, Valleau's, Chatham.*
202 Jesse Miller, r. s., Jordan's, Harris.
203 David L. Braxton, Griffin's, Burke.*
204 Thomas L. Thomas, Heard's, De Kalb.
205 Sherrod M'Carty, Bragaw's, Oglethorpe.*
206 Joseph Bishop, Woodruff's, Campbell.*
207 James Echols, Ware's, Coweta.*
208 Green H. Dukes, 295th, Jasper.
209 John Lovingood, 192d, Elbert.*
210 William Rowel, s. l. w., Harris's, Crawford.
211 Hartwell Lee, Mackleroy's, Clarke.
212 Matthew Hamler's ors., Watson's, Marion.
213 John Cox, Chiles's, Marion.
214 Samuel Carruthers, r. s., Tower's, Gwinnet.*
215 William B. Ballard, 70th, Burke.*
216 Joseph Sawyer, Will's, Twiggs.*
217 Spencer G. Spivey, Wood's, Jefferson.*
218 James A. Larouche, 1st, Chatham.*
219 Thomas Shockley, sol., 537th, Upson.
220 Margaret Buise, w. r. s., Hutson's, Newton.
221 Thomas Vessels, Colquhoun's, Henry.*
222 Johnson M. Houston, Nichols's, Fayette.
223 John Manning, Griffin's, De Kalb.*
224 Eli Garnett, sol., Graves's, Lincoln.
225 Avery Massey's or., Catlett's, Franklin.
226 George Ellis, Lawrence's, Pike.*
227 James G. Conner, sol., Edwards's, Montgomery.*
228 William R. Jordan, Collins's, Henry.*
229 David E. Strong, Williams's, Walton.*

230 Pleasant Perdee, Salem, Baldwin.*
231 William Deason, Bustin's, Pike.*
232 Pitt S. Milner, Covington's, Pike.*
233 Shepherd W. Riley, 735th, Troup.
234 (fr.) Simeon Lawhon, s. l. w., 470th, Upson.*
235 (fr.) William H. Ogilvie, Jenkins's, Oglethorpe.
236 Andrew Scott, sol., Peterson's, Burke.*
237 Francis Jenkins's ors., 364th, Jasper.
238 Barney Rowlins, Coker's, Troup.
239 Jeremiah Walker, Murphy's, Columbia.*
240 Joel W. Pope, 561st, Upson.*
241 William Sanders, Hanner's, Campbell.*
242 Alfred Burch, Wootten's, Telfair.*
243 Thomas Jackson, Mullen's, Carroll.
244 Prosser Horton, 245th, Jackson.
245 John Rutherford, r. s., Perry's, Baldwin.*
246 Lucy Mitchell, w., Gillis's, De Kalb.
247 James Joiner, Crow's, Pike.
248 Mason Walker, Wolfskin's, Oglethorpe.
249 Jefferson Mulkey, Bell's, Columbia.
250 John Averitt, Newman's, Thomas.
251 William Pugh, Roberts's, Hall.
252 Jacob Farmer, Brown's, Habersham.*
253 John Thompson, or., Hines's, Coweta.*
254 Archibald Ramay, Taylor's, Elbert.*
255 Benjamin Burrows, Jr., Valleau's, Chatham.*
256 Harman Adams, York's, Stewart.
257 Elijah Nash, M'Ginnis's, Jackson.
258 Mibzy Strickland, Belcher's, Jasper.
259 Charles Thompson, s. l. w., 559th, Walton.*
260 Stephen Felker, 419th, Walton.
261 Barney Spence, f. a., Loveless's, Gwinnett.*
262 Ebenezer B. Vernon, 561st, Upson.
263 Elizabeth Talbot, w., Morgan's, Clarke.*
264 Mary Taylor, w., 120th, Richmond.
265 John Fullwood, Sweat's, Ware.*
266 William Thomas, Willis's, Franklin.*
267 William W. Broxton, Griffin's, Burke.*
268 Susannah Wilson, w., 9th, Effingham.*
269 Sarah Bray, w., Martin's, Washington.*
270 (fr.) William F. Hudman, Mizell's, Talbot.
271 (fr.) John Starr, 122d, Richmond.
272 Riley Truett's ors., Wilson's, Jasper.*
273 William M'Carthur, Curry's, Wilkinson.*
274 Willis P. Baker, sol., Brooks's, Muscogee.*
275 James Sague, Cleland's, Chatham.
276 Samuel J. Lesaire, Benson's, Lincoln.*

277 John Rainey, 277th, Morgan.
278 Isaac Winship, Mays's, Monroe.
279 Moses Perkins, Gunn's, Jones.
280 Rewal Edwards, Loven's, Henry.*
281 William Arnold, Sanderlin's, Chatham.
282 John Bates, Griffin's, Fayette.
283 John B. Jackson, s. l. w., Atkinson's, Coweta.*
284 George Waller, Peavy's, Bulloch.*
285 William W. Smith, Smith's, Franklin.
286 Isaac W. Hicks, Allen's, Monroe.
287 Theophilus Moseley, Sutton's, Habersham.
288 Adolphus M. Sanford, Robinson's, Putnam.*
289 Caleb Bennett, Mitchell's, Marion.*
290 Joseph W. Griffith, 160th, Greene.
291 William May, Sen., Sparks's, Washington.*
292 Griffith Campbell, Willingham's, Harris.
293 Thomas Leansley, r. s., Ware's, Coweta.
294 Cealson Moreland, sol., 470th, Upson.*
295 A. Johnson's three orphans, Latimer's, De Kalb.*
296 Rowland Johnston, Daniel's, Hall.*
297 Ezekiel Brown, Edwards's, Talbot.*
298 David Megahee, Adams's, Columbia.
299 Robert Hardy, Young's, Wilkinson.
300 James A. Campbell, Wilson's, Pike.
301 James Kenly, Anderson's, Rabun.*
302 Robert H. Sherman, 118th, Hancock.*
303 John S. Strickland, Morgan's, Appling.*
304 Solomon Lockett, sol. 1784–97, Greer's, Warren.*
305 John M'Farland, 3d, Chatham.*
306 (fr.) Ezekiel Painter, Dobbs's, Hall.
307 (fr.) Jesse M. Pinkston, 113th, Hancock.
308 Eli Moore, Coffee's, Rabun.
309 Dempsey Whidden's ors., Barwick's, Washington.
310 Benjamin Bithel's or., 561st, Upson.*
311 Stephen W. Stephens, Allen's, Henry.*
312 Bayles Gills, sol., 318th, Baldwin.*
313 John M. Shelman, sol., Candler's, Bibb.*
314 Samuel Harvell, Hodges's, Newton.
315 Alonzo Scranton, Valleau's, Chatham.
316 Reuben Boatright, sol., 57th, Emanuel.*
317 John Winn, M'Ewin's, Monroe.*
318 Absolem Wallace, 245th, Jackson.*
319 Joseph Scalf, M. Brown's, Habersham.*
320 Joseph Yates, Goulding's, Lowndes.
321 John W. Williams, Maguire's, Gwinnett.
322 Philip R. Younge, 271st, M'Intosh.
323 Daniel Gregory, Curry's, Merriwether.*
324 Jonathan Fielding, Moseley's, Coweta.*

FOURTH DISTRICT, FOURTH SECTION, CHEROKEE

1 Wiley Roberts, Graves's, Lincoln.*
2 William Woodward, Dearing's, Henry.
3 Thomas J. Murdock, 73d, Burke.
4 Thomas J. Gilbert, 555th, Upson.
5 Joseph Moore's ors., Ballard's, Morgan.
6 William M'Clain, Royster's, Franklin.*
7 John M. Ruff, Dearing's, Henry.*
8 James Wade, Turner's, Crawford.*
9 Mary Ann Henderson, or., Thompson's, Henry.*
10 James G. Mayo, Hearn's, Butts.
11 Jeremiah Grisham, Jones's, Lincoln.
12 Jacob Moody, George's, Appling.
13 Milly Highsmith, w., Stower's, Elbert.
14 Matthew Cogger, Allison's, Pike.
15 Alexander W. Wiley, 271st, M'Intosh.*
16 Mark Jackson, sol., 147th, Greene.
17 Thompson Lawson's ors., Graves's, Putnam.*
18 John S. Lavender, Peace's, Wilkinson.
19 Francis Dyer, 4th, Chatham.*
20 John Peacock, sol., Mattox's, Lowndes.*
21 John M. Morgan, Clinton's, Campbell.
22 Hiram Patterson, Sutton's, Habersham.
23 Warren Carpenter, Thompson's, Henry.*
24 Elizabeth Haney, w. r. s., Wynn's, Gwinnett.*
25 Jesse Miller, Allen's, Campbell.
26 Richard Barker, Jennings's, Clarke.*
27 Abner Hammond's ors., 320th, Baldwin.
28 Joseph Lamy, Sewell's, Franklin.
29 Deborah Cook, w. r. s., Lightfoot's, Washington.
30 Hugh Montgomery, Morrison's, Montgomery.
31 Allen J. Mann, Hargrove's, Newton.
32 John M. Lucas, sol., 12th, Effingham.*
33 Reuben Wilks's ors., Groce's, Bibb.
34 Joel Warnack, Rhodes's, De Kalb.
35 John W. Germos, Allen's, Campbell.*
36 Josiah Houston, Jr., Nichols's, Fayette.
37 Emily Denton, w. r. s., Hart's, Jones.*
38 John Hunt's four orphans, 138th, Greene.
39 William Davidson, Sinclair's, Houston.*
40 David Sutley, Moore's, Randolph.*
41 James Robinson, 406th, Gwinnett.

42 Lewis S. Nobles, r. s., Peterson's, Montgomery.*
43 Sarah Glazier, w. r. s., Hampton's, Newton.
44 Henry Cook, M'Culler's, Newton.
45 Edmund W. Jackson, Thompson's, Henry.*
46 Enoch Callaway, 166th, Wilkes.*
47 Richard Footman's ois., 15th, Liberty.
48 William C. Hill, Few's, Muscogee.
49 John Sher d, York's, Stewart.
50 William M'Carra, 589th, Upson.
51 Larkin Barnett, Gittens's, Fayette.
52 James F. Gibson, Derrick's, Henry.*
53 Joseph Oliphant, Young's, Jefferson.*
54 Thomas Malone, Sen., Grubbs's, Columbia.
55 William Neely, Oliver's, Twiggs.*
56 Burdett Leach, r. s., Hammond's, Franklin.
57 Matthew Gilbert, Loven's, Henry.
58 John E. Gernigan, 107th, Hancock.
59 Martin Beliles, Hamilton's, Gwinnett.
60 Albert May, Howard's, Oglethorpe.
61 Josiah Nichols, Kellum's, Talbot.*
62 Mason S. Parker, Martin's, Washington.*
63 Hugh T. Whitemore, M. Brown's, Habersham.
64 Thomas Childress, Jr., Martin's, Newton.*
65 William Cook, Mackleroy's, Clarke.*
66 David Chambers, Pollard's, Wilkes.*
67 Warren Stow, Jr., White's, Franklin.
68 William Hightower, Candler's, Bibb.*
69 Charles W. Evans, Howell's, Troup.
70 Humphrey Hurt, sol., Loveless's, Gwinnett.*
71 Kimbro Standard, M'Ewin's, Monroe.*
72 John Cockram, Jones's, Hall.
73 James W. A. Blackstone, Culbreath's, Columbia.
74 John M. & Elizabeth Coley, f. a., Dobbs's, Hall.*
75 William Seals, Young's, Wilkinson.*
76 Robert Gray, Harris's, Columbia.*
77 Lindsay Holland, Mimms's, Fayette.
78 Lewis M. Brantley, Colley's, Madison.*
79 Benajah Hodges, Roe's, Burke.*
80 William G. Knight, Hendon's, Carroll.*
81 Lucinda Buzbin, w., Hargrove's, Oglethorpe.*
82 George Lamar, Chambers's, Gwinnett.
83 Washington P. Dunbar, Chambers's, Gwinnett.*
84 Sally Grissam, w. r. s., Trout's, Hall.*
85 Eli Parks, Phillip's, Monroe.
86 James Boggs's ors., 242d, Jackson.
87 William Hays, Few's, Muscogee.
88 Benjamin Tolbert, 319th, Baldwin.

89 William Cochran's ors., Brown's, Habersham.
90 Richard Hughs, Thomas's, Clarke.
91 Hezekiah Mack, Coker's, Troup.
92 Joysey Willis, w., Chambers's, Houston.
93 Mary Dickson, w. r. s., 80th, Scriven.
94 Jane Mosey, w., Sanderlin's, Chatham.*
95 John C. Lang, Dearing's, Henry.*
96 Matthew Phillips's ors., Stewart's, Troup.
97 George D. Anderson, Latimer's, De Kalb.
98 William H. Smith, Howard's, Oglethorpe.
99 Wyatt Voss, Dobbs's, Hall.
100 Chuch Allcock, Edwards's, Montgomery.*
101 Abraham Stow, 103d, Hancock.
102 Terrell Speed, Canning's, Elbert.
103 John B. Barton, 4th, Chatham.
104 John T. Blunt, Walker's, Columbia.
105 Levi Freeman, 295th, Jasper.*
106 John A. Newman, 6th, Chatham.*
107 John M'Donald, r. s., Riden's, Jackson.*
108 Solomon M. Phillips, Park's, Walton.*
109 Caswell Hopson, Tuggle's, Merriwether.*
110 Augustus B. Moore, Higginbotham's, Madison.*
111 Daniel R. Turner, Heard's, De Kalb.*
112 Elias R. Sarten, Rhodes's, Hall.*
113 William Trammell, Peek's, Columbia.*
114 George M'Clendon, sol., 365th, Jasper.*
115 Elijah C. Athens, Chambers's, Gwinnett.*
116 James O. Fitts, Nellum's, Elbert.*
117 Alexander Claghorn's ors., Trout's, Hall.
118 Jacob Fogle, 320th, Baldwin.*
119 John M. Clark, Taylor's, Putnam.*
120 William Mahoughn's ors., 320th, Baldwin.*
121 Dudley Mattox, Hamilton's, Gwinnett.*
122 Frederic Thompson, r. s., 249th, Walton.*
123 Sherwood Stroud, r. s., 249th, Walton.*
124 Joseph S. Chambers, Gittens's, Fayette.*
125 Jacob F. Caver, M'Gill's, Lincoln.
126 John Bankston, Jr., Chambers's, Gwinnett.
127 Charles Hutchings, Sullivan's, Jones.
128 Lucy Rogers, h. a., Bivins's, Jones.
129 Elcanah Rogers, Youngs's, Jefferson.
130 Isham Hammons, Alsobrook's, Jones.
131 Lewis Lancer, Jr., Summerlin's, Bulloch.*
132 Caleb M'Kinney, Sen., Rutland's, Bibb.
133 Richard G. Byars, Baley's, Butts.*
134 Lee Ann Ruddell, w. r. s., Moseley's, Wilkes.
135 Henry Booth, Canning's, Elbert.*

136 Thomas Cardwell, Hendon's, Carroll.*
137 Mary Griffith, w., Valleau's, Chatham.
138 Benjamin Jepson, Flynn's, Muscogee.
139 Hiram Fuller, Sapp's, Muscogee.
140 Thomas Humphrey, Barker's, Gwinnett.*
141 Henry Sturges's ors., Graves's, Lincoln.*
142 Archibald S. Wheatly, 168th, Wilkes.*
143 Ann M. Creamer, w., 2d, Chatham.
144 Nicholas Westmant, Smith's, Habersham.
145 James Vaughn, Oliver's, Twiggs.*
146 Thomas Hanner, Hanner's, Campbell.*
147 M'Grewder Bryan, 162d, Greene.
148 Stephen King, Wynn's, Gwinnett.*
149 James Coleman, Gittens's, Fayette.*
150 Richard Myrick, sol., Madden's, Pike.*
151 Silas Cason, Folsom's, Lowndes.*
152 John M. Baker, 537th, Upson.*
153 Mary Owen, w., Baismore's, Jones.
154 John F. Thompson, Lane's, Morgan.
155 Priscilla Nugent, w., 120th, Richmond.*
156 Henry J. B. Phillips, M'Gehee's, Troup.*
157 George Lumpkin, Sen., Blackstock's, Hall.
158 Benjamin Cook, sol., Silman's, Pike.
159 James King, s. i. w., Bailey's, Camden.
160 Gideon H. Burke, Talley's, Troup.
161 John Carroll, Lamberth's, Fayette.*
162 Patrick M'Swain, sol., Davis's, Jones.*
163 Davidport Corly, Craven's, Coweta.
164 Wiley J. Heflin, Smith's, Henry.*
165 Andrew M'Gill, Chambers's, Gwinnett.
166 John Wood, Daniel's, Hall.*
167 William Copeland, Henson's, Rabun.*
168 Leonard Phillips, Allen's, Campbell.
169 Uriah Slappy, Marshall's, Crawford.
170 Allen Pye's ors., Guice's, Oglethorpe.
171 Mary King, w. r. s., Phillips's, Talbot.
172 Eliza A. Taliaferro, w. r. s., Hinton's, Wilkes.
173 Obadiah M. Colbert, 561st, Upson.
174 Arthur Frasier's ors., Stokes's, Lincoln.*
175 John G. Turner's ors., 362d, Jasper.*
176 Samuel Wilkins, sol., Thompson's, Henry.*
177 Lazarus Jones, Wynn's, Gwinnett.*
178 Peyton R. Clements, Taylor's, Jones.*
179 John Wright's ors., Roe's, Burke.*
180 Oliver M. Porter, 137th, Greene.
181 Samuel W. Settles, Britt's, Randolph.*
182 Geraldus King, Young's, Jefferson.*

42

183 Jacob Reid, 177th, Wilkes.*
184 Vincent Davis, Downs's, Warren.*
185 Arthur C. Foil, Alexander's, Jefferson.*
186 Ananias Westbrooks, Lamberth's, Fayette.*
187 Harriet Brock, or., Whelchel's, Hall.
188 John C. P. Kenemore, 672d, Harris.
189 Eli Carlisle, 535th, Dooly.*
190 Henry B. Bailey, Guice's, Oglethorpe.
191 Alexander Mackey, 398th, Richmond.*
192 Dickson Chesnut, Jones's, Thomas.
193 Nancy Denham, w., Pace's, Putnam.
194 James Smith, Whelchel's, Hall.
195 Abden Bradley, Smith's, Madison.*
196 John Low, 398th, Richmond.
197 Gideon V. Holmes, sol., Whitehead's, Habersham
198 William Florence, M'Millon's, Lincoln.
199 Simeon Edwards, Baley's, Butts.
200 William Brazel, Coxe's, Talbot.
201 William A. Black, 10th, Effingham.*
202 George G. Smith, Newsom's, Warren.
203 Harriet White, or., Evans's, Laurens.
204 Moses Brooks, Baugh's, Jackson.
205 Elias M. Countryman, Sutton's, Habersham.
206 Edward Kidd, 69th, Burke.
207 Ellinnor Wilkins, w., Stanfield's, Campbell.
208 Mary Garner, w., Collier's, Monroe.
209 Isaac Carter, Coward's, Lowndes.
210 Lucy Haterway, Allen's, Campbell.*
211 Williamson S. Mercer, Phillips's, Jasper.
212 David Bray, Bower's, Elbert.*
213 William Lancaster, 735th, Troup.*
214 Bernard M. Campbell, Pierce's, Houston.*
215 Selha Moore, w., Night's, Morgan.*
216 Godwin Solomon, Fryer's, Telfair.*
217 William Mooneyham, Taylor's, Putnam.*
218 Joseph Rucker, or., Thomason's, Elbert.*
219 Applin Worsham, Rooks's, Putnam.*
220 Obedience Bass, w., Parham's, Warren.*
221 William P. Truitt, Nesbit's, Newton.*
222 Henry T. Anderson, 318th, Baldwin.
223 Polly Howard, 365th, Jasper.*
224 Charles E. Atkins, Mizell's, Talbot.*
225 James Modeset, Bivens's, Jones.
226 Grief Felton, Burgess's, Carroll.*
227 William C. Whaley, Harralson's, Troup.*
228 Lawrence Jenkins, Will's, Twiggs.*
229 Glass's five orphans, 559th, Walton.

230 William Harris, Haygood's, Washington.
231 Eliza Greene, w., Bush's, Burke.*
232 Peter J. Bagget, Jones's, Thomas.
233 Miles F. Gathwright, Dyer's, Habersham.*
234 John Daniel, Justice's, Bibb.*
235 Moses Wheat, s. l. w., 470th, Upson.*
236 Sebourn Pickett, Holt's, Talbot.
237 William Phillips, Thaxton's, Butts.*
238 James Bell, Morgan's, Madison.
239 John Wright, sol., Graves's, Lincoln.
240 James Bridges, Gunn's, Henry.*
241 John S. Simpson, Johnson's, De Kalb.*
242 Robert Jennings, Jennings's, Clarke.
243 James Griner's ors., Slater's, Bulloch.
244 John Tuggle, Jr., Trout's, Hall.*
245 Joseph H. Lee, Candler's, Bibb.
246 Hezekiah Lamb, or., Watson's, Marion.*
247 William D. Smith, 672d, Harris.*
248 Elijah Griffin, Willis's, Franklin.*
249 Daniel Sparrow's or., Wheeler's, Pulaski.*
250 John Jordan, Jordan's, Harris.*
251 Sarah Paty, w., Gillis's, De Kalb.*
252 James V. Reddin, Cockspur Island, Chatham.*
253 Harrison Gipson, Beasley's, Oglethorpe.
254 John Nablet, Dyer's, Habersham.*
255 Mary Spence, w. r. s., 74th, Burke.*
256 James L. Green, Athens, Clarke.*
257 John M'Killgon, Anderson's, Wilkes.*
258 Charles G. Johnson, Oliver's, Twiggs.*
259 Luke Ross, Candler's, Bibb.
260 Charlotte Herndon, w., Martin's, Washington.*
261 Silas Scarborough, 59th, Emanuel.*
262 Benjamin Powell Gwinnett, Park's, Walton.
263 Elizabeth Hicks, h. a., Rainey's, Twiggs.
264 Samuel R. Anderson, Athens, Clarke.
265 Neal R. Wilkinson, 656th, Troup.
266 George Duncan, Davis's, Jones.*
267 Dawson Bailey, sol., Strickland's, Merriwether.
268 Joel H. Casper, Barker's, Gwinnett.
269 Murdock Shaw, Martin's, Pike.*
270 Nathaniel May, Varner's, Merriwether.*
271 Archibald M'Kinnon, Wilcox's, Telfair.*
272 T. Adams's ors., Walker's, Columbia.*
273 Willias Champin, Griffin's, Fayette.*
274 Elzey Thompson, Hobbs's, Laurens.
275 Dr. John Carter, 120th, Richmond.
276 Solomon Dobbs, Chandler's, Franklin.

277 John Barnett, s. l. w., 693d, Heard.
278 Lazarus G. Howel, Lynn's, Warren.*
279 Nathan Jones, Peavy's, Bulloch.*
280 Moses Chapman, Martin's, Pike.*
281 Webb's orphans, Coker's, Troup.*
282 John Allison, Bower's, Elbert.*
283 Daniel Spraggins, Moseley's, Coweta.*
284 James Sumervill, Welche's, Habersham.*
285 John B. Brazelton, 248th, Jackson.*
286 Simeon Taylor, Brewer's, Monroe.*
287 Washington Baker, Hobbs's, Laurens.*
288 Wright Willis, Bush's, Pulaski.*
289 Jabez Wilkins's two ors., Latimer's, De Kalb.*
290 James M. Turner, M'Korkle's, Jasper.*
291 John Marshal's ors., 289th, Jasper.
292 Isaac Gardner, Dean's, Clarke.*
293 Alfred Hodges's ors., Holt's, Pulaski.*
294 Green Hamby, d. & d., Reid's, Gwinnett.*
295 Polly Shoffut's children, Chastain's, Habersham.*
296 James Rackley, Hatton's, Baker.*
297 John Richards, Whitehead's, Habersham.*
298 Martha Brantley, w., Robertson's, Telfair.*
299 Joel M. Bryan, Tower's, Gwinnett.*
300 John B. Ayres, sol., Griffin's, De Kalb.*
301 Elizabeth R. Jones, w., Smith's, Henry.*
302 William Cone, sol., 140th, Greene.*
303 John P. Hamilton, s. l. w., Lay's, Jackson.*
304 E. Thomas's orphans, 72d, Burke.*
305 Elizabeth H. Morris, w., Walker's, Columbia.*
306 James Smith, r. s., c. r., Guice's, Oglethorpe.
307 James Walker, Brown's, Camden.
308 Absolem S. Smith, Morrison's, Appling.*
309 Reubin Earley, Burgess's, Carroll.*
310 Michael Pilgrim, sol., Field's, Habersham.*
311 Thomas Newman, r. s., 121st, Richmond.*
312 Sampson Black, Burnett's, Habersham.*
313 Elizabeth Greene, w. s. i. w., Bailey's, Laurens.*
314 Jesse Snellgrove, sol.. 574th, Early.*
315 Elizabeth Wood, h. a., Woodruff's, Campbell.*
316 Robert Thompson, Holton's, Emanuel.*
317 Andrew Nelson, Price's, Hall.*
318 Thomas Bowman, Sen., 249th, Walton.
319 William White, Givins's, De Kalb.*
320 Cordy Drake, House's, Henry.*
321 James Skaggs, Chesnut's, Newton.*
322 Jacob W. Miller, Perryman's, Warren.*
323 Josiah P. Ellington, Blackshear's, Laurens.
324 Oliver T. Hockell, Vale's, Campbell.*

FIFTH DISTRICT, FOURTH SECTION, CHEROKEE.

1 Thornton Sims, Mobley's, De Kalb.*
2 William E. Akin, Collier's, Monroe.*
3 Michael Higgins, Foote's, De Kalb.*
4 Robert Carnine's ors., 243d, Jackson.*
5 M. C. & N. Doolittle, f. a., Jennings's, Clarke.*
6 George Kellum, r. s., Kellum's, Talbot.
7 John D. White, 118th, Hancock.
8 Whitlock Arnold, Field's, Habersham.*
9 James S. King, Colquhoun's, Henry.*
10 John Wright's ors., Marshall's, Putnam.
11 Willey S. Armstrong, Davis's, Jones.*
12 Mark Evans, Seay's, Hall.*
13 Heddy's two orphans, Ellis's, Rabun.*
14 Robert R. Holland, Huey's, Harris.*
15 Levi Blesard, Everett's, Washington.*
16 Memory Crump, Smith's, Franklin.
17 Isaac C. Butterworth, Price's, Hall.
18 Joseph L. Brooker, 26th, Glynn.*
19 Joseph Camp, Allen's, Henry.
20 Birde Yarewood, Whitehead's, Habersham.
21 Charles Brantly, 510th, Early.
22 John Heard, Hearn's, Butts.*
23 John Thweatt, Sen., 484th, Upson.*
24 Thomas F. M'Gehee, Greer's, Merriwether.
25 Daniel H. Bryson, Jones's, Habersham.*
26 John F. Redding, Groover's, Thomas.
27 Abraham Guidians, Lyman's, Pulaski.
28 John Goldsmith, s. i. w., Atkinson's, Coweta.
29 George Hammond, 406th, Gwinnett.
30 Martha Lewis, w., 108th, Hancock.
31 William Tidwell, Garner's, Coweta.
32 Samuel T. Loggins, Hamilton's, Hall.*
33 Ivy Hill, Belcher's, Jasper.
34 Albert M. Wingfield, 143d, Greene.*
35 Leroy M. Wilson, Wilson's, Jasper.*
36 Felix T. Williams, Lawrence's, Pike.*
37 Tucker Mouldin, Oliver's, Twiggs.
38 Joseph Watson, Candler's, Bibb.*
39 Elmore Carter, Edwards's, Montgomery.
40 Benjamin Gardner, 72d, Burke.*
41 Jesse White, 779th, Heard.*

42 Esther Ann Wilmoth, or., Clark's, Elbert.
43 Patrick Harris, s. l. w., 307th, Putnam.
44 William Flanagan, r. s., Martin's, Hall.
45 Thomas Satterwhite, s. i. w., 419th, Walton.
46 Edward Lamberth, sol., Lamberth's, Fayette.*
47 Presly Yates, Burnett's, Habersham.
48 E. C. Johnson, w. s. 1784–97, Latimer's, De Kalb*
49 James Griffin, Griffin's, Emanuel.*
50 Richard Banks, Clark's, Elbert.
51 Malcom Mathewson, sol., Burk's, Stewart.
52 Magdalane Blois, w., Cleland's, Chatham.
53 William Martin, 494th, Upson.
54 Charles W. Hearn, 735th, Troup.*
55 John Haddock, 318th, Baldwin.*
56 John A. Smith, or., 555th, Upson.
57 Ezekiel Johnson, Pounds's, Twiggs.*
58 Henry Hayman, r. s., Blair's, Lowndes.*
59 Aaron Turner, Sen., Thompson's, Henry.*
60 Samuel Nichols, Roberts's, Hall.
61 Richard P. Sasnett, 118th, Hancock.
62 Henry Swinney, Bishop's, Henry.
63 Benjamin H. Denson, Gittens's, Fayette.
64 William T. King, 277th, Morgan.*
65 Jason Tomlin, Shattox's, Coweta.
66 Alexander Leggett's ors., Brewer's, Monroe.
67 William J. Ronaldson, 756th, Sumter.
68 Benjamin Joiner, r. s., Covington's, Pike.
69 William Marable, Hall's, Oglethorpe.*
70 Charles Gee's ors., Pounds's, Twiggs.
71 William James,* Edwards's, Franklin.
72 Mary M'Cowen, w., Jordan's, Harris.
73 William Ellison, Hughes's, Habersham.
74 Georgianna Stokes, or., Williams's, Washington.
75 William Byng, Edwards's, Franklin.*
76 Richard Guinn, M'Culler's, Newton.*
77 Samuel Miller, sol., Mitchell's, Pulaski.*
78 John G. Fry, Atkinson's, Coweta.*
79 John L. Park, 788th, Heard.
80 Jonathan C. Fentress, 113th, Hancock.
81 Richard Methune, sol., Mashburn's, Pulaski.
82 Benjamin Shiny, Robison's, Washington.*
83 John B. Bussey, Collier's, Monroe.*
84 Celia Stringer, w. r. s., Peterson's, Burke.
85 Rosanna Johnson, w. r. s., Harris's, De Kalb.
86 William Lackey, Jr., Williams's, Walton.
87 John H. Smith, Ware's, Coweta.*
    a See Executive Order of 11th July, 1833.

88 John Cubbedge, 4th, Chatham.*
89 Henry Bennett, Morgan's, Appling.
90 James M. Bridges, Bridges's, Gwinnett.
91 Richard Gregory, Marsh's, Thomas.
92 James W. Burdett, 175th, Wilkes.*
93 John Seal, Polhill's, Burke.*
94 Odean Castleberry, Sen., Herndon's, Hall.*
95 Joseph Roderick, 516th, Dooly.*
96 Seth P. Pool, M'Ewin's, Monroe.*
97 Littleton Spivey, sol., Chambers's, Houston.
98 William Morgan, Jones's, Madison.
99 Albert Roberts, Sanderlin's, Chatham.*
100 Joseph Byers, Stephens's, Habersham.*
101 Morgan Christian, Hatton's, Baker.*
102 Robert Alexander, sol., 1st section, Cherokee.*
103 Jane Flood, w. r. s., Allen's, Henry.
104 Samuel Henderson's or., Orr's, Jackson.
105 J. Jordan, Seas's, Madison.
106 Balus H. Staten, Dobbs's, Hall.
107 Nicholas P. Gunn, s. l. w., 588th, Upson.
108 Samuel T. Loggins, Hamilton's, Hall.*
109 Littleberry Edwards's ors., Derrick's, Henry.
110 John O'Brian, 1st, Chatham.
111 Jesse Rawls, Sinclair's, Houston.
112 John J. Tanner, 250th, Walton.*
113 Dudley M. Jones, Jones's, Madison.
114 Jeremiah S. Davis, Griffin's, De Kalb.*
115 Charles Haddock, Barrow's, Houston.*
116 Robert Biggins, Foote's, De Kalb.*
117 John Harrell, Bostick's, Twiggs.
118 Thomas Folk, Blackshear's, Laurens.*
119 Elizabeth Albritton, Williams's, Washington.*
120 Joseph Park, 166th, Greene.
121 Thomas Cobbett, r. s., Clark's, Elbert.*
122 David O. Morgan, 785th, Sumter.*
123 John Coffee's or., Keener's, Rabun.
124 Harrison Arnold, Wynn's, Gwinnett.
125 John Moreland, Ellsworth's, Bibb.*
126 Nancy Irwin, w., Peacock's, Washington.*
127 John Stephen Kelly, minor, Leverett's, Lincoln.*
128 Phebe Park, w. r. s., 161st, Greene.
129 Ebenezer Harris, 334th, Wayne.*
130 Kader Fairchild's or., Gibson's, Decatur.*
131 James Arnold's ors., Clark's, Elbert.*
132 Reuben Brock, M. Brown's, Habersham.*
133 Thomas B. Clayton, Covington's, Pike.
134 William W. Lanier, Tuggle's, Merriwether.

135 John S. Walker, Comer's, Jones.*
136 John L. Richardson, Allen's, Campbell.
137 Thomas Hampton, Peterson's, Montgomery.*
138 Sebourn Pate, Griffin's, Fayette.*
139 Anderson Dabney's 3 ors., Johnson's, De Kalb.*
140 John F. Hillyer, 419th, Walton.
141 Thomas Harris, 161st, Greene.*
142 Isaac Johnson's ors., Peacock's, Washington.
143 John Chapman, Smith's, Liberty.
144 William H. Wilson, Head's, Butts.
145 Elijah Dean, sol., Chambers's, Houston.
146 Newman Matthews, Sen., M'Donald's, Lincoln.*
147 Robin & William Barton, ors., Watson's, Marion.*
148 Samuel Smith, sol., 756th, Sumter.*
149 Aulsey A. Vincent, Latimer's, De Kalb.*
150 John Norman, Sen., r. s., Hinton's, Wilkes.*
151 Mary Nixon, w., Dearing's, Butts.*
152 Cheely's four orphans, 114th, Hancock.
153 James Hope, Jones's, Hall.*
154 Nathaniel B. Mercer, Linam's, Pulaski.*
155 James V. Brown, Collier's, Monroe.*
156 Daniel Aycock's ors., Mizell's, Fayette.
157 Henry F. Harden, Silman's, Pike.*
158 William F. Stevy, Jr., Craven's, Coweta.
159 Isaac Sewell, Night's, Morgan.
160 Mary Ann Broughton, or., Baley's, Butts.
161 Augustus D. Statham, Fulks's, Wilkes.
162 Josiah Beall, 561st, Upson.
163 Isaac T. Head, Talley's, Troup.
164 James H. Davidson, Say's, De Kalb.
165 Washington Mark, Calhoun's, Harris.
166 William Dunham, 1st, Chatham.
167 Elias Walker, Williams's, Ware.*
168 Jesse Lecroy, Sen., Brackett's, Newton.*
169 John W. Jordan, 601st, Taliaferro.*
170 Tilmon S. Hood, Orr's, Jackson.
171 William Brownjohn, sol., 1st, Chatham.*
172 Graves's children, f. in p., Valleau's, Chatham.
173 Emanuel J. Brumbeloe, 555th, Upson.
174 David Bird, 113th, Hancock.*
175 Daniel Bartlett, 574th, Early.
176 Edward O'Conner, 600th, Richmond.*
177 Osburn Reeves, Griffin's, Hall.
178 Henry Fitzsimmons, Chambers's, Gwinnett.*
179 Thomas H. Wamack, 35th, Scriven.*
180 Thomas Langston, Holley's, Franklin.*
181 Thomas R. Smilie, 34th, Scriven.*

182 Justian M'Kinney, w., Monk's, Crawford.*
183 William Crews, Perry's, Habersham.*
184 Eliza Ryal's ors., Everett's, Washington.
185 Mary Jernigan, w. r. s., 106th, Hancock.*
186 William Hester, sol., Polhill's, Burke.*
187 William T. Rutledge, Givins's, De Kalb.*
188 Hannah Holland, w., Allison's, Pike.*
189 Abel Gower, r. s., Reed's, Gwinnett.*
190 Richard A. Hall, Durham's, Talbot.*
191 Green B. Williamson, Sanders's, Jones.
192 William Vicey, s. i. w., Woodruff's, Campbell.
193 Robert Killewbrew's ors., Rooks's, Putnam.
194 William H. Avrea, Gittens's, Fayette.*
195 Alfred Tilly, Keener's, Rabun.
196 Wiley Hutchins, 243d, Jackson.*
197 Thomas Gorley, sol., 116th, Hancock.
198 Silas M. Johnson, 608th, Taliaferro.*
199 Peter Wiggins, sol., Brown's, Camden.*
200 Susannah Saire, w., 602d, Taliaferro.
201 Elijah Clark, M'Culler's, Newton.*
202 Mark M. Fleming, Edwards's, Talbot.*
203 Seaborn Nally, Brown's, Habersham.*
204 John Tait, Hughes's, Habersham.
205 Daniel Davis, ———, Montgomery.*
206 Sarah Dougle, w., Wynn's, Gwinnett.*
207 James J. Dickson, Goodwin's, Houston.
208 Martha A. J. Curtis, or., Greer's, Oglethorpe.*
209 Samuel F. Alexander, Chambers's, Gwinnett.*
210 James H. Williamson, Nichols's, Fayette.*
211 Ransom Foster, Jones's, Hall.*
212 James R. King, Daniel's, Hall.*
213 Polly Boggs, w., Hendon's, Carroll.*
214 William Hicks, Walker's, Harris.*
215 Benjamin Watson, Perryman's, Warren.
216 William D. Harrill, Williams's, Decatur.*
217 John D. Wilks, 640th, Dooly.*
218 William Williams, Jones's, Madison.*
219 William Chapman, Phillips's, Jasper.*
220 Benjamin Thompson, r. s., 113th, Hancock.*
221 William Baker, M'Millon's, Lincoln.*
222 Martha Night, h. a., Crow's, Pike.*
223 Elizabeth Boatwright, w., Moseley's, Coweta.
224 Phebe Park, w., 161st, Greene.
225 Hiram Favor, M'Clendon's, Putnam.
226 Robert Cox, Tower's, Gwinnett.
227 Jeremiah Williams, or., 606th, Taliaferro.
228 Sarah H. Ash's ors., Sanderlin's, Chatham.

229 Caswell Branan, Mayo's, Wilkinson.*
230 Martha Wimberly, or., Gunn's, Jefferson.
231 Elizabeth M'Daniel, w. r. s., Gunn's, Jones.*
232 Alexander L. Carruth, Higginbotham's, Madison.
233 Josiah Horn's ors., Hobbs's, Laurens.
234 Lewis Shepherd, Garner's, Washington.*
235 Abraham Massey, Sullivan's, Jones.
236 William Catching, Gray's, Henry.*
237 Riley Findley, sol., M'Korkle's, Jasper.*
238 Henry Evans, Shattox's, Coweta.*
239 Zilpha Bray, h. a., Mimms's, Fayette.
240 Ledia Rousseau, w., Kendrick's, Putnam.*
241 Clenoth Callaway, 165th, Wilkes.*
242 Miles Ellis, Liddell's, Jackson.*
243 Urill Crosby, r. s., Lunceford's, Wilkes.
244 James Pearce, Griffin's, De Kalb.
245 Simpson Montgomery, 785th, Sumter.*
246 Joseph Allen, 602d, Taliaferro.*
247 William Aldrige, r. s., Norman's, Wilkes.*
248 Asher Lane, Hinton's, Wilkes.*
249 George M. Weekley, or., Edwards's, Talbot.*
250 Hezekiah Beall, Grubbs's, Columbia.*
251 Samuel H. Watson's ors., 454th, Walton.*
252 David Pursell, Bragaw's, Oglethorpe.*
253 Thomas Shaw, 406th, Gwinnett.*
254 Asa Reeves, Curry's, Merriwether.
255 Gideon H. Allen, Alberson's, Walton.
256 Young Wilkinson, Winter's, Jones.*
257 John A. D. Childress, Mobley's, De Kalb.*
258 Jesse Williams, s. l. w., Fulks's, Wilkes.*
259 Phillip Lanier, 516th, Dooly.*
260 Wily W. Goss, 406th, Gwinnett.*
261 Thomas G. Lang, Stanfield's, Campbell.*
262 John Jenkins, 34th, Scriven.*
263 Celia Lewis, w. r. s., 406th, Gwinnett.*
264 Benjamin Harrison, Hearn's, Butts.*
265 William D. Whitehead, Buck's, Houston.
266 Sampson Wiggins's five ors., Morton's, De Kalb.
267 John Richard, Sen., Whisenhunt's, Carroll.*
268 George Kenox, 119th, Richmond.*
269 Newson Harper, Cleveland's, Habersham.*
270 Richard Conine, Jr., 307th, Putnam.
271 Mary and John Rozar, ors., 34th, M'Intosh.
272 William Tary, Chastain's, Habersham.
273 Bazil M. Davis, Hill's, Harris.
274 Edwin Dasher, 11th, Effingham.*
275 John Philan, 120th, Richmond.
276 Jonathan Brook, Beasley's, Oglethorpe.*

277 Zubulon P. Gathright, Riden's, Jackson.*
278 Nathan Moore, Anderson's, Rabun.*
279 Benjamin H. Guine, Kelly's, Jasper.*
280 James Calhoun's ors., Braddy's, Jones.
281 Reuben Newcomb, 3d, Chatham.*
282 John Morgan, Morgan's, Madison.*
283 Winny Verdin, w. r. s., Goodwin's, Houston.*
284 John Kent, r. s., Bostick's, Twiggs.*
285 Reuben Cumbo, Tuggle's, Merriwether.*
286 Henry Born, id., 415th, Walton.*
287 Carey Jones, 404th, Gwinnett.
288 John Crouch, Jr., Dawson's, Jasper.
289 Nathan Bird, Price's, Hall.
290 Joseph Brawner, Sen., s. i. w., Howell's, Elbert.
291 Zachariah Carpenter, Thompson's, Henry.*
292 Jarrat Weaver, Thaxton's, Butts.*
293 James Holden, Brock's, Habersham.
294 Newton Sims, 249th, Walton.*
295 John Hickman, r. s., Kendrick's, Monroe.*
296 John Lay, 2d section, Cherokee.*
297 Josiah Jackson, Streetman's, Twiggs.*
298 Henry W. Anderson, Walden's, Pulaski.*
299 Allen J. Jackson, 146th, Greene.
300 James Harrison, 672d, Harris.*
301 William Spier, 10th, Effingham.*
302 Peter Brown's ors., M'Clendon's, Putnam.
303 Jesse M. Roberts, Camp's, Warren.*
304 Anthony Seal, r. s., Huey's, Harris.*
305 William Lunsford, M'Clure's, Rabun.
306 Charles Varner, Harris's, De Kalb.*
307 Lewis Barton, sol., Sutton's, Habersham.*
308 David Caldwell, Strickland's, Merriwether.*
309 Bloomer White, 374th, Putnam.
310 Jesse Lovel, M'Clure's, Rabun.
311 Margaret Morel, w., Valleau's, Chatham.
312 William Hicks, Garner's, Washington.*
313 Matthew Merit, Dixon's, Irwin.*
314 Mekins Huff, Curry's, Merriwether.*
315 William Atkins, Wynn's, Gwinnett.*
316 James Sharpe, Heymes's, Chatham.*
317 Richard H. M. Swan, Butts's, Monroe.*
318 James R. Carlton, Athens, Clarke.
319 Elizabeth Hanson, w., Nesbit's, Newton.*
320 Wily Hood, Hughes's, Habersham.*
321 Richard Adams, Morgan's, Clarke.*
322 Daniel Greene, r. s., Green's, Ware.
323 Francis F. Lewis, 102d, Hancock.
324 Thomas S. Holt, M'Gehee's, Troup.

SIXTH DISTRICT, FOURTH SECTION, CHEROKEE.

1 Joel Edwards, 373d, Jasper.*
2 William Burgamy, Sen., Garner's, Washington.*
3 John Little, Clifton's, Tatnall.*
4 Alexander Freeman, Hill's, Monroe.*
5 Redford B. Giles, 279th, Morgan.*
6 Charles Smith, 3d section, Cherokee.*
7 Seaborn J. Herron, Chastain's, Habersham.*
8 John Wood, 373d, Jasper.*
9 Stognor Harris, Hand's, Appling.
10 John Batchelor, Miller's, Jasper.*
11 William Wiggins, M'Culler's, Newton.*
12 Seaborn Summers, Mackleroy's, Clarke.*
13 Benj. C. Wafford, minor, Sutton's, Habersham.*
14 Isaac St. John, Hutson's, Newton.*
15 Aaron T. Fields, or., Brown's, Habersham.*
16 David E. Twiggs, sol., 123d, Richmond.*
17 Archibald Gaddis, Sen., Chastain's, Habersham.*
18 Malcolm Buies's ors., Killen's, Decatur.*
19 Rachel Leavitt, or., Johnson's, De Kalb.*
20 Middle Thompson, Morgan's, Clarke.*
21 William Cooper, Peterson's, Burke.*
22 John Bennett, Sanderlin's, Chatham.*
23 Hamilton Raiford, 600th, Richmond.*
24 Christopher Franklin, 271st, M'Intosh.*
25 Larkin G. Hubbard, Beasley's, Oglethorpe.*
26 Benj. and John Barnett, ors., 119th, Richmond.*
27 William Pearce's ors., Harris's, Columbia.
28 James Morgan, Davis's, Franklin.*
29 Josiah H. Duke, Greer's, Merriwether.*
30 Beverly L. Culbreath, sol., Sealey's, Talbot.*
31 Isom Moore, Monk's, Crawford.*
32 William Bates, Griffin's, Fayette.
33 William S. Johnson, 279th, Morgan.*
34 Jacob Pitman, Clifton's, Tatnall.*
35 Thomas Doggett, Allen's, Campbell.*
36 Charles Strozier, sol., Ross's, Monroe.*
37 William Edmondson, sol., 138th, Greene.*
38 John Henderson, Chambers's, Houston.*
39 John Kirk, sol., Reid's, Gwinnett.*
40 Mary & Louisa Williams, ors., 271st, M'Intosh.*
41 Stephen Tarver, sol., Williams's, Washington.*

42 Henry Graham, Morgan's, Madison.*
43 Matthew Holland, or., 35th, Scriven.
44 James Linton, Will's, Twiggs.
45 William Fears, 294th, Jasper.*
46 Robert Howe, 334th, Wayne.*
47 Charles Evans, 35th, Scriven.*
48 Polly Oxford, f. a., Stewart's, Troup.
49 John M'Dade, r. s., Reid's, Gwinnett.*
50 Hampton Liles, Bostick's, Twiggs.*
51 Thomas Stubbs, Allen's, Henry.*
52 Lemuel M'Michell, sol., Flynn's, Muscogee.*
53 Sabra Agerton, w., Roberts's, Hall.*
54 Benj. Marshall, Mizell's, Talbot.*
55 Joseph Gouge, Sen., Barker's, Gwinnett.*
56 Isaac Brinson's ors., Gunn's, Jefferson.*
57 Isaac Welden, Gunn's, Henry.*
58 Robert Tate, Herndon's, Hall.*
59 Cyprian Mayo,ᵃ sol., Peace's, Wilkinson.*
60 Shimmy Black, 374th, Putnam.*
61 M. Buller's ors., Welche's, Habersham.*
62 James White, Varner's, Merriwether.*
63 John P. Duke's ors., Coxe's, Morgan.
64 Stanton Porter's ors., Dozier's, Columbia.*
65 Sherrod Peacock, Curry's, Wilkinson.*
66 Elijah Pittard, Buck-branch, Clarke.*
67 William Edwards's ors., 693d, Heard.
68 John C. M'Beth, Silman's, Pike.
69 Samuel Carruthers, 71st, Burke.*
70 Kissa Henry, w., 672d, Harris.
71 George M. Paine, 108th, Hancock.*
72 George Montzingo, Goodwin's, Houston.*
73 John Robertson, Coxe's, Talbot.
74 James P. Thompson, 36th, Scriven.
75 Sarah Woodcock, w., Peavy's, Bulloch.*
76 Garland Coldwell, Merck's, Hall.*
77 Joseph E. Davis, 142d, Greene.
78 Philo Smith, Mullen's, Carroll.*
79 Jane Reynolds, w., Britt's, Randolph.*
80 Samuel Black, Hutson's, Newton.
81 Bryan Newell, Curry's, Merriwether.*
82 Christopher Vicky, Herndon's, Hall.*
83 John Kimball, 2d section, Cherokee.*
84 John S. Taylor, Johnson's, Bibb.*
85 William Pace, sol., Collins's, Henry.*
86 David Langley, 404th, Gwinnett.*
87 Samuel C. Bennett, Barker's, Gwinnett.*

a See Executive Order.

88 Allen Tower, Polhill's, Burke.*
89 Amos Rhan, Holton's, Emanuel.*
90 Elias Bryan, sol., Goodwin's, Houston.*
91 Mark Anthony, s. l. w., Benson's, Lincoln.*
92 Charles Dodson, Belcher's, Jasper.
93 George Eubanks, Sen., r. s., Dearing's, Butts.*
94 Standly Jones's ors., Clarke's, Elbert.
95 Millington S. Johnson, 118th, Hancock.*
96 Simeon Whatly, Hodges's, Newton.*
97 Peter M'Intyre, 334th, Wayne.*
98 Alexander Bearfield, M'Clain's, Newton.*
99 Francis Smith, 510th, Early.*
100 Arnold Johnson's ors., Thaxton's, Butts.
101 Emanuel Roberson's widow, Cleland's, Chatham.*
102 John S. Collins, Brackett's, Newton.*
103 Lodwick P. Alford, Talley's, Troup.*
104 Joseph Adams Eve, 398th, Richmond.*
105 William Slaughter, 537th, Upson.*
106 Thomas Jones, Wynn's, Gwinnett.
107 Samuel Morris, or., Hargrove's, Oglethorpe.*
108 William Mitchell, Jr., Willis's, Franklin.*
109 Samuel Henderson, Allen's, Henry.*
110 Philip Johnson, Jr., Seay's, Hall.*
111 Elias G. Gower, Williams's, Decatur.*
112 John J. Fox, Sims's, Troup.*
113 William Wilder, 34th, Scriven.*
114 William Graham, son of Neil, Wilcox's, Telfair.*
115 Bennett Candle, Sutton's, Habersham.*
116 Moses W. Liddell, Tower's, Gwinnett.*
117 Mary Phillips, w. r. s., Sam Streetman's, Twiggs*
118 Hannah Carry, w., Smith's, Madison.*
119 Richard King, Kendrick's, Monroe.*
120 David Smith, Lyner's, Warren.*
121 Isham Daniel, 693d, Heard.*
122 John C. Price, Whisenhunt's, Carroll.*
123 Pheraby Newman, w., Stewart's, Warren.*
124 T. Duke's ors., 70th, Burke.
125 John Hays, 415th, Walton.
126 Abraham Seabolt, Hughes's, Habersham.*
127 John M'Donald, Winter's, Jones.
128 Sherwood Holcomb, Welche's, Habersham.
129 William Dee, 320th, Baldwin.*
130 Thomas G. Crawford, Keener's, Rabun.*
131 Thomas J. Bryce, Whisenhunt's, Carroll.
132 William Cleming's ors., Baismore's, Jones.
133 William G. Jennings, Greer's, Oglethorpe.
134 Dennis Durden, 59th, Emanuel.

135 John W. Jackson, Stewart's, Warren.*
136 Ezekiel O. Guin, Walker's, Houston.*
137 Reece Watkins, White's, Franklin.
138 Annaorna Hill, w., 249th, Walton.*
139 Solomon Williams, r. s., Rick's, Laurens.*
140 Wiley Hood, Haygood's, Washington.*
141 Thomas Dyall, Williams's, Ware.*
142 John Brutenbough, 600th, Richmond.*
143 Willey P. Bush, Greer's, Merriwether.*
144 James N. Bethune, 320th, Baldwin.
145 Shem Thompson, Allison's, Pike.*
146 Nicholas Sewell, Edwards's, Franklin.*
147 Alfred Franklin, M'Clendon's, Putnam.*
148 Thomas Turner, Morrison's, Appling.*
149 Walker R. Thornton, Fleming's, Franklin.*
150 Whitlock Arnold, Field's, Habersham.*
151 Abel Borge, sol., Allen's, Henry.
152 George M. Lewis, 320th, Baldwin.*
153 Jesse Scarborough, 687th, Sumter.
154 Randolph Pierson, Burk's, Stewart.*
155 George W. Haynie, 242d, Jackson.*
156 Gilead Spriggs, White's, Franklin.*
157 Sarah Jones, w., Ware's, Coweta.*
158 George L. Bledsoe, 561st, Upson.
159 James T. Paine, Riden's, Jackson.
160 William Hodges, Sims's, Troup.*
161 J. Chandler's five orphans, Bryant's, Burke.
162 Richard Thomas, 672d, Harris.*
163 Dr. David Jamison, sol., Buck's, Houston.*
164 John P. Atchison, 404th, Gwinnett.
165 Josiah Houston, Sen., Nichols's, Fayette.
166 Milley Willis, Canning's, Elbert.
167 Garvis Cross, Roberts's, Hall.
168 David Carter, Sen., Royster's, Franklin.
169 Richard Robinson, Phillips's, Jasper.
170 Judith M'Fail, w. r. s., Goulding's, Lowndes.
171 Dennis Hopkins, Gillis's, De Kalb.
172 David Finley, Athens, Clarke.*
173 Henry Collier, sol., 510th, Early.*
174 Abegal R. Porter, id., Smith's, Wilkinson.
175 Joseph Gaddis, 470th, Upson.*
176 Joseph M. Crews, sol., Hopkins's, Camden.*
177 William Bell, 242d, Jackson.
178 George D. Rice, 3d section, Cherokee.*
179 Jesse Mobley, Morrison's, Appling.
180 Henry Mitchell, sol., Collier's, Monroe.*
181 George W. Chisholm, s. s., Alberson's, Walton.*

182 William Hawthorn, sol., Sinclair's, Houston.*
183 Jonathan Tyner, 12th, Effingham.*
184 Alexander B. Stephens, Hargrove's, Oglethorpe.*
185 Mary Pope, w., Stewart's, Jones.
186 John Clark, Gay's, Harris.*
187 Mary M'Coy, w., 588th, Upson.
188 John M. Daniel, Clark's, Morgan.*
189 Henry Durham's ors., Elder's, Clarke.
190 Jarratt Tarples, or., Hill's, Monroe.
191 Echo Thacker, sol., Griffin's, Hall.
192 R. B. Bradford's 2 orphans, Latimer's, De Kalb.
193 James Coile, Hardman's, Oglethorpe.
194 Young W. White, Hill's, Baldwin.*
195 William Johnson, Jordan's, Bibb.*
196 Christian Thomas, w., Welche's, Habersham.*
197 George Lang, Hopkins's, Camden.*
198 Elizabeth Newborn, w., Hutson's, Newton.
199 John Chissem's ors,, 38th, Scriven.
200 Kendrick Shinnon, Robison's, Washington.*
201 Elisha Herndon, s. s., Cleggs's, Walton.*
202 Joshua Mercer, s. l. w., 734th, Lee.*
203 Robert R. Atkinson, Bryant's, Burke.*
204 John S. Cash, Orr's, Jackson.
205 Benjamin T. Chastain, lu., Daniel's, Hall.
206 Edmund Shackelford's ors., 601st, Taliaferro.
207 Eaton Bass, sol., Harralson's, Troup.*
208 James Clay, Mullen's, Carroll.*
209 Newton Purdue, Young's, Jefferson.*
210 William Dunnaway, Lynn's, Warren.
211 William Allen's ors., Covington's, Pike.
212 Mary Hicks, w., Blackshear's, Laurens.*
213 Starlin Sisson, Rhodes's, De Kalb.*
214 William B. Mede's or., M'Coy's, Clarke.
215 James Carlisle, Liddell's, Jackson.
216 William B. Allred, Chesnut's, Newton.*
217 Sampson Bracewell, Bailey's, Laurens.*
218 William Lord, M'Ginnis's, Jackson.*
219 Jesse Mercer's ors., Linam's, Pulaski.
220 Seaborn K. Turner, Kelly's, Jasper.*
221 William Bradberry, Echols's, Clarke.
222 Abraham Bruce, Stephens's, Habersham.
223 Hardy Porker, Peacock's, Washington.*
224 William M'G. Williams, Stewart's, Troup.
225 Jeremiah Smith, 121st, Richmond.
226 Elizabeth Peddy, w., Barrow's, Houston.*
227 James Cantrell, Herndon's, Hall.
228 Rhoda Countryman, w., Hitchcock's, Muscogee.
229 James E. Williams, Britt's, Randolph.*

230 Jeremiah M. Park, Higginbotham's, Madison.*
231 John Keen, House's, Henry.*
232 Lodowick M. Thompson, 137th, Greene.*
233 Benjamin F. Harris, 113th, Hancock.
234 Littleberry Daniel, r. s., 693d, Heard.*
235 James Hanes, Jr., Compton's, Fayette.*
236 John Meacham, sol., M'Gehee's, Troup.*
237 Alexander M'Coy, Jones's, Hall.
238 Henry Cole, Perry's, Habersham.*
239 Mary Deson, w., Cleggs's, Walton.*
240 Mallindy Sutherland, w., Chastain's, Habersham.*
241 John Matley, 702d, Heard.*
242 Levi Palmer, Herndon's, Hall.
243 Robert Sansom's ors., Russell's, Henry.*
244 John A. Germa, Valleau's, Chatham.*
245 Stephen Frasier, Sparks's, Washington.*
246 Elijah Martin, Jr., Belcher's, Jasper.
247 George W. Yarbrough, 785th, Sumter.
248 John Venrable, minor, f. a., Boynton's, Twiggs.
249 William Chesnut, Pearce's, Houston.
250 Sarah Brooks, w., Edwards's, Talbot.*
251 David Redding, Linam's, Pulaski.
252 Edward R. Harden, Athens, Clarke.*
253 Elizabeth Barham, w., Cliett's, Columbia.*
254 Dempsy Farmer, w., Givins's, De Kalb.
255 James M. Miller, Catlett's, Franklin.*
256 John Gillespie, 120th, Richmond.*
257 Reuben Jordan, Reid's, Gwinnett.*
258 James Carroll, Field's, Habersham.
259 Lawrence Joyner, Will's, Twiggs.
260 Charles S. Henry, 4th, Chatham.*
261 Jeremiah Smith's ors., Cleggs's, Walton.
262 Lewis Griffin's ors., Downs's, Warren.*
263 William D. Harrison, Garner's, Washington.*
264 Thomas Kersey, Jr., 59th, Emanuel.
265 Sarah Wesson, w. r. s., Lightfoot's, Washington.*
266 Thomas B. Morton, Dean's, Clarke.*
267 Moses Staten, 161st, Greene.*
268 William Wall, 601st, Taliaferro.*
269 Barnabas Pace, Martin's, Newton.*
270 Richard Freeman, Marsh's, Thomas.*
271 Allen Highsmith, 335th, Wayne.*
272 Francis Moreland, w. r. s., Rooks's, Putnam.*
273 Arthur S. Simpson, 585th, Dooly.*
274 John S. Harris, Butts's, Monroe.*
275 John Jones, Taylor's, Houston.*
276 Michael Buff, Smith's, Madison.*

277 Merick H. Ford, Deavours's, Habersham.*
278 Julia M. Truman, h. a., 165th, Wilkes.*
279 William Hopkins, Huey's, Harris.*
280 Elizabeth Elton, w., Sinquefield's, Washington.*
281 Aaron Goolsbee, s. i. w., 510th, Early.*
282 William Watts, Keener's, Rabun.
283 Edward H. White, 417th, Walton.*
284 Davidson Blackwell, Young's, Carroll.
285 James A. Blanton, Newman's, Thomas.*
286 Rebecca Turner, w., 55th, Emanuel.
287 Allen Grubbs, Allen's, Campbell.*
288 Nancy Langston, w., Mullen's, Carroll.*
289 Henry Jones, 165th, Wilkes.*
290 John H. Leverton, Wynn's, Gwinnett.*
291 John S. Wray, Hall's, Oglethorpe.*
292 James R. Starr, Coker's, Troup.
293 Thomas W. Burford, Jones's, Hall.
294 Edward Neufville, Valleau's, Chatham.*
295 William Mackay, Oatland Island, Chatham.
296 Starland K. Hardridge, Walker's, Harris.*
297 William Holliman, Sapp's, Muscogee.*
298 William R. Grimes, Chambers's, Houston.*
299 Holida Newrane, or., Jones's, Morgan.*
300 John Farror, Royster's, Franklin.*
301 Nehemiah Summerlin, Loveless's, Gwinnett.*
302 Albert G. Bealy, Miller's, Jackson.*
303 Green B. Williams, Allen's, Bibb.
304 Eli Gaither, 559th, Walton.*
305 James A. Wright, 368th, Putnam.*
306 Jonathan Brook, Beasley's, Oglethorpe.*
307 Henry Hisler, sol., Smith's, Wilkinson.*
308 Henry Merk, Miller's, Jackson.
309 Peyton L. Wade, 38th, Scriven.*
310 George Doss, sol., Barker's, Gwinnett.*
311 George L. Hudgins, Blackstock's, Hall.*
312 Albert Rose, Candler's, Bibb.*
313 Abel Palmer's ors., 37th, Emanuel.*
314 Lewis Wold, Gillis's, De Kalb.*
315 Redding Jones, Mitchell's, Marion.*
316 Thomas Veasey's ors., 318th, Baldwin.
317 John Sergeant, Burnett's, Habersham.*
318 Bradford Brooks, Brewer's, Walton.*
319 Solomon Kemp, 404th, Gwinnett.
320 Christian D. Sebey's ors., Cleland's, Chatham.*
321 Israel Miller, Dean's, De Kalb.*
322 Niel M'Leod, Peterson's, Montgomery.
323 Jesse Harris, Huey's, Harris.
324 Henry Merk, Miller's, Jackson.*

SEVENTH DISTRICT, FOURTH SECTION, CHEROKEE.

1 Samuel Thornington, Morrison's, Appling.*
2 Reuben Slaughter's ors., 494th, Upson.
3 Daniel Saunders, M'Ginnis's, Jackson.*
4 David Elmore, Herndon's, Hall.*
5 Thomas Welch, Strickland's, Merriwether.*
6 Dudley Lawson, or., 109th, Hancock.
7 Elizabeth Price, w., Stanton's, Newton.*
8 Jesse Brown, 59th, Emanuel.*
9 Thomas P. M'Rees's ors., Barnett's, Clarke.*
10 William Goode, Mangum's, Franklin.*
11 Joel A. Wilson, 470th, Upson.*
12 Mary Ann Fuller, 15th, Liberty.*
13 George W. Blake, or., Crow's, Merriwether.*
14 Joseph Poythress, sol., Tally's, Troup.
15 Edmund Knoles, sol. 1784–97, Gittens's, Fayette.
16 John Day, Culbreath's, Columbia.
17 Isaac D. Vaughn, Wilhite's, Elbert.
18 William Chambers, 458th, Early.
19 James Miller, Herndon's, Hall.
20 Thomas Smith, sol., Wilson's, Jasper.*
21 Wilson Nelson, sol., 735th, Troup.*
22 John Rosu's ors., Talley's, Troup.
23 James Booth, 417th, Walton.
24 Thomas B. Caper, Loveless's, Gwinnett.*
25 Jesse Johnson, sol., 141st, Greene.*
26 William Blauset, Candler's, Bibb.*
27 Temple Morris, Deavours's, Habersham.*
28 William W. M'Clung, Reid's, Gwinnett.*
29 Abner Y. Densmore, Brock's, Habersham.*
30 Alexander Greenway, Martin's, Hall.*
31 James Rogers, Smith's, Henry.*
32 Henry Burden, Seal's, Elbert.*
33 David M. Collum, Burnett's, Habersham.*
34 Alexander Chamblers, Hill's, Monroe.
35 William Crews, Thomas's, Ware.*
36 Starling Carroll, Hampton's, Newton.
37 Truin Hinton, Norman's, Wilkes.
38 William Morgan, Heard's, De Kalb.
39 William C. Strange, Wynn's, Gwinnett.*
40 Thomas H. H. Rigdon, Slater's, Bulloch.*
41 William Bird's ors., Baismore's, Jones.*

42 William Durham, 249th, Jasper.*
43 Sophia Frances Rebisa, or., Cleland's, Chatham.*
44 Edward Barbarie, Perryman's, Warren.*
45 Samuel J. Shield, Grider's, Morgan.*
46 Martin Dickinson, Deavours's, Habersham.*
47 Thomas P. Swindall, 163d, Greene.*
48 John Holmes, Trout's, Hall.*
49 Thomas Grier, Grier's, Warren.*
50 Memory M'Mullen, Russell's, Henry.
51 John B. Payne, Roberts's, Hall.
52 Leonard Martin, s. i. w., Walker's, Columbia.*
53 John Davidson, Wagnon's, Carroll.*
54 Theophilus Williams, M'Daniel's, Pulaski.*
55 Benjamin Adams, Lightfoot's, Washington.*
56 Thomas J. Jennings, 600th, Richmond.
57 William A. Crumpton, Boynton's, Twiggs.
58 Wilson Baxley, George's, Appling.
59 Elisha T. Hunter, 600th, Richmond.*
60 Lewis Jenkins, r. s., Peacock's, Washington.
61 Johnson Wellborn's ors., 177th, Wilkes.
62 Henry Bankston, Gillis's, De Kalb.*
63 Patrick Fennel, s. l. w., Swiney's, Laurens.*
64 John J. Perkins, or., 162d, Greene.*
65 Calvin Baker, Jr., Fitzpatrick's, Chatham.*
66 Needham Bennefield, Jr., Martin's, Newton.*
67 Nicholas C. Ware, Graves's, Lincoln.*
68 Robert Turner, Deavours's, Habersham.*
69 Benton Spears, Ross's, Monroe.*
70 Alexander Malcolm, 559th, Walton.*
71 John Davis, Sen., r. s., Welche's, Habersham.
72 James Peel, Hitchcock's, Muscogee.
73 John S. Brooks, Peace's, Houston.
74 Hannah Holbrook, w. r. s., Tower's, Gwinnett.
75 Lewis Sale's ors., 735th, Troup.
76 Francis Bates, Smith's, Habersham.*
77 James Curry, or., Graves's, Lincoln.
78 James Jones, Miller's, Ware.*
79 James C. Adams, Winter's, Jones.*
80 Joseph Smith, Hammock's, Jasper.*
81 Isaac Wheaton, Mullen's, Carroll.*
82 Austin Martin, Rhodes's, De Kalb.*
83 Sarah Daniel, w., Mitchell's, Pulaski.*
84 Elizabeth Barr, w., Sinclair's, Houston.
85 Spencer P. Wright, Lane's, Morgan.
86 Zadock Odom, 510th, Early.*
87 William A. Henderson, Belcher's, Jasper.
88 Archibald Lester, Bishop's, Henry.*

89 Stephen C. Pearce, 36th, Scriven.*
90 Ashly Boon, w. of sol., 320th, Baldwin.*
91 Dempsey Barnes, Williams's, Washington.*
92 Burell Bailey, Martin's, Washington.*
93 William Rogers, sol., Brooks's, Muscogee.*
94 John Liverman's ors., 122d, Richmond.
95 John Jackson, sol. 1784–97, Fenn's, Clarke.
96 William Gibson, Wood's, Morgan.
97 William Legrand's ors., Crawford's, Franklin.
98 Elizabeth Bowls, w., Curry's, Merriwether.*
99 James Dickins's ors., Baley's, Butts.
100 John Evers, Smith's, Wilkinson.*
101 Thomas P. Godfrey, Reed's, Gwinnett.*
102 Louis Pitt's ors., Cleland's, Chatham.*
103 William Galpin, 2d, Chatham.*
104 Robert Carter, Barrow's, Houston.
105 Samuel Devereux, Oliver's, Decatur.*
106 Mary Haley, w., Taylor's, Elbert.*
107 Hardy C. Thompson, Griffin's, Emanuel.
108 Archibald Hagan, M'Clain's, Newton.
109 Robert Stoodley, Sullivan's, Jones.
110 Byron Ellis, 470th, Upson.*
111 Noah Ashworth, Taylor's, Elbert.*
112 Obediah Copeland, 162d, Greene.*
113 Joseph Osborn, 243d, Jackson.*
114 John M. C. L. Baker, M'Cleland's, Irwin.*
115 George J. Southerland, 138th, Greene.*
116 John C. Blair, Ellis's, Rabun.*
117 James King, 105th, Baldwin.*
118 Benjamin Gutters, 249th, Walton.*
119 John Nelson's or., Whitaker's, Crawford.
120 Samuel Carruthers, 71st, Burke.*
121 Martha Evans, w., Curry's, Merriwether.*
122 Simon Harrington, Smith's, Liberty.
123 Jempsey D. Baley, Iverson's, Houston.*
124 James B. Akridge, 535th, Dooly.*
125 James Hemby, Loveless's, Gwinnett.*
126 Thomas King, 22d, M'Intosh.*
127 Jacob King, 123d, Richmond.
128 James Walker, Coward's, Lowndes.*
129 Matthew Abbot, Reid's, Gwinnett.
130 Isaac Smith, Lamberth's, Fayette.*
131 Daniel M. Phillips, Hamilton's, Gwinnett.
132 Thomas Hanson, Stanton's, Newton.
133 John B. Salmonds, Stewart's, Troup.*
134 John Irvin's or., 1st, Chatham.
135 Abdallah D. Smith, Moore's, Randolph.

136 Amie Delarouch, 27th, Glynn.*
137 Abijah Overton, Martin's, Newton.*
138 Ferris Green, 417th, Walton.*
139 James S. Graybill, 293d, Jasper.
140 William M'Cook, 114th, Hancock.*
141 Brittian C. Sorrells, Cleggs's, Walton.
142 John Finley, 72d, Burke.
143 William M'Alpin, Say's, De Kalb.*
144 John Drew, Jr., 289th, Jasper.
145 Jacob Priett, Sen., Trout's, Hall.*
146 Jacob Harnage's or., Baker's, Liberty.
147 Thomas Comoham, Bush's, Burke.*
148 Benjamin Vollotton, Hobbs's, Laurens.*
149 John Bucklow, Gibson's, Decatur.*
150 John Stephens, s. l. w., 588th, Upson.*
151 Asa Griffin, Hudson's, Marion.*
152 Charles Key, Nesbit's, Newton.*
153 John Ballard, Prophett's, Newton.
154 Wiley Reuper, Coxe's, Franklin.*
155 Allen Griffith, Echols's, Clarke.*
156 John Campbell, Hopkins's, Camden.
157 John H. Sharp, Payne's, Merriwether.
158 Elias Garner, Varner's, Merriwether.
159 Agnes Anderson, w., Orr's, Jackson.*
160 Richard Fortune, Jones's, Madison.*
161 William Gresham, Coker's, Troup.
162 William Bond, Candler's, Bibb.
163 Hezekiah Mark, Coker's, Troup.
164 T. Riddle, Sen., s.1784–97, Griffin's, Merriwether
165 David Beasley, Thomas's, Clarke.*
166 William P. Hambrick, Wilson's, Pike.
167 John Sanders, Griffin's, De Kalb.
168 John Town's ors., Holley's, Franklin.
169 John Bush, 80th, Scriven.*
170 Sarah Gatewood, w., Hanner's, Campbell.
171 T. Turlington, s. l. w., Whitfield's, Washington.*
172 Samuel K. M'Cutchin, Griffin's, Hall.
173 Mary Trammell, w., 555th, Upson.*
174 John Miess, sol., Kendrick's, Monroe.*
175 Willis Wiggins, M'Culler's, Newton.*
176 Thomas Wade, sol., Barnett's, Clarke.*
177 Matthew Duncan, Shattox's, Coweta.*
178 Rebecca Moore, w., Ballard's Morgan.*
179 Edward Burgess, Chastain's, Habersham.*
180 Moses Coxe's ors., Peterson's, Burke.
181 George Haynie, r. s., M'Ginnis's, Jackson.*
182 Tabitha Waldroup, w., Jones's, Hall.*

183 John Johnson, Rutland's, Bibb.*
184 Peter Hamrick, sol., Jones's, Lincoln.*
185 John Herring, Nichols's, Fayette.*
186 Beverly C. Cook, 190th, Elbert.
187 John F. Achord, Dupree's, Washington.*
188 William Rogers's or., Foote's, De Kalb.
189 Jonathan D. Buffington, Stanfield's, Campbell.*
190 Robert G. Pitts, Crow's, Merriwether.*
191 Ezekiel M'Clendon's ors., Jones's, Thomas.
192 Dominick Luna, Wilmington Island, Chatham.
193 Patrick Rooney, 119th, Richmond.
194 Prior Edwards, 656th, Troup.*
195 Hartwell Johnson, Mason's, Washington.*
196 William Gray, M'Ginnis's, Jackson.*
197 James Sizemore, Hamilton's, Gwinnett.*
198 Isaac Boyet's widow, Lester's, De Kalb.
199 Isaac Hiatt, Jones's, Hall.
200 Jesse Lecroy, Jr., Brackett's, Newton.
201 Chaney M. Lindsey, Loveless's, Gwinnett.*
202 Katharine Daucey, w., Curry's, Wilkinson.*
203 John N. Baley, 494th, Upson.
204 Thomas F. Ward, Crow's, Merriwether.*
205 Daniel G. Spillyard, Young's, Jefferson.
206 Stephen Thorn, Peavy's, Bulloch.*
207 John Conyers, r. s., 37th, Scriven.
208 Seaborn Jones, Jones's, Lincoln.*
209 William P. Ferguson, Barefield's, Jones.
210 James Henderson, Thomason's, Elbert.*
211 Richard Underwood, Camp's, Warren.*
212 John Walley, s. l. w., Hines's, Coweta.*
213 A. B. C. Hough, Mashburn's, Pulaski.*
214 Thomas B. Goodson, 559th, Walton.*
215 John D. H. Brown, s. l. w., 788th, Heard.*
216 Jacob Carter Mizell, Wilcox's, Telfair.*
217 Edmund Smart, Killen's, Decatur.*
218 James W. Fannin, Jr., Flynn's, Muscogee.*
219 Samuel N. Elliot, Dyer's, Habersham.*
220 Josiah Stovall, Candler's, Bibb.*
221 Sina Russell, w., Whitaker's, Crawford.*
222 Asa Eisland, 271st, M'Intosh.*
223 Edward Mays, Morris's, De Kalb.*
224 George J. Lynch, Lawrence's, Pike.
225 David Carnes, Mullen's, Carroll.*
226 Ranson Cooper, Chamber's's, Gwinnett.*
227 Thos. Graham, sol. 1784–97, Baugh's, Jackson.*
228 Nathan Taunton, Mitchell's, Marion.*
229 Isaac Dillard, Howell's, Elbert.

230 William M'Korkle, M'Korkle's, Jasper.*
231 Robert Brown, Hamilton's, Gwinnett.*
232 Charles Warren, M. Brown's, Habersham.
233 Stephen Marchman, Jr., Tompkins's, Putnam.*
234 John T. Rowland, Ellsworth's, Bibb.
235 Arnold Smith, 249th, Walton.
236 William Cavender, Field's, Habersham.*
237 John Harris, sol., Robinson's, Fayette.*
238 Lazarus Henson, 295th, Jasper.*
239 Joseph Summerlin, Head's, Butts.
240 William Garner, 404th, Gwinnett.
241 James W. M'Clain, Say's, De Kalb.*
242 Benjamin Snider, Fitzpatrick's, Chatham.*
243 Robinson's children, f. a., Robison's, Washington.
244 Eli S. Shorter, Few's, Muscogee.*
245 Jesse Pollock, r. s., Buck's, Houston.*
246 Sarah Tweedell, w., Hargrove's, Oglethorpe.
247 Anne R. Carter, w., Greer's, Oglethorpe.
248 Benjamin Stovall, Thomas's, Crawford.*
249 Charles N. Simpson, 175th, Wilkes.*
250 Daniel R. Dees, Miller's, Jackson.*
251 Benjamin Curley, 53d, Emanuel.*
252 George Duren, Martin's, Pike.
253 Jesse Bundy, 7th, Chatham.*
254 Vann Davis, or., Willis's, Franklin.
255 Benjamin S. Jordan, sol., 318th, Baldwin.*
256 Alexander Murphy, Bush's, Burke.*
257 Paschal H. Tailor, 693d, Heard.*
258 James G. Mayo, Hearn's, Butts.
259 Moses S. Guise, 604th, Taliaferro.*
260 Harmon Bolton, Watson's, Marion.
261 Robert White, Tuggle's, Merriwether.*
262 Isaac Hall, sol., Whipple's, Wilkinson.*
263 Michael M'Elwreath, Clinton's, Campbell.*
264 Burrel House, s. i. w., Seas's, Madison.*
265 William B. Crowder, Wolfskin's, Oglethorpe.
266 Henry W. Hamilton, Tuggle's, Merriwether.*
267 Warren B. Massey, Taylor's, Houston.*
268 Hugh Cale, Hart's, Jones.
269 Pannel's children, f. a., Brackett's, Newton.
270 David Anderson's ors., Smith's, Campbell.*
271 Jesse George, Coffee's, Rabun.*
272 Richard Winslett's ors., 307th, Putnam.
273 William H. Wood, Givins's, De Kalb.
274 James Willis, Pounds's, Twiggs.
275 Thomas J. Hall, 190th, Elbert.*
276 William M. Davis, Gillis's, De Kalb.*
277 James Overton, sol., Bishop's, Henry.

278 Elisha Darden, sol. 1784–97, Grier's, Warren.
279 John H. Little, M'Gill's, Lincoln.*
280 John Hawkins, 454th, Walton.*
281 Zachariah Wright, Maguire's, Morgan.*
282 Sion C. Kirkland, 74th, Burke.
283 William Pate, Griffin's, Fayette.
284 Jepthah Alford, sol., Harralson's, Troup.
285 Henry T. Morgan, 11th, Effingham.*
286 Leroy Carruth, Wynn's, Gwinnett.*
287 Zachariah Thompson, Burgess's, Carroll.*
288 James L. Perry, Latimer's, De Kalb.*'
289 James B. Blessit, Perry's, Butts.*
290 John Agnew's ors., 254th, Walton.*
291 Richard G. Barnes, Candler's, Bibb.*
292 James Howard, Mackleroy's, Carroll.*
293 John C. Smith, 470th, Upson.
294 Simeon Castleberry, 307th, Putnam.
295 Friend Freeman, Newman's, Thomas.*
296 Richard Taliaferro, Mobley's, De Kalb.
297 Priscilla Stowers, w. Davis's, Gwinnett.*
298 W. Jones, son of Mason, Jenkins's, Oglethorpe.
299 Mary Dyus, w., Lester's, Monroe.
300 John Cap, Sanders's, Jones.
301 Mary Dunaway, w. r. s., Perryman's, Warren.*
302 William Harn, Jr., 20th, Bryan.*
303 William Owens, Seay's, Hall.
304 John Jones, Jr., Taylor's, Putnam.*
305 Spencer Morris, 243d, Jackson.*
306 Frederic Ward, 307th, Putnam.
307 Martha Caswell, w., Oliver's, Twiggs.*
308 Edward Caleway, sol., 466th, Monroe.*
309 Robert C. Fain, Chambers's, Gwinnett.
310 Henry Shepherd's ors., Wheeler's, Pulaski.
311 James W. Brown, Vining's, Putnam.*
312 Margaret J. Stephens, w., Christie's, Jefferson.*
313 William Everett, 516th, Dooly.
314 Tyrey Jackson, Herndon's, Hall.
315 William Edwards, M. Brown's, Habersham.*
316 Nathan Couch, Hines's, Coweta.*
317 William Bones, Jr., s. s., Jones's, Madison.
318 Thomas Williams, Sen., 1st, Chatham.
319 James M'Neal, M'Korkle's, Jasper.
320 John Conine, Reid's, Gwinnett.*
321 Moses L. Jones, 15th, Liberty.
322 James M'Ree, Berry's, Butts.
323 William L. West, Wood's, Morgan.*
324 James N. M'Lane, Benson's, Lincoln.*

EIGHTH DISTRICT, FOURTH SECTION, CHEROKEE.

1 Hullum Hunt, Seal's, Elbert.
2 Betsey Danielly, w., Mackleroy's, Clarke.
3 Elizabeth Tyler, w., Prophett's, Newton.
4 Labon M. Dodson, Kelly's, Jasper.
5 Sarah Gill, w., Nesbit's, Newton.
6 William Price, Park's, Walton.*
7 Adam M'Loughlin, or., Carswell's, Jefferson.
8 John Whiteside, Flynn's, Muscogee.*
9 James Peead, Seally's, Talbot.
10 Mary Kelly, w., 398th, Richmond.*
11 John F. Huckaby, Collier's, Monroe.*
12 Levi Richardson, Brackett's, Newton.*
13 James Steel, Williams's, Jasper.*
14 James Calhoun's ors., Peterson's, Montgomery.
15 Mark Williams, sol., 254th, Walton.*
16 Christina Garner, w., M'Culler's, Newton.*
17 Matthew Berry, 734th, Lee.*
18 Joseph Coe, Wright's, Tatnall.*
19 John Crow, Perry's, Habersham.*
20 William Brantly, Jr., Peacock's, Washington.
21 Riley S. Baker, 417th, Walton.*
22 Archibald Meacham, Lamberth's, Fayette.
23 Spencer C. Crane, Tuggle's, Merriwether.*
24 Archibald Magruder, Jr., Adams's, Columbia.*
25 Nicholas Bury, 34th, Scriven.*
26 William J. Cleveland, Hall's, Butts.*
27 Pendleton J. Marshall, Silman's, Pike.*
28 Michael Carter, Oliver's, Decatur.*
29 Benjamin Law, id., 15th, Liberty.*
30 George W. Epperson, sol., Hampton's, Newton.*
31 John Cook, sol., Mashburn's, Pulaski.*
32 Lucy Bonner, w., 419th, Walton.
33 James Phillips's ors., Williams's, Jasper.*
34 Edward Seally's ors., Hobbs's, Laurens.*
35 Daniel Dennis, sol., Parham's, Warren.*
36 Rachel M'Gullion, w., Herndon's, Hall.
37 Richard W. Armor, Walker's, Harris.*
38 Mansel Garrett, Stanfield's, Campbell.*
39 Jacob Rodgers, 19th, Bryan.*
40 Robert Cox, Tower's, Gwinnett.*
41 Bedford Duke, Greer's, Merriwether.*

42 William Falkner, sol., Wilhite's, Elbert.*
43 Thomas Penton, or., 26th, Glynn.*
44 George Blythe, Dyer's, Habersham.*
45 Lewis Jarman, Beasley's, Oglethorpe.*
46 West S. Parker, Morgan's, Clarke.*
47 Emberson Davis, Murphy's, Columbia.*
48 Drury M. Cox, Ross's, Monroe.*
49 Ann Morrow, w. r. s., Hampton's, Newton.*
50 Churchill Mason, Head's, Butts.
51 Josiah Freeman's ors., Wilson's, Jasper.
52 Bleuford M. Walton, 289th, Jasper.
53 John Hailey, 589th, Upson.*
54 Abner Nolen, Head's, Butts.*
55 Ricey H. Maynor, Mann's, Crawford.*
56 Daniel Evans, Talley's, Troup.*
57 Redding R. Lewis, Garner's, Washington.*
58 John J. Maxwell, sol., 20th, Bryan.
59 John Thomas, Miller's, Ware.
60 George W. Conine, 307th, Putnam.*
61 Jeptha Pickett, Jones's, Madison.
62 Isham Dison, Howell's, Troup.*
63 Jesse Smith, Jr., sol., Brock's, Habersham.*
64 William Dugger, Sen., r. s., Groover's, Thomas.
65 Jarret P. Moody, Daniel's, Hall.*
66 Robert Culpepper's ors., Harris's, Columbia.
67 John Lanier, sol., 295th, Jasper.*
68 James Kirkpatrick, of Cher., Latimer's, De Kalb.*
69 George W. Voyles, Martin's, Hall.*
70 Sampson Bracewell, Bailey's, Laurens.
71 Thomas Jones, Loveless's, Gwinnett.*
72 James Jordan's ors., Bower's, Elbert.
73 Thomas Hutchison, Tilley's, Rabun.*
74 Benjamin Herrington, 37th, Scriven.
75 Elizabeth Clark, w., Flynn's, Muscogee.*
76 Benjamin Jones, Reid's, Gwinnett.*
77 Francis Wilson, 35th, Scriven.*
78 Jeremiah Spence, Lay's, Jackson.*
79 Geo. Cowan, Sen., sol. 1784-97, Orr's, Jackson.*
80 Elijah Smith, M. Brown's, Habersham.*
81 Thomas S. Dunbar, s. l. w., Barefield's, Jones.*
82 Mitchell Mohon's ors., Bostick's, Twiggs.
83 Miles G. Askew, Ballard's, Morgan.
84 Gasham Stewart's ors., Park's, Walton.
85 Joseph Dickey, Rooks's, Putnam.*
86 Barton C. Pope, Athens, Clarke.*
87 Jesse Warmack, Welche's, Habersham.*
88 Benjamin Davis, sol., Kendrick's, Monroe.*

89 John M'Elroy, 415th, Walton.*
90 David Young, Mason's, Washington.*
91 Jethro Hutson, Staunton's, Newton.*
92 Hardy Burrell, 404th, Gwinnett.*
93 George Nolen, Russell's, Henry.*
94 Uriah Burkett, r. s., 535th, Dooly.*
95 Susannah Monk, w., Kendrick's, Putnam.*
96 William Davis, s. i. w., Colquhoun's, Henry.*
97 John Hudson, r. s., Colquhoun's, Henry.*
98 John T. Cox, 3d section, Cherokee.*
99 Solomon Hadder, Barker's, Gwinnett.*
100 William Harris, sol., Reid's, Gwinnett.*
101 Gabriel Harrison, Garner's, Washington.*
102 Elijah Nash, M'Ginnis's, Jackson.
103 Benjamin Cone, 458th, Early.*
104 William Mullens, Brown's, Habersham.*
105 William Cooper, Walden's, Pulaski.*
106 Kearney Young, Young's, Carroll.*
107 John Peter Arnand, r. s., 3d, Chatham.
108 Larkin Hood, Everett's, Washington.
109 William Johnson, Jr., 114th, Hancock.*
110 William T. Williams, sol., Valleau's, Chatham.*
111 Albert Averett, Flynn's, Muscogee.*
112 Philip Dillard's ors., Odams's, Pulaski.*
113 William M'Collum, Jones's, Habersham.*
114 Joshua Sutton, Sutton's, Habersham.
115 John F. Brantley, Peacock's, Washington.*
116 Josias Boswill's ors., Ellsworth's, Bibb.
117 Joseph M. Cooper, Huey's, Harris.
118 Susannah Cochran, w., 364th, Jasper.
119 James Coventon, Givins's, De Kalb.*
120 Green Posey, Harralson's, Troup.*
121 Samuel Varner, Wynn's, Gwinnett.*
122 Thomas E. Whitfield, Park's, Walton.*
123 Matthew Colson's ors., 36th, Scriven.*
124 Cade Wall, 190th, Elbert.*
125 James M. Riddle, Allen's, Monroe.*
126 Augustus H. Black, Hill's, Baldwin.*
127 Ephraim Young, 248th, Jackson.*
128 Nathan Mathis, Smith's, Houston.*
129 Leonard T. Warner, sol., Newman's, Thomas.*
130 John C. Baldwin, 466th, Monroe.*
131 John Dismukes, Bryan's, Monroe.*
132 Zachariah Batson, 537th, Upson.*
133 Martin Thomas, Martin's, Newton.*
134 William Whitcombe, Cliett's, Columbia.*
135 Reuben Hanes, 419th, Walton.*

136 Marshall Martin, Greer's, Merriwether.
137 Britten Matthews, Roberts's, Hall.
138 John B. Lesueur, Smith's, Elbert.
139 Windsor Graham, Dearing's, Henry.*
140 Levi Simpson, Candler's, Bibb.*
141 William Tackett's ors., Gunn's, Jones.*
142 Green English, Allen's, Monroe.*
143 John Raper's ors., Whisenhunt's, Carroll.*
144 James Rogers, Jr., Johnson's, Warren.*
145 William Green, sol., Allen's, Monroe.*
146 Nancy Stocdale, w., Polhill's, Burke.*
147 John W. Turner, Sullivan's, Jones.*
148 Wade H. Ball, Sinclair's, Houston.*
149 Eliz. Baxter, w. s. i. w., Higginbotham's, Carroll.*
150 William B. Dennis, Parham's, Warren.*
151 Silas Plunkett, 108th, Hancock.*
152 Thomas M. Bagby, Barker's, Gwinnett.
153 Ganaway Malcomb, Coxe's, Morgan.
154 Reader Parker's ors., Parham's, Harris.
155 Walden Griffin, 12th, Effingham.*
156 William Burger, Barnett's, Clarke.*
157 Uriah Taylor, sol., Burk's, Stewart.
158 John W. Fowler, Latimer's, De Kalb.*
159 Matthew T. Caldwell, Allen's, Monroe.*
160 Lewis Maddox, s. i. w., Hobbs's, Laurens.*
161 Alexander Nelson, Hill's, Stewart.*
162 Daniel R. Walton, s. l. w., Waller's, Putnam.
163 John Carter, Rainey's, Twiggs.
164 Allen Stephens, Dyer's, Habersham.
165 Stephen Terry, Foote's, De Kalb.*
166 Charles F. Mills, Fitzpatrick's, Chatham.*
167 William Segraves, Higginbotham's, Madison.*
168 William Riner, Holton's, Emanuel.*
169 William B. Wimberry's ors., 470th, Upson.
170 James W. Shiflet, Taylor's, Elbert.*
171 William Harriss, Robinson's, Fayette.*
172 Churchill Turvin, sol., Parham's, Harris.
173 James Davidson, Whitehead's, Habersham.
174 Thomas Watkins, Henson's, Rabun.
175 Isham Mealer, Scroggins's, Oglethorpe.
176 Lewis Mullens, sol., Mizell's, Talbot.*
177 Willis Boon, s. l. w., Morris's, Crawford.*
178 John Lester, Jr., Seas's, Madison.*
179 John Stewart, Griffin's, De Kalb.*
180 Henry Vaughn, Davis's, Gwinnett.*
181 John Rowell, Miller's, Ware.*
182 Charity Harris, blind, 2d section, Cherokee.*

183 Eliz. P. Kendall, w. r. s., Brooks's, Muscogee.
184 Doct. Robert C. M'Connell's ors., 15th, Liberty.*
185 James M. Willis, Canning's, Elbert.
186 Ransom Shiver, 640th, Dooly.
187 Shadrach R. Felton, Pearce's, Houston.*
188 Isaac Greene, Johnson's, Warren.*
189 Judah Kennedy, w., 121st, Richmond.
190 James Brewer, Brewer's, Monroe.*
191 Milley Brown, w., Hutson's, Newton.*
192 Reuben Jackson, 607th, Taliaferro.*
193 James Loggins, Jr., Hamilton's, Hall.*
194 Hezekiah Smith's ors., Morrison's, Montgomery.
195 Oscar F. Leverett, Curry's, Merriwether.*
196 Philip Tyson, 510th, Early.
197 Benjamin A. Todd, Barefield's, Jones.*
198 William Kendrick, Martin's, Hall.*
199 John Kain, s. 1784–97 & l. w., 687th, Lee.*
200 Henry Jones, Hopkins's, Camden.*
201 Green Murkison, Martin's, Washington.*
202 Henry Knight, Foote's, De Kalb.*
203 Moses Pitman, Martin's, Pike.*
204 Thomas Cowfield, 735th, Troup.
205 James Dorough, s. l. w., Scroggins's, Oglethorpe.
206 Oliver Stephens, M'Korkle's, Jasper.*
207 Gabriel W. Davis, Jordan's, Harris.*
208 Tilmon Niblet, Maguire's, Gwinnett.*
209 William P. Combs, Waltze's, Morgan.*
210 Alfred Doolittle, Hobkerk's, Camden.
211 George W. Craft, Flynn's, Muscogee.
212 Jonathan Smith, Chandler's, Franklin.
213 Thomas Wayne, Morgan's, Clarke.*
214 Richard Osmer's ors., Chisholm's, Morgan.
215 James Carter, h. of f., Iverson's, Houston.
216 Simeon Gray, Whipple's, Wilkinson.*
217 Watson Couch, Justice's, Bibb.*
218 Dawson Hath, Dearing's, Butts.*
219 Allen Geider, Baker's, Liberty.*
220 Penelope Johnson, w., O'Neal's, Laurens.*
221 John S. Higdon's ors., Stewart's, Warren.
222 William Riley, David's, Franklin.
223 Henry Holtzclaw, sol., 165th, Wilkes.*
224 John Bryant, sol., Hart's, Jones.
225 John W. Gordon, Stewart's, Jones.*
226 Pleasant R. Runnels, Lunceford's, Wilkes.*
227 Daniel Campbell, s. l. w., Whitaker's, Crawford.*
228 Pearson B. Monk, Perryman's, Warren.*
229 Henry M'Lendon's ors., Head's, Butts.*

230 Jeremiah D. Land, Lamberth's, Fayette.*
231 Lewis Fitch, Ellsworth's, Bibb.*
232 Solomon W. Monk, Hitchcock's, Muscogee.*
233 Willian Grace, Hitchcock's, Muscogee.*
234 Richard N. Westbrooks, Herring's, Twiggs.
235 James Watkins Harris, Athens, Clarke.*
236 Jefferson Byrd, Summerlin's, Bulloch.
237 Mary Dickson, w. s. l. w., 80th, Scriven.
238 Jonathan Toole, 122d, Richmond.*
239 James Dillard, Howell's, Elbert.*
240 Daniel Sherman, 271st, M'Intosh.*
241 Joseph R. Culpepper, Crow's, Pike.*
242 Robert Harrison, 143d, Greene.*
243 Elizabeth C. Johnson, Latimer's, De Kalb.*
244 James Johnston, M'Gehee's, Troup.*
245 Jeremiah Hardy, Neal's, Campbell.*
246 Martha Fowler, w. r. s., Grider's, Morgan.
247 Stephen Herring, Herring's, Twiggs.*
248 Elizabeth Haney, w., 404th, Gwinnett.
249 John Mitchell, Curry's, Wilkinson.
250 Jonathan Davis, Stephens's, Harbersham.
251 George S. Wilber, Valleau's, Chatham.*
252 Elizabeth York, w., Phillips's, Talbot.
253 Sarah Wright, w. s. i. w., Hardman's, Oglethorpe.
254 Thomas Deaton, Hamilton's, Gwinnett.
255 R. R. Tenbrock, Cleland's, Chatham.
256 Joseph C. Parker, Baley's, Butts.
257 Eli Miller, 555th, Upson.
258 Ausbern Holt, Whitehead's, Habersham.
259 Riley Goss, Jones's, Habersham.
260 James Reynolds, Shattox's, Coweta.*
261 Davis Seaborn, Davis's, Jones.*
262 Rowland A. Tolbert, Higginbotham's, Madison.*
263 Christopher Day, or., 2d, Chatham.
264 Thomas S. & O. Hopkins, ors., 22d, M'Intosh.*
265 Henry Ryals, Jr., sol., 24th, M'Intosh.*
266 Joseph Lloyd, Coxe's, Talbot.*
267 Duke Williams, 494th, Upson.*
268 Orran Whatley, 735th, Troup.
269 William Stone, Hammond's, Franklin.
270 Hugh Manson's ors., Fleming's, Jefferson.
271 Wyly Roberson, Jones's, Morgan.*
272 Thomas R. Clayton, Covington's, Pike.*
273 James Miller's ors., f. d. l. w., 143d, Greene.
274 James M. Bell, or., Watson's, Marion.
275 John Dryden, Baker's, Liberty.*
276 James Whittle, Morris's, Crawford.*

277 Elijah L. Bryant, Sullivan's, Jones.*
278 James Hasly, Craven's, Coweta.*
279 J. W. Castens, or. of J. A., Ellsworth's, Bibb.*
280 Jacob Tinn, Dawson's, Jasper.*
281 Isaac Baldasee, r. s., Wright's, Tatnall.*
282 Thomas Eidson, sol., 147th, Greene.
283 Elisha Davis, Groce's, Bibb.*
284 Ezekiel White's ors., Hill's, Stewart.
285 George Park, Park's, Walton.*
286 Clemmen Jones, 735th, Troup.
287 Jeremiah Stower, Stower's, Elbert.
288 Benjamin Abney, Miller's, Jackson.*
289 Enoch Edwards, Stephens's, Habersham.
290 Stephen M'Ginnis, 404th, Gwinnett.
291 Henry C. Tucker, s. l. w., Mason's, Washington.
292 James H. Martin, Martin's, Laurens.*
293 Charles Kersey, Gunn's, Henry.*
294 David Daniel, sol., Davis's, Gwinnett.
295 Mary Jones, w., Jones's, Hall.*
296 Mary Carmichael, w., Atkinson's, Coweta.*
297 Peyton Clement's ors., 293d, Jasper.*
298 Williamson Bailey, Clark's, Morgan.*
299 Symmecon Adams, Peace's, Wilkinson.*
300 Absolem B. King, Mullen's, Carroll.*
301 Miles Bramblett, White's, Franklin.
302 William Presley's ors., Griffin's, Hall.
303 Asa Upton, Downs's, Warren.
304 Wilson Watkins, Christie's, Jefferson.
305 Nancey Dowell, w., Few's, Muscogee.*
306 John Miller, sol., Mays's, Monroe.
307 James W. Greene, Butts's, Monroe.
308 William C. Bates, Griffin's, Burke.*
309 William Visage, Ellis's, Rabun.
310 Sherod Phillips, 395th, Emanuel.
311 Enoch B. Wallace, Mann's, Crawford.*
312 David M. Stewart's ors., House's, Henry.
313 Isaac Mayfield, Barker's, Gwinnett.*
314 Reuben Moore, Woodruff's, Campbell.*
315 John Kenedy, s. l w., Whitaker's, Crawford.*
316 William A. Hunter, 140th, Greene.*
317 Iray Browning, 394th, Montgomery.*
318 Ambrose H. Perry, sol., 574th, Early.*
319 Thomas Waters's ors., 454th, Walton.
320 Henry Thomas, 555th, Upson.
321 John O. H. Lillibridge, Athens, Clarke.*
322 John Powell's ors., Ball's, Monroe.*
323 John T. Smith, Walker's, Harris.
324 Elijah Teague, Mullen's, Carroll.

NINTH DISTRICT, FOURTH SECTION, CHEROKEE.

1 Celia Giles, w. r. s., Everett's, Washington.
2 John S. Moss, Fulks's, Wilkes.*
3 Susannah Pearce, w., Bridges's, Gwinnett.*
4 William F. Wamble, Haygood's, Washington.*
5 John Murdock, Crawford's, Franklin.*
6 John Jones, Greene's, Oglethorpe.*
7 Edward W. Quarterman, 15th, Liberty.*
8 Job Red, Davis's, Gwinnett.*
9 James Jones, Rick's, Laurens.*
10 Kinchen Martin, Will's, Twiggs.*
11 John Garner, Willis's, Franklin.
12 John Camron, Chambers's, Gwinnett.*
13 Joseph Glisson, Brewton's, Tatnall.*
14 James Murphy, Hines's, Coweta.*
15 Malachi Gillion, Hatton's, Baker.*
16 Churchwell Harris's ors., Haygood's, Washington
17 Hodge Rabun, Neal's, Campbell.*
18 Thomas Wood, Peacock's, Washington.*
19 John Brooks, sol., Whisenhunt's, Carroll.*
20 John G. Powell, s. l. w., Dearing's, Butts.*
21 C. S. Anderson, of Cherokee, Latimer's, De Kalb*
22 Simeon R. Janes, 605th, Taliaferro.*
23 Elbert G. Smith, Seally's, Talbot.*
24 John Harris, 7th, Chatham.*
25 Thomas Harrison, Whitaker's, Crawford.*
26 Joseph Chandler, Durham's, Talbot.*
27 Robert A. Whebell, Cleland's, Chatham.
28 Pleasant J. Allen, 147th, Greene.*
29 John Miller, Hart's, Jones.*
30 William Davis, Price's, Hall.*
31 Elizabeth Robinson, w., Robinson's, Harris.*
32 Wiley Gilmore, Hill's, Baldwin.
33 Ephraim Simpson, Hampton's, Newton.*
34 John St. Johns, Hicks's, Decatur.*
35 William Rieves, Dobb's, Hall.
36 Ovid G. Sparks, Robinson's, Putnam.
37 William H. M'Cormick, Moseley's, Coweta.
38 Thomas H. Sharp, sol., Harp's, Stewart.
39 Henry W. Dorsey, Sullivan's, Jones.*
40 William Bush, Lester's, Pulaski.*
41 James Holder, Phillips's, Monroe.*

42 John Gray, 190th, Elbert.*
43 John L. Elder, Robinson's, Fayette.*
44 Thomas Bellote, Fulsom's, Lowndes.*
45 Thomas S. White, Thomason's, Elbert.
46 James Davis, 604th, Taliaferro.
47 Valentine Young, 243d, Jackson.
48 Jared Wood, s. l. w., Robison's, Washington.*
49 Isaac Williams, Strickland's, Merriwether.*
50 John Eady, or., Martin's, Washington.*
51 Avery Camp, Reid's, Gwinnett.
52 James Bradford, Field's, Habersham.*
53 Samuel G. Locklin, 454th, Walton.
54 Ann Cannon, w. r. s., 417th, Walton.*
55 William Morris, Jr., Gittens's, Fayette.*
56 Thomas F. Gordon, Brock's, Habersham.*
57 Warner Sharbutts, s. l. w., Underwood's, Putnam*
58 Samuel Weathers, Jr., 494th, Upson.
59 John M. Hampton, Hobbs's, Laurens.*
60 John A. Rowell, M'Lane's, Newton.
61 James D. Bludworth, Griffin's, Fayette.
62 Edmund Cason, Kelly's, Elbert.*
63 Rice Henderson, Sen., Hitchcock's, Muscogee.
64 Robert H. Bourquin, Bourquin's, Chatham.*
65 Charity Gamage, w. r. s., Pearce's, Houston.*
66 William A. Baldwin, 559th, Walton.*
67 Gabriel Clemments, Allen's, Bibb.*
68 Henry C. Harris, or., Gunn's, Jones.
69 Ann Vickers, w., Mason's, Washington.*
70 Ann Hendry, w. r. s., Baker's, Liberty.*
71 Zero Perkins, Lay's, Jackson.
72 Martin Skelton, Kelly's, Elbert.*
73 Noah Barnes, 108th, Hancock.
74 Josiah H. Tilus, Ballard's, Morgan.*
75 Silas Grubbs, 373d, Jasper.*
76 Lewis Cannon, Curry's, Merriwether.*
77 Burwell H. Hambrick, Morton's, De Kalb.*
78 William Taynor, Store's, Elbert.*
79 Edward Wilson, 510th, Early.*
80 Pleasant Goldin, Gillis's, De Kalb.*
81 Asahel C. Holmes, Collier's, Monroe.
82 Joseph C. Barksdale, Johnson's, Warren.
83 James N. Martin, sol., Martin's, Stewart.*
84 Richard J. French, or., Bivins's, Jones.*
85 William Blackstock, House's, Henry.*
86 Stephen Baker, Johnson's, De Kalb.
87 Benjamin Spirley, Higginbotham's, Rabun.
88 Stephen Carter, Robinson's, Fayette.

89 Benjamin Borders, Bustin's, Pike.*
90 Lavina Miles, w., Young's, Wilkinson.*
91 James Autrey, Allen's, Monroe.*
92 Benjamin Candley, Catlett's, Franklin.
93 Jesse E. Ham, Houstoun's, Chatham.*
94 Andrew Peter Pillot, 120th, Richmond.*
95 Freeman Williams, Mason's, Washington.*
96 John King, 466th, Monroe.
97 Sarah Waller, w., Ogden's, Camden.*
98 Elisha Douglas, 510th, Early.
99 Herod Raulerson, 333d, Wayne.*
100 Charity Hand, w., 120th, Richmond.
101 James Weatherby, 777th, Randolph.
102 Martin T. Travis, Wood's, Morgan.
103 James Pusser, Haygood's, Washington.*
104 Wiley Davis, 785th, Sumter.
105 Seaborn Gentry, Peurifoy's, Henry.*
106 John Mock, 640th, Dooly.*
107 J. E. Hogue, s. i. w., 779th, Heard.*
108 Keziah Fuller, w. r. s., Adams's, Columbia.
109 James Turner, George's, Appling.*
110 Jason Fain, Barker's, Gwinnett.*
111 Enos N. B. Hill, Grier's, Warren.*
112 Jonathan Milton's ors., Echols's, Clarke.*
113 Robert M. Darnall, 320th, Baldwin.*
114 Rebecca Mays, w., Garner's, Coweta.*
115 John Floyd, M'Linn's, Butts.
116 Charles S. Dodge, 271st, M'Intosh.*
117 John Ellis's ors., Cannon's, Wilkinson.
118 William F. Brown, s. l. w., Taylor's, Putnam.
119 Gideon T. Stewart, Allen's, Henry.
120 Samuel Studdard, Cleggs's, Walton.
121 Abner Smith, or., Allen's, Campbell.
122 James W. Meadows, David's, Franklin.*
123 Thomas Johnson's ors., Hardman's, Oglethorpe.
124 James M'Nabb, Carpenter's, Tatnall.*
125 Edmund Bugg's ors., Few's, Muscogee.*
126 James Hays, 574th, Early.
127 Amariah Daniel, Ellsworth's, Bibb.*
128 Colson Heath, Bryan's, Monroe.*
129 William Veal, Jr., Seay's, De Kalb.
130 John Murph, M'Gill's, Lincoln.*
131 Margery White, w., Allen's, Henry.
132 Hannah Butler, w. r. s., 687th, Lee.*
133 Enos R. Flewellen, Butts's, Monroe.*
134 Susannah Kendrick, w., Gray's, Henry.
135 Leroy Woodard, 175th, Wilkes.*

136 Henry Dennis, Cleggs's, Walton.*
137 Andrew Y. Moore, Gray's, Henry.*
138 William Fowler, sol., Camp's, Warren.
139 Ruth Cantrell, w., Roberts's, Hall.*
140 Allen Bradley, Dobbs's, Hall.*
141 Samuel Taylor, Stone's, Irwin.*
142 John Winn's ors., 15th, Liberty.
143 Caswell Cook, Mann's, Crawford.*
144 Jesse H. Lively, Griffin's, Burke.*
145 Susannah Gremmet, w., M'Lane's, Newton.*
146 William Childs, Sewell's, Franklin.*
147 William Barbary, 537th, Upson.*
148 Allen Proctor, 49th, Emanuel.
149 Demcey Fennel, Newman's, Thomas.*
150 Thomas H. Brown, 119th, Richmond.*
151 John T. Rowland, Ellsworth's, Bibb.*
152 Darcas Horn, w. r. s., Crow's, Pike.
153 Isaac Spence, sol., Jones's, Thomas.
154 John B. Peacock, Whitaker's, Crawford.*
155 George H. Buchannan, Hudson's, Marion.*
156 John W. Hyde, sol., Justice's, Bibb.
157 John Harper, r. s., M. Brown's, Habersham.
158 John Davidson, Hill's, Harris.
159 William Bastin's ors., Grubbs's, Columbia.
160 Nathaniel Burks, Winn's, Gwinnett.*
161 Susannah Alexander, w. r. s., Seally's, Talbot.
162 George W. Gresham, Jenkins's, Oglethorpe.
163 Milley Jones, w., Roberts's, Hall.
164 Elijah Miller, Mullen's, Carroll.*
165 Benjamin E. Gilstrap, Roe's, Burke.*
166 William Clarke, Barron's, Houston.
167 William G. Evans, Chisholm's, Morgan.
168 James Booker, Pollard's, Wilkes.
169 William Wood's ors., Martin's, Newton.
170 Anderson's three orphans, Smith's, Habersham.
171 Thomas J. Robbins, Griffin's, Hall.
172 Joseph Wilson, George's, Appling.
173 J. Alsobrook, Sen., r. s., Alsobrook's, Jones.
174 Joseph E. Maxwell, 15th, Liberty.
175 Robert H. Kilcrease, Hearn's, Butts.*
176 Easley Hunt, Holly's, Franklin.*
177 Spencer Spear, Moffett's, Muscogee.
178 John B. Harris, Kendrick's, Putnam.*
179 Lewis Coffey, Dyer's, Habersham.*
180 John J. Weaver, sol., 2d, Chatham.*
181 Stephen Dodson, Evans's, Fayette.*
182 Willmouth Fox, w. r. s., 362d, Jasper.

183 Henry Jester, Thaxton's, Butts.
184 Charles Hopkins's ors., Chambers's, Gwinnett.
185 Joseph Lawrence, Crow's, Pike.
186 John King, Smith's, Habersham.
187 Jacob Goodson, Smith's, Habersham.*
188 William L. Hughes, Allen's, Bibb.
189 Jonathan L. Weaver's ors, Moore's, Randolph.
190 Thomas Jones's ors., 74th, Burke.*
191 Jesse Weeks, Alexander's, Jefferson.
192 Wilson Faulkner, Rhodes's, De Kalb.*
193 Robert Wood, Silman's, Pike.
194 Robert B. Paul, Newby's, Jones.*
195 William Beavert, Keener's, Rabun.*
196 Richard Knight, Hood's, Henry.*
197 Drury Wall, Jr., Keener's, Rabun.*
198 Linson Bradey, Downs's, Warren.
199 Daniel Walker, Burgess's, Carroll.
200 Peter Rape, Hood's, Henry.*
201 John F. Roberts, 35th, Scriven.*
202 William Chambers, 458th, Early.*
203 William W. M'Clung, Reid's, Gwinnett.*
204 William F. Wigley, Hamilton's, Gwinnett.
205 Singleton Smith, Bower's, Elbert.*
206 James Little, Haygood's, Washington.*
207 Elizabeth Cardin, w., Moore's, Randolph.
208 Joel Coffee, Sen., Coffee's, Rabun.
209 William Tynan, Sanderlin's, Chatham.*
210 Solomon Highsmith, Carpenter's, Tatnall.
211 John Bird, sol., White's, Franklin.*
212 Uriah Fuller, 759th, Sumter.*
213 Josiah Dennis, r. s., Night's, Morgan.
214 James Wise, Peavy's, Bulloch.*
215 Nathaniel Martin, sol., Baker's, Liberty.*
216 James Blanks, 245th, Jackson.*
217 James L. Taylor, 34th, Scriven.*
218 Cornelius B. Williams, Fulks's, Wilkes.*
219 Jemima Fincher, w. r. s., Smith's, Henry.
220 Henry Ash, Field's, Habersham.
221 Elijah Reeder, Curry's, Merriwether.
222 Jeremiah R. Swain, sol., Perryman's, Warren.
223 Rebecca Davis, w. s. i. w., Groce's, Bibb.
224 William Henry, Shearer's, Coweta.
225 John Marshall, Braddy's, Jones.*
226 Johnston Goggins, M'Ewin's, Monroe.
227 Greene Goare, Alsobrook's, Jones.*
228 William Justice, Jr., Ellis's, Rabun.*
229 Martha A. M. Stinson, or., Marshall's, Putnam.*

230 Erastus Bardwell, 122d, Richmond.*
231 Seaborn Harn, Estes's, Putnam.*
232 Henry Hand, sol. 1784, Iverson's, Houston.*
233 Robert T. M. Tucker, Gittens's, Fayette.
234 Abraham Greene, 123d, Richmond.*
235 Benjamin F. Kemp, 589th, Upson.
236 James O'Neal, or., 2d, Chatham.
237 Samuel G. Snow, Jordan's, Bibb.*
238 Nathaniel Austin, Jr., Chambers's, Gwinnett.
239 John Gould, Island, Chatham.*
240 Mark Richardson, Hudson's, Marion.*
241 Stephen Griffin, Bryant's, Burke.*
242 Ephraim Palmer's children, f. a., 470th, Upson.*
243 Daniel Norton, Bailey's, Camden.*
244 Zadoc Cook, sol. 1784–97, Mackleroy's, Clarke.*
245 John J. Johnson, Allen's, Campbell.*
246 William Daniel, son of Geo., Martin's, Newton.*
247 David M. Brown, Gunn's, Jefferson.
248 Matthew Alexander, r. s., Brown's, Habersham.
249 James M'Whorter, Price's, Hall.
250 Susannah Greason, w., Parham's, Warren.
251 Lem Gammond, Mobley's, De Kalb.*
252 Simeon W. Yancey, Edwards's, Talbot.*
253 Abraham Barge, Martin's, Washington.*
254 Vincent A. Smith, Parham's, Warren.*
255 James Millican, Orr's, Jackson.
256 James M'Ardle, Cleland's, Chatham.
257 James Leslie, Young's, Wilkinson.*
258 William P. Irwin, Allison's, Pike.
259 Robert M'Min, Jr., Stephens's, Habersham.
260 James Wilf, Gittens's, Fayette.
261 John H. Waller, Williams's, Washington.*
262 Henry Brown, sol., Adams's, Columbia.*
263 James Adams, Newby's, Jones.*
264 James Taylor, Jr., Morrison's, Appling.*
265 William Reddin, Tuggle's, Merriwether.*
266 James M'Donald's or., Coxe's, Franklin.
267 Anthony F. Story, Orr's, Jackson.*
268 Gilead Spriggs, White's, Franklin.*
269 Evans W. Pinkston, 113th, Hancock.
270 Hubbard Ferril, blind, Muse's, Hancock.*
271 Tilman B. Bobo, Tower's, Gwinnett.*
272 George W. Murray, 320th, Baldwin.
273 Joseph B. Leathers, 1st section, Cherokee.*
274 Madison Frith, Jenkins's, Oglethorpe.*
275 Daniel Lavender, Curry's, Wilkinson.*
276 Amos B. Foster, Harris's, De Kalb.*

277 Mordeica Malden, Fleming's, Franklin.*
278 George Shaw, s. l. w., 559th, Walton.*
279 Stephen Tyson, Peacock's, Washington.*
280 Thomas Giddens, Mattox's, Lowndes.*
281 James W. Mann, Strickland's, Merriwether.*
282 James Adams, Newby's, Jones.*
283 Thomas Coker, Blackstock's, Hall.*
284 Henry Anderson, Nellum's, Elbert.
285 Jesse Brown, Reid's, Gwinnett.
286 John Phinizy, 120th, Richmond.*
287 Joseph Brewer, sol., Night's, Morgan.*
288 Jonathan Griffith's ors., Maguire's, Gwinnett.
289 Alexander Holzendorf, Hopkins's, Camden.
290 Henry Bramlet, Dean's, De Kalb.
291 Thomas S. Pace, Hannah's, Campbell.
292 Stephen Merritt, Smith's, Wilkinson.
293 Curtis Ledford, Hughes's, Habersham.*
294 Bryan Bailey, Taylor's, Houston.*
295 William H. Harrel, M'Daniel's, Pulaski.
296 Robert Smith, 1st, Chatham.*
297 J. T. Kicklighter, Jones's, Bulloch.*
298 Joseph Allen, Hutson's, Newton.*
299 Alexander M'Dougle, M'Clure's, Rabun.*
300 Anderson Mize, s. l. w., Craven's, Coweta.*
301 Mary Thurman, w., Hargrove's, Oglethorpe.*
302 John Dill, 458th, Early.*
303 James B. Click, s. s., Cleggs's, Walton.*
304 John Barnwell, r. s., Dearing's, Henry.
305 John J. Comer, Comer's, Jones.
306 Robert R. Turner, Thompson's, Henry.*
307 Dennis L. Holliday, 74th, Burke.*
308 Bartlett Whorton, Watson's, Marion.*
309 Charles H. Wooten, Anderson's, Wilkes.
310 James Crowder, 106th, Hancock.*
311 Charles Plumb, Allen's, Bibb.*
312 William L. Foster, Ellsworth's, Bibb.*
313 Henry Bulloch, Greer's, Merriwether.*
314 Winright Duncan, Martin's, Pike.*
315 William Fuller, Stanton's, Newton.*
316 Mitchell O'Conner, Valleau's, Chatham.*
317 Mark Jackson, s. i. w., 147th, Greene.
318 Thompson Austin, Winn's, Gwinnett.*
319 Samuel Barrentine, Thompson's, Henry.
320 Tryam Fuller, 249th, Walton.*
321 Charles Smith, Phillips's, Jasper.
322 James M. Gaughf, Evans's, Laurens.*
323 John Oversteel, 57th, Emanuel.*
324 Isham C. Brown, M'Coy's, Houston.

TENTH DISTRICT, FOURTH SECTION, CHEROKEE.

1 David Clarke's ors., 600th, Richmond.
2 Mary White, w., Keener's, Rabun.
3 Josiah Spivey, Thomas's, Crawford.
4 George Dykes, Goodwin's, Houston.*
5 Julius M. Robinson, Oliver's, Decatur.
6 Millon A. Beall, Hendon's, Carroll.
7 Gresham Scogin, sol., Stewart's, Troup.*
8 Bryan Yelverton's ors., Herring's, Twiggs.
9 George W. Bostwick, Boynton's, Twiggs.*
10 Willis Tate, Ross's, Monroe.*
11 Philip Stinchcomb, sol., Fenn's, Clarke.*
12 James S. Russell, Tower's, Gwinnett.
13 Walter Shropshire, or., 255th, Jasper.
14 Hawthorn's two orphans, Nesbit's, Newton.
15 Elias Turner, Hughes's, Habersham.
16 Sarah Mercer, w., Loven's, Henry.*
17 Betty Birdsong, w., Bragaw's, Oglethorpe.*
18 Dennis Lindsey, Whipple's, Wilkinson.*
19 Jarrel Crenshaw's ors., Peurifoy's, Henry.
20 Ely Hendry, Goulding's, Lowndes.
21 John Hollingsworth, Candler's, Bibb.*
22 Othneel M'Cook, Johnson's, Bibb.*
23 Samuel Wilkinson, s. l. w., Dearing's, Butts.*
24 John Fort, Jr., 334th, Wayne.*
25 James Horton, Vining's, Putnam.
26 William Ferguson, Watson's, Marion.*
27 Mary Lewis, w., 111th, Hancock.*
28 Andrew Derrick, Derrick's, Henry.*
29 William James Ray, 15th, Liberty.*
30 Garrett Spinks, Brackett's, Newton.*
31 Reuben Baxter, Dearing's, Henry.
32 Anderson Sears, Mizell's, Talbot.*
33 John H. Booth, Mizell's, Talbot.
34 Samuel Chambers, Griffin's, Fayette.
35 Asa Simmons's ors., Lawrence's, Pike.
36 Michael Hartley, Thames, Crawford.
37 John Grant, s. l. w., Moore's, Randolph.
38 Jane Ash, w., David's, Franklin.*
39 John Swann, sol., 140th, Greene.
40 Richard Levins, Jr., Fryer's, Telfair.
41 James J. Groce, Groce's, Bibb.

42 Isam Fennel's ors., Evans's, Laurens.
43 Elijah Chasteen, Jr., Ellis's, Rabun.
44 John Cash, r. s., Peurifoy's, Henry.*
45 Thomas Clinton, Houston's, Chatham.
46 Mary Wence, w. r. s., 1st, Chatham.*
47 Wesley H. Pattello, House's, Henry.*
48 Benjamin Culpepper, sol., Edwards's, Talbot.*
49 John R. Robertson, Harp's, Stewart.*
50 John Crim, Bell's, Columbia.*
51 Lewis Smith, Mayo's, Wilkinson.*
52 John Williams, Flynn's, Muscogee.*
53 John Himley's ors., 601st, Taliaferro.
54 James H. Fielder, Mullen's, Carroll.
55 Mary Bowen, w., Shearer's Coweta.
56 William Prescott's ors., Adams's, Columbia.
57 William B. Fourman, sol., M'Culler's, Newton.*
58 John Jones, Hampton's, Newton.*
59 Larkin C. Wimpey, Griffin's, Fayette.*
60 John Cliett, sol., Cliett's, Columbia.*
61 Elvy Langston's ors., Murphy's, Columbia.*
62 John Quigley, Smith's, Houston.*
63 James M'Farlin, 458th, Early.*
64 William Waterer, Oliver's, Twiggs.
65 Mary Wilkinson, w., Chastain's, Habersham.*
66 Robert Allen Johnson, Hargrove's, Newton.*
67 Mary Ann Dickey, or., 404th, Gwinnett.
68 Christopher Sewell, s. i. w., Brock's, Habersham.
69 John Watley, 702d, Heard.*
70 Thomas Moland, sol., 362d, Jasper.
71 Solomon Chaney, Allison's, Pike.*
72 Richard Brinkley, s. l. w., 494th, Upson.
73 Hickman Dixon, s. l. w., Underwood's, Putnam.
74 Fleming F. Adrian, sol., Burgess's, Carroll.
75 William Fowler, Lester's, Monroe.
76 Washington H. Brantly, 112th, Hancock.
77 Enoch Dickson, sol., Jones's, Habersham.*
78 James Billingslea's ors., Sullivan's, Jones.
79 Almeida Hill, orphan of Isaac, 419th, Walton.
80 Spear's four orphans, Griffin's, Burke.
81 Mansfield Hinton, Lay's, Jackson.*
82 George Read's ors., Fenn's, Clarke.
83 John W. Wade, Herring's, Twiggs.*
84 Benjamin Donnaway, Norman's, Wilkes.*
85 Richard D. Clinton, Ellsworth's, Bibb.*
86 Gibson West, Bell's, Burke.*
87 Isaac Strickland, 404th, Gwinnett.
88 Thomas J. Voss, M'Clendon's, Putnam.

89 Henry Funderburk, 602d, Taliaferro.
90 Joseph Lee, 36th, Scriven.*
91 William E. Fullwood, 672d, Harris.
92 William W. Edwards, sol., Dobbs's, Hall.
92 Rowlin L. Horn, Newman's, Thomas.*
94 Osborn Eley, Moffett's, Muscogee.
95 Bartholomew Still, Baley's, Butts.*
96 John Grace, r. s., Carpenter's, Tatnall.*
97 Benjamin Hopkins, Hobkerk's, Camden.*
98 John Pounds, Wynn's, Gwinnett.
99 Wade Chapman, 245th, Jackson.*
100 Benjamin Sikes, or., Ellis's, Pulaski.
101 Allen Bridges, Chambers's, Houston.*
102 Thomas B. Evans, Arrington's, Merriwether.
103 John Powell, Jr., Martin's, Washington.*
104 Henry Futch, Jones's, Bulloch.*
105 Thomas Baisden, 318th, Baldwin.*
106 Robert Watson, Burnett's, Habersham.
107 Robert S. Dill, 120th, Richmond.
108 Stephen Boutwell, Camp's, Baker.
109 William H. D. Page, 470th, Upson.
110 Michael M. Mattox, Southwell's, Tatnall.
111 Elizabeth Latimer, w., 154th, Warren.*
112 James M'Naughton, Show's, Muscogee.*
113 Henry Casey, sol., M'Lane's, Newton.*
114 Alexander Hendry, s. i. w., Harrison's, Decatur.*
115 William Bennett, 71st, Burke.
116 Alexander Parker's ors., Cook's, Telfair.
117 Fanny Hill, w., Davis's, Gwinnett.*
118 Abraham Rowan, Rooks's, Putnam.*
119 Eliza Jenks, w., Woodruff's, Campbell.*
120 John Harrell, 756th, Sumter.
121 Martha Hood, or., M'Culler's, Newton.
122 John Strozier's ors., Lunceford's, Wilkes.
123 Charles T. Culpepper, Buck's, Houston.
124 Jordan Bell's ors., Bell's, Burke.
125 Asa Barnes, 103d, Hancock.
126 Willis Kirbee, 162d, Greene.
127 Napoleon B. Potts, Howard's, Oglethorpe.
128 Austin Ellis, Winter's, Jones.
129 Hilliard Mills, id., Arrington's, Merriwether.
130 Thomas W. Davis's ors., Roe's, Burke.
131 Reuben Underwood, Ball's, Monroe.
132 Dupree Postell, Valleau's, Chatham.*
133 Joseph L. B. Richardson, 788th, Heard.*
134 William Jones, Talley's, Troup.
135 Matthew M. Moxley, 71st, Burke.*

136 Noah Walker, s. l. w., Martin's, Laurens.*
137 Henry Cosnard, 120th, Richmond.*
138 Samuel Quinton, Sen., 2d section, Cherokee.*
139 William Williams, 163d, Greene.*
140 Samuel B. Gaston, Cleland's, Chatham.*
141 Lewis W. Whitehead, Herndon's, Hall.*
142 Jesse M'Neill, r. s., Johnson's, Bibb.*
143 Abraham Lake, Hill's, Monroe.
144 Jesse Kent, 120th, Richmond.*
145 Jeremiah Cartledge, Huchinson's, Columbia.*
146 John Austin, Sen., r. s., 250th, Walton.
147 Kendrick Garner, Dean's, De Kalb.*
148 Argen Parham, w., Ross's, Monroe.*
149 Major Johnson, Hudson's, Marion.
150 Alexander Jones, Guice's, Oglethorpe.*
151 Ann Mitchell, w., Marsh's, Thomas.
152 William Bonds, Griffin's, De Kalb.*
153 Edmund Samuel, Graves's, Lincoln.*
154 Doctor R. Malone, 146th, Greene.*
155 Wilie P. Dickson, Ware's, Coweta.*
156 Bryant Bowen, 535th, Dooly.
157 James Branham, Dyer's, Habersham.
158 William B. Bird, Vining's, Putnam.
159 George W. Carter, Moseley's, Wilkes.*
160 David Maddux, Baismore's, Jones.*
161 Robert Carson, Bivins's, Jones.
162 Laban Beckham, Streetman's, Twiggs.
163 John Gross, Williams's, Jasper.*
164 Amos Bedsole, Downs's, Warren.*
165 Eliocnai Mathews, Parham's, Harris.
166 Alexander Kaykendall, Sutton's, Habersham.
167 John Jay, Dobbs's, Hall.*
168 Stephen Williams's ors., Tuggle's, Merriwether.
169 William A. M'Curdy, Smith's, Madison.
170 Charity Davis, h. a., Allen's, Monroe.*
171 William Cleland, 466th, Monroe.
172 David Bell, Mattox's, Lowndes.*
173 Nancy Hiner, w. r. s., Lay's, Jackson.
174 Louisa Hartsfield, or., Allen's, Monroe.
175 John J. Taylor, Wheeler's, Pulaski.*
176 James White, Maguire's, Morgan.*
177 Charles W. F. Buchanon, Alberson's, Walton.
178 William Glasgow, r. s., Wilson's, Madison.*
179 R. Brown's chil., f. a., Welche's, Habersham.
180 John J. M. Willis, or., Gray's, Henry.
181 Charles W. F. Buchanon, Alberson's, Walton.
182 William Robertson, Sen., Daniel's, Hall.

183 Williamson Zuba, Hall's, Oglethorpe.
184 James B. Head, Loveless's, Gwinnett.*
185 Enoch J. Power, Talley's, Troup.*
186 Isaac Turner, Summerlin's, Bulloch.*
187 Alexander Martin, r. s., Mantooth's, Oglethorpe.*
188 John J. Barnell, Jones's, Morgan.*
189 John Oversteel, 24th, M'Intosh.*
190 Isaac Bailey, Strickland's, Merriwether.*
191 William M'Bride Lewis, 271st, M'Intosh.
192 Elijah Jordan, Crow's, Merriwether.*
193 William Vaughn, Sewell's, Franklin.
194 Charles H. Tait, 192d, Elbert.
195 Mastin H. Bray, Wilhite's, Elbert.
196 Thomas Grubbs, Allen's, Bibb.
197 Samuel Owens, Mashburn's, Pulaski.
198 Richard Coleman, sol., 2d section, Cherokee.*
199 Griffin L. Roberts, 419th, Walton.
200 Jeremiah Morris's ors., Hart's, Jones.
201 Martha Duke, or., 70th, Burke.
202 Alexander G. Slappey, Bryan's, Monroe.*
203 John Shackleford, Hammond's, Franklin.
204 William Kinsey, Jones's, Harris.
205 Irby King, Mullen's, Carroll.
206 Randall Hearn, Butts's, Monroe.
207 Daniel M. Smith, Bridges's, Gwinnett.*
208 Martha Sutherland, w., Field's, Habersham.
209 Richard Edmundson, Beaseley's, Oglethorpe.*
210 Greenberry Akridge, Swain's, Thomas.
211 John Sockwell, son of Wm., Martin's, Newton.*
212 Benjamin Melton, 415th, Walton.*
213 Martin G. Slaughter, Kendrick's, Putnam.*
214 John Attmon, Rutland's, Bibb.*
215 James Pennington, Gay's, Harris.
216 Jesse Smith, Ellsworth's, Bibb.*
217 Elizabeth Allen, w., 320th, Baldwin.
218 David Lasley, 163d, Greene.*
219 Charles N. Drury, s. l. w., Ogden's, Camden.*
220 Thomas Pass, Whelchel's, Hall.*
221 Randal Campbell, Peterson's, Montgomery.*
222 William Morgan, Allen's, Henry.*
223 Isam M'Bee's five orphans, Dean's, De Kalb.*
224 Jesse J. Wall, Justice's, Bibb.
225 Crispen Davis, Sen., Thaxton's, Butts.*
226 John Newberry, Butts's, Monroe.*
227 Thomas Crosby, Culbreath's, Columbia.
228 Isaac Gillion, Jr., Hatton's, Baker.
229 William Jordan, 458th, Early.*

230 John Lester, Butts's, Monroe.*
231 Alexander Garden, 365th, Jasper.
232 Thomas Dixon, Dupree's, Washington.*
233 Lindsey Park, Kelly's, Elbert.
234 Wilson Williams, sol., Sims's, Troup.*
235 Braxton P. Smith, Mimms's, Fayette.
236 Hezekiah Miller, 404th, Gwinnett.
237 John Reed, Arrington's, Merriwether.
238 George W. Richardson, 293d, Jasper.
239 James Scott's ors., 34th, Scriven.
240 Henry G. Peterman, Jenkins's, Oglethorpe.
241 George Wolf, 175th, Wilkes.
242 Ann E. White, w., Athens, Clarke.
243 Samuel Fleming, s. l. w., Christie's, Jefferson.
244 Eda Fowler, w., Lamberth's, Fayette.
245 John Reeves, Nichols's, Fayette.
246 Ephraim W. Prior, d. & d., Ballard's, Morgan.
247 Wilson Shivers, Lynn's, Warren.*
248 Catharine R. Goddard, w., Ellsworth's, Bibb.
249 Count P. Fleming, Mashburn's, Pulaski.*
250 Elizur Miller, w., Lightfoot's, Washington.*
251 Amos Edmonds, 295th, Jasper.*
252 Abram Posey, Mitchell's, Marion.*
253 James W. Daniel, Mizell's, Talbot.
254 Daniel O. Saffold, Sam Streetman's, Twiggs.*
255 Matthew Knight, Mobley's, De Kalb.*
256 Mary Willingham, w., Durham's, Talbot.*
257 Martha Evans, w., York's, Stewart.*
258 Mathew Gentry, Willis's, Franklin.*
259 William Dowdy, 1st section, Cherokee.
260 James Baber, r. s., 406th, Gwinnett.
261 Linsey Roberts, Hardman's, Oglethorpe.*
262 Simeon H. Terrell, Griffin's, Hall.
263 John Cockerell, Hargrove's, Newton.
264 John Smith, Merck's, Hall.
265 Berryman G. Merritt, Davis's, Clarke.
266 James Kelly, Hatton's, Baker.
267 James Langston, Jr., Harris's, Columbia.
268 Daniel L. Trussell, 373d, Jasper.
269 Miller's four orphans, 458th, Early.
270 James Griggs, s. l. w., Rooks's, Putnam.*
271 James Holmes, 561st, Upson.*
272 David Palmer, 243d, Jackson.*
273 Robert A. Reid, Whisenhunt's, Carroll.
274 Elam Smith, 588th, Upson.
275 Moses J. Isdale, Perryman's, Warren.
276 John Yarbrough, Baugh's, Jackson.

277 Aaron Williams, Fitzpatrick's, Chatham.*
278 Nancy Wilson, w. s. 1784–97, 295th, Jasper.
279 James Rabun, Newsom's, Warren.
280 Harry B. Miller, Martin's, Stewart.
281 Philip Cloud, Oliver's, Decatur.
282 John Stewart's ors., Craven's, Coweta.
283 Hugh Morrison, Sen., Morrison's, Montgomery.
284 Bunyan Rhodes, Sapp's, Muscogee.*
285 Gabriel Toombs, 165th, Wilkes.*
286 Wilie Clark, Walker's, Houston.*
287 Andrew Norwood, Edwards's, Franklin.*
288 Elisha Tucker, Wallis's, Irwin.*
289 Stephen Tillman, 398th, Richmond.*
290 Willis House, Price's, Hall.*
291 Peter Shick, 1st, Chatham.*
292 Jesse Smith, Wilson's, Madison.*
293 David Burks, Groce's, Bibb.*
294 Penelope Frashier, w., Swain's, Thomas.*
295 John B. White, Martin's, Newton.
296 Nathan F. Hooker, sol., Barron's, Houston.
297 Riley Mitchell, Edwards's, Franklin.
298 Jacob Stephens's ors., Salem, Baldwin.
299 Joseph Habersham's ors., Fitzpatrick's, Chatham*
300 William Murray, or., Edwards's, Talbot.
301 Grey Harris, Pace's, Putnam.*
302 George Renty, 15th, Liberty.
303 Richard Bennett, 271st, M'Intosh.
304 Wiatt Hewell, r. s., Hargrove's, Newton.
305 Patience Rialls, w., 24th, M'Intosh.*
306 Josa Ragan, Park's, Walton.*
307 Washington Redman, or., Griffin's, Hall.
308 Thomas Norris, Pate's, Warren.
309 James H. Farrow, 72d, Burke.
310 James C. Steele, Peurifoy's, Henry.
311 Anthony Ladaveze, 120th, Richmond.
312 Lewis G. Dunsett, Valleau's, Chatham.
313 Benjamin B. Hill, Say's, De Kalb.
314 Everett Ridley, Blount's, Wilkinson.*
315 Joseph Mitchell, 27th, Glynn.
316 David Talley, Mobley's, De Kalb.
317 John T. Penn, Butts's, Monroe.
318 Mary and Ann Abbott, ors., 25th, Glynn.
319 Larkin Johnson, Rooks's, Putnam.
320 Kenneth M'Lennan, Morrison's, Montgomery.*
321 Robert Robinson, Lightfoot's, Washington.
322 Timothy Ranew, Rutland's, Bibb.*
323 Andrew C. Williams, 537th, Upson.*
324 Edmund Raynes, Stewart's, Jones.*

11th DISTRICT, FOURTH SECTION, CHEROKEE.

1 Josiah W. Pope's or., 166th, Wilkes.*
2 Charles S. Dodge, 271st, M'Intosh.*
3 Groves Morris, Brock's, Habersham.*
4 Matthew Varner, Sen., r. s., Hall's, Oglethorpe.
5 James J. Mayo, Dilman's, Pulaski.*
6 Willis Hancock, Bustin's, Pike.*
7 John T. Hamby, Chandler's, Franklin.
8 Philip Lightfoot, Lightfoot's, Washington.*
9 Lewis Montgomery, s. i. w., 516th, Dooly.
10 William A. Jeter, or., 458th, Early.
11 Thomas Lee, Covington's, Pike.
12 Joseph N. Miller, 105th, Baldwin.*
13 Richard Sewett, or., Wood's, Morgan.
14 Kinchen Greer, Brooks's, Muscogee.*
15 John Burkett, Fryer's, Telfair.
16 John W. M'Dermot, Jones's, Morgan.*
17 Alfred M. Wilson, Chambers's, Gwinnett.*
18 Wiley Webb, s. l. w., Monk's, Crawford.*
19 Benjamin Brundege, Sanderlin's, Chatham.*
20 Elias Story, Griffin's, Fayette.*
21 Thomas Moreman, Jr., 177th, Wilkes.
22 Thomas T. Daniel, Atkinson's, Coweta.
23 William H. Burke, Coxe's, Morgan.
24 Asa Jordan, sol., Garner's, Washington.*
25 Haskin Jones, blind, Smith's, Madison.
26 Joseph R. Martin, Nelson's, Pike.
27 Richard N. Smith, 555th, Upson.
28 William Deane, 364th, Jasper.*
29 George W. Edenfield, Griffin's, Emanuel.
30 Peter Murray, Sanderlin's, Chatham.
31 Zachariah Davis, Hill's, Monroe.
32 John Q. Tanner, 250th, Walton.
33 Ashley Alvis, Chisholm's, Morgan.
34 Arthur Fuller, Willingham's, Harris.
35 Hugh Vallotton, sol., Polhill's, Burke.
36 Nancy Jones, w. r. s., Griffin's, Fayette.*
37 Mary M'Donald, w., Merck's, Hall.
38 John Lee, s. l. w., Estes's, Putnam.*
39 Mary Gay, w. s. i. w., Higginbotham's, Madison.
40 John F. Ball, Oliver's, Twiggs.*
41 Wade Harris, Johnson's, Bibb.*

42 John Jones, Baley's, Butts.
43 Littleberry Hutchings, 1st section, Cherokee.
44 Josiah Baismore, Baismore's, Jones.*
45 James Douthill, Mullen's, Carroll.
46 Ralph C. Armstrong, Moseley's, Wilkes.
47 Stephen A. Gray, Cleland's, Chatham.*
48 James Price, Barwick's, Washington.*
49 Elijah Miers, Blackstock's, Hall.
50 James Miller, sol., Harp's, Stewart.
51 William B. Calhoun, 109th, Hancock.
52 Marceller Andrews, h. a., 112th, Hancock.
53 James Keith, Say's, Hall.
54 Robert Smith, Jr., Hearn's, Butts.*
55 Elijah Beardin, Heard's, De Kalb.*
56 Jesse O'Neal, Killen's, Decatur.*
57 John Drigger, Peavy's, Bulloch.
58 Hugh Graham Adams, Wilcox's, Telfair.
59 James R. Greene, Newman's, Thomas.
60 Elijah Tucker, Wallis's, Irwin.*
61 Willeford Jackson, Daniel's, Hall.
62 Milley Watson, w., Price's, Hall.
63 William F. Owen, Say's, Hall.
64 John G. Robertson, 277th, Morgan.
65 Zachariah Chancey, Morgan's, Appling.
66 William Griffin, Hammock's, Jasper.
67 Thomas H. Lary, Ball's, Monroe.
68 James Carter, r. s., Thomason's, Elbert.
69 Jennings Odom, Brewer's, Walton.
70 Jacob Hodge, Hicks's, Decatur.*
71 John Pucket, Trout's, Hall.
72 Thomas Mooney, or., Wilcox's, Telfair.
73 David Langley, 404th, Gwinnett.
74 Mary H. Neyland, w., Roe's, Burke.
75 Solomon Parker, Smith's, Liberty.*
76 James Plunkett, Brackett's, Newton.
77 Moncraft Posey, Whisenhunt's, Carroll.
78 William Germany, Cliett's, Columbia.
79 Elijah Thornton, Martin's, Pike.
80 Stephen Phillips, 395th, Emanuel.
81 Robert Smith, Sen., Hearn's, Butts.
82 Keader Keaton, Baker's, Liberty.
83 Alsa J. Harris, w., Grider's, Morgan.
84 William H. Smith, Morrison's, Appling.
85 Richard Ward's ors., Deavours's, Habersham.
86 Littleberry Daniel, Baker's, Liberty.*
87 John Ferguson's ors., Wynn's, Gwinnett.
88 Odery Watson, Hampton's, Newton.

89 Mary M'Millon, w., 374th, Putnam.
90 David Owens, 559th, Walton.*
91 William Tackett, Mizell's, Talbot.
92 William C. Dickinson, Williams's, Decatur.*
93 John W. Hay, Moseley's, Wilkes.*
94 William Williams, Jr., Coffee's, Rabun.
95 Rachel Collins, w., Young's, Wilkinson.*
96 Samuel D. White, Silman's, Pike.*
97 Abram M. Jackson, Loveless's, Gwinnett.
98 Bryan Renfroe, Everett's, Washington.*
99 Manson Turner, sol., Belcher's, Jasper.
100 Isaac Norris, Sullivan's, Jones.
101 Moses S. Guise, 604th, Taliaferro.
102 Thomas Camp, 417th, Walton.*
103 Benjamin Ray, Harris's, Crawford.
104 William Wilson's ors., 7th, Chatham.
105 John Odina, 271st, M'Intosh.*
106 Isam A. Freeman, Bustin's, Pike.
107 Turner Smith, 10th, Houston.
108 Caleb Stephens, Hannah's, Jefferson.*
109 Nathan E. Batchelor, Maguire's, Morgan.*
110 Bobert Beall, Shattox's, Coweta.
111 Josiah Chadcorck, Bridges's, Gwinnett.
112 Zachariah Sanders, Payne's, Merriwether.*
113 William E. Britton, Barnett's, Clarke.
114 John G. York, Chandler's, Franklin.
115 Jordan Allen, Robinson's, Putnam.
116 Walter Wilson, Perryman's, Warren.
117 Charles Isham, s. i. w., Harris's, De Kalb.
118 Richard Holden, 1st section, Cherokee.
119 Edmund Dell, 34th, Scriven.
120 Alexander Graham, Jr., Cook's, Telfair.*
121 Judith Waters, w. r. s., Royster's, Franklin.*
122 Ditha Williams, w. r. s., Bostick's, Twiggs.*
123 Moses Holland, Dearing's, Henry.
124 Thomas Ansley, Stanton's, Newton.
125 Henry Martin, Martin's, Jones.
126 John M. Walker, Mobley's, De Kalb.
127 James Bannister, Ellis's, Pulaski.
128 Joseph H. Harper, Brackett's, Newton.
129 Samuel Morton, Martin's, Newton.
130 Thomas W. M'Gee, Brewton's, Tatnall.
131 Thomas Brannan, Head's, Butts.
132 Guthridge Ivey, sol., Stewart's, Warren.*
133 John N. R. Greene, 12th, Effingham.*
134 Enos Powell, Pounds's, Twiggs.*
135 Drucilla Godby, w., Griffin's, Burke.*

136 David Griffith, 605th, Taliaferro.*
137 Lemon W. Teat, 366th, Jasper.*
138 William Landrum, Herndon's, Hall.
139 Thomas Willy, Jr., Sanderlin's, Chatham.*
140 William Brown, Silman's, Pike.
141 Robert Poppell, Smith's, Liberty.*
142 William F. Lewis, Mullen's, Carroll.
143 Willoby Barton, Sutton's, Habersham.
144 Andrew Craver, Maguire's, Morgan.*
145 Nathan S. Tucker, Candler's, Bibb.
146 Clayton Bradshaw, Mashburn's, Pulaski.
147 Samuel Wallace's ors., Chambers's, Gwinnett.
148 Polly Jarvis's, minors, f. a., Guice's, Oglethorpe.
149 Isaac Anthony's ors., 120th, Richmond.
150 Sebastion Watters, Jones's, Habersham.
151 Francis W. Atha, s. l. w., Park's, Walton.
152 Charles Cantrell, r. s., Higginbotham's, Rabun.*
153 William Williams, Jr., Hinton's, Wilkes.*
154 Thomas G. Conts, sol., Hampton's, Newton.
155 Burrell J. Webb, Shearer's, Coweta.
156 Rossean Jackson, Mason's, Washington.
157 Richard Grimsby, s. i. w., 458th, Early.
158 John R. Ingram, Derrick's, Henry.*
159 John Pearce, Streetman's, Twiggs.*
160 Guilford Jordan, House's, Henry.*
161 Benjamin Raine, Wilcox's, Telfair.
162 Nicholas Guise, M'Millon's, Lincoln.
163 Wyly Parish, Harrison's, Decatur.*
164 George W. Hinton, Strickland's, Merriwether.*
165 William Jones, Britt's, Randolph.
166 Thomas Davis, Talley's, Troup.*
167 James Sullivin, or., Whitehead's, Habersham.
168 Harriet E. Hill, Valleau's, Chatham.
169 Andrew Gibson, Collins's, Henry.*
170 Bartlett M. Rogers, Coxe's, Talbot.*
171 Jeremiah Skelton's ors., Royster's, Franklin.
172 William P. Evans, Chesnut's, Newton.
173 William Cox, Gunn's, Jones.*
174 Robert M. Harden, Clifton's, Tatnall.*
175 James Bell, 106th, Hancock.
176 Edmund Knowles, r. s., 160th, Greene.
177 William Gaskins, M'Craney's, Lowndes.
178 Edlo Lynch, sol., Maguire's, Morgan.
179 Larkin Smith, Smith's, Habersham.
180 Edward B. Broadnax, sol., M'Culler's, Newton.
181 Richard Homes, Brooks's, Muscogee.*
182 Archibald Beggarly, 293d, Jasper.

183 James Cochran, Wynn's, Gwinnett.
184 Thomas M. Duke, Tompkins's, Putnam.*
185 Daniel Sanford, Jr., Mays's, Monroe.
186 Richard Bostick, Jr., 406th, Gwinnett.
187 Absalom Adams's ors., Chandler's, Franklin.
188 Bolar D. C. Moon, 242d, Jackson.
189 Clara Richardson, w. r. s., Hill's, Monroe.
190 Jourdan Kinnebrew, 177th, Wilkes.*
191 Thomas Walker Jones, 1st, Chatham.
192 John A. Rogers, Brewer's, Monroe.
193 John M. Smith, Canning's, Elbert.*
194 Caleb White, Cleggs's, Walton.*
195 John S. Westbrook, Herring's, Twiggs.*
196 Sylvanus S. Bryan, Lester's, Monroe.*
197 John Sissom, r. s., Liddell's, Jackson.*
198 Charles Z. Brooks, Winter's, Jones.*
199 William R. Miller, Morris's, Crawford.*
200 Enoch Greene, sol., Johnson', Bibb.*
201 William Smith, M'Clure's, Rabun.*
202 Tabitha Norman, h. a., Riden's, Jackson.*
203 Alsey W. Powell, Derrick's, Henry.*
204 Thomas Hendley, 608th, Taliaferro.*
205 Ann A. Irving, d. & d., Ballard's, Morgan.
206 James Robinson, 72d, Burke.
207 Mary Buchannan, w., Wilson's, Jasper.
208 John Benton, sol., Ross's, Monroe.
209 William H. Ellison, or., Jordan's, Bibb.
210 Mary Jackson, w., Ross's, Monroe.
211 Bethsheba Dillard, w., Williams's, Washington.
212 Washington Hinton, Taylor's, Elbert.*
213 Adam Alexander's ors., 293d, Jasper.
214 George W. Johnson, Lunceford's, Wilkes.
215 William A. Crombie, Allen's, Henry.
216 Charles Bogle, Griffin's, Hall.
217 Redman Rees's ors., Parham's, Warren.
218 Jonathan Burks, Dearing's, Henry.
219 John Tankersley, sol., Heard's, De Kalb.*
220 William B. Smith, Smith's, Houston.
221 Louisa Long, w. r. s., Candler's, Bibb.
222 Zebulon Wren, Higginbotham's, Carroll.*
223 Leonard W. Dozier, Streetman's, Twiggs.
224 John Freeman, Jr., 34th, Scriven.
225 Allen Burch, Morrison's, Montgomery.
226 John Adkins, Martin's, Washington.
227 John Page, Mason's, Washington.*
228 Silas Sellars, Williams's, Jasper.
229 George M'Clendon, 365th, Jasper.*

230 Nelson Harris's ors., 103d, Hancock.
231 John Lewin, 120th, Richmond.*
232 Alfred Long's ors., Lynn's, Warren.
233 William Bush, Jr., Martin's, Laurens.*
234 William B. Hamilton, Fleming's, Franklin.*
235 Michael V. Nash, Simmons's, Crawford.*
236 Jacob G. Dunn, Taylor's, Houston.*
237 John Jones, brickmaker, Mashburn's, Pulaski.*
238 Warren W. Martin, Silman's, Pike.*
239 Edward Plummer, Maguire's, Gwinnett.*
240 Jeremiah Gosnell's ors., Higginbotham's, Rabun.*
241 William Epps, sol., Jennings's, Clarke.
242 Augustus Culver, 111th, Hancock.
243 Cooper M'Elhannon, Robinson's, Fayette.
244 John Lewis's ors., Parham's, Warren.
245 William Belknap, 1st, Chatham.
246 Joseph Albrit, 789th, Sumter.*
247 Hail Maxey, Hall's, Oglethorpe.
248 Stephen Reans, Mizell's, Talbot.*
249 Thomas K. Wilson's ors., 608th, Taliaferro.
250 Hillory Alligood, Jr., Evans's, Laurens.*
251 Richard J. Winn, 419th, Walton.
252 John J. Boynton, Mizell's, Talbot.
253 Randol Tillory, Moffett's, Muscogee.
254 Tillman Barnett, Haygood's, Washington.
255 Sally Baogs, w., Hill's, Baldwin.*
256 Joshua Covey, 320th, Baldwin.*
257 Nathan Marsh, Jr., Newsom's, Warren.
258 Eliphalet S. Barber, 122d, Richmond.
259 Hugh Brown, Ogden's, Camden.
260 Abram Reddick, r. s., 365th, Jasper.
261 Jesse Wall, Watson's, Marion.
262 Frederic Smith, Candler's, Bibb.
263 Elizabeth C. Reid, w., Kellum's, Talbot.*
264 William Prothro, Kelly's, Elbert.*
265 Hugh Donaldson, Newman's, Thomas.*
266 Robert Miller, Morton's, De Kalb.
267 Tarply Turvalyvill, Duke's, Carroll.*
268 Obadiah Garrat, sol., Brown's, Camden.*
269 Daniel R. Mitchell, Price's, Hall.*
270 Willis Cason, Sen., r. s., Lester's, Pulaski.*
271 James M. Holsey, 101st, Hancock.
272 Nancy Colman, w. r. s., George's, Appling.*
273 George Dudley's ors., 37th, Scriven.*
274 Giles Jennings, Jennings's, Clarke.*
275 M'Carty Oliver, sol., Smith's, Elbert.*
276 Stephen Evers, George's, Appling.

277 George Pinkard, Ellsworth's, Bibb.*
278 Lawrence Smith, Williams's, Ware.*
279 Leonard Hornesby, Allison's, Pike.*
280 Blake's five orphans, Britt's, Randolph.
281 James Bond, Phillip's, Talbot.
282 Wiley Thaxton, Thaxton's, Butts.
283 Archibald Turner, 734th, Lee.*
284 Arthur Long, Crow's, Pike.
285 William C. Hammond, 1st section, Cherokee.*
286 Prior Edwards, 656th, Troup.*
287 Jesse Warren, Say's, De Kalb.
288 Thos. N. M'Williams, sol., Chambers's, Houston*
289 Mat. and Mary E. Nash, ors., Howell's, Elbert.*
290 Patience Trice, w., Silman's, Pike.*
291 Elias Levans, Douglass's, Telfair.
292 William Thompson, sol., Wilson's, Madison.
293 Benjamin Ganas, Polhill's, Burke.*
294 Robert Boutwell, M'Daniel's, Pulaski.
295 William H. Tarpley, Wolfskin's, Oglethorpe.
296 Charley Dowdy, 1st section, Cherokee.
297 Avy Bray, id., Bower's, Elbert.
298 William Shoemaker, Mimms's, Fayette.*
299 Elijah L. Christian, sol., Wilhite's, Elbert.*
300 Samuel M'Coy, Studstill's, Lowndes.*
301 William Parker, Payne's, Merriwether.*
302 John Hardiman, s. l. w., Shearer's, Coweta.*
303 Thomas H. Chivers, 604th, Taliaferro.*
304 Samuel Slate, Moore's, Randolph.*
305 Harmon Howard's ors., 687th, Lee.
306 James Lewis's ors., Perry's, Baldwin.*
307 Drury Strickland, sol., Chambers's, Gwinnett.*
308 Allen Brown, Lane's, Morgan.*
309 Benjamin K. Taber, Lunceford's, Elbert.*
310 Lewis Lanier, r. s., 36th, Scriven.*
311 James T. Burton, 559th, Walton.
312 William Robuck, Thomason's, Elbert.*
313 Paton Tiller, Loveless's, Gwinnett.*
314 Robert R. Mancell, Pounds's, Twiggs.*
315 Matthew W. Coleman, 779th, Heard.*
316 Green Hill's ors., Rutland's, Bibb.
317 George Wilson, Jones's, Habersham.*
318 Robert Wood, Whelchel's, Hall.
319 Joseph L. Holland, 295th, Jasper.
320 Isaac A. L. Skinner, Cobb's, Muscogee.
321 John Miller, Green's, Oglethorpe.*
322 Samuel Price, Smith's, Henry.
323 John Anderson, 656th, Troup.*

324 Robert S. Langford, d. & d., Wynn's, Gwinnett.
325 (fr.) Bryant Obunion, Blount's, Wilkinson.*
326 (fr.) William Reid, 73d, Burke.
327 (fr.) William M'Dowell, Stewart's, Jones.
328 (fr.) Green Hill, Bridges's, Gwinnett.
329 (fr.) Jedediah S. Miller's ors., 192d, Elbert.
330 (fr.) James Patridge, Kendrick's, Monroe.
331 (fr.) W. D. Holsenbake, Rhodes's, Richmond.*
332 (fr.) Jeremiah Darby, Cliett's, Columbia.
333 (fr.) John Cartwright, 141st, Greene.
334 (fr.) Ermine Case, Hall's, Butts.
335 (fr.) Robert D. Lumpkin, M'Clain's, Newton.*
336 (fr.) Ladrick Strickland, Allen's, Campbell.
337 (fr.) Terril Perry's ors., Rainey's, Twiggs.
338 (fr.) Joseph F. Greene, Phillips's, Talbot.
339 (fr.) John Burket, 537th, Upson.*
340 (fr.) Holland Red, Bryant's, Burke.
341 (fr.) Robert B. Williams, Moseley's, Wilkes.
342 (fr.) Nicholas Whitton, Cleland's, Habersham.*

12th DISTRICT, FOURTH SECTION, CHEROKEE.

1 Henry Key, s. l. w., 512th, Lee.
2 David Hern, 656th, Troup.
3 Ezra L. Crane, Candler's, Bibb.
4 John S. Foster, 7th, Chatham.
5 Thomas Kendrick, Grubbs's, Columbia.
6 Gracey Baley, w., 11th, Effingham.*
7 James G. Snipes, 494th, Upson.
8 Robert C. Bugg, Field's, Habersham.
9 William Dowers, Dobbs's, Hall.
10 Sarah Ginn, w. r. s., Bower's, Elbert.
11 Robert M. Douglass, Harris's, Crawford.
12 Robert H. Fretwell, 277th, Morgan.
13 Jesse C. Smith, Durham's, Talbot.*
14 Josiah Hodges, Streetman's, Twiggs.*
15 David Emanuel, 720th, Decatur.*
16 John H. Thomson, s. l. w., Martin's, Washington.
17 David Hollaway, 260th, Scriven.*
18 Asa Griffin, s. i. w., 114th, Hancock.
19 Henry Crawford, 242d, Jackson.*
20 Ulysses Lewis, Few's, Muscogee.
21 John J. Parkhurst, f. a., Buck's, Houston.*
22 Pleasant T. Hulsey, Dobbs's, Hall.

23 Abel Cain, sol., Rutland's, Bibb.*
24 Jackson Hightower, f. a., Bishop's, Henry.
25 Lodowick Rascow, Crow's, Pike.
26 Pheriby Moody, w., Hand's, Appling.*
27 Calvin Harman, Arrington's, Merriwether.
28 Polly Haygood, wid., Griffin's, De Kalb.
29 Samuel C. Houston, Tower's, Gwinnett.
30 Wilson Brown, Whisenhunt's, Carroll.
31 David A. Parker, 761st, Heard.*
32 Gilbert Watson, 672d, Harris.*
33 Robert Moseley, Gray's, Henry.
34 Britton Sims, sol., 107th, Hancock.
35 Francis E. Miller, Sanderlin's, Chatham.
36 Ratlif Echols's ors., Barron's, Houston.
37 Eli K. Clark, Athens, Clarke.
38 William Hicks, Martin's, Laurens.
39 Marshall B. Guill, 138th, Greene.
40 James Whetton, M'Gill's, Lincoln.*
41 Elizabeth Fulton, 15th, Liberty.*
42 Daniel Thomas, Bridges's, Gwinnett.
43 Nathan Martin, Rhodes's, De Kalb.
44 Michael Mooney, Clark's, Morgan.
45 Robert Hart, sol., Hart's, Jones.
46 William Shirling, Allen's, Monroe.
47 Darling P. Blalock, Moffett's, Muscogee.
48 Brockman W. Henderson, Moore's, Randolph.
49 Archibald Dancy, Curry's, Wilkinson.
50 Joseph J. Pinson, Hargrove's, Oglethorpe.*
51 Roger Hawkins, 3d section, Cherokee.
52 Hiram Booth, lu., Talley's, Troup.
53 William W. Stephens, Braddy's, Jones.
54 James Canaday, Gay's, Harris.*
55 Augustus Satterwhite, 141st, Greene.
56 James A. Middleton, Barker's, Gwinnett.
57 Thomas Walton, Newby's, Jones.
58 Clarissa Walker, w., Burgess's, Carroll.
59 James C. Eckles, s. l. w., 605th, Taliaferro.*
60 James Tool, sol., Winter's, Jones.
61 William Slay, Dean's, De Kalb.
62 James M. Bedgood, Barwick's, Washington.
63 Nancy Sexton, w., Edwards's, Franklin.
64 James Downs, Nellum's, Elbert.
65 Gary F. Parish, 122d, Richmond.
66 Lucy Glynn, w. r. s., 141st, Greene.
67 Peter Holland, M'Ginnis's, Jackson.
68 Anderson Troy, 789th, Sumter.
69 John A. Duncan, Nesbit's, Newton.

70 William Blair, Sen., Phillips's, Monroe.
71 John Hodges, Echols's, Clarke.
72 Jacob Lightsey, Morrison's, Appling.
73 Anderton Stafford, 588th, Upson.
74 Henry Bohannon, s. l. w., Bailey's, Laurens.
75 Darcas Hall, w., Mangham's, Franklin.
76 Daniel J. Purvis, 11th, Chatham.*
77 Fleming Manley, Hill's, Harris.
78 Mary Mackleroy, h. a., Riden's, Jackson.
79 William Willingham, Sanders's, Jones.
80 Daniel Smart, Perry's, Habersham.
81 James George, s. l. w., Alsobrook's, Jones.
82 Silas G. Easton, Lamberth's, Fayette.
83 Joseph Morgan, Coffee's, Rabun.
84 Henry F. Harden, Silman's, Pike.*
85 E. L. M'Carty, Candler's, Bibb.*
86 Abel Pierson, Herndon's, Hall.
87 Elias Scott, Bell's, Columbia.
88 Duncan Campbell, Trout's, Hall.
89 Henry Walker's ors., Parham's, Harris.
90 Andrew Jester, Loveless's, Gwinnett.
91 James W. Carson, Moseley's, Coweta.
92 Thomas Jarrell, Jr., Roberson's, Fayette.
93 George Vinson, Everett's, Washington.
94 Joel Gathright's ors., Athens, Clarke.*
95 Jonathan C. Coker, s. l. w., Moseley's, Coweta.
96 Abraham Hickman, Kendrick's, Monroe.
97 William M. Spence, Wynn's, Gwinnett.*
98 Henry S. Sylvester, Ellsworth's, Bibb.
99 Guilford Lastinger, Slater's, Bulloch.
100 Edward D. Watters,, Wheeler's, Pulaski.
101 Isaac Lindsey, Sen., r. s., Jones's, Hall.
102 Agrippa Whalay, Wynn's, Gwinnett.
103 William Robinson, Sparks's, Washington.
104 Eliza S. Roberts, w., 1st, Chatham.
105 William B. Bulloch, sol., Valleau's, Chatham.
106 I. Cummings, w. r. s., Garner's, Washington.*
107 William Mickler, Hobkerk's, Camden.
108 Martin Graham, Baugh's, Jackson.
109 John Harris, Roberts's, Hall.
110 Pearce's three orphans, 404th, Gwinnett.
111 Starling Acree, s. l. w., 607th, Taliaferro.
112 William P. Simmons, Lester's, Monroe.
113 Thomas Mayes, r. s., David's, Franklin.*
114 Joroyal Barnett, Seay's, Hall.
115 Nancy Black, w., Harris's, Crawford.
116 Julius G. Darby, 454th, Walton.

117 John S. Evans, 788th, Heard.
118 James Thompson, Jr., Shearer's, Coweta.
119 Jacob Readwine, r. s., Bower's, Elbert.
120 Jacob Wolfe, Heard's, De Kalb.*
121 Benjamin F. Fuller, 318th, Baldwin.
122 Eli Whaley, Compton's, Fayette.
123 Howell W. Jenkins, Talley's, Troup.
124 Emanuel Parker, sol., 142d, Greene.
125 Osburn Wilkes, M'Gehee's, Troup.
126 George Fox, 417th, Walton.*
127 Benjamin Willis, Jr.; Wallis's, Irwin.
128 Davis Seaborn, Davis's, Jones.
129 William M'Leod, Burnett's, Lowndes.
130 Frances Swan, w., 466th, Monroe.
131 Roger Bell, s. l. w., 559th, Walton.
132 Jeremiah Walker, Greene's, Ware.*
133 Isaac S. Dedge, Morrison's, Appling.*
134 Nancy Bell, w., Clark's, Elbert.
135 Benjamin F. Dickerson, Williams's, Decatur.
136 Eli H. Moxley, 71st, Burke.*
137 Malcomb Currie, Peterson's, Montgomery.*
138 James Jones, Shearer's, Coweta.*
139 David J. Apperson, Payne's, Merriwether.
140 Ervin Askew, Thompson's, Henry.
141 Middleton B. Montgomery, 404th, Gwinnett.*
142 Joseph Tanner, 250th, Walton.
143 Jonathan Penley, 1st section, Cherokee.*
144 Spencer W. Riley, Martin's, Stewart.
145 Thomas Worthy, Cannon's, Wilkinson.
146 Mary Davis, w. r. s., Peterson's, Montgomery.
147 Matthew Dance, Hall's, Oglethorpe.
148 Henry Bludworth, Griffin's, Fayette.
149 John H. Gresham, sol., Chambers's, Gwinnett.*
150 Abel Griffin, lun., 114th, Hancock.*
151 Bird L. Newton, Groover's, Thomas.*
152 John C. Crump, 59th, Emanuel.
153 Rachel Brooks, w. r. s., Rhodes's, De Kalb.*
154 Jabed Hearn, Heard's, De Kalb.
155 James Karr, Merck's, Hall.
156 Elijah Martin, Wolfskin's, Oglethorpe.*
157 John Gregory, Marsh's, Thomas.*
158 Zacheys Smith, Moore's, Randolph.*
159 Mark Maberry, Fleming's, Franklin.
160 Thomas Chamberlane, M'Gill's, Lincoln.
161 Brice H. Bishop, 149th, Greene.
162 Littleberry W. Baker, Crow's, Merriwether.
163 William Mackey, Blount's, Wilkinson.*

164 Green Brantley, Lightfoot's, Washington.
165 Hartwell Jackson, Morgan's, Clarke.*
166 Anderson Wheeler, Loveless's, Gwinnett.
167 Thomas Smith's ors., Ellis's, Pulaski.
168 Thomas Ramey, Coffee's, Rabun.*
169 Richard H. Watts, 419th, Walton.*
170 Hugh Montgomery, 404th, Gwinnett.*
171 Rachel Hinton, w., Davis's, Clarke.*
172 Henry Harriss, 279th, Morgan.
173 John Martin, Simmons's, Crawford.
174 Bailey Harris's ors., Jordan's, Bibb.'
175 Thomas Mahaffee, Hendon's, Carroll.'
176 Johnson Rowell, Burgess's, Carroll.*
177 Benjamin G. Smith, Smith's, Houston.*
178 Washington Pearce, Smith's, Madison.*
179 Josiah Jordan's ors., ———, Oglethorpe.
180 Hardy Jernigan, sol., 104th, Hancock.*
181 John L. Baird, 672d, Harris.*
182 Jesse B. Buchannan, Williams's, Jasper.*
183 Elizabeth Phillips, w., Madden's, Pike.*
184 Powell Vincent, Williams's, Washington.*
185 Jeremiah Burnett's ors., Echols's, Clarke.
186 Thomas L. Robertson, Alberson's, Walton.*
187 Benjamin Cogburn, 588th, Upson.
188 Alander L. Hill, Givins's, Fayette.*
189 Sarrah Batty, w., Valleau's, Chatham.
190 John Binion's ors., 102d, Hancock.
191 Thomas Mosley, sol., Peterson's, Montgomery *
192 Vixon Cureton, Coxe's, Talbot.*
193 William Egnew, 373d, Jasper.*
194 William H. Betts's ors., 419th, Walton.
195 James G. Chappell, Willingham's, Harris.
196 William Bell, Goodwin's, Houston.
197 Daniel Moulder, Edwards's, Franklin.
198 George W. Barrett, M'Korkle's, Jasper.*
199 Marshall Parks, Kelly's, Elbert.
200 Mary Twilley, w., Foote's, De Kalb.
201 David S. Boulet, 120th, Richmond.
202 Plares Ray, Marshall's, Putnam.
203 Barbara Lee, w., Marshall's, Crawford.
204 Samuel Field, Hammond's, Franklin.
205 Tryon Elkins, 2d, Chatham.
206 James Welsh, Athens, Clarke.
207 James Q. Wills, Crow's, Merriwether.*
208 Elisha Payne's ors., 672d, Harris.*
209 Robert Johnson, Johnson's, Bibb.*
210 James & Alfred M'Keen, ors., 398th, Richmond.*

211 James Holderness, Taylor's, Houston.*
212 James M. Lane, 510th, Early.*
213 Amzi Gailey, Griffin's, Hall.*
214 William J. Wightman, 398th, Richmond.*
215 J. J. E. & L. Williams, ors., 404th, Gwinnett.*
216 Isham White, Whitfield's, Washington.*
217 Martha Singletary, w. r. s., Harrison's, Decatur.*
218 Jethro Norris, Jr., Brewer's, Walton.*
219 Rhadford Bridges, 415th, Walton.*
220 Theophilus Scarbor, Lockhart's, Bulloch.*
221 William F. Mitchell, Barker's, Gwinnett.*
222 Thomas J. Parmelee, 120th, Richmond.*
223 Aaron Johnson, sol., Smith's, Houston.
224 John Holley, Martin's, Washington.
225 Christian's four orphans, Jones's, Madison.
226 John R. T. Lingo, Will's, Twiggs.
227 Mary Hunt, w., Streetman's, Twiggs.
228 Henry Powell, Mason's, Washington.*
229 John O. Dickson, Gittens's, Fayette.
230 John M. Born, Maguire's, Gwinnett.
231 Joshua Ellis, Park's, Walton.
232 Lot Wheeler, Newman's, Thomas.*
233 John Blackman, Lockhart's, Bulloch.
234 Ephraim Peebles, Newsom's, Warren.
235 Cornelius Hardy, Williams's, Jasper.*
236 Mills Howell, 118th, Hancock.
237 Henry Sanford, sol., 143d, Greene.
238 Permidas Reynolds, Stanton's, Newton.
239 Alvan E. Whitten, Hammond's, Franklin.
240 Joshua Miller, sol., 10th, Effingham.
241 Meredith Sneed, Athens, Clarke.*
242 William Tate, Hughes's, Habersham.
243 Abner F. Gibson, Ross's, Monroe.
244 James H. Cobb, Lester's, Pulaski.
245 Martin Defurr, White's, Franklin.
246 Johnson Norman, 166th, Wilkes.*
247 William B. Noles, White's, Franklin.
248 Benjamin Ansley, Stanton's, Newton.
249 John Moses, Allen's, Campbell.*
250 Lovett M'Donald, Cannon's, Washington.
251 John Way's ors., Sen., 15th, Liberty.
252 James T. Connally, Seay's, Hall.
253 Matthew W. Coleman, 779th, Heard.*
254 Goodson's four orphans, Smith's, Habersham.
255 William Tucker, Nellum's, Elbert.*
256 Samuel Smith's ors., Holley's, Franklin.
257 Hardy Coker, 250th, Walton.*

258 Aaron Formon's or., of Cher., Latimer's, De Kalb.
259 John Tucker, Harrison's, Decatur.
260 Abner Chastain, Chastain's, Habersham.
261 Henry Mattux, 192d, Elbert.
262 Seth K. Adams, 373d, Jasper.
263 Susannah Wall, w., Ellsworth's, Bibb.*
264 Meade Lesueur, Ross's, Monroe.
265 William Kinsey's six ors., Jones's, Habersham.
266 Ann Wade, w., Royster's, Franklin.
267 Horris Vann, Gibson's, Decatur.
268 George Slaton, Lay's, Jackson.*
269 William Taunton, Garner's, Washington.*
270 Josiah Gibson, sol., Gittens's, Fayette.*
271 Doctor James B. Stephens, 15th, Liberty.*
272 Stewart M'Elhannan, Lay's, Jackson.*
273 Barney L. Freeman, Jones's, Habersham.*
274 James S. Jones, Stewart's, Warren.*
275 Pen. Ashmore's ors., Strickland's, Merriwether.
276 Duncan M'Arthur, 394th, Montgomery.
277 Ralph Lamaster, Chastain's, Habersham.
278 Michael Cowart, wid'r., Wood's, Jefferson.
279 Isaac Howell, 608th, Taliaferro.
280 John Bagby, sol., Hodges's, Newton.
281 James R. Spear's three orphans, 271st, M'Intosh.
282 Edward W. Wright, Ellsworth's, Bibb.
283 Robert Jerkins, Whipple's, Wilkinson.*
284 Dennis Darden, 59th, Emanuel.*
285 Arnold B. Fassell, Sweat's, Ware.*
286 Eliza Crow, w., Mobley's, De Kalb.
287 Jonathan H. Jenkins, Moffett's, Muscogee.
288 John M. Woolsey, sol., Butts's, Monroe.
289 Jesse Murphy, Chambers's, Gwinnett.
290 William M'Mullen, Liddell's, Jackson.
291 G. D. Hightower, Mason's, Washington.
292 Gabriel Besinger, 271st, M'Intosh.*
293 Thomas J. Smith, 293d, Jasper.
294 William Jordan, s. l. w., 732d, Dooly.
295 John S. Wood, Brock's, Habersham.
296 William Parker, Davis's, Jones.
297 Joseph Crockett, s. l. w., 788th, Heard.
298 James Kerkes, Chambers's, Gwinnett.
299 Moses Broome, 601st, Taliaferro.*
300 Wiley Bearden, Whelchel's, Hall.
301 Abraham Petterjohn, sol., Chastain's, Habersham*
302 James L. Norman, 27th, Glynn.*
303 Jacob M. Cleveland, Clark's, Elbert.*
304 Robert Marks, Parham's, Warren.*

305 Duncan M'Swain's ors., Covington's, Pike.*
306 Jeptha Gilbert, sol., Killen's, Decatur.*
307 George Head, 294th, Jasper.*
308 Thomas R. Dupree, Mizell's, Talbot.*
309 Charles A. Grant's ors., Morris's, Crawford.
310 A. B. Linton, sol., Athens, Clarke.*
311 Job Magee, Ellsworth's, Bibb.
312 Caleb A. Lindley, Hearn's, Butts.
313 Mitchell Story, Norris's, Monroe.
314 Albert G. Bagwell, or., Hammond's, Franklin.*
315 John Gimble, Robinson's, Putnam.
316 Micajah Dyer, Colley's, Oglethorpe.*
317 William Dunn, 364th, Jasper.
318 Nancy Jenkins, w., 404th, Gwinnett.
319 John Sparks, sol., Chambers's, Gwinnett.
320 John T. Edmundson, Dyer's, Habersham.
321 Stroud Milton, Park's, Walton.
322 Lawrence Smith, Williams's, Ware.*
323 Green L. M'Bee, Baugh's, Jackson.
324 Benjamin Woolsey, sol., Hill's, Baldwin.

13th DISTRICT, FOURTH SECTION, CHEROKEE.

1 Joel Forrester, Sen., s. i. w., 140th, Greene.
2 Catharine Phillips, w., Williams's, Walton.*
3 Emanuel Britton, Moffett's, Muscogee.*
4 John Hill, Jr., Baugh's, Jackson.
5 Frazer F. Wood, Nesbit's, Newton.
6 Isaac Mitchell, sol., Seas's, Hall.
7 Daniel Wagnon, 141st, Greene.
8 Moses W. Ways's or., 15th, Liberty.*
9 Mary Myers, w. r. s., 271st, M'Intosh.
10 Frances Duke, w., 788th, Heard.*
11 James Ramsey, sol., David's, Franklin.*
12 Martha Dees, w., Brown's, Camden.
13 William Collins, s. i. w., 720th, Decatur.*
14 William Turner, 734th, Lee.
15 Joseph Weldon, Gay's, Harris.*
16 Edmund Smart, Killen's, Decatur.*
17 William C. Wallis, s. l. w., Mann's, Crawford.*
18 Quinton Hoy, sol., Johnson's, Bibb.*
19 Lovick P. Hodnett, 656th, Troup.*
20 Elizabeth Miles, w., Evans's, Laurens.*
21 William Neal, 149th, Greene.*

22 Thomas C. Kendrick, Robinson's, Putnam.*
23 Elizabeth Swearingen, w., 516th, Dooly.*
24 John Nealson's ors., Evans's, Fayette.
25 Jane Sparks, w. r. s., Stewart's, Troup.
26 James Holland, Nesbit's, Newton.
27 Isaac Bailey, Strickland's, Merriwether.*
28 David N. Quin, Collier's, Monroe.*
29 Joel Caver, M'Gill's, Lincoln.*
30 William Cole, 55th, Emanuel.*
31 Beverly A. Freeman, Peurifoy's, Henry.*
32 Elizabeth M'Kee, w., Seas's, Madison.*
33 Orsamus Spraggins, Sen., Moseley's, Coweta.*
34 Richard Garner, Mitchell's, Pulaski.*
35 William Hall, Atkinson's, Coweta.*
36 Albert Jones, Robinson's, Putnam.*
37 Henry H. Wall, Boynton's, Twiggs.
38 Bryant White, Baismore's, Jones.*
39 George Hunt, s. l. w., Mattox's, Coweta.*
40 Theophilus Pearce, 144th, Greene.*
41 Donald M'Donald, Madden's, Pike.*
42 William Doby, 1st, Chatham.*
43 Nancy Hart, w., Peacock's, Washington.*
44 Shadrack T. Williams, Perryman's, Warren.
45 Thomas W. Henderson, sol., Rainey's, Twiggs
46 Moses Justice, Ellis's, Rabun.
47 Rice Henderson, Hitchcock's, Muscogee.*
48 Elizabeth Ball, w., Mitchell's, Pulaski.*
49 William Branham, 404th, Gwinnett.*
50 Mary Nichols, w., Bostick's, Twiggs.*
51 Susannah Black, w., Jones's, Habersham.*
52 Simeon Humphrey, Cleggs's, Walton.*
53 James B. Holcomb, 466th, Monroe.*
54 John Anderson, Field's, Habersham.*
55 Hester Reese, w., 119th, Richmond.*
56 Edward Mires, Young's, Wilkinson.*
57 Daniel M'Millan, Robertson's, Telfair.
58 Elizabeth Holland, w., 604th, Taliaferro.*
59 Henry Bush, Bryan's, Pulaski.*
60 Elizabeth Jennings, w., Heard's, De Kalb.*
61 Noah Mercer, Braddy's, Jones.*
62 Turner Hunt, Jr., sol., Norris's, Monroe.*
63 Isaac Laroche's ors., 122d, Richmond.
64 Paschal H. Jackson, Griffin's, De Kalb.*
65 Elias Grouver, 11th, Effingham.
66 Larkin W. Woodruff, Jenkins's, Oglethorpe.
67 Martin Dial, Jr., Alberson's, Walton.*
68 George Watts, r. s., Mobley's, De Kalb.*

69 Thomas Bell, Martin's, Hall.*
70 Alston Clark Hallums, Herndon's, Hall.
71 Robert Owen, 365th, Jasper.*
72 Nathan C. Monroe, Ellsworth's, Bibb.*
73 John E. Disheroon, Edwards's, Talbot.*
74 Lee R. Miller, Dupree's, Washington.*
75 William H. Bailey, Clark's, Morgan.*
76 Isaiah L. Swain, Hand's, Appling.*
77 James Lewis's ors., 6th, Chatham.
78 Moses Bridges, Hargrove's, Oglethorpe.
79 Thomas Anthony, M'Ginnis's, Jackson.
80 Abram Smith, Griffin's, Merriwether.
81 David Lowrey, m. s., Seay's, Hall.*
82 Joshua M'Entyre, Edwards's, Franklin.*
83 Josiah Thrower, Mayo's, Wilkinson.*
84 Nathan Dobbs, r. s., Hamilton's, Gwinnett.*
85 Edmund Swint, Haygood's, Washington.*
86 Josiah Watson, sol., 245th, Jackson.*
87 Benjamin Richerson, m. s., 160th, Greene.*
88 James B. Allen, Covington's, Pike.*
89 Benjamin Oscar, sol., Kendrick's, Monroe.*
90 Thomas O'Kelly, Alberson's, Walton.*
91 William Brown, Smith's, Henry.
92 Hannah E. Crews, w., 11th, Effingham.
93 Sheldon Swift, Hitchcock's, Muscogee.*
94 James Cooper, Harp's, Stewart.*
95 Robert Bond, Everett's, Washington.*
96 James D. Jarratt, 318th, Baldwin.*
97 James Stephens, 561st, Upson.*
98 Lewis Day, 559th, Walton.
99 James B. Rouse, Hudson's, Marion.*
100 Lewis Bagley, 318th, Baldwin.*
101 John Hemby, Phillip's, Talbot.*
102 Elizabeth Moore, w., Loven's, Henry.
103 Robert M. Simms, Compton's, Fayette.*
104 Elizabeth Johnson, w., Pounds's, Twiggs.
105 William H. Morrow's ors., Stanton's, Newton.
106 William Hunt, Athens, Clarke.*
107 William S. Sharp, Payne's, Merriwether.
108 Patrick M. Thomas, 734th, Lee.*
109 Luke Gravitt, Roberts's, Hall.*
110 Matthew Elmore, Ross's, Monroe.*
111 Fennel Hendricks, M'Ginnis's, Jackson.*
112 Orphans of Wesley Knight, Pearce's, Houston.
113 Thomas B. Wynn, Hatchett's, Oglethorpe.
114 Willett W. Snell, Mashburn's, Pulaski.*
115 Gideon Powledge, Edwards's, Talbot.

116 Jacob Reed, sol., Beasley's, Oglethorpe.*
117 Ashton B. Cox, 398th, Richmond.*
118 Wiley Auders, Welche's, Habersham.*
119 William Winslow, Williams's, Decatur.*
120 John Pierce, Willis's, Franklin.*
121 William D. Tinsley, Greer's, Merriwether.*
122 William Hill's or., Mattox's, Lowndes.
123 Dunham Singletary, Johnson's, Bibb.*
124 Mary Wills, w., Phillip's, Talbot.
125 James T. Robertson, sol., 143d, Greene.*
126 Wayne Wise, Echols's, Clarke.
127 Edwin Calier, Mizell's, Talbot.
128 John Witcher, Sen., 4th section, Cherokee.
129 David Garrison's ors., Reid's, Gwinnett.
130 John Worsham, 362d, Jasper.
131 Mary Brown w., 271st, M'Intosh.*
132 John Gilbert, r. s., 243d, Jackson.*
133 Uriah Sappy, Marshall's, Crawford.
134 Robert Garrett, Curry's, Wilkinson.
135 Jesse Pitts, 364th, Jasper.*
136 Elias Fincher, Barker's, Gwinnett.*
137 William M'Leroy, Scroggins's, Oglethorpe.*
138 James Armstrong, 320th, Baldwin.*
139 Ganaway Malcombe, Coxe's, Morgan.
140 Elijah Anglin, s. i. w., Will's, Twiggs.*
141 Edward Kelly, r. s., Bush's, Pulaski.
142 Joseph Morrow, Heard's, De Kalb.
143 Elijah Owens, Sutton's, Habersham.
144 Benjamin T. Standard, M'Ewin's, Monroe.*
145 Abram Smith, 2d section, Cherokee.
146 Joseph Williams, Shearer's, Coweta.
147 Nathaniel Bibby, Calhoun's, Harris.*
148 Joseph C. Higginbotham, House's, Henry.*
149 Robert L. Harris, Jones's, Morgan.*
150 John Walker, Hearn's, Butts.*
151 Charles Underwood, Brown's, Camden.*
152 Mary E. Peeble's ors., 318th, Baldwin.*
153 Henry Harned Baker, Valleau's, Chatham.*
154 William Cleveland, sol. 1784–97, 295th, Jasper.*
155 James Stone, 250th, Walton.*
156 Daniel M'Red, Whisenhunt's, Carroll.*
157 John Wynn's ors., 15th, Liberty.*
158 Wilson Weaver, Hudson's, Marion.*
159 Pleasant Roberts, 374th, Putnam.
160 Patrick C. Haine's ors., 398th, Richmond.*
161 Thomas B. Harwell, 295th, Jasper.
162 Renne Fitzpatrick, r. s., 779th, Heard.

163 Rebecca Bagwell, w., Wynn's, Gwinnett.*
164 Solomon Gross, sol. 1784–97, 294th, Jasper.*
165 Milton W. Gillespie, Mangum's, Franklin.*
166 Asa Whitby, Mullen's, Carroll.
167 John P. Hutchins, Chambers's, Gwinnett.
168 William M. Coulter, Thaxton's, Butts.
169 Mary Williams's children, 34th, Scriven.
170 James Clark, Streetman's, Twiggs.*
171 James Carpenter, sol., Stower's, Elbert.*
172 William Morrow, Chandler's, Franklin.*
173 Midas L. Greybill, Ellsworth's, Bibb.*
174 Wyat Williams, sol., Beasley's, Oglethorpe.*
175 Elizabeth Haney, w., Wynn's, Gwinnett.*
176 William Guess, Gillis's, De Kalb.*
177 M'Gregor Baisden, 25th, Glynn.*
178 John Hawkins, s. i. w., Howard's, Oglethorpe.
179 Enoch Morriss, Johnson's, De Kalb.*
180 William Freeman, 38th, Scriven.
181 John Smith's ors., M'Cleland's, Irwin.
182 Nancey Williams, w. r. s., 177th, Wilkes.
183 John T. Duke, Coxe's, Morgan.*
184 Martin Stedham, M'Clain's, Newton.*
185 Joseph C. Higginbotham, House's, Henry.*
186 Evan Davis, Dozier's, Columbia.*
187 Elisha Delong's ors., Reid's, Gwinnett.
188 Pinkney H. Edge, id., Whitehead's, Habersham.*
189 John Bellamy, Garner's, Coweta.*
190 John Holton, Barron's, Houston.*
191 Jesse Berry, 672d, Harris.
192 Jesse Cohom, Campbell's, Wilkes.
193 Hardy H. Acree, Hatton's, Baker.*
194 Henry Davis, Peavy's, Bulloch.*
195 John Hill, Griffin's, Merriwether.
196 Eli C. Norton, Griffin's, Fayette.*
197 Jacob A. H. Reviere, Dozier's, Columbia.
198 Samuel M'Lendon, s. i. w., Dearing's, Henry.*
199 James Bennett's ors., 734th, Lee.
200 Turner A. Cleaves, Peurifoy's, Henry.
201 David K. Roach, Lynn's, Warren.
202 John Parrott, Hobbs's, Laurens.*
203 Andrew R. Moore, Peurifoy's, Henry.
204 Charles Matthews, Pate's, Warren.*
205 William M'Collock, Lawrence's, Pike.
206 Jane Hudgepeth, w., Allen's, Monroe.
207 Jeremiah B. Covington, Silman's, Pike.*
208 Benjamin J. Rolls, Harrison's, Decatur.*
209 Thomas Smalley, Tankersley's, Columbia.

210 Joseph B. Hunt, Fenn's, Clarke.*
211 Jeremiah S. Tucker, Phillips's, Jasper.
212 Luke Johnson, Collins's, Henry.*
213 William Edge, Whitehead's, Habersham.*
214 Yancy R. M'Vey, Dilman's, Pulaski.*
215 George W. Roberts, Folsom's, Lowndes.*
216 Lewis Packer, 555th, Upson.*
217 Thomas J. Johnson, sol., Marsh's, Thomas.*
218 Connaway's three orphans, Hargrove's, Newton.*
219 Charles T. Power, Smith's, Madison.*
220 Robert G. Gilmer, Howard's, Oglethorpe.*
221 Claiborn Osborn, Loveless's, Gwinnett.*
222 David Thompson, Sen., sol., 249th, Walton.
223 Philip Cook, sol., M'Gehee's, Troup.*
224 John C. Hamilton, Candler's, Bibb.
225 Pledge Price, Sparks's, Washington.
226 Isaac Justus, Ellis's, Rabun.
227 Benjamin Hill's ors., M'Clain's, Newton.
228 Elisha Perryman, Jr., sol., Perryman's, Warren.
229 Allen Reaves, Nichols's, Fayette.
230 Augustus W. Tipper, Peurifoy's, Henry.
231 Jacob Swearingen, 516th, Dooly.*
232 Wiatt R. Smith, 295th, Jasper.
233 Enoch Jackson, Watson's, Marion.
234 Axam Bailey, Burk's, Stewart.
235 Edmund Pryor, or., 69th, Burke.
236 Joseph Byars, Dearing's, Butts.
237 James Dixon, 1st, Chatham.
238 David Boland, Hines's, Coweta.
239 Jane Goolsby, or., Guice's, Oglethorpe.
240 Elias Allison, Sen., sol., 278th, Morgan.
241 James J. Dooly, Bell's, Columbia.
242 Joseph A. Wishard, Hitchcock's, Muscogee*
243 John Rainwater, 142d, Greene.*
244 Frederic Pope, Martin's, Laurer*.
245 James Hubbard, 149th, Greene.
246 Henry Matthews, Parham's, Harris
247 Samuel Hall, Hill's, Baldwin.*
248 Chappell's three orphans, 454th, Walton.
249 Matthew Warnock, Rhodes's, De Kalb.*
250 James Lindsey, or., Strickland's, Merriwether.*
251 Edward Brown, Groce's, Bibb.*
252 David Carter, Morrison's, Appling.*
253 Elijah Perth, Trout's, Hall.*
254 John T. Thornton, Gay's, Harris.*
255 James Echols, Loven's, Henry.*
256 James Powell, Candler's, Bibb.*

257 Edward H. Saterfield, Jones's, Habersham.
258 James O. Ragland, sol., Ellis's, Rabun.
259 Herndon Harralson, 141st, Greene.
260 Michael Ryley's ors., Collins's, Henry.
261 Grissom Dekle, Newman's, Thomas.
262 Floyd Winslett, 160th, Greene.
263 James Hardy, Payne's, Merriwether.
264 Shatteen C. Mitchell, M'Korkle's, Jasper.
265 John D. Gordon, Hannah's, Campbell.*
266 Lewis S. Nobles, r. s., Peterson's, Montgomery.*
267 William Yawn, 720th, Decatur.
268 William L. Alfriend, 162d, Greene.
269 James M. Nellums, Seal's, Elbert.
270 Benjamin Williamson, York's, Stewart.
271 John E. Sewell, Heard's, De Kalb.*
272 Andrew J. Griffith, Maguire's, Gwinnett.*
273 Wm. M'Canless's ors., Williams's, Washington.
274 Selah Spears, w. r. s., Hines's, Coweta.
275 Thomas White's ors., Gunn's, Jones.
276 James Palen, sol., Cleland's, Chatham.*
277 Thomas M'Clure, Mullen's, Carroll.
278 George W. Sanders, Alberson's, Walton.
279 Butler S. Turner, Alberson's, Walton.*
280 Jeremiah Darby, Cliett's, Columbia.
281 James Kilgore, Harp's, Stewart.
282 Sarah Smith, w., Whitehead's, Habersham.
283 Joseph D. Baker, Dobbs's, Hall.
284 John Treadaway, Brewer's, Walton.*
285 Edwin Duke, minor, f. a., Brackett's, Newton.
286 William Bradberry, Madden's, Pike.*
287 Nevill M. Lumpkin, Howard's, Oglethorpe.*
288 (fr.) Sampson P. Mobley, Simmons's, Crawford.*
289 (fr.) Lemuel Dwitte, 600th, Richmond.*
290 (fr.) James English, Burnett's, Lowndes.
291 (fr.) Samuel Wright, sol., Martin's, Jones.*
292 James F. Allen, Sanders's, Jones.
293 Ezekiel Clements, Barwick's, Washington.
294 Azmond R. Almand, Mobley's, De Kalb.
295 Mason Chumbler, Miller's, Jackson.*
296 James D. Hudson, Madden's, Pike.
297 William Phillips's minors, Swain's, Thomas.
298 William M. C. Neel, Jr., Williams's, Decatur.
299 John Gallman, Allen's, Henry.
300 Frederic Land, sol., Stone's, Irwin.
301 James H. M'Ewin, sol., M'Ewin's, Monroe.
302 William Parker, Brown's, Habersham.
303 John Clark, r. s., Collier's, Monroe.*

304 Seaborn Downs, 10th, Effingham.*
305 John Parrish, 537th, Upson.
306 Thomas Edmonson, Chandler's, Franklin.
307 Windsor Graham, Dearing's, Henry.*
308 Daniel Dunn, 406th, Gwinnett.
309 William Loftley, 640th, Dooley.
310 Abraham Greene, 123d, Richmond.*
311 (fr.) Austin Kenman, Martin's, Washington.*
312 (fr.) John Reynolds, Harris's, Columbia.
313 (fr.) George W. Snow, Wagnon's, Carroll.
314 (fr.) Benjamin Brock's ors., 74th, Burke.
315 (fr.) Solomon Williams, 735th, Troup.
316 (fr.) John Jenkins, 122d, Richmond.
317 (fr.) James V. Drake, Hatchett's, Oglethorpe.
318 John Dawner, 177th, Wilkes.*

14th DISTRICT, FOURTH SECTION, CHEROKEE.

1 Henry T. Bumley, Newsom's, Warren.*
2 Jesse Liptrot, 74th, Burke.*
3 John Higgs, Daniel's, Hall.*
4 Moses Wilson, sol., Espy's, Clarke.*
5 Richard Hutchinson, 417th, Walton.*
6 Jerry Warner's ors., Jordan's, Bibb.*
7 Jesse Bowden, Monk's, Crawford.*
8 Sampson Gibbs, Stone's, Irwin.
9 Thompson Hawk, Hutson's, Newton.*
10 Littleton R. Brewer, Echols's, Clarke.*
11 John Oliver, Sen., Thomas's, Clarke.*
12 Silas Misser, Linam's, Pulaski.*
13 John Grizzle, Chastain's, Habersham.*
14 William M. Harrison, 607th, Taliaferro.*
15 Seaborn D. Slatham, Stone's, Irwin.*
16 Elizabeth Cohom, w. r. s., 603d, Taliaferro.*
17 Wiley Rhodes, 601st, Taliaferro.*
18 Thomas S. Satterwhite, Simmons's, Crawford.*
19 Thomas Sherby, Johnson's, Lowndes.
20 Seth Armes, 295th, Jasper.*
21 Erwin Strickland, Gillis's, De Kalb.*
22 Luke M'Glaughen, Carswell's, Jefferson.*
23 Nancy Wilks, w. r. s., Howell's, Elbert.*
24 Littleton Baker, 406th, Gwinnett.*
25 Robert Cooper, Whisenhunt's, Carroll.
26 Isaac Bowen, Walker's, Columbia.*

27 Edmund Gross's ors., 34th, Scriven.*
28 Rebecca Mooneyham, or., Taylor's, Putnam.*
29 David Brown, Ogden's, Camden.*
30 (fr.) Guilford Kent, Wheeler's, Pulaski.*
31 (fr.) Henry Harrison, 293d, Jasper.*
32 John Sparrow, Wheeler's, Pulaski.*
33 Absolem Kenedy, sol., Lester's, Monroe.*
34 Collin Shackelford, Hampton's, Newton.*
35 Isaac Hughes, Mobley's, De Kalb.
36 Richard Strother, s. i. w., 111th, Hancock.
37 Samuel Sellars, Hatton's, Baker.*
38 John Springer, sol., Candler's, Bibb.*
39 John Buckner, Catlett's, Franklin.*
40 John Temples, Royster's, Franklin.*
41 James Boyd, Reid's, Gwinnett.*
42 Joseph Austin, 15th, Liberty.*
43 James Hardwick, Roe's, Burke.*
44 Charles C. Whitehead, Streetman's, Twiggs.*
45 Coleman C. Gibbs, Alberson's, Walton.*
46 William Hamilton, sol., Prescott's, Twiggs.*
47 William Johnston, Robinson's, Harris.*
48 Susannah Craft, w., 320th, Baldwin.*
49 James Hudpeth's ors., Allen's, Monroe.
50 Joseph B. Williams, Higginbotham's, Rabun.*
51 Stephen Petty, Heard's, De Kalb.*
52 James Belk, Sen., 604th, Taliaferro.*
53 Thomas A. Gordon's ors., Gunn's, Jones.
54 Thomas Davis, Welche's, Habersham.*
55 Hiram Holston, Strickland's, Merriwether.*
56 Rebecca Hood, or., Norris's, Monroe.
57 John & Martha Jenkins, ors., 119th, Richmond.
58 John Spencer, sol., 192d, Elbert.*
59 Edmund Rix, Woodruff's, Campbell.
60 (fr.) Oran W. Young's ors., Evans's, Laurens.*
61 (fr.) Francis S. Johnson, Candler's, Bibb.
62 Joseph Phillips, Ellsworth's, Bibb.*
63 Elizabeth Henry, w. r. s., 106th, Hancock.
64 Uriah Sumner, Hart's, Jones.*
65 Isaac Perdue, sol., Kendrick's, Monroe.*
66 Felix D. Woodyard, 277th Morgan.*
67 William Andrews, Whisenhunt's, Carroll.*
68 James Fleming's two ors., 138th, Greene.
69 Jepthal V. Davis, 138th, Greene.*
70 George Houston, Kellum's, Talbot.*
71 John M. Rayford, Clark's, Elbert.*
72 William Stone, Higginbotham's, Rabun.*
73 Asa M'Clusky, Norris's, Monroe.*

74 Whitfield Williams, Chiles's, Marion.*
75 Martin Mixon, Hand's, Appling.*
76 William Lunsford, sol., Seal's, Elbert.
77 Jane Henderson, w., Lunceford's, Wilkes.
78 Jonathan Williams, Coffee's, Rabun.*
79 John Fussell, Dixon's, Irwin.*
80 Uriah Skinner, Jr., Roe's, Burke.*
81 Rufus Ray, Adams's, Columbia.*
82 Julius Clark, 561st, Upson.*
83 Joshua Morris, Morgan's, Clarke.*
84 Benjamin Couger, Barker's, Gwinnett.*
85 Antonio Lewis, Cliett's, Columbia.
86 John Holland, Sen., Jones's, Hall.*
87 Elam Smith, 588th, Upson.
88 Jesse Godwin, Blair's, Lowndes.
89 Elijah Hammond, Sen., Hannah's, Campbell.
90 (fr.) William M. Gilmore, Robinson's, Harris.
91 Jonathan Hall, Hill's, Harris.
92 William Skinner, Roe's, Burke.*
93 Walter Mitchell, 242d, Jackson.*
94 John Clifton's ors., Loven's, Henry.*
95 Frederic Nance's three orphans, 138th, Greene.
96 Richard Iley, sol., Sewell's, Jackson.*
97 John Jacobs's ors., 335th, Wayne.
98 Benjamin H. Cameron, Talley's, Troup.*
99 B. Triewett, Sinclair's, Houston.*
100 Mary W. Patterson, id., Hart's, Jones.*
101 Edward Rhyner, 56th, Emanuel.*
102 John B. Turner, Whisenhunt's, Carroll.*
103 Thomas Harriss, 279th, Morgan.
104 John Dial, Alberson's, Walton.
105 William N. Touchstone, Bustin's, Pike.
106 N. Bridges's ors., Candler's, Bibb.*
107 Benjamin Bell's ors., Davis's, Jones.
108 Delila Davidson, Martin's, Jones.*
109 William Fauste, 759th, Sumter.*
110 Mountain Greene, Lawrence's, Pike.*
111 Alexander J. Huie, Evans's, Fayette.*
112 Joel Matthews, Whitaker's, Crawford.
113 John Harmon, Sen., r. s., Lunceford's, Elbert.
114 Sarah Jackson, w., 109th, Hancock.*
115 Lewis Sheppard, 561st, Upson.*
116 Henry H. Lowe, 672d, Harris.
117 (fr.) Arthur Johnson, Brewer's, Monroe.
118 (fr.) John D. Pitts, Jordan's, Bibb.*
119 Josiah Hamilton, Peterson's, Montgomery.*
120 Lemuel Cobb, Foote's, De Kalb.*

121 Thomas Whitehead, 672d, Harris.
122 James A. Jordan, 656th, Troup.*
123 Stephen Johnson, Goodwin's, Houston.
124 William Reid, M'Clure's, Rabun.*
125 Sarah Coleman, w., Hatton's, Baker.*
126 George James's ors., Tower's, Gwinnett.*
127 Joseph B. Anthony, Braddy's, Jones.*
128 Augustus H. Findley, Frasier's, Monroe.*
129 George Barr, Canning's, Elbert.
130 Thomas Wilson's ors., 398th, Richmond.*
131 William Masengate, Buck's, Houston.*
132 Levin Clifton, sol., Foote's, De Kalb.*
133 James Lawrence, Loveless's, Gwinnett.*
134 David Delk, Jr., 404th, Gwinnett.
135 Aaron S. Harris, 333d, Wayne.*
136 David M. Bulloch, 71st, Burke.*
137 Ezekiel Gilbert, sol., Calhoun's, Harris.*
138 Benjamin Grainger, 120th, Richmond.*
139 William Brock, s. l. w., Moseley's, Coweta.*
140 Asa B. Mitchell, Robinson's, Fayette.
141 Thomas Brade, Goodwin's, Houston.
142 Thomas D. Johnson, Mangum's, Franklin.
143 Josiah Watson, 245th, Jackson.*
144 John Robinson, Vining's, Putnam.*
145 (fr.) George P. Wagnon, Ellsworth's, Bibb.
146 (fr.) Susannah Willis, w. r. s., 168th, Wilkes.
147 Robert Quarles, sol., Higginbotham's, Rabun.*
148 John Bezbun, s. l. w., Hargrove's, Oglethorpe.*
149 Mason H. Hamlin, Ball's, Monroe.
150 John W. Lyle, Coker's, Troup.
151 Nancy Whitfield, w., Roe's, Burke.*
152 Mary Penn, w., Nellum's, Elbert.
153 John F. Preston, Hearn's, Butts.*
154 David Presley, Hamilton's, Hall.*
155 Seaburn Staten, Dobbs's, Hall.*
156 Arthur Fort's ors., Royster's, Twiggs.*
157 Toliver Weathington, 537th, Upson.*
158 Thomas H. Swift, Edwards's, Franklin.*
159 William Payton, Nellum's, Elbert.*
160 Jordan Hancock, M'Craney's, Lowndes.*
161 Benjamin H. Bobo, Kelly's, Elbert.*
162 Edmund Dalrymaple, Griffin's, Hall.*
163 Benjamin Holland, s. l. w., Britt's, Randolph.
164 Jesse M. Callaway, 466th, Monroe.*
165 Joseph Beavers's ors., Aderhold's, Campbell.*
166 Mary Parish, w., Blount's, Wilkinson.*
167 Thomas Bigg's or., Barnett's, Clarke.*

168 John Cason, Park's, Walton.*
169 Joseph Richardson, Williams's, Ware.*
170 Richard Goode, Lay's, Jackson.*
171 Jethro Thompson, Hughes's, Habersham.
172 John Dunn, 105th, Baldwin.
173 (fr.) Charles A. Brown, 245th, Jackson.
174 Mason Walker, Wolfskin's, Oglethorpe.
175 ——— Wade's orphans, Allison's, Pike.
176 John T. Roper, Reid's, Gwinnett.
177 John S. Linton, Athens, Clarke.*
178 Charles S. Sorrells, 419th, Walton.*
179 James Carmichael, Davis's, Clarke.*
180 Eliza Lyons, w., 120th, Richmond.
181 Edward Hawkins, 374th, Putnam.
182 Mary Owens, w., 589th, Upson.
183 Sarah A. Stephens's ors., Bryant's, Burke.
184 Caleb Sappington, Anderson's, Wilkes.*
185 James Barton's ors., 120th, Richmond.
186 Thomas R. Knowles, 160th, Greene.
187 Drewry Christian, Wilhite's, Elbert.
188 William Coats, 168th, Wilkes.
189 James Roberts, Jr., 555th, Upson.
190 Reuben Woodruff, sol., Nesbit's, Newton.*
191 William Whitehead, sol., 672d, Harris.*
192 Isaiah Barrer, Bryant's, Burke.*
193 Jeremiah Innman, 74th, Burke.*
194 Nathaniel H. Rhodes, 454th, Walton.*
195 Dempsey Grice, Kelly's, Elbert.*
196 Francis H. Oliver, Thomas's, Clarke.*
197 William Thomas, Kellum's, Talbot.*
198 (fr.) Asa Scott, Willis's, Franklin.
199 (fr.) Temperance Dial, h. a., Smith's, Madison.
200 David G. Jones, Hobkerk's, Camden.*
201 Eli Ason, Valleau's, Chatham.*
202 Hardiman Holmes, Trout's, Hall.*
203 William R. Busby, Rutland's, Bibb.*
204 Carrington Wheeler's ors., Loveless's, Gwinnett.
205 John G. Price, Whisenhunt's, Carroll.*
206 James Johnson, Hudson's, Marion.
207 William Ledbetter, Estes's, Putnam.
208 Solomon Barfield, 687th, Lee.
209 Vernon Smoot, Kellum's, Talbot.
210 William Webb, Hardman's, Oglethorpe.*
211 Ezekiel Wall, 555th, Upson.*
212 Thomas H. Brewer, 12th, Effingham.*
213 Blanchey M. Lawrence, w., Mizell's, Talbot.
214 Philip Hudgins, sol., Dyer's, Habersham.*

215 William Tuggle, Jr., 140th, Greene.*
216 John M. Cooper, s. l. w., 122d, Richmond.*
217 Elijah S. Boynton, s. i. w., Russell's, Henry.*
218 Lucrecy Buckner, w., Bryan's, Monroe.*
219 Philip F. Combs, 174th, Wilkes.*
220 Andrew Gilliam, Chambers's, Gwinnett.*
221 Asa Lewis's ors., Derrick's, Henry.*
222 Alfred Jonson, Martin's, Pike.*
223 James Finley, M'Culler's, Newton.*
224 (fr.) Thomas K. Hanson, 693d, Heard.
225 (fr.) Orange Davis, Newby's, Jones.
226 James Guire, M'Dowell's, Lincoln.*
227 Caleb Oliver's ors., Clark's, Elbert.*
228 John Johnston, Coxe's, Franklin.*
229 Hillory H. Corley, or., 406th, Gwinnett.
230 Fuquay Holladay, Hart's, Jones.*
231 David Andriss, Jr., sol., Hanner's, Campbell.*
232 John F. L. Cain, Hamilton's, Gwinnett.*
233 James Green, 702d, Heard.*
234 Henry B. Thornton, 735th, Troup.*
235 William Barber, Peacock's, Washington.*
236 Elizabeth Downs, w., Cliett's, Columbia.*
237 Delphia Pace, w., Bishop's, Henry.*
238 Micajah Pope, Mobley's, De Kalb.
239 Green Allen, Prescott's, Twiggs.*
240 Charles Sims, s. i. w., Seas's, Madison.
241 John Cargill, Tuggle's, Merriwether.*
242 Solomon P. Kent, Jennings's, Clarke.
243 Rachel & Presley Hill, ors., 123d, Richmond.*
244 Rhody Whiddon, w., Barwick's, Washington.*
245 Ignatius Scott, s. l. w., 601st, Taliaferro.*
246 Charles Hook's ors., Vining's, Putnam.*
247 Isaiah Golding, 74th, Burke.*
248 Reding Rass, Latimer's, De Kalb.*
249 George W. Hanson, Nesbit's, Newton.*

15th DISTRICT, FOURTH SECTION, CHEROKEE.

1 (fr.) Harris Ricks, Hicks's, Decatur.
2 John Dickey, Lunceford's, Elbert.*
3 Eli H. Baxter, 102d, Hancock.*
4 L. D. Posey, Whisenhunt's, Carroll.*
5 John M. Johnson, Young's, Wilkinson.*
6 Buckner Abernethy, Hughes's, Habersham.*
7 David Merce Elliott, Candler's, Bibb.*
8 Jeremiah Cloud, 3d section, Cherokee.*
9 Thomas Coston, Williams's, Washington.*
10 James Clary, Williams's, Decatur.
11 Edward A. Ballard, s. l. w., Moore's, Randolph.*
12 Jacob W. Eberhart, Colley's, Oglethorpe.*
13 Jones Davis, Jordan's, Harris.
14 Thomas Justice, Ellis's, Rabun.
15 Nelson Gunn's ors., Prescott's, Twiggs.
16 William J. Harper, Whitebluff, Chatham.*
17 William Chappell, Sen., 417th, Walton.
18 Pittman Carrington, Smith's, Madison.
19 Green M. Wiggins, Dean's, Clarke.
20 John Benford, Martin's, Jones.
21 Sterling Adams, Higginbotham's, Carroll.*
22 Valentine Breazwell, Mullen's, Carroll.*
23 Richard Smith, sol., Iverson's, Houston.*
24 Sarah Beavers, w., Aderhold's, Campbell.
25 George W. M'Call, Carpenter's, Tatnall.*
26 John Luckie, Adams's, Columbia.
27 Thomas V. Miller, Durham's, Talbot.*
28 Sally Morris, h. a., Hines's, Coweta.
29 Hay T. Landrum, Howard's, Oglethorpe.*
30 John Hog, Harralson's, Troup.
31 James Cooper, Mullen's, Carroll.
32 Sardis E. Cross, 73d, Burke.*
33 Daniel M'Gahee, Strickland's, Merriwether.*
34 Reuben Bankston, Martin's, Pike.*
35 Reuben Alewine, Belcher's, Jasper.*
36 Isaac D. Read, Fenn's, Clarke.*
37 William Freeman, Jones's, Hall.
38 William Wallace, Sen., Herndon's, Hall.*
39 James A. Landcaster, Williams's, Washington.
40 Mary Pettis, w., 398th, Richmond.
41 Edward L. Thornton, Newman's, Thomas.*

42 John C. Lanier, 3d section, Cherokee.*
43 John Higdon, 37th, Emanuel.*
44 William Bayles, Camp's, Warren.
45 James Spence, or., Wynn's, Gwinnett.
46 John T. Thomas, Dearing's, Henry.*
47 Polly Owens's ors., 406th, Gwinnett.*
48 Ephraim M. Johnson, Price's, Hall.
49 (fr.) William Lee's ors., Will's, Twiggs.
50 (fr.) John Phillips, 574th, Early.
51 William Gibson, 175th, Wilkes.*
52 Josiah Johnson, Johnson's, Bibb.*
53 Hamblin Hudgens, Martin's, Newton.*
54 Duet C. Rutledge, Maguire's, Gwinnett.*
55 James Anderson, Brock's, Habersham.
56 Anna Thompson, w., M. Brown's, Habersham.
57 William Lane, Brewer's, Walton.
58 Juda Foster, w., Clark's, Elbert.
59 Michael M'Lane, sol., Iverson's, Houston.
60 John L. Veazey, 142d, Greene.
61 Thomas Fenn, sol., Killen's, Decatur.*
62 John M'Cullock, of Cher., Latimer's, De Kalb.
63 Joseph Rice, Herndon's, Hall.*
64 William Tindall's ors., Harris's, Columbia.
65 Lott Williams's ors., 120th, Richmond.*
66 George Freeman's ors., Edwards's, Talbot.
67 Temperance Manly, w. r. s., Crawford's, Franklin.
68 Elizabeth Tate, w., Willis's, Franklin.
69 George W. Hay, 417th, Walton.*
70 Pittman M. Lumpkin, Beasley's, Oglethorpe.
71 John Barnes, Chastain's, Habersham.
72 William Willson, Ellis's, Rabun.
73 (fr.) Moses J. M'Clendon, 364th, Jasper.
74 (fr.) William Walker, Hall's, Oglethorpe.
75 Josiah Sterling's ors., Hardman's, Oglethorpe.
76 Solomon Howard, Jordan's, Harris.*
77 Robert Robinson, Hobbs's, Laurens.
78 John M. Miller, 37th, Scriven.
79 David Henderson's ors., Lay's, Jackson.
80 John Buffington, Lawrence's, Pike.
81 Elizabeth Hunter, w. r. s., Reid's, Gwinnett.
82 John K. Fitchett's or., 333d, Wayne.
83 David Sisson, Smith's, Habersham.
84 Domineck Luna, Wilmington, Chatham.
85 Benjamin Lokey, sol., Foote's, De Kalb.
86 James M. Warren, Brewer's, Walton
87 Isaac S. S. Barker, Johnson's, De Kalb.
88 John Pate, Compton's, Fayette.*

89 Joseph G. Chappell, 494th, Upson.*
90 Leroy Pollard's ors., Silman's, Pike.
91 Avis Shannon, w., Holley's, Franklin.
92 Thomas James, sol., Crawford's, Franklin.
93 Elija Stanford, Stewart's, Warren.*
94 John S. Smith, Griffin's, Hall.*
95 Seaborn Milligan, Anderson's, Wilkes.*
96 William J. Parks, Daniel's, Hall.
97 (fr.) Thomas Vaughan, 406th, Gwinnett.
98 Jarrett Wright's ors., Cannon's, Wilkinson.
99 Nathaniel Callyhan, Sims's, Troup.*
100 Garris Cross, Roberts's, Hall.*
101 Keader Keaton, Baker's, Liberty.*
102 Daniel Fullbright, Hendon's, Carroll.
103 Levi Kinks's ors., Parham's, Harris.
104 Darias Purcell, Smith's, Franklin.
105 Elizabeth Daniel, d. & d., Dearing's, Henry.*
106 Thomas Caraway's ors., Moore's, Randolph.
107 Nathaniel Olmstead's ors., Valleau's, Chatham.*
108 Leroy Broom, 144th Greene, Taliaferro.*
109 Jane Ward, w., 190th, Elbert.
110 John Prescott, Morgan's, Appling.
111 Charles Harper, 20th, Bryan.
112 Halcom Hagans, Hand's, Appling.
113 Mary Dean, 15th, Liberty.*
114 James Spurlock, M'Ginnis's, Jackson.*
115 S. Cone, Sen., of Cherokee, Latimer's, De Kalb.*
116 Zachariah Timmons, 27th, Glynn.*
117 William H. Dunaway, M'Gill's, Lincoln.*
118 Sarah E. Hearn, or., M'Clendon's, Putnam.
119 (fr.) Ezekiel Wimberly, sol., Pounds's, Twiggs.
120 (fr.) Henry R. Deadwiler, Wilhite's, Elbert.*
121 Susan J. Phillips, w., Sanderlin's, Chatham.*
122 Asbury Lynch, Maguire's, Morgan.*
123 Hugh M. Hardin, Sanderlin's, Chatham.*
124 Littleton Thomason, s. l. w., Thaxton's, Butts.*
125 Jesse Parker, Lay's, Jackson.*
126 Bartholomew Still, Baley's, Butts.*
127 John Summer's ors., Davis's, Jones.
128 Edward White, Burk's, Stewart.*
129 Allen Blackburn, 35th, Scriven.*
130 John F. Achord, s. l. w., Dupree's, Washington.*
131 John Mallory, Bourquin's, Chatham.*
132 George J. Dodd, Barker's, Gwinnett.*
133 Susan Campbell, w., Morrison's, Appling.*
134 James J. Oquin, Show's, Muscogee.*
135 Elisha Rogers, 588th, Upson.*

136 John M. Bruce, 561st, Upson.*
137 Sarah Lowe, w., House's, Henry.*
138 William W. Hayes, Craven's, Coweta.*
139 John B. Gilbert's ors., 3d, Chatham.*
140 Martin O. Thompson, 379th, Jasper.*
141 (fr.) Abner Harralson, Night's, Morgan.*
142 Editha Wright, w., Curry's, Merriwether.
143 J. M'Cranie, Sen., sol., M'Craney's, Lowndes.*
144 George W. Mackleroy, Burk's, Stewart.*
145 John H. Moore, Lunceford's, Wilkes.
146 Ralph Ressengine, sol., 3d, Chatham.
147 Stephens Roberts, Folsom's, Lowndes.*
148 James Taylor, Sen., Morrison's, Appling.*
149 Hugh C. Boyle, Deavours's, Habersham.*
150 Charles A. Rosier, Linam's, Pulaski.*
151 Joseph J. Martin, Mobley's, De Kalb.*
152 Paley Winters, h. a., Brown's, Habersham.*
153 Wesley W. Reese, Peterson's, Burke.*
154 Lewis M. Madison, Stanfield's, Campbell.*
155 Elizabeth Allen, w., Covington's, Pike.*
156 Reddle Sperger's ors., Hill's, Harris.
157 John Hill, Jones's, Wilkes.*
158 Benjamin Oliver, 72d, Burke.*
159 Collins Waters's ors., Trout's, Hall.
160 Francis A. Menard, Ellsworth's, Bibb.*
161 George W. Willis, 166th, Wilkes.
162 (fr.) Clarissa Jackson, w., Bishop's, Henry.
163 Elbert Miller, Burk's, Stewart.
164 Richard Williamson, Orr's, Jackson.*
165 James Luke, son of Reuben, Peek's, Columbia.*
166 Samuel Metz, Allen's, Henry.*
167 Moses Cantrell, Jones's, Habersham.*
168 Thomas Stephens, Coxe's, Talbot.
169 John Brown, sol., Edwards's, Talbot.
170 William Jackson, sol., Latimer's, De Kalb.*
171 Reuben Gunter, M'Ginnis's, Jackson.*
172 Wesley Raines, Herndon's, Hall.
173 Isaac N. Davis, Canning's, Elbert.*
174 Hugh Roney, Jones's, Thomas.*
175 Josiah Kitchens, Hood's, Henry.
176 William Coulter, Blair's, Lowndes.*
177 James A. Bush, Peace's, Wilkinson.*
178 James B. Griffith, Jr., Morgan's, Madison.*
179 George Baldwin's ors., Burk's, Stewart.*
180 Elizabeth Mayfield, w., Holley's, Franklin.
181 (fr.) Roger Greene, 248th, Jackson.
182 (fr.) J. & H. Huff, ors., Greene's, Oglethorpe.

183 Thomas W. Chipman, Kendrick's, Monroe.
134 Jacob Crow, Gittens's, Fayette.*
185 James M. Lesueur, Ross's, Monroe.*
186 William F. Sweat, Peavy's, Bulloch.*
187 Benj. Fannin, of Cherokee, Latimer's, De Kalb.*
188 William Grimes, Alexander's, Jefferson.
189 John B. Smith, s. i. w., Smith's, Henry.
190 Benj. Tarver, s. l. w., Robinson's, Washington.
191 George L. Alexander, 293d, Jasper.
192 Stephen Potts's ors., Belcher's, Jasper.
193 Nancy Adams, w., Hughes's, Habersham.
194 Sarah Vickers, w. r. s., 118th, Hancock.*
195 Daniel Huff, Arrington's, Merriwether.*
196 Richard F. Bush, 122d, Richmond.*
197 Henry Holmes, Boynton's, Twiggs.*
198 Augustus B. Longstreet, 119th, Richmond.*
199 R. H. H. Burke, Athens, Clarke.*
200 William G. Fitzpatrick, Frasier's, Monroe.*
201 (fr.) Hugh Curry's ors., Smith's, Wilkinson.

. 18th DISTRICT, FOURTH SECTION, CHEROKEE.

1 William Myhand, sol., Kellum's, Talbot.*
2 Samuel Standridge, Chastain's, Habersham.
3 George W. Owens, 494th, Upson.
4 Sarah Abbot, w., Groce's, Bibb.
5 William F. Crew, Peurifoy's, Henry.*
6 Levina E. Brady, w., Harp's, Stewart.
7 John Spears, r. s., Nesbit's, Newton.*
8 William Hobbs, Coxe's, Talbot.*
9 John T. Webb, 687th, Lee.*
10 Robert Wood, s. i. w., Colley's, Madison.
11 William J. Wright, Norris's, Monroe.
12 Elizabeth Walker, w. r. s., Mason's, Washington.
13 Wiley G. Sammons, Lamp's, Jefferson.
14 Andrew Lay's ors., 607th, Taliaferro.
15 (fr.) George Nead, Sen., r. s., 9th, Effingham.
16 Willis Roberts, Seal's, Elbert.
17 Thomas Baker, Johnson's, De Kalb.
18 Edward Williams, Burnett's, Habersham
19 Charles Warren, M. Brown's, Habersham.*
20 John Epperson, sol., Mangum's, Franklin.*
21 Catharine Patten, w. s. i. w., Colley's, Madison.
22 William R. M'Canless, Hughes's, Habersham.*

23 Francis M'Waters, M'Culler's, Newton.*
24 Joshua Rainwater, Burgess's, Carroll.*
25 Lewis Johnson, Gibson's, Decatur.
26 Thomas Clark's ors., Edwards's, Franklin.*
27 Ann Leslie, w., Sullivan's, Jones.
28 (fr.) Jeremiah M. Williams, Griffin's, Fayette.
29 (fr.) Cullen Cowart, 49th, Emanuel.
30 Irby Gilder, Britt's, Randolph.*
31 William Smith, Waltze's, Morgan.*
32 Jacob Little, 687th, Sumter.
33 John Gray's ors., Russell's, Henry.*
34 Jacob Beck, M'Gehee's, Troup.*
35 William Pitts, Kellum's, Elbert.*
36 Mary Smith, w. r. s., Newsom's, Warren
37 Silas S. Baker, Dyer's, Habersham.
38 Benjamin Long, Herndon's, Hall.*
39 Joseph M'Brayer, Mullen's, Carroll.*
40 James Gilmer, Sen., r. s., Martin's, Hall.*
41 David C. Rosie, Few's, Muscogee.
42 Cyrus W. Cotton, Allen's, Bibb.*
43 Thomas C. Brown, 106th, Hancock.
44 Seaborn J. Weaver, Hines's, Coweta.*
45 Anderson Barrett, 249th, Walton.*
46 William Stotsberry, or., Valleau's, Chatham.
47 Nancy Richardson, w., Adams's, Columbia.
48 John Holder, Reid's, Gwinnett.*
49 Harman Kirkpatrick, Hargrove's, Newton.*
50 Livingston Gaines's ors., 365th, Jasper.
51 William Gibson's ors., 588th, Upson.
52 Hardy Pace, sol., Harris's, De Kalb.
53 (fr.) Elizabeth Lane, w., Stanton's, Newton.
54 (fr.) Mary H. Brown, w., 1st, Chatham.*
55 James Edmondson, M'Craney's, Lowndes.
56 Job Bird, Morgan's, Madison.*
57 Jane Jones, w., Young's, Wilkinson.*
58 John A. Bachelor, or. of Eli, 454th, Walton
59 John Hare, Pounds's, Twiggs.*
60 Quilley Taylor, Clinton's, Campbell.
61 James Brown, Graves's, Lincoln.*
62 Thomas C. Weekley, Edwards's, Talbot.*
63 Charles H. Rice Houston, Candler's, Bibb.
64 John U. Fletcher, Huey's, Harris.*
65 (fr.) William Mecombs, Mimms's, Fayette.
66 (fr.) Robert Hamilton, Hamilton's, Hall.
67 Milley Coleman, 72d, Burke.*
68 Owen F. Jackson, 672d, Harris.
69 Thomas Brice, Daniel's, Hall.

70 Solomon Birdwall, 320th, Baldwin.*
71 Marving Whatley, Sen., Few's, Muscogee.
72 Thomas Smith's ors., Phillips's, Talbot.
73 James Mulkey's or., Ballard's, Morgan.
74 William S. Bell, 271st, M'Intosh.*
75 John Rogers, sol., Johnson's, Warren.*
76 William Watson, M'Ewin's, Monroe.*
77 Josiah Daniel, Rainey's, Twiggs.
78 Eliza A. Cooler, or., Cleland's, Chatham.*
79 Asa Thompson's 4 orphans, Sutton's, Habersham.
80 Wiley K. Jones's ors., Tuggle's, Merriwether.*
81 John Rainey, Dean's, De Kalb.
82 David B. Butler, Candler's, Bibb.*
83 Thomas H. Baker, Sparks's, Washington.*
84 James Boyd's ors., 248th, Jackson.*
85 James Fuller, Adams's, Columbia.*
86 (fr.) William Owenby's ors., Phillips's, Jasper.*
87 (fr.) Norman M'Donald, Crow's, Merriwether.
88 Angus M'Leod, Blair's, Lowndes.
89 William S. M'Cord, Hampton's, Newton.
90 Joshua Barnes, Thomas's, Crawford.*
91 Robert W. Carlisle, Stanton's, Newton.*
92 James Walker, M'Clain's, Newton.*
93 Jesse Ammons, Copeland's, Houston.*
94 Peggy Collom, w., Hamilton's, Hall.*
95 James Ballard, 74th, Burke.*
96 (fr.) Caleb Garrison, s. l. w., Garner's, Coweta.
97 (fr.) James Lankford, Miller's, Ware.
98 Marcus N. Ellis, Ellsworth's, Bibb.
99 John Brewster, 406th, Gwinnett.*
100 Maria Smith, w., Newby's, Jones.*
101 Desier Stroud, Bostick's, Twiggs.*
102 John M. Linn, Bishop's, Henry.*
103 Levi Phillips, r. s., Higginbotham's, Carroll.*
104 Joshua Spooner, 35th, Scriven.*
105 John Turner, George's, Appling.
106 Augustus Myddelton, 22d, M'Intosh.*
107 Levin Walker, Atkinson's, Coweta.*
108 James Miller, Monk's, De Kalb.
109 John Hopkins's ors., 175th, Wilkes.*
110 Mary Stevens, h. a., Barker's, Gwinnett.*
111 James Barton, Seay's, Hall.*
112 William M'Elhenney, Jr., 373d, Jasper.*
113 (fr.) Larkin Satterfield, Jones's, Habersham.*
114 (fr.) John Wilson M'Gehee, Taylor's, Jones.*
115 Robert Berry, Evans's, Fayette.*
116 Benjamin Clemments, Price's, Hall.

117 Joseph Robinson, 141st, Greene.
118 Francis O. Black, Holton's, Emanuel.
119 Arthur S. Cook, Polhill's, Burke.*
120 Mary Tubberville, or., Cleland's, Chatham.*
121 (fr.) Daniel Mayor, Thomas's, Clarke.
122 (fr.) Ebenezer Harris, 334th, Wayne.*
123 Matthew T. Phillips, 555th, Upson.*
124 Charles C. M'Kinley, 588th, Upson.
125 William G. Jones, M'Coy's, Houston.*
126 Eldrid T. Jordan, Colley's, Oglethorpe.
127 George W. R. Stone, Miller's, Ware.
128 Nancy Lee, w., 148th, Greene.
129 (fr.) Ford Butler, sol., Griffin's, Merriwether.*
130 John Abney, Miller's, Jackson.*
131 Alfred Hicks, Sutton's, Habersham.*
132 William Burge, 404th, Gwinnett.
133 Isaac Waldravin, sol., 656th, Troup.
134 (fr.) Samuel Garlick's ors., Roe's, Burke.
135 (fr.) Roger Q. Dickinson, 606th, Taliaferro.
136 Nathan E. Batchlor, Maguire's, Morgan.*
137 James A. Murray's or., 2d, Chatham.
138 Zachariah Williamson, Sullivan's, Jones.
139 William Whilton, Mays's, Monroe.
140 (fr.) Anderson F. Thomason, Smith's, Campbell.
141 Lydia Thompson, w., Burnett's, Habersham.
142 John Townsend, Studstill's, Lowndes.
143 Henry W. Ross, 417th, Walton.*
144 Edwin Goodson, Robison's, Washington.*
145 (fr.) Thomas Grimsley, Tuggle's, Merriwether.
146 Henry Haynes, Sutton's, Habersham.
147 Wiley P. Heard, Lane's, Morgan.
148 (fr.) James V. Martin, 145th, Greene.
149 (fr.) Martha Murrill, Valleau's, Chatham.*
150 Simeon Gutry, Hutson's, Newton.
151 John P. Buckelew, Derrick's, Henry.*
152 (fr.) Henry S. Ray, Johnson's, Bibb.
153 Henry Claibone, Edwards's, Talbot.
154 Hannah Deason, w. r. s., Clinton's, Campbell.

19th DISTRICT, FOURTH SECTION, CHEROKEE.

1 (fr.) Ephraim C. Blocker, Hudson's, Marion.
2 Benjamin Jones, Jr., Taylor's, Putnam.*
3 John W. Smith, Craven's, Coweta.*
4 Absolem Williams, Dyer's, Habersham.*
5 Wiley Reed, Howard's, Oglethorpe.
6 Jonathan Ewing, 102d, Hancock.
7 William O. Bowman, Chastain's, Habersham.
8 Robert Pugely's ors., Gunn's, Jefferson.
9 Isaac Tower's ors., Latimer's, De Kalb.
10 Edward P. Nixon, Robinson's, Fayette.*
11 John Simmons, sol., Wilson's, Pike.
12 Merriam Traywick, or., 118th, Hancock.
13 Alexander Mobley, Dixon's, Irwin.
14 Amelia C. Mattox, w. r. s., Campbell's, Wilkes.*
15 Gideon Elvington, r. s., Folsom's, Lowndes.
16 John Phillips, Allen's, Campbell.*
17 Benajah Thornton, Flynn's, Muscogee.
18 Jet S. Skidmore, Williams's, Walton.
19 Samuel Glenn, Hatchett's, Oglethorpe.*
20 Jabez J. Holcomb, 2d section, Cherokee.
21 Thomas Bealy, Sen., r. s., Allen's, Henry.
22 Anthony Winter, 1st, Chatham.*
23 J. Oliver, of Gum Swamp, Mashburn's, Pulaski.
24 James Mathis, Wynn's, Gwinnett.*
25 John Wayne, Gunn's, Coweta.
26 Francis Hardaway, sol., Allen's, Monroe.
27 Burrell Bales, Woodruff's, Campbell.*
28 Philip Young, Sutton's, Habersham.
29 William Avery's ors., Norris's, Monroe.
30 William S. Thompson, Salem, Baldwin.
31 Ezekiel M'Cravey, sol., Brock's, Habersham.*
32 Wylie Maxwell, 166th, Wilkes.
33 John Wilkins, Sanderlin's, Chatham.
34 Coonrod Weaver, Henson's, Rabun.
35 Abraham Powell, Chastain's, Habersham.
36 John Wansley, 672d, Harris.
37 Charles Slatham, Fulks's, Wilkes.*
38 Joshua Ammons, Park's, Walton.*
39 Allen Rhodes, 607th, Taliaferro.
40 John J. Steadly, Brewton's, Fayette.
41 (fr.) John Dorton, Gunn's, Henry.

42 (fr.) Mary Wood, w., Everett's, Washington.
43 Caleb Smith, Mizell's, Talbot.*
44 William Moore, sol., Collins's, Henry.
45 Edward D. Craft, Coker's, Troup.
46 Jackson Ward, Hall's, Oglethorpe.*
47 Allen Bradley, Dobbs's, Hall.*
48 Thomas Edge, Whitehead's, Habersham.*
49 Ambrose D. Brown, Hamilton's, Gwinnett.
50 James Thrower, Hood's, Henry.
51 Aaron Turner, Jr., Thompson's, Henry.*
52 Sterling G. Barrow, Chambers's, Houston.
53 Elias Sconyers, 73d, Burke.
54 Joseph Patterson, Whelchel's, Hall.
55 Joshua Bailey, Hampton's, Newton.
56 Matthew Stephens, Hammond's, Franklin.
57 Charles Baldwin's ors., 141st, Greene.
58 Aquilla Bruice, Hughes's, Habersham.
59 Giles Webb's ors., Mason's, Washington.
60 Caleb Hall, Sen., Bridges's, Gwinnett.
61 (fr.) Washington Harris, Jordan's, Bibb.
62 (fr.) Samuel Karr, s. i. w., Bower's, Elbert.
63 William Jones, Coffee's, Rabun.
64 Orphans of Britton L. Pearce, Roe's, Burke.
65 Robert E. Martin, 143d, Greene.*
66 John Mallon, 4th, Chatham.*
67 Pierson Ivy, Perryman's, Warren.
68 John W. Pelham, 785th, Sumter.*
69 Hillary Moore, Chambers's, Gwinnett.
70 Jacob Cleonkloy, Lamberth's, Fayette.*
71 Lewis Sawyer, Morris's, Crawford.*
72 John Akins, Clark's, Morgan.*
73 Rebecca Faris, w. r. s., 404th, Gwinnett.
74 William Whitfield's ors., Roe's, Burke.*
75 John Phelan, 120th, Richmond.
76 James Love, Russell's, Henry.
77 William Ballard, Moseley's, Coweta.
78 Peter Lingo, Garner's, Washington.
79 John King, s. i. w., Butts's, Monroe.
80 Thomas Florance, Levrett's, Lincoln.
81 Ney Peugh, Bustin's, Pike.
82 Jonathan Williams, Liddell's, Jackson.
83 Isham Turner, Gittens's, Fayette.
84 Patience Hamilton, w., 102d, Hancock.
85 Richard Coggin, Smith's, Habersham.
86 Edward D. Tracey, Candler's, Bibb.
87 James H. Chapman, Givins's, De Kalb.
88 James Blackstock, House's, Henry.

89 Lewis Brown, r. s., Butts's, Monroe.
90 William C. Kilgore, 415th, Walton.
91 Joseph Brown, r. s., Henson's, Rabun.
92 William Almon, Wood's, Morgan.
93 William Wood, Trout's, Hall.
94 Washington Goin, Herndon's, Hall.
95 David Wilson's ors., Perryman's, Warren.
96 Joseph R. Sasnett, sol., 118th, Hancock.
97 William M. Craig, 702d, Heard.
98 (fr.) Hope H. Parnell, Athens, Clarke.
99 (fr.) Joseph Smith, Will's, Twiggs.
100 Mary Morris, w., 295th, Jasper.
101 Patrick Holt, Baismore's, Jones.
102 John Gregory, Jordan's, Bibb.
103 William Carrol, sol., Culbreath's, Columbia.
104 John E. Petigrue, 320th, Baldwin.
105 Susannah Watts, w., 111th, Hancock.*
106 Francis O'Kelly, 417th, Walton.
107 Briton Buttrill, Perry's, Butts.
108 Moses Tullis, Jr., Watson's, Marion.
109 Edward H. Norwood, Kellum's, Talbot.*
110 Sarah Stucky, w., 124th, Richmond.*
111 M'Neal's five orphans, Hargrove's, Newton.
112 Russell Williams, h. d., Herndon's, Hall.
113 Horis Calton, 656th, Troup.
114 Windal Bower, Christie's, Jefferson.
115 William Wood, 734th, Lee.*
116 (fr.) John Hooper, Gillis's, De Kalb.
117 (fr.) Drury Bradley, or., Wood's, Morgan.
118 Walter Stewart, s. i. w., Colquhoun's, Henry.*
119 Jane Patterson, w. r. s., 466th, Monroe.
120 Proctor Berry, 606th, Taliaferro.*
121 Matthew Pirtle, Trout's, Hall.
122 James M'Bee, Mangum's, Franklin.
123 John Britt, Hampton's, Newton.
124 William M. Hart, 143d, Greene.
125 Francis Hernandy, Cleland's, Chatham.*
126 John J. Heard, 374th, Putnam.
127 Henry Bennett's ors., Morgan's, Appling.
128 Edwin J. Vardaman, Greer's, Merriwether.*
129 William Bailey, 174th, Wilkes.*
130 Clark Howell, 406th, Gwinnett.
131 William S. Morgan, 785th, Sumter.
132 Joseph Brady's ors., Winter's, Jones.
133 Samuel Freeman, M'Millon's, Lincoln.*
134 Howell Moseley, Evans's, Fayette.
135 John L. Shelly, 535th, Dooly.

136 Mary Ann Crawford, w. r. s., Grubbs's Columbia.
137 Benajah Cain, sol., 574th Early
138 William G. W. Richardson, Rooks's, Putnam.*
139 Sarah English, w. r. s., Fleming's, Franklin.
140 George Booth's ors., Wilhite's, Elbert.
141 Richard Tatum, Watson's, Marion.
142 William L. West, Wood's, Morgan.*
143 Lely Magness, h. a., 70th, Burke.*
144 Paul Patrick, Sen., 249th, Walton.
145 F. J. Jennings, Latimer's, De Kalb.
146 George M. Hays, Hodges's, Newton.
147 Samuel Biltison's ors., 3d, Chatham.
148 Zephaniah Franklin, r. s., Parham's, Warren.*
149 (fr.) Noah Powell, Dilman's, Pulaski.
150 (fr.) Joseph Angle, Valleau's, Chatham.
151 Elijah Watson, Taylor's, Houston.
152 William Alford, 278th, Morgan.
153 Joel Barton, 277th, Morgan.*
154 Vinson Cooper, Mullen's, Carroll.
155 Samuel Clay, sol., 672d, Harris.
156 Absolem Vaughn, Mitchell's, Pulaski.
157 George Taylor, Jordan's, Harris.
158 Stephen M'Pherson, Reid's, Gwinnett.*
159 Henry Barges, M'Korkle's, Jasper.
160 Lewis H. Plant, Alsobrook's, Jones.
161 Jane Dickinson, or., Deavours's, Habersham.
162 Oliver Palmer, Valleau's, Chatham.
163 Allen Stephens, Colley's, Oglethorpe.*
164 Sarah F. Vernon, or., Colley's, Oglethorpe.
165 (fr.) Aaron Baker, 561st, Upson.
166 (fr.) Samuel Howard Fay, Groce's, Bibb.
167 Zachariah Goulding, Cleland's, Chatham.*
168 John R. M'Mahan, Dearing's, Butts.
169 Elizabeth Lewis, w., 245th, Jackson.*
170 James A. Courvoice, or., Valleau's, Chatham.
171 Edwin L. Lucas, Flynn's, Muscogee.*
172 John H. Lumpkin, Wolfskin's, Oglethorpe.
173 Charles R. Wiseman, sol., Thompson's, Henry.*

APPENDIX.

The following Names were accidentally omitted at the time these sheets passed through the press until too late to insert them in their proper place under the head of Fourth District, Second Section. See page 73.

323 (fr.) Anthony Jones, Lynn's, Warren.
324 (fr.) Wilie A. Thomas, Jordan's, Bibb.*
325 (fr.) Rev. Patin P. Smith, Dyer's, Habersham.
326 (fr.) Delilah Fields, w., Lamp's, Jefferson.
327 (fr.) Robert Chandler, sol., Wynn's, Gwinnett.
328 (fr.) Vincent L. Lee, 24th, M'Intosh.*
329 (fr.) John Walker, Mizell's, Talbot.
330 (fr.) Thomas Reynolds's ors., Park's, Walton.
331 (fr.) John Reno, Jr., Merck's, Hall.
332 (fr.) Jesse Vincent, Martin's, Hall.*
333 (fr.) Johnson M. Hooper, Aderhold's, Campbell.
334 (fr.) Cyntha Beasley, w., Gillis's, De Kalb.
335 (fr.) Frederic M'Giddery, Mattox's, Lowndes.*
336 (fr.) John H. Blalock, or., 398th, Richmond.
337 (fr.) Samuel Fulton, 295th, Jasper.
338 (fr.) William F. Ingram, Gunn's, Jones.
339 (fr.) Albert B. Harris, M'Millon's, Lincoln.*
340 (fr.) Abraham Luke, Hill's, Monroe.
341 (fr.) William Williams, Jr., Coffee's, Rabun.
342 (fr.) William Havener, 120th, Richmond.

THE END.

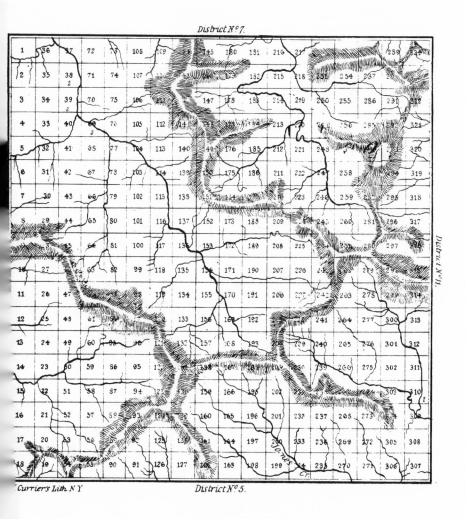

District Nº 7.

Currier's Lith. N.Y.   District Nº 5.

A MAP of the 6th DISTRICT 1st SECTION

of originally Cherokee, now

UNION & LUMPKIN COUNTIES

James F. Smith

Scale of 160 chains to an inch

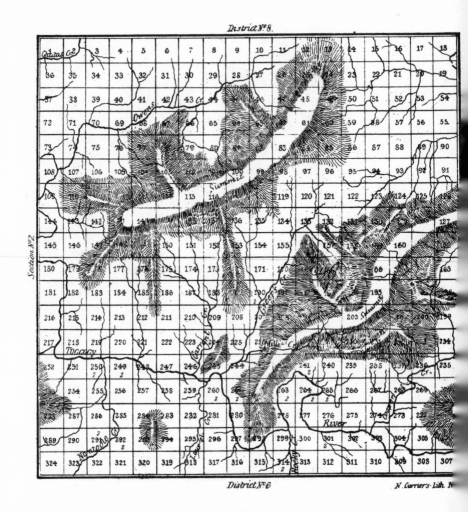

A MAP of the 7th DISTRICT 1st SECTION

of originally Cherokee, now

UNION COUNTY

James F. Smith

Scale of 160 chains to an Inch

NORTH CAROLINA

District No 7.

N Currier's Lith N.Y.

A MAP of the *8th* DISTRICT *1st* SECTION

of originally Cherokee, now

UNION COUNTY

James F. Smith

Scale of 100 chains to an inch

District Nº 10.

N. Currier's Lith. N.Y.

A MAP of the 9th DISTRICT 1st SECTION

of originally Cherokee, now

UNION COUNTY

James F. Smith

Scale of 160 chains to an inch

District Nº 9.

Chestee River

A MAP of the 10th. DISTRICT 1st SECTION

of originally Cherokee, now

UNION COUNTY.

James F. Smith

District Nº 11.

N. Currier's Lith. N.Y.

Scale of 160 chains to an inch

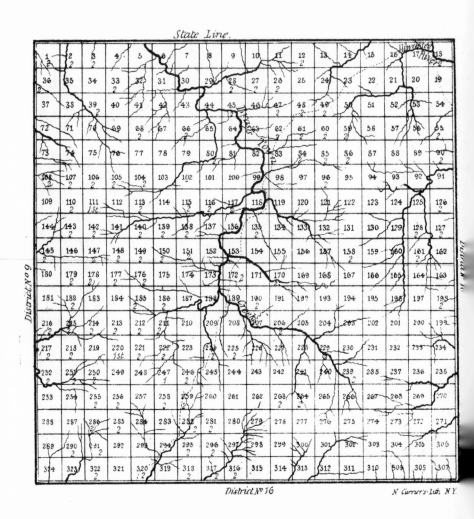

A MAP of the *17th* DISTRICT *1st* SECTION

of originally Cherokee, now

UNION COUNTY

James F. Smith

Scale of 100 chains to an Inch

A MAP of the 18th DISTRICT 1st. SECTION

of originally Cherokee, now

UNION COUNTY.

James F. Smith

Scale of 100 chains to an inch

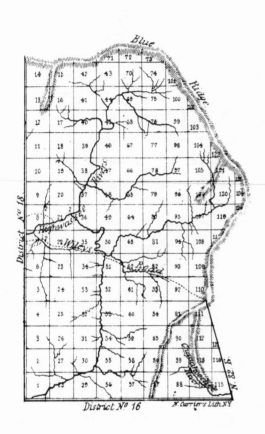

A MAP *of the* **19th.** *DISTRICT* **1st** *SECTION*

of originally Cherokee.now

UNION COUNTY

James F. Smith

Scale of 100 chains to an inch

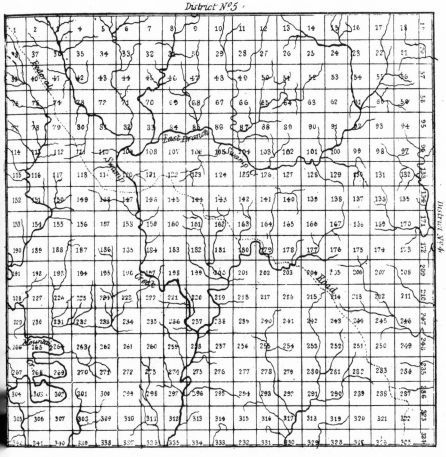

A MAP of the 4th DISTRICT 2d SECTION

of originally Cherokee, now

CHEROKEE COUNTY

James F. Smith

Scale of 180 chains to an inch

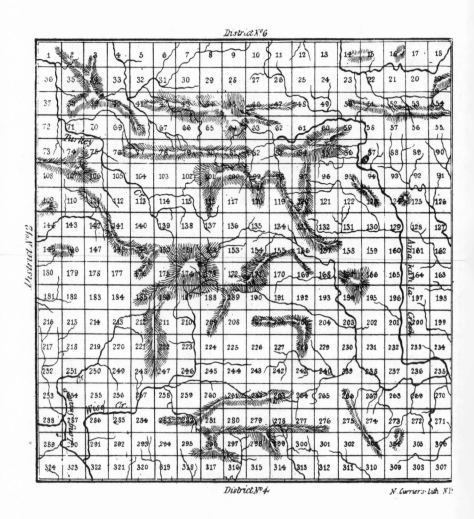

A MAP of the 5th DISTRICT 2d SECTION

of originally Cherokee, now

GILMER COUNTY.

James F. Smith

Scale of 100 chains to an Inch

District Nº7

1	2	3	4	5	6	7	8	9	10	11	12	13	14	15	16	17	18
36	35	34	33	32	31	30	29	28	27	26	25	24	23	22	21	20	19
37	38	39	40	41	42	43	44	45	46	47	48	49	50	51	52	53	54
72	71	70	69	68	67	66	65	64	63	62	61	60	59	58	57	56	55
73	74	75	76	77	78	79	80	81	82	83	84	85	86	87	88	89	90
108	107	106	105	104	103	102	101	100	99	98	97	96	95	94	93	92	91
109	110	111	112	113	114	115	116	117	118	119	120	121	122	123	124	125	126
144	143	142	141	140	139	138	137	136	135	134	133	132	131	130	129	128	127
145	146	147	148	149	150	151	152	153	154	155	156	157	158	159	160	161	162
180	179	178	177	176	175	174	173	172	171	170	169	168	167	166	165	164	163
181	182	183	184	185	186	187	188	189	190	191	192	193	194	195	196	197	198
216	215	214	213	212	211	210	209	208	207	206	205	204	203	202	201	200	199
217	218	219	220	221	222	223	224	225	226	227	228	229	230	231	232	233	234
252	251	250	249	248	247	246	245	244	243	242	241	240	239	238	237	236	235
253	254	255	256	257	258	259	260	261	262	263	264	265	266	267	268	269	270
288	287	286	285	284	283	282	281	280	279	278	277	276	275	274	273	272	271
289	290	291	292	293	294	295	296	297	298	299	300	301	302	303	304	305	306
324	323	322	321	320	319	318	317	316	315	314	313	312	311	310	309	308	307

Cartica[r]y

Cr.

Section Nº1.

District Nº5.

N. Currier's Lith. N.Y.

A MAP of the 6th DISTRICT 2d SECTION

of originally Cherokee, now

GILMER COUNTY

James F. Smith

Scale of 100 chains to an inch

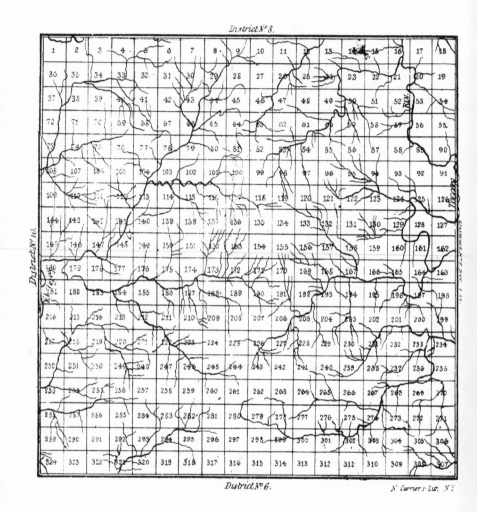

District Nº 8.

District Nº 6.

N. Currier's Lith. N.Y.

A MAP of the 7th DISTRICT 2d SECTION

of originally Cherokee, now

GILMER COUNTY

James F. Smith

Scale of 180 chains to an Inch

NORTH CAROLINA

District Nº 7.

N. Currier's Lith. N.Y.

A MAP of the 8 th DISTRICT 2 d SECTION

of originally Cherokee, now

GILMER COUNTY

James F. Smith

Scale of 160 chains to an Inch

TENNESSEE and N. CAROLINA.

District N° 10.

N. Currier's Lith. N.Y.

A MAP of the 9th DISTRICT 2d SECTION

of originally Cherokee, now

GILMER COUNTY

James F. Smith

Scale of 100 chains to an inch

District Nº 9.

District Nº 1.

District Nº 11.

N. Currier's Lith. N.Y.

A MAP of the 10th DISTRICT 2d SECTION

of originally Cherokee, now

GILMER COUNTY

James F. Smith

Scale of 160 chains to an Inch

District Nº 10.

1	2	3	4	5	6	7	8	9	10	11	12	13	14	15	16	17	18
36	35	34	33	32	31	30	29	28	27	26	25	24	23	22	21	20	19
37	38	39	40	41	42	43	44	45	46	47	48	49	50	51	52	53	54
72	71	70	69	68	67	66	65	64	63	62	61	60	59	58	57	56	55
73	74	75	76	77	78	79	80	81	82	83	84	85	86	87	88	89	90
108	107	106	105	104	103	102	101	100	99	98	97	96	95	94	93	92	91
109	110	111	112	113	114	115	116	117	118	119	120	121	122	123	124	125	126
144	143	142	141	140	139	138	137	136	135	134	133	132	131	130	129	128	127
145	146	147	148	149	150	151	152	153	154	155	156	157	158	159	160	161	162
180	179	178	177	176	175	174	173	172	171	170	169	168	167	166	165	164	163
181	182	183	184	185	186	187	188	189	190	191	192	193	194	195	196	197	198
216	215	214	213	212	211	210	209	208	207	206	205	204	203	202	201	200	199
217	218	219	220	221	222	223	224	225	226	227	228	229	230	231	232	233	234
252	251	250	249	248	247	246	245	244	243	242	241	240	239	238	237	236	235
253	254	255	256	257	258	259	260	261	262	263	264	265	266	267	268	269	270
288	287	286	285	284	283	282	281	280	279	278	277	276	275	274	273	272	271
289	290	291	292	293	294	295	296	297	298	299	300	301	302	303	304	305	306
324	323	322	321	320	319	318	317	316	315	314	313	312	311	310	309	308	307

District Nº 25

Ellijay

District Nº 12.

N. Currier's Lith. N.Y.

A MAP of the 11th DISTRICT 2d SECTION

of originally Cherokee, now

GILMER COUNTY

James F. Smith

Scale of 10 chains to an inch

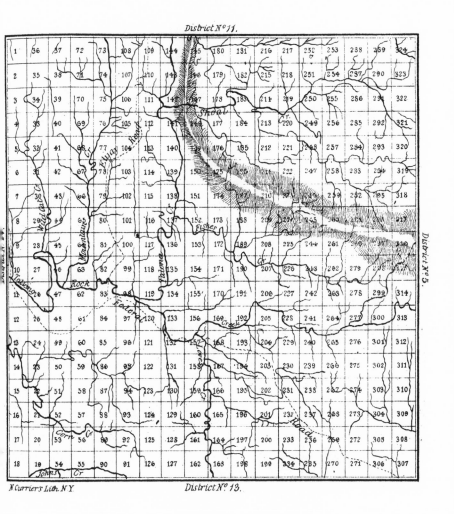

A MAP of the *12th* DISTRICT *2d* SECTION

of originally Cherokee, now

GILMER COUNTY

James F. Smith

Scale of 160 chains to an inch

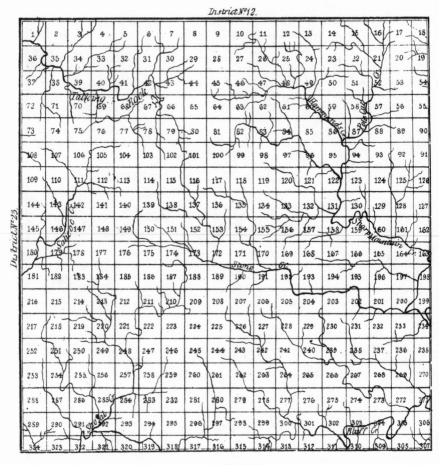

A MAP of the 13th DISTRICT 2d SECTION

of originally Cherokee, now

CHEROKEE COUNTY

James F. Smith

Scale of 100 chains to an inch

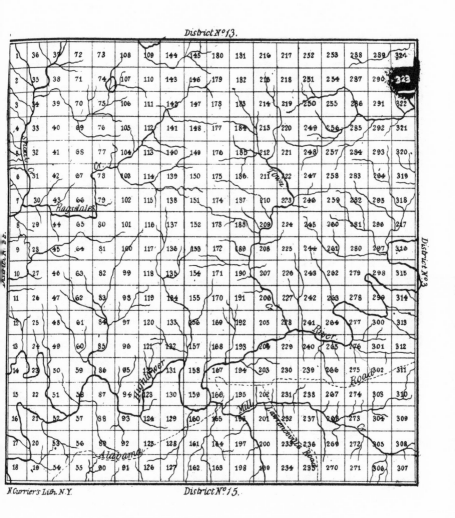

A MAP of the 14th DISTRICT 2d SECTION

of originally Cherokee, now

CHEROKEE COUNTY.

James F. Smith

scale of 160 chains to an inch

20.

A MAP of the 20th DISTRICT 2d SECTION

of originally Cherokee, now

COBB COUNTY

James F. Smith

Scale of 160 chains to an Inch

A MAP of the 20th DISTRICT 2d SECTION

of originally Cherokee, now

COBB COUNTY

James F. Smith

Scale of 160 chains to an inch

A MAP of the 22ND **DISTRICT** 2ND **SECTION**

of originally Cherokee, now

CASS & CHEROKEE COUNTIES

James F. Smith

Scale 160 Chains to an Inch

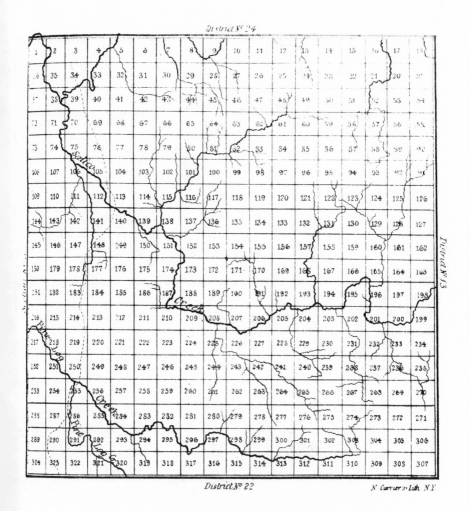

District Nº 24

District Nº 22

District Nº 13

N. Currier's Lith. N.Y.

A MAP of the 23rd DISTRICT 2nd SECTION

of originally Cherokee, now

CASS & CHEROKEE COUNTIES

James F. Smith

Scale 160 Chains to an Inch.

160   320

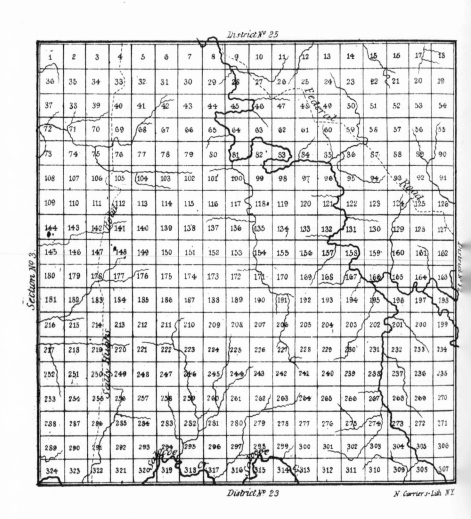

District N° 25

District N° 23

N. Currier's Lith. N.Y.

A MAP of the 24th DISTRICT 2nd SECTION

of originally Cherokee, now

MURRAY & GILMER COUNTIES

James F. Smith

Scale 160 Chains to an Inch.

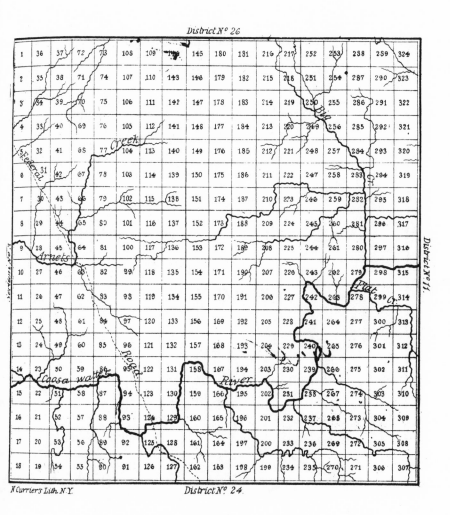

District Nº 26

District Nº 11.

District Nº 24

N Currier's Lith. N.Y.

A MAP of the 25th DISTRICT 2nd SECTION

of originally Cherokee, now

MURRAY & GILMER COUNTIES

James F. Smith

Scale 160 Chains to an Inch.

160   320

District N.º 27.

Holly C.º

Section N.º 3

District N.º 25.

N. Currier's Lith. 8

A MAP of the 26th DISTRICT 2d SECTION

of originally Cherokee, now

MURRAY & GILMER COUNTIES

James F. Smith

Scale 160 Chains to an Inch.

160   320

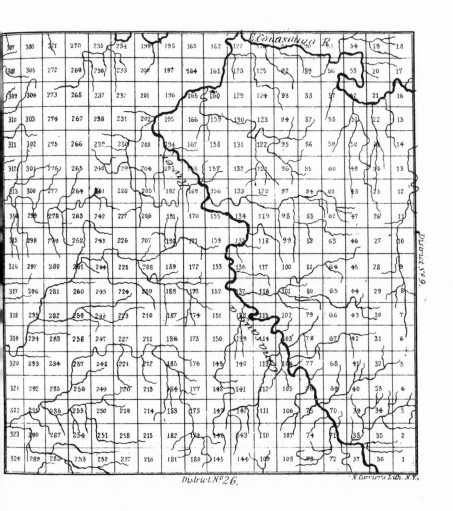

District N⁰26.

A MAP of the 27th DISTRICT 2d. SECTION

of originally Cherokee, now

MURRAY & GILMER COUNTIES

James F. Smith

Scale 160 Chains to an Inch

160   320

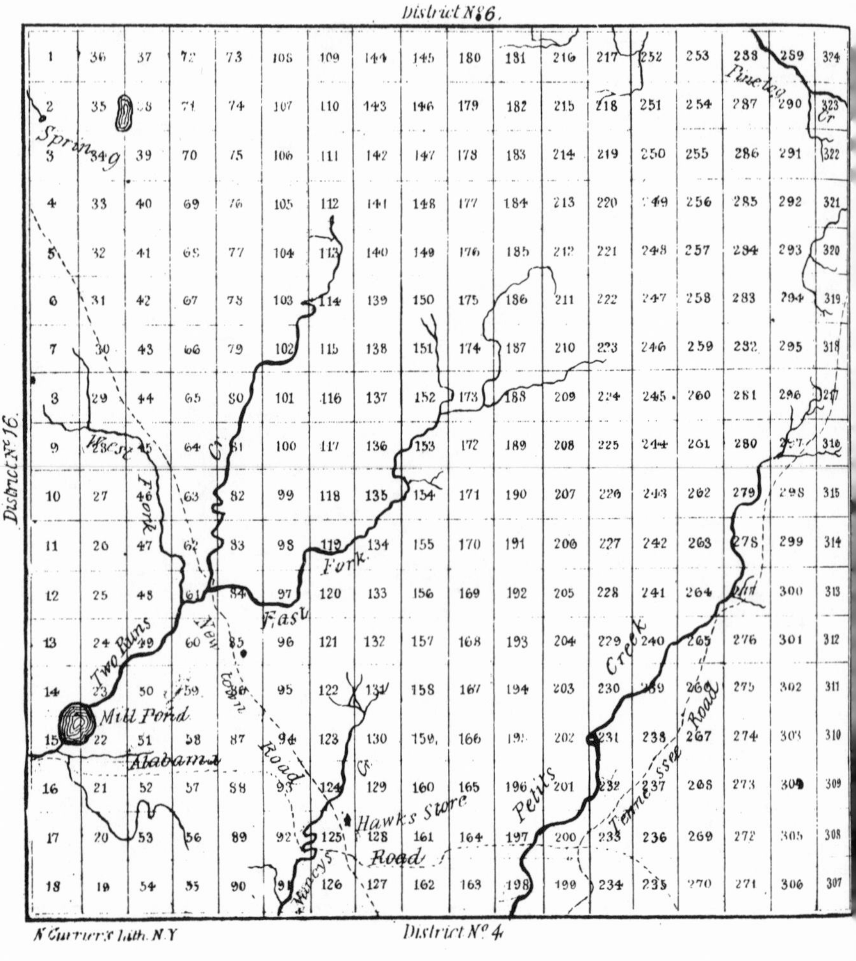

District N 6.

District N 16.

Springs

Horse

Fork

Two Runs

New town

Mill Pond

Alabama

Hawks Store
Road

Nancys

Fast

Fork

Creek

Petts

Pine tree

Cr

Tennessee Road

District N 4.

N Currier's lith. N.Y.

A MAP of the 5th DISTRICT 3d SECTION

of originally Cherokee, now

CASS COUNTY

James F. Smith

Scale 160 Chains to an Inch

160   320

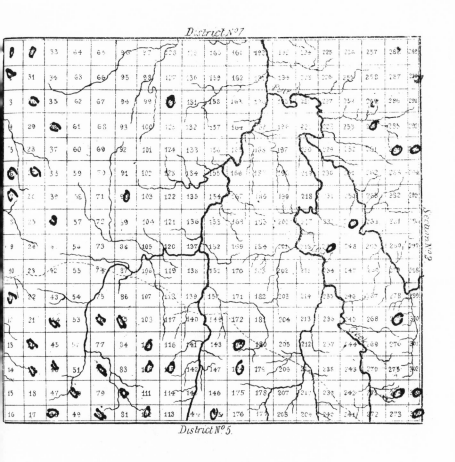

District Nº 7.

District Nº 5.

A MAP of the 6th DISTRICT 3d SECTION

of originally Cherokee, now

CASS COUNTY

James F. Smith

Scale 160 Chains to an Inch.

160   320

District Nº 8

Coosawatee Riv.

Saloga

District Nº 6.

N. Currier's Lith. N.Y.

A MAP of the 7th DISTRICT 3d SECTION

of originally Cherokee, now

MURRAY COUNTY

James F. Smith

Scale. Chains to an Inch.
160
320

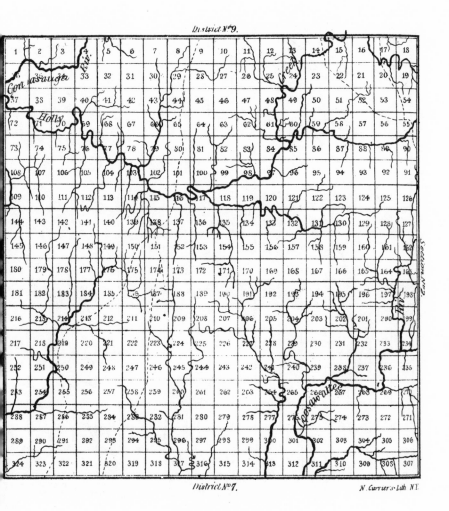

District N°9.

District N°7.

N. Currier's Lith NY.

A MAP of the 8th DISTRICT 3d SECTION

of originally Cherokee, now

MURRAY COUNTY

James F. Smith

Scale 160 Chains to an Inch

District Nº 10

1	2	3	4	5 6	7	8	9	10	11	12	13	14	15	16	17	18
36	35	34	33	32 31	30	29	28	27	26	25	24	23	22	21	20	19
37	38	39	40	41 42	43	44	45	46	47	48	49	50	51	52	53	54
72	71	70	69	68 67	66	65	64	63	62	61	60	59	58	57	56	55
73	74	75	76	77 78	79	80	81	82	83	84	85	86	87	88	89	90
108	107	106	105	104 103	102	101	100	99	98	97	96	95	94	93	92	91
109	110	111	112	113 114	115	116	117	118	119	120	121	122	123	124	125	126
144	143	142	141	140 139	138	137	136	135	134	133	132	131	130	129	128	127
145	146	147	148	149 150	151	152	153	154	155	156	157	158	159	160	161	162
180	179	178	177	176 175	174	173	172	171	170	169	168	167	166	165	164	163
181	182	183	184	185 186	187	188	189	190	191	192	193	194	195	196	197	198
216	215	214	213	212 211	210	209	208	207	206	205	204	203	202	201	200	199
217	218	219	220	221 222	223	224	225	226	227	228	229	230	231	232	233	234
252	251	250	249	248 247	246	245	244	243	242	241	240	239	238	237	236	235
253	254	255	256	257 258	259	260	261	262	263	264	265	266	267	268	269	270
288	287	286	285	284 283	282	281	280	279	278	277	276	275	274	273	272	271
289	290	291	292	293 294	295	296	297	298	299	300	301	302	303	304	305	306
324	323	322	321	320 319	318	317	316	315	314	313	312	311	310	309	308	307

District Nº 8

District Nº 2

creek

creek

Mill

Cona sauga

Road

N. Currier's Lith. N.Y.

A MAP of the 9th. DISTRICT 3rd. SECTION

of originally Cherokee, now

MURRAY COUNTY.

James F. Smith

Scale 160 Chains to an inch.

160   320

Tennessee Line.

1	2	3	4	5	6	7	8	9	10	11	12	13	14	15	16	17	18
36	35	34	33	32	31	30	29	28	27	26	25	24	23	22	21	20	19
37	38	39	40	41	42	43	44	45	46	47	48	49	50	51	52	53	54
72	71	70	69	68	67	66	65	64	63	62	61	60	59	58	57	56	55
73	74	75	76	77	78	79	80	81	82	83	84	85	86	87	88	89	90
108	107	106	105	104	103	102	101	100	99	98	97	96	95	94	93	92	91
109	110	111	112	113	114	115	116	117	118	119	120	121	122	123	124	125	126
144	143	142	141	140	139	138	137	136	135	134	133	132	131	130	129	128	127
145	146	147	148	149	150	151	152	153	154	155	156	157	158	159	160	161	162
180	179	178	177	176	175	174	173	172	171	170	169	168	167	166	165	164	163
181	182	183	184	185	186	187	188	189	190	191	192	193	194	195	196	197	198
216	215	214	213	212	211	210	209	208	207	206	205	204	203	202	201	200	199
217	218	219	220	221	222	223	224	225	226	227	228	229	230	231	232	233	234
252	251	250	249	248	247	246	245	244	243	242	241	240	239	238	237	236	235
253	254	255	256	257	258	259	260	261	262	263	264	265	266	267	268	269	270
288	287	286	285	284	283	282	281	280	279	278	277	276	275	274	273	272	271
289	290	291	292	293	294	295	296	297	298	299	300	301	302	303	304	305	306
324	323	322	321	320	319	318	317	316	315	314	313	312	311	310	309	308	307

Sugar or

River

Coosawattee

Conasauga

District No 9

N Currier's Lith NY

A MAP of the 10th DISTRICT 3d SECTION

of originally Cherokee, now

MURRAY COUNTY

James F. Smith

Scale 160 Chains to an Inch

160   320

Tennessee Line.

1	2	3	4	5	6	7	8	9	10	11	12	13	14	15	16	17	18
36	35	34	33	32	31	30	29	28	27	26	25	24	23	22	21	20	19
37	38	39	40	41	42	43	44	45	46	47	48	49	50	51	52	53	54
72	71	70	69	68	67	66	65	64	63	62	61	60	59	58	57	56	55
73	74	75	76	77	78	79	80	81	82	83	84	85	86	87	88	89	90
108	107	106	105	104	103	102	101	100	99	98	97	96	95	94	93	92	91
109	110	111	112	113	114	115	116	117	118	119	120	121	122	123	124	125	126
144	143	142	141	140	139	138	137	136	135	134	133	132	131	130	129	128	127
145	146	147	148	149	150	151	152	153	154	155	156	157	158	159	160	161	162
180	179	178	177	176	175	174	173	172	171	170	169	168	167	166	165	164	163
181	182	183	184	185	186	187	188	189	190	191	192	193	194	195	196	197	198
216	215	214	213	212	211	210	209	208	207	206	205	204	203	202	201	200	199
217	218	219	220	221	222	223	224	225	226	227	228	229	230	231	232	233	234
252	251	250	249	248	247	246	245	244	243	242	241	240	239	238	237	236	235
253	254	255	256	257	258	259	260	261	262	263	264	265	266	267	268	269	270
288	287	286	285	284	283	282	281	280	279	278	277	276	275	274	273	272	271
289	290	291	292	293	294	295	296	297	298	299	300	301	302	303	304	305	306
324	323	322	321	320	319	318	317	316	315	314	313	312	311	310	309	308	307

District Nº 12.

N. Currier's Lith N

District Nº 78.

A MAP of the 11th DISTRICT 3d SECTION

of originally Cherokee, now

MURRAY COUNTY.

James F. Smith

Scal: 160 Chains to an Inch.

160   320

District Nº 11

District Nº 13

A MAP of the *12th* DISTRICT *3d* SECTION

of originally Cherokee, now

MURRAY COUNTY

James F. Smith

Scale 160 Chains to an Inch.

160   320

District Nº 12

1	2	3	4	5	6	7	8	9	10	11	12	13	14	15	16	17	18
36	35	34	33	32	31	30	29	28	27	26	25	24	23	22	21	20	19
37	38	39	40	41	42	43	44	45	46	47	48	49	50	51	52	53	54
72	71	70	69	68	67	66	65	64	63	62	61	60	59	58	57	56	55
73	74	75	76	77	78	79	80	81	82	83	84	85	86	87	88	89	90
108	107	106	105	104	103	102	101	100	99	98	97	96	95	94	93	92	91
109	110	111	112	113	114	115	116	117	118	119	120	121	122	123	124	125	126
144	143	142	141	140	139	138	137	136	135	134	133	132	131	130	129	128	127
145	146	147	148	149	150	151	152	153	154	155	156	157	158	159	160	161	162
180	179	178	177	176	175	174	173	172	171	170	169	168	167	166	165	164	163
181	182	183	184	185	186	187	188	189	190	191	192	193	194	195	196	197	198
216	215	214	213	212	211	210	209	208	207	206	205	204	203	202	201	200	199
217	218	219	220	221	222	223	224	225	226	227	228	229	230	231	232	233	234
252	251	250	249	248	247	246	245	244	243	242	241	240	239	238	237	236	235
253	254	255	256	257	258	259	260	261	262	263	264	265	266	267	268	269	270
288	287	286	285	284	283	282	281	280	279	278	277	276	275	274	273	272	271
289	290	291	292	293	294	295	296	297	298	299	300	301	302	303	304	305	306
324	323	322	321	320	319	318	317	316	315	314	313	312	311	310	309	308	307

District Nº 26

District Nº 14.

N. Currier's Lith N

A MAP of the 13th DISTRICT 3d SECTION

of originally Cherokee, now

MURRAY COUNTY.

James F. Smith

Scale 160 Chains to an Inch.

160   320

District Nº 13.

District Nº 15.

A MAP of the *14th DISTRICT 3d. SECTION*

of, originally Cherokee, now

MURRAY COUNTY.

James F. Smith

Scale 160 Chains to an Inch.

160   320

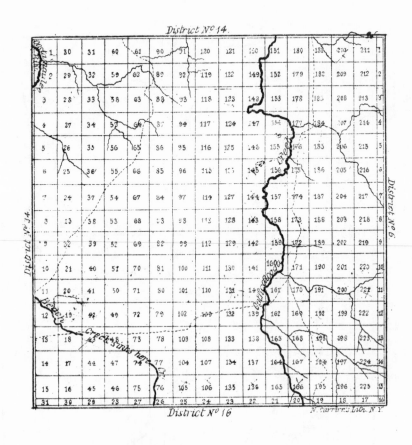

District Nº 14.

District Nº 16

District Nº 6

N. Currier's Lith. N.Y.

A MAP of the 15th DISTRICT 3rd SECTION

of originally Cherokee, now

CASS COUNTY

James F. Smith

Scale 160 Chains to an Inch
160   320

District Nº 16.

1	2	3	4	5	6	7	8	9	10	11	12	13	14	15
30	29	28	27	26	25	24	23	22	21	20	19	18	17	16
31	32	33	34	35	36	37	38	39	40	41	42	43	44	45
60	59	58	57	56	55	54	53	52	51	50	49	48	47	46
61	62	63	64	65	66	67	68	69	70	71	72	73	74	75
90	89	88	87	86	85	84	83	82	81	80	79	78	77	76
91	92	93	94	95	96	97	98	99	100	101	102	103	104	105
120	119	118	117	116	115	114	113	112	111	110	109	108	107	106
121	122	123	124	125	126	127	228	129	130	131	132	133	134	135
150	149	148	147	146	145	144	143	142	141	140	139	138	137	136
151	152	153	154	155	156	157	158	159	160	161	162	163	164	165
180	179	178	177	176	175	174	173	172	171	170	169	168	167	166
181	182	183	184	185	186	187	188	189	190	191	192	193	194	195
210	209	208	207	206	205	204	203	202	201	200	199	198	197	196
211	212	213	214	215	216	217	218	219	220	221	222	223	224	225
240	239	238	237	236	235	234	233	232	231	230	229	228	227	226
241	242	243	244	245	246	247	248	249	250	251	252	253	254	255
270	269	268	267	266	265	264	263	262	261	260	259	258	257	256

District Nº 23

District Nº 5

Mcbees Creek

Thomas Cr.

Connesena Cr.

Alabama

Conasena

Road

Hurl Iron Creek

Ploughs

District Nº 17.

N. Currier's Lith. N.Y.

A MAP of the 16th DISTRICT 3rd SECTION

of originally Cherokee, now

CASS COUNTY

James F. Smith

Scale 160 Chains to an Inch

160   320

District Nº 23.

A MAP of the 22d DISTRICT 3d SECTION

of originally Cherokee, now

FLOYD COUNTY

James F. Smith

N. Curriers Lith. N.Y.

District Nº 21.

Scale 1? Chains to an Inch.

District Nº 24.

Oostanaulee Riv.

Etowah

River

District Nº 22.

N. Currier's Lith S.

A MAP of the 23d DISTRICT 3d SECTION

of originally Cherokee, now

FLOYD COUNTY

James F. Smith

Scale 160 Chains to an Inch.

160   320

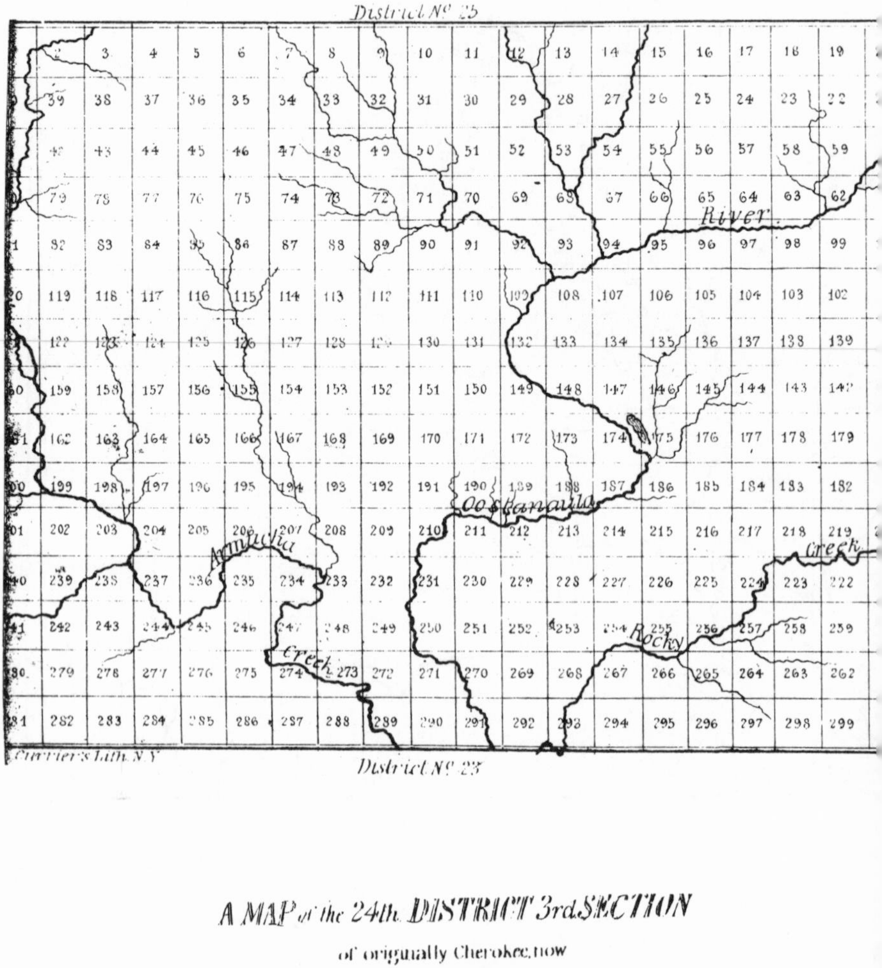
District No. 25
River
Oostanaula
Armuchia
Creek
Rocky
Creek
Currier's Lith. N.Y.
District No. 23

A MAP of the 24th. DISTRICT 3rd. SECTION

of originally Cherokee, now

FLOYD COUNTY

James F. Smith

Scale 160 Chains to an Inch

160 320

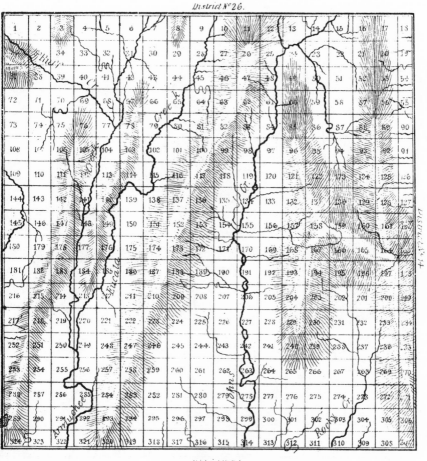

District N⁰ 26.

District N⁰ 24.

N Currier's Lith N Y

A MAP of the 25th DISTRICT 3d SECTION

of originally Cherokee, now

WALKER COUNTY

James F. Smith

Scale 160 Chains to an Inch.

160   320

District Nº 27.

District Nº 25

N Currier's Lith. N.Y.

A MAP of the 26th. DISTRICT 3rd SECTION

of originally Cherokee, now

WALKER COUNTY

James F. Smith

Scale 160 Chains to an Inch.

160   320

District Nº 28.

1	2	3	4	5	6	7	8	9	10	11	12	13	14	15	16	17	18
36	35	34	33	32	31	30	29	28	27	26	25	24	23	22	21	20	19
37	38	39	40	41	42	43	44	45	46	47	48	49	50	51	52	53	54
72	71	70	69	68	67	66	65	64	63	62	61	60	59	58	57	56	55
73	74	75	76	77	78	79	80	81	82	83	84	85	86	87	88	89	90
108	107	106	105	104	103	102	101	100	99	98	97	96	95	94	93	92	91
109	110	111	112	113	114	115	116	117	118	119	120	121	122	123	124	125	126
144	143	142	141	140	139	138	137	136	135	134	133	132	131	130	129	128	127
145	146	147	148	149	150	151	152	153	154	155	156	157	158	159	160	161	162
180	179	178	177	176	175	174	173	172	171	170	169	168	167	166	165	164	163
181	182	183	184	185	186	187	188	189	190	191	192	193	194	195	196	197	198
216	215	214	213	212	211	210	209	208	207	206	205	204	203	202	201	200	199
217	218	219	220	221	222	223	224	225	226	227	228	229	230	231	232	233	234
252	251	250	249	248	247	246	245	244	243	242	241	240	239	238	237	236	235
253	254	255	256	257	258	259	260	261	262	263	264	265	266	287	268	269	270
288	287	286	285	284	283	282	281	280	279	278	277	276	275	274	273	272	271
289	290	291	292	293	294	295	296	297	298	299	300	301	302	303	304	305	306
324	323	322	321	320	319	318	317	316	315	314	313	312	311	310	309	308	307
325	326	327	328	329	330	331	332	333	334	335	336	337	338	339	340	341	342

East Chickamauga River

Faughts Cr.

Chickamauga

District Nº 26.

A MAP of the 27th DISTRICT 3d SECTION

of originally Cherokee, now

WALKER COUNTY

James F. Smith

Scale 160 Chains to an Inch

160   320

TENNESSEE.

District Nº 27.

N. Currier's Lith

A MAP of the 28th DISTRICT 3d SECTION

of originally Cherokee, now

WALKER COUNTY

James F. Smith

Scale 160 Chains to an Inch.

160   320

District Nº 5

1	2	3	4	5	6	7	8	9	10	11	12	13	14	15	16	17	18
36	35	34	33	32	31	30	29	28	27	26	25	24	23	22	21	20	19
37	38	39	40	41	42	43	44	45	46	47	48	49	50	51	52	53	54
72	71	70	69	68	67	66	65	64	63	62	61	60	59	58	57	56	55
73	74	75	76	77	78	79	80	81	82	83	84	85	86	87	88	89	90
108	107	106	105	104	103	102	101	NW	99	98	97	96	95	94	93	92	91
109	110	111	112	113	114	115	116	117	118	119	120	121	122	123	124	125	126
144	143	142	141	140	139	138	137	136	135	134	133	132	131	130	129	128	127
145	146	147	148	149	150	151	152	153	154	155	156	157	158	159	160	161	162
180	179	178	177	176	175	174	173	172	171	170	169	168	167	166	165	164	163
181	182	183	184	185	186	187	188	189	190	191	192	193	194	195	196	197	198
216	215	214	213	212	211	210	209	208	207	206	205	204	203	202	201	200	199
217	218	219	220	221	222	223	224	225	226	227	228	229	230	231	232	233	234
252	251	250	249	248	247	246	245	244	243	242	241	240	239	238	237	236	235
253	254	255	256	257	258	259	260	261	262	263	264	265	266	267	268	269	270
288	287	286	285	284	283	282	281	280	279	278	277	276	275	274	273	272	271
289	290	291	292	293	294	295	296	297	298	299	300	301	302	303	304	305	306
324	323	322	321	320	319	318	317	316	315	314	313	312	311	310	309	308	307

Section Nº 3

Road

Alabama

Coosa

Tar-Bob

Coosa River

District Nº 3

N. Currier's Lith. N.Y.

A MAP of the 4th DISTRICT 4th SECTION

of originally Cherokee, now

FLOYD COUNTY

James F. Smith

Scale 160 Chains to an Inch.

160   320

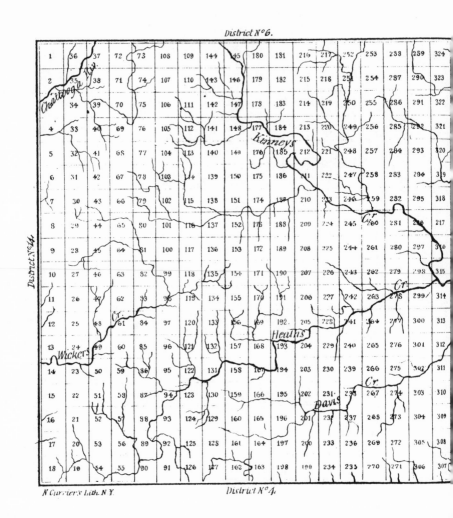

A MAP of the 5th DISTRICT 4th SECTION

of originally Cherokee, now

FLOYD COUNTY.

James F. Smith

Scale 160 Chains to an Inch.

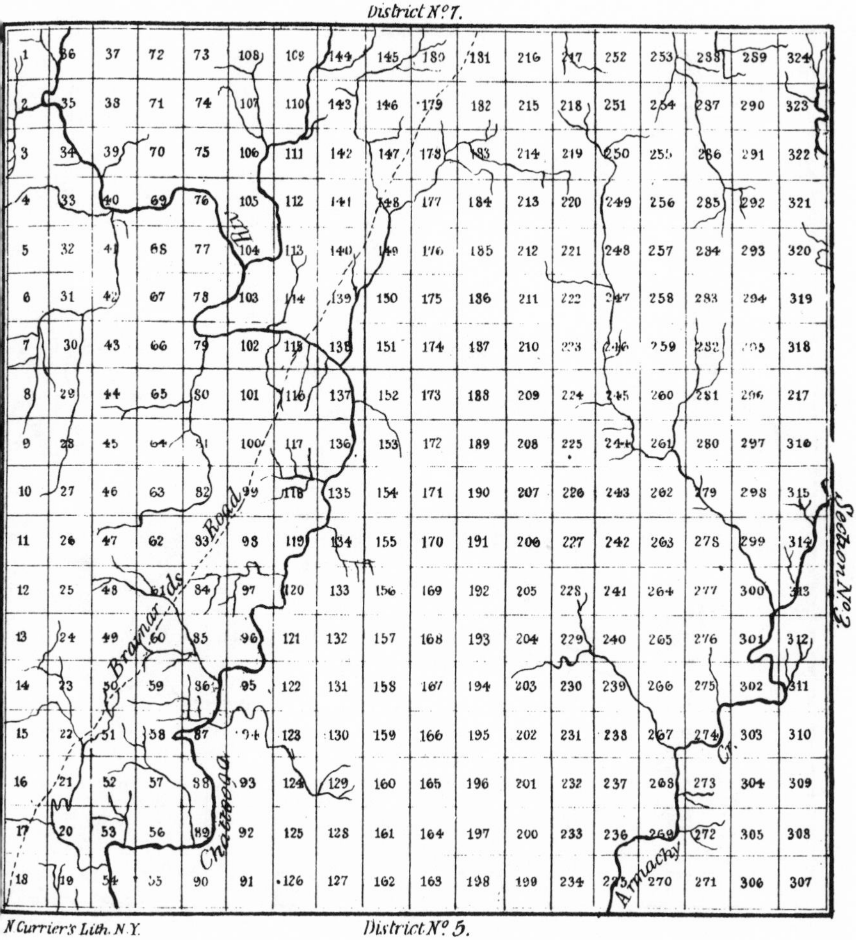
District No. 7.
Section No. 3.
Brainards Road
Riv.
Chattooga
Armachy Cr.
District No. 5.
N Currier's Lith. N.Y.

A MAP of the 6th DISTRICT 4th SECTION

of originally Cherokee, now

WALKER COUNTY

James F. Smith

Scale 160 Chains to an Inch.

160 320

District N° 8.

1	2	3	4	5	6	7	8	9	10	11	12	13	14	15	16	17	18
36	35	34	33	32	31	30	29	28	27	26	25	24	23	22	21	20	19
37	38	39	40	41	42	43	44	45	46	47	48	49	50	51	52	53	54
72	71	70	69	68	67	66	65	64	63	62	61	60	59	58	57	56	55
73	74	75	76	77	78	79	80	81	82	83	84	85	86	87	88	89	90
108	107	106	105	104	103	102	101	100	99	98	97	96	95	94	93	92	91
109	110	111	112	113	114	115	116	117	118	119	120	121	122	123	124	125	126
144	143	142	141	140	139	138	137	136	135	134	133	132	131	130	129	128	127
145	146	147	148	149	150	151	152	153	154	155	156	157	158	159	160	161	162
180	179	178	177	176	175	174	173	172	171	170	169	168	167	166	165	164	163
181	182	183	184	185	186	187	188	189	190	191	192	193	194	195	196	197	198
216	215	214	213	212	211	210	209	208	207	206	205	204	203	202	201	200	199
217	218	219	220	221	222	223	224	225	226	227	228	229	230	231	232	233	234
252	251	250	249	248	247	246	245	244	243	242	241	240	239	238	237	236	235
253	254	255	256	257	258	259	260	261	262	263	264	265	266	267	268	269	270
288	287	286	285	284	283	282	281	280	279	278	277	276	275	274	273	272	271
289	290	291	292	293	294	295	296	297	298	299	300	301	302	303	304	305	306
324	323	322	321	320	319	318	317	316	315	314	313	312	311	310	309	308	307

District N° 12.

District N° 6

N. Currier's Lith. N.

A MAP of the 7th DISTRICT 4th SECTION

of originally Cherokee, now

WALKER COUNTY

James F. Smith

Scale 160 Chains to an Inch.

160   320

District Nº 9.

1	2	3	4	5	6	7	8	9	10		12	13	14	15	16	17	18
36	35	34	33	32	31	30	29	28	27	26	2	24	23	22	21	20	19
37	38	39	40	41			44	45	46	47	48	49	50	51	52	53	54
72	71	70	69	68	67		65	64	63	62	61	60	59	58	57	56	55
73	74	75	76	77	78	79	80	81	82	83	84	85	86	87	88	89	90
108	107	106	105	104	103	102	101	100	99	98	97		95	94	93	92	91
109	110	111	12	113	114	115	116	117		119		121	122	123	124	125	126
144	143	142	141	140	139	138	137	136	135	124	133	132	131	130	129	128	127
145	146	147	148	149	150	151		153	154	155	156	157	153	152	160	161	162
180	179	178	177	176	175	174		172	171	170	169	168	167	166	165	164	163
181	182	183	184	185	186	187	188	189	190	191	192	193	194	195	196	197	198
216	215	214	213	212	211	210	209	208	207	206	205	204	203	202	201	200	199
217	218	219	220			223	224	225	226	227	228	229	230	231	232	233	234
252	251	250	249	248	247	246	245	244	243	242	241	240	239	238	237	236	235
253	254	255	256		258	259	260	261	262	263	264	265	266	267	268	269	270
288	287	286	285	284	283	282	281	280	279	278	277	276	275	274	273	272	271
289	290	291	292	293	294	295	296	297	298	299	300	301	302	303	304	305	306
324			321	320	319	318	317	316	315	314	313	312	311	310	309	308	307

District Nº 7.

Section Nº 3.

N. Currier's Lith. N.Y.

A MAP of the 8 th DISTRICT 4 th SECTION

of originally Cherokee, now

WALKER COUNTY

James F. Smith

Scale 160 Chains to an Inch
160   320

Tennessee Line

Rossville

Federal Road

District N° 8

N Currier's Lith N Y

A MAP of the 9th DISTRICT 4th SECTION

of originally Cherokee, now

WALKER COUNTY.

James F Smith

Scale 160 Chains to an Inch.

160   320

Tennessee Line

District N° 11

N. Currier's Lith. N.Y.

A MAP of the 10th DISTRICT 4th SECTION

of originally Cherokee, now

WALKER COUNTY

James F. Smith

Scale 160 Chains to an Inch

160   320

A MAP of the 11th. DISTRICT 4th. SECTION

of originally Cherokee, now

WALKER COUNTY.

James F. Smith

Scale 160 Chains to an Inch.

District Nº 11

1	36	37	72	73	108	109	144	145	180	181	216	217	252	253	288	289	324
2	35	38	71	74	107	110	143	146	179	182	215	218	251	254	287	290	323
3	34	39	70	75	106	111	142	147	178	183	214	219	250	255	286	291	322
4	33	40	69	76	105	112	141	148	177	184	213	220	249	256	285	292	321
5	32	41	68	77	104	113	140	149	176	185	212	221	248	257	284	293	320
6	31	42	67	78	103	114	139	150	175	186	211	222	247	258	283	294	319
7	30	43	66	79	102	115	138	151	174	187	210	223	246	259	282	295	318
8	29	44	65	80	101	116	137	152	173	188	209	224	245	260	281	296	317
9	28	45	64	81	100	117	136	153	172	189	208	225	244	261	280	297	316
10	27	46	63	82	99	118	135	154	171	190	207	226	243	262	279	298	315
11	26	47	62	83	98	119	134	155	170	191	206	227	242	263	278	299	314
12	25	48	61	84	97	120	133	156	169	192	205	228	241	264	277	300	313
13	24	49	60	85	96	121	132	157	168	193	204	229	240	265	276	301	312
14	23	50	59	86	95	122	131	158	167	194	203	230	239	266	275	302	311
15	22	51	58	87	94	123	130	159	166	195	202	231	238	267	274	303	310
16	21	52	57	88	93	124	129	160	165	196	201	232	237	268	273	304	309
17	20	53	56	89	92	125	128	161	164	197	200	233	236	269	272	305	308
18	19	54	55	90	91	126	127	162	163	198	199	234	235	270	271	306	307

Pigeon or Look out Mountain

Green Creek Gap

Look out Mountain

Sink

District Nº 7

N Currier's Lith. N.Y.

District Nº 13

A MAP of the 12th DISTRICT 4th SECTION

of originally Cherokee, now

WALKER COUNTY

James F. Smith

Scale 160 Chains to an Inch

160   320

District No 12

313	304	303	271	270	235	234	199	198	163	162	127	126	91	90	55	54	19	18
317	305	302	272	269	236	233	200	197	164	161	123	125	92	89	56	53	20	17
316	306	301	273	268	237	232	201	196	165	160	129	124	93	88	57	52	21	16
	307	300	274	267	238	231	202	195	166	159	130	123	94	87	58	51	22	15
	308	299	275	266	239	230	203	194	167	158	131	122	95	86	59	50	23	14
	309	298	276	265	240	229	204	193	168	157	132	121	96	85	60	49	24	13
	310	297	277	264	241	228	205	192	169	156	133	120	97	84	61	48	25	12
	311	296	278	263	242	227	206	191	170	155	134	119	98	83	62	47	26	11
	312	295	279	262	243	226	207	190	171	154	135	118	99	82	63	46	27	10
		294	280	261	244	225	208	189	172	153	136	117	100	81	64	45	28	9
		293	281	260	245	224	209	188	173	152	137	116	101	80	65	44	29	8
		292	282	259	246	223	210	187	174	151	138	115	102	79	66	43	30	7
		291	283	258	247	222	211	186	175	150	139	114	103	78	67	42	31	6
			284	257	248	221	212	185	176	149	140	113	104	77	68	41	32	5
		285	256	249	220	213	184	177	148	141	112	105	76	69	40	33	4
		286	255	250	219	214	183	178	147	142	111	106	75	70	39	34	3
		287	254	251	218	215	182	179	146	143	110	107	74	71	38	35	2
		288	253	252	217	216	181	180	145	144	109	108	73	72	37	36	1

Line

Alabama

Mountain

District No 14.

N. Currier's Lith. N

A MAP of the 13th. DISTRICT 4th. SECTION

of originally Cherokee, now

WALKER COUNTY

James F. Smith

Scale 160 Chains to an Inch.

160   320

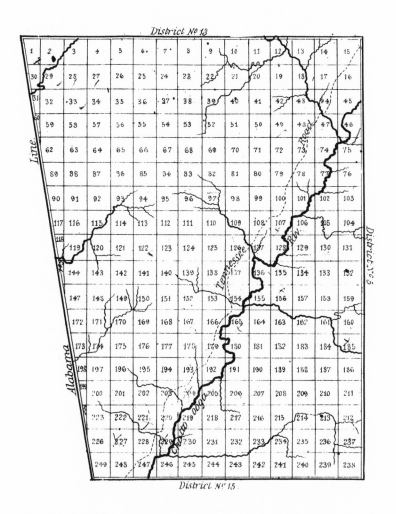

A MAP of the 14th DISTRICT 4th SECTION

of originally Cherokee, now

FLOYD COUNTY.

James F. Smith

Scale 160 Chains to an Inch.

District Nº 14.

District Nº 4

District Nº 16.

N. Currier's Lith. N.Y.

A MAP of the 15th DISTRICT 4th SECTION

of originally Cherokee, now

FLOYD COUNTY.

James F. Smith

Scale 160 Chains to an Inch.

160.   320

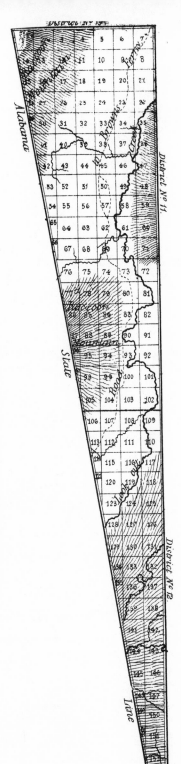

A MAP of the 18th. DISTRICT 4th.SECTION

of originally Cherokee; now

WALKER COUNTY

James F. Smith

Scale 180 Chains to an Inch.

A MAP of the *19th* DISTRICT 4th SECTION

of originally Cherokee, now

WALKER COUNTY.

James F. Smith

Scale 160 Chains to an Inch.

160   320

Anthony, Anslem L. 124;
David 293; Harison 102;
Jas. M. 143; Jno. 9,282;
Jos. B. 399; Mark 342:
Mark S. 48; Thos. 391;
Willis 77
Anthony's, Isaac(ors) 378
Apperson, David J. 385
Appleby, Wm. 223
Applewhite, Jno. 308;
Robt. 131
Archer, Ann 116; Lucy 316;
Mary 139; Wm. Jr. 78
Ard, Margaret 114
Argo, David 151,185; Hil-
ary H. 34; Willis 311
Arkins, Jas. 128
Arline, Jethew 41
Armes, Seth 396
Armor, Rchd. W. 354; Wm.
256
Armour, Robt. 91
Arms, Seth 90
Armsted, Jno. 76
Armstrong, Francis 190;
Jas. 26,392; Jno. 180;
Martin W. 139; Ralph C.
376; Willey S. 333; Wm.
217
Arnand, Jno. Peter 356
Arnett, Kno. 153; Mary 53:
Thos. 108
Arnett's, Robt.(ors) 80
Arnold, Chas. 292; David
287; Eliz. 251; Ezekiel
177; Harrison 335; Jas.
30; Jno. Jr. 162; Over-
ton 16; Whitlock 333,
343; Wm. 22,41,42,325
Arnold's, Jas.(ors) 72,335;
Jno.(ors) 179; Wm.(ors)
98,224
Arnow, Jos. C. 103
Arnstorff, Solomon 12
Aron's, Jno.(ors) 111
Arrant, Allen 151; Eliz.
62; Osborn 151; Reddick
28
Arria, Thos. 232
Arrington, Robt. R. 130;
Wm. 217
Arthur, Matthew 315; Tol-
bert 40
Arundale, Thos. 145
Asbel, Evin 56
Asbell, Elisha 199
Ash, Henry 365; Jane 368
Ash's, Sarah H.(ors) 337
Ashburn, Geo. W. 127
Ashfield, Frederic 117;
Jos. 126
Ashley, Thompson 249
Ashley's, Jas., Barbary
& C. 60
Ashly, Jno. 281; Susannah
229
Ashmore, Jeremiah 208
Ashmore's, Pen.(ors) 388
Ashworth, Noah 274,349
Askew, David 114; Ervin
385; Hillard J. 69; Jas.
P. 69; Miles G. 355;
Thos. 124; Wm. 70,288;
Wm. H. 134
Askew's, Jas.(ors) 234
Askey, Jno. 259
Aslin, Clarissa 97
Ason, Eliz. 400
Astin, Wm. L. 36
Atchison, Jesse H. 121;
Jno. P. 195,343; Wm. 55
Atha, Francis W. 378; Thos.
O. 228
Athens, Elijah C. 328

Atkerson's, Thos.(ors) 211
Atkins, Chas. 236; Chas.
E. 330; Hillery 164;
Ica 280; Wm. 339
Atkinson, Armsted 60;
Green 225; Robt. R. 344;
Saml. C. 223; Washn. G.
43,317
Attaway, David 215; Jesse
232
Attmon, Jno. 372
Atwater, Rdmon 245
Atwell, Jeremiah 209
Atwood, Henry 201; Thos.
191
Auders, Wiley 392
Aughtry, David 42
Augley, Conrod 46; Corod
104
Auldridge, Absalom 127
Austin, Celia 28; Gilbert
237; Harrison 128; Jas.
172; Jno. 371; Jno. C.
295; Jno. G. 210; Jno.
W. 192: Jos. 397; Nathl.
366; Seaborn J. 46;
Starling T. 113; Thomp-
son 367
Autrey, Jas. 363; Jno. 47;
Wm. 81
Autry, Alexr. Jr. 141
Avary, Elias R. 207; Robt.
95.115
Avent, Benj. 44,86; Peter
83
Avera, Danl. 142
Avera's, Chas.(ors) 319
Averatt, Albert 356; Chas.
J. 120
Averette, Matthew 312
Averitt, Jno. 324
Avery's, Wm.(ors) 410
Avory, Madison 52
Avrea, Jno. Jr. 121; Wm.
H. 337
Avria, Alexr. 227
Awood, Jas. 42
Awtry, Jacob 313
Axon, Olivia 55
Aycock, Burwell 196
Aycock's, Danl.(ors) 336
Ayers, Baker 149,159;
Ishmael 238; Jediah 213;
Jno. 144; Wm. 127
Ayer's, Asa (ors) 75
Ayres, Jno. B. 332
Aytry, Henry S. 107

Baas, Danl. 222
Babb, Jno. 315; Sanford
211; Wm. 318
Baber, Ambrose 244; Jas.
373; Wm. 11
Bacchus, Wesley 25
Bachelder, Josiah W. 281;
Nancy 195
Bachellor, Cordy 171,315
Bachellor's, Thos.(ors)
28,64
Bachelor, Jno. A. 407;
Sarah 103; Thos. W. 19
Backley, Mary 48
Bacon, Alfred C. 247;
Francis 296; Jno. E.
48; Wm. 56,104
Badolet, Mary 66
Bagby, Jno. 388; Thos. M.
357
Baggas, Jeremiah 251
Bagget, Elias 85; Peter
J. 331
Baggett, Jno. 61; Laurence
99

Bagley, Benj. 17; Jno. 110;
Lewis 391; Wiley 67
Bagnell's, Danl.(ors) 249
Bags, Lavisa 37
Baggs, Jas. 198
Bagg's, Edmund(ors) 174
Bagwell, Albert 389; Bla-
kely 125; Larkin 147;
Rebecca 393
Bailey, Axam 394; Bryan
367; Burell 349; Dawson
331; Ephrian 154; Green
75; Henry B. 330; Henry
B. 330; Hezekiah 148,
241; Horatio C. 100:
Hosea 68; Isaac 372,390;
Jas. 270; Jas. R. 13;
Joshua 411; Jos. 284;
Keziah 302; Moses P. 308;
Nancy 313; Stephen P.
182,309; Thos. 281; Ur-
bin C. 322; Wm. 93,412;
Wm. H. 391; Williamson
360; Woody 259; Zacha-
riah 46
Bailey's, Henry(ors) 112;
Preston (ors) 146
Baird, Jas. 204; Jno. L.
386
Baisden, Marjam B. 281;
M'Gregor 393; Thos. 370
Baismore, Josiah 231,376
Baker, Aaron 413; Absalom
209; Benj. 154; Calvin,
Jr. 348; Chas. 301; Dan'l
D. 89; Dempsey 176;
Henry Harned 392; Jane
51; Jeremiah 23; Jethro
292; Jno. 26,209; Jno. M.
329; Jno. M.C.L. 349;
Jno. O. 95; Jos. D. 395;
Littleberry W. 385;
Littleton 396; Madison
86; Nathl. 126; Nicholas
282; Riley S. 354; Rus-
sell 197; Silas S. 407;
Solomon 41,144; Stephen
362; Thos. 205,406; Thos.
E. 38; Thos. H. 408;
Wash. 332; Wm. 112,337;
Willis P. 324
Baker's, (ors) 37
Baldasee, Isaac 360
Baldwin, Christopher S.
321; David 267; Jno. C.
306,356; Lydia M. 69;
Saml. B. 81; Wm. A. 362;
Wm. D. 132
Baldwin's, Chas.(ors) 411;
Geo.(ors) 405; Robt.(ors)
119; T.W. 233
Baldy, Wm. 55
Bales, Burrell 410
Baley, Alexr. 50; Gracey
382; Jempsey 349; Jno.
N. 351
Balinger, Jno. 147,198;
Jno. Jr. 245
Ball, Eliz. 116,390; Henry
33,106; Jno. F. 375;
Peter 262; Tuscan H. 186,
278; Wade H. 357
Ball's, Frederic(ors) 285
Ballah, Thos. W. 20
Ballard, Edward A. 402:
Jackson 141; Jas. 408;
Jesse 114,134; Jno. 279,
350; Mary 231; Wiley 120;
Wm. 411; Wm. B. 323
Ballard's, Wm.(ors) 245
Ballinger, Rebecca 310
Bandy, Absalom 61; Mary
389
Bangor, Nathl. 312

Bankley, Jno. 25
Banks, Allen 49; Dunston
296; Elie 266; Rchd.
334; Robt. T. 215; Thos.
31; Thos. A. 16; Thompson 250
Bankston, Henry 348: Jasper 181; Jno. 214,328;
Reuben 402
Bannister, Jas. 377
Bar's, Arthur(ors) 233
Barbarie, Edward 348
Barbary, Wm. 364,401
Barbee, Benj. 239
Barber, Eliphalet S. 380;
Elisha 20; Jno. 196;
M'Gilbrey 67; Reese 153;
Robt. 199; Saml. R. 189;
Solomon 71; Truman 133;
Wiley 238
Barbre, Peter 219
Barden, Arthur 181; Bronson 296
Bardich, Elam C. 170
Bardwell, Erastus 366
Barefield, Chapman 88;
David 116; Jas. M. 188;
Jno. 204,244,261; Luke
J. 139; Saml. 53; Solomon 36,40,400
Barefoot, Wm. 183
Barentine, Jacob 179;
Wash. 177
Barge, Abram 366; Hamilton
92; Jno. 43
Barges, Henry 413
Barham, Eliz. 345
Baring, Lovick 111
Barington, Wm. B. 307
Barker, Anderson 321; Danl.
D. 288; Edmund 197; Isaac S.S. 403; Jno. 220;
Jos. 197; Rchd. 326;
Saml. 289; Wm. 227,300,
319
Barkesdale, Mary 102; Wm.
291
Barkley, Jane 320
Barks, Robt. 10
Barksdale, Jos. C. 362;
Saml. 117
Barley, Celia 239; Jno. B.
55; Wm. 25
Barlow, David R. 24; Elias
72; Geo. 9; Henry 149;
Jno. 118; Wm. 211
Barmoill, David A. 25
Barnard, Edward 53
Barnell, Jno. J. 372
Barnham, Jas. 371
Barnhill, Clarissa 280
Barnley, Henry T. 114
Barnes, Abel 272; Asa 370;
Bedy 277; Colman 224;
Dempsey 349; F. & Clarissa 160; Geo. W. 44,
150; Jesse 248; Jethro
H. 125; Jno. 270,313,
403; Jno. A. 183; Jno.
J. 20; Jno. T. 11; Joshua 27,408; Lewis 161;
Lewis R. 140; Neal 84;
Noah 362; Rchd. G. 353;
Robt. C. 179; Solomon
29; Thos. J. 31
Barne's, Jos.(ors) 237;
Wm.(ors) 66
Barnett, Abel M. 101; Anabella 228; Caroline 248;
David 91,116; Elias 157:
Elisha C. 42; Green D.
249; Jas. 255; Jas. H.
256; Joel 218; Jno. 169,
185,250,332;

Barnett cont'd.
Jno. G. 108,164; Joroyal
384; Larkin 327; Margarett 38,251; Martha 81;
Nathan B. 195; Thos. 25;
Tillman 380; Wm. 239;
Zadoc 197
Barnett's, Benj. J.(ors)
71; Benj. Jno.(ors) 340
Barns, Gilliard 130
Barnton, Elbert 35
Barnwell, David A. 39;
Jno. 367; Michael 57,
121,206,230; Robt. 272;
Wm. 160
Barr, Eliz. 219,319; Geo.
399; Jno. 36,319; Michael O. 171; Roger D. 116;
Sidney 265
Barratte, B. 304
Barrentine, Saml. 367
Barrenton, Jno. 286
Barrer, Isaiah 400
Barrett, Anderson 407;
Frances 13; Geo. W. 386;
Ninian 98; Saml. 17,316;
Wm. F. 76,281
Barringer, Danl. 88
Barringtine, Wm. 269
Barrington, Willis 186
Barron, Andrew J. 316;
Barnabas 184; Benj. 81;
Bennett 308: Frances 18;
M.L. 148; Robt. 60;
Thos. 94
Barrow, Haywood 230; Henry
44; Robt. 51; Sterling
G. 411
Barry, G.L. 317
Barthetoit, Jas. A. 273
Bartlett, Burwell 130;
Cosom Emer 119; Danl.
336; Thos. 81
Barton, Benj. 297; Henry
53; Jas. 408; Joel 413;
Jno. 46,173; Jno. B.
328; Lewis 339; Larkin
157; Robt. P. 85; Robin
& Wm.(ors) 336; Willoby
378
Barton's, Jas.(ors) 400
Basley, Wm. 56
Bass, Eaton 344; Hartwill
70; Ingram 72; Jno. 147;
Josiah 244; Obedience
242,230; Wm. 157
Bass's, Edward(ors) 194
Basse, Jno. 290
Bassett, Jas. 119; Jno.
G. 31; Rchd. 229
Bastian's, Wm.(ors) 84,364
Batchelor, Jno. 204,340;
Nathan E. 377
Bachlor, Nathan E. 409
Bateman, Clara 210; Jesse
94; Joshua B. 121;
Tabitha 260,289
Bateman's, Jacob(ors) 34
Bates, Elisa E. 302; Francis 29,348; Jno. 164,
325; Jno. C. 118; Julius R. 148; Rhoda 321;
Wm. 106,340; Wm. C. 360
Batson, Zachariah 356
Batterell, Burwell 39
Battle, Jos. B. 20; Sarah
203
Batton, Isom 16
Batty, Sarrah 385
Baugh, Pleasant 90
Baughan, Payton 72
Baun, Martha 74
Baxley, Aaron 211; Edmund
104; Wilson 348

Baxley's, Job(ors) 209
Baxly, Wm. 293
Baxter, Eliz. 357; Eli H.
402; Hannah 288; Martha
206; Reuben 368
Baxter's, Jas.(ors) 235
Bayer, Ann 69; Wm. M. 253
Bayles, Hamilton 237;
Larkin 261; Sarah 147;
Wm. 403
Baynes, Alfred J. 115;
Jno. H. 102
Baysmore, Starkey 246
Bazemore, Jefferson 105;
Washn. 278
Beach, Asahel 254,316
Beadles, Jos. 294
Beal, Alpheus 259; Hillery
99; Josiah 170
Beall, Alpheus 111; Andrew H. 24; Bobert 377;
Elias 130; Hezekiah 338;
Josiah 336; Millon A.
268; Nathl. 317; Saml.
177; Susan Ann 55
Beals, Ann 33
Bealy, Albert G. 346;
Thos. 410
Beam, Jesse 195
Bean, Alexr. 84
Beard, Edmund C. 95; Hannah & Jas. 142; Isaac
299; Jas. 145; Jas. A.
63; Moses 15; Sarah 216;
Thos. 239; Wm. 154;
Wm. M. 145
Bearden, Humphrey 148;
Wiley 388
Beardin, Elijah 376;
Jacob 11
Bearfield, Alexr. 342
Beasley, Adam 292; Cyntha
414; David 350; Garret
M. 258: Jas. 118,146,
149,254,318; Jno. Jr.
144; Jno. A. 151; Thos.
Jr. 215; Wm. 17; Wm. P.
170
Beasly, Wright M. 274
Beates, Alfrod 272
Beaty, Albert G. 233;
Alfred 180
Beauford, Henry W. 15,113;
Jos. P. 104
Beaver, Baty 83; Wm. 365
Beavers, Chas. B. 255;
Jno. M. 41; Mary 289;
Sarah 402; Wm. 190;
Willis 47
Beaver's, Jos.(ors) 399;
Peter(ors) 181; Thos.
(ors) 21
Beck, Jacob 184,407; Sarah
59; Thos. J. 198; Thos.
S. 141; Wm. 151
Beckham, Archd. 208; Laban 371
Beddell, Pendleton T. 203
Beddingfield, Bryan 50;
Hiram 285; Jas. 157;
Jno. H. 54
Bedenbock, Joshua 47
Bedgood, Jas. M. 383
Bedsole, Amos 371
Beels, Emesley 247
Beeman, Susan 64
Been, Walter 314
Beesley, Enoch 171; Moses
171; Nathan 217; Renslear 297; Wm. 144
Beggarly, Archd. 378
Beggs, Jno. 56
Beland, Jno. M. 190
Belcher, Jno. 133

417

Belcher's, Wiley(ors) 85
Belflower, Saml. 146
Belgrew, Berry 254
Beliles, Martin 327
Belk, Jas. 397
Belknap, Moses 206; Wm.380
Bell, Allis 123; Anderson
   W. 264; Asbun B. 367;
   David 63,371; Eliz. 191;
   Green 103; Hester 218;
   Jas. 44,225,232,331,378;
   Jas. H. 246; Jas. M.
   359; Jesse 177,317; Jno.
   S. 64; Nancy 385; Reason
   A. 165; Roger 200,385;
   Saml. 114; Sylvanus Jr.
   201; Thos. 97,229,305,
   391; Wm. 283,301,343,
   386; Wm. B. 274; Wm. O.
   315; Wm. S. 408; Wm. T.
   108; Willie R. 47
Bell's, (children) 220;
   Benj.(ors) 398; Jas.(ors)
   9,10; Jno.(ors) 192,211;
   Jordan(ors) 370; Thos.
   (ors) 29
Bellamy, Jno. 393; Lucy 199
Bellew, Jas. H. 29
Bellote, Thos. 362
Beman, Saml. H. 10,25
Bemmington, Jas. 116
Benett, Rchd. 70
Benford, Jno. 402
Bennefield, Hardy 84; Need-
   ham Jr. 348; Wm. 168
Bennett, Ann 125; Caleb
   325; Demsy C. 261; Eliza
   31; Elizabeth 61; Henry
   335; Jno. 100,245,340;
   Lydia 190; Mary 117;
   Micager 294; Mitchell
   254; Mitchell & D.(ors)
   248; Neavil 283; Rchd.
   374; Saml. C. 341; Sarah
   86; Solomon 269; Thos.
   189; Wm. 370
Bennett's, Henry(ors) 412;
   Jas.(ors) 393; Reuben
   (ors) 287; Rchd.(ors)
   72; Thos.(ors) 109
Bennison, Abram D. 273
Benson, M(children) 51
Bentley, Elijah 55; Isaac
   13; Jas. J. 279; Jas. M.
   244; Jesse 179; Jno. 291;
   Nancy 195; Wm. 145
Benton, Aron J. 135; Jesse
   124; Jno. 31,379; Moses
   267
Benton's, Isaac (ors) 135
Berger, Mary C. 40
Berman, Ellis 248
Bernard, Sentus 90
Berrien, Thos. M. 232
Berrin, Jas. W.M. 245
Berry, Albert M. 316; An-
   drew J. 77; David Jr.
   129; Geo. 78; Jesse 393;
   Jno. H. 78; Little 225;
   Martin W. 14; Matthew
   354; Nicholas 234; Proc-
   tor 412; Robt. 408; Saml.
   61; Sarah 280; Wm. P.
   111
Berry's, Dabner (ors) 233;
   Hiram (ors) 206,218
Berryhill, Alexr. 89
Berthelot, Mary E. 152
Besinger, Gabriel 388
Bessent, Robt. 295
Bethel, Thos. F. 82
Bethune, Jas. N. 343; Jno
   G. 107

Betts, Elisha 55; Jno. W.
   78; Nancy 258
Bett's, Lloyd(ors) 119,
   213; Wm.(ors) 386
Beverly, Abner 185; Hester
   62; Jas. 242
Bevil, Jas. 162
Bevill, Zachariah 227
Bezbun, Jno. 399
Biaz, Rachael 303
Bibby, Nathl. 392
Bickers, Jno. 91
Biddell, Jno. 137
Biddy, Mashack 111
Bidell, Absalom 35
Biggard, David 263
Biggers, Nathan E. 318
Biggins, Robt. 335
Biggs, Freeman 94; Thos.
   264; Wm. J. 310
Bigg's, Thos.(ors) 399
Bigham, Jas. 55,319
Biles, Enoch 188
Billingsby, Howell 199;
   Mary 299
Billingsleas's, Jas.(ors)
   119,369
Billup's, Thos.A.(ors)126
Biltison's, Saml.(ors)413
Bingham, Green 112
Binion's, Jno.(ors) 386;
   Wm.(ors) 176
Binnion, Robt. B. 304
Bird, Adam 15; Andrew Jr.
   316; Buford 33; Danl.
   311; David 336; Doctor
   26; Elijah 293; Faith
   207; Jas. H. 204; Jas.
   W. Jr. 323; Job 407;
   Jno. 120,277,365; Lewis
   309; Nathan 339; Parker
   157; Sarah 322; Wm. 165;
   Wr. B. 371; Wm. M. 210;
   Wilson 209
Bird's, Stephen(ors) 228;
   Wm.(ors) 188,195,347;
   Wm. M.(ors) 155; William-
   son (ors) 276
Birdman, Francis 318
Birdsong, Betty 368; Robt.
   35
Birdwall, Solomon 408
Bishop, Abner 51; Asa 302;
   Asa J. 136; Brice H. 385;
   David 270; Graer 82;
   Jos. 323; Matthew 134;
   Reuben 235,321; Rhoda
   178; Simeon 83; Wiley
   11; Wm. 111; Wyley 39
Bishop's, Jas. S.(ors)169
Bissell, Leonard 201
Bithel's, Benj.(or) 325
Bivins, Saml. 213; Shad-
   rach 189
Bivin's, Jno. (ors) 321
Black, Augustus H. 356;
   Carlile 127; Chas. 47;
   Edward 232; Francis C.
   232; Francis O. 409;
   Govy 297; Jas. 236; Jon.
   W. 199; Mark 196; Nancy
   384; Robt. 153; Sampson
   332; Shimmy 341; Susan-
   nah 390; Thos. 107; Wm.
   95; Wm. A. 330
Black's, Lewis(ors) 125;
   Saml.(ors) 259
Blackburn, Allen 404; Jas.
   R. 248; Jno. 23; Martin
   247; Thos. 221
Blackman, Burrel 225; Jno.
   387; Wm. 123
Blackshear, Emily G. 255;
   Wm. T. 233

Blackstock, Ashley 64; Jas.
   411; Jas. Jr. 144; Rchd.
   57; Wm. 362; Wilson F.
   13,155
Blackstone, Jas. W.A. 327
Blackwell, Ambrose K. 43;
   David 148,232; Davidson
   346; Hensley 186; Je-
   royal 275; Joel 181;
   Rosedy 229; Saml. H. 149;
   Theophilus 70
Bladen, Eliz. 235
Blailock's, Gilbert(ors)57
Blair, Adam 289; Eliz. 308;
   Geo. W. 170; Jas. 9,145;
   Jemima 41; Jno. C. 349;
   Jno. D. 218,268; Thos.
   H. 237; Thos. R. 244;
   Wm. 193,384
Blake, Anny 271; Geo. W.
   347; Jno. T. 238; Moses
   65; Wm. 229
Blake's, (ors) 381
Blakely, Jno. 252
Blakey, Churchill 322
Blaleck, Jno. 310
Blalock, Darling P. 383;
   Eleanor 11; Jas. 281;
   Jno. H. 414; Jno. S. 85;
   Milton N. 263; Reuben
   173; Wm. 209,217
Blan, Jas. E. 235
Blanchard, Wm. 225
Blanchett, Henry 16
Blanchett's, Philip(ors)
   245
Bland, Jno. 68
Blangett's, Jere,(ors) 87
Blankenship, Eli 188
Blankinship, Wm. 193
Blanks, Jas. 365; Jno. 206
Blans, Alfred G.P. 249
Blanset, Jas. 241
Blanton, Jas. A. 346
Blasengane, Benj. W. 89
Blassingame, Jas. 94
Blauset, Wm. 347
Blaylock, David 249; Sarah
   312
Bleach, Jno. 35
Bledsoe, Geo. L. 343; Jno.
   162,170; Robt. 273; Thos.
   W. 148
Bledsoe's, Jesse(ors) 104
Blesard, Levi 333
Blissel's, Elisha(ors) 260
Blessit, Jas. B. 353
Blitch, Geo. 40; Thos. 255
Blocker, Ephraim C. 410
Blocker's, Jacob (ors) 154
Blodgett, Foster 186
Blois, Magdalane 334
Blois's, Peter (ors) 106
Blome, Mary E. 134
Blount, David E. 122; Jas.
   292; Jno. B. 51; Wm. 106
Blount's, Jas.(ors) 142;
   Jno. (ors) 87
Blow, Wm. 201
Bludworth, Henry 385; Jas.
   D. 362
Blue, Danl. 118
Blunt, Jno. T. 328
Bluster, Jas. R. 162
Blythe, Geo. 221,355
Boags, Sally 380
Boalt, Jas. 181
Boatright, Jas. 14,118;
   Reuben 103,325
Boatwright, Danl. 90,233;
   Drury 91; Eliz. 337
Bobb, Joel H. 307
Bobo, Benj. H. 399; Jno.
   S. 81; Lewis 194;

413

Chappell cont'd.
Jos. G. 404; Wilkes 177;
Wm. 402; Willie B. 96
Chappell's, (ors) 394
Charlyon's, Jno. K.M.(ors)
159,252
Charro, Andrew 177
Chastain, Abner 388; Allen
B. 125; Benj. 238; Benj.
F. 246; Benj. T. 344;
Elijah 237,369; Jno. 80,
210; Jos. 177
Chasten, S. & N Jane (ors)
55
Chatfield, Sebiah 178
Chatham, Geo. K. 163
Chatham's, Jas.(ors) 286;
Stephen(ors) 57
Chavers, Jno. 50; Wm. 40
Cheatham, Josiah 218
Cheek. Isaac V. 58; Isaiah
284; Wm. B. 200
Cheely's, (ors) 336
Cheeves, Jas. 204
Cheeves's, Jno.(ors) 92
Cherry, Abner 274; Frede-
ric 43; Spencer 319;
Willie 262
Chesher, Philip 98
Cheshire, Jno. 293; Sarah
28
Chesnut, David 172; Dick-
son 330; Gilson 314;
Isaac W. 179; Jas. 236;
Needham 103,155; Wm.
285,345
Chesser, Easter 219; Thos.
107   ,
Chestein, Sarah 282
Chester, Martin 64
Chewning's, Wm.(ors) 300
Chicoming, Mary 320
Childers, A.(Doctor) 140,
319
Childress, Jno. A.D. 338;
Thos. 26,47,316,327; Wm.
155
Childress's, Robt.(ors)291
Childs, Eliz. 249; Gabriel
173; Henry 106; Rapha
292; Wm. 364
Chiles, Lesis G. 133
Chiney, Wm. M. 65
Chipman, Thos. W. 406
Chisholm, Geo. W. 343;
Murdock 9,210
Chosholm's, Andrew (ors)
100
Chissem's, Jno.(ors) 344
Chitwood, Rchd. 72; Wm.
214
Chivers, Thos. H. 381
Choice, Jesse 153; Tully
120
Christian, Drewry 400;
Elijah L. 381; Elijah W.
100; Ira 96; Jesse G.
179; Jno. 33; Marshall
132; Morgan 335; Nancy
143; Wm. 132
Christian's, (ors) 387;
Drury(ors) 161
Christie, Hannah 32; Jos.
B. 128; Nathan G. 101;
Sarah 31
Christmas, Sarah 31
Christopher, Beverly 152;
David 252; Thos. 251
Cjumbler, Mason 395
Chunn, Amos Jr. 180
Church. Lemuel 128; Robt.
89
Churchwell, Jane 303; Jno.
174

Churchwell's, (ors) 23
Cinibron, Jno. H. 125
Clack. Geo. W. 35
Claghorn's, Alexr.(ors)
328
Claibone, Henry 409
Clark, Allen 289; Alexr.
119; Andrew 246; Arthur
261; Benj. B. 126; Danl.
20; Danl. M. 138; David
A. 159; Drury 140,143;
Elijah 102.337; Elijah
Jr. 310; Eli K. 383;
Eliz. 226,355; Henry 78;
Horace 213; Jacob 72;
Jas. 393; Jane 42; Jere.
221; Joab Jr. 64; Jno.
13,45,245,273,286,344,
395; Jno. G. 93; Jno. M.
328; Joshua 276; Julius
398; Leonard H. ?; Lit-
tleberry 102; Marshall
P. 100; Mary 313; Rchd.
314; Thos. 192,219;
Thos. J. 193; Wiley 28;
Wilie 374; Wm. 46,77,
135; Wilson B. 105
Clark's, Danl.(ors) 211;
Davids(ors) 233; John-
son(ors) 120; Luke T.
(ors) 85; Thos.(ors) 407
Clarke, Elisha 315; Geo.
W. 55; Gilbert 87; Hen-
ry E.W. 258; Presby. R.
179; Wm. 315,364
Clarke's, David(ors) 368
Clary, Danl. 214; Jas.
118,402; Wyton 75
Clary's, Jno.(ors) 16
Clasedge, Peter 272
Claxton, Jno. P. 181
Clay, Edmund 262; Green
103; Jas. 344; Jno. 16,
264; Saml. 413; Silas
N. 282; Wm. 274
Clayton, Balaam 31; Jas.
198,271; Jno. 84; Lem-
uel 111; Philip A. 249;
Thos. B. 335; Thos. R.
359; Wm. 235; Wm. W. 192
Cleaves, Turner A. 393
Cleckser, Elijah 270
Clefton, Jno. 112
Cleghorn, Avington 209
Cleitte, Thos. C. 300
Cleland, Wm. 371
Clements, Aasron 226;
Anderson 58; Benj. 408;
Chas. Jr. 118; David G.
71; Ezekiel 395; Gabriel
362; Gabriel M.C. 264;
Israel 55; Jacob A. 183;
Jesse 51; Jno. F. 321;
Lovick P. 162; Mary M.
14; Peyton R. 329; Sarah
43; Wiley S. 99; Wiley
L. 138; Wm. 42.194,288
Clement's, Archd.(ors) 16;
Peyton(ors) 360
Cleming's, Wm.(ors) 342
Clemman's, Mary M. 71
Clemmons, Wm. 305
Clenault, Frances 211
Clensey, Sarah 149
Cleonkloy, Jacob 17,411
Cleveland, Allen 117,213;
Benj. F. 53; Jacob M.
388; Oliver C. 192; Wm.
164,392; Wm. J. 354
Clewis, Geo. 153
Cleyton, Stephen 15
Cliborn, Temperance 31
Click. Jas. B. 367
Cliett, Jno. 369

Clifford, Jas. A. 170
Clifton, Alanson 75; Jas.
G. 140; Levin 399
Clifton's, Jno.(ors) 398
Clinch, Eliz. 151
Cline, Danl. 176; Jacob
240; Wm. 316
Clines, Wm. 176
Clinton, Rchd. D. 369;
Thos. 369
Cloud, Elijah 94; Elisha
102; Ezekiel 289; Jere.
402; Levi 303; Philip
374; Reuben 224
Clubb, Wm. 113
Coalson, Isaac 15; Thos.
86
Coates, Jno.D. 70; Lemuel
133,297; Wm. 110
Coats, Thos. 268; Wm. 400
Cobb, Amon 163; Benj. 45;
Eliz. 24; Ellison 147;
Enoch 80; Jas. 233; Jas.
H. 387; Jno. 79; Lemuel
398; Mary H. 88; Thos.
258; Wm. 238
Cobb's, Henry(ors) 272;
Jno. Jr. 178
Cobbett, Thos. 335
Cochran, Jas. 242.271,379;
Susannah 356; Wm. 244
Cochran's, Wm.(ors) 328
Cochrane, Benj. 262; Neal
F. 240
Cochron, Jacob 81
Cock's, Aaron(ors) 65
Cockerell, Jno. 175.373
Cockram, Jas. 81; Jno. 327
Cockran's, Lucinda 319
Cockran, Hezekiah 163
Cockrell, Saml. 299
Cocroft, Jas. 264; Rchd.
H. 19
Cody, Edmund 68; Ethelred
W. 116; Jas. 103
Cody's, Jas.(ors) 233;
Michael(ors) 144
Coe, Jos. 89,354
Coe's, Wm. H. (ors) 170
Cofer, Jno. 114; Matthew
53
Coffee, Joel 33,365
Coffee's, Jno.(or) 335
Coffey, Edmund 61; Jesse
99; Lewis 208,364
Cofiela, Willis 207
Cogburn, Benj. 386
Coggens, Jno. 287
Cogger, Matthew 326
Coggin, Rchd. 411
Cohen, Aaron 184; Jno. J.
77
Cohom, Eliz. 396; Jesse 393
Cohron, Jesse 214
Coile, Jas. 344
Coiles, Warren 15
Coker, Hardy 387; Isaac
311; Jonathan C. 384;
Sterling 305; Thos. 85,
367
Coker's, Caull(ors) 202
Colbert, Obadiah M. 329;
Peyton H. 141; Thos. 198
Colclough, Charity 205
Coldwell, Eleanor 61; Gar-
land 341; Grabella 70;
Jno. 314
Cole, Hambleton 286; Henry
345; Hosea 69; Jemima 141
Coleman, Abner 216; Chris
256; David 135,298; Eliz.
185; Jas. 329; Jas. L.
240,284; Jas. W. 165;
Jesse 59,310;

Coleman cont'd.
Jno. 20,66,274; Jos. 72;
Matthew W. 381,387; Milley 245,407; Philip 61;
Rebecca 86; Rchd. 372;
Rchd. B. 259; Sarah 87,
275,399; Washn. 267; Wm.
A. 246
Coley, Donaldson 90; Gabriel G. 49; Jas. 21; Jno.
67; Jno. B. & Mary F.
81; Jno. M. & Eliz. 327
Collatt's, Jno.(ors) 13,30
Colley, David 179; Jas.
309
Colley's, Thos.(ors) 216
Collier, Benj.F. 182;
Bryan W. 105; Chloe C.
149; Geo. W. 56; Hardaway 229; Henry 343;
Nancy L. 36; Nathl. H.
31
Collier's, Rchd.(ors) 178;
Wm.(ors) 319
Collins, Cornelius 170;
Danl. 58; David K. 249;
Edmund 14,25; Eli 109;*
Felix 177; Isaac 64; Jacob
218; Jas. 245; Jas. M.
111; Jason 129; Jno. 66,
124,148,260; Jno. D.
212; Jno. S. 342; Jos.
252; Jos. J. 235; Nathan
101; Rachel 377; Riley
169; Robt. 317; Seaborn
J. 212; Sikes 177; Stephen 235; Thos. J. 294;
Wm. 105,389; Wilson 163
Collin's, Benj.(ors) 236;
Wyat(ors) 250
Collom, Peggy 408
Collum, David 347; Solomon
152
Colman, Nancy 380; Rchd.
299
Colquette, Jno. S. 251
Colquitt, Jno. 202; Jos.
E. 294; Robt. 172
Colsom, Eliz. G. 118
Colson's, Matthew(ors) 356
Colston, Frances 175
Colton, Anna M. 152; Henry
204; Valentine 166
Colwell, Margaret 133;
Wm. 96
Combic, P. 119
Combs, Francis H. 48; Geo.
D. 62; Jas. 63; Margaret
129; Mary 137; Permelia
69; Philip F. 401; Wm.
193; Wm. P. 358
Comer, Hugh M. 120,314;
Jas. 21; Jno. F. 212;
Jno. J. 367; Mary B. 100
Commins, Sarah 26
Comoham, Thos. 350
Compton, Jas. I. 116
Conaway, Eliz. 310
Conder, Jno. 191
Condle, Rebecca 217
Cone, Benj. 356; Jno. H.
301; Jas. 225; Knotley
W. 130; Mary 171; S. 404;
Wm. 19,332
Cone's, Jno.(ors) 286
Conger, Jnoas 200
Conier, Rchd. 66
Conine, Geo. W. 355; Jno.
353; Rchd. Jr. 338; Wm.
19
Conn, Jno. 29,235; Wm. M.
138

Conn's, Thos.(ors) 253
Connally, Cornelius 314;
Jas. T. 387; Wm. L. 174,
226
Connaway's, (ors) 394
Connell, Jno. 54,114; Thos.
H. 68
Connell's, Newby(ors) 147
Connelley's, Nathl.(ors)
255
Conner, Benj. 251; Henry
180; Jas. G. 323; Jno.
22,96,156; Martin 75;
Millington 293; Rachel
L. 168; Thos. 181; Thos.
H. 53; Wm. 12; Wm. L.
257; Zephaniah T. 140
Connolly, Jane 312
Conts, Thos. G. 378
Conyers, Harriet D. 171;
Jehew 319; Jno. 351;
Wm. D. 225
Cook, Arthur S. 409; Benj.
329; Beverle C. 351;
Casewell 364; Clark J.
86; David 239; David R.
188; Deaborah 326; Geo.
75,276; Henry 327; Henry
S. 117; Jas. 114; Jas.
R. 238; Jas. W. 271;
Jane 60; Jno. 55,146,
159,196,200,354; Julias
317; Lydia 109; Mary 92;
Mary Ann 214; Nathan 93,
155; Obed 201; Owen 26;
Philip 394; Rebecca 67;
Robt. B. 46; Sarah 239;
Smith 159; Solomon 20;
Starling 15,206; Thos.
162,298; Thos. G. 246;
Tilman 182; Wm. 54,327;
Zadoc 366
Cook's, Jas.(ors) 16; Jos.
(ors) 306; Saml.(ors)
209
Cooke, Ann 74; Francis H.
275
Cooksey, Jno. 233; Wm. W.
152
Cooler, Eliza A. 408
Cooley, Ethenton 219;
Hollis 53
Coon, Henry 172
Cooper, Alexr. H. 104;
Bennett 79; David 271;
Geo. P. 218; Humphrey
187; Jas. 391,402; Jno.
256,274,305; Jno. M.
401; Jno. M'Kinne 38;
Jos. M. 356; Lewis J.
313; Lydia 238; Milton
53,110; Peter 122; Ranson 351; Robt. 396;
Salome 76; Vinson 413;
Wm. 189,340,356; Wm. H.
311
Cooper's, Jno. M.(ors) 93;
Wm.(ors) 133
Coothen, Hiram 278
Cope, Jno. 302; Jno. L. 26
Cope's, Christain(ors) 40
Copeland, Jno. 139; Jno.
D. 104; Jno. M. 23;
Martha 75; Obediah 27,
349; Stephen 31; Wm. 329
Coplin, Archd. H. 137
Copp, Danl. D. 121,137
Coppage, Chas. 99
Coppedge, Clark R. 272;
Eliza Jos. 151
Coram, Wm. M. 295
Cordey, Johnathan P. 234

Coriell, Abram S. 40
Corken, Drury 256
Corley, Davidpert 119;
Elijah 137; Hillory H.
401; Isham 241; Mountraville 267
Corly, Davidport 329
Cornally's, Nath.(ors) 312
Cornell, Tunison 77
Cornwall, Martin 68
Cornwell, Danl. E. 90
Cosby, Chas. R. 45; Jas.
E. 62
Coseys, Alfred 227
Cosnard, Henry 371
Costly, Pierce 260
Coston, Thos. 402
Cotes, Pleasant 62
Cothron, Ezekiel 183
Cotney, Jas. 28
Cotton, Wm. W. Jr. 209
Cotton, Cyrus W. 407; Geo.
32; Stephen G. 115
Cotton's, Jos. J.(ors) 102
Couch, Elijah W. 82; Nathan
353; Saml. 96; Watson
358
Couger, Benj. 92,398
Coulter, Wm. 405; Wm. M.
393
Countryman, Elias M. 330;
Rhoda 344
Couper, Jas. H. 46
Coursey, Jno. A. 130
Courvoice, Jas. A. 413
Coutteau, Margaret A. 85
Coventon, Jas. 356
Covert, Isaac 218
Covey, Joshua 380
Covington, Anderson 170;
Jere. B. 393; Marshall
34,265
Cowan, Franklin 298; Geo.
355; Jas. K. 150; Jno.
Wood 114; Wm. A. 233
Coward, Jas. 202; Polly
273
Cowart, Azariah 173; Cullen
407; Hardy 213; Michael
388; Seaborn 26; Zachariah 238,320
Cowart's, (ors) 171; J.
(ors) 251
Cowen, Robt. 79; Wm. R. 98
Cowfield, Green 66; Thos.
358
Cowper, Jno. 178
Cowsert, Ann 108
Cox, Amos. 212; Ashley 140;
Ashton B. 392; Chas. 95,
278; Darius 323; Drury
M. 355; Eldridge Harris
21; Eli 58; Frederic 205;
Jas. 144; Jas. P. 261;
Jno. 148,287,323; Jno.
T. 45,356; Jno. W. 184;
Mordecai 314; Nancy M.
125; Randal 242; Robt.
318.337,354; Seaborn 223;
Wm. 283,378
Cox's, Rchd. & Frank (ors)
191
Coxe, Lucinda 294; Saml.
181; Thos. W. 256; Wm.
J. 234
Coxe's, Abram(ors) 60;
Moses(ors) 350; Stephen
(ors) 310; Wm.(ors) 122
Coxwell, Benj. 37,145
Cozart, Green P. 64
Craal, Jos. R. 146

*Elisha Collins of Twiggs County was granted land lot #15 of the 20th District, 3rd
section of Cherokee containing 40 acres(Gold) on 10-14-1836;see mms.file on Collins,
Elisha.

Craddock, Mary 209; Wm. 178,238
Crafford, Wm. S. 203,224
Craft, Edward D. 411; Geo. W. 358; Susannah 397
Craft's, Jno.(ors) 53
Crafton, Bennett 112; Wm. 38
Craig, Alexr. 20,275; Elbert E. 144; Wm. 306; Wm. M. 60,412
Craige, Allen 27
Crain, Josiah 95
Crambey, Stephen K. 16
Crane, David 91; Ezra L. 382; Spencer C. 354; Wm. 87; Wm. H. 160
Crandall, Smith 23
Cratin, Sylvester B.J. 285
Craven, Isaac N. 75; Thos. W. 297
Craver, Andrew 378
Craw, Wm. Jackson 270
Crawford, Alexr. 240; Alexr. P. 50; Benj. B. 167; Burton E. 315; Chas. 20,76; Geo. 282; Geo. W. 113; Henry 382; Jesse 283; Jno. 247; Leroy K. 27; Levi M. 239; Lucy 25; Margaret 85; Mary 140; Mary Ann 413; Mashack V. 68; Nathl. M. 250; Noel 45; Oliver 26; Philips 66; Silas 71; Thos. J. 210; Thos. G. 342; Watson A. 292; Wm. 169; Wm. C. 158
Crawford's, Elijah(ors)220
Crawley, Mary 20; Wm. 251
Crawley's, Spencer(ors)70
Cray, Wm. 101
Crayton, Wm. L. 137
Creamer, Ann M. 329; Robt. 163,264
Creddille, Ellington 197; Wm. 210
Creel, Geo. 97
Creemmy, Rebecca 136
Crenshaw, Jos. 109
Crenshaw's, Jarrel(ors) 368
Crew, Margaret 26; Wm. F. 299,406
Crews, Elias 49; Hannah 391; Jas. 88; Jno. 59; Jos. M. 343; Micajah 313; Petsey 217; Wm. 337, 347
Crider, Solomon 164
Crim, Aaron 269; Jno. 369
Crimm, David 230
Crisler, Benj. 14
Critenton, Elijah 294; Pryor 276
Crittentun, Elijah 210
Crittenden, Jno. 205
Crockett, David A. 94; David M. 12; Jos. 388; Wm. H. 216
Croft, Ralph 131; Saml. 86
Crofton, Saml. 237
Crombie, Wm. A. 139,379
Crompton's, Jehu(ors) 293
Cronan, Jas. S. 150
Cronick, Hayle 167; Rachel 181
Crooks, Hugh 27
Crosby, Garner 299; Thos. 372; Urill 338
Cross, Aenon 289; Garris 404; Garvis 343; Jno. 212; Sardis E. 402; Silas 54,69; Wm. 301

Crossley, Edward 66
Crosby, Jacob 212
Crossley, Jno. 148
Crotwell, Adam 271; Geo. 127,235; Jacob 41
Crouch. Jno. Jr. 339; Thos. 268
Crow, Colmon W. 69; Denson 144; Eliza 388; Jacob 406; Jas. 28; Jas. M. 27; Jno. 354; Jno. W. 206; Marlin T. 86; Martin 36; Norman M. 15; Peter Y. 38; Randolph 220; Wm. 217
Crow's, Jonathan(ors) 215; Saml.(ors) 24; Mary (widow) 131
Crowder, Geo. 95; Jas. 367; Wm. B. 352
Crowell, Henry 286
Crowley, Jas. 231
Crumbey, Anthony 224
Crumby, Jno. 43,311; Thos. 245
Crummey, Jesse 162
Crump, Jno. C. 385; Memory 333
Crumpler, Jno. B. 258
Crumpton, Jos. 106; Wm. A. 348
Crumpton's, David(ors)168
Crutchfield, Jno. 322; Robt. 110,274; Ulysses 28
Cryer, Mary 191
Cubbedge, Jno. 335
Culberson, David H. 164; Jas. H. 148; Polly 208
Culbertson, Celia 79
Culbreath, Beverly L. 340; Jno. 229
Culler's, Jno. & Nancy (ors) 246
Cullins, Rchd. 71
Culpepper, Benj. 369; Chas. T. 287,370; David W. 35; Francis 142; Geo. W. 28,197; Jas. 207; Jno. 157,279,299; Jos. R. 359; Rachel 231; Selah 30
Culpepper's, Henry (ors) 25; Robt.(ors) 355; Wm. (ors) 277
Culver, Augustus 380; Hannah 120; Nancy 174, 279; Tabman A. 132
Culverhouse, Chas. 159
Culwell's, Wm.(or) 276
Cumbaa, Gordon M. 199
Cumbert, Jas. 111
Cumbo, Reuben 93,339
Cummens's, Gideon(ors)269
Cummings, I. 384
Cummins, Margaret 267; Wm. 112
Cummin's, Gideon(ors) 76
Cunningham, Eliz. 296; Jno. 79,303; Jos. H. 230; Nancy 144; Patrick 259; Robt. 292; Wm. R. 285
Cupps, Jno. 163
Curbon, Jno. 246
Curbow, Henry 101,318
Curd, Edward 170
Curdy, Jno. S.M. 311
Cureton, Dixon 242; Henry 322; Vixon 386
Cureton's, Thos.(ors) 28
Curl, Kinchen 236
Curley, Benj. 352
Curlie, Mary 285

Currey, Lolsey 121
Currie, Malcomb 385
Curry, Alexr. 249; Jacob 125; Jas. 82,348; Peter M. 158; Saml. T. 143; Sarah 178; Wylie 135; Willis 239
Curry's, Hugh(ors) 406
Curtis, Martha A.J. 337; Robt. 266; Thos. J. 112; Wm. B. 290
Cushman, Rachael 217
Cuslion, Elisha 293
Cutlaw's, Bentley(ors) 194
Cutts, Maford 320

Dabney, Anderson B. 120; Garland 318; Wm. O. 239
Dabney's, Anderson(ors)336
Daggett, Thos. J. 133
Dailey, Jno. Jr. 91; Thos. P. 375
Daily, Vines 32
Dake, Henry Jr. 273
Dalrymaple, Edmund 399
Dame, Mary 191
Dames's, Chas.(ors) 37
Dance, Matthew 385
Dancy, Archd. 383
Dancy's, Francis(ors) 230
Danely, Jas. 66; Margaret 220
Daniel, Allen C. 148; Amariah 363; Amos 183; Beverly 233; David 360; Edward 52; Echols 277; Eli 96,404; Ezechael 27; Frederic 138; Hopkins 280; Isaac 158; Isham 269,342; Jas. J. 275; Jas. M. 22; Jas. S. 17; Jas. W. 373; Jesse 46; Jno. 184,232,331; Jno. K. 219; Jno. M. 344; Josiah 408; Kenneth 90.189; Lewis 282; Littleberry 345,376; Martha 279; Martin B. 125; Mary 162, 190; Moses 15,187,291; Nancy 301; Robt. 302; Sarah 306,348; Stephen 16; Thos. T. 375; Wm. 40, 174,176,186,189,366; Zachariah 286
Daniel's, Aaron(ors) 261; Jno.(ors) 17; Jno. A. (ors) 306; Stephen (ors) 304
Danielly, Betsy 354
Danman, Mary Ann 187
Dannally, Sarah 236
Danner, Geo. 85
Danull, Geo. W. 138
Darbey, Canpey 251; Jas. 183
Darby, Jere. 382,395; Julius G. 384
Darden, Abner 134; Dennis 388; Elisha 353; Reuben R. 233
Darnald, Henry 100,307
Darnall, Robt. M. 363; Saml. 128
Darnell, Dickson W. 153; Henry 26
Darracatt, Jas. B. 174
Darrence, Francis 41
Darris, Eliz. 122
Darsey, Francis 161; Rezin 136
Dasher, Christian H. 309; Edwin 338
Daucey, Katherine 351

Dindy, Youngsett 149,176
Dingler, Saml. 18; Thos.
P. 39; Wm. N. 213
Dinman, Felix G. 294
Dinmons, Allen 161
Discomb, Marg.Caroline 129
Disheroon, Jno. E. 391
Dismuke's, Edmund(ors) 93
Dismukes, Bethene 308;
Jas. 97; Jno. 78,356
Dison, Isham 355; Wm. 57
Dison's, Dempsey(ors) 322
Dix, Gabriel 232
Dixon, Barnes T. 135; Eli-
as J. 273; Hickman 369;
Hickman Jr. 309; Isaac
162: Jas. 394; Jno. 64,
247,294; Micajah 273;
Roland 261; Rolin H.
203; Thos. 373; Wm. 181;
Wm. S. 191
Doane, Isaiah 110
Dobbins, Miles G. 87;
Moses B. 74
Dobbs, Cyrus 20; Fortuna-
tus 179; Jas. G. 23;
Martin 298; Morton 182;
Nathan 391; Sarah 198;
Solomon 331; Wiley 202
Dobson, Henry 74,227,276
Doby, Derrel 205; Jno.
216; Wm. 390
Dodd, Aaron 205,233; Eli-
jah 185; Geo. J. 404;
Lemuel 105
Dodds, Geo. 16; Wm. 279
Dodge, Chas. S. 363,375
Dodgen, Larkin 192
Dodson, Chas. 298,342;
Isaiah 245; Labon M.
354; Stephen 364
Doggeel, Shadrack 270
Doggett, Geo. 115; Nancy
G. 173; Thos. 340
Dokens, Alfred 125
Doles, Eliz. 187; Jesse
180
Dollar, Wm. 312
Dolton, Claiborn 251; Geo.
248; Jno. 298
Doming, Andrew 175
Donaldson, Baylis 107; Eli
109; Geo. 97; Hugh 153,
380; Jas. 223; Robt. G.
F. 220; Wm. 28,131,161
Donalson, Reuben 279
Doney, Frederic F. 256
Donham, Amster 254
Donnan, Jas. R. 43
Donnaway, Jno. M. 96
Dooley, Wm. 62
Doolittle, Alfred 358;
M. C. & N. 333
Dooly, Jas. J. 394; Wm. M.
300
Dopson, Averilla 67
Dorch's, Henry(ors) 208
Dorety, Jno. 56
Dorherty, Eliz. 318
Dorman's, Callan(ors) 316
Dormany, Jno. 16
Dorough, Jas. 358; Nathan
S. 193
Dorrough, Jno. L. 314
Dorsett, Jas. 178; Sus-
annah 178
Dorsey, Andrew 133; Edmund
287; Henry W. 361; Jno.
177; Lemuel 82
Dorton, Benj. 57,145,315;
Jno. 410
Doss, Geo. 346
Doster, Jas. 237
Dotton, Jesse 280

Doughterty, Archd. 94;
Jas. 170; Jno. 154;
Michael 283; Wm. 251
Doughtee, Wm. Jr. 233
Douglas, Elisha 363; Jones
85; Mary Ann 119; Robt.
M. 382
Douglass, Asa 199; Elisha
155; Geo. 247; Geo. L.
243; Jones T. 154; Jos.
202; M.A. 300; Robt. 23,
304; Thos. 264; Tilmon
252
Douglass's, Saml.(ors)
191; Willis(ors) 156
Dougles, Sarah 337
Dourville, Rebecca 192
Dousset, Virginia M.F. 30
Douthet, Thos. J. 279
Douthill, Jas. 376
Dove, Jacob A. 149
Dowd, Jno. 263
Dowdell, Jas. 173
Dowdey, Rchd. 236
Dowdy, Chas. 158; Charley
381; Jno. W. 292; Mary
155; Wm. 60,373; Willis
W.M. 18
Dowell, Nancey 360; Peter
303; Thos. 144
Dowers, Wm. 382
Downey, Caleb 14; Jas. W.
210
Downman, Beverly O. 228,
277
Downs, Crawford 212; Eliz.
401: Isaac 92; Jas. 383;
Seaborn 54,396; Shelbey
222; Thos. 190; Wm. 21;
Wm. J. 80
Doyal, Jno. L. 311
Doyall, Eliz. S. 181
Dozier, Abner C. 66; Leo-
nard W. 379; Rchd. 150;
Richmond 238
Dozier's, Jas. P.(ors) 62
Drake, Cargel 148; Cordy
332; Jas. V. 396; Joshua
119; Pleasant 85; Rebec-
ca 271; Turner 103;
Vines 186; Wm. A. 298
Drake's, Elias(ors) 161
Drane, Benj. 287,316
Draper, Jno. 71
Draughon, Rchd. 304
Dreggors, Jacob 106
Dregors, Henry 253
Drennan, Jos. W. 296
Drew, Jno. Jr. 350; Wm.
146
Drigger, Jno. 376
Driggers, Jas. 99,102
Driggors, Ephraim 73;
Matthew 61
Drinchard, Edward 141
Drinkard, Lucy 102
Driskill, Wm. 17,105
Driskill's, Jno.(ors) 226
Driver, Jordan 273
Drummond, Danl. 257; Wm.
197; Wm. H. 296
Drury, Chas. N. 372
Dryden, Joel 240; Jno.
260,359
Dubois, Walter 9
Dubose, Sarah 86,159; Wm.
E. 35
Dubs, Jno. W. 267
Ducker, Nimrod E. 35,310
Duckworth, Almond 31
Dudley, Eden 161; Joab
133; Jno. B. 153; Wiley
163; Wm. B. 119

Dudley's, Geo.(ors) 151,
380
Due, Wm. J. 201
Duff, Jane 320
Duffil, Lucy 178
Dufour, Jno. J. 137
Dugas, Lewis A. 322
Dugger, Jas. P. 302; Jno.
175; Wm. 355
Duke, Bedford 354; Chas.
251; Edwin 395, Frances
389; Ferdinand 18: Fre-
deric 120; Henry M. 74;
Jas. 298; Jas. H. 26;
Jno. 306; Jno. T. 393;
Josiah H. 340; Martha
372; Nancy 18,57; Reu-
ben 73; Thos. M. 379;
Wm. 229,284,317
Duke's, Jno.(ors) 341; T.
(ors) 201,342
Dukes, Green H. 323;
Matthew C. 239; Robt. W.
47
Dule, Jno. 242
Dumas, Jas. H. 232; Uriah
85
Dunagan, Benj. 294
Dunaway, Benj. 304; Mary
353; Wm. H. 404
Dunbar, Thos. S. 355;
Wash. P. 327
Duncan, Abram. 201; Danl.
264; Dennis 17; Elijah
284; Geo. 137,331; Jas.
91,93,250; Jesse 9; Jno.
194; Jno. A. 383; Jno.
J. 192: Matthew 174,350;
Perason Jr. 270; Simeon
L. 245; Thos. B. 19;
Walker 117; Winright 367
Duncan's, Edmund(ors) 118
Dunham, Geo. C. 28; Geo.
W. 162; Wm. 336
Dunkin, Elias 76; Jno. 80
Dunlap, Saml. C. 280
Dunlop, Enoch 206
Dunman, Thos. 93
Dunn, Ann H. 182; Danl.
396; Drury 157,175; Ja-
cob G. 380; Jno. 22,285,
400; Jno. M. 12; Jno. T.
214; Levicy 159; Michael
270; Saml. 148; Sarah
211; Stephen 201; Thos.
A. 303; Waters 62,89;
Wm. 313,389
Dunnagan, Isaiah 317
Dunnaway, Wm. 344
Dunner, Abram 259
Dunsett, Lewis C. 374
Dunston, Geo. W. 203
Dupon, Paul 243
Dupree, Chas. L. 9; Eliz.
134; Jas. 304; Jessea
283; Thos. R. 389; Thos.
W. Jr. 303
Dupree's, Jno.(ors) 122
Durance, Jas. 177
Durden, Benj. 182; Dennis
342; Francis 220; Riley
19
Duren, Geo. 38,352: Thos.
9,293
Durham, David 209; Isaac
63,236; Jas. H. 128:
Jere. 95; Jno. 137; Jno.
P. 101; Patsey 147; Saml.
D. 162: Shelman 313;
Thos. 258; Wm. 9,384;
Wm. J. 287
Durham's, Henry(ors) 344
Durkee, Louisa 84
Durr, Jno. C. 19

428

Garrison cont'd.
Salsbury 265; Sarah M.
30
Garrison's, David(ors) 392
Garrott, Wm. 258
Gartman, Danl. 211
Gartrell, Jos. 144
Garven, Jno. 125
Garvin, Micajah 160
Gaskins, Wm. 378
Gassett, Wm. 197,228
Gastin, Jno. W. 249
Gaston, Jas. 285; Matthew
217; Saml. B. 371
Gatchett's, Benj.(ors) 131
Gates, Bennett H. 302;
Chas. 95,253
Gatewood, Sarah 350
Gatright, Zubulon 339
Gatright's, Joel(ors) 384
Gathwright, Miles F. 331
Gattin's, Zachariah(ors)
319
Gaughf, Jas. M. 367
Gaulding, Nancy 268; Wm.
73
Gault, Jos. 189
Gauting, Jno. 225
Gay, Gilbert 55; Jno. 141,
191; Joshua 98; Josiah
Jr. 321; Mary 375; Robt.
122
Gee's, Chas.(ors) 334
Geider, Allen 358
Geiger, Cornelius 107;
Jno. J. 314
Gentry, Archd. W. 117;
Cornelius 257; Eliz. 124;
Jere. 88; Jno. 133,243;
Matthew 312,373; Ransom
125; Seaborn 363; Wm. 84
George, Caleb 141; Jas.
93,384; Jesse 323,352;
Mark 158
George's, Jos. W.(ors) 128
Germa, Jno. A. 345
Germany, Jas. 289; Wm. 376;
Wm. C. 274
Germos, Jno. W. 326
Gernett, Nancy D. 194
Gernigan, Jno. E. 327
Geyer, Geo. F. 37
Gheesling, Benj. Jr. 64
Gholston, Benj. 262; Wm.
139
Gibbins, Jno. 284
Gibbons, Rodey 244; Step-
hen 119,282,311
Gibbs, Coleman C. 397;
Cornelius 285,322; Cor-
nelius, Jr. 35; Sampson
23,396
Gibb's, Miles(ors) 134
Gibson, Abner F. 387; An-
drew 378; Austin 81;
Chinchell 12; Dexter N.
54; Geo. W. 222; Isaac
256; Jas. F. 96,327;
Job B. 269; Jonathan
213; Josiah 388; Lewis
39; Luke 260; Polly 296;
Sampson 18; Sylvanus 269;
Wm. 80,349,403; Wm. T.
202
Gibson's, Thornton(ors)
132; Wm.(ors) 154,407
Gidden, Duncan 313
Giddens, Jno. 126; Thos.
367
Gideon, Jno. 228
Gideons, Eliz. 113,142
Gidions, Jesse 114
Gieu, Philip C. 46

Gilbert, Dryry 215; Eze-
kiel 399; Jas. 39,228;
Jas. R. 43; Jeptha 389;
Jno. 14,123,172,272,392;
Jourden 216; Matthew
327; Nancy 169; Robt. M.
137; Robt. R. 63; Thos.
100; Thos. J. 326; Thos.
W. 92,313; Wm. 241
Gilbert's, Jno. B.(ors)
405
Gilder, Irby 407; Jacob
175; Joanna 178; Wiley
178
Giles, Celia 69,361; Jno.
240; Redford B. 340;
Wm. 228
Gilham, Wm. C. 164
Gilkeyson, Robt. E. 130
Gill, Edward W. 173; Jno.
199; Lucy 143; Peter
108; Sarah 178,354;
Thos. 261
Gillam, Robt. 73,128
Gillespie, Christ. 283;
Jas. 157; Jno. 345;
Milton W. 393; Pickens
H. 132
Gillespy, David 313
Gilliam, Andrew 401; Wm.
321
Gilliland, Jno. 272,301;
Wm. 288; Wm. Jr. 227
Gillion, Isaac Jr. 372;
Malachi 361
Gillis, Jno. 172: Kenneth
87: Norman 299; Wm. 65
Gillis's, Murdock(ors) 146
Gillispie's, Saml.(ors)
146
Gills, Bayles 325
Gillstrap, Wm. J. 134
Gilmer, Jas. 407; Robt.
G. 394
Gilmer's, (ors) 81
Gilmore, Eliz. 193; Fran-
cis 156; Jas. 241; Jas.
241; Jas. H. 142; Wiley
361; Wm. M. 398
Gilmore's, S.H.(ors) 45
Gilpin, Wm. 44
Gilstrap, Benj. E. 364
Gilstrop, Eliz, 270
Gimble, Jno. 389
Gimdains, Abram. 301
Gindrat, Jos. H.C. 110
Ginn, Arthur 275; Joshua
203; Sarah 382; Wm. 185
Gipson, Harrison 331;
Littleton 114; Stafford
98
Gisert, Jno. A. 167
Glanton, Abner 52
Glascock, Thos. O. 282
Glasgow, Robt. 104; Wm.
371
Glass, Henry J. 265;
Littleton D. 322; Rchd.
224
Glass's, (ors) 306,330
Glasson, Jas. 148; Wm. 47
Glatigny, Jno. F. 218
Glaver, Jas. P. 255
Glawn's, Edmund(ors) 13
Glaze, Eli 251; Jacob 301;
Jno. 97; Thos. G. 65;
Wm. S. 222
Glaze's, David(ors) 138
Glazier, Chas. R. 51,223;
Sarah 327
Glenn, Ann 290; Eliz. 285,
294; Jas. 134; Jehu J.
199; Jno. 43; Nicey
288: Saml. 410;

Glenn cont'd.
Simeon 52; Thos. 150,
295; Wm. B. 17
Glisson, Jos. 361
Glore, Geo. W. 131
Glover, Allen 175; Drewry
169; Geo. 130; Henry 88;
Jaret 177; Jno. 63; Jno.
J. 27,180; Jos. 173;
Starling 160; Wilie 208
Glozier, Wm. 133,146
Glynn, Lucy 383
Gnann, Timothy T. 49
Goare, Greene 365
Gober, Craddock 86; Wm.
216; Wm. J. 238
Goble, Cornelius 125; Jno.
221; Wm. 144
Godard, Joel 137
Godbay's, (ors) 312
Godbey, Jas. 212
Godbey's, (ors) 314
Godby, Drucilla 377; Henry
294; Stephen 247
Goddard, Catharine R. 373
Goddard's, Bailey(ors) 112
Godden, Frances 122
Goddin's, Barnaby(ors) 248
Godfrey, Ansel 179; Jno.
115; Thos. P. 349; Tur-
ner B. 205; Wm. 42,75
Godfrey's, Thos.(ors) 272
Godley, Jno. M. 172
Godman, Elias 131
Godwin, David 148; Jesse
398; Stephen 12
Godwin's, Jas.(ors) 147
Goen, Hugh 90
Goff, Wm. 46
Goggins, Isaac 189; Jno. F.
318; Johnston 365
Goin, Wash. 412
Going, Jno. 307
Golden, Elender 315;
Frances B. 73; Martin 299
Goldin, Pleasant 362: Tim
C. 148
Golding, Isaiah 401;
Susan 237
Goldsmith, Jno. 333; Jno.
T. 51; Matthew 254
Golightly, Jas. 306; S.
311
Gonder, Jas. E. 290
Good, Priscilla 253
Goodbread, Saml. 206
Gooddown, Jacob V. 220
Goode, Jas. Terrell 61;
Noah 246; Rchd. 400;
Wm. 347
Goodgame, Geo. 101
Goodman, Danl. 23; Jas.
212; Jno. 37; Wm. 274
Goodrich, Luther 281
Goodson, Edwin 409; Jacob
365; Jno. 42; Jordan
135; Thos. B. 351
Goodson's, (ors) 387
Goodwin, Jesse 304; Joel
T. 116; Lewis 83,216;
Sanford 233; Wm. 76,285
Goolsbee, Aaron 346
Goolsby, Anson 132: Elijah
207; Jane 394; Kirby 29;
Mary 44,141; Zachariah
76
Goowin, Rchd. 282
Gorday, Elijah 69
Gorden, Abram. 45
Gordman, Aaron 139; Danl.
62
Gordon, Cornelius 89;
Elijah 302; Jas. 99;
Jno. 199; Jno. D. 395;

433

434

Hinton, Geo. W. 378; Jas.
164; Mansfield 369; Noah
316; Pester 275; Rachael
386; Truin 347; Wm. 17,
249,259,379
Hisler, Henry 346
Hitchcock, Andrew J. 51;
Jno. 20,31,60
Hitt, Chas. B. 190
Hix, Susannah 128
Hobbs, Berry 236; Bowling
292; Margary 296; Thos.
38; Wm. 406; Wm. H. 137
Hobby, Francis J. 194;
Jesse 159
Hockell, Oliver T. 332
Hodge, Allen L. 78; Duke
H. 292; Elisha 50; Har-
riet 268; Jacob 376;
Jas. 286,319
Hodgekirk's, Jno.(ors) 168
Hodgen, Jas. N. 72
Hodges, Alexr. 295; Augus-
tus G.W. 146; Benajah
327; Benj. B. 55; Billy
W. 55; Ellert 298; Henry
16,112; Jas. 168; Jesse
139; Jno. 384; Jno. Ir-
vin 98; Jos. 155,161;
Joshua F. 184; Josiah
382; Judge R. 205; Phile-
mon 175; Robt. 235; Saml.
226; Sarah 141; Wiley T.
237,320; Wm. 18,36,343;
Willis 295
Hodges's, Alfred(ors) 332;
Jas.(ors) 178
Hodnett, Jas. 168; Lovick
P. 389; Thos. 261
Hog, Jno. 402
Hogan, Alexr. 19,223; Eli-
jah 149; Jno. H. 57;
Shadrach Jr. 117; Thos.
238; Thomase 11 214;
Winfred E. 322
Hogg, Jas. V. 145,262
Hoggie, Matthias 57
Hogins, Sarah 281
Hogue, Clement A. 69; J.E.
363; Louis 48
Holbrook, Hannah 197,348;
Green B. 62
Holcomb, Anson 216; Chas.
L. 236; Jabez J. 410;
Jas. B. 390; Moses 84;
Sherwood 342; Theophilus
43
Holcombe, Deskin 55; Fran-
ces 17; Henry 30; Joel
193; Jno. 193
Holdege, Jno. H. 296
Holden, Jas. 183,339; Jos.
10; Rchd. 377
Holder, Abram. 41; David
242; Jas. 361; Jane 92;
Jno. 77,407; Jno. H.
310; Thos. 148; Wm. 171
Holderness, Jas. 387
Holeman, David 106
Holiday, Robt. 320
Holifield, Geo. W. 320
Holiman, Mary 114
Holladay, A.E. 81; Fuquay
401; Jno. M. 35; Wm. 181
Holladay's, Jno.(ors) 38
Holland, Benj. 399; David
257; Elisha 155; Eliz.
21,390; Hannah 337; Henry
50; Isaac 240; Jas. 323,
390; Jno. 279,398; Jno.
H. 278; Jos. 252; Jos.
L. 381; Lindsey 262,327;
Margaret 160; Margaret
S. 15; Matthew 341;

Holland cont'd.
Moses 377; Nancy 138;
Peter 383; Randolph 99;
Robt. R. 333; Robias 49
Holland's, (ors) 212;
Sidney S.(ors) 285
Hollaway, David 382; Geo.
217
Hollaway's, Wm.(ors) 231
Holley, Allen G. 13,246;
David 105; Jno. 387;
Wm. 112,226
Holiday, Andrew 256; Den-
nis L. 367; Firney 177;
Nathan 269; Rchd. J.
121
Holliday's, Jos.(ors) 294
Hollier, Cuthbert S. 93
Hollifield, Green 79
Holliman, Saml. 161; Wm.
346
Hollimon's, Jas.(ors) 234
Hollingsworth, Jno. 184,
368; T. 128
Hollingsworth's, A.(ors)
253
Hollis, Jas. 298; Jno. 13;
Silas 97; Wm. 272; Wil-
lis 264
Holliway, Wm. 161
Holloman, David 131,254;
Levicey 306; Saml. M.
228; Wm. 242
Holloway, David 230
Holloway's, Asa(ors) 169
Holly, Ely 242; Greenlee
177; Jno. 126; Wm. 168
Holly's, Presley(ors) 187,
228
Holmes, Arthur G. 16; As-
hel C. 362; Gideon V.
330; Hardiman 400; Henry
94,406; Isaac 323; Jas.
162,322,373; Jas. S.
264; Jno. 348; Jno. J.
263; Julius 56; Margaret
120; Rchd. 276; Solomon
219; Thos. 234
Holmes's, Robt.(ors) 130
Holms, Jno. 307
Holsenbale, W.D. 382
Holsey, Gideon 42; Jas.
M. 380
Holston, Asa 181; Hiram
397
Holt, Ausbern 359; Elisha
151; Hines 321; Jas. B.
15; Jesse 13; Jno. 244;
Jno. S. 231; Lawrence
37; Patrick 412; Peyton
274; Robt. A. 67,136;
Susannah 290; Tarpley
T.P. 76; Thos. 339; Wm.
W. 157
Holt's, Jno.(ors) 253
Holton, Averitt 136; Jno.
393; Mary Ann 201;
Nathl. 132; Saml. 54;
Wm. 19,284
Holton's, Stephen(ors)
198,199
Holtzclaw, Danl. 143;
Elijah 215; Henry 358;
Horace 221; Hozea 113
Holtzclaw's, Hozea(ors)
128
Holzendorf, Alexr. 367;
Geo. 245; Jas. 34
Homes, Rchd. 378
Homker, Jacob 11
Honeycut, Augustus M. 268
Honeycut's, Meredith(ors)
50

Hood, Edward 310; Eliz.
177; Iccabud 65; Jesse
218; Jos. 131; Larkin
356; Martha 370; Rebecca
397; Tilmon S. 336; Wm.
34; Wily 339,343
Hooker, Nathan F. 374
Hook's, Chas.(ors) 162,
401; Wm.(ors) 108
Hooks, Hilery 320; Hillary
153; Robt. S. 222
Hooper, Harrison 134; Jno.
412; Johnson M. 414;
Rchd. 190; Rchd. Jr. 12
Hoopugh, Jas. 95,129
Hope, Jas. 336; Wm. C. 150
Hopkins, Bedford 136; Benj.
370; Caroline 123; Den-
nis 343; Edward 240;
Isaac 274; Jos. W. 17;
Thos. 191; Thos. S. & O.
(ors) 359; Wm. 131,154,
178,346; Wm. B. 136;
Wm. P. 213
Hopkins's, Chas.(ors) 365;
Jno.(ors) 408
Hopper, Crawford 197; Jor-
dan 205; Mitchell B. 78;
Saml. 48; Thos. 46
Hopping, Ephriam S. 27
Hopson, Brigs W. 242.264;
Caswell 251.328; Nathan
298; Zachariah 197
Horasy, Mary 310
Horn, Abner 48,154; Amelia
41; Benj. 301; Darcas
364; Howell L. 84,258;
Jesse 29; Joab W.E. 31;
Joshua 38; Rchd. 251;
Rowlin L. 370; Mary 258
Horn's, Edward(ors) 13;
Elisha (ors) 124; Josiah
(ors) 338; Laurence(ors)
303
Horne, Mary 169; Thos. 93
Hornesby, Leonard 381
Hornsby, Jno. Jr. 284;
Jno. & Eliza 85; Thos.
176; Wm. 34
Horriss, Moses S. 219
Horseley, Theophilus T. 283
Horsey, Eunice 128
Horsley, Smith 177; Valen-
tine 222
Hortman, Wm. 86
Horton, Abram. 96; Alfred
82; Alfred M. 178; Chas.
167.241; Danl. 19; Henry
B. 40,210; Howell 238;
Isaac 28; Jas. 199,368;
Jere. F. 151; Josiah
283; Memucan 237; Pros-
ser 324; Saml. 13; Sarah
R. 246; Thos. C. 22; Wm.
P. 302
Horton's, Fred K.(ors) 190,
227
Hoskins, Jno. W. 262;
Lemuel P. 127
Hotton, E. 65
Hough, A.B.C. 351
Houghton, Alexr. 11; Eliz.
319; Jere. 226; Robt. B.
126
House, Burrel 135,352;
Elias 65; Jas. 129;
Leister 303; Thos. 74;
Thos. P. 72; Willia 316,
374
Houseworth, Abram. 37
Housley, Wm. 99
Houston, Chas. H. Rice 407;
Edward 60; Geo. 397;
Geo. W. 76; Jas. 199;

436

Houston cont'd.
Jno. 34; Johnson M. 323;
Josiah 343; Josiah Jr.
326; Mossman 228; Robt.
23,314; Saml. C. 383
Houze, Jas. M. 58; Jno. 10
Howard, Abner 252; Brice
301; Chas. 20; Edward T.
148; Hampton H. 169;
Hawkins 161; Jas. 151,
353; Jane 278; Jno. 280;
Jno. A. 285; Jno. H. 172;
Jno. T. 199; Jonathan
159; Luzer 270; Michael
139; Nancy 71; Polly 330;
Robt. 69; Saml. 244;
Starling 215; Solomon
403; Thos. 23,168; Wm.
38; Wm. H. 25,294; Wm.
J. 124,255; Wm. T. 193:
Wm. W. 73; Zebulon 164
Howard's, Harmon(ors) 381
Howe, Andrew A. 274; Robt.
341
Howe's, David(ors) 281
Howel, Lazarus G. 332
Howell. Alfred 105; Byrum
315; Clark 412; Danl. C.
113; Danl. W. 187; David
18,91; Elisha 181; Ethe-
ridge 211; Frances 42;
Frederic L. 261; Hiram
79; Isaac 388; Jas. 177;
Jesse W. 271; Jno. 76,
197; Jno. J. 38: Jos.
294; Mills 387; Phillip
183; Richmond 34; Thos.
61,253; Wm. 111
Howze, Jas. M. 23
Howze's, Henry(ors) 177
Howzi's, Henry(ors) 268
Hoy, Jas. C. 176; Quinton
389
Hoyet, Jas. 80
Hoyle, Spicey 220
Hoyt, Nathan 126
Hubanks, Jas. 218
Hubbard, Eliz. 203; Jas.
394; Jno. 293,318; Jno.
H. 313; Jos. 291; Lar-
kin G. 340; Peterson 20;
P.W. 14; Sarah F. 289;
Susannah 304; Wm. 151;
Zenus 199
Hubbert, Hiram 177
Hubboard, Elisha 12
Hutchinson, Jas. L. 98
Huckabay, Chas. P. 252;
Geo. W. 48
Huckaby, Jas. 89; Jno. F.
354
Hudgens, Benj. 141.159;
David 48; Hamblin 403;
Jas. 149
Hudgeon, Thos. 61
Hudgpeth, Jane 393
Hudgins, Geo. L. 54,346;
Jas. 14; Jno. 40,81,247;
Philip 400; Wm. 292:
Zacheus 52,109
Hudgins's, David(ors) 218
Hudman, Eliz. 98; Garrett
190; Ichabud 248; Thos.
24; Wm. F. 324
Hudnett, Thos. 169
Hudpeth's, Jas.(ors) 397
Hudson, Eliz. 267; Enoch
B. 46; Henry F. 156;
Jas. Jr. 122; Jas. D.
395; Jno. 276,356; Jno.
J. 14; Jos. H. 101;
Milton 267; Mitchell G.
287; Rchd. 61; Ward 87;
Wm. C. 90

Hudson's, Chas.(ors) 95.
268; Wm.(ors) 107
Hudspeth. Cortis 244
Huestin, David R. 122
Huey, Henry 291; Jas. 126
Huff, Andrew 220; Danl.
406; Hamblin 310; Henry
219; J. & H.(ors) 405;
Jno. 116,257; Littleber-
ry 153; Mekin 272,339;
Wm. H. 27; Winney 19,130
Huff's, Wash.(or) 19
Hughes, Aley 158; Benajah
201; Edward 54,126; Eli
136; Goodman 240; Isaac
246,397: Jno. 157; Jno.
W. 32; Rchd. 244; Wm.
33,68,91; Wm. L. 365
Hughs, Emery B. 265;
Littleberry 298; Matthew
L. 323; Rchd. 328;
Willis 264
Huggens, Frances 164
Huggins, Abram. 207: Eli
13
Hugins, Martha 88
Huguenin, Jas. D. 191
Huguly, Amos 21
Huie, Alexr. J. 398; Geo.
295; Jos. 153
Huil, Jos. 277
Huling, Jas. 215
Hullman, Geo. 86
Hulling, Saml. H. 80
Hulmes's, Wm.(ors) 267,
279
Hulsay, Chas. T. 319; Wm.
321
Hulsey, Pleasant T. 382
Hulsy, Chas. 222
Humbert, Jas. 271
Humphrey, Erastus 286; Jno.
227; Jonathan 155; Sime-
on 390; Thos. 329
Humphrey's, Wm.(ors) 302
Humphreys, Chas. F. 54;
Jas. C. 237
Humphries, Berry 254;
Battey 124; Jno. 103:
Joshua 285; Madison 170;
Nancy 258
Hungerford, Wm. S. 195
Hunt, Danl. H. 308:
Easley 364; Elender 294;
Geo. 390; Helm 283;
Jullum 354; Jas. 58:
Joel Jr. 122; Jno. 301;
Jno. J. 297; Jno. R.
176; Jos. 394; Judkins
88: Lucinda 321; Mary
387; Thos. 179,222;
Thos. S. 220; Turner Jr.
390; Welburn 263; Wiatt
60: Wilkins 219; Wm.
122,391
Hunt's, Geo.(ors) 223;
Jno.(ors) 326
Hunter, Andrew 52: Archd.
R.S. 62; Catharine 315;
Chas. 42; David 316;
Elisha 307; Elisha T.
348; Eliz. 403; Geo. W.
59; Hardy E. 131; Jas.
289; Jesse 11,51; Leo-
nard C. 206; Moses 117;
Saml. G. 280: Seth 22;
Wm. A. 105,360
Huntington, Chris. C. 146;
Frederic 25,202
Hunton's, Jas.(ors) 36
Hurb, Jno. T. 247
Hurpe's, Wm. C.(ors) 14
Hursey, Thos. 111
Hursley, Alfred 258

Hurst, Benj. 253; Geo. 83;
Harmond 198; Ibby 108:
Jesse 166; Thos. 94;
Wm. 191: Willis 36
Hurst's, (ors) 122; Chas.
B.(ors) 259
Hurt, Humphrey 327
Huse, Hardy 209
Huskett, Isham 289
Huskette, Isham 89
Huskey, Rebecca 193
Huson, Thos. 257
Hussey, Jno. J. 154
Hussie's, Jno.(ors) 284
Huston, Jno. 133
Hutchens, Littleberry 84
Hutcheson's, N.(ors) 227
Hutchings, Chas. 328;
Littleberry 376
Hutchins, Chas. 281; David
275; Jas. 63; Jno. 128;
Jno. P. 274,393; Levi
222; Wiley 337
Hutchinson, Adam 109; David
G. 239; Jno. 301; Joshua
R. 79; Rchd. 396; Robt.
A. 187
Hutchinson's, Jas.(ors) 188
Hutchison, Moses 269; Thos.
355
Hutson, Eliz. 183; Jethro
356; Jno. 130; Peter 30
Hyde, Jno. W. 364
Hyman, Henry 217; Wm. 37
Hyman's, Aaron(ors) 285
Hyott, Jesse 163

Ikener, Sampson 177
Ilby's, Jon(ors) 279
Iley, Rchd. 113,398
Indson, Mary 193
Indsor, Jas. D. 284
Ingerville, Henry 131
Ingraham, Jesse 212; Thos.
281
Ingram, Bryant 134; Eliz.
126; Hugh Jr. 28; Jack-
son 91; Jas. L. 188;
Jno. 60,136,267; Jno. R.
378; Jno. S. 75; Marga-
ret 43: Martin 261; Matt-
hew 138; Rebecca 167:
Ruth 72; Thos. 277;
Wm. F. 414
Inman, Joel 199
Inman's, Joshua(ors) 196
Innman, Jere. 400
Inzer, Robt. D. 203
Irbey's, Jno. S. 137: Henry
90
Irby's, Jno.(ors) 114
Irons, Hiram Mill 38
Irven, Absalem 78
Irvin, Edwin 112
Irving, Ann A. 379
Irwin, Alexr. 63,130;
Archd. 226; Dulson 125;
Eliz. A. 254; Hugh L. 16,
101; Jas. 322; Jno. 349;
Mary 77; Nancy 335; Oba-
diah 78; Wm. P. 366
Isbell, Jas. 167
Isdale, Moses J. 373
Iseley, Geo. 316; Philip
141
Isham, Chas. 377
Isler, Michael B. 55;
Nathan W. 272
Ivens, Jno. 102
Ivey, Bethan 178; Guthridge
377; Henry 187; Hilson
W. 68; Jere. 161; Lewis
24,247; Montillon 128;
Myrack 98; Robt. 228;

Ivey cont'd.
Seaborn 67; Wm. 204
Ivey's, Jesse(ors) 292
Ivie, Willis R. 36
Ivins, Jno. 58
Ivy, Alexr. 280; Bryant
97; Myrack 287; Nancy
15; Pierson 411

Jack, Wm. 142
Jackson, Abram M. 377;
Allridge 142; Allen J.
339; Ansalum S. 277;
Ashur 35; Barnett 240;
Benj. Warren 273; Brink-
ley 195; Chas. H. 239;
Clarissa 405; Colby R.
167; Ebebezer 52; Ed-
mund 55; Edmund W. 327;
Enoch 394; Hartwell 386;
Hillard 61; Irvin 296;
Jas. 86,225; Jas. W. 294;
Jehit 308; Jesse 74;
Jno. 97,298,349; Jno.
Jr. 234; Jno. B. 325;
Jno. J. 62; Jno. S. 54;
Jno. W. 343; Jordan 161;
Jos. 114; Josiah 339;
Levi 270; Little B. 233;
Littleberry 54; Little-
berry B. 231; Lucandes
174; Mark 326,367; Mary
237,309,379; Matthew
28; Owen F. 407; Paschal
H. 390; Pryent E. 68;
Pyent E. 130; Reuben
358; Robt. 26; Rossean
378; Saml. 97; Sarah 170,
398; Seaborn 258; Step-
hen 59,244; Susy 237;
Thos. P. 52,146,225,228,
259,316,324; Timothy 65;
Tyrey 353; Wm. 62,67,83,
99,114,176,198,243,293,
405; Willieford 376;
Woody 97; Zadock 25
Jackson's, Damaris(or)284;
Danl.(ors) 192; Jas.(ors)
118; Jno.(ors) 174; Robt.
(ors) 32
Jacobs, Jno. A. 185;
Morris 213
Jacobs, Jno.(ors) 398
Jamerson, Geo. T. 65
James, Benj. 89; Cary 230;
Jno. A. 281; Jno. B.
183; Jno. M. 55; Joshua
297; Robt. 282; Thos.
404; Wm. 205,334
James's, Geo.(ors) 399;
Jos.(ors) 104,117;
Michael(ors) 56
Jamison, David (Dr) 343;
Jas. 21; Saml. 186; Wm.
262
Janes, Archd. G. 19;
Simeon R. 361
Janson, Jos. 40
Jarell, Margaret 246
Jarman, Lewis 355; Trus-
sey 113
Jarrad, Thos. W. 272
Jarrard, Josiah 66
Jarratt, Alexr. 155; Jas.
D. 391; Orron 313
Jarrell, Thos. Jr. 384
Jarrett, Whitsen 232
Jarroll's, Nancy(ors) 303
Jarvis's, Polly (mi) 378
Jaseph, Bartemas 162
Jay, Jno. 371
Jean, Benj. 197; Hardy H.
241
Jeannevette, Mary Ann 66

Jeffers, Jas. D. 26; Jno.
F. 187; Jonathan 296;
Thos. 65; Wm. 150
Jeffres, Thos. H. 201
Jeffreys, Drewry 45
Jeffries, Burkett 146;
Wm. 147
Jeiner, Larkin 293
Jemison's, Rial(ors) 51
Jemmison, Rosannah 55
Jenkins, Chas. 93; Danl.
58; Eliz. 85; Howell W.
385; Jesse 80,229; Jno.
338,396; Jonathan H.
388; Lawrence 330; Lewis
91,202,276,348; Nancy
389; Nicholas 289;
Pleasant C. 50; Polly
313; Robt. 165; Rosanna
107; S.D. 17; Starling
279; Walter A. 107; Wm.
173; Willis C. 49; Young
B. 268
Jenkins's, (ors) 30; Fran-
cis(ors) 324; Jno.(ors)
70; Jno. & Martha(ors)
397; Little B.(ors) 214;
Saml.(ors) 193
Jenks, Ebenezer, Jr. 261;
Eliza 370
Jenks's, Garland(ors) 28
Jennings, Chas. 279; Eliz.
390; F.J. 413; Geo. W.
105; Giles 380; Henry
120; Jno. 180; Robt.
240,331; Solomon 258;
Thos. 69; Thos. J. 348;
Wm. G. 342
Jepson, Benj. 329; Esther
278; Wm. M.C. 34
Jerkins, Robt. 147,388
Jerkins's, Wm.(ors) 179
Jerman, Jno. 251; Thos. 37
Jernigan, Hardy 386; Mary
337
Jerril, Josiah 158
Jessop, Saml. 321
Jessup, Young 77
Jester, Andrew 384; Benj.
289; Burgess 29,230;
Henry 365; Levi 86,92,
196
Jeter, Jno. R. 296; Mary
235; Robt. 22; Saml.
251; Wm. A. 375; Wm. L.
131
Jeter's, Wm.(ors) 102
Jewell, Henry 189;
Zacharia 34
Jewett, Jonathan 162
Jinks, Gales 181
Jinnins, Stephen 39
Jobell, Jno. 226
John's, Thos.(ors) 247
Johns, Arthur 40: Chas.
R. 268; Jno. 278; Jona-
than 203; Mary 76; Tarl-
ton 190; Wm. W. 174;
Zechariah 271
Johnson, Aaron 387; Abram.
71,252; Adam T. 229;
Ahashaby 89; Alexr. 9,
62,82; Alfred 49,76;
Angus 105; Anthony 262;
Arthur 398; Bonatte C.
59; Britton 101; Chas.
G. 269,331; Danl. 293;
David 90,187; Dempsey
98,277; E.C. 336; Ed-
ward 104; Eliz. 391;
Eliz. C. 369; Ephraim
M. 403; Eurick Jr. 105;
Ezekiel 334; Francis S.
397; Gafen 73;

Johnson cont'd.
Geo. W. 94,244,379;
Green 115; Hardy 30,106;
Hartwell 351; Hiram 159;
Hugh G. 267; H.V. 118;
Isaac 11; Jacob 58; Jas.
44,134,197,210,262,270,
271,359,400; Jas. B. 91;
Jason 47; Jess 271;
Jesse 79,347; Joel, Jr.
274; Jno. 48,184,212,
351; Jno. Jr. 216; Jno.
F. 63; Jno. H. 48; Jno.
J. 366; Jno. M. 402;
Johnathan Jr. 93; Jos. S.
242; Joshua 98; Josiah
403; Julius 323; Larkin
374; Levy 97; Lewis 407;
Lucy H. 242; Luke 394;
Malchel 247; Major 371;
Martha 36; Martha W. 154,
201; Mary 235; Meshack
65; Millington S. 148,
342; Moses 320; Nancy
320; Nathan 284; Oliver
168; Penelope 358; Peter
82; Philip Jr. 342; R.
67; Randel 294; Rebecca
53; Rchd. 245; Riley 50;
Robt. 269,386; Robt.
Allen 369; Robt. G. 249;
Robt. M. 224; Rosanna
334; Ruffin L. 269; Saml.
29; Saml. S. 267; Sarah
101,299; Silas M. 12,
337; Solomon 160; Solo-
mon R. 316; Stephen 177,
183,399; Susannah 84,187;
Thos. 257,269; Thos. B.
76; Thos. D. 399; Thos.
J. 394; Thos. R. 31;
Travis 320; Wm. 34,293,
344; Wm. Jr. 356; Wm. A.
152; Wm. J. 110; Wm. L.
132; Wm. M. 72; Wm. P.
137; Wm. S. 340; Zacha-
riah 100
Johnson's, Alexr.(ors) 87;
Arnold(ors) 342; Henry
(ors) 18; Isaac (ors) 74,
336; Jas.(ors) 143,167;
Rchd.(ors) 255; Robt.
(ors) 187; Thos.(ors)
363; Thos. W.(ors) 133;
Wm.(ors) 258
Johnston, Albert 229; Al-
sey 266; Jas. 314; Jas.
T. 239; Jno. 178,401;
Luke 20; Rowland 325;
Wm. 397; Wm. H. 140;
Wm. S. 167; Wm. W. 228
Johnston's, A.(ors) 325;
Thos.(ors) 27
Joiner, Absalum 77; Benj.
334; Jain 28; James 324;
Jno. 51; Meredith 294;
Meshack 151,300; Wm. 206
Joiner's, Abram(ors) 267
Joines, Edward W. 317; Jas.
114; Jared 234; Wm. 190
Jolly, Jno. 10; Wm. C. 102
Jones, Aaron 118,199; Adam
196,282; Albert 390;
Alexr. 371; Allen 185,
241; Ambrose 235; Anna
J.C. 106; Anthony 414;
Arthur Jr. 190; Benj.
210,288,355; Benj. Jr.
410; Benj. H. 160; Benj.
o. 229; Berry 148; Ber-
shaba 305; Bryan W. 191;
Carey 339; Clemmen 360;
Clemmew 67; Danl. 178,
211; Davi H. 42;

438

441

Martin cont'd.
Jno. 148,214,221,386;
Jno. B. 144; Jno. J.
405; Jos. R. 375; Kin-
chen 46,361; Lemuel 292;
Leonard 348; Levi 76,
206; Lucretia 221; Mar-
garet 70; Marshall 133,
357; Micajah 162; Milley
236; Moses 306; Nancy
242; Nathl. 365,383;
Payton 183; Rachael 257;
Rachael 257; Robt. E.
411; Saml. J. 71; Saml.
L. 59; Spencer 142; Thos.
121,178; Thos. B. 164,
288; Thos. S. 198; War-
ren W. 380; Wm. 159,201,
208,222,334; Yearly 144
Martin's, Alexr.(ors) 93,
198; Benj.(ors) 76,277;
Cluff(ors) 163; Danl.
(ors) 47; Jno.(ors) 67,
139,284
Martindale, Mary 15
Masengate, Wm. 399
Mashburn, Benj. 132
Mask, Delaney 192
Mason, Alfred C. 233; Chas.
98; Churchill 355; Eliz.
111; Ezekiel 98; Jno.
82; Jno. M. 150; Martha
J. 301; Rchd. S. 204;
Wm. 204
Mass's, Jno.(ors) 22
Massengale, Deberry C.
308; Theodosius E. 99;
Wm. H.H. 98
Massey, Abram. 338; Alston
S. 322; Mary 34; Rchd.
P. 61; Warren B. 129.352
Massey's, Avery(or) 323;
Jas.(ors) 266; Sampson
(ors) 10,35
Massingil, Jno. 300
Masters, Levi 56
Mathews, Chas. L. 48;
Eliochai 371; Eliz. 33;
Frederic 10; Jas. 63;
Noe 11
Mathewson, Malcolm 334
Mathias, Jas. 160
Mathis, Elisha 53; Ezekiel
116; Francis D. 99;
Griffin 27,284; Howell
176; Jas. 410; Johnson
148; Mary S. 41; Nathan
356; Rice 267; Thos. 202
Mathis's, Jno.(ors) 279
Mathison, Jas. 267
Matley, Jno. 345
Matthew, Thos. 194
Matthews, Abram. M. 317;
Archd. 109,222; Benj.
253; Britten 357; Chas.
393; Elijah W. 157; Eliz.
112; Henry 394; Hugh 158;
Isaac 259; Jere. 267;
Jesse 40; Joel 398; Lewis
M. 145; Liberty 86;
Littleberry 265; Newman
321,336; Thos. 81,131,
237; Wm. 12,83,312
Matthew's, Henry(ors) 194,
234; Philip(ors) 40
Mattox, Aaron 137,157,260;
Amelia C. 410; Dudley
328; E.(Judge) 56; Hardy
16; Jno. 257; Jno. A.
164; Jno. W. 214; Michael
M. 370; Thos. 198; Wm. 64
Mattox's, Michael P. 316
Mattux, Henry 338

Maulden, Epps 43; Tucker
303
Mauldin, Rucker 131
Maury, Henry 136
Maxey, Hail 97,380; Jno.
W. 109
Maxwell. Berry 251; Jas.
68; Jno. J. 355; Jos. E.
364; Robt. 38; Thos.
165; Uriah 27; Wm. M.W.
151; Wm. P. 220; Wylie
410
May, Albert 327; Amasa
212; Edmund 38; Gilbert
111; Jas. E. 78; Jno.
174; Nathl. 331; Perry-
man 211; Saml. 23; Thos.
178,234; Wm. 325; Wm.
Jr. 182
Mayes, Thos. 384; Wm. 217
Mayfield, Eliz. 405; Fran-
cis 42; Isaac 360
Maynor, Ricey H. 355;
Willise 21
Mayo, Danl. 312; Cyprian
341; Jas. G. 326,352;
Jas. J. 375; Jesse 254;
Jno. 207; Pleasant R.
240; Richardson 129;
Stephen D. 163; Wm. S.
382s, Benj.(ors) 111
Mayor, Danl. 409
Mays, Benj. D. 14; Edward
351; Harvey M. 37,239;
Jemime 309; Levi 323;
Mary 9; Rebecca 363;
Robt. C. 59
Maztin, Absolem 305
M'Adams, Bradford 229
M'Afee, Robt. G. 158
M'Afer, Morgan W. 240
M'Affee, Arthur 75
M'Alister, (ors) 88
M'Allister, Geo. W. 292
M'Alpin, Wm. 350
M'Ardle, Jas. 366
M'Arthur, Duncan 388
M'Arty, Susannah 143
M'Bee, Green L. 389; Jas.
412; Susannah 138
M'Bee's, Isaac(ors) 174;
Isam(ors) 372
M'Beth, Jno. C. 341
M'Brayer, Jos. 407
M'Bride, Jas. 194,255;
Wm. G. 271
M'Bryde, Jno. J. 24
M'Bryer, Jos. H. 260
M'Burnet, Wm. 162
M'Cain, Hugh M. 317
M'Calhene, Thos. 229
M'Call, Allen 296; Geo. W.
402; Jas. 96; Jno. 146;
Sarah Ann 137; Susan N.
291; Thos. 270
M'Callister, Geo. W. 203;
Jno. W. 281
M'Callum, Patrick 239;
Wm. 146
M'Canless, Jno. 126; Wm.
R. 406
M'Canless's, Wm.(ors) 395
M'Canley, Merdock 280
M'Cans, Jno. 211
M'Cant's, Alexr. R.(ors)
245
M'Cants, David 225
M'Carra, Wm. 327
M'Carter, Jas. H. 71; Jno.
229
M'Carthur, Wm. 324
M'Carthy, Alexr. 58; Robt.
E. 47
M'Carty, Allen 238;

M'Carty cont'd.
Dennis 283; E.L. 384;
Samson 48; Sherrod 323
M'Carty's, (ors) 201
M'Cay's, Wm.(ors) 293
M'Celvale, Wm. 52
M'Celvy, Jno. 145
M'Cibben, Margarette 282
M'Clain, Ephraim 155; Jas.
W. 352; Jno. 47,226; Mary
193; Wm. 96,326
M'Clane, Augustus C. 256
M'Clean, Danl. 229
M'Cleland, Gabriel 194;
Jas. 25; Silas 161,245
M'Clendon, Benj. 251; Den-
nis 85,210; Gabriel 97;
Geo. 328,379; Haley 205;
Hugh 76; Jesse 173; Joel
281; Jno. 213,230; Moses
J. 403; Simeon 35; Simp-
son 14; Zachariah 230
M'Clendon's, (chi) 299;
Ethelred(ors) 93; Ezekiel
(ors) 351
M'Clennon, Sarah 272
M'Clenny's, Wm.(ors) 320
M'Clesky, Benj. G. 27;
Eusebius J. 108; Jas. W.
107
M'Cliskey, Thos. J. 200
M'Cloud, Danl. 300
M'Clung, Jere. A. 141; Luel
M. 288; Wm. W. 347,365
M'Clure, Nancy 131; Saml.
B. 96; Thos. 116,217,395
M'Clusky, Asa 397
M'Coe, Adaline 265
M'Colester's, Jno.(ors) 44
M'Collock, Wm. 393
M'Collum, Danl. 182; Geo.
B. 35; Harvey 292; Joab
293; Jordan 187; Marga-
ret 104; Wm. 12,356
M'Collum's, Abram.(ors) 76
M'Common, Chas. 17
M'Connel, Henry 296
M'Connell, Jas. 207; Joshua
128
M'Connell's, Robt. C.(ors)
358
M'Cook, Danl. 223; Hamil-
ton 245; Othneel 368; Wm.
350
M'Cool, Lucretia 276
M'Corcle, Jno. 144
M'Cord, Jno. 21; Robt. B.
270; Wm. 212; Wm. Jr.
220; Wm. S. 408
M'Cormack's, Jere.(ors)
127; Jno.(ors) 31
M'Cormick, Matthias 39;
Wm. H. 361
M'Cowen, Mary 334
M'Coy, Alexr. 345; Ann 259;
Benj. R. 227; Chas. 306;
Danl. 127; Danl. S. 177;
David 100; Elijah 42;
Harrison 28; Jas. 112;
Jno. 83; Mary 179,344;
Saml. 381; Wm. 271
M'Crackin, Alexr. 250
M'Craine, Archd. 221
M'Cranie, J. 405
M'Crary, Ezra 259,281;
Jasper 258; Jno. Jr. 64;
Jonathan B. 158; Peggy
254; Peleg R. 106; Saml.
267; Thos. B. 142
M'Crary's, Wm.(ors) 289
M'Cravey, Ezekiel 410
M'Cray, Stephen G. 153
M'Cray's, Jno.(ors) 57
M'Crinmon, G. 206

M'Croan, Eli 99
M'Culler, David 307
M'Cullers, Abigail 277; Andrew 25; Burrell 44, 74; Nancy 140
M'Cullock. Jno. 403; Jos. P. 256
M'Cullough, Jacob 189
M'Cully, Josiah 90
M'Cune, Micajah F. 132
M'Curdy, Wm. A. 371
M'Currey, Lauchlin 126
M'Curry, Lauchlin 202
M'Cutchen, Jane 130; Robt. 191
M'Cutchin, Saml. K. 350
M'Cade, Franklin 305; Jno. 222,311,341
M'Daff, Alfred 310
M'Daniel, Allen 239; Ann 196; Barbara 174; Buckner 126; Danl. 160,233; David 173; Eliz. 338: Jno. 54,147,272; Malcolm 308; Margaret 25; Philip A. 102; Wm. 192
M'Dermed, Jno. 172
M'Dermot, Jno. W. 375
M'Dermott, Owen 303
M'Dill, Geo. 265; M.S.E. & N.(ors) 242
M'Doffee, Jno. 271
M'Donald, Alexr. 140; Alexr. H. 96; Benj. 101; Donald 68,390; Geo. W. 278; Green 78,88; Hellen 84; Hugh 247; Jackson 108; Jas. 298; Jno. 15, 113,124,295,328,342; Jno. S.C. 45; Lovett 387; Lovic P. 172; Lovick P. 240; Mary 375; Nicholas P. 215; Norman 408; Randol 168; Sarah 251; Smith 265; Wm. 100
M'Donald's, Allen(ors) 105; Jas.(or) 366
M'Donnell, Henry 241; Neal 149
M'Dougle, Alexr. 367
M'Dow, David 310; Jno. 126
M'Dowell, Mary Ann 21; Wm. 382
M'Duff, Alfred 156; Rchd. 43
M'Duffee, Geo. 224; Jno. 166; Mary 37; Nancy 108
M'Duffee, Neel 285
M'Dugal, Ananias 23; Sarah 101
M'Dugald, Dugald 310
M'Dugall, Danl. 62
M'Durman, Abner 233
M'Eachin, Archd. 167
M'Elhannon, Isiah 156; Stewart 108,388
M'Elhenney, Hezekiah C. 159; Wm. 230; Wm. Jr. 408
M'Ellhannon, Cooper 66,380
M'Elroy, Andrew 44; Jno. 356; Johnston 41
M'Elvy, Archd. 189
M'Elwreath, Jno. 96; Mark 198; Michael 214,352
M'Ennis, Angus 199
M'Entyre, Joshua 391
M'Ever, Andrew 271; Brice 25; Brice C. 234,301; Martha 272
M'Ewen, Jas. H. 38
M'Ewin, Eliz. 82; Isaac A. 112; Jas. H. 395
M'Fadding's, David(ors)189

M'Fail, Judith 343
M'Farlan, Wm. 54
M'Farland, J.D. 322; Jno. 325; Thos. G. 261
M'Farland, Danl.(ors) 13
M'Farlin, Jas. 369
M'Gaha, Jane 29
M'Gahee, Danl. 402
M'Gaher, Josiah 129
M'Garrety, Delila 58
M'Garrity, Jno. 254
M'Gee, Patrick 148; Thos. W. 377
M'Gee's, Jno.(ors) 113
M'Gehee, Jno. S. 294; Jno. Wilson 408; Miles H. 48; Thos. 235; Thos. F. 333; Wm. 235
M'Giddey, Frederic 414
M'Gill, Andrew 329: Jas. 158,299; Morris 65
M'Gillis's, (ors) 282
M'Gilvary, Jno. 168
M'Ginley, Hugh 157
M'Ginnis, Ambrose 300; Jos. L. 247; Levi H.; Stephen 360
M'Ginty, Isaac 63: Jas. C. 103; Meshack 263; Shaderick 100
M'Glann, David 269
M'Glaughen, Luke 396
M'Glawn, Wm. 34
M'Gough, David 305; Nancy 82; Thos. 160
M'Govern, Jno. 179
M'Gowan, Louisa 301
M'Gran, Thos. 233
M'Grath, Roger 92
M'Graw, Jno. 81,102; Timothy 146
M'Gruder, Wm. R. 32
M'Guffey, Jas. 41
M'Guire, Jos. S. 175
M'Gullion, Rachel 354
M'Gullion's, Thos.(ors) 167
M'Hargue, Seaborn 88
M'Innis, Flora 197
M'Intire, Jno. 256
M'Intosh, Jno. N. 185,317; Jno. V. 296; Martha 57; Wm. 111
M'Intosh's, David(ors) 169
M'Intyre, Peter 342
M'Invale, Jno. 134,208
M'Iver, Alexr. 93
M'Junkin, Francis M. 318; Saml. 211
M'Kaskill, Allen 145; Murdock 257
M'Kay, Jonathan 9,70
M'Kean, Sarah 109
M'Kee, Eliz. 390
M'Kee's, Jno.(ors) 306
M'Keen, Jas. & Alfred 386; Robt. W. 9
M'Keller, Peter 202,277
M'Kenney, Chas. 69; Jane 116; Stephen S. 121
M'Kenzie, Wm. 197,262
M'Killgon, Jno. 331
M'Kindley, Jos. 156; Chas. C. 409
M'Kinne, Valentine 250
M'Kinnee, Wm. 264
M'Kinney, Benj. Jr. 249; Caleb 328; Jos. 34; Justin 337; Mordecai 104; Wm. 203
M'Kinni, Murdock 268
M'Kinnon, Ann 298; Archd. 331

M'Kinzie, Danl.(mi) 42; Jno. 312
M'Konky, Jno. 173
M'Korkle, Jas. 33: Jno. F. 278; Wm. 352
M'Kutchen, Saml. K. 205
M'Lain, Jno. 306
M'Lane, Bennett H. 51; Jas. N. 353; Michael 403
M'Larty, Alexr. 155
M'Lauchlin, Duncan 147
M'Lead's, Angus(ors) 236
M'Lean, Allen 273; Geo. 207; Jno. 45
M'Lelion, Jno. 163,194
M'Lemore, Chas. 275
M'Lendon, Dennis 262: Saml. 393
M'Lendon's, Eldad(ors) 269; Henry(ors) 358
M'Lennan, Kenneth 28,374
M'Leod, Angus 408: Charlotte 43; Jas. 33; Murdock 11; Neal 260; Niel 346; Norman W. 59; Wm. 385
M'Leran, Neill 43
M'Leroy, Nathan 97; Wm.392
M'Lewreath, Jno. R. 14
M'Lin, Hugh 48
M'Linn, Hugh 106; Robt. N. 265
M'Lochlin, Wm. 254
M'Loughlin, Adam 354; Alexr. R. 227; Margaret 270
M'Mahan, Jno. 141; Jno. R. 413
M'Mannus, Jas. 209
M'Manus, Jno. 200
M'Math, Andrew 35
M'Mellon, Jas. 10
M'Michael, Ashley 56; Eliz. 181; Silas 304
M'Millan, Danl. 390: Jno. 121; Jno. R. 253
M'Millan's, Archd.(ors) 313
M'Millen, Littleberry 227; Wm. 88
M'Millian, Drury 132; Duncan 290; Henry 171; Jno. R. 62
M'Millon, Danl. 77; Jas. 30; Littleberry 58: Mary 377
M'Min, Robt. Jr. 346
M'Minn, Jane 21; Jesse 166
M'Mitchell, Griffin 244; Lemuel 341
M'Mullan, Thos. J. 68
M'Mullen, Jas. 20; Mary 127; Memory 348; Wm. 265, 388
M'Mullians, Jno. R. 236
M'Mullin, Mary 155; Jos. 153
M'Murphy, Jas. 286
M'Murrain, Wm. 85
M'Murran, David 233; Jesse 24
M'Nabb, Jas. 363
M'Nair, Danl. 113
M'Nal, Danl. 92
M'Naughton, Jas. 370
M'Neal, Andrew 232: Archd. G. 135; Jas. 353
M'Neal's, (ors) 412
M'Neely, Mary 238
M'Neill, Jesse 371
M'Pherson, Archd. 260: Stephen 123,413
M'Queen, Jno. 244
M'Rae, Danl. 95; Mary C.W. 184

M'Rai, Jno. 316
M'Red, Danl. 392
M'Ree, Jas. 353; Mary 319
M'Rees's, Thos. P.(ors)
347
M'Right, Jno. 165
M'Swain, Patrick 329
M'Swain's, Duncan(ors) 389
M'Uin, Jno. T. 184
M'Vay, Jno. 35,37
M'Vey, David 70; Yancy R.
394
M'Vickers, Jno. 103
M'Walker, Allen 231
M'Walters, Jas. 111,252
M'Waters, Francis 69,407;
Wm. 151
M'Watley, Thos. 216
M'Whorter, Helena 163;
Jas. 96,366; Marg. 184
M'Williams, Thos. N. 381
Meacham, Archd. 354; Jno.
354
Mead, Miner 174; Thornton
84,263
Meades, Solomon 301
Meador, Edward 45; Rchd.
122; Wm. 19
Meador's, Jno.(ors) 198
Meadow, Vastl 261
Meadows, Barnabas 255;
Danl. 295; Elijah 176;
Enoch 284; Hiram 85;
Jas. W. 363; Jno. 248,
259; Noah W. 73
Meagher's, Timothy D.(ors)
207
Meeks, Shadrick 147
Mealer, Isham 357; Thomp-
son 312
Means, Alexr. 283
Mearse, Henry B. 154
Mecombs, Wm. 407
Mede, Mary 277
Mede's, Wm. B.(or) 344
Medford, Dempsey B. 294;
Wm. 187
Medlin, Riley 66
Medlock, Jno. 301; Jno. R.
97
Medlock's, A.H.(ors) 226
Meek, Asa T. 280; Jas. S.
74; Robt. 245
Meeks, Allen 74; Josiah
73,219; Nancy 102; Wiley
95
Meeler, Wm. 31
Megahee, David 325
Meigs, Jno. Adams 91
Mell, Simeon 266
Mellevee, Wm. 217
Melton, Benj. 372; Cathern
205; Eli 245; Matthew
93; Strous 46
Melvin, Cotmon 205
Menard, Francis A. 405
Meneeley, Wm. 29
Menefee, Geo. 145; Tatum
105
Mercer, Edwin 173; Henry
314; Hyram 32; Jno. W.H.
243; Joshua 47,344;
Josiah D. 286; Lott 237;
Malacha 53; Mary 178;
Nathl. B. 336; Noah 390;
Sarah 368; Silas 57;
Williamson S. 330
Mercer's, Jesse(ors) 344
Mercier, Benj. P. 178;
Jos. 51
Merck, Geo. 96
Mercks, Geo. W. Jr. 323
Meredith, Catharine 27;
Jno. 302

Merit, Matthew 29,339
Merk. Geo. 278; Henry 346
Merkerson, Duncan 275
Merrell, Benj. 209
Merrill, Maria 320
Merrill's, Jas.(ors) 240
Merriman, Wm. P. 88
Merritt, Barbara 44; Benj.
97; Berryman G. 373;
Hiram 287; Hyram 147;
Jas. 79; Lovic 10; Luke
161; Stanford 270;
Stephen 80,87,367; Wm.
119,133
Merritt's, Aaron(ors) 103
Merriwether, Chas. J. 76;
Thos. 137
Merryfield, Warren 137
Messer, Griffin 258; Jno.
H. 251; Jos. 49; Peter
212
Messick, Jere. 184
Metcalf's, Anthony(ors) 26
Methune, Rchd. 234
Methvin, Wm. 62
Metts, Frederic 134
Metz., Geo. 247; Saml. 405
Miars's, No.(ors) 33
Mickle, Thos. F. 155
Mickler, Peter 80; Wm. 384
Middlebrooks, Milley 194;
Milly 214; Thos. S. 256
Middleton, Jas. 39; Jas.
A. 383; Jno. 264
Midley, Jas. 208
Miers, Elijah 376; Jno.
224; Wm. R. 99
Miess, Jno. 350
Miher's, Wm.(ors) 14
Mikell, Jas. 67,229; Sea-
born 134
Milam, Wiley 188
Miles, David 300; Edward
43,117; Elijah 138;
Eliz. 389; Jared 197;
Lavina 363; Thos. 188;
Wm. 273
Miles's, (ors) 91,310
Miller, Ailey 74; Bazil
94; Bright 205; David
J. 219; Edward 231; El-
bert 405; Elijah 67,364;
Eliz. 101,359; Elizur
373; Ezekiel 88; Eze-
kiel G. 141,203; Fran-
cis E. 383; Francis E.R.
125; Goodwin 38; Harry
B. 374; Henry J. 131;
Hezekiah 373; Isaac 230;
Israel 346; Jacob W.
332; Jas. 44,144,202,
347,376,408; Jas. M.
345; Jas. S. 188; Jere.
29; Jesse 323,326; Jno.
311,360.261,381; Jno. A.
227; Jno. J. 54; Jno.
K. 9; Jno. M. 403; Jno.
M.C. 295; Jonathan 80;
Jos. 163,253,294; Jos.
N. 375; Joshua 387;
Leanah 309; Lee R. 391;
Lucinda & Henry 26;
Lucretia 124; Nathl.
202,244; Obadiah 176;
Rhody 183; Robt. 94,380;
Saml. 334; Sarah 191;
Sarah Ann 155; Thos.
229; Thos. V. 402; Wm.
73,314,318; Wm. R. 379;
Zealous 38
Miller's, (ors) 47,373;
Jas.(ors) 156,359; Jede-
diah S.(ors) 382; Jno.
(ors) 200; Nancy (or)264

Millen, Geo. 95
Millener, Jas. M. 139
Millican, Andrew 54; Jas.
366; Susannah 248; Thos.
69; Wm. 210
Milligan, Lemuel 314; Sea-
born 404
Millink, Henry F. 242
Mill Irons, Geo. W. 129,
244; Jesse 252
Milloun, Athijah 266
Mills, Abram. 20; Chas.
180; Chas. F. 357; Danl.
115; Elijah 258; Henry
162,322; Hilliard 370;
Hugh 158; Jacob 79; Jno.
15,56; Stephen H.H. 214;
Thos. R. 138; Wm. 293
Mills's, Jesse(ors) 84;
Jno.(ors) 150
Milner, Joshua 88; Pitt S.
324
Milton, Benj. 152; Chas.
201; Jas. 150; Jno. 179;
Stroud 389; Tabitha 161
Milton's, Jonathan (ors)
363
Mimms, David D. 117; Elias
55; Eliz. 126; Jos. 299
Mims, Chas. E. 238
Mincey, Aaron 209
Ming, Alfrederic 135
Mingledorf, Jno. 170; Jno.
G. 103
Minis, Isaac 75
Minor's, Nicholas(ors) 112
Minshew, Jno. A. 134
Minter's, Uriah(ors) 111
Minzies, Wm. J. 302
Miras's, Francis(ors) 25
Mires, Edward 390; Joshua
52; Sarah 296
Mires's, (ors) 83
Mirick, Andrew 171
Misser, Silas 396
Mitchell, Andrew 313; Ann
371; Asa B. 399; Chris-
chens 278; Danl. R. 194,
380; Edwin T. 28; Eliz.
273; Geo. 151; Hardy 201;
Henry 42,92,163,343;
Henry D. 71,120; Isaac
389; Jas. L. 150; Jas. M.
240; Joel 227; Jno. 359;
Jno. G. 144; Jno. S. 123;
Jonathan 303; Jos. 374;
Joshua L. 208; Lucy 324;
Martha 91; Morning 54;
Riley 374; Robt. 153;
Roland 128; Saml. 207;
Shatteen Br. 295,395;
Thos. 296; Walter 398;
Wm. 39,58,60,90,101,120,
289,317; Wm. Jr. 74,342;
Wm. F. 65,387; Wm. S.
258
Mitzer, David 251
Mixen, Amelia 104
Mixon, Elijah 31; Jesse
158,318; Martin 398; Wm.
W. 185
Mize, Anderson 367; Warren
61
Mizell, Jacob Carter 351;
Jno. 293; Mary 77; Matt-
hew 90; Wm. 280
Mobbs, Jesse 37
Mobley, Alexr. 410; Benj.
E. 19; Danl. 84; Jesse
243; Jas. N. 313; Jesse
343; Jno. 312; Ledford
55; Merrada 29; Reuben
R. 244; Sampson P. 395;
Thos. 247; Wm. 77

O'Neal's, Edmon(ors) 236;
Wm.(ors) 204
Onsley, Rebecca 198
Oquin, Jas. J. 404
O'Riley, Patrick 42
Ormler, (Oemler) Augustus
G. 308
Orplis, Heggins 253
Orr, Andrew 20; Nancy 44;
Robt. 10; Thos. 173;
Wm. 98; Wm. J. 154
Orr's, Jno.(ors) 233
Orran, Donoho 73
Osborn, Amos 116; Claiborn
394; Jos. 25,138,349;
Rollen 319
Osbourn, Geo. 141
Osburn, Brittain S. 28;
Jas. 152; Jno. W. 243;
Matthew 309; Nicholas
225; Wm. K. 26,280
Oscar, Benj. 391
Oshields, Jethro 10,14
Osmer, Susan 172
Osmer's, Rchd.(ors) 358
Otwell, Guifford R. 204;
Paul M. 10; Solomon W.
23
Ousley, Pleasant 143
Oustead, Jno. 287
Overbay, Saml. R. 310
Oversheet's, Danl.(ors)
310
Oversteel, Jno. 367,372
Overstreet's, Wm.(ors)286
Overton, Abijah 350; Jas.
352; Thos. 244
Owdonis's, J.(ors) 245
Owen, Aner 42; Ann 149;
Benj. F. 180; Jas. 87;
Jno. 41; Jno. G. 168;
Mary 329; Newsom 93;
Owen W. 165; Robt. 391;
Vines H. 94; Wm. F. 376;
Wm. J. 91
Owens, Anderson 262; An-
drew J. 208; David 377;
Dilly 190; Elijah 392;
Geo. W. 406; Jas. S.
238; Jno. 197,265; Male-
kiah R. 83; Martin 162;
Mary 400; Owen 22; Saml.
34,372; Uriah 48; Vines,
H. 24; Wm. 353
Owen's, Polly(ors) 403
Owensby's, Wm.(ors) 274,
408
Owings, Jas. 194
O'Winslett, Jno. M. 209
Oxford, Jacob 14,213;
Polly 341
Ozmore, Robt. 309

Pace, Barnabas 345; Bryant
251; Delphia 401; Hardy
302,407; Jas. 162: Jno.
S. 341; Nathl. G. 288;
Noah 300; Thos. S. 201,
367; Wm. 242
Paces's, Thos.(ors) 28
Pacetty, Dennis 129
Packer, Lewis 394
Padget, Jesse 144
Page, Dicy 96; Eliz. 175,
241; Jno. 379; Lucinda
192; Mary 234; Solomon
Je. 281; Wm. H.D. 212,
370; Winship S. 58
Page's, Allen(ors) 183;
Jesse(ors) 321
Pain, Brastus 177; Geo.
M. 341; Jas. T. 343;
Jno. 267
Paine, Winefred 323

Painter, Ezekiel 325
Pair, Jas. L. 233
Palen, Jas. 395
Palery's, Wm.(ors) 314
Palman, David W. 230
Palmer, Aaron 9; Augustus
H. 34; Danl. 141; David
197,373; Edmund 54;
Frederic & Martha 53;
Levi 345; Martin 35,
215; Oliver 413; Stephen
231; Wm. 321; Wm. H. 195;
Wilson 65
Palmer's, Abel(ors) 346;
Ephraim (chil) 366; G.
(ors) 43; Jos.(ors) 208;
Robt.(ors) 85
Palmore, Solomon 181
Pane, Henry D. 38; Larkin
51,179
Panlette, Rchd. 127
Pannell, Berry 311
Pannell's, (chil) 352
Paples, Jno. 81
Paramore, Everett 83; Wm.
C. 9
Pardue, Sidney M. 261
Parham, Argen 371; Geo.
W. 261; Jno. 123,129;
Joshua 261; Mathew 66;
Wiatt 11; Wm. B. 19
Parham's, Rowland(ors) 18
Paris, Jane 243; Manervy
Ann 219
Paris's, Francis(ors) 234;
Philander O.(ors) 61
Parish, Edward H. 195;
Eliz. 308; Gary F. 383;
Hezekiah J. 81; Jonathan
D. 215; Mary 399; Pros-
ser 120; Wm. 97; Wyley
34; Wyly 378
Park, Andrew 303; Andrew
M. 97; Columbus M. 283;
Ezekiel E. 10; Geo. 360;
Jere. M. 345; Jno. L.
334; Jos. 74,335; Lind-
sey 373; Moses 17; Phebe
335,337
Park's, Jas. G.(ors) 95;
174; Rchd. M.(ors) 28;
Wm.(ors) 290
Parker, Ashley G. 67;
Austin 308; Benj. F.
21; Bryant 44; Caleb
135; Danl. 177; David
A. 383; Emanuel 385;
Geo. W. 109; Gustavus
A. 18; Isaac H. 160;
Jacob 183; Jas. 69,139,
197,227; Jas. A. 53;
Jeptha P. 228; Jesse
404; Jno. 220; Jno. H.
127; Jos. C. 359; Lovey
280; Mason S. 327; Mos-
es 226; Nancy 18; Need-
ham 25; Peter 124;
Rchd. 99; Sarah 89;
Solomon 376; Squire 222;
Susan 22; Wade 79; West
S. 355; Wm. 109,192,381,
388,395
Parker's, Alexr.(ors) 370;
Gabriel(ors) 17; Reader
(ors) 357; Stephen (ors)
303
Parkerson, Jno. C. 269,
295
Parkes, Jas. 133
Parkhurst, Jno. J. 382
Parkins, Thos. 186
Parks, Eliz. 186,327;
Jane 224; Jno. 60; Jno.
W. 199; Marshall 386;

Parks cont'd.
Sarah D. 242: Thos. H.
45; Wilborn 50; Wm. C.
168; Wm. J. 404; Wyatt
R. 33
Parmalee, Alberbert O. 221;
Thos. J. 387
Parmer, Edmon 216; Green
B. 266; Jas. M. 291;
Jos. 24
Parnell, Hope H. 412
Parnell's, Thos.(ors) 41
Parr, Benj. 244; Chas. D.
304
Parr's, Ingram(or) 41
Parris, Emanuel 57
Parris's, Philander O.
(ors) 142
Parrish, Jno. 396; Prosser
322; Robt. N. 323
Parrott, Danl. 81; Jno.
393
Parsons, Jno. 278; Thos.
313; Thos. A. 201; Wm.
M. 91
Parsons's, Thos.(ors) 322
Partan, Henry 143
Partin, Allen 123; Jno.
311; Kindred 215
Partridge, Payton 26
Passmore, Jno. J. 184
Pass, Dicey 221; Matthew
J. 45; Thos. 189,372
Passmore, Henry 73
Pate, Hannah 181; Hollis
M. 231; Jno. 403; Sea-
bourn 336; Wm. 353;
Zaccheus 152; Zeachens
303
Pate's, Danl.(ors) 309;
Edward(ors) 120; Jas.
(ors) 185; Robt.(ors)
18
Patello, Benj. F. 187
Patillo, Chas. 10; Jas.
162
Patman's, Watson(ors) 13
Patrick. David 41,322;
Jos. 124; Paul 64,413;
Wm. 209
Patridge, Jas. 382: Jesse
167
Pattello, Simeon 230;
Wesley H. 369
Patten, Catharine 406;
Robt. 302
Pattershall. Eliz. 102
Patterson, Alexr. 142,277;
Eliz. 198; Francis M.
256; Geo. 109,164; Hiram
326; Jane 412; Jno. 121;
Jno. Jr. 18; Jos. 411;
Mary W. 398; Nathl. J.
27; Nimrod 80; Pleasant
B. 147; P.W. 247; Robt.
J. 10; Tryon 204; Wiley
98; Wm. 81,223
Pattersib's, Jno. R.(ors)
253
Pattison, Jno. 247
Patton, Margaret 244; Wm.
K. 275
Paty, Miles 96; Sarah 331
Paul, Abram. M. 279;
Archd. Y. 204; Jacob 12:
Jas. E. 106; Robt. 191;
Robt. B. 365
Paxon, Saml. 213
Paxton, Milton 131,245
Payne, Absalom 201; Chas.
P. 192; C.S.M. 147;
David 70; Jas. 113:
Jno. 158; Jno. B. 348;
Jos. 231,253;

Pittman, Albert 158; Alfred
T. 278; Benj. D. 30;
Jere. 129; Malachi 134;
Mordica B. 150; Rchd.
264; Silvanus 63; Wm. A.
313; Zilpha 283
Pitts, Geo. 135; Jesse 274,
392; Jno. D. 398; Laban
183; Lizya 254; Robt. G.
351; Wesley 130; Wm. 407;
Wm. C. 295; Willis 104
Pitt's, Louis(ors) 349
Plant, Lewis H. 413
Player, Saml. 233
Pledger, Mary S. 85; Thos.
113
Pless, Augustus 95
Plufer, Jno. 224
Plumb, Chas. 367
Plummer, Edward 194,380;
Jas. W. 275; Jno. R. 227
Plumket, Jas. 225,376;
Silas 84
Plunkett, Jas. 216; Silas
357
Pluute, Jason 255
Poage, Jas. 22
Poarch, Patience 70
Poe, Thos. W. 268
Pogue, Alfred G. 257;
Azariah 173; Wm. D. 141
Pointer, Fleming 32
Polk, Archd. 40; Archd. L.
159; Jonathan A. 83;
Levi 51; Wm. R. 132
Pollard, Abner B. 53;
Elias 80; Josiah 234;
Leroy 272; Royston 131;
Thos. 104; Wm. A. 194
Pollard's, Leroy(ors) 404
Pollock, Jesse 352
Poncil, Michael 226
Ponder, Isham 180
Ponge, Jas. 113
Pool, David V.T. 37; Dicey
237; Jacob 92; Jas. 115;
Jno. H. 134; Seth P. 234,
335; Seymore Spencer 283;
Thos. A. 247; Wm. P. 118
Pool's, Jos.(ors) 106
Poole, Ephraim M. 98;
Young P. 114
Poore's, Wm.(or) 172
Pope, Barton C. 355; Benj.
28; Burrell 45; Burwell
91; Collin 255; Frederic
394; Henry 297; Henry N.
272; Joel W. 324; Mary
344; Micajah 401; Mikel
290; Robt. 14; Thos. 292;
Thos. L. 98,314; Wiley
308; Zedekiah 105
Pope's, Henry(ors) 131;
Josiah W.(or) 375
Popham, Emeriah 112; Jno.
54
Poppell, Robt. 378
Popup's, Benj.(ors) 290
Popwell, Eliz. 264
Porch, David J. 71
Porker, Hardy 344
Porl, Jno. 100
Porter, Abegal R. 343;
Bartholomew 156; Benj.
F. 18; Chas. H. 218;
Eliz. 282; Geo. 110;
Henry H. 186; Hugh 167;
Isaac R. 206; Jas. M.
271; Jane 111; Jno. 147;
Oliver M. 261,329; Sarah
283; Thos. C. 58; Thos.
R. 157
Porter's, Jadethani(ors)
180; J.S.(ors) 116;

Porter's cont'd.
Lavinia & Jane(ors) 180;
Stanton(ors) 341; Wm. G.
(ors) 81
Porterfield, Allen 112;
David Jr. 315
Posey, Abram. 373; Dru-
silly 100; Green 255,
356; L.D. 402; Micajah
297; Moncraft 376; Tel-
fair 277
Poss, Elijah 53
Poss's, Andy(ors) 95
Post, Jno. B. 132,182
Postell, Dupree 370; Jane
E. 171
Potter, Wm. H. 127
Pottle, Jos. 230
Potts, David 310; Hiram
162; Isaac 81; Jas. M.
33; Jno. 153,295; Napo-
leon B. 370; Peter 313;
Thos. 155
Pott's, Stephen(ors) 120,
406
Poulks's, Jno.(ors) 113
Poullere, Ann 181
Poullin's, Jno.(ors) 273
Pounds, Jno. 187,370
Powell, Abram. 410; Abram
F. 131; Alfred 149; Al-
sey W. 379; Ambrose 211;
Benj. M. 132; Chas. 216;
Danl. 51; Enos. 377;
Geo. 27; Henry 387; Jas.
99,278,394; Jas. W. 96;
Jno. 370; Jno. A. 282;
Jno. G. 361; Jonathan
108; Loami 166; Noah
413; Rchd. 179; Rchd. L.
19; Stephens 42; Wm. 26,
253; Wm. H. 57,281
Powell's, Alexr.(ors) 291;
Jno.(ors) 138,360; Ran-
son(ors) 265
Power, Chas. T. 394; Enoch
J. 372; Jas. 31; Saml.
J. 261
Powers, Clem 202; Esther
316; Francis 307
Powill, Wm. Jr. 96
Powledge, Gideon 391
Powry, Elisha 208
Poythress, Jno. 347
Poytress, Sarah E. 204
Prater, Jno. D. 36
Prather, Jas. 151,298;
Jno. S. 267
Prator, Josiah 69
Pratt, Basdel 108; Chas.
M. 118; Danl. 86; Henry
50
Preast, Martin 84; Thos.
64
Prescott, Jas. 235; Jno.
307,404; Mary & Henry
(ors) 245
Prescott's, Wm.(ors) 369
Prescotte, Benajah 279
Presley, Chas. F. 121;
David 399; Moses 166;
Thos. 60
Presley's, Wm.(ors) 360
Pressley, Jno. Jr. 46
Prestage's, Jno.(ors) 61
Preston, Jno. 208; Jno.
F. 399; Sarah 114
Preston's, Gilliam(ors)
164
Prewett, Ansel B. 138;
Jacob 38; Naome 51;
Wm. 226
Prewit, Jno. 70; Jonathan
37

Price, Eliz. 347; Jas. 127,
376; Jas. B. 300; Jno.
310; Jno. C. 342; Jno. G.
400; Lewis 20; Mary 145;
Obedience 289; Pledge
394; Rchd. 300; Robt. W.
246; Saml. 56,381; Wm.
194,262,354; Wm. O. 192;
Wm. P. 46
Prichard, Dolison 36;
Elisha B. 15; Philip 89
Prickett, Elisha 58; Wm. E.
49
Pridgen, Mary 254
Pridgeon, Nathl. 228,229
Priett, Jacob 350
Prigett, Gideon 178
Prim, Abram. 204
Prince, Jas. 52; Jno. 75;
Jos. 29
Prior, Allen W. 15; Eliz.
41; Ephraim W. 373
Pritchett, Gelford 83
Procton, Rchd. 268
Proctor, Allen 364; Biddy
160; David 27; Frederic
B. 176; Hiram 149; Julian
R. 180
Prosser's, Jesse(ors) 127
Prothro, Geo. 141; Wm. 120,
380
Pruett, David 9
Pruett's, Saml.(ors) 66
Pruiett, Mastin 39
Pruit, Hail 222
Pruitt, David 12; Jno. W.
257; Peny 17,145; Saml.
93
Pryor, Edmund 394; Robt.
71
Pucket, Jno. 376
Puckett, Bird 267; Jno.
116; Jno. B. 276; West-
ley 187; Wm. W. 96
Puckett's, Aaron B.(ors)
181
Pugely's, Robt.(ors) 410
Pugh, David G. 204; Jesse
187; Samson 131; Wm. 137,
324
Pullen, Tilman 151; Wm. J.
35; Zelah 294
Pullin, Jno. G. 45; Wm. 48
Pullium, Jas. 77
Purcell, Abigail 137; Dar-
ias 404; Jno. 13
Purdain, Thos. 279
Purdon, Geo. H. 176
Purdue, Newton 344
Purris, Godfrey 100
Pursell, David 338
Purser, Rchd. 49
Purvis, Danl. J. 384
Puryear, Wm. H. 291
Pusser, Jas. 363
Putman, Jas. M. 163; Jas.
N. 24
Pye, Curtis 306; Paschal
P. 220
Pye's, Allen(ors) 329

Qualls, Thos. 82
Quarles, Robt. 399
Quarterman, Edward W. 361
Quick, Evander 151; Nathl.
288; Zachariah 120
Quigley, Jno. 369
Quill, Jos. W. 51
Quillian, Henry K. 80
Quillion, Henry K. 120
Quinn, David N. 390
Quinn, Alfred 136; Stephen
O. 22
Quinnd, Sarah 195

Quintin, Jas. 156
Quinton, Jos. 222; Saml.
371; Wm. 182

Rabb's, Jas.(ors) 101
Raboy's, Burrel(ors) 81
Rabun, Hodge 361; Jas. 374;
Jno. 263; Willis 96,180
Rackley, Jas. 332
Raden, Geo. 258
Radford, Bolin 161; Jno.
132
Radin, Wiley 130
Radney, Robt. M. 22; Wm.
A. 246
Ragan, Abram B. 161; Josa
374; Mark 64
Ragland, Jas. O. 395;
Nancy 99; Wm. 75,317
Ragsdale, Elijah 25: Jno.
C. 179; Rchd. 139
Rahn, Jas. 90
Raiford, Hamilton 340;
Jno. S. 23; Patience 183;
Wm. H. 179
Raiford's, Isaac W.(ors)47
Raine, Benj. 291,378
Raines, Alexr. 185; Edmond
37; Eliz. 76; Jno. 133:
Jno. G. 136; Jno. W. 74;
Rebecca 49; Wesley 405
Rainey, Jno. 205,325,408;
Matthew 306; Pitmilner
144
Rainwater, Abner 126; Jno.
193,394; Joshua 407
Rainy, Thos. 253
Rakestraw, Wm. 252
Raley, Jno. Floyd 308
Ralls, Sally 271
Ralston, Alexr. R. 250
Ramay, Archd. 324
Rambo, Jesse 75; Kinchen
170
Ramey, Eliz. P. 302: Jas.
118; Nancy 178
Ramey's, Sanford(ors) 267
Ramsay, Isaac 24; Mary 36;
Randall 118; Rchd. 72
Ramsey, Alexr. 312: Allen
C. 136; Jas. 389; Lewis
J. 25; Randolph H. 139;
Thos. 386
Ramy, Amalia 200; Milledge
273; Silas 271
Randle, Jas. D. 243: Jno.
S. 271; Wm. 148
Randle's, Wm.(ors) 175
Randolph, Dorothy 213,224;
Jos. 15; Joshua H. 70;
Wash. 145
Ranew, Jno. 122; Timothy
182,374
Raney, Harbert H. 317;
Saml. 151
Rankin, Wm. 103
Rankins, Jno. 122
Rannals, David 109
Ransey, Jas. H. 77
Ransom, Jno. T. 288
Ranson, Jas. 201; Jordan
D. 265
Rape, Henry 30,102; Peter
365
Raper, Delilah 55; Exa 197;
Wm. 304
Raper's, Jno.(ors) 103,357
Rapp, Chas. F. 40
Rasberry, Lovick 321
Rasberry's, Jas.(ors) 116
Rascow, Lodowick 383
Rash, Jas. 65
Rass, Reding 401

Ratchford, Ezekiel 176;
Jos. 204
Ratliff, Geo. 202
Taulerson, Herod 363
Rawlins, J. 108; Peter
139: Thos. W. 185
Rawls, Jas. 79; Jas. C.
185; Jesse 335; Silas 99
Ray, Anderson 248: Barbery
84; Benj. 377; Duncan
108; Eliz. M. 265; Geo.
W. 119; Henry S. 115,
409; Jane 176; Jerusia
246; Jno. 58; Jno. S.
272; Nancy 223; Plares
386; Rufus 398: Silas
104; Solomon 174; Thos.
64,229,291; Wm. 50,280;
Wm. D. 109; Wm. Jas. 368
Ray;s, Elijah(ors) 72
Rayford, Jno. M. 397
Raynalds, Dickerson 114
Raynes, Edmund 374
Read, Isaac D. 402
Read's, Geo.(ors) 369
Readwine, Jacob 385
Reans, Stephen 380
Reaves, Allen 394; Jas. M.
188
Rebisa, Sophia Frances 348
Red, Dudley 281; Holland
382; Job 361; Martha
320; Noah 43
Reddew, Jas. 176
Reddick, Abram 380; Jno.
40
Reddick's, Shadrack(ors)
303
Reddin, Jas. 219; Jas. V.
331; Wm. 366
Redding, David 345; Jno.
F. 333; Thos. 42; Sarah
314
Redding's, Henry H.(ors)
166
Reddingfield, Hiram 285
Redenhour, Danl. 170
Redman, Wash. 374
Redwin, Susannah 229
Redwine, Danl. 72,279
Reed, Augustin 171; Danl.
33; Geo. S. 81; Jacob
258.392; Jno. 373; Owen
30; Toliver 186; Violet
162; Wiley 410
Reeder, Elijah 365
Reedy, Mary 301
Reeks, Andrew M. 175
Rees, Joel 132
Ree;s, David(ors) 190;
Redman(ors) 216,379
Reese, Alfred B. 43; Cuth-
bert 285; Eliz. 45;
Evenezer S. 165; Hester
390; Isum 173; Silva
189; Wesley W. 405
Reeve, Silas 228
Reeves, Abner 139; Asa
338; Coleman 226; Edi-
son 108; Grant B. 275;
Jas. A. 133; Jno. 373;
Jno. B. 191; Jno. S. 99,
163; Jonathan 156; Lof-
tin 265; Osburn 336;
Rhoda 52,114; Robt. 276;
Stephens G. 298; Thos.
320
Rebester, Benj. 129
Reggins, Wm. G. 281
Register, Abram. 150; Jas.
156; Jno. 71; Susannah
75
Reid, Ann 125; Davis B.
263; D.H. 164; Eliz. 68;

Reid cont'd.
Eliz. C. 380: Geo. 292;
Hamilton 75; Hannah 9;
Jacob 330: Jas. 132;
Jas. H. 306; Joel 95;
Margaret 288; Nathl. 209;
Robt. A. 373; Wm. 382,399
Reid's, Edmund(ors) 96
Reikman, Jno. 104
Reins, Jno. R. 270; Tabitha
160
Renfroe, Bryan 377; Camp-
bell 96; Jas. M. 73,202:
Jno. 323; Nathl. 91;
Stephen 51
Renfroe's, Jared(ors) 267;
Peter(ors) 109
Reno, Jno. 414
Renty, Geo. 374
Respass, Rchd. 120
Ressengine, Ralph 405
Reuper, Wiley 350
Rever's, Jno.(ors) 131
Reviere, Jacob A.H. 393;
Milton 52
Reynolds, Anson 13: Edmond
W. 266; Geo. W. 189;
Hugh M. 100; Jas. 31,240,
359; Jane 112,341; Jeff-
erson G. 154; Jeptha V.
165; Jno. 396; Mary 218;
Nancy 251; Patrick M.
288; Permidas 387; Reuben
Y. 293; Thos. 154,229:
Thos. P. 146; Wm. 137:
Wm. Jr. 278
Reynolds's, (ors) 100,196;
Josiah(ors) 143: Thos.
(ors) 414
Rhan, Amos 342; Jonathan
271
Rhodes, Absalom W. 98;
Allen 410; Benj. 191;
Bunyan 374; Dorothy 302;
Eliz. 252; Henry 160;
Henry B. 23: Horace 95;
Mary Ann 13; Mercer 235;
Nathl. H. 400; Rchd. N.
178; Sally 31; Wiley
396; Wm. 224; Wm. H. 53
Rhodes's, Wm.(ors) 184,222
Rhymes, Wm. A. 142
Rhyner, Edward 285,398
Rialls, Patience 374
Rice, Arthur 143; Benj. 89:
Benj. H. 86; Evin 196;
Geo. D. 343; Jas. 159:
Jas. Jr. 161; Jas. W.
201; Jno. L. 58.224; Jno.
W.H. 159; Jos. 403:
Nathl. G. 322; Shadrack
148; Thos. Jr. 179; Thos.
W. 15
Rice's, Barton(ors) 98
Richard, Jno. 338; Uriah
292
Richards, Dexter F. 233;
Ira 214; Jas. W. 156; Jno.
138,311,332; Wm. S. 296
Richardson, Amos 191; Aug.
& Nancy 30; Chas. 106;
Clara 379; Eliza 279;
Geo. W. 373; Jas. 199;
Jesse 172; Jno. 73,97.
262; Jno. L. 336; Jno. R.
146; Jos. 400; Jos. L.B.
370; Levi 354; Mark 366;
Mary Ann 240; Nancy 407;
Peter 76; Robt. 11; Robt.
W. 158; Wm. 290; Wm. G.W.
413
Richardson's, David(ors)
197; Jas. M.(ors) 123;
Laurence(ors) 158

Richerson, Benj. 391
Richey, Wm. R. 215
Richters, Jno. P. 296
Ricketson, Jesse 37
Ricks, Harris 402; Johan-
non 121
Riddell, Presley 281
Riddle, David 314; Jas. M.
356; Marthy 279; T. 350;
Thos. 97
Riddlespurger, Erasmus 194
Riden, Elijah B. 66
Rider, Chris Jr. 269
Ridgedell, Lott N. 184
Ridgway, Saml. T. 221
Ridley, Everett 374
Rielecy, Chas. 42
Rieves, Wm. 19,361
Rigby, Enoch 241
Rigdon, Jno. 104; Thos. H.
H. 347
Riggins, Wm. 291
Right, Geo. W. 215; Jas.
N. 233
Right's, Robt.(ors) 102
Rigil. Jason 140; Wythel
141
Rigsby, Allen J. 193
Riley, David F. 135,250;
Jas. 298; Martin 294;
Sarah 34; Shepherd W.
324; Spencer W. 385; Wm.
358; Wm. M. 123
Riley's, Jas.(ors) 116,266;
Jos.(ors) 9
Riner, Wm. 357
Ringgold, Sarah 221
Ripley's, (ors) 36
Rison, Rchd. A. 254
Rittenberry, B. 119
Rivers, Nancy 220; Robt.
133; Thos. J. 33
Riviere, Francis 250
Rix, Edmund 397
Roach, David K. 393; Jno.
223; Saml. 48
Roads, Josephas 116
Robberson, Jno. 276
Robbins, Major E. 30; Mary
107; Thos. J. 364; Wm.
152
Roberson, Wm. 13,36; Wyly
359
Roberts, Abel 18; Albert
335; Anderson 277; Arm-
stead 126; Bryan J. 105;
Eliz. 57; Eliza S. 384;
Geo. 309; Geo. W. 394;
Griffin L. 372; Hardin
Jr. 197; Jas. 53,309;
Jas. Jr. 400; Jas. C.
296; Jas. M. 287; Jeff-
erson 59,190; Jesse M.
339; Jno. 65,140,255,
296,303; Jno. F. 365;
Jno. G. 100; Jos. 248;
Linsey 373; Mary 253;
Millicent 113; Moses 163;
Nathan 42; Nimrod 163;
Pleasant 145,392; Pres-
ley B. 281; Sansom W.
306; Stephens 405; Wiley
326; Wiley A. 71; Wm. 73,
166,317; Wm. B. 234;
Willis 406; Wilson 73;
Wootson 48
Robert's, Simon(ors) 146;
Wm.(ors) 196
Robertson, Alexr. 71; An-
drew 24; Archd. 26; Benj.
39; David 12,234; Howard
58; Isaac 320; Jas. A.
188; Jas. T. 392; Jno.
97,238,341; Jno. G. 376;

Roberts cont'd.
Jno. R. 369; Jos. 102;
Saml. 160; Sutherland
W. 217; Thos. L. 386;
Turner 233; Wm. 20,132,
141,160,313,371; Wm. H.
228
Robertson's, Emanuel 342;
L.(ors) 227; Wm.(ors)79
Robeson's, Frederic (ors)
281
Robey's, Timothy(ors) 25
Robins, Wm. R. 200
Robinson, Alexr. 59; An-
derson 286; Charlotte
107; David P. 273; David
P. 273; Eliz. 361; Geo.
62; Jas. 258,325,379;
Jeptha 53,215; Jeptha
Jr. 144; Jno. 12,72,74,
323,399; Jno. Bee 177,
228; Jno. W. 44; Jos.
138,409; Jos. L. 315;
Julius M. 368; Manoah
D. 225; Miles 64; Polly
310; Rchd. 343; Robt.
374,403; Sam. 131; Thos.
247,260,261; Wm. 298,
384; Wm. G. 271
Robinson's, (or) 275
(Chil) 352; Aaron(ors)
171; Henry(Or) 313
Robison, Robt. 254; Thos.
128
Robison's, (Chil) 252
Robuck, Julius 194; Martha
46; Wm. 381
Roche, Jno. 203
Rockwell, Wm. S. 81
Roderick, Jos. 238,335
Rogers, Edward 97; Henry
R. 157; Jacob 354; Matt-
hew C. 158
Roe, Enoch 169; Hilliard
321; Jno. 205; Jos. 185;
Wm. D. 322
Roffe, Rchd. W. 155
Roger, Danl. P. 268
Rogers, Bartell M. 378;
Chas. 299; David G. 195.
232; Elcanah 328; Elijah
297; Elisha 404; Henry
111; Jas. 260,347; Jas.
Jr. 357; Jas. C. 207;
Jno. 30.70.408; Jno. A.
379; Jno. C. 9; Johnston
C. 75; Lucy 328; Michael
252; Pleasant H. 184;
Robt. 254; Statley 112;
Simeon 322; Thos. 55;
Wm. 349; Wm. M. 59; Wm.
P. 70
Roger's, (Chil) 286; Jos.
(ors) 303; Wm.(ors) 351
Roland, Maston 32
Rolls, Ann Eliz. 19; Benj.
J. 393
Rolston, Edward S. 286;
Jno. T. 298
Roman's, Peter(ors) 205
Ronaldson, Wm. J. 334
Roney, Hugh 405; Jos. L.
318
Rooks, Mary 28,310; Silas
74; Wm. 308
Rooney, Patrick 351
Root, Chiles 318
Roper, Aaron 173; Chas.
154; Jas. 262; Jno. T.
167,400; Jos. F. 63
Roquemore, Zachariah 220
Rose, Albert 346; Ann 148;
Milton 92; Simri 250,282
Roser, Henry 232

Rosie, David C. 407
Rosier, Anderson 202; Chas.
A. 405
Ross, David 178; Henry W.
409; Luke 247,331; Mary
206; Wm. 277; Wm. M. 107
Rosseau's, Jas.(ors) 18
Rossenbury, Francis J. 316
Rosser, Lewis W. 173
Rosser's, David(ors) 267
Rosu's, Jno.(ors) 347
Roswell, Elsey 19
Rosy, Gasper 318
Roughton, Wm. 84
Roundham, Peter 307
Roundtree, Cutdon 84; El-
bert 48; Jno. 318; Jno.
W. 175; Raba 24
Rouse, Benj. P. 170; Jas.
B. 391; Martin 256; Wm.
320
Rousseau, Geo. 178; Henry
101; J. 230; Ledia 338
Rowan, Abram. 370; Elsey
A. 160; Jno. 214
Rowe, Asa 135; Jacob 244;
Jas. 77; Martha 62
Rowell. Charlotte 184; Danl.
C. 112; Jno. 357; Jno. A.
362; Johnson 386; Wm.
323
Rowland, Andrew 226; Jno.
T. 352,364; Saml. 100
Rowland's, Mary J.(ors) 216
Rowlin, Bazzel 136
Rowlings, Matthew 307
Rowlins, Barney 324; Thos.
W. 259
Rowls, Wm. 285
Rowsey, Foster 259
Rowzee, Jas. M. 15
Royal, Alfred 116; Hardy
127; Moses 146; Wm. T.
212
Royalls, Wm. 209
Rozar, Mary & Jno.(ors) 338
Rozier, F., Wm. & J. 319
Ruarbe, Dennis Jr. 319
Ruark, Berry A. 12; Jesse
317
Rucker, Jos. 330; Rchd. B.
17
Rucks, A.D. & E.W.(ors) 187
Ruddell, Lee Ann 328
Rudling, Danl. 270
Rudulph, Eliz. 316; Jno. T.
265; Michael H. 28
Ruff, Jno. M. 326; Martin
L. 11
Ruffin's, Jas.(ors) 246
Rumbley, Wm. 187
Rump, Jacob 209
Runnells, Marshall M. 207
Runnels, Geo. 232; Harmon
253; Jno. 230; Jno. W.
286; Pleasant R. 358;
Radford 184; Terry 304
Rush, Jas. M. 140; Levi 247
Rusheon, Specey 215
Rushing, Sarah 279
Rushton's, Robt.(ors) 172
Rusk, Thos. 43
Russ, Eleazar 217
Russell, Anna 123; Benj. J.
322; Benj. T. 25; Forgus
107; Jas. 149,266; Jas.
Jr. 19; Jas. H. 205; Jas.
J. 47; Jas. R. 225; Jas.
S. 368; Jno. 16,243,247;
Jno. H. 139; Mark 42;
Martha 161; Mary 230;
Miles B. 210; Nancy 67;
Nathl. 230; Perry G. 260;
Phebe 273; Rebecca 297;

453

Strickland's, Aaron(ors)
197
Stricklin, Calvin 163
Strickling, Kinbird 160
Stringer, Alexr. 63;
Celia 334
Stringfellow, Wm. 55
Stripling, Robt. 62
Stroger, Bennett M. 241
Strong, Allen B. 224; David E. 323; Geo. W. 77;
Jas. M. 105
Strother, Jno. W. 203,293;
Rchd. 397
Stroud, Archd. L.W. 269;
Desier 408; Eliz. Ann
209; Jno. M. 71; Sherwood 140,328
Stroud's, Thos.(ors) 60,
307
Strozer, Peter 16
Strozier, Chas. 156,340;
Jno. W. 320
Struion, Jackson 223
Strozier's, Jno.(ors) 370
Stubblefield, Catharine
147
Stubbs, Jas. 237; Jas. W.
& A.F.(ors) 244; Thos.
305,341; Wm. J. r. 300
Stucky, Sarah 412
Studdard, Ann 33; Jos. 67;
Saml. 88,363
Studdard's, Jas.(ors) 92
Studstill, Jonathan 239;
Wm. 211
Sturdevant, Allen C. 278;
Anderson 27; Edward 286;
Edward H. 185; Jas. 84;
Jno. 123; Jos. 73
Sturges, Benj. B. 183;
Eliz. 186; Rachel 203
Sturges's, Henry(ors) 329;
Jno.(ors) 146; Saml.
(ors) 25
Subers, Amos. 196
Suddeth, Jerid S. 290;
Jno. 183; Lewis 159
Sudduth, Chas. A. 205
Suggs, M'Kinley 315
Sugler, Wm. 227
Sullivan, Elijah 74; Jas.
C. 35,209; Sarah 36
Sullivan's, Danl. F.(ors)
223
Sullivin, Jas. 378
Sulter, Jos. R. 228
Sumervill, Jas. 332
Summer, Alexr. 196
Summer's, Jno.(ors) 404
Summerall, Allen 307
Summerlin, Jas. J. 145;
Jos. 352; Nehemiah 346
Summers, Robt. 245; Seaborn 340
Summons, Lewis 264
Lumner, Eliz. 156; Holland
301; Jesse K. 83; Uriah
397
Sumner's, (ors) 103
Surcell, Abram. 280
Surrency, Jacob 190
Sutherland, Jno. 256;
Mallindy 345; Martha 372
Sutherland's, Jno.(ors)236
Sutley, Danl. R. 231; David
41,326; Jas. 296
Suttle, Edward D. 309
Suttles, Wm. 263
Sutton, Blanset 31; Eliz.
79; Joshua 356; Phebe
125; Sarah 225
Sutton's, Jno.(ors) 113,
310

Swain, Isaiah L. 391; Jas.
G. 99; Jere. R. 365;
Stephen 126,227
Swan, Elijah 214; Frances
385; Lee 315; Rchd. H.M.
339
Swann, Jno. 368; Stephen
252
Swanson, Abdallah 226;
Henry 300; Jno. 123
Swearingen, Baley 196;
Eliz. 390; Jacob 394
Swearingin, Jno. 298
Sweat, Gilbert 81; Solomon
183; Wm. F. 406
Sweet, T. W. 322
Swetman, Geo. W. 100
Swift, Sheldon 77,391;
Thos. H. 399; Tyre 307;
Wm. A. 193
Swilly's, Saml.(ors) 74,
306
Swindall, Thos. P. 348
Swindell, Hannah 98;
Julia 288
Swinney, Henry 334; Jesse
268; Marcus B. 123; Mary
58;
Swint, Edmund 391
Swords, Jas. 178; Jno. 223
Sykes, Jno. P. 260
Sylvester, Henry S. 384

Tabb. Edmund 96; Sarah 316
Taber, Benj. K. 381; Jno.
F. 47
Tabor, Eliz. 36
Tackett, Ezekiel L. 77;
Wm. 377
Tackett's, Wm.(ors) 357
Tackwell, Benj. 88
Taff, Harriett 195
Tailer, Grant 275
Tailor, Paschal H. 352
Tait, Chas. H. 372; Hannah
214; Jno. 337; Wm. 186;
Wm. H. 120
Taiter, Jno. S. 54
Talbert, Benj. 156
Talbot, Eliz. 53,324
Taliaferro, Eliza A. 329;
Rchd. 353
Tallant, David 113; Saml.
26
Talley, David 374; Elkanah
184; Jno. W. 183; Jos.
T. 244
Talley's, Wm. S.(ors) 85
Tallis, Henry Jno. 172
Tally, Jas. B. 241
Tammons, Zipporah 127
Tamplin, Jno. 195
Tankersley, Eliz. 75; Geo.
G. 28,263; Jno. 379;
Jno. G. 40; Lemuel R.
135; Wm. 92
Tankesley, Chas. 302
Tanner, Green 232; Jas.
185; Jno. J. 335; Jno.
Q. 375; Jos. 385; Pencint 251; Sila 11; Thos.
262; Thos. J. 297; Wm.
H. 132; Wilson 86
Tant, Jno. 79; Roden 33
Tapley, Wm. 317
Taply, Jordan 322
Tarples, Jarrat 344
Tarpley, Robt. W. 313;
Wm. H. 381
Tarver, Benj. 406; Etheldred 284; Stephen 340
Tarver's, (Chil) 299; Elijah(ors) 83; Jacob(ors)
108; Starling(ors) 153

Tarvin, David D. 226
Tary, Jos. 200; Lewis 185;
Wm. 338
Tate, Cooper B. 235; Eliz.
403; Jere. 198; Jno.
111,168; Jonathan 25;
Perryman Mackey 188;
Robt. 341; Sarah 36;
Wm. 387; Willis 368;
Zimry W. 195
Tatom, Absalom T. 167;
Jesse D. 185,192
Tatom's, Peter(ors) 148
Tatum, Albert 258; Allen
M. 210; Milley 36; Peter 20; Rchd. 413; Sarah 32
Taunton, Eli 208; Nathan
351; Newsom 256; Wm. 388
Taylor, Abner 144; Abner
F. 47,200; Arthur 166;
Benj. 19,283; Canly 267;
Caraway 194; Chas. E.
223; Chris. 122; D. 152;
Ephraim 282; Frances N.
46; Francis S. 107;
Franklin 235,296; Geo.
14,413; Geo. M. 207;
Giles B. 127; Isaac 299;
Isaiah 179; Jas. 405;
Jas. Jr. 366; Jas. L.
365; Jas. N. 96; Jane
F. 139; Jared Jefferson
156; Jere. 280; Jere,
Jr. 268; Jno. 151,260,
272,295,302,317; Jno. J.
371; Jno. S. 341; Jno.
T. 223; Jno. W. 107;
Mary 319,324; Nancy 47;
Nesbit P.J. 115; O.E.
180; Oliver 17; Quilley
407; Reuben 49; Robt.
198; Robt. H. 190; Saml.
364; Sarah 40,232; Seaborn 190; Simeon 332;
Spencer 169; Turner W.
216; Uriah 357; Warren
34; Wm. 33.58.198,229;
Wm. A. 207; Wm. S. 190;
Wm. W. 39
Taylor's, Jno.(mi) 25;
Jno.(ors) 250,294; Thos.
(ors) 159
Taynor, Wm. 170,362
Teague, Elijah 360
Teasdale, (ors) 100
Teasler, Sarah 210
Teasley, Joshua 95
Teat, Lemon W. 378; Nancy
185; T.B. 198
Tebow's, Jno.(ors) 79
Tedder, Littleton 55; Ransom 37; Robt. 213; Wm.
22,245
Teel, Geo. W. 135
Temple, Frederic 215; Jas.
Jr. 304
Temples, Abner 166; A.F.
267; Eliz. 91; Jno. 397
Tenbrock, R.R. 359
Tenbroeck, R.R. 78
Tendall, Wm. B. 103
Tengle, Thos. I. 268
Tenison, Matthias 314
Tennell, W.A. 267
Tennell's, Isham(ors) 243
Tennille, Alex. St.C. 270
Tennison, Saml. 59
Tenrell, Absolem 285; Ansel 75; Edward T. 90;
Jas. 138; Jno. 192;
Sarah 37,268,316; Simeon 373; Wm. 182; Wm. B.
268

457

459

Vickry, Sampson Jr. 152
Vicky, Chris. 341
Ville's, Jas. Be(ors) 96
Vinant, Kimbrought H. 252
Vincent, Aulsey A. 336;
Henry 95; Henry Jr. 36;
Jesse 414; Larkin 128;
Mary 145; Nathl. 150;
Powell 386; Powel P.
233; Wm. 260
Vines, Parnell 101
Vining, Jno. 270; Lewis
M. 82: Reuben 12
Vinson, Chas. M. 62; Geo.
11,384; Jno. Jr. 83;
Mary 310; Willie 195;
Wm. 291
Vinzant, Mary 209
Visage, Eliz. 217; Wm. 360
Volotton, Benj. 350
Voss, Thos. J. 369; Wyatt
328
Voyles, Geo. W. 355; Jas.
209,232

Wadal, Thos. 226
Waddall, Jos. 254
Waddle, Amaziah 207
Wade, Ann 388; Edward 227;
Henry 116; Jas. 72,181,
251,326; Jno. 57; Jno.
W. 369; M'Guder 297;
Peyton 249; Peyton L.
346; Thos. 350
Wade's, (ors) 400
Wadesworth, Thos. 277
Wadkins, Jas. 141
Wadson, Abner 181
Wadsworth, Alfred E. 85;
Bryan 194; Jas. 162;
Murdock M'Swain 253;
Walter 99; Wm. 204
Wafford, Benj. C. 340; Wm.
304
Wages, Andrew 47; Rchd.
153
Waggoner, David 109
Wagoner, Amos 169
Wagnon, Danl. 389; Geo. P.
399; Sarah 153
Wainwright, Jos. 54
Waites, Jno. 306
Waits, Jno. 224; Saml. 230
Walden, Chas. 231; Eli 219;
Elisha 315; Green 118;
Ira 260
Walder, Saml. 72
Waldravin, Isaac 409;
Littleberry White 218
Waldrip, Jesse 130; Patil-
la 208; Wm. 281
Waldron, Jno. 241
Waldrop, Isaac 19
Waldroup, Tabitha 350
Waldrup, Jos. 71
Walker, Asa 137; Clarissa
383; Danl. 211,249,365;
Danl. Jr. 307; David 174;
Elias 336; Eliz. 406;
Freeman 67; Hardage 156;
Harrison 10; Hezekiah
86,93; Jas. 85,240,278,
288,315,332,349,408;
Jas. B. 280; Jas. C. 110;
Jas. J. 45; Jas. S. 234;
Jas. W. 319; Jere. 324,
385; Jno. 392,414; Jno.
M. 377; Jno. S. 158,336;
Jno. W. 281; Jonathan
258,279; Jos. 78,117;
Jos. W. 54; Leonard 168;
Levin 150,408; Martha
295; Mary G. 239; Mason
324,400; Noah 371;

Walker cont'd.
Robt. 39,178,218; Saml.
P. 75; Solomon 25,282;
Thos. 180,313; Wm. 91,
248,301,403; Wm. Elisha
307; Wm. H. 302; Wm. R.
167
Walker's, (ors) 132,231;
Alfred(ors) 72; David
(ors) 13; Henry(ors)
384; Loxley(ors) 74;
Wm.(ors) 33
Walkins, Elisha 232
Wall, Adam 237; Bud C.
181; Cade 356; Danl. D.
124; Drury Jr. 365;
Ezekiel 400; Henry H.
390; Jas. J. 208: Jesse
380; Jesse C. 271; Jesse
J. 372; Jno. M. 317;
Jos. 258; Miall 100;
Reuben 219; Susannah
388; Wm. 345
Wallace, Absolem 325; El-
lias 303; Enoch B. 360;
Jno. 10; Jno. B. 136;
Jno. H. 195,197; Sophia
195; Wm. 298,402; Wm.
B. 140; Wm. J. 213
Wallace's, Saml.(ors) 17,
378: Wm.(ors) 16
Waller, Geo. 325; Geo. W.
200; Hope Hall 153; Jno.
H. 366; Jno. K.C. 151;
Martha Ann 130; Robt. R.
122; Sarah 363; Smith
305; Thos. 323
Walley, Jno. 351
Wallice, Jesse 304
Walling, Danl. 45; Jas.
15; Lucy 63; Elijah 165;
Gabriel 276; Geo. H.
147; Isaiah C. 105: Jere.
166; Jno. A. 164; Mit-
chell C. 26; Mortimore
R. 22; Wm. 86; Wm. C.
389
Walraven, Jno. 207; Wm.
100
Walsingham, Chas. 142
Walson, David 93
Walters, Jere. 127; Jesse
301
Walthall, Chas. F. 80;
Nancy 291
Walthall's, Edward(ors)153
Walton, Benton 102; Bleu-
ford M. 355; Danl. R.
357; Eliz. 107; Hugh
288; Josiah 202.308;
Susannah W.H. 180; Thos.
383; Thos. S. 68
Walton's, Jno.(or) 276;
Noah(ors) 215
Wamack, Jno. 79; Sarah 69;
Thos. H. 336; Wiley 286;
Wm. 261
Wamble, Lucretia 300;
Wm. F. 361
Wammock, Eliz. 103; Jas.
250; Jno. E. 251
Wamock, Thos. H. 237
Wannack, Jesse 283
Wansley, Jno. 410
Wansloca, Larkin 277
Ward, Ann 287; Eliz. 180,
209; Ezekiel 203; Fred-
eric 166,353; Geo. 92:
Hannah 264; Ignitius 39:
Jackson 411; Jas. 59;
Jane 265,404; Jeptha H.
178; Jno. 80; Jno. L.D.
87; Mark 199,275; Mary
24; Saml. 282; Simon 119;

Ward cont'd.
Solomon 312; Thos. F.
351; Wade 273; Wm. 44,
194
Ward's, Rchd.(ors) 57,376;
T.(ors) 79; Wm.(ors)126
Warden, Chas. 167; Saml.
13
Ware, Ezekiel P. 168; Jas.
M. 156; Jos. 96; Molly
205; Nicholas C. 348;
Philip 155; T. 261; Wm.
86; Wm. M. 274
Ware's, Nicholas(ors) 187
Warker, Jos. V. 249
Warmack, Jesse 355
Warnack, Joel 326
Warner, Benj. 155; Leonard
T. 356
Warner's, Jerry(ors) 396;
Jno. D.(ors) 15
Warnock, Ella 121; Matthew
394; Simeon 130
Warren, Arthur 155; Chas.
352,406; Isaiah 100;
Jas. M. 403; Jesse 381;
Jno. 181,182; Mary 98,
217; M.W. 96; Reuben 39;
Robt. 221; Robt. B. 219;
Samson 281; Waldrup 106;
Wash. 250
Warren's, Archd.(ors) 30;
Bray(ors) 73; Josiah
(ors) 275
Warrington, Peter 202
Warthen, Wm. 39
Warthen's, (ors) 103
Warwick, Jno. H. 206
Wasden, Bryant 119
Wash, Wm. W. 138
Washburn, Arba 108
Washington, Dicy 110; Geo.
H. 128,218
Wasson, Jno. F. 67.230
Waterer, Wm. 283,369
Waters, Allen 146; Clement
274; Henry 49; Isaac
302; Jas. 26; Jubal E.
26; Judith 377; Rchd. H.
289; Simeon 299; Thos.
79,217; Wm. 35,146;
Wm. F. 316
Waters's, Collins(ors) 405;
Needham(ors) 94; Thos.
(ors) 360
Waterson, Geo. 299
Watkins, Alfred 60,230;
Andrew G. 319; Beverly
241; Coleman 68; Elias
311; Jno. 241,255; Jno.
R. 44; M. 278; Moses 40;
Nancy 105; P. 74; Polly
268: Reece 343; Ruse 61;
Solomon 134; Thos. 357;
Wm. 244; Wilson 360
Watkins's, David(ors) 223;
Henry(ors) 91,145; Mar-
tin S.(ors) 91
Watley, Jno. 351,369
Watson, Ansel 263; Arthur
P. 185; Benj. 337; David
301; Elias 61; Elijah
286,413; Eliz. 269,293;
Gideon 82; Gilbert 383;
Griffin 95; Isam 125,
226; Jas. 124; Jere. G.
60; Jesse 37,82; Jesse
H. 125; Jno. 239; Jno.
M. 136; Jno. Osburn (?);
Jno. R. 322; Jno. W. 25;
Jonathan 183; Jordan G.
272; Jos. 176,333; Josiah
391.399; Labun 228; Mary
77; Milley 376;

Whitlock, Jno. 159
Whitlow, Jno. 32; Wm. 70
Whitman, Chris. 159
Whitmire, Stephen 264
Whitmore, Michael 299
Whitney, Carleton 131;
  Priscilla 199
Whittemore's, P.(ors) 24
Whitten, Alvan E. 387; Jas.
  46; Littleton 129,146;
  Wm. S. 40
Whittimore, Barbara 110
Whittle, Jas. 30,359
Whitton, Nicholas 382
Whitworth, Mary H. 89
Whotten, Thos. 219
Whorter, Moses E. 216
Whorton, Bartlett 367;
  Nancy 276
Wick, Jno. B. 271
Wicked, Eliz. 287
Wicker, Matthew 137
Wicker's, Allen(ors) 129
Widner, Giles 208
Wiett, Lewise 195
Wiggins, Baker 126; Elijah
  133; Green M. 402; Jas.
  A. 176; Jesse 98,137,
  229; Joel P. 221; Jno.
  117,211,310; Nancy 176;
  Osburn 272; Peter 337;
  Wm. 340; Willis 350
Wiggins's, Sampson(ors)
  338
Wiggs, Danl. 323
Wightman, Wm. J. 297,387
Wigley, Allen 36; Danl.
  121; Geo. W. 46; Wm. F.
  365
Wilbanks, Abijah 152
Wilber, Geo. S. 359
Wilcher, Eliz. 105
Wilcox, Geo. 117,243; Ja-
  cob 72; Jas. 165; Jno.
  Jr. 78; Lewis 104; T.
  Jr. 76,115; Uriah 317
Wilde, Wm. 42
Wilder, Ezekiel 192; Jno.
  106; Jos. 286; Sampson
  166; Wm. 342; Willis 170
Wilder's, Robt.(ors) 104
Wiley, Alexr. W. 326;
  Jacob 214; Jane 102; Jno.
  104; Jno. P. 297; John-
  son 13; Moses 107; Wm. H.
  10,257
Wilf, Jacob 280; Jas. 281,
  366
Wilhite, Lewis 26
Wilkerson, Lemuel 66
Wilkes, Jas. 11; Reuben
  299; Orsburn 228; Osburn
  385
Wilkie, Geo. 142,207
Wilkins, Archd. 154; Bishop
  317; David 69; David L.
  41; Drewry 293; Ellin-
  nor 330; Jno. 410; Luc-
  retia 47; Saml. 329;
  Thos. P. 111; Wm. Jr. 60
Wilkins's, Jabez(ors) 332
Wilkinson, Calvin 143;
  Danl. M.G. 57; Jas. O.
  263; Jesse 186; Jno. 143;
  Jno. C. 48; Levi 27;
  Margaret 179; Mary 369;
  Neal R. 331; Neill 143,
  189; Reuben 138; Saml.
  368; Sarah 286; Young
  338
Wilkinson's, J.(ors) 183
Wilkison, Wm. A. 61
Wilks, Nancy 396; Saml.
  269; Wm. D. 337

Wilks's, Reuben(ors) 326
Willaford's, Starling
  (ors) 235
Willard, Wm. 259
Willbanks, Wm. T. 224
Willeford, Saml. 316
Willer, Wm. 262
Willey, Alexr. W. 172;
  Gardner 291
Willf, Jno. 167; Jno. Jr.
  278
Willford, Wm. 78
Williams, Aaron 374;
  Abram. 198; Absolem 410;
  Al-xr. 156; Andrew C.
  374; Ann 263; Bartimeus
  142; Benajah 96; Benj.
  147; Benj. F. 217; Ben-
  nett 190; Betsey 292;
  Calliway 110; Chas. D.
  219; Chas. G. 304; Clia
  91; Cornelius B. 365;
  Crawford B. 93,308; Danl.
  H. 85; David 268; Ditha
  377; Duke 111,359; Ed-
  ward 129,406; Elijah
  277; Felix T. 333; Free-
  man 363; Geo. 154; Geo.
  M. 274; Green B. 31,346;
  Henry H. 191; Hubbard
  267; Isaac 166,362; Is-
  ham 62; Jas. 109,218;
  Jas. E. 344; Jas. S. 132;
  Jere. 337; Jere. M. 407;
  Jesse 166,172,255,280,
  338; Jno. 91,101,180,
  289,369; Jno. B. 294;
  Jno. G. 52; Jno. T. 312;
  Jno. W. 325; Jonathan
  398,411; Jos. 392,397;
  Jos. B. 200; Jos. J. 108;
  Joshua 183; Josiah 188;
  Julia 134; Leroy 305;
  Littleberry A. 185; Louis
  92; Luke 257; Madison
  140; Maria 75; Mark 354;
  Mary 91,175,178; Mary &
  Louisa(ors) 340; Matthew
  J. 217; Membrence 203;
  Nancey 393; Rebecca 96,
  154,271; Reuben K. 305;
  Robt. 255,281; Robt. B.
  382; Robt. L. 308; Row-
  land 158; Russell 412;
  Ruth 86; Sampson G. 14;
  Saml. 52,265; Saml. B.
  123; Sarah 190; Shadrack
  T. 390; Simeon 132; Sin-
  ah 171; Sol 60,71; Solo-
  mon 152,343,396; Staf-
  ford 64; Stephen 86;
  Stephen K. 240; Stephen
  M. 83; Theophilus 348;
  Thos. 16,116,303,353;
  Thos. J. 83; W. 214;
  Wash. 88; Whitfield 398;
  Whitmill 319; Wm. 92,
  140,234,263,268,337,
  371,377; Wm. Jr. 378,
  414; Wm. H. 310; Wm. K.
  39; Wm. M. 228; Wm. M'G
  166,344; Wm. T. 356;
  Wm. W. 209; Wilson 373;
  Wright 12; Wyat 393
William's, Denton(ors) 214;
  Edward W.(ors) 244;
  Frederic H.(ors) 146;
  J.J.E. & L.(ors) 387;
  Jno.(ors) 240; Lott(ors)
  403; Mary (Chil) 393;
  M.L. & E.J.(ors) 49
Williamson, Alexr. 134,282;
  Allen 154; Ann F. 288;
  Benajah 209;

Williamson cont'd.
  Benj. 207,395; Curtis
  263; Green B. 337; Green
  B. 79; Isaac B. 46; Jas.
  246; Jas. H. 207,337;
  Jno. 15,48,88,118,137;
  Jno. C. 78; M'Allister
  194; Nancy 46; Proctor
  232; Rchd. 405; Stephen
  275; T.J. 51; Wm. 19,
  73,88; Wm. R. 289; Zachariah 409
Williamson's, Robt.(ors)
  180; Stephen(ors) 371
Williford, Chas. 98; Malichi 202; Wm. 100,249;
  Wilson P. 92
Willingham, Archd. 260;
  Cash 184; Geo. W. 110;
  Jas. 107; Jane 103; Jno.
  H. 65; Mary 373; Riley
  M. 131; Wm. 384; Wm. T.
  218
Willingham's, Jesse(ors)
  192
Willis, Benj. Jr. 385; Ed-
  win 125; Geo. W. 405;
  Jas. 244,352; Jas. L.
  104; Jas. M. 358; Jane
  10; Jno. 147,152,259;
  Jno. J.M. 371; Joysey
  328; Milley 343; Rchd.
  79; Stephen H. 184; Su-
  sannah 399; Thos. 72,
  252; Thos. J. 117; Wal-
  ter J. 275; Wm. 204; Wm.
  Jr. 152; Wm. J. 260;
  Wright 332
Willis's, Jno.(ors) 19;
  Jonathan(ors) 125
Willmaker, Elias 184
Willoughby, Ellis 253;
  Jas. 96; Randol 57;
  Unity 143
Wills, Anon 256; Henry M.
  303; Jas. Q. 386; Jno.
  A. 229,254; Leonard 25,
  110; Mary 392; Mary W.
  302; Thos. 89,304
Willson, Saml. 14; Wm. 403
Willy, Thos. 378
Wilmoreland, Jas. 231
Wilmoth, Esther Ann 334
Wilson, Alexr. 51; Alfred
  M. 375; Andrew S. 144;
  Ann 272,319; Ann E. 24;
  Augustin 248; Danl. 46;
  Edward 81,362; Edward
  & J.(ors) 198; Elkanah
  69; Ephraim 64; Francis
  75,259,355; Geo. 126,
  258,381; Henry 34; Jas.
  17,110,174,175; Jas. H.
  216; Jere. 269; Jesse M.
  195; Joel A. 347; Jno.
  115,128,183,305; Jno.
  N. 195; Jno. S. 260;
  Jno. Starkley 34; Jos.
  83,218,221,364; Josiah
  N. 138; Larkin 81; Leander 109; Leroy M. 333;
  Moses 396; Nancy 174,
  374; Newman 75; Orpha
  123; Rebecca 161; Rely
  277; Robt. 78; Saml. 27;
  Susannah 324; Tennel H.
  265; Thos. 67,102,159,
  231; Thos. B. 21; Thos.
  H. 130; Walter 377; Wm.
  86,116,159,277,305,312,
  318; Wm. E. 198; Wm. H.
  336; Wm. P. 11; Zacha-
  riah K. 20

Wilson's, David(ors) 412;
Jno.(ors) 259; Robt.
(ors) 201; Thos.(ors)
399; Thos. K.(ors) 380;
Thos. M.(ors) 12; Wm.
(ors) 377
Wilt, Chas. 183
Wimberley, Jas. 32,167
Wimberley's, Isaac(ors)249
Wimberly, Ezekiel 404;
Henry 164; Martha 338;
Wimberry's, Wm. B.(ors)357
Wimbush, Wm. M. 66
Wimpey, Larkin C. 369
Wimpy, Archd. 293
Winbush, Jno. M. 73
Wincey, Jas. E. 35
Winchel, Jas. H. 320
Windham, Lucy 14; Reuben
127
Wingate, Amos. 188,201;
Mary 186
Wingate's, Amos.(ors) 140
Winger, Rchd. 264
Wingfield, Albert M. 333
Winkler, Susan 105
Winn, Elisha 183; Jno. 325;
Rchd. J. 380; Seaton 18
Winn's, Jno.(ors) 364
Winningham, Abel 318
Winship, Isaac 325
Winslet, Floyd 395; Randol
200
Winslett, Jonathan 206
Winslett's, Rchd.(ors) 352
Winslow, Wm. 392
Winstell, Jonathan 117
Winston, Thos. 132
Winter, Anthony 410; Jere.
46
Winter's, Rchd.(ors) 15
Winters, Paley 405
Winzer, Austin 83
Wirthington, Dennia 198
Wise, Abijah 285; Hugh 69;
Jas. 365; Preston 191;
Walden 223; Wayne 392
Wise's, Jno.(ors) 35
Wiseman, Chas. R. 413
Wisenbaker, Jas. 285; Jno.
172
Wishard, Jos. A. 394
Witcher, Ambrose 39; Benj.
M. 285; Jno. 392; Lecey
264
Witherspoon, Jno. H. 104
Witt, Martin 189; Middle-
ton 186
Wofford, Absalom 87; Eliza
125; Jas. 12; Jere. 50;
Jno. 22
Wold, Lewis 346
Woldrup, Levi 303
Wolf, Council B. 47; Geo.
50,373; Georgianna 161;
Henry 22
Wolfe, Jacob 113,385
Wollis, Jefferson 118
Womac, Chas. 41
Womble, Enoch W. 130:
Littleberry 210
Woolbot, Noah 298
Wood, Abram 110; Aristar-
cus 183; Caleb 200; Col-
lin 106; David 133; David
H. 29; Eliz. 95,131,183,
332; Fountain 286,299;
Frazier F. 389; Geo. B.
123; Geo. W. 196; Green
184; Henry 63,181; Heza-
kiah 32; Ira 41; Isaac
60; Jas. 30,283,295: Jas.
Jr. 222; Jas. C. 224;
Jared 362;

Wood cont'd.
Jno. 161,329,340; Mar-
garet 272; Mary 191,411;
Nancy 276; Owen 74;
Paschal H. 110; Rchd. N.
308; Rchd. W. 108; Rchd.
W. Jr. 242; Robt. 76,
108,156,365,381,406;
Robt. S. 243; Sterling
263; Thos. 255,361; Thos.
G. 146; Wiley E. 23; Wm.
89,231,412: Wm. H. 23,
191,352
Wood's, Allen(ors) 49;
Jno.(ors) 101; Jos.(ors)
213,284; Thos.(ors) 214;
Wm.(ors) 116,364
Woodall, David 303: Elihu
237,248; Henry T. 268:
Isaac 194; Stephen 72;
Talbot 192; Tolbert 185;
Thos. R. 190
Woodard, Leroy 363
Woodcock, Sarah 341; Sea-
born 141
Woodruff, David 174; Lar-
kin W. 390; Reuben 400;
Rchd. 172,208; Saml. 239;
Wm. B. 169
Woods, Archd. 59; Benj. W.
110; Jno. 55; Martha
114; Thos. 124,266;
Timothy C. 301; Willis
A. 274
Woodson, Creed T. 127
Woodward, Kyeah 215; Orren
S. 112; Wm. 326
Woodward's, (ors) 75:
Mills(ors) 77
Woody, Temperence 226
Woodyard, Felix D. 23,397:
Jas. M. 156
Woolbright, Jno. P. 124
Wooley, Margaret 166
Woolfolk, Robt. H. 23
Woolf's, Jno. 66
Woolsey, Abram M. 147;
Benj. 389; Jno. M. 388
Wooten, Aaron 33; Chaney
35; Chas. H. 367; Danl.
21; Jas. B. 17; Jennett
200; Jno. R. 200; Lewis
262; Simeon 136
Wootten's, Benj.(or) 247
Word, Jas. 231,309; Nathl.
R. 71; Wm. 119,264
Worley, Pleasant 223,275;
Silas 162,182; Woodson
253; Wm. 24
Worly, Jas. H. 232; Silas
J. 268
Worrell, Kinchen 70
Worrill, Edmund H. 252
Worsham, Applin 330; Jno.
392; Jno. S. 159; Mary
204; Wm. 280
Wortham, Geo. 14; Jos. W.
141; Saml. 318; Wm. C.
20
Worthy, Billington S. 193:
Jno. 61,159,259; Milton
125; Saml. 12,242; Thos.
385; Wm. 117; Wm. Jr.
27
Wosham, Jno. S. 112: Leo-
nard 160
Wozencroft, Jas. B. 68
Wray, Jno. S. 346; Silas
36
Wren, Geo. W. 282; Zebu-
lon 379
Wright, Abram 235; Agnes
111; Amis 150; Burton
H. 94;

Wright cont'd.
Charlotte A. 163; David
61; Edith 405; Edward W.
388; Geo. B. 280: Henry
187; Hiram 52; Jas. 34,
282; Jas. A. 346; Jas.
T. 85; Jesse 212; Jno.
44,250,331; Lawson 151;
Legrands S. 261; Matthew
H. 84; Milicart 154;
Millicent 113; Nathan 78:
Saml. 13,49,395; Sarah
141,359; Spencer P. 348;
Stith H. 99: Susan 296;
Willie 57; Wm. 182,298:
Wm. G. 65; Wm. J. 195,
406; Wm. R. 271; Willis
161,248; Zachariah 353
Wright's, David(ors) 155,
171,265; Geo. W.(ors) 31;
Jarrett(ors) 404; Jett
(ors) 215: Jno.(ors) 329,
333
Wyatt, Elijah 314; Eliz.
139; Jno. 284; Philip H.
172; Wm. 68,270; Wm. H.
149
Wyche, Alfred 267; Geo.
168; Henry 257; Susannah
137
Wylie, Peter 248; Saml. B.
73
Wylly, Elisha 284; T. 82
Wynce, Mary 110
Wynn, Jno. A. 20; Jno. C.
10; Thos. B. 391; Thos.
H. 157
Wynn's, Jno.(ors) 256,392;
Jones(ors) 37
Wynne, Frances 203; Jno.
208; Nancy 13; Wm. J. 260
Wytcher, Alexr. 122

Yancey, Jas. 218: Simeon
W. 366; Wm. 285
Yancy, Elijah 296; Levi
208; Lewis D. 63; Miens
134; Simeon W. 49
Yarber's, Jno. 40,201
Yarber's, Pinkey(ors) 32
Yarbraw's, Westley(ors) 259
Yarbrough, Benj. 32; Eliz.
235; Geo. 61; Geo. W.
345; Isaac 183; Jas. 57;
Jno. 373; Jno. W. 115;
Nathan 309; Rachel 195;
Rchd. 26; Silas 46; Thos.
H. 294; Wyatt 189
Yarbrough's, Bealle(ors)55;
Benj.(ors) 18: J.(ors)
139
Yarewood, Birdie 333
Yates, Jos. 325: Peter 175;
Presly 334; Susannah 129,
315; Wm. 10,106
Yaun, Chesley A. 224; Henry
247
Yawn, Wm. 395
Yeager, Abner 303
Yeales, Jno. 219; Mary 285
Yearty, Elsbury 123
Yearwood, Jerry 157
Yeates's, Jas.(ors) 69
Yellowby, Eliz. 136
Yelverton's, Bryan(ors) 368
Yomans, Saml. P. 239
Yonks, Jacob D. 63
York, Archd. 99; Eliz. 359;
Jno. G. 377; Wm. 183
York's, Jno.(ors) 20
Youn, Jos. 189
Young, Andrew 221; Danl.
108; David 221,356; Enoch
94; Ephriam 356;